# CONTENTS

# Eleventh Edition

# HUMAN COMMUNICATION

## THE BASIC COURSE

### JOSEPH A. DEVITO

Hunter College of the City University of New York

PEARSON

Boston   New York   San Francisco
Mexico City   Montreal   Toronto   London   Madrid   Munich   Paris
Hong Kong   Singapore   Tokyo   Cape Town   Sydney

Editor in Chief: Karon Bowers
Project Manager: Lisa Sussman
Series Editorial Assistant: Susan Brilling
Marketing Manager: Susan Czajkowski
Associate Editor: Jennifer DeMambro
Editorial Production Service: Tom Conville for Nesbitt Graphics, Inc.
Composition Buyer: Linda Cox
Manufacturing Buyer: JoAnne Sweeney
Electronic Composition: Nesbitt Graphics, Inc.
Interior Design: Nesbitt Graphics, Inc.
Photo Researcher: Nesbitt Graphics, Inc.
Cover Administrator: Linda Knowles

For related titles and support materials, visit our online catalog at www.ablongman.com.

Between the time website information is gathered and then published, it is not unusual for some sites to have closed. Also, the transcription of URLs can result in typographical errors. The publisher would appreciate notification where these errors occur so that they may be corrected in subsequent editions.

Library of Congress Cataloging-in-Publication Data

DeVito, Joseph A.
  Human communication: the basic course / Joseph A. DeVito.—11th ed.
     p. cm.
  Includes bibliographical references and index.
  ISBN-13: 978-0-205-52259-0
  ISBN-10:    0-205-52259-9
  1. Communication. I. Title.

P90.D485 2009
302.2—dc22                                                    2007047717

ISBN-13: 978-0-205-52259-0    ISBN-10: 0-205-52259-9

Credits appear on page 496, which constitutes an extension of the copyright page.

Printed in the United States of America

10 9 8 7 6 5 4 3 2 1 RRD-OH 11 10 09 08

## Welcome to

# HUMAN COMMUNICATION:

## THE BASIC COURSE

### Eleventh Edition

It is indeed a pleasure to write a preface to this eleventh edition. It's an honor really to have the opportunity to teach so many students about this amazing and fascinating subject of human communication. With this edition, I hope to continue serving that important function.

Here I'd like to introduce (1) the general nature of the text, (2) the book's major features, (3) the major changes in this edition, and (4) the supplements and ancillaries that are available with this text.

## The Book (In Brief)

*Human Communication: The Basic Course* is designed for the introductory college course that covers the major areas and skills of the broad field of human communication. It offers comprehensive coverage of the fundamentals of human communication.

- Part One (Foundations of Human Communication) covers the fundamental concepts and principles of human communication, the self and perception, listening, and verbal and nonverbal messages (Units 1–6).
- Part Two (Interpersonal, Small Group, and Organizational Communication) covers interpersonal interaction and relationships, small group membership and leadership, conflict, and organizational communication (Units 7–13).
- Part Three (Public Speaking) covers the preparation and presentation of public speeches, including informative, persuasive, and special occasion speeches (Units 14–19).

Because some courses cover interviewing but others do not, the interviewing material formerly included in this textbook is now a separate book, *The Interviewing Guidebook*.

The text covers classic approaches and new developments; it covers research and theory but gives coordinate attention to communication skills. This book is addressed to students who have little or no prior background in communication. If this will be your only communication course, *Human Communication* will provide you with a thorough foundation in the theory, research, and skills of this essential liberal art. For those of you who will take additional and advanced courses or who are beginning a major in communication, it will provide the essential foundation for more advanced and more specialized study.

## Major Features of *Human Communication*

The eleventh edition builds on the successful features of previous editions but also incorporates much that is new. Consequently, I'd like to explain here the major features of the text; in the next section I'll explain what's new.

### Balance of Theory/Research and Skills

The eleventh edition continues the pattern of the previous edition in giving equal emphasis to research and theory, on the one hand, and practical communication skills, on the other. Supplementing

ix

the discussions of theory and research throughout the text, **Understanding Theory and Research** boxes focus on just a small sampling of the many theories and research findings in communication. These boxes explain how we know what we know about communication, describe how researchers go about expanding our knowledge of communication in all its forms, and introduce a variety of interesting theories and research findings.

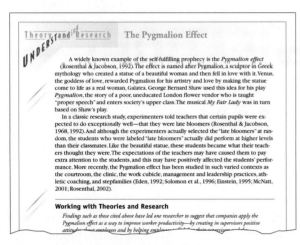

In a similar way, communication skills are not only integrated throughout the text but also emphasized in special **Building Communication Skills** boxes throughout the text. Each of these skills boxes contain an exercise that offers you the opportunity to practice important communication skills and a summary statement of the essential skill derived from the experience.

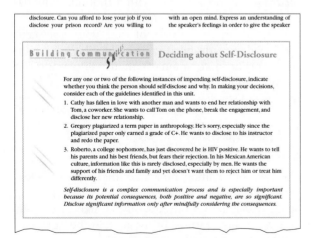

A third and related feature, introduced in the previous edition, **Ask the Researcher**, is designed to combine the text's two major emphases: theory/research and skills. In Ask the Researcher boxes, nationally and internationally known theorists and researchers respond to questions typical of students' queries about practical aspects of human communication. You'll find the experts' responses—19 in all (one per unit)—most interesting.

## Expanded Coverage of Public Speaking

The book devotes six full units to public speaking. The first three of these units cover the 10 essential steps for preparing and presenting a public speech.

- Unit 14, Public Speaking Topics, Audiences, and Research, introduces the study of public speaking, shows you how to manage your fear, and explains the first three steps for speech preparation: selecting the topic and purpose; analyzing the audience; and researching the topic.

- Unit 15, Supporting and Organizing Your Speech, covers the next four steps: formulating the thesis and main points; supporting the main points; organizing the speech; and constructing the conclusion, introduction, and transitions.

- Unit 16, Style and Presentation in Public Speaking, covers the remaining three steps: wording the speech; rehearsing the speech; and presenting the speech.

The next three units (Units 17, The Informative Speech; Unit 18, The Persuasive Speech; and Unit 19, The Special Occasion Speech) cover informative, persuasive, and special occasion speeches in detail—the types of speeches and the strategies for informing, persuading, and performing a variety of other public speaking functions such as presenting an award or giving a eulogy or a toast.

Introduced in the previous edition and expanded here are **Public Speaking Sample Assistant** boxes that present sample speeches and outlines, often with suggestions for critical analysis. These PSSAs feature excellent speeches and outlines that illustrate what you'll want to do in your own public speeches. In addition, two purposely poorly written speeches are included to illustrate what you'll want to avoid. The aims of this feature are (1) to provide specific examples of what you should and what you shouldn't do and (2) to enable you to see clearly the steps involved in preparing and presenting a public speech.

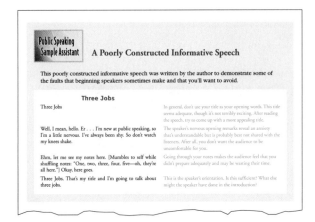

**Public Speaking Sample Assistant**

**A Poorly Constructed Informative Speech**

This poorly constructed informative speech was written by the author to demonstrate some of the faults that beginning speakers sometimes make and that you'll want to avoid.

**Three Jobs**

Three Jobs

Well, I mean, hello. Er . . . I'm new at public speaking, so I'm a little nervous. I've always been shy. So don't watch my knees shake.

Ehm, let me see my notes here. [Mumbles to self while shuffling notes: "One, two, three, four, five—oh, they're all here."] Okay, here goes.

Three Jobs. That's my title and I'm going to talk about three jobs.

In general, don't use your title as your opening words. This title seems adequate, though it's not terribly exciting. After reading the speech, try to come up with a more appealing title.

The speaker's nervous opening remarks reveal an anxiety that's understandable but is probably best not shared with the listeners. After all, you don't want the audience to be uncomfortable for you.

Going through your notes makes the audience feel that you didn't prepare adequately and may be wasting their time.

This is the speaker's orientation. Is this sufficient? What else might the speaker have done in the introduction?

## Emphasis on Cultural Issues

Like the previous editions, this edition reflects the crucial role of culture and intercultural differences in all forms of human interaction. There are few communications that are not influenced by culture in some way. Thus, a cultural consciousness is essential in any communication text. In this eleventh edition this cultural consciousness and coverage takes several forms.

An entire unit (Unit 2, Culture and Communication) explains the nature of culture, some of the ways in which cultures differ from one another and the influences these differences have on communication, and some of the ways you can improve your own intercultural communication.

Cultural issues also are integrated throughout the text. Here are major examples:

- Unit 1 establishes the central role of the cultural context in all forms of communication and also considers the role of culture and gender differences in the principles of communication.
- Unit 2 focuses entirely on culture, as already noted.
- Unit 3 considers the roles of cultural scripts and of culture in implicit personality theory and in uncertainty, as well as the role of culture in self-concept and its influence in self-disclosure.
- Unit 4 considers cultural and gender differences in listening.
- Unit 5 looks at cultural and gender rules in verbal messages (e.g., "rules" about directness and politeness); at sexist, heterosexist, and racist language; and at the cultural identifiers people prefer.
- Unit 6 looks at cultural influences on nonverbal communication channels such as facial expression, color, touch, silence, and time.
- Unit 7 examines cultural influences on conversational rules, cultural sensitivity as a general conversational skill, and cultural differences in turn taking and in the qualities of conversational effectiveness.
- Unit 8 looks at cultural influences on the stages of interpersonal relationships and on relationship rules and the cultural bias in relationship research.
- Unit 9 considers the roles of culture and gender in friendship, love, and family relationships.
- Unit 10 examines the small group as a culture, looks at the role of norms in small group communication, and examines the distinctions between high- and low-power-distance groups.
- Unit 11 looks at small group membership and leadership in cultural perspective.
- Unit 12 discusses the influence of cultural and gender differences on interpersonal and small group conflict and conflict resolution strategies, as well as the importance of face-saving in different cultures.
- Unit 13 discusses the nature of culture in the organization.
- Unit 14 covers cultural sensitivity and speech topics, the roles of culture and gender in audience analysis, and secular and sacred cultures.
- Unit 15 discusses cultural considerations in speech organization (high- and low-context cultures) and cultural sensitivity in presentation aids.
- Unit 16 covers the role of culture in emotional display.
- Unit 17 discusses the cultural implications of the "knowledge gap" hypothesis.
- Unit 18 explains some of the cultural differences in the ways people use and respond to persuasive strategies.
- Unit 19 covers the cultural context of special occasion speeches and the cultural distinction between individualist and collectivist cultures.

People with disabilities also may be viewed from a cultural perspective. Four special tables offer suggestions for improving communication between people with and without disabilities. These tables provide tips for communication between people with and without visual problems (Unit 1), between people with and without mobility problems, for example, people with cerebral palsy or who use wheelchairs (Unit 2), between people who have hearing difficulties and those who don't (Unit 4), and between people with and without speech or language disorders (Unit 7).

## Coverage of Media Literacy

This edition of *Human Communication* focuses its discussion of mass communication on media literacy, a topic that is (as it should be) a crucial part of the study of human communication. Each unit contains a **Media Watch** box that explains some important aspect of mass media and suggests ways to increase your own media literacy—defined as the ability to understand, analyze, evaluate, and produce mass communication messages.

**MEDIA WATCH**
**OUTING**

In self-disclosure, as already noted, you reveal information about yourself to others. Although at times you may be forced to disclose, normally you control what you reveal. There is, however, another type of disclosure—the disclosure that occurs when someone else takes information from your hidden self and makes it public. Although this third-party disclosure can concern any aspect of your hidden self, the media have made a special case out of revealing information about affectional orientation, or "outing."

Outing as a media process began in a relatively obscure gay magazine, *Outweek. Outweek's* article on "The Secret Gay Life of Malcolm Forbes" made public the homosexuality of one of the world's richest men; it "outed" him (Gross, 1991; Johansson & Percy, 1994). On March 3, 1995, the *Wall Street Journal* ran a front-page story on Jann Wenner, the multimillionaire owner and publisher of *Rolling Stone, Us, Men's Journal,* and *Family Life.* The story was basically financial and focused on the possible effects Wenner's marital breakup would have on his media empire. Somewhat casually noted in the article—without Wenner's per-

mission and against his wishes (Rotello, 1995)—was the fact that the new person in Wenner's life was a man. This article, although not the first to discuss Wenner's gay relationship, has been singled out because of the prestige of the *Wall Street Journal* and because of the many issues this type of forced disclosure raises.

Outing raises a privacy issue that is not easy to resolve. If Wenner had been dating a woman, the media would have mentioned it, but few would have raised the privacy issue—because Wenner is a public figure, and divorce was a relevant issue that would likely affect his financial empire. However, if the media reported only on heterosexual extramarital relationships, it would imply that homosexual relationships are illegitimate and not to be spoken of openly.

*Increasing Media Literacy*

*How do you feel about outing? What guidelines should the media follow in dealing with individuals that individuals wish to keep private? At what point should the media be allowed to consider a person a public figure who has no right to privacy?*

**REFLECTIONS ON ETHICS**

**Information Ethics**

One approach to ethics revolves around the notion of choice and argues that you have the right to information relevant to the choices you make. In this view, communication is ethical when it facilitates your freedom of choice by presenting you with accurate information. Ethical communication provides you with the kind of information that will help you make your own choices. Unethical communications interfere with your freedom of choice by preventing you from securing information that will help you make those choices. Communications are also unethical when they give you false or misleading information that will lead you to make choices you would not make if you had accurate and truthful information.

In this ethical system, you have the right to information about yourself that others possess and that influences the choices you will make. Thus, for example,

you have the right to face your accusers, to know the witnesses who will be called to testify against you, to see your credit ratings, and to know what Social Security benefits you will receive. On the other hand, you do not have the right to information that is none of your business, such as information about whether your neighbors are happy or argue a lot or receive food stamps.

**Ethical Choice Point**

*Your best friend's husband is currently having an extramarital affair with a 17-year-old girl. Your friend, suspecting this, asks if you know anything about it. Would it be ethical for you to lie and say you know nothing, or are you obligated to tell your friend what you know? Are you obligated to tell the police? What would you do?*

used to refer to the conscious revealing of information, as in the statements "I'm afraid to compete; I guess I'm afraid I'll lose," or "I love you."

2. In self-disclosure you reveal "information" about yourself; it is "information" in that it involves something that the receiver did not know about you. This information may vary from the relatively commonplace ("I'm really scared about

**Who You Are**

Highly sociable and extroverted people self-disclose more than those who are less sociable and more introverted. People who are comfortable communicating also self-disclose more than those who are apprehensive about talking in general. And competent people engage in self-disclosure more than less-

## Coverage of Computer-Mediated Communication

Numerous sections throughout the text cover computer-mediated communication. Examples include the ways in which online communication and face-to-face communication are similar and different; the role of technology in easing intercultural communication; the ease of misperception in Internet interactions; self-disclosure on the Internet; politeness (netiquette) on the Net; e-mail as a form of conversation; the advantages and disadvantages of online relationships; how online and face-to-face relationships differ; listservs and chat groups as small groups; leadership on the Internet; online conflicts; how to conduct and evaluate research using e-mail, newsgroups, and the Web; and computer-assisted presentations in public speaking.

## Coverage of Ethical Issues

Ethics is central to all forms of communication and because of this a **Reflections on Ethics** box appears in each of the 19 units. These discussions raise ethical principles and pose ethical dilemmas. The purpose of this feature is to connect ethical issues with the various topics of human communication and to encourage you to think about your own ethical system. Among the ethical issues considered are censoring messages and interactions; making ethical choices; listening, speaking, and criticizing ethically; the ethics of lying, gossip, and emotional appeals; ethics on the job; and the leader's ethical responsibility.

## Interactive Pedagogy

Of course, a printed textbook cannot literally be interactive. Yet *Human Communication*, together with the accompanying MyCommunicationLab (www.mycommunicationlab.com) comes amazingly close. This edition continues to emphasize new and useful pedagogical aids, especially those that are interactive, to help you better understand the theory and

research and to enable you to effectively build and polish your communication skills.

**Boxed Interactives.** The Reflections on Ethics discussions, the Media Watch boxes, and the Understanding Theory and Research boxes throughout the text contain interactive experiences designed to encourage you to interact with the concepts and to relate these insights to your own everyday communication.

**Self-Tests.** Interactive self-tests titled Test Yourself appear throughout the text and are designed to help personalize the material. Each self-test ends with a two-part discussion: How did you do? (which contains the scoring instructions and often general norms) and What will you do? (which asks about the appropriate course of action that you might take, given the insight the test provided).

**TEST YOURSELF**

**How Accurate Are You at People Perception?**

Respond to each of the following statements with T for true if the statement is usually or generally accurate in describing your behavior, or with F for false if the statement is usually or generally inaccurate in describing your behavior.

_____ 1. When I know some things about another person, I can pretty easily fill in what I don't know.

_____ 2. I make predictions about people's behaviors that generally prove to be true.

_____ 3. I base most of my impressions of people on the first few minutes of our meeting.

_____ 4. I generally attribute people's attitudes and

**Critical Thinking Questions.** These questions, appearing at the end of each unit, focus on the central concepts and skills of the unit. You can use these questions to expand on, evaluate, and apply the concepts, theories, and research findings discussed in the text and to stimulate lively classroom discussion.

**Key Terms and Glossaries.** A list of key terms at the end of each unit will help you review the major terms discussed in the unit. These terms are now accompanied by references to the pages of the text on which they're introduced and defined. In addition, two glossaries appear at the back of the book: (1) a traditional glossary of communication concepts, which provides brief definitions of the significant concepts in the study of human communication, and (2) a glossary of communication skills.

**Unit Openers.** The opening paragraph of each unit identifies the major topics covered in the unit and the learning goals (both theory and skills) you should be able to achieve.

**Summary Statements.** At the end of each unit, a summary reviews the essential concepts and principles covered in the unit.

**Photo Captions.** All photo captions ask for your active involvement, presenting a communication situation in which you need to act.

## What's New

Although the basic orientation and point of view of the previous edition remain in this edition, there is much that is new.

### New Unit on Organizational Communication

Unit 13, Communication in the Workplace: Organizational Communication, introduces the expanding area of organizational communication. This unit replaces the previous edition's Communication@Work boxes, and adds a great deal more to the discussion of communication in the workplace.

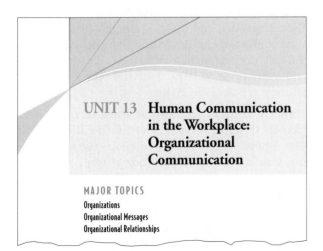

**UNIT 13  Human Communication in the Workplace: Organizational Communication**

MAJOR TOPICS
Organizations
Organizational Messages
Organizational Relationships

### New Unit on Special Occasion Speaking

Unit 19, The Special Occasion Speech, provides guidance on a wide variety of special occasion speeches

including the speech of presentation or acceptance, the eulogy, the commencement address, the farewell speech, the speech to secure goodwill, and the toast.

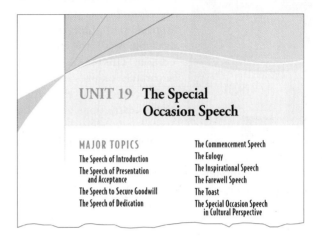

**UNIT 19  The Special Occasion Speech**

MAJOR TOPICS
The Speech of Introduction
The Speech of Presentation and Acceptance
The Speech to Secure Goodwill
The Speech of Dedication

The Commencement Speech
The Eulogy
The Inspirational Speech
The Farewell Speech
The Toast
The Special Occasion Speech in Cultural Perspective

## New Boxed Features and Text Discussions

Many of the boxed items are new, and many have been restructured and rewritten; the primary objectives here were to update the information and make it more practical.

Among the new **Understanding Theory and Research** boxes are discussions of Online Relationship Theories (Unit 8), Approaches to Organizations and Peter and Dilbert (both in Unit 13), and A Blurring of Purposes and Humor (both in Unit 19). In addition, Intimacy and Risk and Love Styles and Personality have been recast as theory and research boxes.

A variety of new **Building Communication Skill** boxes appear here; for example, Distinguishing Content from Relationship Messages and Resolving Ambiguity (both in Unit 1), Exploring Cultural Attitudes (Unit 2), Till This Do Us Part and Using Affinity Seeking Strategies (both in Unit 9), Combating Groupthink (Unit 11), Workplace Analysis (Unit 13), and exercises on developing the speech of introduction and the speech of presentation/acceptance (Unit 19).

New **Media Watch** boxes include: What Is Media Literacy? (Unit 1), Principles of Media Literacy Listening (Unit 4), Interpersonal Relationships and the Media (Unit 9), and Product Placement (Unit 15). Advertising and Public Relations (formerly separate boxes) are now combined and appear with the new unit on Organizational Communication.

Two new **Reflections on Ethics** cases are those on organizational ethics and telling the truth.

Among the new **self-tests** are those on cultural orientation (Unit 2), self-esteem (Unit 3), relationship violence (Unit 9), group membership (Unit 11), approaches to organizational management (Unit 13), and individualism versus collectivism (Unit 19).

## Interviewing

A new 112-page book on interviewing, *The Interviewing Guidebook*, replaces the 40-page pamphlet that was available with the previous edition. This book is sold separately or packaged with new copies of this text. Some restrictions apply. The expanded discussion of informative and employment interviewing now contains worksheets for preparing for these interviews along with sample résumés and letters to accompany the résumé.

## Structural Changes

Units 1 (preliminaries) and 2 (principles) of the previous edition have been combined into one unit (Unit 1, Preliminaries to Human Communication). Similarly, Units 4 (perception) and 6 (the self) have been combined into one unit (Unit 3, The Self and Perception). The purpose here was to reduce redundancy and to allow for greater expansion of the units on interpersonal relationships, organizational communication, and public speaking.

## Photo Program

A new and enlarged photo program is used in this edition. A total of 40 additional photos have been added to this edition (an increase from 55 to 95). Also, each of the interior photos is now accompanied by a communication dilemma that asks, "What would you say?" These photos are designed to relate the content of the chapter to a wide variety of specific communication situations.

## Some Unit-by-Unit Improvements

### Part One: Foundations of Human Communication

**Unit 1: Preliminaries to Human Communication.** Additional information on computer-mediated communication, including an extensive table comparing face-to-face and computer-mediated communication. The benefits of human communication study are spelled out in some detail in the opening of the unit. In fact, throughout the text an effort was made to stress the benefits, the payoffs, of all forms of communication.

**Unit 2: Culture and Communication.** A new 15-item self-test on cultural orientation now introduces the five major dimensions of culture.

**Unit 3: The Self and Perception.** An expansion of the self-esteem discussion including a new self-test.

**Unit 4: Listening.** New discussions of barriers to listening and fallacies of language.

**Unit 5: Verbal Messages.** Distinctions between individual and institutional racism, heterosexism, ageism, and sexism are introduced here.

**Unit 6: Nonverbal Messages.** A revised and expanded section on culture and nonverbal communication.

### Part Two: Interpersonal, Small Group, and Organizational Communication

**Unit 7: Interpersonal Communication: Conversation.** Dialogic and monologic communication is now included with the discussion of conversational skills. Expanded discussions of feedback and feedforward (formerly discussed in Unit 1) are presented as part of the conversation process.

**Units 8 and 9: Interpersonal Relationship Stages and Theories; Friends, Lovers, and Families.** The former Unit 10 on interpersonal relationships has been divided into two units that include expanded discussions of relationships generally; a new section, The Dark Side of Interpersonal Relationships; and a new self-test on violence in relationships.

**Units 10 and 11: Small Group Communication; Members and Leaders.** These units on small group communication contain a new self-test on group membership—to parallel the self-test on leadership—and an explanation of the influence of high- and low-context cultures on small group interaction.

**Unit 12: Interpersonal and Small Group Conflict.** Expanded and updated discussion of the cultural context of conflict. In addition, the widely used self-test on argumentativeness has been included and an abbreviated 10-item self-test on verbal aggressiveness replaces the 20-item test.

**Unit 13: Human Communication in the Workplace: Organizational Communication.** This unit is new to this edition and makes use of some of the Communication@Work boxes from the previous edition but expands on these considerably. Among the topics covered are the importance, nature, and characteristics of organizations; organizational messages, both formal and informal; and organizational relationships, romance, mentoring, and networking.

The new boxed items include discussions of approaches to organizations and the "theories" of Peter and Dilbert.

## Part Three: Public Speaking

**Unit 14: Public Speaking Topics, Audiences, and Research.** This chapter has been totally revised to include a discussion of the benefits of public speaking, an expanded discussion of topics and purposes, and an updated presentation of research. A new and extensive table on the oral citation should answer most questions about how to cite a source orally.

**Unit 15: Supporting and Organizing Your Speech.** A new speech replaces the PowerPoint speech on culture shock, which has been moved to the MyCommunicationLab website (www .mycommunicationlab.com). Analogies and definitions as supporting material have been added here. New speech excerpts appear throughout.

**Unit 16: Style and Presentation in Public Speaking.** This unit now includes an extended discussion on the nature of and strategies for speech criticism in the classroom.

**Unit 17: The Informative Speech.** A new excellent informative speech on social entrepreneurship is included here with annotations to guide the student through the public speaking process.

**Unit 18: The Persuasive Speech.** A new excellent persuasive speech on false confessions is included here with annotations.

**Unit 19: The Special Occasion Speech.** This new unit includes a variety of special occasion speeches.

# Ancillaries/Supplementary Materials

## Supplements for the Instructor

### Print Resources

- **Instructor's Manual and Test Bank,** prepared by Karen Anderson, University of North Texas, and Richard Pineda, University of Texas, El Paso. This text-specific ancillary includes a sample syllabus, chapter-by-chapter outlines, summaries, objectives, discussion questions, and classroom activities. The test bank contains multiple-choice, true/false, fill in the blank, matching, short answer and essay questions for each chapter.

- **A&B Public Speaking Transparency Package, version II,** contains one hundred full-color transparencies created with PowerPoint software.

- **The Blockbuster Approach: Teaching Interpersonal Communication with Video, 3/e,** by Thomas Jewell, Bergen Community College. This guide provides lists and descriptions of commercial videos that can be used in the classroom to illustrate interpersonal concepts and complex interpersonal relationships.

- **Great Ideas for Teaching Speech (GIFTS), 3/e,** by Raymond Zeuschner, California Polytechnic State University, San Luis Obispo. This instructional booklet provides descriptions of and guidelines for assignments successfully used by experienced public speaking instructors in their classrooms.

- **A Guide for New Teachers of Introduction to Communication, 2/e,** by Susanna G. Porter, Kennesaw State University. This instructor's guide is designed to help new teachers effectively teach the introductory communication course. Topics such as choosing a text, structuring your course, effectively using group work, dealing with classroom challenges, and giving feedback are included.

### Electronic Resources

- **MyCommunicationLab** (www.mycommunicationlab.com). Where students learn to communicate with confidence! As an interactive and instructive online solution designed to be used as a supplement to a traditional lecture course or completely administered as an online course, MyCommunicationLab combines multimedia, video, communication activities, research support, tests, and quizzes to make teaching and learning more relevant and enjoyable. (Access code required.)

- **Computerized Test Bank.** The printed test questions are also available electronically though our computerized testing system, TestGen EQ. The user-friendly interface enables instructors to view, edit, and add questions; transfer questions to tests; and print tests in a variety of fonts. Search and sort features allow instructors to locate questions quickly and arrange them in a preferred order.

- **PowerPoint Presentation Package,** prepared by Aleshia Panbamrung, Indiana Purdue University, Fort Wayne. This text-specific package consists of a collection of lecture outlines and graphic images keyed to every chapter in the text. Available on the Web at www.ablongman.com/irc (access code required).

- **Allyn & Bacon Communication Digital Media Archive, version 3.0,** available on CD-ROM, offers more than 200 still images, video excerpts, and PowerPoint slides that can be used to enliven classroom presentations.

- **VideoWorkshop for Introduction to Communication, version 2.0** (www.ablongman.com/ videoworkshop), by Kathryn Dindia, University of

Wisconsin. *VideoWorkshop for Introduction to Communication* is a new way to bring video into your course for maximized learning. This total teaching and learning system includes quality video footage on an easy-to-use CD-ROM, plus a *Student Learning Guide* and an *Instructor's Teaching Guide*.

- **Lecture Questions for Clickers: Introduction to Communication,** by Keri Moe, El Paso Community College. An assortment of questions and activities covering culture, listening, interviewing, public speaking, interpersonal conflict, and more are presented in PowerPoint and can be used along with the Personal Response System to get students more involved in the material. Available on the Web at www.ablongman.com/irc (access code required).

- **PowerPoint Presentation for Public Speaking.** This course-specific PowerPoint outline includes 125 slides and a brief User's Guide. Available on the Web at www.ablongman.com/irc (access code required).

### Video Materials

- **A&B Communication Video Libraries.** Adopters can choose appropriate video material from Allyn & Bacon's video libraries for Public Speaking, Interpersonal Communication, and Small Group Communication. Please contact your Pearson representative for a list of available videos. Some restrictions apply.

## Supplements for Students

### Print Resources

- **Brainstorms,** by Joseph A. DeVito. Students find 19 practical, easy-to-use creative thinking techniques along with insights into the creative thinking process.

- **The Interviewing Guidebook,** by Joseph A. DeVito. See page xiv for a detailed description.

- **ResearchNaviagtor.com Guide: Speech Communication.** This updated booklet by Steven L. Epstein of Suffolk County Community College includes tips, resources, and URLs to aid students conducting research on Pearson Education's research website, www.researchnavigator.com. The guide contains a student access code for the Research Navigator database, offering students unlimited access to a collection of more than 25,000 discipline-specific articles from top-tier academic publications and peer-reviewed journals, as well

as the *New York Times* and popular news publications. The guide is available packaged with new copies of the text.

- **Study Card for Introduction to Communication.** Course information is distilled down to the basics, helping students quickly master the fundamentals, review a subject for understanding, or prepare for an exam. Because they are laminated for durability, students can keep these study cards for years to come and pull them out whenever needed for a quick review.

- **Speech Preparation Workbook,** by Jennifer Dreyer and Gregory H. Patton, San Diego State University. This workbook takes students through the stages of speech creation—from audience analysis to writing the speech—and includes guidelines, tips, and easy-to-complete pages.

- **Preparing Visual Aids for Presentations, 4/e,** by Dan Cavanaugh. This brief booklet provides a host of ideas for using today's multimedia tools to improve presentations, including suggestions for how to plan a presentation, guidelines for designing visual aids and storyboarding, and a walkthrough that shows how to prepare a visual display using PowerPoint.

- **Public Speaking in the Multicultural Environment, 2/e,** by Devorah Lieberman, Portland State University. This two-chapter essay focuses on speaking and listening to a culturally diverse audience and emphasizes preparation, delivery, and how speeches are perceived.

- **Multicultural Activities Workbook,** by Marlene C. Cohen and Susan L. Richardson, both of Prince George's Community College. This workbook is filled with hands-on activities with a multicultural focus, such as checklists, surveys, and writing assignments.

- **The Speech Outline: Outlining to Plan, Organize, and Deliver a Speech: Activities and Exercises,** by Reeze L. Hanson and Sharon Condon, of Haskell Indian Nations University. This brief workbook includes activities, exercises, and answers to help students develop and master the critical skill of outlining.

### Electronic Resources

*MyCommunicationLab* (www.mycommunicationlab.com). See page xv for a detailed description.

- **Introduction to Communication Study Site,** accessible at www.abintrocommunication.com. This website features communication study materials for students, including flashcards and a complete set of practice tests for interpersonal communication, group communication, and public speaking. Students also will find Web links to valuable sites for further exploration of major topics.

- ■ **VideoLab CD-ROM.** This interactive study tool for students can be used independently or in class. It provides digital video of student speeches. A series of drills to help students analyze content and delivery follows each speech.

- ■ *Speech Writer's Workshop CD-ROM, version 2.0.* This exciting public speaking software includes a *Speech Handbook* with tips for researching and preparing speeches; a *Speech Workshop*, which guides students step-by-step through the speech-writing process; a *Topics Dictionary*, which gives students hundreds of ideas for speeches; and the *Documentor* citation database, which helps students format bibliographic entries in either MLA or APA style.

- ■ *VideoWorkshop for Introduction to Communication, version 2.0* (www.ablongman.com/videoworkshop). See pages xv–xvi for complete details.

## Acknowledgments

It's a pleasure to thank three groups of people who contributed greatly to this new edition.

First, I want to thank my colleagues for taking time from their busy schedules and responding to the Ask the Researcher questions. Thank you for making this undertaking enjoyable for me—your e-mails were always interesting and stimulating—

and for helping to illustrate the practical skills that can be derived from theory and research. I thank you for your contributions to communication and for your willingness to contribute to this feature. Thank you (in order of appearance): Mark Hickson III, Melbourne S. Cummings, Ann Bainbridge Frymier, Judi Brownell, Richard A. Fiordo, Don W. Stacks, Gust A. Yep, Walid A. Afifi, Sandra Metts, Carole A. Barbato, Katherine Hawkins, Charles J. Wigley III, Pam Shockley-Zalabak, Virginia P. Richmond, Bruce E. Gronbeck, Joseph Chesebro, Timothy P. Mottet, Jon F. Nussbaum, Melissa BeKeLja Wanzer.

I also want to thank the reviewers who shared insights and classroom experiences with me and have commented on the previous editions. Your suggestions have helped me improve this text significantly. Thank you:

Karen Anderson, University of North Texas; Kimberly Berry, Ozarks Technical Community College; Judy Cannady, Ozarka College; Cynthia Graham, University of Wisconsin, Superior; Gwen A. Hullman, University of Nevada; Aleshia Panbamrung, Indiana University–Purdue University, Fort Wayne; Rachel C. Prioleau, University of South Carolina, Spartanburg; Charles V. Roberts, East Tennessee State University; Jill Tyler, University of South Dakota; and Alan Zaremba, Northeastern University.

I'm indebted to the many people at Allyn & Bacon who worked to turn my manuscript into the book you now hold. Thank you: Karon Bowers, editor; Jessica Cabana, editorial assistant; Kristen Desmond LeFevre, developmental editor; Suzan Czajkowski, marketing manager; Poyee Oster, photo researcher; Jay Howland, copy editor; and Tom Conville, project manager. All contributed significantly to the finished book.

**Joseph A. DeVito**

jadevito@earthlink.net
http://tcbdevito.blogspot.com

# Part 1

## Foundations of Human Communication

## UNIT 1    Preliminaries to Human Communication

### MAJOR TOPICS

The Benefits, Forms, and Purposes of Human Communication
The Elements of Human Communication
The Principles of Human Communication

### Special Features

Of all the knowledge and skills you have, those concerning communication will prove the most useful. Your ability to communicate will always influence and play a crucial part in how effectively you live your personal and professional lives. It's vital to your success to learn how communication works and to master its most essential skills.

**In this unit you'll learn about:**
- the benefits, forms, and purposes of human communication.
- the major elements in the human communication process.
- the essential principles that explain how communication works.

**You'll learn to:**
- communicate with a clear understanding of the essential elements and how they relate to one another.
- use the essential principles of human communication to increase your own effectiveness in interpersonal, small group, and public speaking.

Let's begin this unit with a clear explanation of what you'll get out of this text and course and what forms of communication you'll study.

## THE BENEFITS, FORMS, AND PURPOSES OF HUMAN COMMUNICATION

You'll benefit greatly from studying the forms of communication covered in this course. So let's begin our exploration with an introduction of these benefits. Next we'll preview the forms of human communication you'll cover and look at some of the purposes served when you communicate.

### The Benefits of Human Communication

A perfectly legitimate question to ask before beginning your study of any subject is "why?" You may ask yourself, "Why should I learn about human communication? What will it do for me? What will I be able to do after taking this course that I wasn't able to do before? In short, how will I benefit from the study of human communication presented in this course and in this text?"

Actually, you'll benefit in lots of ways. Your knowledge of human communication and your mastery of many of its skills will enable you to better:

■ **Present yourself as a confident, likable, approachable, and credible person.** Your effectiveness in just about any endeavor depends heavily on your *self-presentation*—your ability to present yourself in a positive light, through your verbal and nonverbal messages. Incidentally, it is also largely through your skills of self-presentation (or lack of them) that you display negative qualities as well.

■ **Build friendships, enter into love relationships, work with colleagues, and interact with family members.** These are the *interpersonal and relationship skills* for initiating, maintaining, repairing, and sometimes dissolving relationships of all kinds. And unless you're going to be living totally alone, these are skills you'll use every day, in every encounter. These are the skills that businesses of all kinds have on their lists of most important competencies for organizational success; they are an essential part of business competence (Bassellier & Benbasat, 2004).

■ **Interview to gain information, to successfully present yourself to get the job you want, and to participate effectively in a wide variety of other interview types.** *Interviewing skills* will help get you the job you want and ultimately the career you're preparing for in college.

■ **Participate effectively in relationship and task groups—informative, problem-solving, and brainstorming groups, at home or at work.** These *group interaction and leadership skills* will help you both as a group member and as a leader. In a workplace world that operates largely on group interaction, these skills are increasingly essential if you are to be an effective organizational member and will help you rise in the organization. After all, people in power will often come to know you best through your group (that is, communication) performance.

■ **Communicate information to and influence the attitudes and behaviors of small and large audiences.** These *presentation* or *public speaking skills* will enable you to manage your fear and make it work for you rather than against you.

## COMMUNICATION CHOICE POINTS

Throughout this text you'll find marginal items, labeled What Do You Say? that identify a communication choice point, a point at which you need to make a decision and say something (or, of course, decide to remain silent). These What do you say? items are designed to encourage you to apply the skills discussed in the text to a wide variety of communication situations.

Effective public speaking is essential in leadership positions of all kinds; whether in politics, business, education, or medicine, leaders speak publicly.

- **Use the media critically and with awareness of the techniques media use to influence you.** *Media literacy skills* will make you a more informed and empowered user of the many media that you encounter on a daily basis. Without such skills, you risk being used by the media for their ends alone. Much as a lack of media literacy will disempower you, competence in media literacy—the aim of the discussions of media literacy throughout this text—will empower you and put you in charge. The first of these Media Watch boxes appears on page 7 and explains in more detail what media literacy is.

You'll learn these skills and reap the benefits as you learn the various areas or forms of communication, to which we now turn.

## The Forms of Human Communication

The forms of human communication vary from one-person communication (in which you talk to yourself) to communication with millions (as in public speaking, mass communication, and computer-mediated communication). Here we look briefly at each of these forms.

## Intrapersonal Communication

**Intrapersonal communication** is communication you have with yourself. Through intrapersonal communication you talk with, learn about, and judge yourself. You persuade yourself of this or that, reason about possible decisions to make, and rehearse messages that you plan to send to others. In intrapersonal communication you might, for example, wonder how you did in an interview and what you could have done differently. You might conclude you did a pretty good job but that you need to be more assertive when discussing salary. Increasing your self-awareness, your mindfulness, and your ability to think critically about all types of messages will aid you greatly in improving your own intrapersonal communication. And this information—on the self, perception, listening, and verbal and nonverbal messages—will provide a foundation for learning about the various forms of human communication.

## [Interpersonal Communication]

**Interpersonal communication** is communication between two persons or among a small group of persons. Most often, the communication emphasized in the study of interpersonal communication is communication of a continuing personal (rather than temporary and impersonal) nature; it's communication between or among intimates or those involved in close relationships—friends, romantic partners, family, and coworkers, for example. These relationships are interdependent, meaning that the actions of one person have some impact on the other person; whatever one person does influences the other person. Sometimes interpersonal communication is pleasant, but sometimes it erupts into conflict, making each person's communication especially significant for the other.

Interpersonal communication can take place face-to-face as well as through electronic channels (as in e-mail, instant messaging, or chat rooms, for example) or even via traditional letter-writing. Whether you e-mail your friends or family about your plans for the weekend, ask someone in class for a date, or confront a colleague's racist remarks at the water cooler, you're communicating interpersonally.

## Interviewing

**Interviewing** is communication that proceeds by question and answer. Through interviewing you learn about others and what they know; you counsel or get counseling from others; or you get or don't get the job you want. Today much interviewing (especially initial interviews) takes place through e-mail and (video) phone conferencing.

## Small Group Communication

**Small group communication** is communication among members of groups of about 5 to 10 people. Small group communication serves both *relationship needs* such as those for companionship, affection, or support and *task needs* such as balancing the family budget, electing a new chairperson, or designing a new ad campaign. Through small group communication you interact with others, solve problems, develop new ideas, and share knowledge and experiences. You live your work and social life largely in groups, from school orientation meetings to executive board meetings, from informal social groups to formal meetings discussing issues of local or international concern. You also may live a good part of your life in online chat rooms, where you may interact with people from different cultures living thousands of miles away, and in social network chat (for example, MyFace, MySpace, Facebook, Xanga) where you learn about and chat with others.

## Organizational Communication

**Organizational communication** is communication that takes place within an organization among members of the organization. Conferencing with colleagues, working in teams, talking with a supervisor, or giving employees directions are just a few examples of organizational communication. The study of organizational communication offers you guidelines for improving your own formal and informal communication in an organizational setting.

## Public Speaking

**Public speaking**, also termed *public communication* or *presentational speaking*, is communication between a speaker and an audience. Audiences range in size from several people to hundreds, thousands, and even millions. Through public communication others inform and persuade you. And you, in turn, inform and persuade others—to act, to buy, or to think in a particular way.

Much as you can address large audiences face-to-face, you also can address such audiences electronically and through the mass media. Through newsgroups, blogs, or social networks, for example, you can post a "speech" for anyone to read and then read their reactions to your message. And with the help of the more traditional mass media of radio and television, you can address audiences in the hundreds of millions as they sit alone or in small groups scattered throughout the world.

## Computer-Mediated Communication

The term **computer-mediated communication** refers to communication between people that takes place through some computer connection. E-mail, chat room, newsgroup, instant messaging, website, and blog communication are all examples of computer-mediated communication, often abbreviated CMC. In large part, the principles of face-to-face and computer-mediated communication are similar; if you're effective in one mode, you're likely to be effective in others. The principles and skills we'll discuss will prove applicable to all forms of communication. Table 1.1 presents a summary of some of the ways in which computer-mediated communication differs from face-to-face communication. As you continue reading about these elements in this chapter, you may want to return to this table and add your own ideas to those presented here.

### Table 1.1 Face-to-Face and Computer-Mediated Communication

Throughout this text, face-to-face and computer-mediated communication are discussed, compared, and contrasted. Here is a brief summary of some communication concepts and some of the ways in which face-to-face and computer-mediated communication are similar and different.

| Human Communication Element | Face-to-Face Communication | Computer-Mediated Communication |
|---|---|---|
| Sender [presentation of self, impression management, speaking turn] | • Visual appearance communicates who you are; personal characteristics (sex, approximate age, race, etc.) are overt and open to visual inspection; receiver controls the order of what is attended to; disguise is difficult. | • You present the self you want others to see; personal characteristics are covert and are revealed when you want to reveal them; speaker controls the order of revelation; disguise or anonymity is easy. |
| | • You compete for the speaker's turn and time with the other person(s); you can be interrupted. | • It's always your turn; speaker time is unlimited; you can't be interrupted. |

| Human Communication Element | Face-to-Face Communication | Computer-Mediated Communication |
|---|---|---|
| Receiver [number, interests, third party, impression formation] | • One or a few who are in your visual field.<br>• Limited to those you have the opportunity to meet; often difficult to find people who have the same interests you do especially in isolated communities with little mobility.<br>• Your messages can be overheard by or repeated to third parties, but not verbatim and not with the same accuracy as online.<br>• Impressions are based on the verbal and nonverbal cues receiver perceives. | • One, a few, or as many as you find in a chat room, have on your e-mail list, or who read your bulletin board posts.<br>• Virtually unlimited; you can more easily and quickly find people who match your interests.<br>• Your messages can be retrieved by others or forwarded verbatim to a third party or to hundreds of third parties (with or without your knowledge).<br>• Impressions are based on text messages (usually) receiver reads. |
| Context [physical, temporal] | • Where you both are; together in essentially the same physical space.<br>• As it happens; you have little control over the context once you're in a communication situation.<br>• Communication is *synchronous*—messages are exchanged at the same time. | • Where you and receiver each want to be, separated in space.<br>• You can more easily choose the timing—when you want to respond.<br>• Communication may be synchronous, as in chat rooms and instant messaging, or *asynchronous*—messages are exchanged at different times, as in e-mail and bulletin board postings. |
| Channel | • Auditory plus visual plus tactile plus proxemic (related to distance)<br>• Two-way channel enabling immediate interactivity. | • Visual for text (though auditory and visual for graphics and video are available).<br>• Two-way channels, some enabling immediate and some delayed interactivity. |
| Messages [verbal, nonverbal, permanence] | • Spoken words along with gestures, eye contact, accent, paralinguistic (vocal but nonverbal) cues, space, touch, clothing, hair, and all the other nonverbal cues.<br>• Temporary unless recorded; speech signals fade rapidly.<br>• Rarely are abbreviations verbally expressed. | • Written words in purely text-based CMC, though that's changing.<br>• Messages are permanent unless erased.<br>• Limited nonverbal cues; some can be created with emoticons or words, and some (like smells and touch) cannot.<br>• Use lots of abbreviations. |
| Feedforward | • Conveyed nonverbally and verbally early in the interaction. | • In e-mail it's given in the headings and subject line, as well as in the opening sentences. |
| Ethics and Deception | • Presentation of false physical self is more difficult, though not impossible; presenting false psychological and social selves is easier.<br>• Nonverbal leakage cues often give you away when you're lying. | • Presentation of false physical self as well as false psychological and social selves is relatively easy.<br>• Can probably lie more easily. |

## Mass Communication

**Mass communication** is communication from one source to many receivers, who may be scattered throughout the world. Mass communication takes place via at least the following media outlets:

- *newspapers*
- *television*
- *radio*
- *film and video*
- *music*
- *the Internet, the Web, and blogs*

The coverage of mass communication in this book focuses on media literacy and aims to help you to become a wiser, more critical user of the media (see the first Media Watch box below).

As you can see if you glance through your college catalogue, each of these forms of communication is likely to be covered in separate and more detailed courses in public speaking, small group communication, interpersonal communication, mass communication, and so on. In this course and in this text, the essentials of these communication forms are introduced, giving you the knowledge and skills to become a more effective communicator, and at the same time the background to move on to more detailed study, whether in more in-depth courses or in your own reading. Table 1.2 on pages 8–9 gives you an overview of these varied forms of human communication.

Through these varied forms of communication, you'll accomplish a number of different purposes. Let's take a look at several of these purposes.

## The Purposes of Human Communication

The purposes of human communication may be conscious or unconscious, recognizable or unrecognizable. And although communication technologies are changing rapidly and drastically—we send e-mail, work at computer terminals, and telecommute, for example—the purposes of communication have remained essentially the same throughout the computer revolution and are likely to continue

### WHAT IS MEDIA LITERACY?

*[I]t is precisely because they [the mass media] are so familiar that we need to study them. Familiarity, for example, may blind us to the distinct kind of communication that takes place through the mass media, and especially to the processes by which they influence us.*

*—Kathleen Hall Jamieson and Karlyn Kohrs Campbell*

*Media literacy—as you'll discover in this first Media Watch box—covers a range of skills that are vital to dealing with the mass media. Because these skills are so important, Media Watch boxes are presented throughout the text, reminding you that the media are influencing you in ways you need to be aware of.*

*Media literacy* may be defined as your ability to understand, analyze, evaluate, and produce mass communication messages (television, film, music, radio, billboards, advertising, public relations, newspapers and magazines, books, websites and blogs, newsgroups and chat rooms).

Because the media influence you in numerous ways (only some of which you may be conscious of), it's crucial that you learn how this influence is exerted so that you, rather than the media, can determine what influences you and what doesn't. Looked at in this way, media literacy is a form of empowerment. It can help you to use the media more intelligently; to understand, analyze, and evaluate media messages more effectively; to influence the messages that the media send out; and to create your own mediated messages.

#### Increasing Media Literacy

*Increase your sensitivity to media by examining your own use of media. If possible, keep a record or log of all the time you spend on media in one day, the media you use most often, the purposes you use the media for, the rewards you get from the media, and especially the ways in which the media might be influencing you. Also, increase your sensitivity by supplementing these Media Literacy boxes with visits to some interesting websites; try, for example, Citizens for Media Literacy at* www.main.nc.us/cml *and the Media Education Foundation at* www.mediaed.org.

## Table 1.2 **Forms of Human Communication**

This table identifies and arranges the forms of communication in terms of the number of persons involved, from one (on intrapersonal communication) to thousands and millions (in mass communication). It also previews (in general) the progression of topics in this book.

| Forms of Human Communication | Some Common Purposes | Some Theory-Related Concerns | Some Skills-Related Concerns |
|---|---|---|---|
| Intrapersonal: communication with the self  | To think, reason, analyze, reflect | How does a person's self-concept develop? How does the self-concept influence communication? How can problem-solving and analyzing abilities be improved and taught? What is the relationship between personality and communication? | Enhancing self-esteem, increasing self-awareness, improving problem solving and analyzing abilities, increasing self-control, reducing stress, managing intrapersonal conflict |
| Interpersonal: communication between two persons  | To discover, relate, influence, play, help | What is interpersonal effectiveness? Why do people develop relationships? What holds friends, lovers, and families together? What tears them apart? How can relationships be repaired? | Increasing effectiveness in one-to-one communication, developing and maintaining effective relationships (friendship, love, family), improving conflict resolution abilities |
| Interviewing: communication that proceeds through questions and answers  | To learn, evaluate, influence | What are the legal issues in interviewing? How can interview responses be analyzed? What is the role of nonverbal communication? | Phrasing questions to get at the information you want, presenting your best self, writing résumés and cover letters |
| Small group: communication within a small group of persons 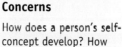 | To share information, generate ideas, solve problems, help | What makes a leader? What type of leadership works best? What roles do members play in groups? What do groups do well, and what do they fail to do well? How can groups be made more effective? | Increasing effectiveness as a group member, improving leadership abilities, using groups to achieve specific purposes (for example, solving problems, generating ideas) |
| Organizational: communication within an organization 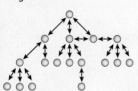 | To inform, persuade, relate | What leadership styles work best in organizations? How and why do organizations grow and deteriorate? What role does culture play in the organization? | Transmitting information, motivating workers, dealing with feedback, dealing with the grapevine, increasing satisfaction |

| | | | |
|---|---|---|---|
| Public: communication of speaker with audience 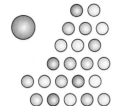 | To inform, persuade, entertain | What kinds of organizational structure work best in informative and persuasive speaking? How can audiences be most effectively analyzed and adapted to? How can ideas be best developed for communication to an audience? | Communicating information more effectively; increasing persuasive abilities; developing, organizing, styling, and delivering messages with greater effectiveness |
| Computer-mediated: communication between people through computers  | To discover, relate, influence, play, help | Are there gender differences? In what ways is CMC more efficient? How can modalities be combined? | Increasing security in e-communications, combining CMC with face-to-face communication |
| Mass: communication addressed to an extremely large audience, mediated by audio and/or visual means 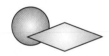 | To entertain, persuade, and inform | What functions do the media serve? How do the media influence us? How can we influence the media? In what ways is information censored by the media for the public? How does advertising work? | Improving your ability to use the media to greater effectiveness, increasing our ability to control the media, avoiding being taken in by advertisements and tabloid journalism |

through whatever revolutions follow. Five general purposes of communication can be identified: To discover, to relate, to help, to persuade, and to play (see Figure 1.1 on page 10).

### To Discover

One of the major purposes of communication concerns personal discovery. When you communicate with another person, you learn about yourself as well as about the other person. In fact, your self-perceptions result largely from what you've learned about yourself from others during communications, especially your interpersonal encounters. Communication also helps you discover the external world—the world of objects, events, and other people. Communication enables you to reduce your uncertainty about people and about the world, and reducing uncertainty in turn enables you to communicate more effectively.

### To Relate

You probably spend much of your communication time and energy establishing and maintaining social relationships. You communicate with your close friends in school, at work, on the phone, and over the Internet. You talk with your parents, children,

and brothers and sisters. You interact with your relational partner. All told, this takes a great deal of your time and attests to the importance of the relational purpose of communication.

### To Help

You fulfill the helping purpose when you constructively criticize, express empathy, work with a group to solve a problem, or listen attentively and supportively to a public speaker. Not surprisingly, obtaining and giving help are among the major functions of Internet communication and among the major reasons people use the Internet (Meier, 2000, 2002).

### To Persuade

In your everyday interpersonal and group encounters, you often try to persuade—to change the attitudes and behaviors of others. You try to get people to vote a particular way, try a new diet, buy a particular item, see a movie, visit a website, take a specific course, believe that something is true or false, value or devalue some idea, and so on. In interviews, you may try to persuade a company to hire you; in public speaking, you may try to persuade your audience that you should be elected to hold a certain office or position. Some researchers, in fact, argue that all communication is persuasive and that all our communications seek some persuasive goal (Canary, Cody, & Manusov, 2000).

### To Play

Communication as play includes motives of pleasure, escape, and relaxation (Barbato & Perse, 1992; Rubin, Perse, & Barbato, 1988). You tell jokes, say clever things, and relate interesting stories largely for the pleasure it gives to you and your listeners. Similarly, you may communicate because it relaxes you, allowing you to get away from pressures and responsibilities.

These five purposes are the reasons you communicate. The next section will help explain *how* you communicate by exploring the elements involved in the communication act.

## THE ELEMENTS OF HUMAN COMMUNICATION

Before examining the definition of the term *communication* and its various elements, take a moment to think about your beliefs about communication by taking the self-test on page 11.

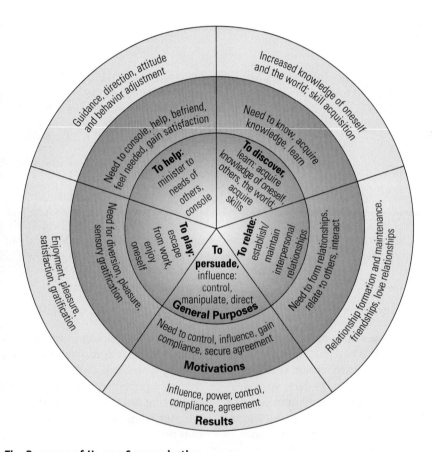

**FIGURE 1.1** **The Purposes of Human Communication**

Shown here are the five general purposes of communication—but the aims of communication also can be looked at from at least two other perspectives. First, purposes may be seen as motives for engaging in communication. That is, you engage in communication to satisfy your need for knowledge or to form relationships. Second, these purposes may be viewed in terms of the results you want to achieve. That is, you engage in interpersonal communication to increase your knowledge of yourself and others or to exert influence or power over others. Any communication act serves a unique combination of purposes, is prompted by a unique combination of motives, and can produce a unique combination of results. A similar typology of purposes comes from research on motives for communicating. In a series of studies, Rubin and her colleagues (Rubin & Martin, 1998; Rubin, Fernandez-Collado, & Hernandez-Sampieri, 1992; Rubin & Martin, 1994; Rubin, Perse, & Barbato, 1988; Rubin & Rubin, 1992; Graham, 1994; Graham, Barbato, & Perse, 1993) have identified six primary motives for communication: pleasure, affection, inclusion, escape, relaxation, and control. How do these compare to the five purposes discussed here?

## ASK THE RESEARCHER

### Values of a Human Communication Course

*These brief Q&As are designed to illustrate the close connection between theory and research on the one hand and practical skills on the other. In each Ask the Researcher box, a question is posed to a national or international expert, who responds as if speaking directly with a student.*

*I'm taking this course in human communication. I am not certain what practical uses this course will have for me. Why should I be taking this course?* You interact with others every day in a variety of contexts. In most contexts, you have a purpose in mind: To learn or to persuade. In job interviews, you need to know what factors the employers are seeking in nonverbal behavior, language use, attitude, level of knowledge, amount of enthusiasm, and personal motivation. In learning situations, you need to know when to ask a question as well as how to frame your question. As a manager of others, you need to know what kinds of messages will motivate your subordinates to perform at their highest levels. Human communication is significant for every aspect of your life from learning at school to obtaining positions in corporations to soliciting a salary increase. Socially, human communication is at the core of what makes relationships work or fail. This course and this book may be among the most important instruments in developing you as a more sensitive and effective person.

For further information: Hickson, M., III, Stacks, D. W., & Padgett-Greely, M. (1998). *Organizational communication in the personal context: From interview to retirement.* Boston: Allyn & Bacon.

**Mark Hickson III** (Ph.D., Southern Illinois University) is a professor of communication studies at the University of Alabama at Birmingham. He teaches courses in communication theory, nonverbal communication, and organizational communication.

## TEST YOURSELF

### What Do You Believe about Communication?

Respond to each of the following statements with T (true) if you believe the statement is usually true or F (false) if you believe the statement is usually false.

_____ 1. Good communicators are born, not made.

_____ 2. The more a couple communicates, the better their relationship will be.

_____ 3. When two people are in a close relationship for a long period of time, one person should not have to communicate his or her needs and wants; the other person should know what these are.

_____ 4. Complete openness should be the goal of any meaningful interpersonal relationship.

_____ 5. Interpersonal or group conflict is a reliable sign that the relationship or group is in trouble.

_____ 6. Like good communicators, leaders are born, not made.

_____ 7. Fear of speaking in public is detrimental and must be eliminated.

**HOW DID YOU DO?** As you may have figured out, all seven statements are generally false. As you read this text, you'll discover not only why these beliefs are false but also the trouble you can get into when you assume they're true. Briefly, here are some of the reasons why each of the statements is generally false:

1. Effective communication is a learned skill; although some people are born brighter or more extroverted than others, all can improve their abilities and become more effective communicators.

2. If you practice bad communication habits, you're more likely to grow less effective than to become more effective; consequently, it's important to learn and follow the principles of effectiveness.

3. This assumption is at the heart of many interpersonal difficulties: People aren't mind readers, and to assume that they are merely sets up barriers to open and honest communication (see Units 8 and 9).

4. Although you may feel ethically obligated to be totally honest, this is generally not an effective strategy. In fact, "complete" anything is probably a bad idea.

5. Interpersonal conflict does not have to involve a winner and a loser; both people can win, as demonstrated in Unit 12.

6. Leadership, like communication and listening, is a learned skill that you'll develop as you learn the principles of human communication in general and of group leadership in particular (Unit 11).

7. Most speakers are nervous; managing, not eliminating, the fear will enable you to become effective regardless of your current level of fear (Unit 14).

**WHAT WILL YOU DO?** Consider how these beliefs about communication influence the way you communicate. Then, as you read this book and participate in class discussions and activities, reexamine your beliefs about communication and consider how new beliefs would influence the way you communicate. The theories and research discussed in this text will help you reconsider your own beliefs about communication, and the skill-building activities will help you practice new ways of communicating. Three excellent websites containing a variety of self-tests on emotional intelligence, personality, knowledge, relationships, careers, and more are **www.allthetests.com**, **www.queendom.com/tests**, and **www.psychologytoday.com**.

## Defining Communication

**Communication** occurs when one person (or more) sends and receives messages that are distorted by noise, occur within a context, have some effect, and provide some opportunity for feedback. Figure 1.2 illustrates the elements present in all communication acts, whether intrapersonal, interpersonal, small group, public speaking, or mass communication—or whether face-to-face, by telephone, or over the Internet: (1) context, (2) sources-receivers, (3) messages, (4) channels, (5) noise, and (6) effects. In addition, we'll examine the role of ethics in communication.

## Communication Context

All communication takes place in a **context** that has at least four dimensions: (1) physical, (2) social-psychological, (3) temporal, and (4) cultural (Figure 1.3, page 14). The *physical context* is the tangible

or concrete environment in which communication takes place—the room or hallway or park. This physical context exerts some influence on the content of your messages (what you say) as well as on the form (how you say it).

The *social-psychological context* includes, for example, the status relationships among the participants, the roles and the games that people play, and the cultural rules of the society in which people are communicating. It also includes the friendliness or unfriendliness, formality or informality, and seriousness or humorousness of the situation. For example, communication that would be permitted at a graduation party might not be considered appropriate at a funeral.

The *temporal (or time) context* includes the time of day as well as the time in history in which the communication takes place. For many people, the morning is not a time for communication. For others, the morning is ideal. Historical context is no less important—because the appropriateness and impact of messages depend, in part, on the time in which they're uttered. Consider, for example, how messages on racial, sexual, or religious attitudes and values would be differently framed and responded to in different times in history. Still another aspect of time is how a message fits into the sequence of communication events. For example, consider the varied meanings a "simple" compliment paid to a friend would have depending on whether you said it immediately after your friend paid you a compliment, immediately before you asked your friend for a favor, or during an argument.

The *cultural context* has to do with your (and others') **culture**: the beliefs, values, and ways of behaving that are shared by a group of people and passed down from one generation to the next. Cultural factors affect every interaction and influence what you say and how you say it. As you'll see throughout this book, the communication strategies and principles that work with members of one culture may not work with members of other cultures. Further, research shows that you lose approximately 50 percent of information communicated in an *inter*cultural situation (communication between members of different cultures) and only 25 percent in an *intra*cultural situation (communication between members of the same culture) (Li, 1999). These are just some reasons why **intercultural communication** is so difficult and why culture is so crucial to communication.

These four dimensions of context interact with one another. For example, arriving late for an appointment (temporal context) might violate a cultural rule, which might lead to changes in the social-psychological context, perhaps creating ten-

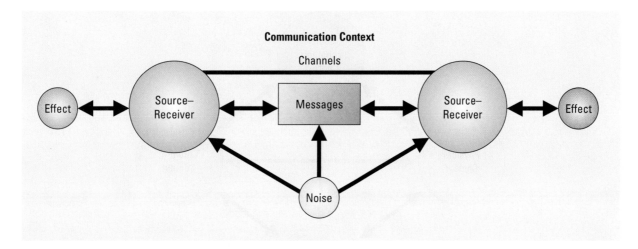

**FIGURE 1.2** **The Elements of Human Communication**

This is a simplified view of the elements of human communication and their relationship to one another. Messages (including feedforward and feedback) are sent simultaneously through a variety of channels from one source-receiver to another. The communication process takes place in a context (physical, cultural, social-psychological, and temporal) and is subjected to interference by noise (physical, psychological, and semantic). The interaction of messages with each source-receiver leads to some effect.

sion and unfriendliness, which in turn might lead to changes in the physical context—for example, choosing a less intimate restaurant for your lunch meeting.

## Sources–Receivers

The compound term *sources-receivers* emphasizes that each person involved in communication is both a **source** (or speaker) and a **receiver** (or listener). You send messages when you speak, write, gesture, or smile. You receive messages in listening, reading, smelling, and so on. As you send messages, however, you're also receiving messages. You're receiving your own messages (you hear yourself, you feel your own movements, you see many of your own gestures), and you're receiving the messages of the other person—visually, aurally, or even through touch or smell. As you assign meaning to these verbal and nonverbal signals, you're performing receiving functions.

### Source–Receiver Encoding–Decoding

The act of producing messages—for example, speaking or writing—is called **encoding**. By putting your ideas into sound waves or into a computer program you're putting these ideas into a **code**, hence encoding. The act of receiving messages—for example, listening or reading—is called **decoding**. By translating sound waves or words on a screen into ideas you take them out of code, which is decoding. Thus, speakers or writers are called **encoders**, and listeners or readers, **decoders**.

As with sources-receivers, the compound term *encoding-decoding* emphasizes that you perform these functions simultaneously, at least in face-to-face communication. As you speak (encoding), you're also deciphering the responses of the listener (decoding). In computer communication this simultaneous exchange of messages occurs only sometimes. In e-mail (as well as snail mail) and newsgroup communication, for example, the sending and receiving may be separated by several days or much longer. In chat groups and instant messaging, on the other hand, communication takes place in real time; the sending and receiving take place (almost) simultaneously.

### Source–Receiver Competence

The term **communication competence** refers to your knowledge of the social aspects of communication (Rubin, 1982, 1985; Spitzberg & Cupach, 1989). Communication competence includes knowledge of such factors as the role of context in influencing the content and form of communication messages—for example, the knowledge that in certain contexts and with certain listeners one topic is appropriate and another is not. Knowledge about the rules of nonverbal behavior—for example, the appropriateness of touching, vocal volume, and physical closeness—is also part of communication competence.

Communication competence also includes your ability to apply this knowledge in communicating. So when you read about communication competence,

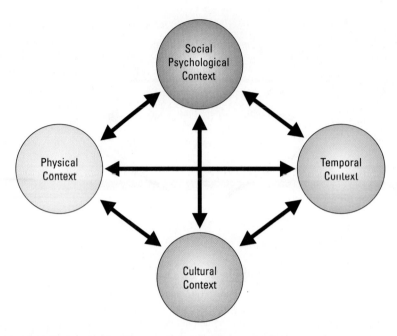

**FIGURE 1.3** **The Communication Context**

This figure is intended to illustrate that the communication context is not a single entity but consists of a variety of contexts that affect communication—and, perhaps most important, to remind you that each dimension of context influences each other dimension.

realize that it includes both an understanding of how communication works, *and* the ability to use this understanding in communicating effectively. Keep in mind, however, that communication competence is culture specific; the way communication works and the elements that make it effective differ from one culture to another.

## Messages

Communication **messages** take many forms. You send and receive messages through any one or any combination of sensory organs. Although you may customarily think of messages as being verbal (oral or written), you also communicate nonverbally. Everything about you communicates. For example, the clothes you wear and the way you walk, shake hands, tilt your head, comb your hair, sit, and smile all communicate messages.

In face-to-face communication the actual message signals (the movements in the air) are evanescent; they fade almost as they're uttered. Some written messages, especially computer-mediated messages such as those sent via e-mail, are unerasable. E-mails that are sent among employees in a large corporation, for example, are often stored on disk or tape.

Two special types of messages include *feedback* (the messages you send that are reactions to other messages) and *feedforward* (the messages you send as

preface to your "main" messages). Both feedback and feedforward are **metamessages**—messages that communicate about other messages. Such communication about communication, or **metacommunication**, may be verbal ("I agree with you" or "Wait until you hear this one") or nonverbal (a smile or a prolonged pause). Or, as is most often the case, it's some combination of verbal and nonverbal signals.

### Feedback Messages

Throughout the listening process, a listener gives a speaker **feedback**—messages sent back to the speaker reacting to what is said. Feedback tells the speaker what effect he or she is having on the listener(s). This can take many forms: A frown or a smile, a yea or a nay, a pat on the back or a punch in the mouth are all types of feedback. Sometimes feedback is easy to identify, but sometimes it isn't (Skinner, 2002).

Part of the art of effective communication is the ability to discern feedback and to adjust messages on the basis of that feedback. For example, on the basis of feedback, a speaker may adjust messages by strengthening, deemphasizing, or changing the content or form of the messages. These adjustments then serve as feedback to the receiver—who, in response, readjusts his or her feedback messages. The process is circular, with one person's feedback serving as the stimulus for the other person's feed-

## NEGATIVE COMMUNICATION EFFECTS

An e-mail that you wrote to a close friend in anger (but never intended to send) was sent. You want to reduce the negative effects of such an e-mail.

WHAT DO YOU SAY?

back, just as any message serves as the stimulus for another person's message.

Another type of feedback is the feedback you get from listening to yourself: You hear what you say, you feel the way you move, you see what you write. On the basis of this self-feedback you adjust your messages; for example, you may correct a mispronunciation, shorten your story, or increase your volume.

You can view feedback in terms of five important dimensions: positive–negative, person-focused–message-focused, immediate–delayed, low-monitored–high-monitored, and supportive–critical.

- *Positive–negative.* **Positive feedback** (smiles, applause, and head nods signifying approval) tells the speaker that the message is being well received and that he or she should continue speaking in the same general mode. **Negative feedback** (frowns, boos, puzzled looks, gestures signifying disapproval) tells the speaker that something is wrong and that some adjustment needs to be made.
- *Person-focused–message-focused.* Feedback may center on the person ("You're sweet," "You've got a great smile") or on the message ("Can you repeat that phone number?" "Your argument is a good one").
- *Immediate–delayed.* In interpersonal situations feedback is most often conveyed immediately after the message is received. In other communi-

cation situations, however, the feedback may be delayed; for example, feedback from an interview may come weeks after the interview took place. In media situations some feedback comes immediately—for example, through Nielsen ratings; other feedback comes much later, through consumers' viewing and buying patterns.

- *Low-monitored–high-monitored.* Feedback varies from the spontaneous and totally honest reaction (low-monitored feedback) to the carefully constructed response designed to serve a specific purpose (high-monitored feedback). In most interpersonal situations you probably give feedback spontaneously; you allow your responses to show without any monitoring. At other times, however, you may be more guarded, as when your boss asks you how you like your job or when your grandmother asks what you think of her holiday fruitcake.
- *Supportive–critical.* Supportive feedback confirms the worth of a person and of what that person says; it occurs when, for example, you console another or when you encourage the other to talk; it often involves **affirmation** of the person's self-definition. Critical feedback, on the other hand, is evaluative. When you give critical feedback you judge another's performance—as in, for example, evaluating a speech or coaching someone learning a new skill.

Each feedback opportunity, then, presents you with choices along at least these five dimensions. To use feedback effectively, you need to make educated choices along these dimensions. Realize that these categories are not exclusive. Feedback does not have to be either critical or supportive; it can be both. For example, in teaching someone how to become a more effective interviewer, you might critically evaluate a practice interview but you might also express support for the effort. Similarly, you might respond to a friend's question immediately and then after a day or two elaborate on your response.

## Feedforward Messages

**Feedforward** is information you provide before sending your primary messages; it reveals something about the messages to come (Richards, 1951). Feedforward includes such diverse examples as the preface or the table of contents in a book, the opening paragraph of a chapter, movie previews, magazine covers, and introductions in public speeches. Feedforward has four major functions: (1) to open the channels of communication, (2) to preview the message, (3) to altercast, and (4) to disclaim.

■ **To open the channels of communication.** Often we preface our messages with comments whose only function is to open the channels of communication (Malinowski, 1923; Lu, 1998). The infamous "opening line" ("Do you come here often?" or "Haven't we met before?") is a clear example of this type of feedforward. Another type of feedforward serving this function of opening the channels is **phatic communication** or "small talk." It's the "how are you" and "nice weather" greetings that are designed to maintain rapport and friendly relationships (Placencia, 2004; Burnard, 2003). Similarly, listeners' short comments that are unrelated to the content of the conversation but that indicate interest and attention may also be considered phatic communication in that they keep the channels of communication open (McCarthy, 2003).

■ **To preview future messages.** Feedforward messages frequently preview other messages. Feedforward may, for example, preview the content ("I have news for you"), the importance ("Listen to this before you make a move"), the form or style ("I'll be brief"), or the positive or negative quality of subsequent messages ("You're not going to like this, but here's what I heard").

■ **To altercast.** The type of feedforward known as **altercasting** asks the receiver to approach your message in a particular role or even as someone else (McLaughlin, 1984; Weinstein & Deutschberger, 1963; Johnson, 1993; Pratkanis, 2000). For example, you might ask a friend, "As a single mother, what do you think of the new child care proposals?" This question casts your friend into the role of single mother (rather than that of teacher, Democrat, or Baptist, for example). It asks your friend to assume a particular perspective.

■ **To disclaim.** A **disclaimer** is a statement that aims to ensure that your message will not reflect negatively on you. Disclaimers entice the listener to hear your message as you wish it to be heard rather than through some assumption that might reflect negatively on you (Hewitt & Stokes, 1975). For example, to ensure that people listen to you fairly, you might disclaim any thought that you're biased against one gender: "I'm no sexist, but. . . ." (The disclaimer is discussed in greater detail in Unit 7.)

## Channels

The communication **channel** is the medium through which the message passes. Communication rarely takes place over only one channel; you may use two, three, or four different channels simultaneously. For example, in face-to-face interactions you speak and listen (vocal channel), but you also gesture and receive signals visually (visual channel). In chat groups, you type and read words and use various symbols and abbreviations to communicate the emotional tone of the message. If your computer system is especially sophisticated, you may communicate via the Internet through audio and visual means as well. In addition, in face-to-face communication you emit and detect odors (olfactory channel). Often you touch another person, and this too communicates (tactile channel).

At times, one or more channels may be damaged. For example, in individuals with visual difficulties, the visual channel is impaired, and so adjustments have to be made. Table 1.3 gives you an idea of how such adjustments between those with and without visual impairments can make communication more effective.

## Noise

**Noise** is anything that interferes with your receiving a message. At one extreme, noise may prevent a message from getting from source to receiver. A roaring noise or line static can easily prevent entire messages from getting through to your receiver. At the other extreme, with virtually no noise interference, the message of the source and the message received are almost identical. Most often, however, noise distorts some portion of the message a source sends as it travels to a receiver. Like messages that may be auditory or visual, noise comes in both auditory and visual forms. Four types of noise are especially relevant:

■ *Physical noise* is interference that is external to both speaker and listener; it interferes with the physical transmission of the signal or message. Examples include the screeching of passing cars, the hum of a computer, sunglasses, extraneous messages, illegible handwriting, blurred type or fonts that are too small or difficult to read, misspellings and poor grammar, and popup ads.

■ *Physiological noise* is created by barriers within the sender or receiver such as visual impairments, hearing loss, articulation problems, and memory loss.

■ *Psychological noise* is mental interference in speaker or listener and includes preconceived ideas, wandering thoughts, biases and prejudices, closed-mindedness, and extreme emotionalism. You're likely to run into psychological noise when you talk with someone who is closed-minded or who refuses to listen to anything he or she doesn't already believe.

---

**Table 1.3** **Interpersonal Communication Tips**

Between People with and People without Visual Impairments

People vary greatly in their visual abilities; some people are totally blind, some are partially sighted, and some have unimpaired vision. Ninety percent of individuals who are "legally blind" have some vision. All of us, however, have the same need for communication and information. Here are some tips for making communication between blind and sighted people more effective.

If you're the sighted person and are talking with a blind person:

1. *Identify yourself.* Don't assume the blind person will recognize your voice.

2. *Face your listener; you'll be easier to hear.* At the same time, don't shout. People who are visually impaired are not hearing impaired. Speak at your normal volume.

3. Because your gestures, eye movements, and facial expressions cannot be seen by the visually impaired listener, *encode into speech all the meanings-both verbal and nonverbal-that you wish to communicate.*

4. *Use audible turn-taking cues.* When you pass the role of speaker to a person who is visually impaired, don't rely on nonverbal cues; instead, say something like "Do you agree with that, Joe?"

5. *Use normal vocabulary, and discuss the same kinds of topics you would discuss with sighted people.* Don't avoid terms like "see" or "look" or even "blind." Don't avoid discussing a television show, or a painting, or the way your new car looks; these are normal conversational topics for all people.

If you are a visually impaired person and are interacting with a sighted person:

1. *Help the sighted person meet your special communication needs.* If you want your surroundings described, ask. If you want the person to read the road signs, ask.

2. *Be patient with the sighted person.* Many people are nervous talking with people who are visually impaired for fear of offending. Put them at ease in a way that also makes you more comfortable.

These suggestions were drawn from www.cincyblind.org/what_do_you_do_.htm and www.rnib.org/uk/ (both accessed October 23, 2004).

---

- *Semantic noise* is created when the speaker and listener have different meaning systems; it includes language or dialectical differences, the use of jargon or overly complex terms, and ambiguous or overly abstract terms whose meanings can be easily misinterpreted. You see this type of noise regularly—for example, in the medical doctor who uses "medicalese" without explanation or in the insurance salesperson who speaks in the jargon of the insurance industry.

As you can see from these examples, all communications contain noise. Noise cannot be totally eliminated, but its effects can be reduced. Making your language more precise, sharpening your skills for sending and receiving nonverbal messages, and improving your listening and feedback skills are some ways to combat the influence of noise.

## Communication Effects

Communication always has some **effect** on one or more persons involved in the communication act. For every communication act, there is some consequence. Generally three types of effects are distinguished.

- **Intellectual (or cognitive) effects** are changes in your thinking. When you acquire information from a class lecture, for example, the effect is largely intellectual.

- **Affective effects** are changes in your attitudes, values, beliefs, and emotions. Thus, when you become frightened when watching the latest horror movie, its effect is largely affective. Similarly, after a great experience with, say, a person of another culture, your feelings about that culture may change. Again, the effect is largely affective (but perhaps also intellectual).

- **Psychomotor effects** are changes in overt behaviors such as, for example, learning new bodily movements such as how to throw a curve ball or how to paint a room or learning to use different verbal and nonverbal behaviors.

These effects are not as separate as they might at first seem. In many cases, a single message—say a public speech on homelessness—may inform you (intellectual effect), move you to feel differently (affective effect), and lead you to be more generous when you come upon a homeless person (psychomotor effect).

## Ethics

Because communication has consequences, it also involves questions of **ethics**, of right and wrong (Bok, 1978; Jaksa & Pritchard, 1994). For example, while it might be (temporarily) effective to exaggerate or even lie in order to sell a product or get elected, it would not be ethical to do so.

The ethical dimension of communication is complicated because ethics is so interwoven with our personal philosophy of life and with the culture in which we have been raised that it's difficult to propose general guidelines for specific individuals. Nevertheless, ethical responsibilities need to be considered as integral to any communication act. The decisions you make concerning communication must be guided by what you consider right as well as by what you consider effective.

In thinking about the ethics of communication, you can take the position that ethics is objective or that it's subjective. In an *objective view* you'd claim that the morality of an act—say, a communication message—is absolute and exists apart from the values or beliefs of any individual or culture. This objective view holds that there are standards that apply to all people in all situations at all times.

In this way of thinking, if lying, advertising falsely, using illegally obtained evidence, and revealing secrets, for example, are considered unethical, then they'll be considered unethical regardless of the circumstances surrounding them or of the values and beliefs of the culture in which they occur.

In a *subjective view* you'd claim that the morality of an act depends on the culture's values and beliefs as well as on the particular circumstances. Thus, from a subjective position you would claim that the end might justify the means—a good result can justify the use of unethical means to achieve that result. You would further argue that lying is wrong to win votes or sell cigarettes, but that lying can be ethical if the end result is positive (such as trying to make someone who is unattractive feel better by telling them they look great, or telling a critically ill person that they'll feel better soon).

To emphasize the central role of ethics in all aspects of communication, each unit of this text includes a Reflections on Ethics box. The first such discussion continues explaining the nature of ethics and discusses the three major areas of ethics (below).

---

# REFLECTIONS
## ON ETHICS

## The Areas of Ethics

According to the Internet Encyclopedia of Philosophy (www.iep.utm.edu/e/ethics.htm), the field of ethics consists of three areas:

- *Metaethics* concerns itself with the origins of ethical principles (where they come from—God? Social conventions? Cultural norms?) and with the meanings of various ethical concepts (What is responsibility? What is right? What is wrong?).
- *Normative ethics* concerns itself with articulating the standards of right and wrong; this is the area that proposes specific ethical principles (for example, Don't lie; Don't willfully hurt another person). It is from normative ethics that we learn the principles governing what is ethical and what is unethical.
- *Applied ethics* concerns itself with the ethical implications of controversial issues (Is capital punishment ethical? Is preventing marriage by same-sex couples ethical? Is it ethical to engage in war?).

These three areas often intersect. For example, the ethics of capital punishment is clearly *applied ethics*, as it focuses on a controversial issue. But this topic also draws on the insights of *metaethics* (Where do the rights to kill another person come from? Who has the right to kill another human being?) and on *normative ethics* (By what standard does one person claim the right to kill another person? Under what conditions might it be justifiable to kill another person?).

## Ethical Choice Point

*In a class discussion of ethics, your instructor presents the following possible ethical guidelines: (1) Behavior is ethical when you feel in your heart that you're doing the right thing; (2) Behavior is ethical when it is consistent with your religious beliefs; (3) Behavior is ethical when it's legal within the society; (4) Behavior is ethical when the majority of people would consider it ethical; and (5) Behavior is ethical when the end result is in the interest of the majority. How would you respond to these guidelines? Would you accept any as an accurate statement of what constitutes ethical behavior? Would you reject any? Why?*

## The Elements in Transaction

Communication is **transactional**, which means that the elements in communication are interdependent. Each person in the communication act is both speaker and listener; each person is simultaneously sending and receiving messages (see Figure 1.4 below) (Barnlund, 1970; Watzlawick, 1977, 1978; Watzlawick, Beavin, & Jackson, 1967; Wilmot, 1987).

There are several implications and ramifications of this transactional view.

- First, "transactional" means that *communication is an-ever changing process.* It's an ongoing activity; all the elements of communication are in a state of constant change. You're constantly changing, the people with whom you're communicating are changing, and your environment is changing. Nothing in communication ever remains static.

**Linear View**

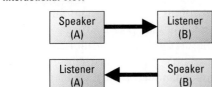

**Interactional View**

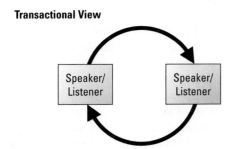

**Transactional View**

**FIGURE 1.4  Three Views of Communication**

The top diagram represents a linear view of communication, in which the speaker speaks and the listener listens. The middle diagram represents an interactional view, in which speaker and listener take turns speaking and listening; A speaks while B listens, then B speaks while A listens. The bottom diagram represents a transactional view. This is the view that most communication theorists hold. In the transactional view, each person serves simultaneously as speaker and listener; at the same time that you send messages, you're also receiving messages from your own communications and also from the messages of the other person(s).

- Second, in any transactional process, *each element relates integrally to every other element*; each exists in relation to the others. For example, there can be no source without a receiver. There can be no message without a source. There can be no feedback without a receiver. Because of this interdependence, a change in any one element of the process produces changes in the other elements. For example, you're talking with a group of your friends when your mother enters the group. This change in "audience" will lead to other changes. Perhaps you or your friends will adjust what you're saying or how you say it. The new situation may also influence how often certain people talk, and so on. Regardless of what change is introduced, other changes will be produced as a result.

- Third, *each person in a communication transaction acts and reacts on the basis of a multitude of factors.* For example, the way you act in a communication situation will naturally depend on the immediate context, which in turn is influenced by your history, past experiences, attitudes, cultural beliefs, self-image, future expectations, emotions, and a host of related issues. One implication of this is that actions and reactions in communication are determined not only by what is said, but also by the way each person interprets what is said. Your responses to a movie, for example, don't depend solely on the words and pictures in the film but also on your previous experiences, present emotions, knowledge, physical well-being, and other factors. Similarly, two people listening to the same message will often derive two very different meanings. Although the words and symbols are the same, each person interprets them differently because each is influenced differently by their history, present emotions, and so on.

## THE PRINCIPLES OF HUMAN COMMUNICATION

Here we'll explore several important principles that govern how communication works and that have important implications for your own communication effectiveness: (1) Communication is a package of signals; (2) communication is a process of adjustment; (3) communication involves content and relationship dimensions; (4) communication is ambiguous; (5) communication sequences are punctuated; (6) communication involves symmetrical and complementary transactions; and (7) communication is inevitable, irreversible, and unrepeatable. Before reading these principles, take a look at the Understanding Theory and Research box on "Communication Theories" on page 21.

## Communication Is a Package of Signals

Communication behaviors, whether they involve verbal messages, gestures, or some combination thereof, usually occur in "packages" (Pittenger, Hockett, & Danehy, 1960). Usually, that is, verbal and nonverbal behaviors reinforce or support each other. All parts of a message system normally work together to communicate a particular meaning. You don't express fear with words while the rest of your body is relaxed. You don't express anger through your posture while your face smiles. Your entire body works together—verbally and nonverbally—to express your thoughts and feelings.

In any form of communication, whether interpersonal, small group, public speaking, or mass media, you probably pay little attention to this "packaging." It goes unnoticed. But when there's an incongruity—when the weak handshake belies the confident verbal greeting, when the nervous posture belies the focused stare, when the constant preening belies the verbal expressions of being comfortable and at ease—you take notice. Invariably you begin to question the credibility, the sincerity, and the honesty of the individual.

Often, contradictory messages are sent over a period of time. Note, for example, that in the following interaction the employee is being given two directives—use initiative and don't use initiative. These **mixed messages** place the employee in a "double bind"—regardless of what he or she does, rejection will follow.

EMPLOYER: You've got to learn to take more initiative. You never seem to take charge, to take control.

EMPLOYEE: [Takes the initiative, makes decisions.]

EMPLOYER: You've got to learn to follow the chain of command and not do things just because you want to.

EMPLOYEE: [Goes back to old ways, not taking any initiative.]

EMPLOYER: Well, I told you. We expect more initiative from you.

Contradictory messages may be the result of the desire to communicate two different emotions or feelings. For example, you may like a person and want to communicate a positive feeling, but you may also feel resentment toward this person and want to communicate a negative feeling as well. The result is that you communicate both feelings; for example, you say that you're happy to see the person but your facial expression and body posture communicate your negative feelings (Beier, 1974). In this example, and in many similar cases, the socially acceptable message is usually communicated verbally while the less socially acceptable message is communicated nonverbally.

## Communication Is a Process of Adjustment

Communication can take place only to the extent that the communicators use the same system of signals (Pittenger, Hockett, & Danehy, 1960). You will not be able to communicate with another person to the extent that your language systems differ. In reality, however, no two persons use identical signal systems, so a process of **adjustment** is relevant to all forms of communication. Parents and children, for example, not only have largely different vocabularies but also have different meanings for the terms they do share. Different cultures, even when they use a common language, often have greatly different nonverbal communication systems. To the extent that these systems differ, meaningful and effective communication will not take place.

Part of the art of communication is identifying the other person's signals, learning how they're used, and understanding what they mean. Those in close relationships will realize that learning the other person's signals takes a great deal of time and often a great deal of patience. If you want to understand what another person means (by smiling, by saying "I love you," by arguing about trivia, by making self-deprecating comments), rather than simply acknowledging what the other person says or does, you have to learn that person's system of signals.

This principle of adjustment is especially important in intercultural communication, largely because people from different cultures use different signals—and sometimes also use the same signals to signify quite different things. Focused eye contact means honesty and openness in much of the United States. But in Japan and in many Hispanic cultures, that same behavior may signify arrogance or disrespect if, say, engaged in by a youngster with someone significantly older.

### Communication Accommodation

Generally, you're likely to view someone who is similar to you more positively and to see that person as more attractive than someone who is dissimilar. For example, in one study roommates who had similar communication attitudes (both were high in their willingness to communicate and low in their verbal aggressiveness) liked each other better and were more satisfied with their status as roommates than those with dissimilar attitudes (Martin & Anderson, 1995). Similarly, you're likely to judge a speaker as more believable when his or her language intensity is similar to your own (Aune & Kikuchi, 1993). And you're likely to see those whose speech rate is similar to yours as more sociable and intimate than those

---

**Theory and Research** UNDERSTANDING **Communication Theories**

*In addition to the theory and research discussed throughout the text, two Understanding Theory and Research boxes appear in each unit to highlight a particular theory or hypothesis about communication and to focus attention on the nature and function of theory and research in the study of human communication.*

A **theory** is a generalization that explains how something works—for example, gravity, blood clotting, interpersonal attraction, or communication. In academic writing, the term *theory* is usually reserved for a well-established system of knowledge about how things work or how things are related. A theory is still fundamentally a generalization, but it's often supported by research findings and other well-accepted theories.

The theories you'll encounter in this book try to explain how communication works—for example, how you accommodate your speaking style to your listeners, how communication works when relationships deteriorate, how friends self-disclose, how problem-solving groups communicate, how speakers influence audiences, and how the media affect people. As you can see from even these few examples, theories provide general principles that help you understand an enormous number of specific events.

One great value of communication theories is that they help you predict future events. Because theories summarize what's been found, they can offer reasonable predictions for events that you've never encountered. For example, theories of persuasion will help you predict what kinds of emotional appeals will be most effective in persuading a specific audience. Or theories of conflict resolution will enable you to predict what strategies would be effective or ineffective in resolving differences.

Despite their many values, theories don't reveal truth in any absolute sense. Rather, theories reveal some degree of accuracy, some degree of truth. In the natural sciences (such as physics and chemistry), theories are extremely high in accuracy. If you mix two parts of hydrogen to one part of oxygen, you'll get water—every time you do it. In social and behavioral sciences such as communication, sociology, and psychology, the theories are far less accurate in describing the way things work and in predicting how things will work.

This failure to reveal truth, however, does not mean that theories are useless. In increasing your understanding and your ability to predict, theories are extremely helpful. Theories often have practical implications as you work on developing your own communication skills. For example, theories of interpersonal attraction offer practical insights into how to make yourself more attractive to others; theories of leadership offer practical advice on how you can more effectively exert your own leadership. This interrelationship between theories and skills is a theme you'll find throughout this book. The more you know about how communication works (that is, the theories and research), the more likely you'll be able to use it effectively (that is, build your communication skills).

### Working with Theories and Research

*Log on to one of the academic databases to which you have access and browse through issues of* Quarterly Journal of Speech, Communication Monographs, *or* Communication Theory *(or scan similar journals in your own field of study); you'll be amazed at the breadth and depth of academic research and theory.*

**RELATIONSIHP AMBIGUITY**

You've been dating someone on and off for a year or so and you'd like to invite your date to meet your parents (you're anxious to see what they think about your partner) but aren't sure how your date will perceive this invitation.

WHAT DO YOU SAY?
*In what context?*

who speak much more slowly or more rapidly than you do (Buller, LePoire, Aune, & Eloy, 1992). In interethnic interactions, people who saw themselves as similar in communication styles were attracted to each other more than to those they perceived as having different communication styles (Lee & Gudykunst, 2001). These findings, and many more like them, support **communication accommodation theory**, the theory that you adjust to or accommodate to the speaking style of your listeners in order to gain a variety of benefits—not only believability and likeability, as already noted, but also general social approval and even communication efficiency (Giles, Mulac, Bradac, & Johnson, 1987).

## Communication Involves Content and Relationship Dimensions

Communications, to a certain extent at least, refer to the real world, to something external to both speaker and listener. At the same time, however, communications also refer to the relationships between the parties (Watzlawick, Beavin, & Jackson, 1967). In other words, communication has both **content and relationship dimensions**.

For example, an employer may say to a worker, "See me after the meeting." This simple message has a content aspect and a relational aspect. The **content message** refers to the behavioral response expected—namely, that the worker see the employer after the meeting. The **relationship message** tells how the communication is to be dealt with. For example, the use of the simple command says that there's a status difference between the two parties: The employer can command the worker. This aspect is perhaps seen most clearly if you imagine the worker giving this command to the employer; to do so would be awkward and out of place, because it would violate the expected relationship between employer and worker.

In any communication situation, the content dimension may stay the same but the relationship aspect may vary. For example, the employer could say to the worker either "You had better see me after the meeting" or "May I please see you after the meeting?" In each case, the content is essentially the same; that is, the message being communicated about the behaviors expected is the same. But the relationship dimension is very different. The first example signifies a definite superior–inferior relationship and even a put-down of the worker. In the second, the employer signals a more equal relationship and shows respect for the worker.

Similarly, at times the content may be different but the relationship essentially the same. For example, a teenager might say to his or her parents, "May I go away this weekend?" or "May I use the car tonight?" The content of the two messages is clearly very different. The relationship dimension, however, is essentially the same. It clearly denotes a superior–inferior relationship in which permission to do certain things must be secured.

### Ignoring Relationship Dimensions

Problems may arise when the distinction between the content and relationship levels of communication is ignored. Consider a couple arguing over the

## Theory and Research  UNDERSTANDING  Communication Research

Research is usually conducted on the basis of some theory and its predictions—although sometimes the motivation to conduct research comes from a simple desire to answer a question. Communication research is a systematic search for information about communication, the very information that is discussed throughout this text; for example, information about perception and listening, verbal and nonverbal messages, interpersonal interactions, small group encounters, and public speaking situations.

Some research is designed to explore what exists; for example, *What do people say after getting caught in a lie?* Other research is designed to describe the properties of some communication behavior; for example, *What are the various types of excuses?* Still other research aims to predict what will happen in different situations; for example, *What types of excuses will work best in a business relationship?* Research findings bearing on these questions help explain how communication works and suggest ways to use communication more effectively.

In evaluating communication research (or any kind of research), ask yourself three questions:

- **Are the results reliable?** In establishing reliability, a measure of the extent to which research findings are consistent, you ask if another researcher, using the same essential tools, would find the same results. Would the same people respond in the same way at other times? If the answer to such questions is yes, then the results are reliable. If the answer is no, then the results may be unreliable.

- **Are the results valid?** Validity is a measure of the extent to which a measuring instrument measures what it claims to measure. For example, does your score on an intelligence test really measure what we think of as intelligence? Does your score on a test of communication apprehension measure what most people think of as constituting apprehension?

- **Do the results justify the conclusion?** Results and conclusions are two different things. Results are objective findings such as "men scored higher than women on this test of romanticism." Conclusions are the researcher's (or reader's) interpretation of the results and might include, for example, "Men are more romantic than women."

### Working with Theories and Research

*What question about communication would you like answered? Research the question and find out if the question has already been answered. If not, how might you go about conducting your own research to secure the answer?*

---

fact that Pat made plans to study with friends during the weekend without first asking Chris if that would be all right. Probably both would have agreed that to study over the weekend was the right choice to make. Thus the argument is not at all related to the content level. The argument centers on the relationship level. Chris expected to be consulted about plans for the weekend. Pat, in not doing so, rejected this definition of the relationship.

Let me give you a personal example. My mother came to stay for a week at a summer place I had. On the first day she swept the kitchen floor six times,

though I had repeatedly told her that it did not need sweeping: I would be tracking in dirt and mud from outside, so all her effort would be wasted. But she persisted in sweeping, saying that the floor was dirty and should be swept. On the content level we were talking about the value of sweeping the kitchen floor. But on the relationship level we were talking about something quite different. We were each saying, "This is my house." When we realized this (though only after considerable argument), I stopped complaining about the relative usefulness of sweeping a floor that did not need sweeping, and she stopped sweeping it.

**CONTENT AND RELATIONSHIP MESSAGES**

An older relative frequently belittles you, though always in a playful way. But it's uncomfortable and probably not very good for your self-esteem. You're determined to stop the behavior but not lose the relationship.

WHAT DO YOU SAY?
*Through what channel?*

For another insight consider the following interchange:

THOM: I'm going bowling tomorrow. The guys at the plant are starting a team. [He focuses on the content and ignores any relational implications of the message.]

SOFIA: Why can't we ever do anything together? [She responds primarily on a relational level, ignoring the content implications of the message and expressing her displeasure at being ignored in his decision.]

THOM: We can do something together anytime; tomorrow's the day they're organizing the team. [Again, he focuses almost exclusively on the content.]

This example reflects research findings that show that men tend to focus more on content messages, whereas women focus more on relationship messages (Pearson, West, & Turner, 1995). Once we recognize this gender difference, we may be able to develop increased sensitivity to the opposite sex.

## Recognizing Relationship Dimensions

Here's essentially the same situation but with added sensitivity to relationship messages:

THOM: The guys at the plant are organizing a bowling team. I'd sure like to be on the team. Do you mind if I go to the organizational meeting tomorrow? [Although he focuses on content, he shows awareness of the relational dimensions by asking if

this would be a problem. He also shows this in expressing his desire rather than his decision to attend this meeting.]

SOFIA: That sounds great, but I'd really like to do something together tomorrow. [She focuses on the relational dimension but also acknowledges his content message. Note too that she does not respond as if she has to defend herself or her emphasis on relational aspects.]

THOM: How about you meet me at Luigi's for dinner after the organizational meeting? [He responds to the relational aspect without abandoning his desire to join the bowling team—and seeks to incorporate it into his communications. He attempts to negotiate a solution that will meet both Sofia's and his needs and desires.]

SOFIA: Perfect. I'm dying for spaghetti and meatballs. [She responds to both messages, approving of both his joining the team and their dinner date.]

Arguments over content are relatively easy to resolve. You can look something up in a book or ask someone what actually took place. Arguments on the relationship level, however, are much more difficult to resolve, in part because you (like me in the example with my mother) may not recognize that the argument is in fact about your relationship. The accompanying Building Communication Skills box, Distinguishing Content and Relationship Messages, provides additional insight into this important distinction.

---

**Building Communication Skills** — Distinguishing Content from Relationship Messages

Deborah Tannen, in *You're Wearing That?* (2006), gives examples of content and relationship communication and the problems that can result from different interpretations. For example, the mother who says, "Are you going to wear those earrings?" may think she's communicating solely a content message. To the daughter, however, the message is largely relational and is a criticism of the way she intends to dress. (Of course, the mother may have intended criticism.) Often, questions that may appear to be objective and focused on content are perceived as attacks, as in the title of Tannen's book. Identify the possible content and relational messages that a receiver might get in being asked the following questions:

- *You're* calling me?
- Did you say, *you're* applying to *medical* school?
- You're in *love*?
- You paid a *hundred dollars* for that?
- And that's *all* you did?

*Content and relationship messages serve different communication functions. Being able to distinguish between these functions is a prerequisite for using and responding to messages effectively.*

---

## Communication Is Ambiguous

Ambiguous messages are messages with more than one potential meaning. Sometimes this **ambiguity** occurs because we use words that can be interpreted differently. Informal time terms offer good examples; *soon, right away, in a minute, early, late,* and similar terms often mean different things to different people. The terms are ambiguous. A more interesting type of ambiguity is grammatical ambiguity. You can get a feel for this type of ambiguity by trying to paraphrase—rephrase in your own words—the following sentences:

1. What has the cat in its paws?
2. Visiting relatives can be boring.
3. They are flying planes.

You can interpret and paraphrase each of these in at least two different ways:

1. What monster has the cat in its paws? What does the cat have in its paws?
2. To visit relatives can be boring. Relatives who visit can be boring.
3. Those people are flying planes. Those planes are for flying.

Although these examples are particularly striking—and are the work of linguists, or specialists who analyze language—some degree of ambiguity exists in all communication; all messages are ambiguous to some degree. In other words, when you express an idea, you never communicate your meaning exactly and totally; rather, you communicate your meaning with some reasonable accuracy—enough to give the other person a reasonably clear sense of what you mean. Sometimes, of course, you're less accurate than you anticipated: Your listener "gets the wrong idea," or "gets offended" when you only meant to be humorous, or "misunderstands your emotional meaning." Because of this inevitable uncertainty, you may qualify what you're saying, give an example, or ask, "Do you know what I mean?" These tactics help the other person understand your meaning and reduce uncertainty (to some degree).

Similarly, all relationships contain uncertainty. Consider a close relationship of your own and ask yourself the following questions. Answer on a scale ranging from 1 (completely or almost completely uncertain) to 6 (completely or almost completely certain). How certain are you about:

- what you can or cannot say to each other in this relationship? Do you know what the sore spots are or what topics are best avoided?
- whether or not you and your partner feel the same way about each other? Would you each describe your relationship similarly?
- the future of the relationship? Do you each see your future and the relationship's future in the same way?

Very likely you were not able to respond to all four questions with 6s, and it's equally likely that your relationship partner would be unable to respond with all 6s. These questions from a relationship uncertainty scale (Knobloch & Solomon, 1999)—and other similar tests—illustrate that you probably experience some degree of uncertainty about the norms that govern your relationship communication (question 1), the degree to which each of you defines the relationship in similar ways (question 2), and the relationship's future (question 3).

Any communication situation can be ambiguous. In small group or organizational situations, you may be unsure of how you or your ideas are being evaluated. You may be unsure of the hierarchy in the organization. You may be unsure of what style of leadership will prove effective and what style will cause resentment. In public speaking you probably face the greatest ambiguity; namely, how your audience will respond to your speech. Will they be in favor of what you're advocating or against it? Will they understand certain technical terms, or will you have to define them? Will they be willing to pay attention?

By developing the skills of communication presented in this text, you'll be able to reduce ambiguity and make your meanings as unambiguous as possible. In this connection take a look at the accompanying Building Communication Skills box, Resolving Ambiguity (page 28).

## Communication Is Punctuated

Communication events are continuous transactions. There's no clear-cut beginning or ending. As a participant in or an observer of the communication act, you engage in punctuation: You divide up this continuous, circular process into causes and effects, or **stimuli** and **responses**. That is, you segment this continuous stream of communication into smaller pieces. You label some of these pieces causes or stimuli and others effects or responses.

Consider an example: The students are apathetic; the teacher does not prepare for classes. Figure 1.5 (a) illustrates the sequence of events, in which there's no absolute beginning and no absolute end. Each action (the students' apathy and the teacher's lack of preparation) stimulates the other. But there's no initial stimulus. Each of the events may be regarded as a stimulus and each as a response, but there's no way to determine which is which.

Consider how the teacher might divide up this continuous transaction. Figure 1.5 (b) illustrates the teacher's perception of the situation. From this point of view, the teacher sees the students' apathy as the stimulus for his or her lack of preparation, and the lack of preparation as the response to the students' apathy. In Figure 1.5 (c) we see how the students might divide up the transaction. The students might see this "same" sequence of events as beginning with the teacher's lack of preparation as the stimulus (or cause) and their own apathy as the response (or effect).

Take another example: Pat cooks; Chris criticizes the cooking. Pat begins to exert less effort, Chris criticizes more, Pat exerts still less effort, Chris continues to criticize, and so on. Pat may see the argument as beginning with Chris's negative comments—the criticism is the cause and exerting less effort is the effect. Chris may see the argument as beginning with Pat's lousy cooking—lack of effort is the cause and justifiable criticism is the effect.

**FIGURE 1.5** **Punctuation and the Sequence of Events**

Try using this three-part figure, discussed in the text, to explain what might go on when Pat complains about Chris's nagging and Chris complains about Pat's avoidance and silence.

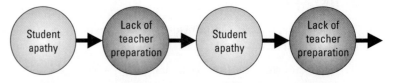

**(a) The sequence of events punctuated by the teacher**

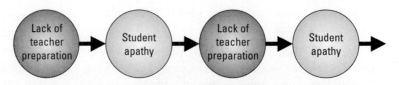

**(b) The sequence of events punctuated by the students**

This tendency to divide up the various communication transactions in sequences of stimuli and responses is referred to as **punctuation of communication** (Watzlawick, Beavin, & Jackson, 1967). People punctuate the continuous sequences of events into stimuli and responses for ease of understanding and remembering. And, as both the preceding examples illustrate, people punctuate communication in ways that allow them to look good and that are consistent with their own self-image.

If communication is to be effective, if you're to understand what another person means from his or her point of view, then you have to see the sequence of events as punctuated by the other person. Further, you have to recognize that your punctuation does not reflect what exists in reality. Rather, it reflects your own unique but fallible perception.

## Communication Involves Symmetrical and Complementary Transactions

Relationships can be described as either symmetrical or complementary (Watzlawick, Beavin, & Jackson, 1967). In a **symmetrical relationship** the two individuals mirror each other's behavior. The behavior of one person is reflected in the behavior of the other. If one member nags, the other member responds in kind. If one member expresses jealousy, the other member expresses jealousy. If one

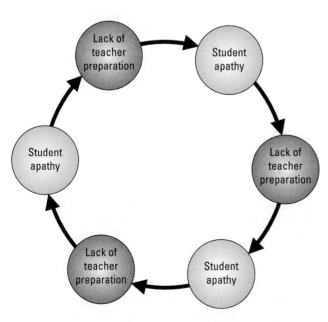

**(c) The sequence of events as it exists in reality**

member is passive, the other member is passive. The relationship is one of equality, with the emphasis on minimizing the differences between the two individuals.

Note, however, the problems that can arise in this type of relationship. Consider the situation of a husband and wife, both of whom are aggressive. The aggressiveness of the husband fosters aggressiveness in the wife; the anger of the wife arouses anger in the husband. As this escalates, the aggressiveness can no longer be contained, and the relationship is consumed by aggression.

In a **complementary relationship**, in contrast, the two individuals engage in different behaviors. The behavior of one serves as the stimulus for the complementary behavior of the other. In complementary relationships the differences between the parties are maximized. One partner acts as the superior and the other as the inferior, one is passive and the other active, one strong and the other weak. At times cultures establish such relationships—as, for example, the complementary relationship between teacher and student or between employer and employee. Early marriages are likely to be complementary relationships in which each person tries to complete himself or herself. When these couples separate and form new partnerships, the new relationships are likely to be symmetrical and to involve a kind of reconfirmation of each partner's own identity (Prosky, 1992). Generally, research finds that complementary couples have a lower marital adjustment level than do symmetrical couples (Main & Oliver, 1988; Holden, 1991; McCall & Green, 1991).

A problem in complementary relationships—familiar to many college students—is the situation created by extreme rigidity. Whereas the complementary relationship between a nurturing and protective mother and a dependent child is at one stage vital and essential to the life of the child, a **rigid complementarity** when the child is older can become a handicap to further development, if the change so essential to growth is not allowed to occur.

## Communication Is Inevitable, Irreversible, and Unrepeatable

Communication is a process that is inevitable, irreversible, and unrepeatable. Communication messages are always being sent (or almost always), can't be reversed or uncommunicated, and are always unique and one-time occurrences. Let's look at these qualities in more detail.

---

Building Communication Skills **Resolving Ambiguity**

*These exercises, presented in Building Communication Skills boxes throughout the text, are designed to stimulate you to think more actively about the concepts and skills covered in the unit and to help you practice your developing communication skills.*

Here are a few ambiguous situations; for each, indicate what you would say to resolve the ambiguity. If possible, try to share your responses with others in a small group and perhaps combine responses to come up with the ideal way to reduce the ambiguity. Or responses from a larger group can be written on index cards (anonymously), collected, and read aloud for the entire group to evaluate.

1. You've been dating Pat on and off for the past six months. Today, Pat asks you to come to dinner and meet the parents. You're not sure if this means that Pat wants to get more serious (which you do not want) or if it's a simple dinner invitation with no additional motives. How might you disambiguate this dinner invitation message?

2. At an appraisal interview, your supervisor says that your work over the last six months has improved considerably—then smiles and says, "But there's always more that we need to do," and then nonverbally indicates that the interview is over and you can return to work. Since you're considering other job offers, you want to know in more detail how your current employer sees you and your prospects for advancement. How might you disambiguate this job appraisal?

3. You receive a written invitation to address the eighth-grade class of your local middle school on careers in communication. The invitation said little more than that a conference on careers is planned and that they are hoping you'll be one of the speakers. This is too ambiguous for you; you need to know in more detail what will be expected of you. How might you disambiguate this invitation to speak?

4. You've been invited to a colleague's house for dinner. Around two hours before you're scheduled to leave for the dinner, it begins to snow, and your colleague calls to say that you shouldn't feel you have to come to dinner in the snow; the roads may get dangerous. The snow is only a light dusting, and your SUV would have no trouble getting there. You wonder what your colleague was really saying—whether it's "I'd like to cancel the dinner and I'm using the snow as an excuse" or "I'm concerned about your safety and I don't want you to travel in potentially dangerous weather just because of this dinner." What do you say?

*Messages and relationships are often ambiguous; instead of assuming one interpretation is right and another wrong, it may be useful to try to disambiguate the message and find out exactly what the speaker means.*

---

## Inevitability

In many instances communication takes place even though one of the individuals does not think he or she is communicating or does not want to communicate. Consider, for example, the student sitting in the back of the classroom with an expressionless face, perhaps staring out the window. Although the student might claim not to be communicating with the teacher, the teacher may derive any of a variety of messages from this behavior; for example, that the student lacks interest, is bored, or is worried about something. In any event, the teacher is receiving mes-

sages even though the student may not intend to communicate. In an interactional situation, you can't avoid communicating (Watzlawick, Beavin, & Jackson, 1967); communication is inevitable. This principle of **inevitability** does not mean, of course, that all behavior is communication. For example, if the student looked out the window and the teacher failed to notice this, no communication would have taken place.

Further, when you're in an interactional situation you can't avoid responding to the messages of others. For example, if you notice someone winking at you, you must respond in some way. Even if you don't re-

## IRREVERSIBILITY

Without thinking you make some culturally insensitive remarks and even though everyone laughs politely, you want to explain that you're really not the kind of person who normally talks this way.

WHAT DO YOU SAY?

spond actively or openly, that lack of response is itself a response, and it communicates. Again, if you don't notice the winking, then obviously communication has not occurred.

## Irreversibility

Notice that you can reverse the processes of only some systems. For example, you can turn water into ice and then the ice back into water. And you can repeat this reversal process as many times as you wish. Other systems, however, are irreversible. You can turn grapes into wine, but you can't turn the wine back into grapes—the process can go in only one direction. Communication is such an irreversible process. Once you say something, once you press the send key on your e-mail, you can't uncommunicate it. You can of course try to reduce the effects of your message by saying, for example, "I really didn't mean what I said" or "I was so angry I couldn't think straight." But regardless of how you try to negate or reduce the effects of a message, the message itself, once it has been sent and received, can't be reversed.

Because of **irreversibility** (and unerasability), be careful not to say things you may be sorry for later. Especially in conflict situations, when tempers run high, avoid saying things you may later wish to withdraw. Commitment messages—"I love you" messages and their variants—also need to be monitored. And in group and public communication situations, when messages are received by many people, it's crucial to recognize their irreversibility. Similarly, online messages that could be interpreted as sexist, racist, homophobic, or ageist, which you thought were private or erased from your computer, may

later be recalled and retrieved by others, creating all sorts of problems for you and your organization.

As a result of the differences between the permanency of electronic communication and the evanescence of face-to-face communication, you may wish to be cautious in your electronic messages. E-mail is probably your most common form of computer communication, though these cautions also apply to all other forms of electronic communication, including newsgroup postings, instant messages, and website messages. In an organizational context, it's important to find out what the e-mail policy of the company is. One survey found that 75 percent of companies had written e-mail policies but that less than half of all companies surveyed trained their workers in e-mail policies (Coombes, 2003).

- E-mails are difficult to destroy. Often e-mails you think you deleted will remain on servers and workstations and may be retrieved by a clever hacker.

- E-mails can readily be made public; the ease of forwarding e-mails to others or of posting your comments on websites makes it especially important that you consider carefully what you write. The message that you intend for one person may actually be received by many others, too.

- E-mails are not privileged communication and can easily be used against you, especially in the workplace. Criticizing a colleague may one day leave you open to accusations of discrimination. Passing along sexist, racist, homophobic, or ageist "jokes" to a friend may one day fuel accusations of a hostile working environment and cost your employer millions, as such "jokes" cost Chevron a few years ago.

- E-mails provide permanent records: They make it impossible for you to say, for example, "That's not exactly what I said," because exactly what you said will be there in black and white.
- E-mail files may be accessed by others, such as a nosy colleague at the next desk or a visiting neighbor, and can then be sent to additional outsiders.

## Unrepeatability

The reason for the **unrepeatability** of communication is simple: Everyone and everything is constantly changing. As a result, you can never recapture the exact same situation, frame of mind, or relationship dynamics that defined a previous communication act. For example, you can never repeat meeting someone for the first time, making a first impression in an interview, or resolving a specific group problem.

You can, of course, try again, as when you say, "I'm sorry I came off so forward, can we try again?" But even after you say this, you have not erased the initial impression. Instead you try to counteract this initial and perhaps negative impression by going through the motions again.

## SUMMARY: PRELIMINARIES TO HUMAN COMMUNICATION

This unit explained the benefits, forms, and purposes of human communication; the major elements of human communication, and several functional principles that explain how human communication works.

1. Communication is the act, by one or more persons, of sending and receiving messages that occur within a context, are distorted by noise, have some effect (and some ethical dimension), and provide some opportunity for feedback.

2. The major skills to be learned here include self-presentation, relationship, interviewing, group interaction and leadership, and presentation.

3. The major types of human communication are intrapersonal, interpersonal, small group, organizational, public, computer-mediated, and mass communication.

4. Communication is multipurposeful; we use communication to discover, to relate, to help, to persuade, and to play.

5. The universals of communication—the elements present in every communication act—are the context, including culture; source–receiver sending or encoding processes and receiving or decoding processes; messages; channels; noise; feedback and feedforward; effects; and ethics.

6. The communication context has at least four dimensions: physical, social–psychological, temporal, and cultural.

7. Culture consists of the collection of beliefs, attitudes, values, and ways of behavior shared by a group of people and passed down from one generation to the next through communication rather than genes.

8. Communication competence is knowledge of the elements and rules of communication, which vary from one culture to another.

9. Communication is a transactional process in which each person simultaneously sends and receives messages.

10. Noise is anything that distorts a message; it's present to some degree in every communication transaction and may be physical, physiological, psychological, or semantic in origin.

11. Feedback is information or messages that are sent back to the source. It may come from the source itself or from the receiver, and may be characterized along such dimensions as positive and negative, person-focused and message-focused, immediate and delayed, low-monitored and high-monitored, and supportive and critical.

12. Feedforward messages preface other messages and may be used to open the channels of communication, to preview future messages, to disclaim, and to altercast.

13. Communication messages may be of varied forms and may be sent and received through any combination of sensory organs. The communication channel is the medium through which the messages are sent.

14. Communication always has an effect. Effects may be cognitive, affective, or psychomotor.

15. Ethics in communication consists of the rightness or wrongness—the morality—of a communication transaction. Ethics is integral to every communication transaction.

16. Communication is normally a package of signals, each reinforcing the other. Opposing communication signals from the same source result in contradictory messages.

17. The double bind, a special kind of contradictory message, may be created when contradictory messages are sent simultaneously.

18. Communication is a process of adjustment and takes place only to the extent that the communicators use the same system of signals.

19. Communication involves both content dimensions and relationship dimensions.

20. Communication is ambiguous and often can be interpreted in different ways.

21. Communication sequences are punctuated for processing. Different people divide up the communication sequence into stimuli and responses differently.

22. Communication involves symmetrical and complementary transactions.

23. In any interaction situation, communication is inevitable; you can't avoid communication, nor can you not respond to communication.

24. Communication is irreversible. You can't uncommunicate.

25. Communication is unrepeatable. You can't duplicate a previous communication act.

# KEY TERMS IN PRELIMINARIES TO HUMAN COMMUNICATION

Here are the essential terms used in this unit and the pages on which they are introduced. Many of these terms are also defined in the glossary at the end of the text. In addition, flash cards are available online at MyCommunicationLab (www.mycommunicationlab.com) to help you further master the vocabulary of human communication.

adjustment (p. **20**)

affirmation (p. **15**)

altercasting (p. **16**)

ambiguity (p. **25**)

channel (p. **16**)

code (p. **13**)

communication (p. **12**)

communication accommodation theory (p. **22**)

communication competence (p. **13**)

complementary relationship (p. **28**)

computer-mediated communication (p. **5**)

content and relationship dimensions (p. **22**)

content messages (p. **22**)

context (p. **12**)

culture (p. **12**)

decoder (p. **13**)

decoding (p. **13**)

disclaimer (p. **16**)

effect (p. **17**)

encoder (p. **13**)

encoding (p. **13**)

ethics (p. **18**)

feedback (p. **14**)

feedforward (p. **15**)

inevitability (p. **28**)

intercultural communication (p. **12**)

interpersonal communication (p. **4**)

interviewing (p. **4**)

intrapersonal communication (p. **4**)

irreversibility (p. **29**)

mass communication (p. **7**)

messages (p. **14**)

metacommunication (p. **14**)

metamessages (p. **14**)

mixed messages (p. **20**)

negative feedback (p. **15**)

noise (p. **16**)

organizational communication (p. **5**)

phatic communication (p. **16**)

positive feedback (p. **15**)

public speaking (p. **5**)

punctuation of communication (p. **26**)

receiver (p. **13**)

relationship messages (p. **22**)

responses (p. **26**)

rigid complementarity (p. **28**)

small group communication (p. **5**)

source (p. **13**)

stimuli (p. **26**)

symmetrical relationship (p. **28**)

theory (p. **21**)

transactional (p. **19**)

unrepeatability (p. **30**)

# THINKING CRITICALLY ABOUT PRELIMINARIES TO HUMAN COMMUNICATION

1. **Reading Feedback.** Based on your own experiences, do you find that instructors who accurately read and respond to student feedback are better liked than instructors who can't read feedback as accurately? Is there a relationship between the ability to read feedback and the ability to communicate information or to motivate or persuade an audience? In what ways might the ability to give effective feedback influence the growth or deterioration of a relationship?

2. **Feedforward.** In this book there are several examples of feedforward; for example, (1) the cover, (2) the "Welcome" section, (3) the tables of contents, (4) each unit's opening page, (5) each unit's opening paragraph, and (6) the section headings within units. What more specific purposes do each of these serve?

3. **Online and Off-line Activities.** A report dated August 11, 2004, by the Pew Internet and American Life Project (The Internet and Daily Life, www.pewinternet.org/PPF/r/131/ report_display.asp, accessed February 10, 2005) noted that people are more likely to "get news, play games, pay bills, send cards, look up phone numbers and addresses, buy tickets, check sports scores, listen to music, schedule appointments, and communicate with friends" off-line than online. Why do you think this is the case? Do you think the items on this list will change over the next 5 years? Over the next 20 years?

4. **Synchronous and Asynchronous Messaging.** In face-to-face and chat room communication, messages are exchanged with virtually no delay; communication is synchronous. In other forms of communication—for example, snail or e-mail and blog posts—the messages may be exchanged with considerable delay; communication here is asynchronous. What differences in communication style can you attribute to synchronicity and asynchronicity?

5. **Inevitability, Irreversibility, and Unrepeatability.** Identify one or two or three rules or guidelines that the concepts of inevitability, irreversibility, and unrepeatability would suggest for each of the following situations: (a) the first day at a new job, (b) asking for a date, (c) a face-to-face job interview, (d) chatting in an online group, (e) meeting with a dying friend, (f) popping the question, (g) introducing yourself in class, (h) arguing with your romantic partner, (i) seeing an old friend after many years, (j) giving a speech to regain the goodwill of the people, and (k) leading a group of colleagues in a brainstorming session.

# LogOn! MyCommunicationLab
## WWW.MYCOMMUNICATIONLAB.COM

MyCommunicationLab will provide you with a broad collection of materials that will help you master the theory and skills of this course and this text; it will also make your experience in this course more enjoyable and more varied. There are practice tests, crossword puzzles, videos, and figures and tables from a variety of books; all of these will prove useful supplements for each unit in the text. At the end of each unit you'll find a brief note of just some of the materials available on MCL that are relevant to the unit.

For Unit 1, visit MCL for such exercises as the following: Using Communication Channels, Modeling Human Communication, Responding to Contradictory Messages, Symmetrical and Complementary Relationships, Applying the Principles, Analyzing an Interaction, Principles of Communication, and Communication Competence.

While in MCL click on the Research Navigator tab and you'll find a wealth of research materials that you can use throughout this course and especially in the public speaking section.

# UNIT 2 Culture and Communication

## MAJOR TOPICS

**What Is Culture?**
**Cultural Differences**
**Intercultural Communication**

## Special Features

When you speak or listen, you're doing so as a member of a particular and unique culture—you're greatly influenced by the teachings of your religion, your racial and national history, the social expectations for your gender, and a host of other factors. This unit explores this topic of culture and its relationship to human communication.

**In this unit you'll learn about:**
- culture's role in human communication.
- the ways cultures differ from one another.
- the forms and principles of intercultural communication.

**You'll learn to:**
- send and receive messages with a recognition of cultural influences and differences.
- communicate successfully in intercultural situations.

## WHAT IS CULTURE?

*Culture* (introduced briefly in Unit 1) consists of (1) relatively specialized elements of the lifestyle of a group of people (2) that are passed on from one generation to the next through communication, not through genes.

(1) Included in a social group's "culture" is everything that members of that group have produced and developed—their values, beliefs, artifacts, and language; their ways of behaving and ways of thinking; their art, laws, religion, and, of course, communication theories, styles, and attitudes.

(2) Culture is passed on from one generation to the next through communication, not through genes. Thus, the term *culture* does not refer to color of skin or shape of eyes, as these are passed on through genes, not communication. But because members of a particular race or country are often taught similar beliefs, attitudes, and values, it's possible to speak of "Hispanic culture" or "African American culture." It's important to realize, however, that within any large group—especially a group based on race or nationality—there will be enormous differences. The Kansas farmer and the Wall Street executive may both be, say, German American, but may differ widely in their attitudes, beliefs, and lifestyles. In some ways the Kansas farmer may be closer in attitudes and values to a Chinese farmer than to the New York financier.

In ordinary conversation *sex* and *gender* are often used synonymously. In academic discussions of culture, they're more often distinguished. **Sex** refers to the biological distinction between male and female; sex is determined by genes, by biology. **Gender**, on the other hand, refers to the "social construction of masculinity and femininity within a culture" (Stewart, Cooper, Stewart, with Friedley, 2003). Gender (masculinity and femininity) is what boys and girls learn from their culture; it's the attitudes, beliefs, values, and ways of communicating and relating to one another that boys and girls learn as they grow up.

Thus, gender—although partly transmitted genetically and not by communication—may be considered a cultural variable, largely because cultures teach boys and girls different attitudes, beliefs, values, and ways of communicating and relating to one another. Thus, you act like a man or a woman in part because of what your culture has taught you about how men and women should act. This is not, of course, to deny that biological differences also play a role in the differences between male and female behavior. In fact, research continues to uncover biological roots of male/female differences we once thought were entirely learned (McCroskey, 1997).

Culture is transmitted from one generation to another through **enculturation**, the process by which you learn the culture into which you're born (your native culture). Parents, peer groups, schools, religious institutions, and government agencies are the main teachers of culture.

A somewhat different process of learning culture is **acculturation**, the process by which you learn the rules and norms of a culture different from your native culture. In acculturation your original or native culture is modified through direct contact with or exposure to a new and different "host" culture. For example, when immigrants settle in the United States (the host culture), their own culture becomes influenced by U.S. culture. Gradually, the values, ways of behaving, and beliefs of the host culture become more and more a part of the immigrants' culture. At the same time, of course, the host culture changes, too, as it interacts with the immigrants' culture. Generally, however, the culture of the immigrant changes more. The reasons for this are that the host country's members far outnumber the immigrant group and that the media are largely dominated by and reflect the values and customs of the host culture (Kim, 1988).

New citizens' acceptance of the new culture depends on many factors (Kim, 1988). Immigrants who come from cultures similar to the host culture will be-

---

**Theory and Research**     **Cultural Theories**

UNDERSTANDING

Consider two very different theories of culture: cultural evolution and cultural relativism. The theory of *cultural evolution* (often called social Darwinism) holds that much as the human species evolved from lower life forms to Homo sapiens, cultures also evolve. Consequently, some cultures may be considered advanced and others primitive. Most contemporary scholars reject this view, because the judgments that distinguish one culture from another have no basis in science and are instead based on individual values and preferences as to what constitutes "advanced" and what constitutes "primitive."

The *cultural relativism* approach, on the other hand, holds that all cultures are different but that no culture is either superior or inferior to any other (Berry, Poortinga, Segall, & Dasen, 1992). This view is generally accepted today and guides the infusion of cultural materials into contemporary textbooks on all academic levels (Jandt, 2004). But this position does not imply that all cultural practices are therefore equal or that you have to accept all cultural practices equally. As noted in the text, there are many cultural practices popular throughout the world that you may find, quite logically and reasonably, unacceptable.

---

**Working with Theories and Research**

*Explore these two positions more fully by consulting one or more of the references cited in this unit, or by logging on to your favorite search engine or database and searching for such concepts as "cultural relativism," "cultural evolution," and "social Darwinism." What might you add to the brief discussion presented here?*

---

come acculturated more easily. Similarly, those who are younger and better educated become acculturated more quickly than do older and less well educated people. Personality factors also play a part. Persons who are risk takers and open-minded, for example, have greater acculturation potential. Also, persons who are familiar with the host culture before immigration—through interpersonal contact or through media exposure—will be acculturated more readily.

Before exploring further the role of culture in communication, consider your own cultural values and beliefs by taking the self-test on page 36. This test illustrates how your own cultural values and beliefs may influence your interpersonal, small group, and public communications—both the messages you send and the messages to which you listen.

## The Importance of Culture in Communication

There are many reasons for the current cultural emphasis in the field of communication. Because of (1) demographic changes, (2) increased sensitivity to cultural differences, (3) economic interdependency, (4) advances in communication technology, and (5) the fact that communication competence is specific to a culture (what works in one culture will not necessarily work in another), it's impossible to communicate effectively without being aware of how culture influences human communication.

### Demographic Changes

Most obvious, perhaps, are the vast demographic changes taking place throughout the United States. Whereas at one time the United States was largely a country populated by northern Europeans, it's now a country greatly influenced by the enormous number of new citizens from Central and South America, Africa, and Asia. And the same is true to an even greater extent on college and university campuses throughout the United States. With these changes have come different customs and the need to understand and adapt to new ways of looking at communication.

Consider these facts (*The New York Times Almanac 2005*; *The World Almanac and Book of Facts 2005*): The foreign-born population of the United States is increasing dramatically. In 1980, the foreign-born population was 14 million (about 6.2 percent of the total population), in 1990 it was 19.8 million (7.9 percent), and in 2000 it was 28.4 million (10.4 percent). Increasingly, frequent communication in a multicultural context is inevitable.

# TEST YOURSELF

## What Are Your Cultural Beliefs and Values?

Here the extremes of eight cultural differences are identified. For each characteristic indicate your own values:

**a.** If you feel your values are very similar to the extremes, then select 1 or 7.

**b.** If you feel your values are quite similar to the extremes, then select 2 or 6.

**c.** If you feel your values are fairly similar to the extremes, then select 3 or 5.

**d.** If you feel you're in the middle, then select 4.

| Left Extreme | Characteristic | Right Extreme |
|---|---|---|
| Men and women are equal and are entitled to equality in all areas. | **Gender Equality** 1 2 3 4 5 6 7 | Men and women are very different and should stick to the specific roles assigned to them by their culture. |
| You should enjoy yourself as much as possible. | **Hedonism** 1 2 3 4 5 6 7 | You should work as much as possible. |
| Religion is the final arbiter of what is right and wrong; your first obligation is to abide by the rules and customs of your religion. | **Religion** 1 2 3 4 5 6 7 | Religion is like any other social institution; it's not inherently moral or right just because it's a religion. |
| Your first obligation is to your family; each person is responsible for the welfare of his or her family. | **Family** 1 2 3 4 5 6 7 | Your first obligation is to yourself; each person is responsible for himself or herself. |
| Romantic relationships, once made, are forever. | **Relationship Permanency** 1 2 3 4 5 6 7 | Romantic relationships should be maintained as long as they're more rewarding than punishing and dissolved when they're more punishing than rewarding. |
| People should express their emotions openly and freely. | **Emotional Expression** 1 2 3 4 5 6 7 | People should not reveal their emotions, especially those that may reflect negatively on them or others or make others feel uncomfortable. |
| Money is extremely important and should be a major consideration in just about any decision you make. | **Money** 1 2 3 4 5 6 7 | Money is relatively unimportant and should not enter into life's really important decisions, such as what relationship to enter or what career to pursue. |

**HOW DID YOU DO?** This test was designed to help you explore the possible influence of your cultural beliefs and values on communication. If you visualize communication as involving choices, then your beliefs will influence the choices you make and thus how you communicate and how you listen and respond to the communications of others. For example, your beliefs and values about gender equality will influence the way in which you communicate with and about the opposite sex. Your group and individual orientation will influence how you perform in work teams and how you deal with your peers at school and at work. Your degree of hedonism will influence the kinds of communications you engage in, the books you read, and the television programs you watch. Your religious beliefs will influence the ethical system you follow in communicating. Review the entire list of characteristics and try to identify one specific way in which each characteristic influences your communication.

**WHAT WILL YOU DO?** Are you satisfied with your responses? If not, how might you get rid of your unproductive or unrealistic beliefs? What beliefs would you ideally like to substitute for these?

In your more immediate environment, consider the number of foreign students who come to the United States to continue their education. For the years 2002-2003, according to the Institute of International Education (www.parstimes.com/news/archive/2003/washfile028.html, accessed February 8, 2005) there were 586,323 international students studying in the United States. The number of students from the top 10 countries, along with the percentage of increase or decrease from the previous year, were:

- India, 74,603 (up 12 percent)
- China, 64,7575 (up 2 percent)
- South Korea, 51,519 (up 5 percent)
- Japan, 45,960 (down 2 percent)
- Taiwan, 28,017 (down 3 percent)
- Canada, 26,513 (unchanged)
- Mexico, 12,801 (up 2 percent)
- Turkey, 11,601 (down 4 percent)
- Indonesia, 10,432 (down 10 percent)
- Thailand, 9,982 (down 14 percent)

Students from the Middle East—especially from Saudi Arabia, Kuwait, and the United Arab Emirates—declined the most, although the absolute numbers were still quite high: from 38,545 during the previous year to 34,803 for 2002-2003.

As you can see from even these few figures, frequent intercultural communication is an inevitable part of college life today.

## Cultural Sensitivity

As a people we've become increasingly sensitive to cultural differences. American society has moved from an *assimilationist perspective* (which holds that people should leave their native culture behind and adapt to their new culture) to a perspective that values *cultural diversity* (which holds that people should retain their native cultural ways). And, with some notable exceptions—hate speech, racism, sexism, homophobia, and classism come quickly to mind—we're more concerned with communicating respectfully and ultimately with developing a society where all cultures can coexist and enrich one another. At the same time, the ability to interact effectively with members of other cultures often translates into financial gain and increased employment opportunities and advancement prospects.

## Economic Interdependency

Today most countries are economically dependent on one another. Our economic lives depend on our ability to communicate effectively across different cultures. Similarly, our political well-being depends in great part on that of other cultures. Political unrest in any part of the world—South Africa, eastern Europe, or the Middle East, to take a few examples—affects our security in the United States. So interdependent have nations become that a new phrase, "spaghetti bowl," has come into use to refer to "the interconnected and tangled economic relationships of a group of nations" (*New York Times*, December 24, 2006, Section 4, p. 4).

U.S. corporations, too, are becoming more and more interculturally oriented. Increasingly you see large and small corporations expanding into foreign countries. Manufacturing, media, information technology, and farming interests depend on foreign markets. Business opportunities, therefore, have an increasingly international dimension, making cultural awareness and intercultural communication competence essential skills for professional success.

## Communication Technology

The rapid spread of communication technology has brought foreign and sometimes very different cultures right into our living rooms. News from foreign countries is commonplace. You see nightly—in vivid color—what is going on in remote countries. Technology has made intercultural communication easy, practical, and inevitable. Daily the media bombard you with evidence of racial tensions, religious disagreements, sexual bias, and all the other problems caused when intercultural communication fails. And, of course, the Internet has made intercultural communication as easy as writing a note on your computer. You can now communicate by e-mail just as easily with someone in Europe or Asia, for example, as with someone in another city or state.

## Communication Competence

Communication competence is specific to a given culture; what proves effective in one culture may be ineffective in another. For example, in the United States corporate executives get down to business during the first several minutes of a meeting. In Japan, however, business executives interact socially for an extended period and try to find out something about one another. Thus, the communication principle influenced by U.S. culture would advise participants to get down to the meeting's agenda during the first five minutes. The principle influenced by Japanese culture would advise participants to avoid dealing with business until everyone has socialized sufficiently and feels well enough acquainted to begin negotiations. Each principle seems effective within its own culture and ineffective outside its own culture. For example, Asians often find that the values they have learned—values that discourage competitiveness and assertiveness—work against them in Western cultures that endorse competition and outspokenness (Cho, 2000).

## The Aim of a Cultural Perspective

Because culture permeates all forms of communication, it is necessary to understand its influences if you are to understand how communication works and master its skills. As illustrated throughout this text, culture influences communications of all types (Moon, 1996). It influences what you say to yourself and how you talk with friends, lovers, and family in everyday conversation. It influences how you interact in groups and how much importance you place on the group versus the individual. It influences the topics you talk about and the strategies you use in communicating information or in persuading. And it influences how you use the media and the credibility you attribute to them.

A cultural emphasis helps distinguish what is *universal* (true for all people) from what is *relative* (true for people in one culture but not for people in other cultures) (Matsumoto, 1994). The principles for communicating information and for changing listeners' attitudes, for example, will vary from one culture to another. If you are to understand communication, then you need to know how its principles vary and how the principles must be qualified and adjusted on the basis of cultural differences.

And, of course, this cultural understanding is necessary to communicate effectively in a wide variety of intercultural situations. Success in communication—on your job and in your social life—will depend on your ability to communicate effectively with persons who are culturally different from yourself.

As demonstrated throughout this text, cultural differences exist across the communication spectrum—from the way you use eye contact to the way you develop or dissolve a relationship (Chang & Holt, 1996). But these should not blind you to the great number of

similarities that also exist among even the most widely separated cultures. Close interpersonal relationships, for example, are common in all cultures, though they may be entered into for very different reasons by members of different cultures. Further, when reading about cultural differences, remember that these are usually matters of degree. Thus, most cultures value honesty, but not all value it to the same degree.

An emphasis on cultural awareness does not imply that you should accept all cultural practices, or that all cultural practices are equal (Hatfield & Rapson, 1996). For example, cockfighting, foxhunting, and bullfighting are parts of the culture of some Latin American countries, England, and Spain, but you need not find these activities acceptable or equal to cultural practices in which animals are treated kindly. Further, a cultural emphasis does not imply that you have to accept or follow even the practices of your own culture. For example, even if the majority in your culture finds cockfighting acceptable, you need not agree with or follow the practice. Similarly, you can reject your culture's values and beliefs; its religion or political system; or its attitudes toward the homeless, the handicapped, or the culturally different. Of course, going against your culture's traditions and values is often very difficult. But it is important to realize that although culture influences you, it does not determine your values or behavior. Often, for example, personality factors (such as your degree of assertiveness, extroversion, or optimism) will prove more influential than culture (Hatfield & Rapson, 1996).

In sum, cultural beliefs exert powerful (often unconscious) influences on your communication. Becoming aware of these beliefs will help you deal more effectively with their influences on your communication interactions, especially when you are communicating with people holding widely different beliefs.

# CULTURAL DIFFERENCES

For effective communication to take place in a global world, goodwill and good intensions are helpful—but they are not enough. If you're going to be effective, you need to know how cultures differ and how these differences influence communication. Research supports five major cultural distinctions that have an impact on communication. Cultures differ in terms of their (1) individualist or collectivist orientation, (2) emphasis on context (whether high or low), (3) power structure, (4) masculinity–femininity, and (5) tolerance for ambiguity. Each of these dimensions of difference has significant impact on all forms of communication (Hofstede, 1997; Hall & Hall, 1987; Gudykunst, 1994). Before reading about these dimensions, take the self-test on page 40; it will help you think about your own cultural orientations and will personalize the text discussion and make it more meaningful.

## Individual and Collective Orientation

Cultures differ in the way in which they promote individualist and collectivist thinking and behaving. An **individualist culture** teaches members the importance of individual values such as power, achievement, hedonism, and stimulation. Examples include the cultures of the United States, Australia, United Kingdom, Netherlands, Canada, New Zealand, Italy, Belgium, Denmark, and Sweden (Hofstede, 1997; Singh & Pereira, 2004). A **collectivist culture** teaches members the importance of group values such as benevolence, tradition, and conformity. Examples of such cultures include Guatemala, Ecuador, Panama, Venezuela, Colombia, Indonesia, Pakistan, China, Costa Rica, and Peru (Hofstede, 1997; Singh & Pereira, 2004). Americans generally have a preference for individualist values; in contrast, many Asian cultures have a preference for collectivist values (Kapoor, Wolfe, & Blue, 1995; Hofstede, 1997).

One of the major differences between these two orientations is the extent to which an individual's goals or the group's goals are given greater importance. Of course, these goals are not mutually exclusive; you probably have both individualist and collectivist tendencies. For example, you may compete with other members of your basketball team for the most baskets or most valuable player award (and thus emphasize individual goals). At the same time, however, you will—in a game—act in a way that will benefit the entire team (and thus emphasize group

goals). In actual practice, both individual and collective tendencies will help you and your team each achieve your goals. Yet most people and most cultures have a dominant orientation; they're more individually oriented or more collectively oriented in most situations, most of the time. In an individualist culture members are responsible for themselves and perhaps their immediate family. In a collectivist culture members are responsible for the entire group.

In some instances these tendencies may come into conflict. For example, do you shoot for the basket and try to raise your own individual score, or do you pass the ball to another player who is better positioned to score and thus benefit your team? You make this distinction in popular talk when you call someone a team player (collectivist orientation) or an individual player (individualist orientation).

Success, in an individualist culture, is measured by the extent to which you surpass other members of your group; you take pride in standing out from the crowd. And your heroes—in the media, for example—are likely to be those who are unique and who stand apart. In a collectivist culture success is measured by your contribution to the achievements of the group as a whole; you take pride in your similarity to other members of your group. Your heroes are more likely to be team players who don't stand out from the rest of the group's members.

In an individualist culture you're responsible to your own conscience, and responsibility is largely an individual matter; in a collectivist culture you're responsible to the rules of the social group, and responsibility for an accomplishment or a failure is shared by all members. Competition is fostered in individualist cultures, whereas cooperation is promoted in collectivist cultures. In small group settings in an individualist culture, you may compete for leadership; there will likely be a very clear distinction between leaders and members. In a collectivist culture leadership will often be shared and rotated; there will likely be little distinction between leader and members. These orientations also influence the kinds of communication members consider appropriate in an organizational context. For example, individualist organization members favor clarity and directness; in contrast, collectivists favor "face-saving" and the avoidance of hurting others or arousing negative evaluations (Kim & Sharkey, 1995).

Distinctions between in-group members and out-group members are extremely important in collectivist cultures. In individualistic cultures, which prize each person's individuality, the distinction is likely to be less important.

Today the nightly news brings stories of suicide bombers—people who will give up their own life in support of a cause in which they believe. In individualistic cultures this is something difficult to understand;

it's so foreign to everything such cultures teach and value. But for those from collectivist cultures, the larger social group is more important than the individual; giving up an individual life for the life of the group is entirely consistent with their cultural orientation.

# TEST YOURSELF

## What's Your Cultural Orientation?

For each of the items below, select either *a* or *b*. In some cases, you may feel that neither *a* nor *b* describes yourself accurately; in these cases simply select the one that is closer to your feeling. As you'll see when you read this next section, these are not *either/or* preferences, but *more-or-less* preferences.

1. Success, to my way of thinking, is better measured by
   a. the extent to which I surpass others.
   b. my contribution to the group effort.

2. My heroes are generally
   a. people who stand out from the crowd.
   b. team players.

3. Of the following values, the ones I consider more important are:
   a. achievement, stimulation, enjoyment.
   b. tradition, benevolence, conformity.

4. Generally, in my business transactions, I feel comfortable
   a. relying on oral agreements.
   b. relying on written agreements.

5. If I were a manager, I would likely
   a. reprimand a worker in public if the occasion warranted.
   b. always reprimand in private regardless of the situation.

6. In communicating, it's generally more important to be
   a. polite rather than accurate or direct.
   b. accurate and direct rather than polite.

7. I'd enjoy working in most groups where
   a. there is little distinction between leaders and members.
   b. there is a clearly defined leader.

8. As a student (and if I feel well informed) I'd feel
   a. comfortable challenging a professor.
   b. uncomfortable challenging a professor.

9. In choosing a life partner or even close friends, I'd feel more comfortable
   a. with just about anyone, not necessarily one from my own culture and class.
   b. with those from my own culture and class.

10. Of the following characteristics, the ones I value more highly are
    a. aggressiveness, material success, and strength.
    b. modesty, tenderness, and quality of life.

11. In a conflict situation, I'd be more likely to
    a. confront conflicts directly and seek to win.
    b. confront conflicts with the aim of compromise.

12. If I were a manager of an organization I would stress
    a. competition and aggressiveness.
    b. worker satisfaction.

13. Generally, I'm
    a. comfortable with ambiguity and uncertainty.
    b. uncomfortable with ambiguity and uncertainty.

14. As a student, I'm more comfortable with assignments in which
    a. there is freedom for interpretation.
    b. there are clearly defined instructions.

15. Generally, when approaching an undertaking with which I've had no experience, I'd feel
    a. comfortable.
    b. uncomfortable.

**HOW DID YOU DO?**

- Items 1–3 refer to the **individualist–collectivist orientation; a** responses indicate an individualist orientation, and **b** responses indicate a collectivist orientation.

- Items 4–6 refer to the **high- and low-context** characteristics; **a** responses indicate a high-context focus, and **b** responses indicate a low-context focus.

- Items 7–9 refer to the **power distance** dimension; **a** responses indicate greater comfort with a low power distance, and **b** responses indicate comfort with a high power distance.

- Items 10–12 refer to the **masculine–feminine** dimen-sion; **a** responses indicate a masculine orientation; **b** responses, a feminine orientation.

- Items 13–15 refer to the **tolerance for ambiguity** or uncertainty; **a** responses indicate high tolerance, and **b** responses indicate a low tolerance.

**WHAT WILL YOU DO?** Understanding your preferences in a wide variety of situations as culturally influenced (at least in part) is a first step to controlling them and to changing them should you wish to do so. This understanding also helps you modify your behavior as appropriate for greater effectiveness in certain situations. The remaining discussion in this section further explains these orientations and their implications.

**Theory and Research** **UNDERSTANDING** Language and Thought

The linguistic relativity hypothesis claims (1) that the language you speak influences the thoughts you have, and (2) that therefore, people speaking widely differing languages will see the world differently and will think differently.

Theory and research, however, have not been able to find much support for this claim. A more modified hypothesis currently seems supported: The language you speak helps you to talk about what you see and perhaps to highlight what you see. For example, if you speak a language that is rich in color terms (English is a good example), you will find it easier to talk about nuances of color than will someone from a culture that has fewer color terms (some cultures, for example, distinguish only two, three, or four parts of the color spectrum). But this doesn't mean that people see the world differently, only that their language helps (or doesn't help) them to talk about certain variations in the world and may make it easier (or more difficult) for them to focus their thinking on such variations.

Nor does it mean that people speaking widely differing languages are doomed to misunderstand one another. Translation enables you to understand a great deal of the meaning in any foreign language message. And, of course, you have your communication skills; you can ask for clarification, for additional examples, for restatement. You can listen actively, give feedforward and feedback, use perception checking, and employ a host of other skills you'll encounter throughout this course.

Language differences don't make for very important differences in perception or thought. Difficulties in intercultural understanding are due more often to ineffective communication than to differences in languages.

### Working with Theories and Research

*Based on your own experience, how influential do you find language differences to be in perception and thought? Can you recall any misunderstandings that might be attributed to a particular language's leading its speakers to see or interpret things differently?*

## High- and Low-Context Cultures

Cultures also differ in the extent to which information is made explicit, on the one hand, or is assumed to be in the context or in the persons communicating, on the other. In a **high-context culture** much of the information in communication is in the context or in the person—for example, information that was shared through previous communications, through assumptions about each other, and through shared experiences. The information is thus known by all participants but it is not explicitly stated in the verbal message.

In a **low-context culture** most of the information is explicitly stated in the verbal message. In formal transactions it will be stated in written (or contract) form.

To appreciate the distinction between high and low context, consider giving directions:

**High-Context Situation**

*A person who knows the neighborhood asks you:* "Where's the voter registration center?"

*You answer:* "Next to the laundromat on Main Street" or "The corner of Albany and Elm."

**Low-Context Situation**

*A newcomer to your city asks you:* "Where's the voter registration center?"

*You answer:* "Make a left at the stop sign. Then go two blocks and turn right. The office is next to a wash-and-dry service called Green's Laundromat."

With someone who knows the neighborhood (a high-context situation), you can assume the person knows local landmarks (like the laundromat). With a newcomer (a low-context situation), you cannot assume the person shares any information with you. So you have to use directions that a stranger will understand; you have to be more explicit and include more information than you would in a high-context situation, where you can assume that you have neighborhood information in common.

High-context cultures are also collectivist cultures (Gudykunst, Ting-Toomey, & Chua, 1988; Gudykunst & Kim, 1992). These cultures (Japanese, Arabic, Latin American, Thai, Korean, Apache, and Mexican are examples) place great emphasis on personal relationships and oral agreements (Victor, 1992). Low-context cultures are also individualist cultures. These cultures (German, Swedish, Norwegian, and American are examples) place less emphasis on personal relationships and more emphasis on verbalized, explicit explanation—for example, on written contracts in business transactions.

Members of high-context cultures spend lots of time getting to know one another interpersonally and socially before any important transactions take place. Because of this prior personal knowledge, a great deal of information is shared by the members and therefore does not have to be explicitly stated. Members of low-context cultures spend a great deal less time getting to know one another and hence don't have that shared knowledge. As a result everything has to be stated explicitly.

A frequent source of intercultural misunderstanding that can be traced to the distinction between high- and low-context cultures can be seen in **face-saving** (Hall & Hall, 1987). People in high-context cultures place a great deal more emphasis on face-saving. For example, they're more likely to avoid argument for fear of causing others to lose face, whereas people in low-context cultures (with their individualist orientation) will use argument to win a point. Similarly, in high-context cultures criticism should take place only in private. Low-context cultures may not make this public–private distinction. Low-context managers who criticize high-context workers in public will find that their criticism causes interpersonal problems—and does little to resolve the difficulty that led to the criticism in the first place (Victor, 1992).

Members of high-context cultures are reluctant to say no for fear of offending and causing the person to lose face. So, for example, it's necessary to understand when the Japanese executive's yes means yes and when it means no. The difference is not in the words used but in the way in which they're used. It's easy to see how the low-context individual may interpret this reluctance to be direct—to say no when you mean no—as a weakness or as an unwillingness to confront reality.

## Power Distances

In some cultures power is concentrated in the hands of a few, and there's a great difference between the power held by these people and the power of the ordinary citizen. These are called **high-power-distance cultures**; examples are Malaysia, Panama, Guatemala, the Philippines, Venezuela, Mexico, China, the Arab world, Indonesia, and Ecuador (Hofstede, 1997; Singh & Pereira, 2004). In **low-power-distance cultures** power is more evenly distributed throughout the citizenry; examples include Austria, Israel, Denmark, New Zealand, Ireland, Norway, Sweden, Finland, Switzerland, and Costa Rica (Hofstede, 1997; Singh & Pereira, 2004). These differences impact communication in numerous ways. For example, in high-power-distance cultures there's a great power distance between students and teachers; students are expected to be modest, polite, and totally respectful. In low-power-distance cultures (and you can see this clearly in U.S. college classrooms) students are expected to demonstrate their knowledge and command of the subject matter, participate in discussions with the teacher, and even challenge the teacher—something many high-power-distance culture members wouldn't even think of doing.

Friendship and dating relationships also will be influenced by the power distance between groups (Andersen, 1991). In India, for example, such relationships are expected to take place within your cultural class. In Sweden a person is expected to select friends and romantic partners on the basis not of class or culture but of individual factors such as personality, appearance, and the like.

In low-power-distance cultures you're expected to confront a friend, partner, or supervisor assertively; there is in these cultures a general feeling of equality that is consistent with assertive behavior (Borden, 1991). In high-power-distance cultures, direct confrontation and assertiveness may be viewed negatively, especially if directed at a superior.

Consider, for example, the war in Iraq. Put in terms of power distance, the United States and some allies are trying to change Iraq from a high-power-distance culture, in which those few in authority made the decisions for the many, to a low-power-distance culture, in which people are relatively equal (that is, a democracy). Yet even in democracies where everyone is equal under the law (or should be), there are still great power distances between those in authority—the employers, the police, the politicians—and the ordinary citizen, as there are between those who are rich and those who are poor.

## Masculine and Feminine Cultures

Especially important for self-concept is the culture's attitude about gender roles; that is, about how a man or woman should act. In fact, a popular classification of cultures is in terms of their masculinity and femininity (Hofstede, 1997, 1998). When denoting cultural orientations, the terms *masculine* and *feminine*, and used by G. Hofstede (1997) to describe this cultural difference, should be taken not as perpetuating stereotypes but as reflecting some of the commonly held assumptions of a sizable number of people throughout the world. In a highly **masculine culture**, people value male aggressiveness, material success, and strength. Women, on the other hand, are valued for their modesty, focus on the quality of life, and tenderness. A highly **feminine culture** values modesty, concern for relationships and the quality of life, and tenderness in both men and women. On the basis of Hofstede's (1997, 1998) research, the 10 countries with the highest masculinity score are (beginning with the highest) Japan, Austria, Venezuela, Italy, Switzerland, Mexico, Ireland, Jamaica, Great Britain, and Germany. The 10 countries with the highest femininity score are (beginning with the highest) Sweden, Norway, the Netherlands, Denmark, Costa Rica, Yugoslavia, Finland, Chile, Portugal, and Thailand. Of the 53 countries ranked, the United States ranks 15th most masculine.

Masculine cultures emphasize success and so socialize their members to be assertive, ambitious, and competitive. For example, members of masculine cultures are more likely to confront conflicts directly and to fight out any differences competitively; they're more likely to emphasize win–lose conflict strategies. Feminine cultures emphasize the quality of life and so socialize their members to be modest and to highlight close interpersonal relationships. Feminine cultures, for example, are more likely to uti-lize compromise and negotiation in resolving conflicts; they're more likely to seek win–win solutions.

Similarly, organizations can be viewed as masculine or feminine. Masculine organizations emphasize competitiveness and aggressiveness. They stress the bottom line and reward their workers on the basis of their contributions to the organization. Feminine organizations are less competitive and less aggressive. They emphasize worker satisfaction and reward their workers on the basis of need; those who have large families, for example, may get better raises than single people, even if they haven't contributed as much to the organization.

Try exploring your own cultural attitudes and ways of looking at things with the accompanying Building Communication Skills box below.

## High-Ambiguity-Tolerant and Low-Ambiguity-Tolerant Cultures

Levels of **ambiguity tolerance** vary widely among cultures. In some cultures people do little to avoid uncertainty, and they have little anxiety about not knowing what will happen next. In some other cultures, however, uncertainty is strongly avoided and there is much anxiety about uncertainty.

### High-Ambiguity-Tolerant Cultures

Members of high-ambiguity-tolerant cultures don't feel threatened by unknown situations; uncertainty is a normal part of life, and people accept it as it

---

**Building Communication Skills**   **Exploring Cultural Attitudes**

One of the best ways to appreciate the influence of culture on communication is to consider the attitudes people have about central aspects of culture. In a group of five or six—try for as culturally diverse a group as you can find—discuss how you think most of the students at your school feel (not how you feel) about each of the following. Use a five-point scale: 5 = most students strongly agree; 4 = most students agree; 3 = students are relatively neutral; 2 = most students disagree; 1 = most students strongly disagree.

_____ 1. Most feminists are just too sensitive about sexism.

_____ 2. Both females and males are victims of sexism.

_____ 3. Gay rights means gay men and lesbians demanding special privileges.

_____ 4. All men and women have a choice to be homosexual or not.

_____ 5. Racism isn't going to end overnight, so minorities need to be patient.

_____ 6. Minorities have the same opportunity as whites to succeed in our society.

*Attitudes strongly influence communication. Understanding your cultural attitudes is prerequisite to effective intercultural communication.*

*Source: These statements were taken from the Human Relations Attitude Inventory (Koppelman, with Goodhart, 2005). The authors note that this inventory is based on an inventory developed by Flavio Vega.*

comes. Examples of such low-anxiety cultures include Singapore, Jamaica, Denmark, Sweden, Hong Kong, Ireland, Great Britain, Malaysia, India, the Philippines, and the United States.

Because high-ambiguity-tolerant cultures are comfortable with ambiguity and uncertainty, they minimize the importance of rules governing communication and relationships (Hofstede, 1997; Lustig & Koester, 2006). People in these cultures readily tolerate individuals who don't follow the same rules or the cultural majority and may even encourage different approaches and perspectives.

Students from high-ambiguity-tolerant cultures appreciate freedom in education and prefer vague assignments without specific timetables. These students want to be rewarded for creativity and readily accept an instructor's lack of knowledge.

## Low-Ambiguity-Tolerant Cultures

Members of low-ambiguity-tolerant cultures do much to avoid uncertainty and have a great deal of anxiety about not knowing what will happen next; they see uncertainty as threatening and as something that must be counteracted. Examples of such low-ambiguity-tolerant cultures include Greece, Portugal, Guatemala, Uruguay, Belgium, El Salvador, Japan, Yugoslavia, Peru, France, Chile, Spain, and Costa Rica (Hofstede, 1997).

Low-ambiguity-tolerant cultures create very clear-cut rules for communication that must not be broken. For example, students from strong-uncertainty-avoidance cultures prefer highly structured experiences with little ambiguity; they prefer specific objectives, detailed instructions, and definite timetables. An assignment to write a term paper on "anything" would be cause for alarm; it would not be clear or specific enough. These students expect to be judged on the basis of the right answers and expect the instructor to have all the answers all the time (Hofstede, 1997).

With these five cultural distinctions in mind, let's now examine intercultural communication.

## MEDIA WATCH

## CULTURAL IMPERIALISM

The theory of *cultural imperialism* affords an interesting perspective on the influence of media, especially the impact of Western media on the cultures of developing countries (Becker & Roberts, 1992; DeZoysa & Newman, 2002). The theory argues that media from developed countries such as those of North America and western Europe dominate the cultures of countries importing such media. This cultural dominance is also seen in computer communication, in which the United States and the English language dominate.

Media products from the United States emphasize the country's dominant attitudes and values—for example, the preference for competition, the encouragement of individual expression, the promotion of capitalism and democracy, and the quest for financial success. An extreme form of the theory of cultural imperialism argues that the attitudes and values of the dominant media culture will eventually become the attitudes and values of the rest of the world.

Television programs, films, and music from the United States and western Europe are so popular and so in demand in developing countries that they may actually inhibit the growth of the native culture's own talent. So, for example, instead of pursuing their own vision by creating an original television drama or film, native writers in developing countries may find it easier to work as translators for products from more developed countries. And native promoters may find it more lucrative to sell, say, U.S. rock groups' CDs than to cultivate native talent. Similarly, the popularity of U.S. and western European media may also lead artists in developing countries to imitate Western cultural artifacts rather than developing their own styles—styles more consistent with their native culture. From another perspective, however, some people might argue that media products from the United States are superior to those produced elsewhere and hence serve as a standard for quality work throughout the world. Also, it might be argued that such products introduce new trends and perspectives and hence enrich the importing cultures.

### Increasing Media Literacy

*What do you think of the influence that media from the United States and western Europe are having on native cultures throughout the world? How do you evaluate this trend? Do you see advantages? How does this influence what you believe and feel about cultures other than your own?*

# INTERCULTURAL COMMUNICATION

Regardless of your own cultural background, you will surely come into close contact with people from a variety of other cultures—people who speak different languages, eat different foods, practice different religions, and approach work and relationships in very different ways. It doesn't matter whether you're a longtime resident of a country or a newly arrived immigrant: You are or you soon will be living, going to school, working, and forming relationships with people who are from very different cultures. Your day-to-day experiences are sure to become increasingly intercultural. Here we look first at the nature and forms of intercultural communication and second at guidelines for improving your own intercultural interactions.

## The Nature and Forms of Intercultural Communication

As discussed in Unit 1, the term *intercultural communication* refers to communication between persons who have different cultural beliefs, values, or ways of behaving. The model in Figure 2.1 illustrates this concept. The larger circles represent the culture of the individual communicators. The inner circles symbolize the communicators (the sources-receivers). In this model each communicator is a member of a different culture. In some instances, the cultural differences are relatively slight—say, between persons from Toronto and New York. In other instances, the cultural differences are great—say, between a farmer from Borneo and a surgeon in Germany.

All messages originate from within a specific and unique cultural context, and that context influences the messages' content and form. You communicate as you do largely as a result of your culture. Culture (along with the processes of enculturation and acculturation) influences every aspect of your communication experience.

The following types of communication may all be considered "intercultural" and, more important, subject to the varied barriers and gateways to effective communication identified in this unit:

- Communication between people of different national cultures—for example, between Chinese and Portuguese individuals, or between French and Norwegian.
- Communication between people of different races (sometimes called *interracial communication*)—for example, between African Americans and Asian Americans.

### DATING AN ETHNOCENTRIC

You've been dating this wonderful person for the last few months but increasingly are discovering that your "ideal" partner is extremely ethnocentric and sees little value in other religions, other races, other nationalities, in short, a bigot. You want to educate your possible life partner.

WHAT DO YOU SAY?
*In what context?*

- Communication between people of different ethnic groups (sometimes called *interethnic communication*)—for example, between Italian Americans and German Americans.
- Communication between people of different religions—for example, between Roman Catholics and Episcopalians, or between Muslims and Jews.
- Communication between nations (sometimes called *international communication*)—for example, between the United States and Argentina, or between China and Italy.
- Communication between smaller cultures existing within the larger culture—for example, between doctors and patients, or between research scientists and the general public.

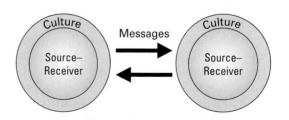

**FIGURE 2.1**   **A Model of Intercultural Communication**

This basic model of intercultural communication is designed to illustrate that culture is a part of every communication transaction. What other ways can you think of to illustrate the process of intercultural communication?

**GETTING YOUR FOOT OUT OF YOUR MOUTH**

At work you tell a homophobic joke only to discover that it was resented and clearly violated the organizational norms for polite and unbiased talk. You want to make this situation a little less awkward and potentially damaging to your work experience.

WHAT DO YOU SAY?

■ Communication between a smaller culture and the dominant culture—for example, between homosexuals and heterosexuals, or between older people and the younger majority.

■ Communication between genders—between men and women. Because gender roles are largely learned through culture, it seems useful to consider male-female communication as intercultural (Tannen, 1994a, b; Payne, 2001). Further, you can view male-female communication as cross-cultural because of the numerous differences in the way men and women speak and listen (Eckstein & Goldman, 2001).

## Improving Intercultural Communication

Murphy's law ("If anything can go wrong, it will") is especially applicable to intercultural communication. Intercultural communication is, of course, subject to all the same barriers and problems as are the other forms of communication discussed throughout this text. In this section, however, we'll consider some suggestions designed to counteract the barriers that are unique to intercultural communications (Barna, 1997; Ruben, 1985; Spitzberg, 1991).

Above all, intercultural communication depends on the cultural sensitivity of both individuals. **Cultural sensitivity** is an attitude and way of behaving in which you're aware of and acknowledge cultural differences. Cultural sensitivity is crucial on a global scale, as in efforts toward world peace and economic growth; it's also essential for effective interpersonal communication and for general success in life (Franklin & Mizell, 1995). Without cultural sensitivity there can be no effective interpersonal communication between people

who are different in gender or race or nationality or affectional orientation. So be mindful of the cultural differences between yourself and the other person. For example, the close physical distance that is normal in Arab cultures may prove too familiar or too intrusive in much of the United States and northern Europe. The empathy that most Americans welcome may be uncomfortable for most Koreans (Yun, 1976).

The following guidelines can help you achieve cultural sensitivity: (1) Prepare yourself, (2) reduce your ethnocentrism; (3) confront your stereotypes; (4) be mindful; (5) avoid overattribution; (6) recognize differences; and (7) adjust your communication. We'll take a look at each guideline in turn.

### Prepare Yourself

There's no better preparation for intercultural communication than learning about the other culture. Fortunately, there are numerous sources to draw on. View a video or film that presents a realistic view of the culture. Read what members of the culture as well as "outsiders" write about the culture. Scan magazines and websites from the culture. Talk with members of the culture. Chat in international chat rooms. Read blogs from members of the culture. Read materials addressed to people who need to communicate with those from other cultures. The easiest way to do this is to search the online bookstores (for example, Barnes and Noble at www.bn.com, Borders at www.borders.com, and Amazon at www.Amazon.com) for such keywords as *culture, international,* and *foreign travel.*

Another part of this preparation is to recognize and face fears that may stand in the way of effective intercultural communication (Gudykunst, 1994; Stephan & Stephan, 1985). For example, you may

# ASK THE RESEARCHER

## Culture Talk

*I'm going to work abroad in a firm where most of the people are members of a culture very different from mine. I know culture is important; what I don't know is when it's appropriate to discuss cultural differences and when it's not. Any general guidelines I could follow? I don't want to do anything stupid, at least not during my first few weeks.*

Your recognizing that culture is important is the first sign that you'll do well abroad. Intercultural communication as an academic discipline developed because of our (Americans') oblivion to other people's cultures, even as guests in their country.

We earned the "ugly American" title because we assumed that American culture was superior to others, and that despite where we visited or worked, people from the host culture had to acquiesce to our desires. Before you move to a foreign country, learn as much about its culture and people as you can; it will help you accept, appreciate, and respect difference.

Talking about cultural difference is inevitable. It's how you do it. When you notice difference, ask, respectfully, about it; for example, "I noticed that your head is always covered, I've never seen your hair. Is there some cultural or religious reason for it?" Instead of, "Why don't you take that scarf off your head, I get tired of looking at it."

For further information: Calloway-Thomas, C., Cooper, P. J., & Blake, C. (1999). *Intercultural communication: Roots and routes.* Boston: Allyn & Bacon and Samovar, L.A., & Porter, R. E. (2003). *Intercultural communication: A reader* (10th ed.). Belmont, CA: Wadsworth.

**Melbourne S. Cummings** (Ph.D., University of California, Los Angeles) is a professor of communication at Howard University and teaches courses in African American communication, nonverbal communication, and intercultural communication.

fear for your self-esteem. You may be anxious about your ability to control the intercultural situation, or you may worry about your own level of discomfort. You may fear saying something that will be considered politically incorrect or culturally insensitive and thereby losing face.

You may fear that you'll be taken advantage of by a member of the other culture. Depending on your own stereotypes, you may fear being lied to, financially duped, or made fun of.

You may fear that members of this other group will react to you negatively. You may fear, for example, that they will not like you or will disapprove of your attitudes or beliefs or perhaps even reject you as a person. Conversely, you may fear negative reactions from members of your own group. They might, for example, disapprove of your socializing with culturally different people.

Some fears, of course, are reasonable. In many cases, however, fears are groundless. Either way, you need to assess your concerns logically and weigh their consequences carefully. Then you'll be able to make informed choices about your communications.

## Reduce Ethnocentrism

As you learn your culture's ways, you develop an **ethnic identity**—that is, a commitment to the beliefs and philosophy of your culture (Chung & Ting-Toomey, 1999). The degree to which you identify with your cultural group can be measured by your responses to such questions as the following (from Ting-Toomey, 1981). Using a scale ranging from 1 (strongly disagree) to 5 (strongly agree), indicate how true about you the following statements are:

- I am increasing my involvement in activities with my ethnic group.
- I involve myself in causes that will help members of my ethnic group.
- It feels natural being part of my ethnic group.
- I have spent time trying to find out more about my own ethnic group.
- I am happy to be a member of my ethnic group.
- I have a strong sense of belonging to my ethnic group.
- I often talk to other members of my group to learn more about my ethnic culture.

High scores (5s and 4s) indicate a strong commitment to your culture's values and beliefs; low numbers (1s and 2s) indicate a relatively weak commitment.

A different type of cultural identification is ethnocentrism. Before reading about this important concept, examine your own cultural thinking by taking the self-test below.

## TEST YOURSELF

### How Ethnocentric Are You?

Here are 18 statements representing your beliefs about your culture. For each statement indicate how much you agree or disagree, using the following scale: Strongly agree = 5, agree = 4, neither agree nor disagree = 3, disagree = 2, strongly disagree = 1.

_____ 1. Most cultures are backward compared to my culture.

_____ 2. My culture should be the role model for other cultures.

_____ 3. Lifestyles in other cultures are just as valid as those in my culture.

_____ 4. Other cultures should try to be like my culture.

_____ 5. I'm not interested in the values and customs of other cultures.

_____ 6. People in my culture could learn a lot from people in other cultures.

_____ 7. Most people from other cultures just don't know what's good for them.

_____ 8. I have little respect for the values and customs of other cultures.

_____ 9. Most people would be happier if they lived like people in my culture.

_____ 10. People in my culture have just about the best lifestyles of anywhere.

_____ 11. Lifestyles in other cultures are not as valid as those in my culture.

_____ 12. I'm very interested in the values and customs of other cultures.

_____ 13. I respect the values and customs of other cultures.

_____ 14. I do not cooperate with people who are different.

_____ 15. I do not trust people who are different.

_____ 16. I dislike interacting with people from different cultures.

_____ 17. Other cultures are smart to look up to my culture.

_____ 18. People from other cultures act strange and unusual when they come into my culture.

**HOW DID YOU DO?** This test was presented to give you the opportunity to examine some of your own cultural beliefs, particularly those cultural beliefs that contribute to ethnocentrism. The person who is low in ethnocentrism would have high scores (4s and 5s) for items 3, 6, 12, and 13, and low scores (1s and 2s) for the other items. The person who is high in ethnocentrism would have low scores for items 3, 6, 12, and 13, and high scores for the other items.

**WHAT WILL YOU DO?** Use this test to bring to consciousness your own cultural beliefs so that you can examine those beliefs logically and objectively. Ask yourself if your beliefs are productive; will they help you achieve your professional and social goals? Or are they counterproductive; will they actually hinder your achieving your goals?

Source: This test is taken from James W. Neuliep, Michelle Chaudoir, and James C. McCroskey (2001). A cross-cultural comparison of ethnocentrism among Japanese and United States college students. *Communication Research Reports*, 18 (Spring), 137–146. Used with permission of Eastern Communication Association.

As you've probably gathered from taking this test, **ethnocentrism** is the tendency to see others and their behaviors through your own cultural filters, often as distortions of your own behaviors. It's the tendency to evaluate the values, beliefs, and behaviors of your own culture as more positive, superior, logical, and natural than those of other cultures. So although ethnocentrism may give you pride in your own culture and its achievements and may encourage you to sacrifice for that culture, it also may lead you to see other cultures as inferior and may foster an unwillingness to profit from the contributions of other cultures. For example, recent research shows a "substantial relationship" between ethnocentrism and homophobia (Wrench & McCroskey, 2003).

Ethnocentrism exists on a continuum. People are not either ethnocentric or not ethnocentric; rather, most are somewhere between these polar opposites. And, of course, your degree of ethnocentrism varies depending on the group on which you focus. For example, if you're Greek American, you may have a low degree of ethnocentrism when dealing with Italian Americans, but a high degree when dealing with Turkish Americans or Japanese Americans. Your degree of ethnocentrism (and we're all ethnocentric to at least some degree) will influence your communication in all its forms, an influence illustrated throughout this text.

### Confront Stereotypes

Stereotypes, especially when they operate below the level of conscious awareness, can create serious communication problems. Originally, *stereotype* was a printing term that referred to the plate that printed the same image over and over. A sociological or psychological **stereotype** is a fixed impression of a group of people. Everyone has attitudinal stereotypes—of national groups, religious groups, or racial groups, or perhaps of criminals, prostitutes, teachers, or plumbers. Ask yourself, for example, if you have any stereotypes of, say, bodybuilders, the opposite sex, a racial group different from your own, members of a religion very different from your own, hard drug users, or college professors. It is very likely that you have stereotypes of several or perhaps all of these groups. Although we often think of stereotypes as negative ("They're lazy, dirty, and only interested in getting high"), they may also be positive ("They're smart, hardworking, and extremely loyal").

If you have these fixed impressions, you might, upon meeting a member of a particular group, see that person primarily as a member of that group. Initially, a stereotype may provide you with some helpful orientation. However, it creates problems when you apply to a person all the characteristics you assign to members of that person's group without examining the unique individual. If you meet a politician, for example, you may tend to apply to the person a series of stereotypical "politician" images. To complicate matters further, you may see in the person's behavior the manifestation of various characteristics that you would not see if you did not know that this person was a politician. In online communication, because there are few visual and auditory cues, it's not surprising to find that people form impressions of their online communication partner with a heavy reliance on stereotypes (Jacobson, 1999).

Consider another kind of stereotype: You're driving along a dark road and are stopped at a stop sign. A car pulls up beside you and three teenagers jump out and rap on your window. There may be a variety of reasons for this: They may need help, they may want to ask directions, or they may be planning a carjacking. Your self-protective stereotype may help you decide on "carjacking" and may lead you to pull away and into the safety of a busy service station. In doing that, of course, you may have escaped being carjacked, or you may have failed to help innocent people who needed your help.

Stereotyping can lead to two major barriers. First, you will fail to appreciate the multifaceted nature of all people and all groups. The tendency to group a person into a class and to respond to that person primarily as a member of that class can lead you to perceive that a person possesses those qualities (usually negative) that you believe characterize the group to which he or she belongs. For example, consider your stereotype of an avid computer user. Very likely it's quite different from the research findings—which show that such users are as often female as male and are as sociable, popular, and self-assured as their peers who are not into heavy computer use (Schott & Selwyn, 2000).

Second, stereotyping also can lead you to ignore the unique characteristics of an individual; you therefore fail to benefit from the special contributions each person can bring to an encounter.

### Increase Mindfulness

Being mindful rather than mindless (a distinction considered in Unit 7) is generally helpful in intercultural communication situations (Burgoon, Berger, & Waldron, 2000). When you're in a mindless state, you behave on the basis of assumptions that would not normally pass intellectual scrutiny. For example, you know that cancer is not contagious, and yet you may still avoid touching cancer patients. You know that people who are blind generally don't have hearing problems, yet you may use a louder voice when talking to persons without sight. When the discrepancies between behaviors and available evidence are pointed out and your mindful state is awakened, you quickly realize that these behaviors are not logical or realistic.

You can look at this textbook and your course in human communication as means of awakening your mindful state about the way you engage in interpersonal, group, and public communication. After completing this course, you should be much more mindful and much less mindless about all your communication behavior.

### Avoid Overattribution

Overattribution is the tendency to attribute too much of a person's behavior or attitudes to one of that person's characteristics (she thinks that way because she's a woman; he believes that because he was raised as a Catholic). In intercultural communication situations, overattribution appears in two ways. First, it's the tendency to see too much of what a person believes or does as caused by the person's cultural identification. Second, it's the tendency to see a person as a spokesperson for his or her particular culture—to assume that because a person is, say, African American, he or she is therefore knowledgeable about the entire African American experience; or that the person's thoughts are always focused on African American issues. People's ways of thinking and ways of behaving are influenced by a wide variety of factors; culture is just one of them.

# REFLECTIONS ON ETHICS

## Culture and Ethics

Throughout history there have been numerous cultural practices that most people today would judge unethical and might well wish to make illegal. Sacrificing virgins to the gods and sending children to fight wars are obvious examples. And even today there are practices woven deep into the fabric of different cultures that many Americans would find unethical. Consider a few examples:

- Some cultures support bronco-riding events at which the bull's testicles are tied so that it will experience pain and try to throw off the rider.

- Some cultures support female circumcision, whereby part or all of a young girl's genitals are surgically altered so that she can never experience sexual intercourse without extreme pain, a practice designed to keep her a virgin until marriage.

- Some cultures support the practice of wearing fur. In some cases this means catching wild animals in extremely painful traps; in others it involves raising captive animals so they can be killed when their pelts are worth the most money.

### Ethical Choice Point

*Imagine that you're talking with a group of work colleagues about cultural differences and diversity. During the discussion one or another of your colleagues expresses approval of each of the above practices, arguing that each culture has a right to its own practices and beliefs and that no one has the right to object to cultural traditions. Given your own beliefs about these issues and about cultural diversity in general, what ethical obligations do you have to respond? What would you say?*

## Recognize Differences

To communicate interculturally you need to recognize the differences between yourself and people from other cultures, the differences within the other cultural group, and the numerous differences in meaning.

**Differences between Yourself and the Culturally Different.** A common barrier to intercultural communication occurs when you assume that similarities exist and that differences do not. This is especially true of values, attitudes, and beliefs. You might easily accept different hairstyles, clothing, and foods. In basic values and beliefs, however, you may assume that deep down all people are really alike. They aren't. When you assume similarities and ignore differences, you'll fail to notice important distinctions and when communicating will convey to others that your ways are the right ways and that their ways are not important to you. Consider this example. An American invites a Filipino coworker to dinner. The Filipino politely refuses. The American is hurt and feels that the Filipino does not want to be friendly. The Filipino is hurt and concludes that the invitation was not extended sincerely. Here, it seems, both the American and the Filipino assume that their customs for inviting people to dinner are the same when, in fact, they aren't. A Filipino expects to be invited several times before accepting a dinner invitation. When an invitation is given only once, it's viewed as insincere.

Here's another example. An American college student hears the news that her favorite uncle has died. She bites her lip, pulls herself up, and politely excuses herself from the group of foreign students with whom she is having dinner. The Russian thinks: "How unfriendly." The Italian thinks: "How insincere." The Brazilian thinks: "How unconcerned." To many Americans, it's a sign of bravery to endure pain (physical or emotional) in silence and without any outward show of emotion. To members of other groups, such silence is often interpreted negatively to mean that the individual does not consider them friends who can share such sorrow. In other cultures, people are expected to reveal to friends how they feel.

**Differences within the Culturally Different Group.** Within every cultural group there are vast and important differences. As all Americans are not alike, neither are all Indonesians, Greeks, Mexicans, and so on. When you ignore these differences—when you assume that all persons covered by the same label (in this case a national or ethnic label) are the same—you're guilty of stereotyping. A good example of this is seen in the use of the term "African American." The term stresses the unity of Africa and of those who are of African descent and is analogous to "Asian American" or "European American." At the same time, it ignores the great diversity within the African continent when, for example, it's used as analogous to "German American" or "Japanese American." More analogous terms would be

## PRIVILEGED LANGUAGE

In discussing your friendship with members of another race, you use terms that members of the race use among themselves but which are normally considered negative. The people you're talking to, however, take offense at your use of these terms. You want to lessen this negative reaction and to let the group know that you don't normally use such racial terms.

WHAT DO YOU SAY?

"Nigerian American" or "Ethiopian American." Within each culture there are smaller cultures that differ greatly from each other and from the larger culture.

**Differences in Meaning.** Meaning exists not in words but in people (a principle we'll return to in Unit 5). Consider, for example, the differences in meaning that exist for words such as woman to an American and a Muslim, religion to a born-again Christian and an atheist, and lunch to a Chinese rice farmer and a Madison Avenue advertising executive. Even though the same word is used, its meanings will vary greatly depending on the listeners' cultural definitions.

Nonverbal differences in meaning also exist. For example, a left-handed American who eats with the left hand may be seen by a Muslim as obscene. To the Muslim, the left hand isn't used for eating or for shaking hands but to clean oneself after excretory functions. So using the left hand to eat or to shake hands is considered insulting and obscene.

### Adjust Your Communication

Intercultural communication (in fact, all communication) takes place only to the extent that you and the person you're trying to communicate with share the same system of symbols. As Unit 1 discussed, your interaction will be hindered to the extent that your language and nonverbal systems differ. Therefore, it's important to adjust your communication to compensate for cultural differences.

---

**Building Communication Skills** — Confronting Intercultural Difficulties

How might you deal with any one or two of the following obstacles to intercultural communication? If you have the opportunity, share your responses with others in the class. You'll gain a wealth of practical insights.

1. You're in an interracial, interreligious relationship. Your partner's family ignores your "couplehood." For example, you and your partner are never invited to dinner as a couple or included in any family affairs. You decide to confront your partner's family.

2. Your parents persist in holding stereotypes about other religious, racial, and ethnic groups. These stereotypes come up in all sorts of conversations. You're really embarrassed by these attitudes and feel you must tell your parents how incorrect you think these stereotypes are.

3. George, a colleague at work, recently underwent a religious conversion. He now persists in trying to get everyone else—you included—to undergo this same religious conversion. You decide to tell him that you find this behavior offensive.

*Confronting cultural insensitivity is not an easy task; most people do not see their own insensitivity. So approach these situations carefully; rely on all the communication skills presented throughout this text and in your course.*

Furthermore, you have to share your own system of signals with others so that they can better understand you. Although some people may know what you mean by your silence or by your avoidance of eye contact, others may not. You cannot expect others to decode your behaviors accurately without help.

Communication accommodation theory, as explained in Unit 1, holds that speakers will adjust or accommodate to the communication style of their listeners in order to interact more pleasantly and efficiently (Giles, Mulac, Bradac, & Johnson, 1987). As you adjust your messages, recognize that each culture has its own rules and customs for communication (Barna, 1997; Ruben, 1985; Spitzberg, 1991).

These rules identify what is appropriate and what is inappropriate. Thus, for example, in U.S. culture you would call a person you wished to date three or four days in advance. In certain Asian cultures you might call the person's parents weeks or even months in advance. In U.S. culture you say, as a general friendly gesture and not as a specific invitation, "come over and pay us a visit sometime." To members of other cultures, this comment is sufficient to prompt the listeners actually to visit at their convenience. Table 2.1 presents a good example of a set of cultural rules—guidelines for communicating with an extremely large and important culture that many people don't know.

## Table 2.1  Communication Tips

### Between People with and without Disabilities

The suggestions offered here are considered appropriate in the United States, though not necessarily in other cultures. For example, although most people in the United States accept the phrase "person with mental retardation," it's considered offensive to many in the United Kingdom (Fernald, 1995).

If you're the one without such a disability:

1. *Avoid negative terms and terms that define the person as disabled such as "the disabled man" or "the handicapped child."* Instead say "person with a disability," always emphasizing the person rather than the disability. Avoid terms that describe the person with a disability as abnormal; for example, when you refer to people without disabilities as "normal," you in effect say that a person with a disability isn't normal.

2. *Treat assistive devices such as wheelchairs, canes, walkers, or crutches as the personal property of the user.* Be careful not to move these out of your way; they're for the convenience of the person with the disability. Avoid leaning on a person's wheelchair, for example; it's similar to leaning on a person.

3. *Shake hands with the person with the disability if you shake hands with others in a group.* Don't avoid shaking hands if an individual's hand is crippled, for example.

4. *Avoid talking about the person with a disability in the third person.* For example, avoid saying, "Doesn't he get around beautifully with the new crutches." Always direct your comments directly to the individual.

5. *Don't assume that people who have a disability are intellectually impaired.* Slurred speech—such as may occur with people who have cerebral palsy or cleft palate—should never be taken as indicating a low-level intellect. Be especially careful not to talk down to such people as, research shows, many people do (Unger, 2001).

6. *When you're not sure of how to act, ask.* For example, if you're not sure if you should offer walking assistance, ask: "Would you like me to help you into the dining room?" And, even more important, accept the person's response. If he or she says no, then that means no; don't insist.

7. *Maintain similar eye level.* If a person is in a wheelchair, for example, it might be helpful for you to sit down or kneel down to get onto the same eye level.

If you're the one with a disability:

1. *Let the other person know if he or she can do anything to assist you in communicating.* For example, if you want someone to speak in a louder voice, ask. If you want to relax and have someone push your wheelchair, say so.

2. *Be patient and understanding.* Many people mean well but may simply not know how to act or what to say. Put them at ease as best you can.

3. *Demonstrate your own comfort.* If you detect discomfort in the other person, you might talk a bit about your disability to show that you're not uncomfortable and that you understand that others may not know how you feel. But don't feel this is something you should or have to do; you're under no obligation to educate the public.

These suggestions are based on a wide variety of sources; for example, www.empowermentzone.com/etiquet.txt (the website for the National Center for Access Unlimited), www.dol.gov/dol/top/disability/index.htm, www.dissvcs.uga.edu/com-peodis.html, and www.ucpa.org/ucp_generaldoc.cfm (all accessed October 23, 2004).

## SUMMARY: CULTURE AND COMMUNICATION

This unit introduced the study of culture and its relationship to communication and considered how cultures differ and some of the theories developed to explain how culture and communication affect each other. In addition, the unit introduced the study of intercultural communication and its nature and principles.

1. Culture consists of the relatively specialized lifestyle of a group of people—their values, beliefs, artifacts, ways of behaving, and ways of communicating—that is passed on from one generation to the next through communication rather than through genes.

2. Enculturation is the process by which culture is transmitted from one generation to the next.

3. Acculturation involves the processes by which one culture is modified through contact with or exposure to another culture.

4. Cultures differ in terms of individualist or collectivist orientations, high and low context, high and low power distance, masculinity and femininity, and tolerance of ambiguity.

5. Individualist cultures emphasize individual values such as power and achievement, whereas collectivist cultures emphasize group values such as co-operation and responsibility to the group.

6. In high-context cultures much information is in the context or the person; in low-context cultures information is expected to be made explicit.

7. In high-power-distance cultures there are large differences in power between people; in low-power-distance cultures power is more evenly distributed throughout the population.

8. Masculine cultures emphasize assertiveness, ambition, and competition; feminine cultures emphasize compromise and negotiation.

9. High-ambiguity tolerant cultures feel little threatened by uncertainty; it's accepted as it comes. Low-ambiguity tolerant cultures feel uncomfortable with uncertainty and seek to avoid it.

10. Intercultural communication is communication among people who have different cultural beliefs, values, or ways of behaving.

11. Ethnocentrism, which exists on a continuum, is our tendency to evaluate the beliefs, attitudes, and values of our own culture positively and those of other cultures negatively.

12. Stereotyping is the tendency to develop and maintain fixed, unchanging impressions of groups of people and to use these impressions to evaluate individual members of these groups, ignoring unique individual characteristics.

13. Among guidelines for more effective intercultural communication are: prepare yourself, recognize and reduce your ethnocentrism, confront your stereotypes, be mindful, avoid overattribution, recognize differences, and adjust your communication.

## KEY TERMS IN CULTURE AND COMMUNICATION

| | | | |
|---|---|---|---|
| acculturation (p. **34**) | ethnic identity (p. **47**) | high-context culture (p. **41**) | low-power-distance |
| ambiguity tolerance | ethnocentrism (p. **48**) | high-power-distance | cultures (p. **42**) |
| (p. **43**) | face-saving (p. **42**) | cultures (p. **42**) | masculine culture (p. **43**) |
| collectivist culture (p. **39**) | feminine culture (p. **43**) | individualist culture (p. **39**) | sex (p. **34**) |
| cultural sensitivity (p. **46**) | gender (p. **34**) | low-context culture (p. **41**) | stereotype (p. **49**) |
| enculturation (p. **34**) | | | |

## THINKING CRITICALLY ABOUT CULTURE AND COMMUNICATION

1. **Cultural Differences.** Cultural differences underlie some of the most hotly debated topics in the news today. For example, consider the following questions. How would you answer these? How do your cultural attitudes, beliefs, and values influence your responses?

   • Should Christian Scientist parents be prosecuted for preventing their children from receiving life-saving medical procedures such as blood transfusions?

   • Should cockfighting be permitted or declared illegal in all states as "cruelty to animals"? Some Latin Americans have argued that cockfighting is a part of their culture and should be permitted even though it's illegal in most of the United States.

   • Should same-sex marriages be legalized? Right now, only one state (Massachusetts) permits same-sex marriage, but other states such as New York have it on their agenda.

2. **Choosing a Mate.** Men and women from different cultures were asked the following question: "If a man (woman) had all the other qualities you desired, would you marry this person if you were not in love with him (her)?" (LeVine, Sato, Hashimoto, & Verma, 1994). Fifty percent of the respondents from Pakistan, 49 percent from India, and 19 percent from Thailand said yes. At the other extreme were respondents from Japan (only 2

percent said yes), the United States (3.5 percent), and Brazil (4 percent). How would you answer this question? How is your answer influenced by your culture?

3. **Sexual Relations.** Some cultures frown on sexual relationships outside of marriage; others consider sex a normal part of intimacy. Intercultural researchers (Hatfield & Rapson, 1996) recall a discussion between colleagues from Sweden and the United States on ways of preventing AIDS. When researchers from the United States suggested promoting abstinence, their Swedish counterparts asked, "How will teenagers ever learn to become loving, considerate sexual partners if they don't practice?" "The silence that greeted the question," note Hatfield and Rapson (1996, p. 36), "was the sound of two cultures clashing." How have your cultural beliefs and values influenced what you consider appropriate relationship behavior?

4. **What's in a Name?** Some researchers prefer to use the term *subculture* to refer to smaller cultures within larger cultures; other researchers do not use the term, feeling that it implies that some cultures are less important than others. Some researchers prefer to use the term *co-culture* to refer to a variety of cultures coexisting side by side, whereas others think this term is imprecise, because all cultures coexist (Lustig & Koester, 2006); these theorists prefer simply to refer to all cultures as *cultures*. How do you feel about the terms "subculture," "co-culture," and just plain "culture"?

5. **Cell Phone Etiquette.** Cell phone users vary widely in how they use their phones in public places, and rules of cell phone etiquette abound (for example, www.microsoft.com/smallbusiness/resources/technology/communications/cell_phone_etiquette_10_dos_and_donts.mspx and www.dmwmedia.com/news/2006/12/14/12-unwritten-rules-of-cell-phone-etiquette, accessed May 2, 2007). What rules of cell phone etiquette do you follow? Where are you most likely to turn off your cell phone? In what public situations are you likely to leave it on?

# LogOn! MyCommunicationLab
## WWW.MYCOMMUNICATIONLAB.COM

Among the materials you'll find on MCL relevant to the discussion of culture and human communication are two self-tests (What's Your Cultural Awareness? and How Open Are You Interculturally?) and exercises including Going from Culture to Gender, The Influence of Cultural Beliefs, and Sources of Your Cultural Beliefs. Also, take a look at American Fact Finder and watch the videos Bikes & Spikes, Vietnamese Culture, Cultural Background, and Tonya in the Classroom.

# UNIT 3  The Self and Perception

## MAJOR TOPICS

The Self in Human Communication
Self-Disclosure
Perception and the Stages of Perception

Perceptual Processes
Increasing Accuracy in Perception

## Special Features

The self is perhaps the most important element in any form of communication. This unit focuses on the ways in which you and others perceive yourself.

**In this unit you'll learn about:**
- self-concept, self-awareness, and self-esteem.
- the process of self-disclosure.
- the nature and workings of perception.

**You'll learn to:**
- communicate with a better understanding of who you are.
- regulate your self-disclosures and respond appropriately to the disclosures of others.
- increase your own accuracy in perceiving other people and their messages.

# THE SELF IN HUMAN COMMUNICATION

Who you are and how you see yourself influence not only the way you communicate, but also how you respond to the communications of others. First we'll explore the self: the self-concept and how it develops; self-awareness and ways to increase it; self-esteem and ways to enhance it; and self-disclosure, or communication that reveals who you are.

## Self-Concept

Your **self-concept** is your image of who you are. It's how you perceive yourself: your feelings and thoughts about your strengths and weaknesses, your abilities and limitations. Self-concept develops from the images that others have of you, comparisons between yourself and others, your cultural experiences, and your evaluation of your own thoughts and behaviors (Figure 3.1 on page 57). Let's explore each of these components of the self-concept.

### Others' Images of You

If you want to see how your hair looks, you probably look in a mirror. But what would you do if you wanted to see how friendly or how assertive you are? According to the concept of the **looking-glass self** (Cooley, 1922), you'd look at the image of yourself that others reveal to you through the way they communicate with you.

Of course, you would not look to just anyone. Rather, you would look to those who are most significant in your life—to your *significant others*, such as your friends, family members, and romantic partners. If these significant others think highly of you, you will see a positive self-image reflected in their behaviors; if they think little of you, you will see a more negative image.

## Comparisons with Others

Another way you develop self-concept is by comparing yourself with others, most often with your peers (Festinger, 1954). For example, after an exam, you probably want to know how you performed relative to the other students in your class. This gives you a clearer idea of how effectively you performed. If you play on a baseball team, it's important to know your batting average in comparison with the batting average of others on the team. You gain a different perspective when you see yourself in comparison to your peers.

## Cultural Teachings

Your culture instills in you a variety of beliefs, values, and attitudes about such things as success (how you define it and how you should achieve it); the relevance of religion, race, or nationality; and the ethical principles you should follow in business and in your personal life. These teachings provide benchmarks against which you can measure yourself. Your ability to achieve what your culture defines as success, for example, contributes to a positive self-concept; in the same way, your failure to achieve what your culture encourages contributes to a negative self-concept.

Especially important in self-concept are cultural teachings about gender roles—about how a man or woman should act. In fact, a popular classification of cultures is in terms of their "masculinity" and "femininity" (Hofstede, 1997). As noted in Unit 2, *masculine cultures* tend to socialize people to be assertive, ambitious, and competitive. For example, members of masculine cultures are more likely to confront conflicts directly and to competitively fight out any differences; they're more likely to emphasize win–lose conflict strategies. *Feminine cultures* socialize people to be modest and to emphasize close interpersonal relationships. Members of feminine cultures, for example, are more likely to utilize compromise and negotiation in resolving conflicts; they're more likely to seek win–win solutions.

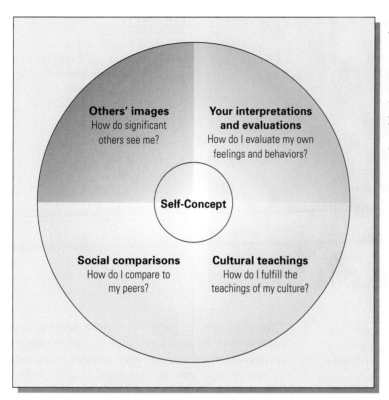

**FIGURE 3.1**  **The Sources of Self-Concept**

This diagram depicts the four sources of self-concept, the four contributors to how you see yourself. As you read about self-concept, consider the influence of each factor throughout your life. Which factor influenced you most as a preteen? Which influences you most now? Which will influence you most 25 or 30 years from now?

When you display the traits that are rewarded by your culture—whether they be masculine or feminine—you're likely to be rewarded and complimented, and this feedback is likely to contribute to a positive self-concept. Displaying contrary traits is likely to result in criticism, which, in turn, will contribute to a more negative self-concept.

## Self-Interpretations and Self-Evaluations

Your *self-interpretations* (your reconstruction of the incident and your understanding of it) and *self-evaluations* (the value—good or bad—that you place on the behavior also contribute to your self-concept. For example, let's say you believe that lying is wrong. If you then lie and you view it as a lie (rather than as, say, a polite way of avoiding an issue), you will probably evaluate this behavior in terms of your internalized beliefs about lying (*lying is wrong*) and you'll react negatively to your own behavior. You may, for example, experience guilt about violating your own beliefs. On the other hand, let's say that you pull someone out of a burning building at great personal risk. You will probably evaluate this behavior positively; you'll feel good about this behavior and, as a result, about yourself.

## Self-Awareness

**Self-awareness**—your knowledge of who you are; of your traits, your strengths and limitations, your emotions and behaviors, your individuality—is basic to all communication. You can achieve self-awareness by examining the several aspects of yourself as they might appear to others as well as to yourself. One tool that is commonly used for this examination is called the Johari window, a metaphoric division of the self into four areas (Figure 3.2 on page 58).

## Your Four Selves

Divided into four areas or "panes," the **Johari window** shows different aspects or versions of the self. The four aspects are the *open self, blind self, hidden self,* and *unknown self.* These areas are not separate from one another but interdependent. As one dominates, the others recede to a greater or lesser degree; or, to stay with our metaphor, as one windowpane becomes larger, one or another becomes smaller.

- The **open self** represents all the information, behaviors, attitudes, and feelings about yourself that you know and that others also know. Such knowledge could include everything from your name, skin color, sex, and age to your religion and political beliefs. The size of the open self varies according to your personality and the people to whom you're relating. You may be more open with some people than you are with others. So, you may have a large open self about your romantic life with your friends (you tell them everything) but a very small open self about the same issues with, say, your parents.

**BLIND SELF**

You're going to enter a new job—one that you hope you'll keep for the major part of your professional career—and you really need honest feedback on your total performance at your present job.

WHAT DO YOU SAY?
*To whom? Through what channel?*

- The **blind self** represents knowledge about you that others have but you don't. This might include your habit of finishing other people's sentences or your way of rubbing your nose when you become anxious. A large blind self indicates low self-awareness and interferes with accurate communication. So it's important to reduce your blind self and learn what others know about you. You can do this by following the suggestions offered below, under "Growing in Self-Awareness."

- The **unknown self** represents those parts of yourself that neither you nor others know. This is information that is buried in your subconscious. You may, for example, learn of your obsession with money, your fear of criticism, or the kind of lover you are through hypnosis, dreams, psychological tests, or psychotherapy.

- The **hidden self** represents all the knowledge you have of yourself but keep secret from others.

This windowpane includes all your successfully kept secrets; for example, your fantasies, embarrassing experiences, and any attitudes or beliefs of which you may be ashamed. You probably keep secrets from some people and not from others; for example, you might not tell your parents you're dating someone of another race or religion, but you might tell a close friend.

Each person's Johari window will be different, and each individual's window will vary from one time to another and from one communication situation to another. By way of example Figure 3.3 illustrates two possible configurations.

## Growing in Self-Awareness

Because self-awareness is so important in communication, try to increase awareness of your own needs, desires, habits, beliefs, and attitudes. You can do this in various ways.

|  | **Known to self** | **Not known to self** |
|---|---|---|
| **Known to others** | **Open self**<br>Information about yourself that you and others know | **Blind self**<br>Information about yourself that you don't know but that others do know |
| **Not known to others** | **Hidden self**<br>Information about yourself that you know but others don't know | **Unknown self**<br>Information about yourself that neither you nor others know |

**FIGURE 3.2**   **The Johari Window**

This diagram is a commonly used tool for examining what we know and don't know about ourselves. It can also help explain the nature of self-disclosure, covered later in this unit. The window gets its name from its originators, *Joseph* Luft and *Harry* Ingham.

Source: Joseph Luft, *Group Process: An Introduction to Group Dynamics* (3rd ed.). Copyright © 1984. New York: McGraw-Hill. Reprinted by permission.

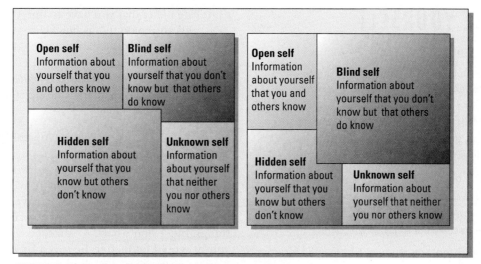

**FIGURE 3.3  Johari Windows of Different Structures**

Notice that as one self grows, one or more of the other selves shrink. Assume that these models depict the self-awareness and self-disclosure of two different people. How would you describe the type of communication (especially self-disclosure) that might characterize each of these two people?

■ **Listen to others.** Conveniently, others are constantly giving you the very feedback you need to increase self-awareness. In every interaction people comment on you in some way—on what you do, what you say, how you look. Sometimes these comments are explicit: "Loosen up" or "Don't take things so hard." Often they're "hidden" in the way others look at you—in the expressionless face that indicates disagreement or disappointment or the broad smile that says, "I think you're wonderful." Sometimes feedback is hidden in the topics that others talk about or avoid: If someone sticks to academic topics and avoids relationship topics, this may reveal the level on which the person sees the relationship between you. Pay close attention to this kind of information.

■ **Increase your open self.** Revealing yourself to others will help increase your self-awareness. As you talk about yourself, you may see connections that you had previously missed. With feedback from others, you may gain still more insight. Also, by increasing your open self, you increase the chances that others will reveal what they know about you.

■ **Seek information about yourself.** Encourage people to reveal what they know about you. Use situations that arise every day to gain self-information: "Do you think I came down too hard on the kids today?" "Do you think I was assertive enough when asking for the raise?" But seek this self-awareness in moderation. If you do it too often, your friends will soon look for someone else with whom to talk.

■ **Dialogue with yourself.** No one knows you better than you know yourself. Ask yourself self-awareness questions: What motivates me to act as I do? What are my short-term and long-term goals? How do I plan to achieve them? What are my strengths and weaknesses?

## Self-Esteem

**Self-esteem** is a measure of how valuable you think you are; people with high self-esteem think very highly of themselves, whereas people with low self-esteem view themselves negatively. Before reading further about this topic, consider your own self-esteem by taking the self-test on page 60.

The basic idea behind building self-esteem is that when you feel good about yourself—about who you are and what you're capable of doing—you will perform better. When you think like a success, you're more likely to act like a success. Conversely, when you think you're a failure, you're more likely to act like a failure. When you get up to give a speech and you visualize yourself being successful and effective, you're more likely to give a good speech. If, on the other hand, you think you're going to forget your speech or mispronounce words or mix up your presentation aids, you are less likely to be successful. Increasing self-esteem will, therefore, help you to function more effectively in school, in interpersonal relationships, and in careers. Here are five suggestions for increasing self-esteem that parallel the questions in the self-test.

# TEST YOURSELF

## How's Your Self-Esteem?

Respond to each of the following five statements with T for true if the statement describes you at least some significant part of the time; write F for false if the statement describes you rarely or never.

_____ 1. Generally, I feel I have to be successful in all things.

_____ 2. Some of my acquaintances are often critical or negative of what I do and how I think

_____ 3. I often tackle projects that I know are impossible to complete to my satisfaction.

_____ 4. When I focus on the past, I more often focus on my failures than on my successes and on my negative rather than my positive qualities.

_____ 5. I make little effort to improve my personal and social skills.

**HOW DID YOU DO?** "True" responses would generally be seen as indicating attitudes that get in the way of building positive self-esteem. "False" responses would indicate that you are thinking much the way a self-esteem coach would want you to think.

**WHAT WILL YOU DO?** The following discussion elaborates on the issues suggested by these five statements and illustrates why each of them creates problems for the development of healthy self-esteem. So the guidelines below are a good starting place. You might also want to log into the National Association for Self-Esteem's website (www.self-esteem-nase.org). There you'll find a variety of materials for examining and bolstering self-esteem.

## Attack Self-Destructive Beliefs

Challenge beliefs you have about yourself that are unproductive or that make it more difficult for you to achieve your goals (Einhorn, 2006). Here, for example, are some beliefs that are likely to prove self-destructive (Butler, 1981):

1. The belief that you have to be perfect; this causes you to try to perform at unrealistically high levels at work, school, and home; anything short of perfection is unacceptable.
2. The belief that you have to be strong; this belief tells you that weakness and any of the more vulnerable emotions like sadness, compassion, or loneliness are wrong.
3. The belief that you have to please others and that your worthiness depends on what others think of you.

4. The belief that you have to hurry up; this compels you to do things quickly, to try to do more than can be reasonably expected in any given amount of time.
5. The belief that you have to take on more responsibilities than any one person can be expected to handle.

**Self-destructive beliefs** set unrealistically high standards and therefore almost always lead to failure. As a result, you may develop a negative self-image, seeing yourself as someone who constantly fails. So replace these self-destructive beliefs with more productive ones, such as "I succeed in many things, but I don't have to succeed in everything" and "It would be nice to be loved by everyone, but it isn't necessary to my happiness."

## Seek Out Nourishing People

Psychologist Carl Rogers (1970) drew a distinction between _noxious_ and _nourishing_ people. Noxious people criticize and find fault with just about everything. Nourishing people, on the other hand, are positive and optimistic. Most important, nourishing people reward us, they stroke us, they make us feel good about ourselves. To enhance your self-esteem, seek out these people—and avoid noxious people, those who make you feel negatively about yourself. At the same time, seek to become more nourishing yourself so that you each build up the other's self-esteem.

Identification with people similar to yourself also seems to increase self-esteem. For example, in one study deaf people who identified with the larger deaf community had greater self-esteem than those who didn't so identify (Jambor & Elliott, 2005). Similarly, identification with your cultural group also seems helpful in developing positive self-esteem (McDonald, McCabe, Yeh, Lau, Garland, & Hough, 2005).

## Work on Projects That Will Result in Success

Some people want to fail (or so it seems). Often, they select projects that will result in failure simply because these projects are impossible to complete. Avoid this trap; select projects that will result in success. Each success will help build self-esteem, and each success will make the next success a little easier. If a project does fail, recognize that this does not mean that _you're_ a failure. Everyone fails somewhere along the line. Failure is something that happens; it's not necessarily something you've created. It's not something inside you. Further, your failing once does not mean that you will fail the next time. So learn to put failure in perspective.

### SELF-ESTEEM

Your best friend at work has hit a new low in self-esteem—a long-term relationship failed, an expected promotion never materialized, a large investment went sour. You want to help your friend regain self-esteem.

*WHAT DO YOU SAY?*
*To whom? Through what channel?*

## Remind Yourself of Your Successes

Some people have a tendency to focus, sometimes too much, on their failures, their missed opportunities, their social mistakes. If your objective is to correct what you did wrong or to identify the skills that you need to correct these failures, then focusing on failures can have some positive value. But if you focus on failure without thinking about plans for correction, then you're probably just making life more difficult for yourself and limiting your self-esteem. To counteract the tendency to recall failures, remind yourself of your successes. Recall these successes both intellectually and emotionally. Realize why they were successes, and relive the emotional experience—the feelings you had when you sank that winning basketball or aced that test or helped that friend overcome a personal problem. And while you're at it, recall your positive qualities.

## Secure Affirmation

An affirmation is simply a statement asserting that something is true. In discussions of self-concept and self-awareness, as noted in this unit, the word *affirmation* is used to refer to positive statements about you, statements asserting that something good or positive is true of you. It's frequently recommended that you remind yourself of your successes with self-affirmations—that you focus on your good deeds; on your positive qualities, strengths, and

virtues; on your productive and meaningful relationships with friends, loved ones, and relatives (Aronson, Cohen, & Nail, 1998; Aronson, Wilson, & Akert, 2002).

Self-affirmations include statements such as "I'm a worthy person," "I'm responsible and can be depended upon," "I'm capable of loving and being loved," "I'm a good team player," and "I can accept my past but also let it go." The idea behind this advice is that the way you talk to yourself will influence what you think of yourself. If you *affirm* yourself—if you tell yourself that you're a success, that others like you, that you will succeed on the next test, and that you will be welcomed when asking for a date—you will soon come to feel more positive about yourself.

Some researchers, however, argue that self-affirmations—although extremely popular in self-help books—may not be very helpful. These critics contend that if you have low self-esteem, you're not going to believe your self-affirmations, because you don't have a high opinion of yourself to begin with (Paul, 2001). They propose that the alternative to self-affirmation is to secure affirmation from others. You'd do this by, for example, becoming more competent in communication and interacting with more positive people. In this way, you'd get more positive feedback from others—which, these researchers argue, is more helpful than self-talk in raising self-esteem.

It is also worth noting that many people who have extremely low self-esteem have become quite successful in their chosen fields. At the other extreme, a surprisingly large number of criminals and delinquents are found to have extremely high self-esteem (Johnson, 1998).

## SELF-DISCLOSURE

**Self-disclosure** is (1) a type of communication in which (2) you reveal information about yourself that (3) you normally keep hidden (Jourard, 1968, 1971a, 1971b; Tardy & Dindia, 2006).

1. You can look at self-disclosure as a type of communication in which you take information from your hidden self and move it to the open self. Overt statements about the self (for example, "I'm getting fat"), as well as slips of the tongue (for example, using the name of an ex instead of your present lover), unconscious non-verbal movements (for example, self-touching movements or eye avoidance), and public confessions (for example, "Well, Jerry, it's like this . . . ) can all be considered forms of self-disclosure. Usually, however, the term *self-disclosure* is

# REFLECTIONS
## ON ETHICS

## Information Ethics

One approach to ethics revolves around the notion of choice and argues that you have the right to information relevant to the choices you make. In this view, communication is ethical when it facilitates your freedom of choice by presenting you with accurate information. Ethical communication provides you with the kind of information that will help you make your own choices. Unethical communications interfere with your freedom of choice by preventing you from securing information that will help you make those choices. Communications are also unethical when they give you false or misleading information that will lead you to make choices you would not make if you had accurate and truthful information.

In this ethical system, you have the right to information about yourself that others possess and that influences the choices you will make. Thus, for example,

you have the right to face your accusers, to know the witnesses who will be called to testify against you, to see your credit ratings, and to know what Social Security benefits you will receive. On the other hand, you do not have the right to information that is none of your business, such as information about whether your neighbors are happy or argue a lot or receive food stamps.

### Ethical Choice Point

*Your best friend's husband is currently having an extramarital affair with a 17-year-old girl. Your friend, suspecting this, asks if you know anything about it. Would it be ethical for you to lie and say you know nothing, or are you obligated to tell your friend what you know? Are you obligated to tell the police? What would you do?*

---

used to refer to the conscious revealing of information, as in the statements "I'm afraid to compete; I guess I'm afraid I'll lose," or "I love you."

2. In self-disclosure you reveal "information" about yourself; it is "information" in that it involves something that the receiver did not know about you. This information may vary from the relatively commonplace ("I'm really scared about that French exam") to the extremely significant ("I'm so depressed, I feel like committing suicide"). For self-disclosure to occur, you must reveal the information to someone else. That is, you cannot self-disclose to yourself—the information must be received and understood by at least one other individual.

3. Generally, self-disclosure—at least the kind that's researched in communication and related fields—involves information that you normally keep hidden. To tell a listener something about yourself that you'd tell anyone is not self-disclosure but rather simply talking about yourself.

## Factors Influencing Self-Disclosure

Many factors influence whether or not you disclose, what you disclose, and to whom you disclose. Among the most important factors are who you are, your culture, your gender, who your listeners are, and your topic and channel.

### Who You Are

Highly sociable and extroverted people self-disclose more than those who are less sociable and more introverted. People who are comfortable communicating also self-disclose more than those who are apprehensive about talking in general. And competent people engage in self-disclosure more than less-competent people. Perhaps competent people have greater self-confidence and more positive things to reveal. Similarly, their self-confidence may make them more willing to risk possible negative reactions (McCroskey & Wheeless, 1976).

### Your Culture

Different cultures view self-disclosure differently. Some cultures (especially those high in masculinity) view disclosing inner feelings as weakness. Among some groups, for example, it would be considered "out of place" for a man to cry at a happy occasion such as a wedding, whereas in some Latin cultures that same display of emotion would go unnoticed. Similarly, it's considered undesirable in Japan for colleagues to reveal personal information, whereas in much of the United States it's expected (Barnlund, 1989; Hall & Hall, 1987).

There is some indication that the political climate today will influence the cross-cultural self-disclosure patterns of all people. Significant self-disclosure between Americans and Muslims, for example, is likely to be more guarded than before September 11, 2001, and the Iraqi war, as are self-disclosures between recent immigrants and other Americans (Barry, 2003).

These differences aside, there are also important similarities across cultures. For example, people from Great Britain, Germany, the United States, and Puerto Rico are all more apt to disclose personal information—hobbies, interests, attitudes, and opinions on politics and religion—than information on finances, sex, personality, and interpersonal relationships (Jourard, 1971a). Similarly, one study showed self-disclosure patterns between American males to be virtually identical to those between Korean males (Won-Doornink, 1991).

## Your Gender

The popular stereotype of gender differences in self-disclosure emphasizes males' reluctance to speak about themselves. For the most part, research supports this view; women do disclose more than men. There are exceptions, however. For example, men and women make negative disclosures about equally (Naifeh & Smith, 1984), and boys are more likely than girls to disclose family information on the Internet (www.CNN.com, accessed May 17, 2000). Another notable exception occurs in initial encounters. Here, men will disclose more intimately than women, perhaps "in order to control the relationship's development" (Derlega, Winstead, Wong, & Hunter, 1985). Still another exception is found in a study of Americans and Argentineans; here males indicated a significantly greater

willingness to self-disclose than females (Horenstein & Downey, 2003).

Women disclose more than men about their previous romantic relationships, their feelings about their closest same-sex friends, their greatest fears, and what they don't like about their partners (Sprecher, 1987). Women also increase the depth of their disclosures as the relationship becomes more intimate, whereas men seem not to change their self-disclosure levels. Women have fewer taboo topics—information that they will not disclose to their friends—than men do (Goodwin & Lee, 1994). Finally, women also self-disclose more to members of their extended families than men (Komarovsky, 1964; Argyle & Henderson, 1984, 1985; Moghaddam, Taylor, & Wright, 1993).

## Your Listeners

Self-disclosure occurs more readily in small groups than in large groups. *Dyads*, or groups of two people, are the most hospitable setting for self-disclosure. With one listener, you can monitor your disclosures, continuing if there's support from your listener and stopping if there's not. With more than one listener, such monitoring becomes difficult, because the listeners' responses are sure to vary.

Research shows that you disclose most to people you like (Derlega, Winstead, Wong, & Greenspan, 1987) and to people you trust (Wheeless & Grotz, 1977). You also come to like those to whom you disclose (Berg & Archer, 1983). At times self-disclosure is more likely to occur in temporary than in permanent relationships—for example, between strangers on a train or plane, in a kind of "in-flight intimacy"

### CORRECTIVE SELF-DISCLOSURE

When you met your current partner—with whom you want to spend the rest of your life—you minimized the extent of your romantic past. You now want to come clean and disclose your "sordid" past.

WHAT DO YOU SAY?
*Through what channel?*

(McGill, 1985). In this situation two people set up an intimate, self-disclosing relationship during a brief travel period, but they don't pursue it beyond that point. In a similar way, you might set up a relationship with one or several people on the Internet and engage in significant disclosure. Perhaps knowing that you'll never see these other people, and that they will never know where you live or work or what you look like, makes it easier to open up to them.

You are more likely to disclose when the person you are with discloses. This **dyadic effect** (what one person does, the other person also does) probably leads you to feel more secure and reinforces your own self-disclosing behavior. In fact, research shows that disclosures made in response to the disclosures of others are generally more intimate than those that are not the result of the dyadic effect (Berg & Archer, 1983). This dyadic effect, however, is not universal across all cultures. For example, although many Americans are likely to follow the dyadic effect and reciprocate with explicit, verbal self-disclosure, Koreans aren't (Won Doornink, 1985). As you can appreciate, this difference can easily cause intercultural difficulties; for example, an American may feel insulted if his or her Korean counterpart doesn't reciprocate with self-disclosures that are similar in depth.

## Your Topic and Channel

You also are more likely to disclose about some topics than others. For example, you're more likely to disclose information about your job or hobbies than about your sex life or financial situation (Jourard, 1968, 1971a). Further, you're more likely to disclose favorable information than unfavorable information. Generally, the more personal and negative the topic, the less likely you are to self-disclose.

Recent research has addressed differences in self-disclosure depending on the channel, whether face-to-face or computer mediated. Some researchers have pointed to a **disinhibition effect** that occurs in online communication; as noted earlier, people seem less inhibited in communicating in e-mail or in chat groups, for example, than in face-to-face situations. Among the reasons for this seem to be that in online communication there is a certain degree of anonymity and invisibility (Suler, 2004). Research also finds that reciprocal self-disclosure occurs more quickly and at higher levels of intimacy online than it does in face-to-face interactions (Levine, 2000; Joinson, 2001).

The self-test "How Willing to Self-Disclose Are You?" focuses on the influences of four of the factors just discussed: you, your culture, your listeners, and your topic.

## TEST YOURSELF

### How Willing to Self-Disclose Are You?

Respond to each statement below by indicating the likelihood that you would disclose such items of information to, say, other members of this class. Use the following scale: 1 = would definitely self-disclose; 2 = would probably self-disclose; 3 = don't know; 4 = would probably not self-disclose; and 5 = would definitely not self-disclose.

____ **1.** My attitudes toward different nationalities and races

____ **2.** My sexual fantasies

____ **3.** My drinking and/or drug-taking behavior

____ **4.** My personal goals

____ **5.** My major weaknesses

____ **6.** My feelings about the people in this group

**HOW DID YOU DO?** There are, of course, no right or wrong answers to this self-test. By considering these topics, however, you may be able to pinpoint more precisely the areas about which you're willing to disclose and the areas about which you aren't willing to disclose. How would your answers have differed if the question had asked you to indicate the likelihood of your self-disclosing to your best friend?

**WHAT WILL YOU DO?** This test, and ideally its discussion with others who also complete it, should get you started thinking about your own self-disclosing behavior and especially the factors that influence it. Can you identify what factors most influence your willingness to disclose or not to disclose each of these items of information?

## The Rewards and Dangers of Self-Disclosure

Self-disclosure often brings rewards, but it can also create problems. Whether or not you self-disclose will depend on your assessment of the possible rewards and dangers. Among the rewards of self-disclosure are:

- **Self-knowledge.** Self-disclosure helps you gain a new perspective on yourself and a deeper understanding of your own behavior.

- **Improved coping abilities.** Self-disclosure helps you deal with problems, especially guilt. Because you feel that problems are a basis for rejection, you may develop guilt. By self-disclosing negative feelings and receiving support rather than rejection, you may be better able to deal with guilt, perhaps reducing or even eliminating it.

- **Communication enhancement.** Self-disclosure often improves communication. You understand the messages of others largely to the extent that you understand the individuals. You can tell what certain nuances mean, when a person is serious or joking, and when a person is being sarcastic out of fear or out of resentment.

- **More meaningful relationships**. By self-disclosing you tell others that you trust, respect, and care enough about them and your relationship to reveal yourself. This, in turn, leads the other individual to self-disclose and forms at least the start of a relationship that is honest and open and allows for more complete communication. Within a sexual relationship, self-disclosure increases sexual rewards and general relationship satisfaction. These two benefits in turn increase sexual satisfaction (Byers & Demmons, 1999).

Among the dangers of self-disclosure are:

- **Personal risks**. The more you reveal about yourself to others, the more areas of your life you expose to possible attack. Especially in the competitive context of work (or even romance), the more that others know about you, the more they'll be able to use against you.

- **Relationship risks**. Even in close and long-lasting relationships, self-disclosure can cause problems. Parents, normally the most supportive people in most individuals' lives, frequently reject children who disclose their homosexuality, their plans to marry someone of a different race, or their belief in another faith. Your best friends—your closest intimates—may reject you for similar self-disclosures.

- **Professional risks**. Sometimes self-disclosure may result in professional or material losses. Politicians who disclose that they have been in therapy may lose the support of their own political party and find that voters are unwilling to vote for them. Teachers who disclose disagreement with school administrators may find themselves being denied tenure, teaching undesirable schedules, and becoming victims of "budget cuts." In the business world self-disclosures of alcoholism or drug addiction often result in dismissal, demotion, or social exclusion.

Remember that self-disclosure, like any other communication, is irreversible (see Unit 1). You cannot self-disclose and then take it back. Nor can you erase the conclusions and inferences listeners make on the basis of your disclosures. Remember, too, to examine the rewards and dangers of self-disclosure in terms of particular cultural rules. As with all cultural rules, following the rules about self-disclosure brings approval, and violating them brings disapproval.

**REGULATING SELF-DISCLOSURE**

You're currently engaged, but over the past few months you've been seeing someone else and have fallen in love. Now you want to break off your engagement and disclose this new relationship.

WHAT DO YOU SAY?
*Through what channel?*

## Guidelines for Self-Disclosure

Because self-disclosure is so important and so delicate a matter, here are some guidelines for (1) deciding whether and how to self-disclose, (2) responding to the disclosures of others, and (3) resisting the pressure to self-disclose.

### Guidelines for Making Self-Disclosures

In addition to weighing the potential rewards and dangers of self-disclosure, consider the following factors as well. These hints will help you raise the right questions before you make what must be your decision.

- **Consider the motivation for the self-disclosure.** Self-disclosure should be motivated by a concern for the relationship, for the others involved, and for yourself. Self-disclosure should serve a useful and productive function for all persons involved. Self-disclosing past indiscretions because you want to clear the air and be honest may be worthwhile; to disclose the same episodes to hurt your partner, however, is likely to damage the relationship.

- **Consider the appropriateness of the self-disclosure.** Self-disclosure should be appropriate to the context and to the relationship between you and your listener. Before making any significant self-disclosure, ask whether this is the right time (Do you both have the time to discuss this in the length it requires?) and place (Is the place free of distractions? Is it private?). Ask, too, whether this self-disclosure is appropriate to the relationship. Generally, the more intimate the disclosure, the closer the relationship should be. It's probably best to resist making intimate disclosures (especially negative ones) with nonintimates or with casual acquaintances, or in the early stages of a relationship.

- **Consider the disclosures of the other person.** During your disclosures, give the other person a chance to reciprocate with his or her own disclosures. If the other person does not reciprocate, reassess your own self-disclosures. It may be that for this person at this time and in this context, your disclosures are not welcome or appropriate. For example, if you reveal your romantic mistakes to a friend but your friend says nothing or reveals only trivial details, it may be a cue to stop disclosing. Generally, it's best to disclose gradually and in small increments so you can monitor your listener's responses and retreat if they're not positive enough.

- **Consider the possible burdens self-disclosure might entail.** Carefully weigh the potential problems that you may incur as a result of your disclosure. Can you afford to lose your job if you disclose your prison record? Are you willing to risk relational difficulties if you disclose your infidelities? Also, ask yourself whether you're making unreasonable demands on the listener. For example, consider the person who swears his or her mother-in-law to secrecy and then discloses having an affair with a neighbor. This disclosure places an unfair burden on the mother-in-law, who is now torn between breaking her promise of secrecy and allowing her child to believe a lie.

The accompanying Building Communication Skills box provides a few examples of impending self-disclosures that illustrate the difficulty involved in deciding what to disclose and how to do it.

## Guidelines for Facilitating and Responding to Self-Disclosures

When someone discloses to you, it's usually a sign of trust and affection. In carrying out this most important receiver function, keep the following guidelines in mind.

- **Practice the skills of effective and active listening.** The skills of effective listening (Unit 4) are especially important when you're listening to self-disclosures: Listen actively, listen for different levels of meaning, listen with empathy, and listen with an open mind. Express an understanding of the speaker's feelings in order to give the speaker

---

## Building Communication Skills  Deciding about Self-Disclosure

For any one or two of the following instances of impending self-disclosure, indicate whether you think the person should self-disclose and why. In making your decisions, consider each of the guidelines identified in this unit.

1. Cathy has fallen in love with another man and wants to end her relationship with Tom, a coworker. She wants to call Tom on the phone, break the engagement, and disclose her new relationship.

2. Gregory plagiarized a term paper in anthropology. He's sorry, especially since the plagiarized paper only earned a grade of C+. He wants to disclose to his instructor and redo the paper.

3. Roberto, a college sophomore, has just discovered he is HIV positive. He wants to tell his parents and his best friends, but fears their rejection. In his Mexican American culture, information like this is rarely disclosed, especially by men. He wants the support of his friends and family and yet doesn't want them to reject him or treat him differently.

*Self-disclosure is a complex communication process and is especially important because its potential consequences, both positive and negative, are so significant. Disclose significant information only after mindfully considering the consequences.*

the opportunity to see his or her feelings more objectively and through the eyes of another. Ask questions to ensure your own understanding and to signal your interest and attention.

- **Support and reinforce the discloser**. Express support for the person during and after the disclosures. Try to refrain from evaluation. Concentrate on understanding and empathizing with the discloser. Make your supportiveness clear to the discloser through your verbal and nonverbal responses: Maintain eye contact, lean toward the speaker, ask relevant questions, and echo the speaker's thoughts and feelings. Men are generally more reluctant than women to show this kind of emotional support, at least to the degree that women do; the reason, recent research shows, is that men don't want their behavior to be seen as feminine (Burleson, Holmstrom, & Gilstrap, 2005).

- **Be willing to reciprocate**. When you make relevant and appropriate disclosures of your own in response to the other person's disclosures, you're demonstrating your understanding of the other's meanings and at the same time a willingness to communicate on this meaningful level. If your colleague discloses embarrassing dating situations and you reveal an experience of your own, you're indicating an understanding on a deeper level than you would if you merely responded with "That's funny" or "I know what you mean."

- **Keep the disclosures confidential**. When someone discloses to you, it's because the person wants you to know about his or her feelings and thoughts. If you reveal these disclosures to others, negative effects are inevitable. But most important, betraying a confidence is unfair; it debases what could be and should be a meaningful inter-

personal experience. It's interesting to note that one of the netiquette rules of e-mail is that you shouldn't forward mail to third parties without the writer's permission. This rule is useful for self-disclosure generally: Maintain confidentiality; don't pass on disclosures made to you to others without the person's permission.

- **Don't use the disclosures against the person**. Many self-disclosures expose some kind of vulnerability or weakness. If you later turn around and use a disclosure against the person who has disclosed to you, you betray the confidence and trust invested in you. Regardless of how angry you may get, resist the temptation to use the disclosures of others as weapons. If your friend confides a fear of cats and you later use this to ridicule or make a joke, you're likely to create relationship problems between you and your friend.

## Guidelines for Resisting Pressure to Self-Disclose

You may, on occasion, find yourself in a position in which a friend, colleague, or romantic partner pressures you to self-disclose. In such situations, you may wish to weigh the pros and cons of self-disclosure, and make your own decision as to whether and what you'll disclose. If your decision is to not disclose and you're still being pressured, then you need to say something. Here are a few suggestions.

- **Don't be pushed**. Although there may be certain legal or ethical reasons for disclosing, generally you don't have to disclose if you don't want to. Realize that you're in control of what you reveal and of when and to whom you reveal it. Remember that self-disclosure has significant consequences.

### DISCLOSURE PRESSURE

You're dating this wonderful person who self-discloses easily and fully and who, unfortunately, is putting pressure on you to reveal more about yourself. You just aren't ready to do so at this time.

WHAT DO YOU SAY?
*Through what channel?*

So if you're not sure you want to reveal something, at least not until you've had additional time to think about it, then don't.

■ **Be indirect and move to another topic.** Avoid the question that asks you to disclose, and change the subject. If someone presses you to disclose your past financial problems, move the conversation to financial problems in general or nationally or change the topic to a movie you saw or to your new job. This is often a polite way of saying, "I'm not talking about it" and may be the preferred choice in certain situations and with certain people. Most often people will get the hint and will understand your refusal to disclose.

■ **Be assertive in your refusal to disclose.** If necessary, say, very directly, "I'd rather not talk about that now," or "Now is not the time for this type of discussion."

With an understanding of the self in human communication, we can explore perception, the processes by which you come to understand yourself and others and, of course, the processes by which others come to understand you.

# PERCEPTION AND STAGES OF PERCEPTION

**Perception** is your way of understanding the world; it is the process by which you make sense out of what psychologist William James called the "booming buzzing confusion" all around you. More technically, perception is the process by which you become aware of objects, events, and especially people through your senses: sight, smell, taste, touch, and hearing. Perception is an active, not a passive, process. Your perceptions result from what exists in the outside world and from your own experiences, desires, needs and wants, loves and hatreds. Among the reasons why perception is so important in communication is that it influences your communication choices. The messages you send and listen to will depend on how you see the world, on how you size up specific situations, on what you think of the people with whom you interact.

Perception is a continuous series of processes that blend into one another. For convenience of discussion we can separate perception into five stages: (1) You sense, you pick up some kind of stimulation; (2) you organize the stimuli in some way; (3) you interpret and evaluate what you perceive; (4) you store your perception in memory; and (5) you retrieve it when needed (Figure 3.4).

## Stage 1: Stimulation

At the first stage of perception, your sense organs are *stimulated*—you hear a new CD, you see a friend, you smell someone's perfume, you taste an orange, you feel another's sweaty palm. Naturally, you don't perceive everything; rather, you engage in selective perception, which includes selective attention and selective exposure.

In **selective attention** you attend to those things that you anticipate will fulfill your needs or will prove enjoyable. For instance, when daydreaming in class, you don't hear what the instructor is saying until he or she calls your name. Your selective attention mechanism focuses your senses on your name being called.

The principle of **selective exposure** states that you tend to expose yourself to information that will confirm your existing beliefs, that will contribute to your objectives, or that will prove satisfying in some way. For example, after you buy a car, you're more apt to read and listen to advertisements for the car you just bought, because these messages tell you that you made the right decision. At the same time, you will tend to avoid advertisements for the cars that you considered but eventually rejected, because these messages would tell you that you made the wrong decision.

You're also more likely to perceive stimuli that are greater in intensity than surrounding stimuli and to perceive stimuli that have novelty value. For example, television commercials normally play at a greater intensity than regular programming to ensure that you take special notice. And you're more likely to notice the coworker who dresses in a novel way than you are to notice the person who dresses like everyone else.

## Stage 2: Organization

At the second stage of perception, you organize the information your senses pick up. Three interesting ways in which you organize your perceptions are (1) by rules, (2) by schemata, and (3) by scripts.

### Organization by Rules

One frequently used rule of perception is that of **proximity**, or physical closeness. The rule says that things that are physically close together constitute a unit. Thus, using this rule, you would perceive people who are often together, or messages spoken one right after the other, as units, as belonging together. You also assume that the verbal and nonverbal signals sent at about the same time are related and constitute a unified whole.

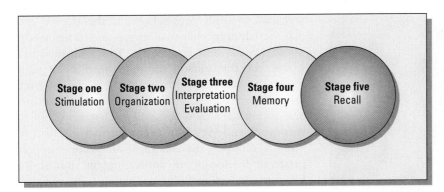

**FIGURE 3.4**
**The Stages of Perception**

Perception occurs in five stages: stimulation, organization, interpretation–evaluation, memory, and recall. Understanding how perception works will help make your own perceptions (of your self and of others) more accurate.

Another rule is **similarity**, a principle stating that things that look alike or are similar in other ways belong together and form a unit. This principle leads you to see people who dress alike as belonging together. Similarly, you might assume that people who work at the same jobs, who are of the same religion, who live in the same building, or who talk with the same accent belong together.

You use the principle of **contrast** when you conclude that some items (people or messages, for example) don't belong together because they're too different from each other to be part of the same unit. So, for example, in a conversation or a public speech, you'll focus your attention on changes in intensity or rate because these contrast with the rest of the message.

## Organization by Schemata

Another way you organize material is by creating **schemata**, mental templates or structures that help you organize the millions of items of information you come into contact with every day as well as those you already have in memory. Schemata may thus be viewed as general ideas about people (Pat and Chris, Japanese, Baptists, New Yorkers); about yourself (your qualities, abilities, and even liabilities); or about social roles (the attributes of police officers, professors, or multimillionaires). (The word *schemata*, by the way, is the plural of *schema* and is preferred to the alternative plural *schemas*.)

You develop schemata from your own experience—actual experiences as well as vicarious experiences from television, reading, and hearsay. Thus, for example, you may have a schema that portrays college athletes as strong, ambitious, academically weak, and egocentric. And, of course, you've probably developed schemata for different religious, racial, and national groups; for men and women; and for people of different affectional orientations. Each group that you have some familiarity with will be represented in your mind in some kind of schema. Schemata help you organize your perceptions by allowing you to classify millions of people into a manageable number of categories or classes. As you'll soon see, however, schemata can also create problems—they can influence you to see what is not there or to miss seeing what is there.

## Organization by Scripts

A **script** is a type of schema. Like a schema, a script is an organized body of information; but a script focuses on an action, event, or procedure. It's a general idea of how some event should unfold; it's the rules governing events and their sequence. For example, you probably have a script for eating in a restaurant with the actions organized into a pattern something like this: Enter, take a seat, review the menu, order from the menu, eat your food, ask for the bill, leave a tip, pay the bill, exit the restaurant. Similarly, you probably have scripts for how you do laundry, how you behave in an interview, the stages you go through in introducing someone to someone else, and the way you ask for a date.

Everyone relies on shortcuts—rules, schemata, and scripts, for example, are all useful shortcuts to simplify understanding, remembering, and recalling information about people and events. If you didn't have these shortcuts, you'd have to treat each person, role, or action differently from each other person, role, or action. This would make every experience totally new, totally unrelated to anything you already know. If you didn't use these shortcuts, you'd be unable to generalize, draw connections, or otherwise profit from previously acquired knowledge.

Shortcuts, however, may mislead you; they may contribute to your remembering things that are consistent with your schemata (even if they didn't occur) and distorting or forgetting information that is inconsistent. Judgments about members of other cultures are often ethnocentric. Because you form schemata and scripts on the basis of your own cultural beliefs and experiences, you can easily (but inappropriately) apply these to members of other

**FIRST IMPRESSION CORRECTION**

You made a bad impression at work—you drank too much at an office party and played the clown. This is not the impression you want to give and you need to change it fast.

WHAT DO YOU SAY?
*Through what channel?*

cultures. It's easy to infer that when members of other cultures do things that conform to your scripts, they're right, and when they do things that contradict your scripts, they're wrong—a classic example of ethnocentric thinking. As you can appreciate, this tendency can easily contribute to intercultural misunderstandings.

A similar problem arises when you base your schemata for different cultural groups on stereotypes that you may have derived from television or movies. So, for example, you may have schemata for religious Muslims that you derived from stereotypes presented in the media. If you then apply these schemata to all Muslims, you risk seeing only what conforms to your script and failing to see or distorting what does not conform to your script.

## Stage 3: Interpretation–Evaluation

The interpretation–evaluation step (a linked term because the two processes cannot be separated) is inevitably subjective and is greatly influenced by your experiences, needs, wants, values, expectations, physical and emotional state, gender, and beliefs about the way things are or should be, as well as by your rules, schemata, and scripts.

For example, when you meet a new person who is introduced to you as a college football player, you will tend to apply your schema to this person and may view him (perhaps) as strong, ambitious, academically weak, and egocentric. You will, in other words, see this person through the filter of your schema and evaluate him according to your schema for college athletes. Similarly, when viewing someone asking for a date, you will apply your script to this event and view the event through the script. You will interpret the actions of the suitor as appropriate or inappropriate depending on your script for date-requesting behavior and on the ways in which the suitor performs the sequence of actions.

## Stage 4: Memory

You store in memory both your perceptions and their interpretations–evaluations. So, for example, you have in memory your schema for college athletes, and you know that Ben Williams is a football player. Ben Williams is then stored in memory with "cognitive tags" that tell you that he's strong, ambitious, academically weak, and egocentric. That is, despite the fact that you've not witnessed Ben's strength or ambitions and have no idea of his academic record or his psychological profile, you still may store your memory of Ben along with the qualities that make up your script for "college athletes."

Now, let's say that at different times you hear that Ben failed Spanish I (normally an A or B course at your school), that Ben got an A in chemistry (normally a tough course), and that Ben is transferring to Harvard as a theoretical physics major. Schemata act as filters or gatekeepers; they allow certain information to be stored in relatively objective form, much as you heard or read it, but may distort or prevent other information from being stored. As a result, these three items of information about Ben may get stored very differently in your memory along with your schema for college athletes.

For example, you may readily store the information that Ben failed Spanish, because it's consistent with your schema; it fits neatly into the template that you have of college athletes. Information that's consistent with your schema—as in this example—will strengthen your schema and make it more resistant to change (Aronson, Wilson, & Akert, 2002). Depending on the strength of your schema, you may also store in memory (even though you didn't hear it) the "information" that Ben did poorly in other courses as well. The information that Ben got an A in chemistry, because it contradicts your schema (it just doesn't seem right), may easily be distorted or lost. The information that Ben is transferring to Harvard, however, is a bit different. This information also is inconsistent with your schema; but it is so drastically inconsistent that you may begin to look at this mindfully. Perhaps you'll begin to question your schema for athletes, or perhaps you'll view Ben as an exception to the general rule. In either case, you're going to etch Ben's transferring to Harvard very clearly in your mind.

What you remember about a person or an event isn't an objective recollection, but is more likely heavily influenced by your preconceptions or your schemata about what belongs and what doesn't belong. Your reconstruction of an event or person contains a lot of information that was not in your original experience and may omit a lot that was in this experience.

## Stage 5: Recall

At some later date, you may want to recall or access information you have stored in memory. Let's say you want to retrieve your information about Ben because he's the topic of discussion among you and a few friends. As you'll see in the discussion of listening in the next unit, memory isn't reproductive;

you don't simply reproduce what you've heard or seen. Rather, you *reconstruct* what you've heard or seen into a whole that is meaningful to you—depending in great part on your schemata and scripts—and it's this reconstruction that you store in memory. Now, when you want to retrieve this information from memory, you may recall it with a variety of inaccuracies. You're likely to:

- recall information that is consistent with your schema. In fact, you may not even recall the specific information you're looking for (say about Ben) but actually just your schema (which contains the information about college athletes and therefore about Ben).

- fail to recall information that is inconsistent with your schema. You have no place to put that information, so you easily lose it or forget it.

- recall information that drastically contradicts your schema, because it forces you to think (and perhaps rethink) about your schema and its accuracy; it may even force you to revise your schema.

**MEDIA WATCH**

**OUTING**

In self-disclosure, as already noted, you reveal information about yourself to others. Although at times you may be forced to disclose, normally you control what you reveal. There is, however, another type of disclosure—the disclosure that occurs when someone else takes information from your hidden self and makes it public. Although this third-party disclosure can concern any aspect of your hidden self, the media have made a special case out of revealing information about affectional orientation, or "outing."

Outing as a media process began in a relatively obscure gay magazine, *Outweek*. *Outweek*'s article on "The Secret Gay Life of Malcolm Forbes" made public the homosexuality of one of the world's richest men; it "outed" him (Gross, 1991; Johansson & Percy, 1994). On March 3, 1995, the *Wall Street Journal* ran a front-page story on Jann Wenner, the multimillionaire owner and publisher of *Rolling Stone, Us, Men's Journal*, and *Family Life*. The story was basically financial and focused on the possible effects Wenner's marital breakup would have on his media empire. Somewhat casually noted in the article—without Wenner's per-

mission and against his wishes (Rotello, 1995)—was the fact that the new person in Wenner's life was a man. This article, although not the first to discuss Wenner's gay relationship, has been singled out because of the prestige of the *Wall Street Journal* and because of the many issues this type of forced disclosure raises.

Outing raises a privacy issue that is not easy to resolve. If Wenner had been dating a woman, the media would have mentioned it, but few would have raised the privacy issue—because Wenner is a public figure, and divorce was a relevant issue that would likely affect his financial empire. However, if the media reported only on heterosexual extramarital relationships, it would imply that homosexual relationships are illegitimate and not to be spoken of openly.

### Increasing Media Literacy

*How do you feel about outing? What guidelines should the media follow in dealing with issues that individuals wish to keep private? At what point should the media be allowed to consider a person a public figure who has no right to privacy?*

# PERCEPTUAL PROCESSES

Before reading about the specific processes that you use in perceiving other people, examine your own perception strategies by taking the following self-test, "How Accurate Are You at People Perception?"

# TEST YOURSELF

## How Accurate Are You at People Perception?

Respond to each of the following statements with T for true if the statement is usually or generally accurate in describing your behavior, or with F for false if the statement is usually or generally inaccurate in describing your behavior.

_____ 1. When I know some things about another person, I can pretty easily fill in what I don't know.

_____ 2. I make predictions about people's behaviors that generally prove to be true.

_____ 3. I base most of my impressions of people on the first few minutes of our meeting.

_____ 4. I generally attribute people's attitudes and behaviors to their most obvious physical or psychological characteristic.

_____ 5. I believe that the world is basically just, that good things happen to good people and bad things happen to bad people.

**HOW DID YOU DO?** This brief perception test was designed to raise questions about concepts to be explored in this section of the text. All statements refer to perceptual processes that you may use but that may get you into trouble, leading you to form inaccurate impressions. These processes include implicit personality theory (statement 1), self-fulfilling prophecy (2), and primacy–recency (3). Statements 4 and 5 typify two kinds of mistakes we often make in attempting to attribute motives to other people's and even our own behaviors: overattribution (4) and the self-serving bias (5), which often involves a belief that the world is fundamentally just. Ideally, you would have responded to all of these statements with "false," indicating that you regularly avoid falling into these potential traps.

**WHAT WILL YOU DO?** As you read this section, think about these perceptual tendencies, and consider how you might avoid them so as to achieve more accurate and reasonable people perception. At the same time, recognize that situations vary widely and that this text's suggestions will prove useful in most but not all cases.

# Implicit Personality Theory

Consider the following brief statements. Note the word in parentheses that you think best completes each sentence:

- Carlo is energetic, eager, and (intelligent, stupid).
- Kim is bold, defiant, and (extroverted, introverted).
- Joe is bright, lively, and (thin, heavy).
- Ava is attractive, intelligent, and (likable, unlikable).
- Susan is cheerful, positive, and (outgoing, shy).
- Angel is handsome, tall, and (friendly, unfriendly).

What makes some of these choices seem right and others seem wrong is your **implicit personality theory**, a system of rules that tells you which personal characteristics go with which other characteristics. Your theory may, for example, have told you that a person who is energetic and eager is also intelligent, although there's no logical reason why a stupid person could not be energetic and eager. The widely documented **halo effect** is a function of the implicit personality theory (Dion, Berscheid, & Walster, 1972; Riggio, 1987). That is, if you believe a person has some positive qualities, you're likely to infer that she or he also possesses other positive qualities. There is also a reverse halo effect: If you know a person possesses several negative qualities, you're likely to infer that the person also has other negative qualities.

When using implicit personality theories, apply them carefully so as to avoid perceiving qualities that your theory tells you should be present in an individual when they actually are not. For example, you may see "goodwill" in a friend's "charitable" acts, when a tax deduction may have been the real motive. Similarly, be careful of ignoring or distorting qualities that don't conform to your theory but that are actually present in the individual. For example, you may ignore negative qualities in your friends that you would easily perceive in your enemies.

As you might expect, the implicit personality theories that people hold differ from culture to culture, from group to group, and even from person to person. For example, the Chinese have a concept called *shi gu*, which refers to a person who is skillful, devoted to family, worldly, and reserved (Aronson, Wilson, & Akert, 2002). This concept isn't easily encoded in English, as you can tell by trying to find a general concept that covers this type of person. In English, on the other hand, we have a concept of the "artistic type," a generalization that seems absent in Chinese languages. Thus, although it is easy for speakers of English or Chinese to refer to specific concepts—such as socially skilled or creative—each language creates its own generalized categories. As a result, in Chinese languages, the qualities that make up *shi gu* are more easily seen as going together than they might be for an English speaker; they're part of the implicit personality theory of more Chinese speakers than of, say, English speakers.

## The Self-Fulfilling Prophecy

A **self-fulfilling prophecy** occurs when you make a prediction that comes true because you act on it as if it were true (Merton, 1957). Put differently, a self-fulfilling prophecy occurs when you act on your schema as if it were true and in doing so you make it true (McNatt, 2001; Eden, 1992; Solomon et al., 1996; Einstein, 1995). For example, suppose you enter a group situation convinced that the other members will dislike you. Almost invariably you'll be proved right; the other members will appear to you to dislike you. You may be acting in a way that encourages the group to respond negatively. In this way you fulfill your prophecies about yourself.

There are four steps in the self-fulfilling prophecy:

1. You make a prediction or formulate a belief about a person or a situation. For example, you expect Pat to be friendly in interpersonal encounters.

2. You act toward the person or situation as if that prediction or belief were true. For example, you act as if Pat were a friendly person.

3. Because you act as if the belief were true, it becomes true. For example, because of the way you act toward Pat, Pat becomes comfortable and friendly.

4. You observe your effect on the person or the resulting situation, and what you see strengthens your beliefs. For example, you observe Pat's friendliness, and this reinforces your belief that Pat is in fact friendly.

A widely known example of the self-fulfilling prophecy is the Pygmalion effect, explained in the Understanding Theory and Research box below.

---

## Understanding Theory and Research   The Pygmalion Effect

A widely known example of the self-fulfilling prophecy is the *Pygmalion effect* (Rosenthal & Jacobson, 1992). The effect is named after Pygmalion, a sculptor in Greek mythology who created a statue of a beautiful woman and then fell in love with it. Venus, the goddess of love, rewarded Pygmalion for his artistry and love by making the statue come to life as a real woman, Galatea. George Bernard Shaw used this idea for his play *Pygmalion*, the story of a poor, uneducated London flower vendor who is taught "proper speech" and enters society's upper class. The musical *My Fair Lady* was in turn based on Shaw's play.

In a classic research study, experimenters told teachers that certain pupils were expected to do exceptionally well—that they were late bloomers (Rosenthal & Jacobson, 1968, 1992). And although the experimenters actually selected the "late bloomers" at random, the students who were labeled "late bloomers" actually did perform at higher levels than their classmates. Like the beautiful statue, these students became what their teachers thought they were. The expectations of the teachers may have caused them to pay extra attention to the students, and this may have positively affected the students' performance. More recently, the Pygmalion effect has been studied in such varied contexts as the courtroom, the clinic, the work cubicle, management and leadership practices, athletic coaching, and stepfamilies (Eden, 1992; Solomon et al., 1996; Einstein, 1995; McNatt, 2001; Rosenthal, 2002).

### Working with Theories and Research

*Findings such as those cited above have led one researcher to suggest that companies apply the Pygmalion effect as a way to improve worker productivity—by creating in supervisors positive attitudes about employees and by helping employees to feel that their supervisors and the organization as a whole value them highly (McNatt, 2001). In what ways might this Pygmalion effect be applied at your own workplace?*

## Primacy–Recency

Assume for a moment that you're enrolled in a course in which half the classes are extremely dull and half extremely exciting. At the end of the semester, you evaluate the course and the instructor. Would your evaluation be more favorable if the dull classes occurred in the first half of the semester and the exciting classes in the second? Or would it be more favorable if the order were reversed? If what comes first exerts the most influence, you have a **primacy effect.** If what comes last (or most recently) exerts the most influence, you have a **recency effect.**

In the classic study on the effects of **primacy–recency** in perception, college students perceived a person who was described as "intelligent, industrious, impulsive, critical, stubborn, and envious" more positively than a person described as "envious, stubborn, critical, impulsive, industrious, and intelligent" (Asch, 1946). Clearly, there's a tendency to use early information to get a general idea about a person and to use later information to make this impression more specific. The initial information helps you form a schema for the person. Once that schema is formed, you're likely to resist information that contradicts it.

One interesting practical implication of primacy-recency is that the first impression you make is likely to be the most important. The reason for this is that the schema that others form of you acts as a filter to admit or block additional information about you. If the initial impression or schema is positive, others are likely to remember additional positive information, because it confirms their schema, and to forget or distort negative information, because it contradicts their schema. They are also more likely to interpret as positive information that is actually ambiguous. You win in all three ways—if the initial impression is positive.

## Attribution

**Attribution** is the process by which you try to explain the reasons or motivations for a person's behavior. One way to engage in attribution is to ask if the person was in control of the behavior. For example, suppose you invite your friend Desmond to dinner for 7 p.m. and he arrives at 9. Consider how you would respond to each of these reasons:

> Reason 1: I just couldn't tear myself away from the beach. I really wanted to get a great tan.
> Reason 2: I was driving here when I saw some young kids mugging an old couple. I broke it up and took the couple home. They were so frightened that I had to stay with them until their children arrived. Their phone was out of order and my cell battery died, so I had no way of calling to tell you I'd be late.
> Reason 3: I got in a car accident and was taken to the hospital.

Depending on the reason, you would probably attribute very different motives to Desmond's behavior. With reasons 1 and 2, you'd conclude that Desmond was in control of his behavior; with reason 3, that he was not. Further, you would probably respond negatively to reason 1 (Desmond was selfish and inconsiderate) and positively to reason 2 (Desmond was a Good Samaritan). Because Desmond was not in control of his behavior in reason 3, you would probably not attribute either positive or negative motivation to his behavior. Instead, you would probably feel sorry that he got into an accident.

You probably make similar judgments based on controllability in numerous situations. Consider, for example, how you would respond to the following situations:

- Doris fails her history midterm exam.
- Sidney's car is repossessed because he failed to keep up the payments.
- Margie is 150 pounds overweight and is complaining that she feels awful.
- Thomas's wife has just filed for divorce and he is feeling depressed.

You would most likely be sympathetic to each of these people if you felt that he or she was not in control of what happened; for example, if the examination was unfair, if Sidney lost his job because of employee discrimination, if Margie had a glandular problem, and if Thomas's wife wanted to leave him for a wealthy drug dealer. On the other hand, you probably would not be sympathetic if you felt that these people were in control of what happened; for example, if Doris partied instead of studying, if Sidney gambled his payments away, if Margie ate nothing but junk food and refused to exercise, and if Thomas had been repeatedly unfaithful and his wife finally gave up trying to reform him.

In sum, in perceiving and especially in evaluating other people's behavior, you frequently ask if they were in control of the behavior. Generally, research shows that if you feel a person was in control of negative behaviors, you'll come to dislike him or her. If you believe the person was not in control of negative behaviors, you'll come to feel sorry for and not blame the person.

Attribution processes can involve several potential errors: (1) the self-serving bias, (2) overattribution, and (3) the fundamental attribution error.

# ASK THE RESEARCHER

## Making a First Impression

*I'm planning on becoming a teacher and want to draw on the insights
of this course to be a better (no, a sensational) teacher. For starters, how can
I make an excellent first impression on high school students?*

The first thing to keep in mind is that your students will have a great deal of uncertainty on the first day. They will be trying to figure out who you are and what kind of teacher you'll be. Students will be interpreting both your verbal and nonverbal messages, so make sure your verbal messages give them information that they need in order to meet your expectations and to succeed. Your nonverbal messages need to communicate that you like them, want to know them as individuals, and want them to succeed. Specific nonverbal behaviors that communicate liking (also referred to as immediacy) are smiling, making eye contact, and moving about the classroom so that you are physically close (but not too close) to as many students as possible. Immediacy and enthusiasm tend to be reciprocated, so make the first move and show your students how much you like them and how enthusiastic you are about the course.

For additional information: Frymier, A. B., & Houser, M. (2000). The teacher–student relationship as an interpersonal relationship. *Communication Education, 49,* 207–219. Also Richmond, V. P. (2002). Teacher nonverbal immediacy: Uses and outcomes. In J. L. Chesebro & J. C. McCroskey (Eds.), *Communication for teachers* (pp. 65–82). Boston: Allyn & Bacon.

**Ann Bainbridge Frymier** (Ed.D., West Virginia University) is associate dean of the Graduate School and an associate professor of communication at Miami University in Oxford, Ohio, and teaches courses in instructional communication, persuasion, interpersonal communication, and research methods. Her research examines how communication functions in the classroom to enhance student learning (frymierab@muohio.edu).

## The Self-Serving Bias

The **self-serving bias** is an error usually made to preserve your self-esteem. You commit the self-serving bias when you take credit for the positive and deny responsibility for the negative. For example, you're more likely to attribute your positive outcomes (say, you get an A on an exam) to internal and controllable factors—to your personality, intelligence, or hard work (Bernstein, Stephan, & Davis, 1979; Duval & Silva, 2002). And you're more likely to attribute your negative outcomes (say, you get a D) to external and uncontrollable factors—to the exam's being exceptionally difficult or unfair.

## Overattribution

**Overattribution** is the tendency to single out one or two obvious characteristics of a person and attribute everything that person does to this one or these two characteristics. For example, if a person is blind or was born into great wealth, there's often a tendency to attribute everything that person does to such factors. And so you might say, "Alex overeats because he's blind," or "Lillian is irresponsible because she never had to work for her money." To prevent overattribution, recognize that most behaviors and personality characteristics result from lots of factors. You almost always make a mistake when you select one factor and attribute everything to it. So when you make a judgment, ask yourself if other factors might be operating here: Are there other factors that might be influencing Alex's eating habits or Lillian's irresponsible behavior?

## The Fundamental Attribution Error

The **fundamental attribution error** occurs when you overvalue the contribution of internal factors (for example, a person's personality) to behaviors and undervalue the influence of external factors (for example, the context or situation the person is in). In other words, the fundamental attribution error is the tendency to conclude that people do what they do because that's the kind of people they are, not because of the situation they're in. When Pat is late for an appointment, you're more likely to conclude that Pat is inconsiderate or irresponsible than to attribute the lateness to a bus breakdown or a traffic accident.

This fundamental attribution error is at least in part culturally influenced (Goode, 2000). For example, in the United States people are more likely to explain behavior by saying that people did what they did because of who they are. When researchers asked Hindus in India to explain why their friends behaved as they did, the respondents gave greater weight to external factors than did respondents in the United States (Aronson, Wilson, & Akert, 2002). Generally, Americans have little hesitation in offering causal explanations of a person's behavior ("Pat did this because..."); Hindus, on the other hand, are generally reluctant to explain a person's behavior in causal terms (Matsumoto, 1994).

# INCREASING ACCURACY IN PERCEPTION

Successful communication depends largely on the accuracy of your perception of yourself, of others, and of the world generally. You now know about barriers that can arise with perceptual processes—barriers such as the self-serving bias, overattribution, and the fundamental attribution error in attribution. There are, however, additional ways to think more critically about your perceptions and thereby to increase your perceptual accuracy. This section will offer some key strategies.

## Analyze Your Perceptions

Become aware of your perceptions and try to subject them to logical analysis and critical thinking. First, recognize your own role in perception. For example, your emotional and physiological state will influence the meaning you give to your perceptions. A movie may seem hysterically funny when you're in a good mood but just plain stupid when you're in a bad mood. Also, beware of your own biases; for example, do you tend to perceive only the positive in

---

## Theory and Research    Understanding    The Just World Hypothesis

Many people believe that the world is just: Good things happen to good people and bad things to bad people (Aronson, Wilson, & Akert, 2002; Hunt, 2000). Put differently, the just world hypothesis suggests that you'll get what you deserve! Even if you mindfully dismiss this assumption, you may use it mindlessly when perceiving and evaluating other people. Consider a particularly vivid example: In certain cultures (for example, in Bangladesh, Iran, or Yemen), a woman who is raped is considered by many (though certainly not all) to have disgraced her family and to be deserving of severe punishment—in many cases, even death. Although most people reading this book will claim that this is unjust and unfair, it's quite common even in Western cultures to blame the victim. Much research, for example, shows that people often blame the victim for being raped (Bell, Kuriloff, & Lottes, 1994). In fact, accused rapists' defense attorneys routinely attack rape victims in court for dressing provocatively. And it's relevant to note that only two states—New York and Florida—currently forbid questions about the victim's clothing.

The belief that the world is just creates perceptual distortions by leading us to deemphasize the influence of situational factors and to overemphasize the influence of internal factors in our attempts to explain the behaviors of other people or even our own behaviors.

Another way in which the belief in a just world distorts perception is through the egocentric fairness bias: People who have strong beliefs in a just world see their own behaviors as fairer and more moral than those of others (Tanaka, 1999). The reasoning goes like this:

- if I am fairer and more moral than others,
- then I will experience more good than bad,
- because the world is just.

---

### Working with Theories and Research

*Take a look at your own behaviors; do you act as you do because of your belief in a just world? For example, do you act fairly because you think you'll be rewarded for it? Do you know people who do act on the basis of this hypothesis—for example, doing good in anticipation of good things happening to them?*

people you like and only the negative in people you don't like? Even your gender will influence your perceptions. Women consistently evaluate other people more positively than men on such factors as agreeableness, conscientiousness, and emotional stability (Winquist, Mohr, & Kenny, 1998).

Second, avoid early conclusions. On the basis of your observations of behaviors, formulate hypotheses to test against additional information and evidence rather than drawing conclusions you then look to confirm. At the same time, seek validation from others. Do others see things the same way you do? If not, ask yourself if your perceptions may be in some way distorted.

## Check Your Perceptions

**Perception checking** is another way to make your perceptions more accurate. The goal of perception checking is not to prove that your initial perception is correct but to explore further the thoughts and feelings of the other person. With this simple technique, you lessen your chances of misinterpreting another's feelings. In its most basic form, perception checking involves two components.

- Describe what you see or hear, recognizing that your perceptions are heavily influenced by who you are, your emotional state, and so on. At the

same time, you may wish to describe what you *think* is happening. For example:

- "You've called me from work a lot this week. You seem concerned about how things are at home."

- "You've not wanted to talk with me all week. You say that my work is fine, but you don't seem to want to give me the same responsibilities that other editorial assistants have."

- Avoid mind reading; avoid trying to deduce the thoughts and feelings of another person from their observable behaviors. A person's motives are not open to outside inspection; you can only make *assumptions* based on behaviors that you observe. So seek confirmation. Ask the other person if your perception is accurate in as supportive a way as possible:

- "Are you worried about me or the kids?"

- "Are you displeased with my work? Is there anything I can do to improve my job performance?"

Try your hand at perception checking by asking yourself how you'd respond to the following statements:

- "Yeah, I finally married; it took me 43 years. And now comes the task of making do."

---

**B u i l d i n g  C o m m u n i c a t i o n  S K I L L S    Perceptual Empathizing**

Try empathizing with each of the individuals involved in these scenarios, indicating how each of the persons might *reasonably* feel about the situation. After completing both scenarios, try formulating a summary statement of your own empathic strengths and weaknesses.

1. Pat, a single parent, has two children ages 7 and 12 who often lack some of the important things children their age should have (e.g., school supplies, sneakers, and toys) because Pat can't afford them. Yet Pat smokes two packs of cigarettes a day.

   Pat sees . . .
   The 12-year-old daughter sees . . .
   The children's teachers see . . .

2. Chris has extremely high standards and feels that getting all A's is an absolute necessity. In fear of that first B (after three and a half years of college), Chris cheats on an examination and gets caught by the instructor.

   Chris sees . . .
   The instructor sees . . .
   The average B or C student sees . . .

*To understand the perspective of another person, try to understand their reasons for their behaviors while resisting defining these reasons from your own perspective.*

- "I can't imagine why I didn't get that job. I knew more about the company and the job than the interviewer."

- "You'll never make it in this company; you're too bright, too dedicated."

## Reduce Your Uncertainty

Earlier, in Unit 1, the concepts of ambiguity and uncertainty were introduced and the differences among cultures were noted. These concepts are also useful in understanding perception. Put simply: Reducing uncertainty enables you to achieve greater accuracy in perception. Not surprisingly, you'll also find greater communication satisfaction if your uncertainty is reduced (Neuliep & Grohskopf, 2000).

A variety of **uncertainty reduction strategies** can help you reduce uncertainty in perception generally and in people perception specifically (Berger & Bradac, 1982; Gudykunst, 1994).

- Observe the person while he or she is engaged in an active task, preferably interacting with others in relatively informal social situations. People are less apt to monitor their behaviors and more likely to reveal their true selves in informal situations.

- Set up situations so as to be able to observe a person in more specific and more revealing contexts. Employment interviews, theatrical auditions, and student teaching placements are examples of situations designed to reduce uncertainty by letting observers see how people act and react.

- Ask others for information. For example, you might ask a colleague if a third person finds you interesting and might like to have dinner with you.

- Interact with the individual. For example, you can ask questions: "Do you enjoy sports?" "What did you think of that computer science course?" "What would you do if you got fired?"

## Increase Your Cultural Awareness

Recognizing and being mindful of cultural differences will help increase your accuracy in perception. For example, Russian or Chinese performers such as ballet dancers will often applaud their audience by clapping. Americans may easily misinterpret this gesture as egotistical. Similarly, a German man will enter a restaurant before the woman in order to see if the place is respectable enough for the woman to enter. This simple custom may appear rude to people from cultures in which it's considered courteous to allow the woman to enter first (Axtell, 1993).

Cultural awareness will help counteract the difficulty most people have in understanding the nonverbal messages of people from other cultures. For example, be aware that it's easier to decode emotions communicated facially by members of your own culture than to read emotions shown by members of other cultures (Weathers, Frank, & Spell, 2002). This "in-group advantage" will assist your perceptional accuracy for members of your own culture but will often hinder your accuracy for members of other cultures (Elfenbein & Ambady, 2002).

Within every cultural group, too, there are wide and important differences. Not all Americans are alike, and neither are all Indonesians, Greeks, Mexicans, and so on. When you make assumptions that all people of a certain culture are alike, as Unit 2 explained, you're thinking in stereotypes. In addition to recognizing differences between another culture and your own, recognizing differences among members of any given culture will help you perceive people and situations more accurately.

## SUMMARY: THE SELF AND PERCEPTION

This unit explored the self, the ways you perceive yourself, and perception, the way you perceive others and others perceive you.

1. Self-concept is the image that you have of yourself, and is composed of feelings and thoughts about both your abilities and your limitations. Self-concept develops from the image that others have of you, the comparisons you make between yourself and others, the teachings of your culture, and your own interpretations and evaluations of your thoughts and behaviors.

2. The Johari window model of the self is one way to view self-awareness. In this model there are four major areas: the open self, the blind self, the hidden self, and the unknown self. To increase self-awareness, analyze yourself, listen to others to see yourself as they do, actively seek information from others about yourself, see yourself from different perspectives, and increase your open self.

3. Self-esteem is the value you place on yourself. To enhance self-esteem, attack self-destructive beliefs, seek out nourishing others, work on projects that will result in success, and secure affirmation.

4. Self-disclosure is a form of communication in which information about the self that is normally kept hidden is communicated to one or more others.

5. Self-disclosure is more likely to occur when the potential discloser (1) feels competent, is sociable and extroverted, and is not apprehensive about communication; (2) comes from a culture that encourages self-disclosure; (3) is a woman; (4) is talking to supportive listeners who also disclose; and (5) talks about impersonal rather than personal topics and reveals positive rather than negative information.

6. The rewards of self-disclosure include increased self-knowledge, the ability to cope with difficult situations and guilt, communication efficiency, and chances for more meaningful relationships. The dangers of self-disclosure include personal and social rejection and professional or material losses.

7. Before self-disclosing, consider the cultural rules operating, the motivation for the self-disclosure, the possible burdens you might impose on your listener or on yourself, the appropriateness of the self-disclosure, and the disclosures of the other person.

8. When listening to disclosures, take into consideration the cultural rules governing the communication situation, try to understand what the discloser is feeling, support the discloser, refrain from criticism and evaluation, and keep the disclosures confidential.

9. When you don't want to disclose, try being firm, being indirect and changing the topic, or assertively stating your unwillingness to disclose.

10. Perception is the process by which you become aware of the many stimuli impinging on your senses. Perception occurs in five stages: Sensory stimulation occurs, sensory stimulation is organized, sensory stimulation is interpreted–evaluated, sensory stimulation is held in memory, and sensory stimulation is recalled.

11. The following processes influence perception: (1) implicit personality theory, (2) self-fulfilling prophecy, (3) primacy–recency, and (4) attribution.

12. Several strategies can increase your accuracy in perceptions: (1) Analyze your perceptions; for example, recognize your role in perception and formulate hypotheses rather than conclusions, looking for a variety of cues. (2) Check perceptions; that is, describe what you see or hear and ask for confirmation, and avoid mind reading. (3) Reduce uncertainty by, for example, collecting information about the person or situation, and interacting and observing the interaction. And (4) be culturally aware, recognizing the differences between you and others as well as the differences among members of the culturally different group.

## KEY TERMS IN THE SELF AND PERCEPTION

attribution (p. **74**)
blind self (p. **58**)
contrast (p. **69**)
disinhibition effect (p. **64**)
dyadic effect (p. **64**)
fundamental attribution error (p. **75**)
halo effect (p. **72**)
hidden self (p. **58**)

implicit personality theory (p. **72**)
Johari window (p. **57**)
looking-glass self (p. **56**)
open self (p. **57**)
overattribution (p. **75**)
perception (p. **68**)
perception checking (p. **77**)
primacy effect (p. **74**)
primacy–recency (p. **74**)

proximity (p. **68**)
recency effect (p. **74**)
schemata (p. **69**)
script (p. **69**)
selective attention (p. **68**)
selective exposure (p. **68**)
self-awareness (p. **57**)
self-concept (p. **56**)
self-destructive beliefs (p. **60**)

self-disclosure (p. **61**)
self-esteem (p. **59**)
self-fulfilling prophecy (p. **73**)
self-serving bias (p. **75**)
similarity (p. **69**)
uncertainty reduction strategies (p. **78**)
unknown self (p. **58**)

## THINKING CRITICALLY ABOUT THE SELF AND PERCEPTION

1. **Self-Esteem.** Popular wisdom emphasizes the importance of self-esteem. The self-esteem camp, however, has come under attack from critics (for example, Bushman & Baumeister, 1998; Baumeister, Bushman, & Campbell, 2000; Bower, 2001; Coover & Murphy, 2000; Hewitt, 1998). These critics argue that high self-esteem is not necessarily desirable: It does nothing to improve academic performance, it does not predict success, and it may even lead to antisocial (especially aggressive) behavior. On the other hand, it's difficult to imagine how a person would function successfully without positive self-feelings. What do you think about the benefits or liabilities of self-esteem?

2. **Predictability and Uncertainty.** As you and another person develop a closer and more intimate relationship, you generally reduce your uncertainty about each other; you become more predictable to each other. Do you think this higher predictability makes a relationship more stable or less stable? More enjoyable or less enjoyable? Are there certain things about your partner (best friend, lover, or family member) that you are uncertain about, and do you want to reduce this uncertainty? What kinds of messages might you use to accomplish this uncertainty reduction?

3. **Self-Disclosure.** Some research indicates that self-disclosure occurs more quickly and at higher levels of intimacy

online than in face-to-face situations (Joinson, 2001; Levine, 2000). In contrast, other research finds that people experience greater closeness and self-disclosure in face-to-face groups than in Internet chat groups (Mallen, Day, & Green, 2003). What has been your experience with self-disclosure in online and face-to-face situations?

4. **Your Public Messages.** Will knowing that some undergraduate and graduate admissions offices and potential employers may examine your postings on sites such as MySpace, Facebook, and Xanga influence what you write?

For example, do you avoid posting opinions that might be viewed negatively by schools or employers? Do you deliberately post items that you want schools or employers to find?

5. **Online dating.** According to a *New York Times* survey, online dating is losing its stigma as an activity for losers (June 29, 2003, p. A1). Why do you think perceptions are changing in the direction of greater acceptance of online relationships? What is your current implicit personality theory of the "online dater"?

## LogOn! MyCommunicationLab

### WWW.MYCOMMUNICATIONLAB.COM

Visit MyCommunicationLab and take a look at some relevant exercises: Perceiving Yourself, Perceiving Your Many Intelligences, Perceiving Others, Taking Another's Perspective, Barriers to Accurate Perception, Paraphrasing, Increasing Self-Awareness, Giving and Receiving Compliments, Timing Self-Disclosure, and Responding to Self-Disclosures. Also take the self-tests How Shy Are You? and How Much Do You Self-Monitor? Take a look at the videos Assisted Learning and Debbie Bank's Commencement Address. A variety of excellent figures and tables will provide additional views of the topics covered here; see the "visualize" category. While you're online also take a look at the website maintained by the popular psychology magazine *Psychology Today*; it covers many of the topics discussed in this unit (www.psychologytoday.com). Of special interest are the self-tests, which can help you learn more about yourself. Log on to this website and take one or more of these self-tests. Other websites containing self-tests include All the Tests (www.allthetests.com) and Queendom.com (www.queendom.com).

# UNIT 4 Listening in Human Communication

## UNIT CONTENTS

## Special Features

There can be little doubt that you listen a great deal. On waking, you listen to the radio or television. On the way to school, you listen to friends, people around you, screeching cars, singing birds, or falling rain. In school, you listen to the instructors, to other students, and to yourself. You listen to friends at lunch and return to class to listen to more instructors. You arrive home and again listen to family and friends. Perhaps you listen to CDs, radio, or television. All in all, you listen for a good part of your waking day.

**In this unit you'll learn about:**
- the benefits of listening.
- how listening works and how it varies with gender and culture.
- the styles of listening you can use.

**You'll learn to**
- avoid the barriers to effective listening.
- adjust your listening so that it's most effective for the specific situation.

According to the International Listening Association, **listening** is "the process of receiving, constructing meaning from, and responding to spoken and/or nonverbal messages" (Emmert, 1994 and cited in Brownell, 2006).

In this unit we will look at the importance of listening, the nature of the listening process, some cultural and gender differences in listening, and the varied styles of listening you might use in different situations. Throughout this unit, we'll identify ways to avoid the major barriers to listening and guidelines for more effective listening.

## THE IMPORTANCE OF LISTENING: TASK AND RELATIONSHIP BENEFITS

Regardless of what you do, listening will prove a crucial communication component and will serve both task and relationship functions. For example, one study concluded that in this era of technological transformation, employees' interpersonal skills are especially significant; workers' advancement will depend on their ability to speak and write effectively, to display proper etiquette, and *to listen attentively*. And in a revealing survey of 40 CEOs of Asian and Western multinational companies, respondents cited a lack of listening skills as *the major shortcoming* of top executives (Witcher, 1999).

An important task benefit of listening is to establish and communicate power. In much the same way that you communicate power verbally and nonverbally—topics we'll consider in the next two units—you also can communicate your power through listening. Here are a few suggestions on how to listen with power.

- Respond visibly, but in moderation. Too little response says you aren't listening, and too much response says you aren't listening critically. Backchanneling cues—head nods and brief oral responses that say you're listening—are especially helpful in communicating power.

- Avoid "adaptors"—behaviors such as playing with your hair or drawing pictures on a Styrofoam cup. Adaptors signal discomfort and hence a lack of power. The absence of adaptors, on the other hand, makes you appear in control of the situation and comfortable in the role of listener.

- Maintain an open posture. When around a table or in an audience, resist covering your face, chest, or stomach with your hands. These postures are often interpreted as signaling defensiveness or vulnerability and hence powerlessness.

- Take modest notes when appropriate. Taking too many notes may communicate a lack of ability to distinguish between what is and what is not important. Taking too few notes may communicate a lack of serious purpose or a reluctance to deal with the material.

- You also can signal power through visual dominance behavior (Exline, Ellyson, & Long, 1975; Burgoon & Bacue, 2003). For example, the average speaker maintains a high level of eye contact while listening and a lower level while speaking. When you want to signal dominance, you might reverse this pattern—maintain a high level of eye contact while talking but a lower level while listening.

It's also interesting to note that the effective listener—to take just a few examples of both task and relationship benefits—is more likely to emerge as group leader, a more effective salesperson, a more attentive and effective health-care worker, and a more effective manager (Johnson & Bechler, 1998; Kramer, 1997; Castleberry & Shepherd, 1993; Lauer, 2003; Stein & Bowen, 2003; Levine, 2004). Recently medical educators, claiming that doctors are not trained to listen to their patients, have introduced what they call "narrative medicine" to teach doctors how to listen to their patients and to help doctors recognize how their perceptions of their patients are influenced by their own emotions (Smith, 2003).

Another way to appreciate the importance of listening is to consider its many benefits. Here are some, built around the purposes of human communication identified in Unit 1:

- **Learning:** Listening enables you to acquire knowledge of others, the world, and yourself, so as to avoid problems and make better-informed decisions. For example, hearing Peter tell about his travels to Cuba will help you learn more about Peter and about life in another country. Listening to the difficulties of your sales staff may help you offer more pertinent sales training.

- **Relating:** Through attentive and supportive listening you can gain social acceptance and popularity. Others will increase their liking of you once they see your genuine concern for them.

- **Influencing:** Listening can help you change the attitudes and behaviors of others. For example, workers are more likely to follow your advice once they feel you've really listened to their insights and concerns.

- **Playing:** Listening can be enjoyable, letting you share pleasurable thoughts and feelings. Really listening to the anecdotes of coworkers will allow you to balance the world of work and the world of play.

- **Helping:** Listening often is vital in efforts to assist others. For example, listening to your child's complaints about her teacher will increase your ability to help your child cope with school and her teacher.

## THE LISTENING PROCESS

Before reading about the process of listening, examine your own listening habits and tendencies by taking the following self-test.

## TEST **YOURSELF**

### How Do You Listen?

Respond to each question with the following scale: 1 = always, 2 = frequently, 3 = sometimes, 4 = seldom, and 5 = never.

_____ **1.** I listen actively, communicate acceptance of the speaker, and prompt the speaker to further explore his or her thoughts.

_____ **2.** I listen to what the speaker is saying and feeling; I try to feel what the speaker feels.

_____ **3.** I listen without judging the speaker.

_____ **4.** I listen to the literal meanings that a speaker communicates; I don't look too deeply into hidden meanings.

_____ **5.** I listen without active involvement; I generally remain silent and take in what the other person is saying.

_____ **6.** I listen objectively; I focus on the logic of the ideas rather than on the emotional meaning of the message.

_____ **7.** I listen critically, evaluating the speaker and what the speaker is saying.

_____ **8.** I look for the hidden meanings: the meanings that are revealed by subtle verbal or nonverbal cues.

`HOW DID YOU DO?` These statements focus on the ways of listening discussed in this unit. All of these ways are appropriate at some times but not at other times. It depends. So the only responses that are really inappropriate are "always" and "never." Effective listening is listening that is tailored to the specific communication situation.

`WHAT WILL YOU DO?` Consider how you might use these statements to begin to improve your listening effectiveness. A good way to start is to review these listening behaviors and try to identify situations in which each behavior would be appropriate and situations in which each behavior would be inappropriate.

The process of listening can be described as a series of five steps: (1) receiving (hearing and attending to the message), (2) understanding (deciphering meaning from the message you hear), (3) remembering (retaining what you hear in memory), (4) evaluating (thinking critically about and judging the message), and (5) responding (answering or giving feedback to the speaker). The process is visualized in Figure 4.1.

Note that the listening process is circular. The responses of person A serve as the stimuli for person B, whose responses in turn serve as the stimuli for person A, and so on. As will become clear in the following discussion of the five steps, listening is not a

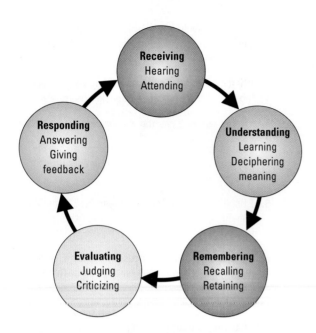

**FIGURE 4.1** **A Five-Stage Model of Listening**

At each stage of listening there will be lapses. Thus, for example, at the receiving stage, a listener receives part of the message but because of noise (and perhaps for other reasons) fails to receive other parts. Similarly, at the stage of understanding, a listener understands part of the message but because of the inability to share another's meanings exactly (see Unit 5 for more on this) fails to understand other parts. The same is true for remembering, evaluating, and responding. This model draws on a variety of previous models that listening researchers have developed (e.g., Alessandra, 1986; Barker & Gaut, 2002; Brownell, 1987; Steil, Barker, & Watson, 1983).

process of transferring an idea from the mind of a speaker to the mind of a listener. Rather, it is a process in which speaker and listener work together to achieve a common understanding.

As you read this discussion of the five stages of listening, realize that listening can go wrong at any of the five stages. At the same time, you can enhance your listening ability by strengthening the skills needed at each listening stage.

## Receiving

Unlike listening, hearing begins and ends with this first stage—receiving. Hearing is something that just happens when you open your ears or when you get within earshot of auditory stimuli.

Listening is quite different. Listening begins, but does not end, with receiving messages the speaker sends. In listening you receive both the verbal and the nonverbal messages—not only the words but also the gestures, facial expressions, variations in vol-

ume and rate, and lots more, as you'll discover when we discuss messages in more detail in Units 5 and 6. For improved reception:

- **Focus attention** on the speaker's verbal and nonverbal messages, on both what is said and what is not said.
- **Look for feedback** in response to previous messages as well as feedforward (Unit 1), which can reveal how the speaker would like his or her message viewed.
- **Avoid distractions** in the environment and focus attention on the speaker rather than on what you'll say next.
- **Maintain your role as listener** and avoid interrupting the speaker until he or she is finished.

In this brief discussion of receiving (and in this entire unit on listening), the unstated assumption is that both individuals can receive auditory signals without difficulty. But for the many people who have hearing impairments, listening presents a variety of problems. Table 4.1 provides tips for communication between those with and those without hearing problems.

## Understanding

Understanding is the stage at which you learn what the speaker means. This understanding must take into consideration both the thoughts that are expressed and the emotional tone that accompanies them—the urgency or the joy or sorrow expressed in the message. For improved understanding:

- **Relate new information** to what you already know.
- **See the speaker's messages** from the speaker's point of view. Avoid judging the message until you've fully understood it—as the speaker intended it.
- **Ask questions** to clarify or to secure additional details or examples if necessary.
- **Rephrase (paraphrase)** the speaker's ideas in your own words.

## Remembering

Messages that you receive and understand need to be remembered for at least some period of time. In some small group and public speaking situations, you can augment your memory by taking notes or by tape-recording the messages. In most interpersonal communication situations, however, such note taking would be considered inappropriate—although you often do write down a phone number, an appointment, or directions.

## Table 4.1  Interpersonal Communication Tips

**Between People with and without Hearing Impairment**

People differ greatly in their hearing ability: Some are totally deaf and can hear nothing; others have some hearing loss and can hear some sounds; still others have impaired hearing but can hear most speech. Although people with profound hearing loss can speak, their speech may appear labored and may be less clear than the speech of those with unimpaired hearing. Here are some suggestions for more effective communication between deaf and hearing people.

If you have unimpaired hearing:

1. *Set up a comfortable context.* Reduce the distance between yourself and the person with a hearing impairment. Reduce the background noise. Turn off the television or even the air conditioner.

2. *Avoid interference.* Make sure the visual cues from your speech are clearly observable; for example, face the person squarely and avoid smoking, chewing gum, or holding your hand over your mouth. Make sure the lighting is adequate.

3. *Speak at an adequate volume.* But avoid shouting, which can distort your speech and may insult the person. Be careful to avoid reducing volume at the ends of your sentences.

4. *Phrase ideas in different ways.* Because some words are easier to lip-read than others, it often helps if you rephrase your ideas in different ways.

5. *Avoid overlapping speech.* In group situations only one person should speak at a time. Similarly, don't talk to a person with a hearing impairment through a third party; direct your comments to the person himself or herself. Elementary school teachers, for example, have been found to direct fewer comments to deaf children than to hearing students (Cawthon, 2001).

6. *Ask for additional information.* Ask the person if there is anything you can do to make it easier for him or her to understand you.

7. *Don't avoid common terms.* Use terms like "hear," "listen," "music," or "deaf" when they're relevant to the conversation. Trying to avoid these common terms will make your speech sound artificial.

8. *Use nonverbal cues.* These can help communicate your meaning; gestures indicating size or location and facial expressions indicating emotions and feelings are often helpful.

If you have impaired hearing:

1. *Do your best to eliminate background noise.*

2. *Move closer to the speaker if this helps you hear better.* Alert the speaker that this closer distance will help you hear better.

3. *Ask for adjustments.* If you feel the speaker can make adjustments to ease your comprehension, ask. For example, ask the speaker to repeat a message, to speak more slowly or more distinctly, or to increase his or her volume.

4. *Position yourself for best reception.* If you hear better in one ear than another, position yourself accordingly; if necessary, clue the speaker in to this fact.

5. *Ask for additional cues.* If necessary, ask the speaker to write down certain information, such as phone numbers or website addresses. Carrying a pad and pencil will prove helpful for this and in the event that you wish to write something down for others.

These suggestions were drawn from a variety of sources: *Tips for Communicating with Deaf People* (Rochester Institute of Technology, National Technical Institute for the Deaf, Division of Public Affairs), www.his.com/&sim;lola/deaf.html, www.zak.co.il/deaf-info/old/comm_strategies.html, and www.agbell.org/information/brochures_communication.cfm (all websites accessed October 23, 2004).

What you remember of a message is not an exact recording of what you hear; your memory doesn't just reproduce what you hear. Rather, your memory *reconstructs* the messages you hear and read, a process considered in more detail in the Understanding Theory and Research box (Reconstructing Memory) on page 86.

You can improve your message memory by:

- **identifying the central ideas** in a message and the major support advanced for them;

- **summarizing the message** in a more easily retained form, being careful not to ignore crucial details or qualifications;

- **repeating names and key concepts** to yourself or, if appropriate, aloud; and

- **asking questions** when in doubt.

## Theory and Research — Reconstructing Memory

### UNDERSTANDING

When you remember a message, do you remember it as it was spoken, or do you remember what you think you heard? The commonsense response, of course, would be that you remember what was said. But before accepting this simple explanation, try to memorize the list of 12 words presented below, modeled on an idea from a research study (Glucksberg & Danks, 1975). Don't worry about the order of the words; only the number of words remembered counts. Take about 20 seconds to memorize as many words as possible. Then close the book and write down as many words as you can remember.

| | | |
|---|---|---|
| dining room | table | milk |
| cafeteria | shopping | hungry |
| green beans | steak | saucer |
| satisfied | knife | menu |

Don't read any further until you've tried to memorize and reproduce the list of words.

If you're like most people, you not only remembered a good number of the words on the list, but also "remembered" at least one word that was not on the list: *eat*. Most people would recall the word as being on the list (whether they read the list as you've done here or hear it spoken)—but, as you can see, it wasn't. What happens is that in remembering you don't simply reproduce the list; you reconstruct it. In this case you gave the list meaning, and part of that meaning included the word *eat*. Memory for speech, then, is not reproductive—you don't simply reproduce in your memory what the speaker said. Rather, memory is reconstructive: You reconstruct the messages you hear into a system that makes sense to you but, in the process, often remember distorted versions of what was said.

### Working with Theories and Research

*Log on to your favorite database or search engine and search for articles dealing with false memory. In what types of situations is false memory found? What are some of its implications for communication?*

## Evaluating

Evaluating consists of judging messages in some way. At times, you may try to evaluate the speaker's underlying intent. Often this evaluation process goes on without much conscious thought. For example, Elaine tells you that she is up for a promotion and is really excited about it. You may then try to judge her intention. Does she want you to use your influence with the company president? Is she preoccupied with her accomplishment and thus telling everyone about it? Is she looking for a pat on the back? Generally, if you know the person well, you'll be able to identify the intention and therefore be able to respond appropriately.

In other situations, evaluation is more in the nature of critical analysis. For example, in listening to proposals advanced in a business meeting, you will at this stage evaluate them. Is there evidence to show that these proposals are practical and will increase productivity? Is there contradictory evidence? Are there alternative proposals that would be more practical and more productive?

In evaluating, try to

- **resist evaluation** until you fully understand the speaker's point of view;
- **assume that the speaker is a person of good-will**, and give the speaker the benefit of any doubt by asking for clarification on issues that you feel you must object to (are there any other reasons for accepting this new proposal?);
- **distinguish facts from inferences** (see Unit 5), opinions, and personal interpretations by the speaker; and
- **identify any biases, self-interests, or prejudices** that may lead the speaker to slant unfairly what is presented

## Responding

Responding occurs in two phases: (1) responses you make while the speaker is talking and (2) responses you make after the speaker has stopped talking. These responses are feedback—information that you send back to the speaker and that tells the

## ASK THE RESEARCHER

### Not Listening

*I appreciate all these suggestions for listening, but what if you don't want to listen? For example, I don't want to hear about my colleagues' relationships, my neighbor's tax problems, or even my partner's frequent and detailed sports updates. Any suggestions?*

It's not unusual to find yourself in a situation where someone is speaking and you don't want to listen. The speaker isn't thinking about you—he or she is talking to sort out a problem or to express an enthusiasm. The way you respond is always your judgment call. Consider whether listening in this case is something that the speaker would greatly appreciate before you take the risk of offending your partner by cutting them off.

If you decide not to listen, take a deep breath and interrupt. Politely. Change the subject by recognizing the speaker's concern and then move on to a different topic: "I'm amazed that Jim hasn't responded. I realize it's very stressful. You know, there's something that I need to discuss with you. . . ." Don't hang in the middle. There's nothing worse than giving the impression that you're listening when you're not. Either listen, or be assertive and change the subject.

For further information: Brownell, J. (2006). *Listening: Attitudes, principles and skills* (3rd ed.). Boston: Allyn & Bacon.

**Judi Brownell** (Ph.D., Syracuse University) is dean of students and a professor of organizational communication in the School of Hotel Administration at Cornell University, where she teaches managerial communication and organizational behavior. Professor Brownell is a past president of the International Listening Association and was inducted into the Listening Hall of Fame.

speaker how you feel and think about his or her messages. Responses made while the speaker is talking should be supportive and should acknowledge that you're listening. These include what researchers on nonverbal communication call **backchanneling cues**: "I see," "yes," "uh-huh," and similar signals that let the speaker know you're attending to the message.

Responses made after the speaker has stopped talking are generally more elaborate and might include expressing empathy ("I know how you must feel"), asking for clarification ("Do you mean that this new health plan is to replace the old one, or will it just be a supplement?"), challenging ("I think your evidence is weak here"), and agreeing ("You're absolutely right on this, and I'll support your proposal when it comes up for a vote"). For effective responding:

- **Be supportive** of the speaker throughout the speaker's talk by using and varying backchanneling cues; using only one backchanneling cue—for example, saying "uh-huh" throughout—may make it appear that you're not really listening.

- **Express support** for the speaker in your final responses.

- **Be honest**; the speaker has a right to expect honest responses, even if these express anger or disagreement.

- **State your thoughts and feelings** as your own, using I-messages. For example, say "I think the new proposal will entail greater expense than you outlined" rather than "Everyone will object to the plan for costing too much."

Table 4.2 on page 88 identifies some types of difficult listeners—listeners who don't follow the suggestions for each of the five listening stages—and their problem-causing ways of responding.

## LISTENING, CULTURE, AND GENDER

Listening is difficult, in part, because of the inevitable differences in the communication systems between speaker and listener. Because each person has had a

## Table 4.2 Some Problem-Causing Ways of Responding in Listening

Review this table and try to see if it includes some of your own listening behaviors.

| Listener Type | Listening (Responding) Behavior | (Mis)interpreting Thoughts |
|---|---|---|
| Static | Gives no feedback, remains relatively motionless, reveals no expression. | Why isn't she reacting? Am I not producing sound? |
| Monotonous | Seems responsive, but the responses never vary; regardless of what you say, the response is the same. | Am I making sense? Why is he still smiling? I'm being dead serious. |
| Overly expressive | Reacts to just about everything with extreme responses. | Why is she so expressive? I didn't say anything that provocative. She'll have a heart attack when I get to the punch line. |
| Reader/writer | Reads or writes while "listening" and only occasionally glances up. | Am I that boring? Is last week's student newspaper more interesting than me? |
| Eye avoider | Looks all around the room and at others but never at you. | Why isn't he looking at me? Do I have spinach on my teeth? |
| Preoccupied | Listens to other things at the same time, often with headphones turned up so loud that the sound interferes with your own thinking. | When is she going to shut that music off and really listen? Am I so boring that my talk needs background music? |
| Waiting | Listens for a cue to take over the speaking turn. | Is he listening to me or rehearsing his next interruption? |
| Thought-completing | Listens a little and then finishes your thought. | Am I that predictable? Why do I bother saying anything? He already knows what I'm going to say. |

unique set of experiences, each person's communication and meaning system is going to be different from each other person's. When speaker and listener come from different cultures or are of different genders, the differences and their effects are naturally so much greater. Let's look first at culture.

## Listening and Culture

In a global environment in which people from very different cultures work together, it's especially important to understand the ways in which cultural differences can influence listening. Four of these listening influences include: (1) language and speech, (2) nonverbal behaviors, (3) feedback, and (4) credibility.

### Language and Speech

Even when speaker and listener speak the same language, they speak it with different meanings and different accents. No two speakers speak exactly the same language. Speakers of the same language will, at the very least, have different meanings for the same terms because they have had different experiences.

Speakers and listeners who have different native languages and who may have learned English as a second language will have even greater differences in meaning. Translations are never precise and never fully capture the meaning in the other language. If your meaning for "house" was learned in a culture in which everyone lived in their own house with lots of land around it, then talking about houses with someone whose meaning was learned in a neighborhood of high-rise tenements is going to be difficult. Although you'll each hear the same word, the meanings you'll each develop will be drastically different. In adjusting your listening—especially in an intercultural setting—understand that the speaker's meanings may be very different from yours even though you're speaking the same language.

In many classrooms throughout this country, there will be a wide range of **accents**. Those whose native language is a tonal one such as Chinese (in which differences in pitch signal important meaning differences) may speak English with variations in pitch that may seem puzzling to their hearers. Those whose native language is Japanese may have trouble distinguishing *l* from *r*, as Japanese does not include this distinction. The native language acts as a filter and influences the accent given to the second language.

## PRINCIPLES OF MEDIA LITERACY LISTENING

*In a day of virtual reality and computer simulations "seeing is NOT believing."*

—*David Considine*

Here are a few basic principles to illustrate the importance of listening in media literacy.

1. Media messages are value-laden, meaning that the media contain the values of the producer and often of the primary audience. And these messages ethicize and socialize you—they give you an ethical standard and teach you the social rules you should follow. Because media messages are (generally) expensive to produce (feature films, television shows), they are likely to reflect the values of the rich and powerful. In contrast, electronic media—blogs, websites, and social networks such as MySpace or Friendster—are free or relatively inexpensive, and through these media people normally without influence voice opinions and send out persuasive messages. So listen to television programs, for example, with a consciousness of the values that are embedded in the production—the sitcom as well as the news broadcast—and how might these influence your thoughts and behaviors.

2. Media messages are informative and persuasive. They inform you of the news and at the same time persuade you that this is in fact the news; that is, that what the newspaper covers are in fact the significant events of the day. And of course media persuade you, on a more obvious level, with advertising. Almost all media messages have some persuasive aim. As a literate media consumer, see these persuasive messages clearly so that you can analyze them and test their validity, rather than letting them influence you without your awareness.

3. Media help construct your view of reality: What you know of the world and its people you probably learned largely from the media. Some media messages are accurate, and some are not; some messages are slanted, and most of them are overly simplified. Listen to the ways in which the media influence how you see the world and to the ways they present distorted pictures of what is supposed to be reality.

### Increasing Media Literacy

*In what ways have the media influenced your beliefs about, for example, the war in Iraq, the economy, or religion in government? How have the media influenced your peers' beliefs about these same issues? What specific media have the most influence on you? Why?*

## Nonverbal Behaviors

Speakers from different cultures have different display rules—cultural rules that govern which nonverbal behaviors are appropriate and which are inappropriate in a public setting. As you listen to other people, you also "listen" to their nonverbal cues. If these are drastically different from what you expect on the basis of the verbal message, you may see them as a kind of noise or interference or even as contradictory messages. Also, of course, different cultures may give very different meanings to the same nonverbal gesture; for example, the thumb and forefinger forming a circle means "OK" in most of the United States, but it means "money" in Japan, "zero" in some Mediterranean countries, and "I'll kill you" in Tunisia.

## Feedback

Members of some cultures give very direct and honest feedback. Speakers from these cultures—the United States is a good example—expect the feedback to be a forthright reflection of what their listeners are feeling. In other cultures—Japan and Korea are good examples—it's more important to be positive than to be truthful, so people may respond with positive feedback (say, in commenting on a business colleague's proposal) even though they don't actually feel positive. Listen to feedback, as you would all messages, with a full recognition that various cultures view feedback very differently.

## Credibility

What makes a speaker credible, or believable, also will vary from one culture to another. In some cultures people would claim that competence is the most important factor in, say, the choice of a teacher for their preschool children. In other cultures the most important factor might be the goodness or morality of the teacher. Similarly, members of different cultures may perceive the credibility of various media very differently. For example, members of a repressive society in which the government controls television news may come to attribute little credibility to

### LISTENING THROUGH GENDER

Your supervisor just doesn't seem to listen to your ideas and your feedback and you have the strong suspicion that it's because of your gender. You want to be listened to more fairly and yet you don't want to alienate your supervisor.

WHAT DO YOU SAY?
*Through what channel?*

such broadcasts. After all, these listeners might reason, television news is simply what the government wants you to know. This reaction may be hard to understand or even recognize for someone raised in the United States, for example, where traditionally the media have been largely free of such political control.

## Listening and Gender

Deborah Tannen opens her chapter on listening in her best-selling *You Just Don't Understand: Women and Men in Conversation* (1990) with several anecdotes illustrating that when men and women talk, men lecture and women listen. The lecturer is positioned as the superior: as the teacher, the expert.

The listener is positioned as the inferior: as the student, the nonexpert.

Women, according to Tannen, seek to build rapport and establish a closer relationship, and so use listening to achieve these ends. For example, women use more listening cues (such as interjecting "yeah," or "uh-huh," nodding in agreement, or smiling) to let the other person know they're paying attention and are interested. Women also make more eye contact when listening than do men, who are more apt to look around and often away from the speaker (Brownell, 2006). Men not only use fewer listening cues but interrupt more, and they will often change the topic to a subject they know more about or that is less relational or people oriented or

---

# REFLECTIONS ON ETHICS

## Listening Ethically

Most often discussions of ethics in communication focus on the speaker. But listeners, too, have ethical obligations.

- Give the speaker an honest hearing. Avoid prejudging the speaker before hearing her or him. Try to put aside prejudices and preconceptions so you can understand and then evaluate the speaker's message fairly.
- Empathize with the speaker. You don't have to agree with the speaker, but try to understand emotionally as well as intellectually what the speaker means. In this way, you'll come to understand the speaker more fully.
- Give the speaker honest responses and feedback. In a learning environment such as a communication class, this means giving honest and constructive criticism to help the speaker improve.

- Reflect honestly on the questions the speaker raises. Much as the listener has a right to expect an active speaker, the speaker has the right to expect a listener who will actively deal with, rather than just passively hear, the message.

## Ethical Choice Point

*You're teaching a class in communication. In the public speaking segment, one of your students, a sincere and devout Iranian Muslim, gives a speech on "why women should be subservient to men." After the first two minutes of the speech, half the class walks out. During the next class you plan to give a lecture on the ethics of listening. What is your ethical obligation in this situation? What would you say?*

Theory and Research   **Cues to Lying**

UNDERSTANDING

In listening, you normally assume that the speaker is telling the truth and seldom even ask yourself if the speaker is lying. When you do wonder about a speaker's truthfulness, research shows, it may be because the speaker exhibits behaviors that often accompany lying. Here are some verbal and nonverbal behaviors that are associated with lying (Knapp & Hall, 1997; O'Hair, Cody, Goss, & Krayer, 1988; Bond & Atoum, 2000; Al-Simadi, 2000; Burgoon & Bacue, 2003). As you review these behaviors, ask yourself if you use these cues in making assumptions about whether or not people are telling the truth. Be careful that you don't fall into the trap of thinking that just because someone emits these cues, he or she is therefore lying; these cues are often used by truth-tellers as well and are not 100 percent reliable in indicating lying. In fact, in one study participants who held stereotypical views of how liars behave (for example, liars don't look at you, or liars fidget) were less effective in detecting lying than were those who did not hold such beliefs (Vrij & Mann, 2001). Generally, however, research finds that liars

- smile less
- respond with shorter answers, often simple yes or no responses
- use fewer specifics and more generalities; for example, "we hung out"
- shift their posture more
- use more self-touching movements
- use more and longer pauses
- avoid direct eye contact with the listener and blink more often than normal
- appear less friendly and attentive
- make more speech errors

### Working with Theories and Research

*Can you recall a situation in which you made the assumption that someone was lying on the basis of such cues (or others)? What happened? Should you want to learn more about lying, search for such terms as "lying," "deception," "poker tells," and "falsehood." It's a fascinating subject of study.*

---

that is more factual, such as sports statistics, economic developments, or political problems. Men, research shows, tend to play up their expertise, emphasize it, and use it in dominating the conversation. Women often play down their expertise.

Now, you might be tempted to conclude from this that women play fair in conversation and that men don't; for example, that men consistently seek to put themselves in a position superior to women. But that may be too simple an explanation. Research shows that men communicate this way not only with women but with other men as well. Men are not showing disrespect for their female conversational partners but are simply communicating as they normally do. Women, too, communicate as they do not only with men but also with other women.

Tannen argues that the goal of a man in conversation is to be accorded respect. Therefore, a man seeks to display his knowledge and expertise, even if to do this he has to change the topic to one he

knows a great deal about. Women, on the other hand, seek to be liked; so they express agreement, rarely interrupt in order to take their turn as speaker, and give lots of cues (verbally and nonverbally) to indicate that they are listening.

There's no evidence to show that these differences represent any negative motives—for example, motives on the part of men to prove themselves superior or on the part of women to ingratiate themselves. Rather, these differences in listening are largely the result of the ways in which men and women have been socialized.

It should be mentioned that not all researchers agree that there is sufficient evidence to make the claims that Tannen and others make about gender differences in listening (Goldsmith & Fulfs, 1999). Gender differences are changing in today's world, and it's best to take generalizations about gender as starting points for investigation and not as airtight conclusions.

# STYLES OF EFFECTIVE LISTENING

As stressed throughout this unit, listening is situational; the type of listening that is appropriate will vary with the situation, and each situation will call for a somewhat different combination of listening styles. The art of effective listening largely consists of making appropriate choices along the following four dimensions:

- empathic and objective listening
- nonjudgmental and critical listening
- surface and depth listening
- active and inactive listening

Let's take a look at each of these dimensions.

## Empathic and Objective Listening

To understand what a person means and feels, listen with **empathy** (Rogers, 1970; Rogers & Farson, 1981). To empathize with others is to feel with them, to see the world as they see it, to feel what they feel. Empathy will enable you to understand other people's meanings, and it will also enhance your relationships (Barrett & Godfrey, 1988; Snyder, 1992).

Empathy is best understood as having two distinct parts: thinking empathy and feeling empathy (Bellafiore, 2005). In *thinking empathy* you express an understanding of what the person means. For example, when you paraphrase someone's comment, showing that you understand the meaning the person is trying to communicate, you're communicating *thinking empathy*. The second part is *feeling empathy*; here you express your feeling of what the other person is feeling. You demonstrate a similarity between what you're feeling and what the other person is feeling. Often you'll respond with both thinking and feeling empathy in the same brief response; for example, when a friend tells you of problems at home, you may respond by saying, for example, *Your problems at home do seem to be getting worse. I can imagine how you feel so angry at times.*

Empathic listening is the preferred mode of responding in most communication situations, but there are times when you need to go beyond it to measure meanings and feelings against some objective reality. It's important to listen to Peter tell you how the entire world hates him and to understand how Peter feels and why he feels this way. But then you need to look more objectively at Peter and perhaps see the paranoia or the self-hatred behind his

## EMPATHIC LISTENING

Your neighbors who've avoided work all their lives and lived off unfairly obtained government disability payments have just won the lottery for $86 million. They want you to share their joy, and they invite you over for a champagne toast and tell you about their plan to move into a mansion.

WHAT DO YOU SAY?

complaints. Sometimes, in other words, you have to put your empathic responses aside and listen with objectivity and detachment.

In adjusting your empathic and objective listening focus, keep the following recommendations in mind:

- **Punctuate from the speaker's point of view** (Unit 1). If you want to understand the speaker's perspective, see the sequence of events as the speaker does, and try to figure out how this can influence what the speaker says and does. Keep your focus (your thoughts and your messages) on the speaker.

- **Engage in equal, two-way conversation**. To encourage openness and empathy, try to eliminate any physical or psychological barriers to equality (for example, step out from behind the large desk separating you from your employee). Avoid interrupting the speaker—a sign that what you have to say is more important.

- **Seek to understand both thoughts and feelings**. Don't consider your listening task finished until you've understood what the speaker is feeling as well as what he or she is thinking.

- **Avoid "offensive listening,"** the tendency to listen to bits and pieces of information that will enable you to attack the speaker or find fault with something the speaker has said.

- **Strive especially to be objective in listening to friends and foes alike**. Be aware that your attitudes may lead you to distort messages—for example, to block out positive messages about a foe or negative messages about a friend. Guard against "expectancy hearing," in which you fail to hear what the speaker is really saying and instead hear what you expect.

- **Avoid trying to solve the problem** or even giving advice when trying to achieve empathy. Being empathic is hard enough, and at this point it's better to communicate your support and understanding rather than your evaluation of the situation.

- **Encourage the speaker to explore his or her feelings further** by demonstrating a willingness to listen and an interest in what the speaker is saying.

The accompanying Building Communication Skills box provides a few situations for you to practice your empathic skills (below).

## Nonjudgmental and Critical Listening

Effective listening includes both nonjudgmental and critical responses. Listen nonjudgmentally (with an open mind and with a view toward understanding) and listen critically (with a view toward making some kind of evaluation or judgment). Listen first for understanding; only when you understand should you be willing to evaluate or judge the messages.

Listening with an open mind will help you understand messages better; listening with a critical mind

**ADJUSTING LISTENING**

Your friend has just broken up a love affair and is telling you about it. "I can't seem to get Chris out of my mind," he says. "All I do is daydream about the stuff we used to do, and all the fun we used to have."

WHAT DO YOU SAY?

will help you analyze and evaluate the messages. In adjusting your nonjudgmental and critical listening, focus on the following guidelines:

- **Keep an open mind.** Avoid prejudging. Delay your judgments until you fully understand the intention and the content the speaker is communicating. Avoid both positive and negative evaluation until you have a reasonably complete understanding.

- **Avoid filtering out or oversimplifying difficult or complex messages.** Similarly, avoid

---

### Building Communication Skills   Expressing Empathy

For any one or two of the following situations, indicate in one sentence (or more) how you'd respond to the speaker with *thinking empathy* and in one sentence (or more) how you'd respond with *feeling empathy*. Assume that all three people are your peers.

1. "I've never felt so alone in my life. Chris left last night and said it was all over. We were together for three years and now—after a 10-minute argument—everything is lost."

2. "I just got $20,000 from my aunt's estate. She left it to me! Twenty thousand! Now I can get that car and buy some new clothes!"

3. "A Camry! My parents bought me a Camry for graduation. What a bummer. They promised me a Lexus."

*Expressing empathy is crucial to meaningful communication, but it is not an easily acquired skill; it takes practice.*

filtering out undesirable messages. Clearly, you don't want to hear that something you believe in is untrue, that people you care for are unkind, or that ideals you hold are self-destructive. Yet it's important that you reexamine your beliefs by listening to such messages.

- **Recognize your own biases**. These may interfere with accurate listening and cause you to distort message reception through the process of **assimilation**—the tendency to integrate and interpret what you hear or think you hear to conform to your own biases, prejudices, and expectations. For example, are your ethnic, national, or religious biases preventing you from appreciating a speaker's point of view?

- **Avoid uncritical listening when you need to make evaluations and judgments**. Recognize and resist the normal tendency to sharpen—a

process in which one or two aspects of a message become highlighted, emphasized, and perhaps embellished. Often the concepts that are sharpened are incidental remarks that somehow stand out from the rest of the message.

- **Recognize fallacies**—ways of using language to subvert instead of clarify truth and accuracy—and don't be persuaded by their pseudo-logic. Table 4.3 identifies some popular language fallacies. In Unit 18, "The Persuasive Speech," we'll consider additional fallacies that are closely related to persuasion.

## Surface and Depth Listening

In Shakespeare's *Julius Caesar*, Marc Antony, in giving the funeral oration for Caesar, says: "I come to bury Caesar, not to praise him. / The evil that men do lives after them; / The good is oft interred with

### Table 4.3 Listening to Fallacies of Language

Here are four language fallacies that often get in the way of meaningful communication and that need to be identified in critical listening. After reviewing these fallacies, take a look at some of the commercial websites for clothing, books, music, or any such product you're interested in. Can you find examples of these fallacies?

| Fallacy | Example | Notes |
|---|---|---|
| *Weasel words* are terms whose meanings are slippery and difficult to pin down (Hayakawa & Hayakawa, 1990). | A commercial claiming that Medicine M works "better" than Brand X but failing to specify how much or in what respect Medicine M performs better. It's quite possible that Medicine M performs better in one respect but less effectively according to nine other measures. | Other weasel words are *help, virtually, as much as, like* (as in "it will make you feel like new"), and *more economical*. Ask yourself, "Exactly what is being claimed?" For example, "What does 'may reduce cholesterol' mean? What exactly is being asserted?" |
| *Euphemisms* make the negative and unpleasant appear positive and appealing. | An executive's reference to the firing of 200 workers as "downsizing" or "reallocation of resources"; Justin Timberlake's reference to the highly publicized act with Janet Jackson during the 2004 Super Bowl as a "wardrobe malfunction." | Often euphemisms take the form of inflated language designed to make the mundane seem extraordinary, the common seem exotic ("the vacation of a lifetime," "unsurpassed vistas"). Don't let words get in the way of accurate firsthand perception. |
| *Jargon* is the specialized language of a professional class. | The language of the computer hacker, the psychologist, or the advertiser. | When used to intimidate or impress, as when used with people who aren't members of the profession, jargon prevents meaningful communication. Don't be intimidated by jargon; ask questions when you don't understand. |
| *Gobbledygook* is overly complex language that overwhelms the listener instead of communicating meaning. | Extra-long sentences, complex grammatical constructions, and rare or unfamiliar words. | Some people just normally speak in complex language. But others use complexity to confuse and mislead. Ask for simplification when appropriate. |

---

**Building Communication Skills**   Regulating Your Listening Style

With specific reference to the four dimensions of effective listening discussed here, what styles would you use in each of the following situations? What types of listening would be obviously inappropriate in each situation?

1. Your steady dating partner for the last five years tells you that spells of depression are becoming more frequent and more long lasting.
2. Your history instructor lectures on the contributions of the ancient Greeks to modern civilization.
3. Your brother tells you he's been accepted into Harvard's MBA program.
4. Your supervisor explains the new computerized mail system.
5. A newscaster reports on a recent Arab–Israeli meeting.

*Regulate your listening on the basis of the specific situation in which you find yourself.*

---

their bones." And later: "For Brutus is an honourable man; / So are they all, all honourable men." But if we listen beyond the surface of Marc Anthony's words, we can see that he does indeed come to praise Caesar, and to convince the crowd that Brutus was dishonorable—despite the fact that at first glance his words seem to say quite the opposite.

In most messages there's an obvious meaning that you can derive from a literal reading of the words and sentences. But there's often another level of meaning. Sometimes, as in these famous lines from *Julius Caesar*, the deeper level is the opposite of the literal meaning. At other times it seems totally unrelated. In reality, most messages have more than one level of meaning. For example, suppose Carol asks you how you like her new haircut. On one level, the meaning is clear: Do you like the haircut? But there's also another, perhaps a more important level: Carol is asking you to say something positive about her appearance. In the same way, the parent who complains about working hard at the office or in the home may, on a deeper level, be asking for an expression of appreciation. The child who talks about the unfairness of the other children in the playground may be asking for comfort and love, for some expression of caring.

To appreciate these other meanings, engage in depth listening. If you respond only to the surface-level communication (the literal meaning), you miss the opportunity to make meaningful contact with the other person's feelings and needs. If you say to the parent, "You're always complaining. I bet you really love working so hard," you fail to respond to the call for understanding and appreciation. In regulating your surface and depth listening, consider the following guidelines:

- **Focus on both verbal and nonverbal messages**. Recognize both consistent and inconsistent "packages" of messages, and use these as guides for drawing inferences about the speaker's meaning. Ask questions when in doubt. Listen also to what is omitted. Remember that speakers communicate by what they leave out as well as by what they include.

- **Listen for both content and relational messages**. The student who constantly challenges the instructor is, on one level, communicating disagreement over content. However, on another level—the relationship level—the student may be voicing objections to the instructor's authority or authoritarianism. The instructor needs to listen and respond to both types of messages.

- **Make special note of statements that refer back to the speaker**. Remember that people inevitably talk about themselves. Whatever a person says is, in part, a function of who that person is. Attend carefully to those personal, self-reference messages.

- **Don't disregard the literal meaning of messages in trying to uncover the more hidden meanings**. Balance your listening between surface and the underlying meanings. Respond to the different levels of meaning in the messages of others, as you would like others to respond to yours—sensitively but not obsessively, readily but not overambitiously.

## Active and Inactive Listening

One of the most important communication skills you can learn is active listening. Consider the following interaction. You say: "I can't believe I have to redo this entire budget report. I really worked hard on this project, and now I have to do it all over again." To this, you get three different responses.

ANDY: That's not so bad; most people find they have to redo their first reports. That's the norm here.

CONNIE: You should be pleased that all you have to do is a simple rewrite. Peggy and Michael both had to completely redo their entire projects.

GREG: You have to rewrite that report you've worked on for the last three weeks? You sound really angry and frustrated.

All three listeners are probably trying to make you feel better. But they go about it in very different ways—and surely with very different results. Andy tries to lessen the significance of the rewrite. This well-intended and extremely common response does little to promote meaningful communication and understanding. Connie tries to give the situation a positive spin. In their responses, however, both Andy and Connie are also suggesting that you should not be feeling the way you do; they're saying that your feelings are not legitimate and should be replaced with more logical feelings.

Greg's response, however, is different from the others. Greg uses active listening. **Active listening** owes its development to Thomas Gordon (1975), who made it a cornerstone of his P.E.T. (parent effectiveness training) technique. It is a process of sending back to the speaker what you as a listener think the speaker meant—both in content and in feelings. Active listening, then, is not merely repeating the speaker's exact words, but rather putting together into some meaningful whole your understanding of the speaker's total message. And, incidentally, when combined with empathic listening, it proves the most effective mode for success as a salesperson (Comer & Drollinger, 1999).

Active listening helps you check your understanding of what the speaker said and, more importantly, of what he or she meant. Reflecting back perceived meanings to the speaker gives the speaker an opportunity to offer clarification and to correct any misunderstandings. Active listening also lets the speaker know that you acknowledge and accept his or her feelings. In the sample responses given above, Greg listened actively and reflected back what he thought you meant while accepting what you were feeling. Note too that he also explicitly identified the feelings ("You sound angry and frustrated"), allowing you the opportunity to correct his interpretation. Still another function of active listening is that it stimulates the speaker to explore feelings and thoughts. Greg's response encourages you to elaborate on your feelings and perhaps to understand them better as you talk them through.

Three simple techniques may help you master the process of active listening: paraphrasing the

## ACTIVE LISTENING

Your life partner comes from work visibly upset, and clearly has a need to talk about what happened . . . but simply says, "Work sucks!" You're determined to use active listening techniques.

WHAT DO YOU SAY?
*Through what channel?*

speaker's meaning, expressing understanding, and asking questions.

- **Paraphrase the speaker's meaning**. Stating in your own words what you think the speaker means and feels helps ensure understanding and demonstrates your interest. Paraphrasing gives the speaker a chance to extend what was originally said. In paraphrasing, be objective; be especially careful not to lead the speaker in the direction you think he or she should go. Also, don't overdo paraphrasing. Paraphrase when you feel there's a chance for misunderstanding or when you want to express support for the other person and keep the conversation going.

- **Express understanding of the speaker's feelings**. In addition to paraphrasing the content, echo the feelings the speaker expressed or implied ("You must have felt horrible"). This expression of feelings will help you further check your perception of the speaker's feelings and will allow the speaker to see his or her feelings more objectively (especially helpful when they're feelings of anger, hurt, or depression) and the opportunity to elaborate on these feelings.

- **Ask questions**. Asking questions ensures your own understanding of the speaker's thoughts and feelings and secures additional information ("How did you feel when you read your job appraisal report?"). Ask questions to provide just enough stimulation and support so that the speaker feels he or she can elaborate on these thoughts and feelings.

Table 4.4 presents a summary of some of the major themes presented in the above suggestions for listening more effectively.

## Table 4.4 Listening Barriers and What to Do about Them

Here are a few general barriers to listening and some suggestions for dealing with these barriers as a listener and as a speaker.

| Barriers | Correctives | |
|---|---|---|
| | **For Listener** | **For Speaker** |
| *Physical barriers*; for example, a chalkboard with a previous speaker's notes; defective hearing | Focus on the speaker; you can look at the room and the audience later. | Try—whenever possible—to remove potential distractions. |
| *Mental distractions*; for example, thinking about your upcoming Saturday night date or becoming too emotional to think (and listen) clearly | Recognize that you can think about your date later; get back to listening. | Make what you say compelling and so relevant to the listener. |
| *Closed-mindedness*; for example, refusing to hear any feminist argument or anything about gay marriage | Assume that what the speaker is saying will be useful in some way. | Anticipate this and ask for open-ness—"I know this seems contrary to what many people think, but let's look at this logically." |
| *Biases and prejudices*; for example, a gender bias that assumes that only one sex has anything useful to say about certain topics | Be willing to subject your biases and prejudices to contradictory information; after all if they're worth having, they should stand up to differences of opinion. | When you feel that your listener(s) may be biased, ask for a suspension of bias—"I know you don't like the XXX, and I can understand that. But just listen to. . . ." |
| *Rehearsing responses*; for example, anticipating what you're going to say and how you're going to phrase your response or even interrupting the speaker | Make a mental note of something and then get back to listening. | When you feel the audience is preparing to argue with you, tell them that you'll return to this point later. |
| *Dismissing the speaker*; for example, because of the way the speaker is dressed, or because of his or her accent, or because his or her last speech was dull, or because the Dems (Reps) are just telling us what we want to hear—therefore, there's no sense listening | Assume that everyone has something of value to say to you; in fact, people who are most unlike you probably have the most to tell you. | Stress the importance of what you will say; dress so as not to detract from your message. |
| *Focusing on irrelevancies*; for example, an especially vivid example | When encountering a particularly vivid example, recall the point, the main idea, that it refers to; don't get hung up on red flags. | Repeat the main points and connect them to your examples and illustrations. Try to avoid language or examples that may divert attention from your main ideas |
| *Excessive self-focus*; for example, listening only to those ideas that have direct relevance to you | Think about how this topic relates to others or to some larger picture. Not everything is about you; avoid interpreting everything in terms of what it means to you; see other perspectives. | Include all listeners; make what you say relevant to everyone. |
| *Faulty assumptions*; for example, assuming you know what the speaker is going to say so there's no need to listen | Let the speaker guide your listening. | If you suspect that listeners will make faulty assumptions, make it clear that what you're saying will be unexpected. |
| *Drawing too-early conclusions or judgments*; for example, not listening after you hear an idea with which you disagree (not waiting for the evidence or argument) | Avoid making judgments before you gather all the information; listen before judging. | Consider giving part of the evidence before stating any idea to which you anticipate serious objection from listeners. |

# SUMMARY: LISTENING IN HUMAN COMMUNICATION

This unit discussed the importance of listening, the process of listening, the influence of culture and gender on the way people listen, and the principles for listening more effectively.

1. Effective listening yields a wide variety of benefits, including more effective learning, relating, influencing, playing, and helping.

2. Listening is a five-part process that begins with receiving, and continues through understanding, remembering, evaluating, and responding.

3. Receiving consists of hearing the verbal signals and perceiving the nonverbal signals.

4. Understanding involves learning what the speaker means, not merely what the words mean.

5. Remembering involves retaining the received message, a process that involves considerable reconstruction.

6. Evaluating consists of judging the messages you receive.

7. Responding involves giving feedback while the speaker is speaking and taking your turn at speaking after the speaker has finished.

8. Listening is influenced by a wide range of cultural factors, such as differences in language and speech, nonverbal behaviors, credibility criteria, and feedback approaches.

9. Listening is influenced by gender: Men and women seem to view listening as serving different purposes.

10. Effective listening involves adjusting our behaviors on the basis of at least four dimensions: empathic and objective listening, nonjudgmental and critical listening, surface and depth listening, and active and inactive listening.

11. The empathic–objective dimension involves the degree to which the listener focuses on feeling what the speaker is feeling versus grasping the objective message.

12. The nonjudgmental–critical dimension involves the degree to which the listener evaluates what is said.

13. The surface–depth dimension has to do with the extent to which the listener focuses on literal or obvious meanings versus hidden or less obvious meanings.

14. The active–inactive dimension involves the extent to which the listener reflects back and expresses support for the speaker.

# KEY TERMS IN LISTENING IN HUMAN COMMUNICATION

accent (p. **88**)
active listening (p. **96**)

assimilation (p. **94**)
backchanneling cues (p. **87**)

empathy (p. **92**)
listening (p. **82**)

# THINKING CRITICALLY ABOUT LISTENING IN HUMAN COMMUNICATION

1. **Your Listening Self.** Using the four dimensions of listening effectiveness discussed here (empathic–objective, nonjudgmental–critical, surface–depth, and active–inactive), how would you describe yourself as a listener when listening in class? When listening to your best friend? When listening to a romantic partner? When listening to your parents? When listening to your superiors at work?

2. **Listening to Complaints.** Would you find it difficult to listen to friends who were complaining that the insurance premium on their Bentley was going up? Would you find it difficult to listen to unemployed friends complain that their rent was going up and that they feared becoming homeless? If there is a difference, why?

3. **Selling by Listening.** Researchers have argued that effective listening skills are positively associated with salespeople's effectiveness in selling (Castleberrry & Shepherd, 1993). Can you think of examples from your own experience that would support this positive association between effective listening and effective selling?

4. **Men and Women Listening.** The popular belief, as noted in this unit, is that men listen the way they do to prove themselves superior and that women listen as they do to ingratiate themselves. Although there is no evidence to support this belief, it persists in the assumptions people make about the opposite sex. What do you believe accounts for the differences in the way men and women listen?

5. **Cell Phone Annoyances.** Some researchers have argued that listening to the cell phone conversations of others is particularly annoying because you can hear only one side of the conversation; cell phone conversations were rated as significantly more intrusive than two people talking face-to-face (Monk, Fellas, & Ley, 2004). Do you find the cell phone conversations of people near you on a bus or in a store annoying, perhaps for the reason given here? For other reasons?

# LogOn! MyCommunicationLab

Visit MCL and take a look at the self-test [When] Is Lying Unethical? and the exercises Passing Information from One Person to Another, Listening Like a Man and a Woman, Reducing Listening Barriers, Practicing Active Listening, and Listening. Also listen to Taking Lessons from a Guru of Listening and participate in the simulation How Good Is Your Memory for Stories.

While you're online visit The International Listening Association, a professional association of people interested in the study and teaching of effective listening (www.listen.org) and check out the Listening Resources. What can you add to the discussion presented in this unit?

# UNIT 5  Verbal Messages

## MAJOR TOPICS

**Principles of Verbal Messages**
**Disconfirmation and Confirmation**
**Using Verbal Messages Effectively**

## Special Features

Y ou can use language to communicate your thoughts and feelings and to create meaningful and lasting relationships. But you can just as easily use language to distort and prevent meaningful dialogue and destroy relationships.

**In this unit you'll learn about:**
- how language works.
- the nature of disconfirmation and confirmation.

**You'll learn to:**
- express confirmation when appropriate.
- use verbal messages more effectively.

A s you communicate, you use two major signal systems—the verbal and the nonverbal. *Verbal messages* are messages sent with words. It's important to remember that the word *verbal* refers to *words*, not to *orality*; verbal messages consist of both oral and written words. In contrast, verbal messages do not include laughter; vocalized pauses you make when you speak (such as *er, hmm,* and *ah*); and responses you make to others that are oral but don't involve words (such as *ha ha, aha,* and *ugh*!). These vocalizations are considered *nonverbal*—as are, of course, facial expressions, eye movements, gestures, and so on.

As explained in Unit 1, your messages normally occur in "packages" consisting of both verbal and nonverbal signals that occur simultaneously. Usually, verbal and nonverbal behaviors reinforce or support each other. For example, you don't usually express fear with words while the rest of your body relaxes. You don't normally express anger with your body posture while your face smiles. Your entire being works as a whole—verbally and nonverbally—to express your thoughts and feelings.

This unit focuses on the verbal system (the next will examine the nonverbal system) and discusses the principles of verbal messages, the concepts of confirmation and disconfirmation, and the ways you can use verbal messages most effectively.

## PRINCIPLES OF VERBAL MESSAGES

As you grew up, you learned the language spoken by the people around you. You learned its phonological, or sound, system; its semantic system, or system of word meanings; and its syntactic system, which enabled you to put words into meaningful sentence patterns. Our concern in this unit is not with the grammatical structure of language (that's the linguist's job), but with the verbal messages you speak and hear. These verbal messages, of course, rely on the rules of grammar; you can't just make up sounds or words or string words together at random and expect to be understood. But, as we'll see, following the rules of grammar is not enough to achieve effective communication. For this we need to understand five key principles of verbal messages: (1) meanings are in people, (2) meanings depend on context, (3) language is denotative *and* connotative, (4) language varies in directness, and (5) messages are influenced by culture and gender.

## Meanings Are in People

If you wanted to know the meaning of the word *love,* you'd probably turn to a dictionary. There you'd find a definition such as Webster's: "the attraction, desire, or affection felt for a person who arouses delight or admiration or elicits tenderness, sympathetic interest, or benevolence." But where would you turn if you wanted to know what Pedro means when he says, "I'm in love"? Of course, you'd ask Pedro to discover his meaning. It's in this sense that meanings are not in words but in people. Consequently, to uncover meaning, you need to look into people and not merely into words.

Also recognize that as you change, you also change the meanings you created out of past messages. Thus, although the message sent may not have changed, the meanings you created from it yesterday and the meanings you create today may be quite different. Yesterday, when a special someone said, "I love you," you created certain meanings. But today, when you learn that the same "I love you" was said to three other people, or when you fall in love with someone else, you drastically change the meanings you perceive from those three words.

As already noted in Unit 2, this principle is especially important in intercultural communication, as meanings for the same words are often drastically different between members of different cultures. This became especially obvious after the tragedy of the World Trade Center attack: Terms like *justice*, *suicide*, and *terrorism* were given totally different meanings by many in Afghanistan and in the United States.

A failure to recognize this important principle is at the heart of a common pattern of miscommunication called bypassing. **Bypassing** is "the miscommunication pattern which occurs when the sender (speaker, writer, and so on) and the receiver (listener, reader, and so forth) miss each other with their meanings" (Haney, 1973). Bypassing can take either of two forms.

### Bypassing: Different Words, Same Meaning

One type of bypassing occurs when two people use different words but give them the same meaning; on the surface there's disagreement, but at the level of meaning there's agreement. The two people actually agree but assume, because they use different words (some of which may actually never be verbalized), that they disagree. Here's an example:

PAT: I'm not interested in one-night stands. I want a permanent relationship. [Meaning: I want an exclusive dating relationship.]

CHRIS: I'm not ready for that. [Meaning: I'm not ready for marriage.]

### Bypassing: Same Words, Different Meaning

The second type of bypassing is more common and occurs when two people use the same words but give the words different meanings. On the surface it looks like the two people agree (simply because they're using the same words). But if you look more closely, you see that the apparent agreement masks real disagreement, as in this example:

PAT: I don't really believe in religion. [Meaning: I don't really believe in God.]

CHRIS: Neither do I. [Meaning: I don't really believe in organized religions.]

Here Pat and Chris assume that they agree, but actually they disagree. At some later date the implications of these differences may well become crucial.

Numerous other examples could be cited. Couples who say they're "in love" may mean very different things; one person may be thinking about

"a permanent and exclusive commitment," whereas the other may be referring to "a sexual involvement." "Come home early" may mean one thing to an anxious parent and quite another to a teenager.

Because of bypassing it is a mistake to assume that when two people use the same word, they mean the same thing, or that when they use different words, they mean different things. Words in themselves don't have meaning; meaning is in the people who use those words. Therefore, people can use different words but mean the same thing or use the same words but mean different things.

## Meanings Depend on Context

Verbal and nonverbal communications exist in a context, and that context to a large extent determines the meaning of any verbal or nonverbal behavior. The same words or behaviors may have totally different meanings when they occur in different contexts. For example, the greeting "How are you?" means "Hello" to someone you pass regularly on the street but means "Is your health improving?" when said to a friend in the hospital. A wink to an attractive person on a bus means something completely different from a wink that says "I'm kidding."

Similarly, the meaning of a given signal depends on the other behavior it accompanies or is close to in time. Pounding a fist on the table during a speech in support of a politician means something quite different from that same gesture in response to news of a friend's death. Focused eye contact may signify openness and honesty in one culture and defiance in another. In isolation from the context, it's impossible to tell what meaning was intended by merely examining the signals. Of course, even if you know the context in detail, you still may not be able to decipher the meaning of the message.

## Language Is Denotative *and* Connotative

**Denotation** refers to the meaning you'd find in a dictionary; it's the meaning that members of the culture assign to a word. **Connotation** refers to the emotional meaning that specific speakers–listeners give to a word. Words have both kinds of meaning. Take as an example the word *death*. To a doctor this word might mean (or denote) the time when brain activity ceases. This is an objective description of a particular event. In contrast, when a mother is informed of her child's death, the word means (or connotes) much more. It recalls her child's youth, ambition, family, illness, and so on. To her it's a highly emotional, subjective, and personal word. These emotional, subjective, or personal reactions are the word's connotative meaning.

Take another example: Compare the term *migrants* (used to designate Mexicans coming into the United States to better their economic condition) with the term *settlers* (used to designate Europeans who came to the United States for the same reason) (Koppelman, 2005). Though both terms describe essentially the same activity (and are essentially the same denotatively), the former is often negatively evaluated and the latter often positively valued—so the two words differ widely in their connotations.

Semanticist S. I. Hayakawa (Hayakawa & Hayakawa, 1990) coined the terms "snarl words" and "purr words" to clarify further the distinction between denotative and connotative meaning. **Snarl words** are highly negative ("She's an idiot," "He's a pig," "They're a bunch of losers"). Sexist, racist, and heterosexist language and hate speech provide lots of other examples. **Purr words** are highly positive ("She's a real sweetheart," "He's a dream," "They're the greatest"). Although they may sometimes seem to have denotative meaning and to refer to the "real world," snarl and purr words are purely connotative in meaning. They don't describe people or events; rather, they reveal the speaker's feelings about these people or events.

## Language Varies in Directness

**Direct speech** communicates your meaning explicitly and leaves little doubt as to the thoughts and feelings you want to convey. **Indirect speech**, on the other hand, communicates your meaning in a roundabout way. In indirect speech you don't really say what you mean, but you imply it. Indirect messages have both advantages and disadvantages.

One of the advantages of indirect speech is that it allows you to express a desire without insulting or offending anyone; it allows you to observe the rules of polite interaction. So instead of saying, "I'm bored with this group," you say, "It's getting late and I have to get up early tomorrow," or you look at your watch and pretend to be surprised by the time. In this way you state a preference but express it indirectly so as to avoid offending someone. Sometimes indirect messages allow you to ask for compliments in a socially acceptable manner; for example, a person who says, "I was thinking of getting a nose job" may hope to get a response such as "A nose job? You? Your nose is perfect."

Indirect messages can also create problems, however. For example, meanings that are expressed too indirectly may be misunderstood; the other person may simply not grasp your implied meaning. When this happens, you may come to resent the other person for not seeing beneath the surface—and yourself for not being more up-front. Another disadvantage is that you may be seen as manipulative; that is, as trying to get someone to do something without really saying it. For example, you might tell a friend, "I really could use a loan until payday, but I really don't want to ask anyone."

## Messages Are Influenced by Culture and Gender

Your verbal messages are influenced in large part by your culture and gender. Let's look first at some of the cultural influences.

### Cultural Influences

Your culture teaches you that certain ways of using verbal messages are acceptable and certain ways are not. For example, you may have learned to address older people by Title + Last Name (Ms. Winter), as with professors and doctors, but to address peers or people much younger than you by their first names. When you follow such cultural principles in communicating, you're seen as a properly functioning member of the culture. When you violate the principles, you risk being seen as deviant or perhaps as insulting. Here are a variety of such principles:

**The Principle of Cooperation.** The principle of **cooperation** holds that in any communication interaction, both parties will make an effort to help each other understand each other. That is, we assume cooperation. The ways in which we assume cooperation are identified in the principle's four corollaries or maxims. As you read down the list, ask yourself how you follow these maxims in your everyday conversation:

- **The maxim of quality:** Say what you know or assume to be true, and do not say what you know to be false.
- **The maxim of relation:** Talk about what is relevant to the conversation.
- **The maxim of manner:** Be clear, avoid ambiguities (as much as possible), be relatively brief, and organize your thoughts into a meaningful pattern. In e-mail and instant messaging, brevity is especially important, and as a result acronyms have become popular. Table 5.1 identifies some of the more popular acronyms.
- **The maxim of quantity:** Be as informative as necessary to communicate the information.

**The Principle of Peaceful Relations.** This principle holds that when you communicate your primary goal is to maintain peaceful relationships. This means that you would never insult anyone and you may even express agreement with someone when you really disagree, a principle that violates

## Table 5.1 Some Popular Acronyms

Here are some popular acronyms used widely in computer-mediated communication. For an ever-increasing list of acronyms see Net Lingua's website at www.fun-with-words.com/acronyms.html.

| Acronym | Meaning |
|---------|---------|
| BTW | By the way |
| IMHO | In my humble opinion |
| IMNSHO | In my not so humble opinion |
| NP | No problem |
| OTT | Over the top |
| OTOH | On the other hand |
| RUOK | Are you okay? |
| TIC | Tongue in cheek |
| TTYL | Talk to you later |
| TVM | Thanks very much |

the principle of cooperation and the maxim of quality (Midooka, 1990).

**The Principle of Face-Saving.** Face-saving messages are those that preserve the image of the other person and do nothing to insult the person or make him or her appear in a negative light. The principle holds that you should never embarrass anyone, especially in public. Always allow people to save face, even if this means avoiding the truth—as when you tell someone he or she did good work although the job was actually poorly executed. Many Asian and Latin American cultures stress the value of indirectness because it helps people avoid overt criticism and the loss of face.

**The Principle of Self-Denigration.** The principle of self-denigration advises you to avoid taking credit for accomplishments and to minimize your abilities or talents in conversation (Gu, 1997). At the same time, you would raise the image of the people with whom you're talking.

**The Principle of Directness.** As discussed earlier, directness and indirectness communicate different impressions. Levels of directness also vary greatly from culture to culture. A somewhat different kind of indirectness is seen in the greater use of intermediaries to resolve conflict among the Chinese than among North Americans, for example (Ma, 1992). In most of the United States, directness is the preferred style. "Be up front" and "Tell it like it is" are commonly

heard communication guidelines. Contrast these with the following two principles of indirectness found in the Japanese language (Tannen, 1994a):

- *Omoiyari*, close to our concept of empathy, says that listeners need to understand the speaker without the speaker's being specific or direct. This style places a much greater demand on the listener than would a direct speaking style.

- *Sassuru* advises listeners to anticipate a speaker's meanings and to use subtle cues from the speaker to infer his or her total meaning.

**The Principle of Politeness.** Most cultures have a politeness principle, but cultures differ in the way they define politeness and in how much they emphasize politeness compared with, say openness or honesty (Mao, 1994; Strecker, 1993). Asian people, especially the Chinese and Japanese, are often singled out because they emphasize politeness more and mete out harsher social punishments for violations than would people in the United States or western Europe (Fraser, 1990). Politeness also varies with the type of relationship, as depicted in Figure 5.1.

A somewhat different type of culture is the Internet culture, which also has its rules for politeness (see Table 5.2 on page 106).

Cultural differences can often create misunderstanding. For example, a person from a culture that values an indirect style of speech may be speaking indirectly in order to be polite. If, however, you're from a culture that values a more direct style of

## POLITENESS

After interacting with a person you're meeting for the first time and whom you want to impress, you quickly and mentally review the rules of politeness. Unfortunately, you violated just about every one. You need to correct this impression of yourself as impolite.

WHAT DO YOU SAY?

speech, you may assume that the person is using indirectness to be manipulative, because this may be how your culture regards indirectness.

## Gender Influences

Gender also influences our verbal communication. For example, studies from different cultures show that women's speech is generally more polite than men's speech, even on the telephone (Brown, 1980; Wetzel, 1988; Holmes, 1995; Smoreda & Licoppe,

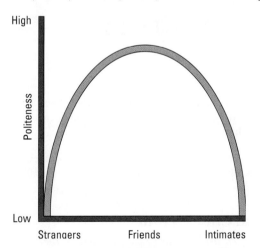

**FIGURE 5.1** **Wolfson's Bulge Model of Politeness**

This figure depicts a proposed relationship between levels of politeness and degrees of intimacy. Politeness, according to this inverted U model, is greatest with friends and significantly less with strangers and intimates. Can you build a case for an opposite theory—that politeness is especially high with both strangers and intimates and least with friends?

Source: *Second Language Discourse: A Textbook of Current Research*, J. Fine. Copyright © 1988. Reproduced with permission of Greenwood Publishing Group, Inc., Westport, CT.

2000). Women seek areas of agreement in conversation and in conflict situations more often than men do. Similarly, young girls are more apt to try to modify disagreements, whereas young boys are more apt to express more "bald disagreements" (Holmes, 1995). Women also use more polite speech when seeking to gain another person's compliance than men do (Baxter, 1984).

The popular stereotype in much of the United States holds that women tend to be indirect in making requests and in giving orders, and that this indirectness communicates a powerlessness and discomfort with their own authority. Men, the stereotype continues, tend to be direct, sometimes to the point of being blunt or rude. This directness communicates men's power and comfort with their authority. Deborah Tannen (1994a) provides an interesting perspective on these stereotypes. Women are, it seems, more indirect in giving orders; they are more likely to say, for example, "It would be great if these letters could go out today" than "Have these letters out by three." But, Tannen (1994a, p. 84) argues, "issuing orders indirectly can be the prerogative of those in power" and does not necessarily show powerlessness. Power, to Tannen, is the ability to choose your own style of communication.

Men also can be indirect, and they are more likely to use indirectness when they express weakness, reveal a problem, or admit an error (Rundquist, 1992; Tannen, 1994a, 1994b). Men are more likely to speak indirectly when expressing emotions (other than anger). They are also more indirect when they refuse expressions of increased romantic intimacy. Men are thus indirect, the theory goes, when they are saying something that goes against the masculine stereotype.

## Table 5.2 The Rules of Netiquette

Much as the rules of etiquette provide guidance for communicating in social situations, the rules of **netiquette** provide guidance for communicating politely over the Net. These rules, as you'll see, are helpful for making Internet communication easier and more pleasant, facilitating greater personal efficiency, and putting less strain on the system and on other users. Here are several guidelines suggested by most computer researchers; also see **www.albion.com/netiquette.**

| Rule of Netiquette | Suggestions |
|---|---|
| Read the FAQs. | Before asking questions about the system, read the Frequently Asked Questions; your question has probably been asked before, and you'll put less strain on the system and on yourself. |
| Don't shout. | Don't write in caps (it's perceived as shouting). Use caps only for emphasis. |
| Lurk before speaking. | Read the posted notices and the conversations before contributing anything yourself; in this way you'll avoid violating any rule of the group. |
| Be brief. | Follow the maxim of quantity by communicating only the needed information; follow the maxim of manner by communicating clearly, briefly, and in an organized way. These suggestions are even more important in business and organizational communication. |

# REFLECTIONS ON ETHICS

## Lying

**Lying** is the act of sending messages designed to make others believe what you know to be untrue (Ekman, 1985; Burgoon & Hoobler, 2002). You can lie by *commission* (making explicitly false statements or deliberately being evasive or misleading) or by *omission* (omitting relevant information and thus allowing others to draw incorrect inferences). Similarly, you can lie *verbally* (in speech or writing) or *nonverbally* (with an innocent facial expression despite the commission of some wrong, or with a knowing nod instead of the honest expression of ignorance). Lies may range from "white lies" and truth stretching to lies that form the basis of infidelity in a relationship, of libel, and perjury. Not surprisingly, lies have ethical implications.

■ Some lies are considered innocent, acceptable, and ethical, such as lying to a child to protect a fantasy belief in Santa Claus or the Tooth Fairy or publicly agreeing with someone to enable the person to save face.

■ Some lies may be considered not merely ethical but required, such as saying your friend looks good to make him or her feel better.

■ Other lies are considered unacceptable and unethical, such as lying to defraud investors or making false accusations.

### Ethical Choice Point

*You've been asked to serve as a witness in the trial of a suspect in the robbery of a local grocery store. You really don't want to get involved; in fact, you're afraid to get involved. Yet you wonder if you can ethically refuse and say you didn't see anything (although you did). There are other witnesses, and your testimony is not likely to make a significant difference. What is your ethical obligation in this situation? What would you do?*

There are also gender similarities. For example, in both the United States and New Zealand, men and women seem to pay compliments in similar ways (Manes & Wolfson, 1981; Holmes, 1995), and both men and women use politeness strategies when communicating bad news in an organization (Lee, 1993). A few theories of gender differences are highlighted in the accompanying Understanding Theory and Research box.

## DISCONFIRMATION AND CONFIRMATION

The terms *confirmation* and *disconfirmation* refer to the extent to which you acknowledge another person. Consider this situation. You've been living with someone for the last six months and you arrive home late one night. Your partner, let's say Pat, is angry and complains about your being so late. Which of the following is most likely to be your response?

1. Stop screaming. I'm not interested in what you're babbling about. I'll do what I want, when I want. I'm going to bed.
2. What are you so angry about? Didn't you get in three hours late last Thursday when you went to that office party? So knock it off.

3. You have a right to be angry. I should have called to tell you I was going to be late, but I got involved in a serious debate at work, and I couldn't leave until it was resolved.

In response 1, you dismiss Pat's anger and even indicate dismissal of Pat as a person. In response 2, you reject the validity of Pat's reasons for being angry but do not dismiss either Pat's feelings of anger or Pat as a person. In response 3, you acknowledge Pat's anger and the reasons for it. In addition, you provide some kind of explanation and, in doing so, show that both Pat's feelings and Pat as a person are important and that Pat has the right to know what happened. The first response is an example of disconfirmation, the second of rejection, and the third of confirmation.

Psychologist William James once observed that "no more fiendish punishment could be devised, even were such a thing physically possible, than that one should be turned loose in society and remain absolutely unnoticed by all the members thereof." In this often-quoted observation, James identifies the essence of disconfirmation (Watzlawick, Beavin, & Jackson, 1967; Veenendall & Feinstein, 1995). **Disconfirmation** is a communication pattern in which we ignore someone's presence as well as that person's communications. We say, in effect, that this

---

**Theory and Research** **Theories of Gender Differences**

UNDERSTANDING

Throughout this text, gender differences are discussed in a wide variety of contexts. One researcher distinguishes three perspectives on gender differences in communication (Holmes, 1995):

- Gender differences are due to innate biological differences. Thus, gender differences in communication, such as differences in politeness or in listening behavior, are the result of these biological differences.

- Gender differences are due to different patterns of socialization, which lead to different forms of communication. Thus, the gender differences that you observe are due to the different ways boys and girls are raised and taught when growing up and throughout life—by being rewarded for "appropriate" gender communication and being punished for "inappropriate" gender communication.

- Gender differences are due to the inequalities in social power. For example, because of women's lesser social power, they're more apt to communicate with greater deference and politeness than are men.

### Working with Theories and Research

*What arguments could you offer in support of or in opposition to any of these positions? How might you go about conducting research to test any one of these hypotheses?*

person and what this person has to say are not worth serious attention or effort—that this person and this person's contributions are so unimportant or insignificant that there is no reason to concern ourselves with her or him. The Amish community practices an extreme form of disconfirmation called "shunning," in which the community members totally ignore a person who has violated one or more of their rules. The specific aim of shunning is to get the person to repent and to reenter the community of the faithful. But it seems that all cultures practice some form of exclusion for those who violate important cultural rules.

Note that disconfirmation is not the same as **rejection.** In rejection, you disagree with the person; you indicate your unwillingness to accept something the other person says or does. In disconfirming someone, however, you deny that person's significance; you claim that what this person says or does simply does not count.

**Confirmation** is the opposite communication pattern. In confirmation you not only acknowledge the presence of the other person but also indicate your acceptance of this person, of this person's self-definition, and of your relationship as defined or viewed by this other person.

Disconfirmation and confirmation may be communicated in a wide variety of ways. Table 5.3 shows just a few examples and the accompanying Building Communication Skills box invites additional examples.

You can gain insight into a wide variety of offensive language practices by viewing them as types of disconfirmation—as language that alienates and separates. Four obvious practices, which we'll consider here, are racism, heterosexism, ageism, and sexism. Extremes of these are often termed *hate speech*, which is examined in the Media Watch box in Unit 16.

Another-ism is *ableism*—discrimination against people with disabilities. This particular practice is

---

## Table 5.3 Confirmation and Disconfirmation

As you review this table, try to imagine a specific illustration for each of the ways of communicating disconfirmation and confirmation (Pearson, 1993; Galvin, Bylund, & Brommel, 2007).

### Confirmation

1. Acknowledge the presence and the contributions of the other by either supporting or taking issue with what the other says.

2. Make nonverbal contact by maintaining direct eye contact, touching, hugging, kissing, or otherwise demonstrating acknowledgment of the other; engage in dialogue—communication in which both persons are speakers and listeners, both are involved, and both are concerned with each other.

3. Demonstrate understanding of what the other says and means, and reflect these feelings to confirm your understanding.

4. Ask questions of the other concerning both thoughts and feelings, and acknowledge the questions of the other; return phone calls; answer e-mail and letters.

5. Encourage the other to express thoughts and feelings, and respond directly and exclusively to what the other says.

### Disconfirmation

1. Ignore the presence and the messages of the other person; ignore or express (nonverbally and verbally) indifference to anything the other says.

2. Make no nonverbal contact; avoid direct eye contact; avoid touching the other person. Engage in monologue—communication in which one person speaks and one person listens, there is no real interaction, and there is no real concern or respect for each other.

3. Jump to interpretation or evaluation rather than working at understanding what the other means; express your own feelings, but ignore the feelings of the other or give abstract, intellectualized responses.

4. Make statements about yourself; ignore any lack of clarity in the other's remarks; ignore the other's requests; fail to answer questions, return phone calls, or answer e-mails and letters.

5. Interrupt or otherwise make it difficult for the other to express him- or herself; respond only tangentially or by shifting the focus in another direction.

## Confirming, Rejecting, or Disconfirming

Here are three practice situations. For each situation, (a) write the three potential responses as indicated; then, (b) after completing all three situations, indicate what effects each type of response is likely to generate.

1. Enrique receives this semester's grades in the mail; they're a lot better than previous semesters' grades but are still not great. After opening the letter, Enrique says: "I really tried hard to get my grades up this semester." Enrique's parents respond:

   With disconfirmation
   With rejection
   With confirmation

2. Elizabeth, who has been out of work for the past several weeks, says: "I feel like such a failure; I just can't seem to find a job. I've been pounding the pavement for the last five weeks and still nothing." Elizabeth's friend responds:

   With disconfirmation
   With rejection
   With confirmation

3. Candi's colleague at work comes to her overjoyed and tells her that she was just promoted to vice president of marketing, skipping three steps in the hierarchy and tripling her salary. Candi responds:
   With disconfirmation
   With rejection
   With confirmation

*Each type of response communicates a different message; generally, however, confirming message are likely to increase relationship satisfaction and disconfirming messages are likely to decrease relationship satisfaction.*

---

handled throughout the text in a series of tables or in-text discussions offering tips for communicating between people with and without a variety of disabilities:

- between blind and sighted people (Unit 1)

- between people with and without disabilities (Unit 2)

- between deaf and hearing people (Unit 4)

- between people with and without speech and language disorders (Unit 7)

## Racism

According to Andrea Rich (1974), "any language that, through a conscious or unconscious attempt by the user, places a particular racial or ethnic group in an inferior position is racist." **Racist language** expresses racist attitudes. It also, however, contributes to the development of racist attitudes in those who use or hear the language. Even when racism is subtle, unintentional, or even unconscious, its effects are systematically damaging (Dovidio, Gaertner, Kawakami, & Hodson, 2002).

Racism exists on both individual and institutional levels, a distinction made by educational researchers and used throughout this discussion (Koppelman, 2005). The term *individual racism* refers to the negative attitudes and beliefs that people hold about specific races. Assumptions such as the idea that certain races are intellectually inferior to others or that certain races are incapable of certain achievements are clear examples of individual racism. Prejudice against American Indians, African Americans, Hispanics, and Arabs have been with us throughout history and are still a part of many people's lives today. Such racism is seen in the negative terms people use to refer to members of other races and to disparage their customs and accomplishments.

*Institutionalized racism* is seen in de facto school segregation, in companies' reluctance to hire members of minority groups, in banks' unwillingness

# ASK THE RESEARCHER

## Family and Cultural Differences

*I'm in a serious romantic relationship with someone who is my cultural opposite. We differ in race, religion, and nationality. Our problem, however, is not with us; rather, it is with our families. Both of our families are narrow-minded, bigoted, and culturally insensitive. What can we do to get our families to accept our relationship and to demonstrate some cultural sensitivity?*

Your complex situation should challenge all of you. An easy answer could be offered but would be wrong. You have communication options for easing the tensions. You may try to see yourself as they see you. Rethink your negative view of them. Ask how your families may actually care about you, despite your disapproving their way of showing it. Do you see them merely as objects to be manipulated? If they are insensitive, do you want to be like them? Assuming they have shortcomings, can you change their attitudes as you would bicycle tires? To harmonize the conflict, you might modify your communication with them in hopes of improving your relationship. Focusing on your relationship, you may be able to model the caring communication you wish them to practice. You might use different communication channels to reduce disharmony. Rather than employing face-to-face communication only, you might also share your tender differences through letters, tapes, computer-mediated messages, and even go-betweens.

For further information: Barnes, S. (2003). *Computer-mediated communication*. Boston: Allyn & Bacon. Also Hall, B. J. (2005). *Among cultures: The challenge of communication*. Belmont, CA: Thompson, and Travis, L., & Violato, C. (2001). *Advances in adolescent psychology*. Calgary, AB: Detselig.

**Richard Fiordo** (Ph.D., University of Illinois–Urbana) is a professor of communication at the University of North Dakota, where he teaches communication courses that strive to reduce individual, group, and cultural conflict (richard.fiordo@und.edu). Much of his research applies to international and multicultural issues. He is a board member for the Society for Adolescentology (which studies diverse aspects of adolescence, including its psychological presence in adulthood) at Ambrosiana University in Milan, Italy (www.adolescence.it).

---

to extend mortgages and business loans to members of some races, or in lenders' charging higher interest rates to members of certain groups.

Examine your own language in regard to racism; do you

- avoid using derogatory terms for members of a particular race?

- avoid interacting with members of other races through stereotypes perpetuated by the media?

- make sure not to refer to race when it's irrelevant, as in "an African American surgeon" or "an Asian athlete"?

- avoid attributing economic or social problems to the race of the individuals rather than to institutionalized racism or to general economic problems that affect everyone?

## Heterosexism

Heterosexism also exists on both an individual and an institutional level. *Individual heterosexism* involves attitudes, behaviors, and language that disparage gay men and lesbians as well as a belief that all sexual behavior that is not heterosexual is unnatural and deserving of criticism and condemnation. These beliefs are at the heart of antigay violence and "gay bashing." Individual heterosexism also includes such beliefs as the notions that homosexuals are more likely than heterosexuals to commit crimes (there's actually no difference) or to molest children (actually, heterosexual, married men are overwhelmingly the child molesters) (Abel & Harlow, 2001; Koppelman, 2005). It also includes the belief that homosexuals cannot maintain stable relationships or effectively raise children, a belief that contradicts research evidence (Fitzpatrick, Jandt, Myrick, & Edgar, 1994; Johnson & O'Connor, 2002).

*Institutional heterosexism* is easy to identify. For example, the ban on gay marriage in many states and the fact that at this time only one state (Massachusetts) allows gay marriage is a good example of institutional heterosexism. Other examples include the Catholic Church's ban on homosexual priests, the United States military's prohibiting openly gay people from serving in the armed forces, and the many laws that prohibit adoption of children by gay people. In some cultures homosexual relations are illegal (for example, in India, Malaysia, Pakistan, and Singapore); penalties range from a "misdemeanor" conviction in Liberia, to life in jail in Singapore, to death in Pakistan.

**Heterosexist language** includes derogatory terms used for lesbians and gay men. For example, surveys in the military showed that 80 percent of those surveyed heard "offensive speech, derogatory names, jokes or remarks about gays" and that 85 percent believed that such derogatory speech was "tolerated" (*New York Times*, March 25, 2000, p. A12). You also see heterosexism in more subtle forms of language usage; for example, when you qualify a reference to a professional—as in "gay athlete" or "lesbian doctor"—and, in effect, say that athletes and doctors are not normally gay or lesbian.

Still another instance of heterosexism is the presumption of heterosexuality. Usually, people assume the person they're talking to or about is heterosexual. And usually they're correct, because most people are heterosexual. At the same time, however, this presumption denies the lesbian or gay identity a certain legitimacy. The practice is very similar to the presumptions of whiteness and maleness that we have made significant inroads in eliminating. Here are a few additional suggestions for avoiding heterosexist (or what some call homophobic) language. Do you:

- avoid offensive nonverbal mannerisms that parody stereotypes when talking about gay men and lesbians? Do you use the "startled eye blink" with which some people react to gay couples (Mahaffey, Bryan, & Hutchison, 2005)?

- avoid "complimenting" gay men and lesbians by saying that they "don't look it"? To gay men and lesbians, this is not a compliment. Similarly, expressing disappointment that a person is gay—often thought to be a compliment, as in comments such as "What a waste!"—is not really a compliment.

- avoid making the assumption that every gay or lesbian knows what every other gay or lesbian is thinking? It's very similar to asking a Japanese person why Sony is investing heavily in the United States or, as one comic put it, asking an African American, "What do you think Jesse Jackson meant by that last speech?"

- avoid denying individual differences? Comments like "Lesbians are so loyal" or "Gay men are so open with their feelings," which ignore the reality of wide differences within any group, are potentially insulting to all members of the group.

- avoid overattribution, the tendency to attribute just about everything a person does, says, and believes to the fact that the person is gay or lesbian? This tendency helps to activate and perpetuate stereotypes.

- remember that relationship milestones are important to all people? Ignoring anniversaries or birthdays of, say, a relative's partner makes a statement that is resented by everyone.

## HOMOPHOBIA

You're bringing your college roommate home for the holidays; she's an outspoken lesbian while your family is extremely homophobic. You want to prepare your family and your roommate for their holiday get-together.

WHAT DO YOU SAY?
*To whom? Through what channel?*

## THE MEDIA AND DISCONFIRMATION

*Whoever controls the media—the images—controls the cultures.*

—*Allen Ginsberg*

In all forms of communication, be especially careful not to rely on media stereotypes. The media are responsible for propagating many discriminatory stereotypes, and a media-literate individual needs to be able to recognize these and to see that such stereotypes are not reality but extreme examples, often created for comic effect or to maintain a viewer's attention. Men and women on comedy shows are often seen in an unpleasant light; most men on television are portrayed as incompetent, relationally inept, absorbed with sports, and ignorant of the important things in life. Men will never learn how to relate to women and are doomed to be insensitive clods. And women are portrayed as complaining, never satisfied, and abnormally thin. Old folks are portrayed as inept, complaining, loud, and offensive. And of course old people have lost and will never again find romance; for older people the kisses, for example, have to be nonsexual.

Racism is rampant in the media's portrayal of Muslims; almost all the Muslims on television are negatively constructed and are much more likely to be terrorists than they are to be teachers or lawyers or store owners or carpenters. Also, consider the negative stereotypes of gay men and lesbians; they're extremes that you rarely see in real life.

### Increasing Media Literacy

*No specific examples were given here to support the accusation of media stereotypes. Examine the current lineup of television situation comedies and dramas and try to identify examples that support or contradict the idea that media engage in stereotyping.*

---

As you think about heterosexism, recognize that heterosexist language will create barriers to communication, whereas its absence will foster more meaningful communication: greater comfort, an increased willingness to disclose personal information, and a greater willingness to engage in future interactions (Dorland & Fisher, 2001).

## Ageism

Although used mainly to refer to prejudice against older people, the term *ageism* can also refer to prejudice against other age groups. For example, if you describe all teenagers as selfish and undependable, you're discriminating against a group purely because of their age, and thus are using **ageist language**. In some cultures—some Asian and some African cultures, for example—the old are revered and respected. Younger people seek them out for advice on economic, ethical, and relationship issues.

*Individual ageism* is seen in negative stereotypes and in the general disrespect many have for older people. *Institutional ageism* is seen in mandatory retirement laws and age restrictions in certain occupations (as opposed to requirements based on demonstrated competence). In less obvious forms, ageism is seen in the media's portrayal of old people

as incompetent, complaining, and, perhaps most clearly evidenced in both television and films, without romantic feelings. Rarely, for example, does television or film show older people working productively, being cooperative and pleasant, and engaging in romantic and sexual relationships.

Popular language is replete with examples of linguistic ageism; terms like "little old lady," "old hag," "old-timer," "over the hill," "old coot," and "old fogy" are a few examples. As with sexism, qualifying a description of someone in terms of his or her age demonstrates ageism. For example, if you refer to "a quick-witted 75-year-old" or "an agile 65-year-old" or "a responsible teenager," you're implying that these qualities are unusual in people of these ages and thus need special mention. You're saying that "quick-wittedness" and "being 75" do not normally go together. The problem with this kind of stereotyping is that it's simply wrong. There are many 75-year-olds who are extremely quick-witted (and many 30-year-olds who aren't).

You also communicate ageism when you speak to older people in overly simple words or explain things that don't need explaining. Nonverbally, you demonstrate ageist communication when, for example, you avoid touching an older person but touch others, or when you avoid making direct eye contact with the older person but readily do so with others, or when you speak at an overly high volume (suggesting that all older people have hearing difficulties).

One useful way to avoid ageism is to recognize and avoid the illogical stereotypes that ageist language is based on. Do you:

- avoid talking down to a person because he or she is older? Older people are not mentally slow; most people remain mentally alert well into old age.

- refrain from refreshing an older person's memory each time you see the person? Older people can and do remember things.

- avoid implying that relationships are no longer important? Older people continue to be interested in relationships.

- speak at a normal volume and maintain a normal physical distance? Being older does not mean being hard of hearing or being unable to see; most older people hear and see quite well, sometimes with hearing aids or glasses.

- engage older people in conversation as you would wish to be engaged? Older people are interested in the world around them.

Even though you want to avoid ageist communication, there are times when you may wish to make adjustments when talking with someone who does have language or communication difficulties. The American Speech and Hearing Association offers several useful suggestions (www.asha.org/public/speech/development/communicating-better-with-older-people.htm, accessed June 3, 2006):

- Reduce as much background noise as you can.

- Ease into the conversation by beginning with casual topics and then moving into more familiar topics. Stay with each topic for a while; avoid jumping too quickly from one topic to another.

- Speak in relatively short sentences and questions.

- Give the person added time to respond. Some older people react more slowly and need extra time.

- Listen actively. Practice the skills of active listening discussed in Unit 4.

## Sexism

Sexism—like all the -isms discussed here—exists on both an individual and institutional level. *Individual sexism* consists of prejudicial attitudes and beliefs about men or women based on rigid beliefs about gender roles. These might include beliefs such as the ideas that women should be caretakers, should be sensitive at all times, and should acquiesce to a man's decisions concerning political or financial matters. Sexist attitudes would also include beliefs that men are insensitive, interested only in sex, and incapable of communicating feelings.

*Institutional sexism*, on the other hand, involves customs and practices that discriminate against people because of their gender. Two very clear examples are the widespread practice of paying women less than men for the same job and the discrimination against women in the upper levels of management. Another clear example of institutionalized sexism is seen in the divorce courts' practice of automatically or near-automatically granting child custody to the mother rather than the father.

Of particular interest here is **sexist language**: language that puts down someone because of his or her gender (a term usually used to refer to language derogatory toward women). The National Council of Teachers of English has proposed guidelines for nonsexist (gender-free, gender-neutral, or sex-fair) language. These guidelines concern the use of the generic word *man*, the use of generic *he* and *his*, and sex-role stereotyping (Penfield, 1987). Consider your own communication behavior. Do you

- avoid using *man* generically? Using the term to refer to both men and women emphasizes maleness at the expense of femaleness. Gender-neutral terms can easily be substituted. Instead of *mankind*, say *humanity*, *people*, or *human beings*. Similarly, the use of terms such as *policeman* or *fireman* and other terms that presume maleness as the norm—and femaleness as a deviation from this norm—are clear and common examples of sexist language.

- refrain from using *he* and *his* as generic? Instead, you can alternate pronouns or restructure your sentences to eliminate any reference to gender. For example, the NCTE Guidelines (Penfield, 1987) suggest that instead of saying, "The average student is worried about his grades," you say, "The average student is worried about grades."

- stay away from sex-role stereotyping? When you make the hypothetical elementary school teacher female and the college professor male or refer to doctors as male and nurses as female, you're sex-role stereotyping; the same is true when you identify the sex of a professional in phrases such as *woman doctor* or *male nurse*.

## Racist, Heterosexist, Ageist, and Sexist Listening

Just as racist, heterosexist, ageist, and sexist attitudes will influence your language, they can also influence your listening. In this disconfirming type of listening, you hear what the speaker is saying through the

## MISUSING CULTURAL IDENTIFIERS

During a conversation, your classmates all use negative self-reference terms. Trying to be one of the group, you too use these terms and almost immediately realize that the linguistic privilege allowing insiders to use [self] derogatory names, does not apply to outsiders. You don't want anyone to think that you normally talk this way.

WHAT DO YOU SAY?

stereotypes you hold. Disconfirmation in listening occurs when you listen differently to a person because of his or her gender, race, affectional orientation, or age even though these characteristics are irrelevant to the message.

Racist, heterosexist, ageist, and sexist listening occurs in lots of situations. For example, when you dismiss a valid argument—or attribute validity to an invalid argument—because the speaker is of a particular race, affectional orientation, age group, or gender, you're listening with prejudice.

But there also are many instances when these characteristics are relevant and pertinent to your evaluation of the message. For example, the sex of a person who is talking about pregnancy, fathering a child, birth control, or surrogate motherhood is, most would agree, probably relevant to the message. So in these cases it is not sexist listening to take the sex of the speaker into consideration. It is, however, sexist listening to assume that only one sex can be

an authority on a particular topic or that one sex's opinions are without value. The same is true in relation to listening through a person's race, affectional orientation, or age.

## Cultural Identifiers

Perhaps the best way to develop nonsexist, non-heterosexist, nonracist, and nonageist language is to examine the preferred cultural identifiers to use in talking to and about members of different groups. Remember, however, that preferred terms frequently change over time, so keep in touch with the most current preferences. The preferences and many of the specific examples identified here are drawn largely from the findings of the Task Force on Bias-Free Language of the Association of American University Presses (Schwartz, 1995).

### Race and Nationality

Generally, most African Americans prefer *African American* to *black* (Hecht, Collier, & Ribeau, 1993), although *black* is often used with *white*, as well as in a variety of other contexts (for example, Department of Black and Puerto Rican Studies, the *Journal of Black History*, and Black History Month). The American Psychological Association recommends that both terms be capitalized, but the *Chicago Manual of Style* (the manual used by most newspapers and publishing houses) recommends using lowercase. The terms *Negro* and *colored*, although used in the names of some organizations (for example, the United Negro College Fund and the National Association for the Advancement of Colored People), are not used outside these contexts.

*White* is generally used to refer to those whose roots are in European cultures and usually does not include Hispanics. Analogous to *African American* (which itself is based on a long tradition of terms such as *Irish American* and *Italian American*) is the phrase *European American*. Few European Americans, however, call themselves that; most prefer their national origins emphasized, as in, for example, *German American* or *Greek American*. This preference may well change as Europe moves toward becoming a more cohesive and united entity. *People of color*—a more literary-sounding term appropriate perhaps to public speaking but awkward in most conversations—is preferred to *nonwhite*, which implies that whiteness is the norm and nonwhiteness is a deviation from that norm. The same is true of the term *non-Christian*: It implies that people who have other beliefs deviate from the norm.

Generally, the term *Hispanic* refers to anyone who identifies himself or herself as belonging to a Spanish-speaking culture. *Latina* (female) and *Latino* (male) refer to persons whose roots are in one of the Latin American countries, such as Haiti, the Dominican Republic, Nicaragua, or Guatemala. *Hispanic American* refers to United States residents whose ancestry is in a Spanish culture; the term includes people from Mexico, the Caribbean, and Central and South America. In emphasizing a Spanish heritage, however, the term is really inaccurate, because it leaves out the large numbers of people in the Caribbean and in South America whose origins are African, Native American, French, or Portuguese. The words *Chicana* (female) and *Chicano* (male) refer to persons with roots in Mexico, although these terms often connote a nationalist attitude (Jandt, 2004) and are considered offensive by many Mexican Americans. *Mexican American* is generally preferred.

*Inuk* (plural *Inuit*), also spelled with two n's (*Innuk* and *Innuit*), is preferred to *Eskimo* (a term the United States Census Bureau uses), which was applied to the indigenous peoples of Alaska and Canada by Europeans and literally means "raw meat eaters."

The word *Indian* technically refers only to someone from India, not to citizens of other Asian countries or to the indigenous peoples of North America. *American Indian* or *Native American* is preferred, even though many Native Americans do refer to themselves as *Indians* and *Indian people*. The word *squaw*, used to refer to a Native American woman and still used in the names of some places in the United States and in some textbooks, is clearly a term to be avoided; its usage is almost always negative and insulting (Koppelman, 2005).

In Canada indigenous people are called *first people* or *first nations*. The term *native American* (with a lowercase n) is most often used to refer to persons born in the United States. Although technically the term could refer to anyone born in North or South America, people outside the United States generally prefer more specific designations such as *Argentinean*, *Cuban*, or *Canadian*. The term *native* describes an indigenous inhabitant; it is not used to indicate "someone having a less developed culture."

*Muslim* (rather than the older *Moslem*) is the preferred form to refer to a person who adheres to the religious teachings of Islam. *Quran* (rather than *Koran*) is the preferred term for the scriptures of Islam. *Jewish people* is often preferred to *Jews*, and *Jewess* (a Jewish female) is considered derogatory.

When history was being written from a European perspective, Europe was taken as the focal point and the rest of the world was defined in terms of its location relative to that continent. Thus, Asia became the East or the Orient, and *Asians* became *Orientals*—a term that is today considered inappropriate or Eurocentric. Thus, people from Asia are *Asians*, just as people from Africa are *Africans* and people from Europe are *Europeans*.

## Affectional Orientation

Generally, *gay* is the preferred term to refer to a man who has an affectional orientation toward other men, and *lesbian* is the preferred term for a woman who has an affectional orientation toward other women (Lever, 1995). (*Lesbian* means "homosexual woman," so the term *lesbian woman* is redundant.) *Homosexual* refers to both gays and lesbians, but more often to a sexual orientation to members of one's own sex. *Gay* and *lesbian* refer to a lifestyle and not merely to sexual orientation. *Gay* as a noun, although widely used, may prove offensive in some contexts, as in "We have two gays on the team." Because most scientific thinking holds that sexuality is not a matter of choice, the terms *sexual orientation* and *affectional orientation* are preferred to *sexual preference* or *sexual status* (for example, www.apa.org/topies/orientation.html; www.pflagatl .org/FandFarticles/APA.htm).

## Age

*Older person* is preferred to *elder, elderly, senior*, or *senior citizen* (which last term technically refers to someone older than 65). Usually, however, language designating age is unnecessary. There are times, of course, when you'll need to refer to a person's age group, but most of the time age is beside the point—in much the same way that racial or affectional orientation terms are usually irrelevant.

## Sex

Generally, the term *girl* should be used only to refer to very young females and is equivalent to *boy*. Neither term should be used for people older than age 17 or 18. *Girl* is never used to refer to a grown woman, nor is *boy* used to refer to people in blue-collar positions, as it once was. *Lady* is negatively evaluated by many because it connotes the stereotype of the prim and proper woman. *Woman* or *young woman* is preferred.

Let's turn now from issues of confirmation to some guidelines for using language effectively by avoiding common mistakes and applying some simple principles.

**OBJECTING TO DISCONFIRMATION**

One of your instructors persists in using all of the inappropriate and culturally insensitive sexist, heterosexist, racist, and ageist language. You want to object to this type of talk.

WHAT DO YOU SAY?
*To whom? Through what channel?*
*What do you say?*

# USING VERBAL MESSAGES EFFECTIVELY

A chief concern in using verbal messages is to recognize what critical thinking theorists call "conceptual distortions"; that is, mental mistakes, misinterpretations, or reasoning fallacies. Avoiding these distortions and substituting a more critical, more realistic analysis is probably the best way to improve your own use of verbal messages (DeVito, 1974). Let's look at several principles of language that are often ignored or misunderstood along with the conceptual distortions that result from such misunderstandings (Korzybski, 1933).

## Language Symbolizes Reality (Partially)

Language symbolizes reality; it's not the reality itself. Of course, this is obvious. But consider: Have you ever reacted to the way something was labeled or described rather than to the actual item? Have you ever bought something because of its name rather than because of the actual object? If so, you were probably responding as if language were the reality, a distortion called intensional orientation.

## Intensional Orientation

**Intensional orientation** (the *s* in *intensional* is intentional) is the tendency to view people, objects, and events according to the way they're talked about—the way they're labeled. For example, if Sally were labeled "uninteresting," you would, responding intensionally, evaluate her as uninteresting even before listening to what she had to say. You'd see Sally through a filter imposed by the label "uninteresting." **Extensional orientation**, on the other hand, is the tendency to look first at the actual people, objects, and events and only afterwards at their labels. In this case, it would mean looking at Sally without any preconceived labels, guided by what she says and does, not by the words used to label her.

To avoid intensional orientation, extensionalize. Never give labels greater attention than the actual thing. Give your main attention to the people, things, and events in the world as you see them and not as they're presented in words. For example, when you meet Jack and Jill, observe and interact with them. Then form your impressions. Don't respond to them as "greedy, money-grubbing landlords" because Harry labeled them this way. Don't respond to George as "lazy" just because Elaine told you he was.

The accompanying Understanding Theory and Research box explores the concept of intensional orientation and its connection with the verb "to be."

## Allness

A related distortion is **allness**: forgetting that language symbolizes only a portion of reality, never the whole. When you assume that you can know all or say all about anything, you're into allness. In reality, you never can see all of anything. You never can experience anything fully. You see a part, then conclude what the whole is like. You have to draw conclusions on the basis of insufficient evidence (because you always have insufficient evidence). A useful **extensional device** to help combat the tendency to think that all can or has been said about anything is to end each statement mentally with **et cetera**—a reminder that there's more to learn, more to know, and more to say and that every statement is inevitably incomplete. Instead of saying, for example, "I wouldn't like her; I saw the way she treated her father," you'd say, "I don't think I'd like her; I saw the way she treated her

father, but I haven't seen her with other people, and I really don't know her father, et cetera." Of course, some people overuse the "et cetera." They use it not as a mental reminder but as a substitute for being specific. This obviously is to be avoided and merely adds to conversational confusion.

To avoid allness, recognize that language symbolizes only a part of reality, never the whole. Whatever someone says—regardless of what it is or how extensive it is—represents only part of the story.

## Language Expresses Both Facts and Inferences

Language enables you to form statements of both facts and inferences without making any linguistic distinction between the two. Similarly, in speaking and listening you often don't make a clear distinction between statements of fact and statements of inference. Yet there are great differences between the two. Barriers to clear thinking can be created when inferences are treated as facts, a tendency called **fact–inference confusion**.

For example, you can say, "She's wearing a blue jacket," and you can say, "He's harboring an illogical hatred." Although the sentences have similar struc-

---

## Theory and Research    The Verb "To Be"

### Understanding

The theory of **E-prime** (or E') argues that if you wrote and spoke English without the verb *to be*, you'd describe events more accurately (Bourland, 1965–1966; Wilson, 1989; Klein, 1992; Bourland & Johnston, 1997). For example, when you say, "Johnny is a failure," the verb *is* implies that "failure" is in Johnny rather than in your observation or evaluation of Johnny. The verb *to be* (in forms such as *is*, *are*, and *am*) also implies permanence; the implication is that because failure is in Johnny, it will always be there; Johnny will always be a failure. A more accurate and descriptive statement might be "Johnny failed his last two math exams."

Consider this theory as applied to your thinking about yourself. When you say, for example, "I'm not good at public speaking" or "I'm unpopular" or "I'm lazy," you imply that these qualities are in you. But these are simply evaluations that may be incorrect or, if at least partly accurate, may change over time (Joyner, 1993).

---

### Working with Theories and Research

*How might you apply the E-prime principle to gain greater understanding of the ways in which you view yourself? To answer this question you might try first to identify your self (who you are, what you are) in a few sentences using forms of the verb to be and then to rephrase these same sentences in E-prime. What different perspectives do these two versions give you?*

tures, they're different. You can observe the jacket and its color, but how do you observe "illogical hatred"? Obviously, this is not a **factual statement** but an **inferential statement**. It's a statement you make on the basis not only of what you observe, but of what you infer. For a statement to be considered factual, it must be made by the observer after observation and must be limited to what is observed (Weinberg, 1958).

There is nothing wrong with making inferential statements. You must make them in order to talk about much that is meaningful to you. The problem arises when you act as if those inferential statements were factual. You can test your ability to distinguish facts from inferences by taking the fact–inference self-test below (based on the tests constructed in Haney, 1973).

## TEST YOURSELF

### Can You Distinguish Facts from Inferences?

Carefully read the following report and the observations based on it. Indicate whether you think the observations are true, false, or doubtful on the basis of the information presented in the report. Write T if the observation is definitely true, F if the observation is definitely false, and ? if the observation may be either true or false. Judge each observation in order. Don't reread the observations after you've indicated your judgment, and don't change any of your answers.

A well-liked college teacher had just completed making up the final examinations and had turned off the lights in the office. Just then a tall, broad figure with dark glasses appeared and demanded the examination. The professor opened the drawer. Everything in the drawer was picked up and the individual ran down the corridor. The dean was notified immediately.

____ 1. The thief was tall and broad and wore dark glasses.

____ 2. The professor turned off the lights.

____ 3. A tall figure demanded the examination.

____ 4. The examination was picked up by someone.

____ 5. The examination was picked up by the professor.

____ 6. A tall, broad figure appeared after the professor turned off the lights in the office.

____ 7. The man who opened the drawer was the professor.

____ 8. The professor ran down the corridor.

____ 9. The drawer was never actually opened.

____ 10. Three persons are referred to in this report.

**HOW DID YOU DO?** Number 3 is true, number 9 is false, and all the rest are "?" Review your answers by referring back to the story. To get you started, consider: Is there necessarily a thief? Might the dean have demanded to see the instructor's examination (statement 1)? Did the examination have to be in the drawer (statements 4 and 5)? How do you know it was the professor who turned off the lights (statement 6)? Need the professor have been a man (statement 7)? Do the instructor and the professor have to be the same person (statement 10)?

**WHAT WILL YOU DO?** Again, recognize that there's nothing wrong with making inferences. When you hear inferential statements, however, treat them as inferences and not as facts. Be mindful of the possibility that such statements may prove to be wrong. As you read this chapter, try to formulate specific guidelines that will help you distinguish facts from inferences.

To avoid fact–inference confusion, phrase inferential statements in such a way as to show that they are tentative. Inferential statements should leave open the possibility of alternatives. If, for example, you treat the statement "Our biology teacher was fired for poor teaching" as factual, you eliminate any alternatives. But if you preface your statement with, say, "Pat told me . . ." or "I'm wondering if . . .," the inferential nature of your statement will be clear. Be especially sensitive to this distinction when you're listening. Most talk is inferential. Beware of the speaker who presents everything as fact. Analyze closely and you'll uncover a world of inferences.

## Language Is Relatively Static

Language changes only very slowly, especially when compared to the rapid change in people and things. **Static evaluation** is the tendency to retain evaluations without change while the reality to which they refer is changing. Often a verbal statement you make about an event or person remains static ("That's the way he is; he's always been that way") while the event or person may change enormously. Alfred Korzybski (1933) used an interesting illustration. In a tank you have a large fish and many small fish, the natural food for the large fish. Given freedom in the tank, the large fish will eat the small fish. If you partition the tank, separating the large fish from the small fish by a clear piece of glass, the large fish will continue to attempt to eat the small fish but will fail, knocking instead into the glass partition.

Eventually, the large fish will learn the futility of attempting to eat the small fish. If you now remove the partition, the small fish will swim all around the big fish, but the big fish will not eat them. In fact, the large fish will die of starvation while its natural food swims all around. The large fish has learned a pattern or "map" of behavior, and even though the actual territory has changed, the map remains static.

The mental **date** is an extensional device that helps you keep your language (and your thinking) up to date and helps you guard against static evaluation. The procedure is simple: date your statements and especially your evaluations. Remember that Pat Smith$_{1995}$ is not Pat Smith$_{2008}$; academic abilities$_{2004}$ are not academic abilities$_{2008}$. T. S. Eliot, in *The Cocktail Party*, said, "What we know of other people is only our memory of the moments during which we knew them. And they have changed since then . . . at every meeting we are meeting a stranger." In listening, look carefully at messages that claim that what was true still is. It may or may not be. Look for change.

## Language Can Obscure Distinctions

Language can obscure distinctions among people or events that are covered by the same label but are really quite different (indiscrimination); it can also make it easy to focus on extremes rather than on the vast middle ground between opposites (polarization).

### Indiscrimination

**Indiscrimination** is the failure to distinguish between similar but different people, objects, or events. This error occurs when you focus on categories or classes and fail to see that each phenomenon is unique and needs to be looked at individually.

Everything is unlike everything else. Our language, however, provides you with common nouns, such as *teacher*, *student*, *friend*, *enemy*, *war*, *politician*, and *liberal*. These lead you to focus on similarities—to group together all teachers, all students, and all politicians. At the same time, the terms divert attention away from the uniqueness of each person, each object, and each event.

---

**Building Communication Skills**  **Talking about the Middle**

Fill in the word that would logically go where the question mark appears, a word that is the opposite of the term on the left.

hot _____?
high _____?
good _____?
popular _____?
sad _____?

Filling in these opposites was probably easy—the words you supplied were probably short, and, if various different people supplied opposites, you'd probably find a high level of agreement among them.

Now fill in the middle positions with words meaning, for example, "midway between hot and cold," "midway between high and low." Do this before reading further.

You probably had greater difficulty here. You probably took more time to think of these middle terms, and you also probably used multiword phrases. Further, you would probably find less agreement among different people completing this same task. From this brief experience what implications can you draw about polarization?

*Although most things, people, and events fall between extremes, the common but illogical tendency is to concentrate on the extremes and ignore the middle.*

This misevaluation is at the heart of stereotyping on the basis of nationality, race, religion, sex, and affectional orientation. A stereotype, as you know, is a fixed mental picture of a group that is applied to each individual in the group without regard to his or her unique qualities. Whether stereotypes are positive or negative, they create the same problem: They provide you with shortcuts that are often inappropriate.

A useful antidote to indiscrimination (and stereotyping) is another extensional device called the **index.** This mental subscript identifies each individual as an individual even though both may be covered by the same label. Thus, politician$_1$ is not politician$_2$, teacher$_1$ is not teacher$_2$. The index helps you to discriminate among without discriminating against. Although the label ("politician," for example) covers all politicians, the index makes sure that each is thought about as an individual. The index would, for example, prevent you from grouping all Muslims or all Christians or all Jews in the same category. Each Muslim, each Christian, and each Jew is unique and needs a unique index number. So at the same time that you have to generalize and appreciate similarities, the index reminds you also to look at differences. Instead of saying, for example, "I don't want you to hang around with Muslims," a parent would discriminate *among* (rather than *against*) Muslims and say something like "I don't want you to hang around with Abdul or with Said."

## Polarization

Another way in which language can obscure differences is in its preponderance of extreme terms and its relative lack of middle terms, a characteristic that often leads to polarization. **Polarization** is the tendency to look at the world in terms of opposites and to describe it in extremes—good or bad, positive or negative, healthy or sick, intelligent or stupid. Polarization is often referred to as the fallacy of "either/or" or "black or white." Most people exist somewhere between the extremes. Yet there's a strong tendency to view only the extremes and to categorize people, objects, and events in terms of polar opposites.

Problems are created when opposites are used in inappropriate situations. For example, "So-and-so is either for us or against us." These options don't include all possibilities. The person may be for us in some things and against us in other things, or may be neutral.

To correct this polarizing tendency, beware of implying (and believing) that two extreme classes include all possible classes—that an individual must be one or the other, with no alternatives ("Are you pro-choice or pro-life?"). Most people, most events, most qualities exist between polar extremes. When others imply that there are only two sides or alternatives, look for the middle ground.

The Building Communication Skills box (page 119) explores the ease of polarizing and the difficulty of talking about the middle.

## SUMMARY: VERBAL MESSAGES

This unit focused on verbal messages, and specifically on the nature of language and the ways language works; the concept of disconfirmation and how it relates to racism, heterosexism, ageism, and sexism; and the ways in which language can be used more effectively.

1. Meanings are in people, not in things.

2. Meanings are context based; the same message in a different context will likely mean something different.

3. Language is both denotative (objective and generally easily agreed upon) and connotative (subjective and generally highly individual in meaning).

4. Language varies in directness; through language you can state exactly what you mean or you can hedge and state your meaning very indirectly.

5. Meanings are influenced by culture and gender; each culture has its own rules identifying the ways in which language should be used, and in some respects males and females use language differently.

6. Disconfirmation is the process of ignoring the presence and the communications of others. Confirmation is accepting, supporting, and acknowledging the importance of the other person.

7. Racist, heterosexist, ageist, and sexist language puts down and negatively evaluates members of various groups.

8. Using language effectively involves eliminating conceptual distortions and substituting more accurate assumptions about language.

9. Language symbolizes reality; it's not the reality itself, so avoid intensional orientation and allness.

10. Language can express both facts and inferences, so learn to make distinctions between them.

11. Language is relatively static, but reality changes rapidly; try to constantly revise the way you talk about people and things.

12. Language can obscure distinctions in its use of general terms and in its emphasis on extreme rather than middle terms, so be careful to avoid indiscrimination and polarization.

## KEY TERMS IN VERBAL MESSAGES

ageist language (p. **112**)
allness (p. **117**)
bypassing (p. **102**)
confirmation (p. **108**)
connotation (p. **102**)
cooperation (p. **103**)
date (p. **119**)
denotation (p. **102**)
direct speech (p. **103**)

disconfirmation (p. **107**)
E-prime (p. **117**)
et cetera (p. **117**)
extensional device (p. **117**)
extensional orientation
   (p. **116**)
fact–inference confusion
   (p. **117**)
factual statement (p. **118**)

heterosexist language
   (p. **111**)
index (p. **120**)
indirect speech (p. **103**)
indiscrimination (p. **119**)
inferential statement
   (p. **118**)
intensional orientation
   (p. **116**)

lying (p. **106**)
netiquette (p. **106**)
polarization (p. **120**)
purr words (p. **103**)
racist language (p. **109**)
rejection (p. **108**)
sexist language (p. **113**)
snarl words (p. **103**)
static evaluation (p. **118**)

## THINKING CRITICALLY ABOUT VERBAL MESSAGES

1. **Changing Communication Styles.** When researchers asked men and women what they would like to change about the communication style of the opposite sex, most men said they wanted women to be more direct, and most women said they wanted men to stop interrupting and offering advice (Noble, 1994). What one change would you like to see in the communication style of the opposite sex? Of your own sex?

2. **Importance of a Concept.** A widely held assumption in anthropology, linguistics, and communication is that the importance of a concept to a culture can be measured by the number of words the language has for talking about the concept. So, for example, in English there are lots of words for money, transportation, or communication, as all these concepts are important in English-speaking cultures. With this principle in mind, consider the findings of Julia Stanley, for example, who researched terms indicating sexual promiscuity. Stanley found 220 English-language terms referring to a sexually promiscuous woman but only 22 terms for a sexually promiscuous man (Thorne, Kramarae, & Henley, 1983). What does this suggest about cultural attitudes and beliefs about promiscuity in men and women?

3. **From Negative to Positive.** It's interesting to note that terms denoting some of the major movements in art—for example, impressionism and cubism—were originally applied negatively. The terms were then adopted by the artists themselves and eventually became positive. A parallel can be seen in the use of the word *queer* by some lesbian and gay organizations. The purpose of these groups in using the term is to cause it to lose its negative connotation. One possible problem, though, is that such terms may not lose their negative connotations and may simply reinforce the negative stereotypes that society has already assigned to certain groups. By using these terms, members may come to accept the labels with their negative connotations and thus contribute to their own stereotyping. What's been your experience with people who refer to themselves with negative terms? How do you feel about this?

4. **Directness.** How would you describe the level of directness you use when talking face-to-face versus the level you use in e-mail and chat rooms? If you do notice differences, to what do you attribute them?

5. **Cell Phone Politeness.** Among the rules of cell phone etiquette are these don'ts: (1) Don't intrude on others with your cell conversations; (2) don't take a cell call during a business meeting; (3) don't use your cell in elevators, libraries, or theaters; and (4) don't use loud or annoying ring tones (see, for example, www.microsoft.com/smallbusiness/resources/technology/communications/cell_phone, accessed June 3, 2006, or www.infoworld.com/articles/op/xml/00/05/26/000526opwireless.html, accessed June 3, 2006; or search for "cell phone etiquette"). What rule do you wish people would follow more often? What is your own code for cell phone etiquette?

# LogOn! MyCommunicationLab
WWW.MYCOMMUNICATIONLAB.COM

Visit MCL for self-tests that measure how confirming, polite, and direct you are—and for a variety of exercises and discussions on verbal messages (Men and Women Talking, Talking with the Grief Stricken, Integrating Verbal and Nonverbal Messages, Using the Abstraction Ladder as a Creative Thinking Tool, Varying Directness, Identifying the Barriers to Communication, "Must Lie" Situations, What Do You Mean? Biased Language Survey, What's in a Name? and Semiotics for Beginners (on connotation and denotation). Also watch the video Having a Baby on supportive communication and Verbal Pitfalls.

While online visit the Institute of General Semantics website, www.time-binding.org. General semantics is an approach to language that emphasizes the connection between the way you speak (on the one hand) and the way you think and behave (on the other). This unit's discussion of Using Verbal Messages Effectively rests on the principles of general semantics.

# UNIT 6 Nonverbal Messages

## MAJOR TOPICS

The Functions of Nonverbal Communication
The Channels of Nonverbal Communication
Culture and Nonverbal Communication

## Special Features

When you smile, nod your head in agreement, or wave your hand to someone, you're communicating nonverbally. In fact, some researchers argue that you actually communicate more information nonverbally than you do with words.

**In this unit you'll learn about:**
- the functions nonverbal communication serves and how nonverbal communication interacts with your verbal messages.
- the channels of nonverbal communication.
- the role of culture and gender in nonverbal communication.

**You'll learn to:**
- communicate more effectively with nonverbal messages.
- respond appropriately to the nonverbal messages of others.
- communicate with an awareness of cultural and gender influences and differences in nonverbal communication.

Nonverbal communication is communication without words. You communicate nonverbally when you gesture, smile or frown, widen your eyes, move your chair closer to someone, wear jewelry, touch someone, raise your vocal volume, or even say nothing. The crucial aspect of nonverbal communication is that the message you send is in some way received by one or more other people. If you gesture while alone in your room and no one is there to see you, then, most theorists would argue, communication has not taken place. The same, of course, is true of verbal messages; if you recite a speech and no one hears it, then communication has not taken place.

Using nonverbal communication effectively can yield two major benefits (Burgoon & Hoobler, 2002). First, the greater your ability to send and receive nonverbal signals, the higher your attractiveness, popularity, and psychosocial well-being are likely to be. Second, the greater your nonverbal skills, the more successful you're likely to be at influencing (or deceiving) others. Skilled nonverbal communicators are highly persuasive, and this persuasive power can be used to help or support another or it can be used to deceive and fool.

Research shows that of the two genders, women are the better senders and receivers of nonverbal messages in most contexts (Hall, 1998; Burgoon & Hoobler, 2002). For example, in a review of 21 research studies, 71 percent of the findings showed women to be superior nonverbal senders. And in a review of 61 studies on decoding, 84 percent showed women to be superior receivers (Hall, 1998).

## THE FUNCTIONS OF NONVERBAL COMMUNICATION

Let's consider the functions of nonverbal communication by looking at (1) the ways in which nonverbal messages are integrated with verbal messages, and (2) the functions that researchers have focused on most extensively.

### Integrating Nonverbal and Verbal Messages

In face-to-face communication you blend verbal and nonverbal messages to best convey your meanings. While speaking, you also smile, frown, or gesture, for example. It's this combination of verbal and nonverbal signals that communicates your meanings. Here are six ways in which nonverbal messages interact with verbal messages: (1) accenting, (2) complementing, (3) contradicting, (4) regulating, (5) repeating, and (6) substituting (Knapp & Hall, 2005):

- Nonverbal communication often serves to *accent* or emphasize some part of the verbal message. You might, for example, raise your voice to underscore a particular word or phrase; bang your fist on the desk to stress your commitment; or look longingly into someone's eyes when saying, "I love you."

- Nonverbal communication may *complement* or add nuances of meaning not communicated by your verbal message. Thus, you might smile when telling a story (to suggest that you find it humorous), or frown and shake your head when recounting someone's deceit (to suggest your disapproval).

- You may deliberately *contradict* your verbal messages with nonverbal movements—for example, by crossing your fingers or winking to indicate that you're lying.

- Movements may be used to *regulate*—to control or indicate your desire to control—the flow of verbal messages, as when you purse your lips, lean forward, or make hand gestures to indicate that you want to speak. You might also put up your hand or vocalize your pauses (for example, with "um" or "ah") to indicate that you have not finished and are not ready to relinquish the floor to the next speaker.

- You can *repeat* or restate the verbal message nonverbally. You can, for example, follow your verbal "Is that all right?" with raised eyebrows and a questioning look, or motion with your head or hand to repeat your verbal "Let's go."

- You may also use nonverbal communication to *substitute for* or take the place of verbal messages. For instance, you can signal "OK" with a hand gesture. You can nod your head to indicate yes or shake your head to indicate no.

## Serving Varied Communication Functions

Although nonverbal communication serves the same functions as verbal communication, nonverbal researchers have singled out several specific functions as especially significant (Burgoon, Buller, & Woodall, 1996; Burgoon & Hoobler, 2002).

### To Manage Self-Impression

It is largely through the nonverbal communications of others that you form impressions of them. Based

## ASK THE RESEARCHER

### Cues for Success

*I'm running for office in a class election, and I want to know what I can do nonverbally to make myself more likable and more credible and hence more likely to be elected. Any suggestions?*

In a campaign speech enhance your physical appearance (if female, moderate makeup; if male, shave) and dress slightly better than expected at your school. You should engage in pleasant facial expressions, use a slightly faster speech rate with a good range of inflection, and speak from your diaphragm. Engage in a moderate amount of gestures, but keep them between your neck and waist and spread them away from your body. Engage your audience with a slight forward lean to show interest in them.

In interpersonal contexts where you have already enhanced your physical appearance, close your distance slightly if your listener agrees with you, but increase your distance slightly if s/he disagrees with you. If you have not enhanced your appearance, maintain your initial distance. Allow your natural emotions to flow (provide positive feedback, unless you totally disagree with the point), reduce your range of gestures, and speak with a confident, slightly faster than normal rate, but at a conversational volume.

For further information: Hickson, M. L., Stacks, D. W., & Moore, N. J. (2003). *Nonverbal communication: Studies and applications*. Los Angeles: Roxbury. And Richmond, V. P., & McCroskey, J. C. (2003). *Nonverbal behavior in interpersonal relations*. Boston: Allyn & Bacon.

**Don W. Stacks** (Ph.D., University of Florida) is a professor of advertising and public relations at the University of Miami. He teaches courses in public relations, research methods, nonverbal communication, persuasion, and communication theory and directs the undergraduate and graduate programs in advertising and public relations.

on a person's body size, skin color, and dress as well as on the way the person smiles, maintains eye contact, and expresses himself or herself facially, you form impressions—you judge who the person is and what the person is like. Nonverbal researchers group these impressions into five categories (Leathers, 1997; Mehrabian, 1971).

- credibility, or how competent and believable you find the person
- likability, or how much you like or dislike the person
- attractiveness, or how attractive you find the person
- dominance, or how powerful the individual is
- status, or relative rank or standing of the person; a relaxed rather than a tense posture and large gestures contribute to an impression of higher status

And, of course, you reveal yourself largely through the same nonverbal signals you use to size up others. But not only do you communicate your true self nonverbally; you also strive to manage the impression that you give to others. For example, you may do your best to appear brave when you're really scared, or to appear happy when you're really sad.

## To Define Relationships

Much of your relationship life is lived nonverbally: Largely through nonverbal signals, you communicate your relationship to another person and that person communicates to you. Holding hands, gazing into each other's eyes, and even dressing alike are ways in which you communicate closeness in your interpersonal relationships.

You also use nonverbal signals to communicate your relationship dominance and status (Knapp & Hall, 1997). The large corner office with the huge desk communicates high status, just as the basement cubicle communicates low status.

## To Structure Interaction

When you're in conversation, you give and receive cues—to speak, to listen, to comment on what the speaker just said. Turn-taking cues regulate and structure the interaction. These turn-taking cues may be verbal (as when you say, "What do you think?"), but most often they're nonverbal—a nod of the head in the direction of someone else, for example, signals that you're ready to give up your speaking turn and want this other person to say something.

You also show that you're listening and that you want the conversation to continue (or that you're not listening and want the conversation to end) largely through nonverbal signals.

## To Influence

Much as you influence others by what you say, you also influence others by your nonverbal signals. A focused glance that says you're committed, gestures that further explain what you're saying, and appropriate dress signaling that "I'll easily fit in with this company" are a few examples of how you influence others with nonverbal signals.

And, of course, with the ability to influence comes the ability to deceive—to lie, to mislead another person into thinking something is true when it's false or that something is false when it's true. Using your eyes and facial expressions to communicate a liking for other people when you're really just interested in gaining their support for your promotion is an often-seen example of nonverbal deception.

Not surprisingly, you also may try to use nonverbal signals to detect deception in others. For example, you may suspect a person of lying if he or she avoids eye contact, fidgets, or sends verbal and nonverbal messages that are inconsistent. But be careful. Research shows that it is much more difficult to tell when someone is lying than you probably think it is. Using nonverbal cues in an effort to detect lying is likely to get you into trouble by leading you to formulate incorrect conclusions (Burgoon & Hoobler, 2002; Burgoon & Bacue, 2003; Knapp & Hall, 2005; Park, Levine, McCornack, Morrison, & Ferrara, 2002). For example, you may judge a person who avoids eye contact as lying when the eye avoidance may really be due to shyness or to a cultural rule that discourages eye contact, as does Japanese culture (Axtell, 1993).

## To Communicate Emotion

Although people often explain and reveal emotions verbally, nonverbal expressions communicate a great part of emotional experience. It is largely through facial expressions that you reveal your level of happiness or sadness or confusion, for example. Of course, you also reveal your feelings by posture (for example, whether tense or relaxed), gestures, and eye movements and even by the extent to which your pupils dilate.

Nonverbal messages often serve to communicate unpleasant messages—messages you might feel uncomfortable saying in words (Infante, Rancer, & Womack, 2002). For example, you might avoid eye contact and maintain large distances between yourself and someone with whom you don't want to interact, or with whom you want to decrease the intensity of your relationship.

# THE CHANNELS OF NONVERBAL COMMUNICATION

Nonverbal communication is probably most easily explained in terms of the various channels through which messages pass. Here we'll survey 10 channels: (1) body, (2) face, (3) eye, (4) space, (5) artifactual, (6) touch, (7) paralanguage, (8) silence, (9) time, and (10) smell.

## The Body

Two areas of the body are especially important in communicating messages. First, the movements you make with your body communicate; second, the general appearance of your body communicates.

### Body Movements

Researchers in **kinesics**, or the study of nonverbal communication through face and body movements, identify five major types of movements: emblems, illustrators, affect displays, regulators, and adaptors (Ekman & Friesen, 1969; Knapp & Hall, 1997).

**Emblems.** **Emblems** are body gestures that directly translate into words or phrases; for example, the OK sign, the thumbs-up for "good job," and the V for victory. You use these consciously and purposely to communicate the same meaning as the words. But emblems are culture specific, so be careful when using your culture's emblems in other cultures. For example, when President Nixon visited Latin America and gestured with the OK sign, intending to communicate something positive, he was quickly informed that this gesture was not universal. In Latin America the gesture has a far more negative meaning. Here are a few cultural differences in the emblems you may commonly use (Axtell, 1993):

- In the United States, to say "hello" you wave with your whole hand moving from side to side, but in a large part of Europe that same signal means "no." In Greece such a gesture would be considered insulting.

- The V for victory is common throughout much of the world; but if you make this gesture in England with the palm facing your face, it's as insulting as the raised middle finger is in the United States.

- In Texas the raised fist with little finger and index finger held upright is a positive expression of support, because it represents the Texas longhorn steer. But in Italy it's an insult that means "Your spouse is having an affair with someone else." In parts of South America it's a gesture to ward off evil, and in parts of Africa it's a curse: "May you experience bad times."

- In the United States and in much of Asia, hugs are rarely exchanged among acquaintances; but among Latins and southern Europeans, hugging is a common greeting gesture, and failing to hug someone may communicate unfriendliness.

**Illustrators.** **Illustrators** enhance (literally "illustrate") the verbal messages they accompany. For example, when referring to something to the left, you might gesture toward the left. Most often you illustrate with your hands, but you can also illustrate with head and general body movements. You might, for example, turn your head or your entire body toward the left. You might also use illustrators to communicate the shape or size of objects you're talking about. Research points to an interesting advantage of illustrators: They increase your ability to remember. In one study people who illustrated their verbal messages with gestures remembered some 20 percent more than those who didn't gesture (Goldin-Meadow, Nusbaum, Kelly, & Wagner, 2001).

**Affect Displays.** **Affect displays** are movements of the face (smiling or frowning, for example) but also of the hands and general body (body tension or relaxation, for example) that communicate emotional meaning. Often affect displays are unconscious; you smile or frown, for example, without awareness. At other times, however, you may smile consciously, trying to convey your pleasure or satisfaction. Not surprisingly, people who smile spontaneously are judged to be more likable and more approachable than people who don't smile or people who pretend to smile (Gladstone & Parker, 2002).

**Regulators.** **Regulators** are behaviors that monitor, control, coordinate, or maintain the speaking of another individual. When you nod your head, for example, you tell the speaker to keep on speaking; when you lean forward and open your mouth, you tell the speaker that you would like to say something.

**Adaptors.** **Adaptors** are gestures that satisfy some personal need, such as scratching to relieve an itch or moving your hair out of your eyes. **Self-adaptors** are self-touching movements (for example, rubbing your nose). **Alter-adaptors** are movements directed at the person with whom you're speaking, such as removing lint from someone's jacket or straightening a person's tie or folding your arms in front of you to keep others a comfortable distance from you. **Object-adaptors** are gestures focused on objects, such as doodling on or shredding a Styrofoam coffee cup.

## Body Appearance

Your general body appearance also communicates. Height, for example, has been shown to be significant in a wide variety of situations. Tall presidential candidates have a much better record of winning the election than do their shorter opponents. Tall people seem to be paid more and are favored by interviewers over shorter job applicants (Keyes, 1980; Guerrero, DeVito, & Hecht, 1999; Knapp & Hall, 2005). Taller people also have higher self-esteem and greater career success than do shorter people (Judge & Cable, 2004).

Your body also reveals your ethnicity (through skin color and tone) and may also give clues as to your more specific nationality. Your weight in proportion to your height will also communicate messages to others, as will the length, color, and style of your hair.

Your general **attractiveness** is also a part of body communication. Attractive people have the advantage in just about every activity you can name. They get better grades in school, are more valued as friends and lovers, and are preferred as coworkers (Burgoon, Buller, & Woodall, 1996). Although we normally think that attractiveness is culturally determined—and to some degree it is—research seems to indicate that definitions of attractiveness are universal (Brody, 1994). A person rated as attractive in one culture is likely to be rated as attractive in other cultures—even in cultures whose people are widely different in appearance.

## Facial Communication

Throughout your interactions, your face communicates various messages, especially your emotions. Facial movements alone seem to communicate the degree of pleasantness, agreement, and sympathy felt; the rest of the body doesn't provide any additional information. But for other emotional messages—for example, the intensity with which an emotion is felt—both facial and bodily cues send messages (Graham, Bitti, & Argyle, 1975; Graham & Argyle, 1975).

So important are these cues in communicating your full meaning that graphic representations are commonly used in Internet communication. In graphic user interface chat groups, buttons are available to help you encode your emotions graphically. Table 6.1 identifies some of the more common "emoticons," icons that communicate emotions.

Some researchers in nonverbal communication claim that facial movements may express at least the following eight emotions: happiness, surprise, fear, anger, sadness, disgust, contempt, and interest (Ekman, Friesen, & Ellsworth, 1972). Facial expressions of these emotions are generally called primary affect displays: They indicate relatively pure, single emotions. Other emotional states and other facial displays are combinations of these various primary emotions and are called affect blends. You communicate these blended feelings with different parts of your face. Thus, for example, you may experience both fear and disgust at the same time. Your

## Table 6.1 Some Popular Emoticons

Here are a few of the many popular emoticons used in computer communication. The first six are popular in the United States; the last three are popular in Japan and illustrate how culture influences such symbols. That is, because Japanese culture considers it impolite for women to show their teeth when smiling, the emoticon for a woman's smile shows a dot signifying a closed mouth. Two excellent websites that contain extensive examples of smileys, emoticons, acronyms, and shorthand abbreviations are www.netlingo.com/smiley.cfm and www.netlingo.com/emailsh.cfm.

| Emoticon | Meaning | Emoticon | Meaning |
|---|---|---|---|
| :-) | Smile; I'm kidding | *This is important* | Substitutes for underlining or italics |
| :-( | Frown; I'm feeling down | <G> | Grin; I'm kidding |
| * | Kiss | <grin> | Grin; I'm kidding |
| {} | Hug | ^.^ | Woman's smile |
| {*****} | Hugs and kisses | ^_^ | Man's smile |
| _This is important_ | Gives emphasis, calls special attention to | ^o^ | Happy |

eyes and eyelids may signal fear, and movements of your nose, cheek, and mouth area may signal disgust.

## Facial Management

As you learned your culture's nonverbal system of communication, you also learned certain **facial management techniques** that enable you to communicate your feelings to achieve the effect you want—for example, ways to hide certain emotions and to emphasize others. Consider your own use of such techniques. As you do so, think about the types of interpersonal situations in which you would use each of the following facial management techniques (Malandro, Barker, & Barker, 1989; Metts & Planalp, 2002). Would you

- *Intensify?* For example, would you exaggerate surprise when friends throw you a party to make your friends feel better?
- *Deintensify?* Would you cover up your own joy about a successful outcome in the presence of a friend who didn't receive such good news?
- *Neutralize?* Would you cover up your sadness to keep from depressing others?
- *Mask?* Would you express happiness in order to cover up your disappointment at not receiving the gift you expected?
- *Simulate?* Would you express an emotion you don't feel?

These tactics of facial management help you display emotions in socially acceptable ways. For example, when someone gets bad news in which you may secretly take pleasure, the cultural display rule dictates that you frown and otherwise nonverbally signal your displeasure. If you place first in a race and your best friend barely finishes, the display rule requires that you minimize your expression of pleasure in winning and avoid any signs of gloating. If you violate these display rules, you'll seem insensitive. So although facial management techniques may be deceptive, they're also expected—in fact required—by the rules of polite interaction.

## Encoding–Decoding Accuracy

One popular question concerns the accuracy with which people can encode and decode emotions through facial expressions. It can be difficult to separate the ability of the encoder from the ability of the decoder, however. Thus, a person may be quite adept at communicating emotions nonverbally, but the receiver may prove insensitive. On the other hand, the receiver may be good at deciphering emotions, but the sender may be inept. For example, introverts are not as accurate at decoding nonverbal cues as are extroverts (Akert & Panter, 1986).

**SMILING**

Sam smiles almost all the time. Even when he criticizes or reprimands a subordinate, he ends with a smile and this dilutes the strength of his message. As Sam's supervisor, you need him to realize what he's doing and to change his nonverbals.

WHAT DO YOU SAY?
*Through what channel?*
*In what context?*

Despite this difficulty, research in 11 different countries shows that women are better than men at both encoding and decoding nonverbal cues (Rosenthal & DePaulo, 1979). It may be argued that because men and women play different roles in society, they've learned different adaptive techniques and skills to help them perform these roles. Thus, in most societies women are expected to be more friendly, nurturing, and supportive and so learn these skills (Eagly & Crowley, 1986).

Accuracy in decoding also varies with the emotions themselves. Some emotions are easier to encode and decode than others. In one study, for example, people judged facial expressions of happiness with an accuracy ranging from 55 to 100 percent, surprise from 38 to 86 percent, and sadness from 19 to 88 percent (Ekman, Friesen, & Ellsworth, 1972).

## Eye Communication

Research on the messages communicated by the eyes (a study known technically as oculesis) shows that these messages vary depending on the duration, direction, and quality of the eye behavior. For example, in every culture there are strict, though unstated, rules for the proper duration for eye contact. In U.S. culture the average length of gaze is 2.95 seconds. The average length of mutual gaze (two persons gazing at each other) is 1.18 seconds (Argyle & Ingham, 1972; Argyle, 1988). When eye contact falls short of this amount, you may think the person is uninterested, shy, or preoccupied. When

---

**Theory** and **Research**  —  **UNDERSTANDING**    The Facial Feedback Hypothesis

The **facial feedback hypothesis** holds that your facial expressions influence physiological arousal (Lanzetta, Cartwright-Smith, & Kleck, 1976; Zuckerman, Klorman, Larrance, & Spiegel, 1981). In one study, for example, participants held a pen in their teeth to simulate a sad expression and then rated a series of photographs. Results showed that mimicking sad expressions actually increased the degree of sadness the subjects reported feeling when viewing the photographs (Larsen, Kasimatis, & Frey, 1992). Further support for this hypothesis comes from a study that compared (1) participants who felt emotions such as happiness and anger with (2) participants who both felt and expressed these emotions. In support of the facial feedback hypothesis, people who felt and expressed the emotions became emotionally aroused faster than did those who only felt the emotion (Hess, Kappas, McHugo, & Lanzetta, 1992).

Generally, research finds that facial expressions can produce or heighten feelings of sadness, fear, disgust, and anger. But this effect does not occur with all emotions; smiling, for example, doesn't seem to make us feel happier (Burgoon & Bacue, 2003). Further, it has not been demonstrated that facial expressions can eliminate one feeling and replace it with another. So if you're feeling sad, smiling will not eliminate the sadness and replace it with gladness. A reasonable conclusion seems to be that your facial expressions can influence some feelings, but not all (Burgoon & Bacue, 2003).

### Working with Theories and Research

*What effect do you observe when you express your emotions? Do your feelings get stronger? Weaker?*

---

the appropriate amount of time is exceeded, you may perceive the person as showing unusually high interest.

The direction of the eye also communicates. In much of the United States, you're expected to glance alternately at the other person's face, then away, then again at the face, and so on. The rule for the public speaker is to scan the entire audience, not focusing for too long on or ignoring any one area of the audience. When you break these directional rules, you communicate different meanings—abnormally high or low interest, self-consciousness, nervousness over the interaction, and so on. The quality of eye behavior—how wide or how narrow your eyes get during interaction—also communicates meaning, especially interest level and such emotions as surprise, fear, and disgust. Some researchers note that eye contact serves to enable gay men and lesbians to signal their homosexuality and perhaps their interest in the other person—an ability referred to as "gaydar" (Nicholas, 2004).

### Eye Contact and Eye Avoidance

Eye contact can serve a variety of functions. One such function is to seek feedback. In talking with someone, we look at her or him intently, as if to say, "Well, what do you think?" As you might predict, listeners gaze at speakers more than speakers gaze at listeners. In public speaking, you may scan hundreds of people to secure this feedback.

A second function is to inform the other person that the channel of communication is open and that he or she should now speak. You see this regularly in conversation, when one person asks a question or finishes a thought and then looks to you for a response. And one study found that eye contact was the most frequently noted nonverbal behavior used to tell library users that the librarian was approachable (Radford, 1998).

Eye movements may also signal the nature of a relationship, whether positive (an attentive glance) or negative (eye avoidance). You can also signal your power through **visual dominance** behavior (Exline, Ellyson, & Long, 1975). The average person, for example, maintains a high level of eye contact while listening and a lower level while speaking. When people want to signal dominance, they may reverse this pattern—maintaining a high level of eye contact while talking but a much lower level while listening.

By making eye contact you psychologically lessen the physical distance between yourself and another person. When you catch someone's eye at a party, for example, you become psychologically close though physically far apart.

Eye avoidance, too, can serve several different functions. When you avoid eye contact or avert your glance, you may help others maintain their privacy. For example, you may do this when you see a couple arguing in public. You turn your eyes away (though your eyes may be wide open) as if to say, "I don't mean to intrude; I respect your privacy," a behavior referred to as **civil inattention** (Goffman, 1971).

Eye avoidance can also signal lack of interest—in a person, a conversation, or some visual stimulus. At times, too, you may hide your eyes to block out unpleasant stimuli (a particularly gory or violent scene in a movie, for example) or close your eyes to block out visual stimuli and thus heighten other senses. For example, you may listen to music with your eyes closed. Lovers often close their eyes while kissing, and many prefer to make love in a dark or dimly lit room.

## Pupil Dilation

In the fifteenth and sixteenth centuries, Italian women put drops of belladonna (which literally means "beautiful woman") into their eyes to enlarge the pupils so that they would look more attractive. Contemporary **pupillometrics** research supports the intuitive logic of these women; dilated pupils are judged more attractive than constricted ones (Hess, 1975; Marshall, 1983). In one study, researchers retouched photographs of women; in half they enlarged the pupils, and in the other half they made them smaller (Hess, 1975). Men were then asked to judge the women's personalities from the photographs. The photos of women with small pupils drew responses such as "cold," "hard," and "selfish"; those with dilated pupils drew responses such as "feminine" and "soft." Interestingly, the male observers could not verbalize the reasons for their different perceptions. Pupil dilation and our reactions to changes in the pupil size of others may function below the level of conscious awareness.

Pupil size also reveals your interest and level of emotional arousal. Your pupils enlarge when you're interested in something or when you are emotionally aroused. When homosexuals and heterosexuals were shown pictures of nude bodies, the homosexuals' pupils dilated more when they viewed same-sex bodies, whereas the heterosexuals' pupils dilated more when they viewed opposite-sex bodies (Hess, Seltzer, & Schlien, 1965). These pupillary responses are also observed in persons with profound mental retardation (Chaney, Givens, Aoki, & Gombiner, 1989). Perhaps we judge dilated pupils as more attractive because we respond to them as indicative of a person's interest in us. And that may be the reason why both models and fuzzy beanbag toys have exceptionally large pupils.

## Space Communication

Space is an especially important factor in interpersonal communication, although we seldom think

---

# Building Communication Skills   Choosing a Seat

Look at the diagram here, which represents a table with 12 chairs, one of which is already occupied by the "boss." Below are listed five messages you might want to communicate. For each of these messages, indicate (a) where you would sit to communicate the desired message, and (b) any other messages that your seating position will make it easier for you to communicate.

1. You want to polish the apple and ingratiate yourself with your boss.

2. You aren't prepared and want to be ignored.

3. You want to challenge your boss on a certain policy that will come up for a vote.

4. You want to be accepted as a new (but important) member of the company.

5. You want to get to know the person already seated at position number 5.

*Every nonverbal (and verbal) message that you send has an impact, even the seat you select at a meeting. Your messages always reveal (to some extent) who you are and what others will think of you.*

about it. Edward T. Hall (1959, 1963, 1976) pioneered the study of spatial communication and called this research area **proxemics**. We can examine this broad area by looking at (1) proxemic distances and (2) territoriality.

## Proxemic Distances

Edward Hall (1959, 1963, 1976) distinguishes four **proxemic distances**, or **spatial distances**: the physical distances that define the types of relationships between people and the types of communication in which they are likely to engage (see Table 6.2).

**Intimate Distance.** In **intimate distance**, ranging from actual touching to 18 inches, the presence of the other individual is unmistakable. Each person experiences the sound, smell, and feel of the other's breath. You use intimate distance for lovemaking, comforting, and protecting. This distance is so short that most people don't consider it proper in public.

**Personal Distance.** **Personal distance** refers to the protective "bubble" that defines your personal space, ranging from 18 inches to 4 feet. This imaginary bubble keeps you protected and untouched by others. You can still hold or grasp another person at this distance, but only by extending your arms; this allows you to take certain individuals such as loved ones into your protective bubble. At the outer limit of personal distance, you can touch another person only if both of you extend your arms. This is the distance at which you conduct most of your interpersonal interactions; for example, talking with friends and family.

**Social Distance.** At **social distance**, ranging from 4 to 12 feet, you lose the visual detail you have at personal distance. You conduct impersonal business and interact at a social gathering at this social distance. The more distance you maintain in your interactions, the more formal they appear. In offices of high officials, the desks are positioned so the official is assured of at least this distance from clients.

**Public Distance.** **Public distance**, from 12 to more than 25 feet, protects you. At this distance you could take defensive action if threatened. On a public bus or train, for example, you might keep at least this distance from a drunken passenger. Although at this distance you lose fine details of the face and eyes, you're still close enough to see what is happening.

The specific distances that we maintain between ourselves and other people depend on a wide variety of factors (Burgoon, Buller, & Woodall, 1996; Burgoon & Bacue, 2003). Among the most significant are *gender* (in same-sex dyads women sit and stand closer to each other than do men, and people approach women more closely than they approach men); *age*

---

## Table 6.2 Relationships and Proxemic Distances

Note that these four distances can be further divided into close and far phases and that the far phase of one level (say, personal) blends into the close phase of the next level (social). Do your relationships also blend into one another? Or are, say, your personal relationships totally separate from your social relationships?

| Relationship | Distance | |
|---|---|---|
| Intimate relationship | Intimate distance | |
| | 0 ———————— 18 inches | |
| | close phase | far phase |
| Personal relationship | Personal distance | |
| | 1 ———————— 4 feet | |
| | close phase | far phase |
| Social relationship | Social distance | |
| | 4 ———————— 12 feet | |
| | close phase | far phase |
| Public relationship | Public distance | |
| | 12 ———————— 25+ feet | |
| | close phase | far phase |

## PROXEMICS

Like the close-talker in an episode of Seinfeld, one of your team members at work maintains an extremely close distance when talking. Coupled with the fact that this person is a heavy smoker and reeks of smoke, you need to say something.

WHAT DO YOU SAY?
*Through what channel?*

(people maintain closer distances with similarly aged others than they do with those much older or much younger); and *personality* (introverts and highly anxious people maintain greater distances than do extroverts). Not surprisingly, we maintain shorter distances with people we're familiar with than with strangers and with people we like than with those we don't like. One theoretical explanation of the dynamics of spatial distances is discussed in the accompanying Understanding Theory and Research box (on page 134).

## Territoriality

One of the most interesting concepts in ethology (the study of animals in their natural surroundings) is **territoriality**, a possessive or ownership reaction to an area of space or to particular objects. Two interesting dimensions of territoriality are territory types and territorial markers.

**Territory Types.**   Three types of territory are often distinguished: primary, secondary, and public (Altman, 1975). **Primary territories** are your exclusive preserve: your desk, room, house, or backyard, for example. In these areas you're in control. The effect is similar to the **home field advantage** that a sports team has when playing in its own ballpark. When you're in these home territories, you generally have greater influence over others than you would in someone else's territory. For example, in their own home or office, people generally take on a kind of leadership role; they initiate conversations, fill in silences, assume relaxed and comfortable postures, and maintain their positions with greater conviction. Because the territorial owner is dominant, you stand a better chance of getting your raise approved, your point accepted, or a contract resolved in your favor if you're in your own primary territory (home, office) rather than in someone else's (Marsh, 1988).

**Secondary territories**, although they don't belong to you, are associated with you—perhaps because you've occupied them for a long time or they were assigned to you. For example, your desk in a classroom may become a secondary territory if it is assigned to you or if you regularly occupy it and others treat it as yours. Your neighborhood turf, a cafeteria table where you usually sit, or a favorite corner of a local coffee shop may be secondary territories. You feel a certain "ownership-like" attachment to the place, even though it's really not yours in any legal sense.

**Public territories** are areas that are open to all people, such as a park, movie house, restaurant, or beach. European cafés, food courts in suburban malls, and the open areas in large city office buildings are public spaces that bring people together and stimulate communication.

The electronic revolution, however, may well change the role of public space in stimulating communication (Drucker & Gumpert, 1991; Gumpert & Drucker, 1995). For example, home shopping clubs make it less necessary for people to go downtown or to the mall, and shoppers consequently have less opportunity to run into other people and to talk and exchange news. Similarly, electronic mail permits us to communicate without talking and without leaving the house to mail a letter. Perhaps the greatest change is telecommuting (Giordano, 1989), in which workers can go to work without leaving their homes. The face-to-face communication that normally takes place in an office is replaced by communication via computer.

Territoriality is closely linked to **status**. Generally, the size and location of your territories signal your status within your social group. For example, male animals will stake out a particular territory and consider it their own. They will allow prospective mates

**Expectancy violations theory**, developed by Judee Burgoon, explains what happens when you increase or decrease the distance between yourself and another person in an interpersonal interaction (Burgoon, 1978; Burgoon & Bacue, 2003). Each culture has certain expectancies for the distance that people are expected to maintain in their conversations. And, of course, each person has certain idiosyncrasies. Together, these determine expected distance. If you violate the expected distance to a great extent (small violations most often go unnoticed), the relationship itself comes into focus; the other person begins to turn attention away from the topic of conversation to you and to your relationship with him or her.

If this other person perceives you positively—for example, if you're a high-status person or you're particularly attractive—then you'll be perceived even more positively if you violate the expected distance. If, on the other hand, you're perceived negatively and you violate the norm, you'll be perceived even more negatively.

### Working with Theories and Research

*Do your own experiences support this theory of space expectancy violations? What do you see happening when space expectations are violated?*

to enter but will defend the territory against entrance by others, especially by other males of the same species. The larger the animal's territory, the higher the status of animal within the herd. The size and location of human territories also say something about status (Mehrabian, 1976; Sommer, 1969). An apartment or office in midtown Manhattan or downtown Tokyo, for example, is extremely high-status territory. The cost of the territory restricts it to those who have lots of money.

**Territory Markers.** Much as animals mark their territory, humans mark theirs with three types of **markers**: central markers, boundary markers, and earmarkers (Hickson, Stacks, & Moore, 2003). **Central markers** are items you place in a territory to reserve it. For example, you place a drink at the bar, books on your desk, or a sweater over the chair to let others know that these territories belong to you.

**Boundary markers** set boundaries that divide your territory from "theirs." In the supermarket checkout line, the bar placed between your groceries and those of the person behind you is a boundary marker. Similarly, the armrests separating your seat from those of the people on either side at a movie theater and the molded plastic seats on a bus or train are boundary markers.

**Earmarkers**—a term taken from the practice of branding animals on their ears—are those identifying marks that indicate your possession of a territory or object. Trademarks, nameplates, and initials on a shirt or attaché case are all examples of earmarkers. Some teenagers, for example, perhaps because they can't yet own territories, often use markers to indicate a kind of pseudo-ownership or appropriation of someone else's or a public territory for their own use (Childress, 2004). Examples of graffiti and the markings of gang boundaries come quickly to mind.

## Artifactual Communication

**Artifactual communication** is communication via objects made by human hands. Thus, color, clothing, jewelry, and the decoration of space would be considered artifactual. Let's look at each of these briefly.

### Color Communication

There is some evidence that colors affect us physiologically. For example, respiratory movements increase with red light and decrease with blue light. Similarly, eye blinks increase in frequency when eyes are exposed to red light and decrease when exposed to blue. These responses seem consistent with our intuitive feelings about blue being more soothing and red more arousing. When a school changed the color of its walls from orange and white to blue, the blood pressure of the students decreased and their academic performance increased (Ketcham, 1958; Malandro, Barker, & Barker, 1989).

Color communication also influences perceptions and behaviors (Kanner, 1989). People's acceptance of a product, for example, is largely determined by its packaging, especially its color. In one study the very same coffee taken from a yellow can was described as weak, from a dark brown can as too strong, from a red can as rich, and from a blue can as mild. Even your acceptance of a person may depend on the colors he or she wears. Consider, for example, the comments of one color expert (Kanner, 1989): "If you have to pick the wardrobe for your defense lawyer heading into court and choose anything but blue, you deserve to lose the case." Black is so powerful it could work against the lawyer with the jury. Brown lacks sufficient authority. Green would probably elicit a negative response.

## Clothing and Body Adornment

People make inferences about who you are, at least in part, from the way you dress. Whether these inferences are accurate or not, they will influence what people think of you and how they react to you. Your socioeconomic class, your seriousness, your attitudes (for example, whether you're conservative or liberal), your concern for convention, your sense of style, and perhaps even your creativity will all be judged in part by the way you dress (Molloy, 1975, 1977, 1981; Burgoon, Buller, & Woodall, 1996; Knapp & Hall, 2005). In the business world, your clothing may communicate your position within the hierarchy and your willingness and desire to conform to the norms of the organization. It also may communicate your professionalism, which seems to be the reason why some organizations favor dress codes (Smith, M. H., 2003). On campus, college students will perceive an instructor dressed informally as friendly, fair, enthusiastic, and flexible; they will see the same instructor dressed formally as prepared, knowledgeable, and organized (Malandro, Barker, & Barker, 1989).

Try personalizing this brief discussion by considering, for example, how you'd dress in each of such situations as these:

- to interview for a job at a prestigious and conservative law firm
- to appear friendly but serious as you teach your first college class
- to appear as the trendiest partygoer at the trendiest spot in town
- to make your romantic partner's parents (you've been dating about six months), about whom you know very little, think you're absolutely wonderful
- to attend a parent–teacher conference (you're the parent) at your child's preschool and appear very

## CLOTHING COMMUNICATION

One of your friends has been passed over for promotion several times and you think you know the reason: Your friend dresses inappropriately, though generally not as bad as the guy in the photo. You want to help your friend.

*WHAT DO YOU SAY?*
*Through what channel? In what context?*

concerned and involved, though in truth you've not participated in any of the school's activities

Very likely you'd dress very differently in each of these situations, attesting to the importance of clothing in impression formation.

The way you wear your hair says something about your attitudes—from a concern about being up to date, to a desire to shock, to perhaps a lack of interest in appearances. Men with long hair will generally be judged as less conservative than those with shorter hair. Your jewelry also communicates about you. Wedding and engagement rings are obvious examples that communicate specific messages. College rings and political buttons likewise communicate specific messages. If you wear a Rolex watch or large precious stones, others are likely to infer that you're rich. Men who wear earrings will be judged differently from men who don't. What judgments are made will depend on who the receiver is, the communication context, and all the factors identified throughout this text.

Body piercings are now common, especially among the young. Nose, nipple, tongue, and belly button jewelry (among other piercings) send a variety of messages. Although people wearing such jewelry may wish to communicate positive meanings, research indicates that those interpreting these messages seem to infer that the wearer is communicating an unwillingness to conform to social norms and a willingness to take greater risks than people without such piercings (Forbes, 2001). It's worth noting that in a study of employers' perceptions, applicants with eyebrow piercings were rated and ranked significantly lower than those without such piercings (Acor, 2001). In another study, nose-pierced job candidates were scored lower on measures of credibility such as character and trust as well as sociability and hirability (Seiter & Sandry, 2003). And in health care situations, tattoos and piercings may communicate such undesirable traits as impulsiveness, unpredictability, and a tendency toward being reckless or violent (Rapsa & Cusack, 1990; Smith, M. H., 2003).

Tattoos whether temporary or permanent, likewise communicate a variety of messages—often the name of a loved one or some symbol of allegiance or affiliation. Tattoos also communicate to the wearers themselves. For example, tattooed students see themselves (and perhaps others do as well) as more adventurous, creative, individualistic, and risk-prone than those without tattoos (Drews, Allison, & Probst, 2000).

The accompanying Media Watch box continues this discussion of clothing by looking at clothing with specific verbal messages.

## Space Decoration

The way you decorate your private spaces also communicates about you. The office with a mahogany desk and bookcases and oriental rugs communicates your importance and status within an organization, just as a metal desk and bare floor indicate a worker much farther down in the hierarchy.

Similarly, people will make inferences about you based on the way you decorate your home. The expensiveness of the furnishings may communicate your status and wealth; their coordination may convey your sense of style. The magazines may reflect your interests, and the arrangement of chairs around a television set may reveal how important watching television is to you. The contents of bookcases lining the walls reveal the importance of reading in your life. In fact, there's probably little in your home that will not send messages from which others will draw inferences about you. Computers, wide-screen televisions, well-equipped kitchens, and oil paintings of great-grandparents, for example,

## MEDIA WATCH

# LEGIBLE CLOTHING

Legible clothing is anything that you wear that displays some verbal message; it's clothing that literally can be read. In some instances the message proclaims status; it tells others that you are, for example, rich or stylish or youthful. The Gucci or Louis Vuitton logos on your luggage communicate your financial status. In a similar way your sweatshirt with the word "Bulls" or "Pirates" emblazoned across it communicates your interest in sports and your favorite team.

Legible clothing is being bought and worn in record numbers. Many designers and manufacturers have their names integrated into the design of the clothing: DKNY, Calvin Klein, Armani, L. L. Bean, the Gap, and Old Navy are just a few examples. At the same time that you're paying extra to buy the brand name, you're also providing free advertising for the designer.

T-shirts and sweatshirts are especially popular as message senders. One study surveyed 600 male and female students as to the types of T-shirt messages they preferred (Sayre, 1992). Four messages were cited most often:

- Affiliation messages, such as a club or school name, communicate that you're a part of a larger group.

- Trophy names, such as those of a high-status concert or perhaps a ski lodge, say that you were in the right place at the right time.

- Metaphorical expressions, such as pictures of rock groups or famous athletes, reveal that you're part of a current trend.

- Personal messages, such as statements of beliefs or philosophies, tell others that you're willing to express your beliefs publicly.

## Increasing Media Literacy

*Affiliation messages may create problems when they identify the wearer as a member of a gang, because wearing gang colors can contribute to violence, especially in schools (Burke, 1993; Zimmerman, 2000). How do you feel about these and other provocative types of clothing messages? Do you feel that some clothing messages should be prohibited? If so, which ones? Or do you feel that such messages should be protected by the First Amendment to the Constitution, which guarantees freedom of speech?*

## TOUCH BOUNDARIES

A colleague at work continually touches you in passing—your arm, your shoulder, your waist. These touches are becoming more frequent and more intimate. You want this touching to stop.

WHAT DO YOU SAY?
*To whom? Through what channel?*

all say something about the people who live in the home.

Similarly, the absence of certain items will communicate something about you. Consider what messages you'd get from a home where no television, phone, or books could be seen.

People will also make judgments as to your personality on the basis of room decorations. Research finds, for example, that people will make judgments about your openness to new experiences (distinctive decorating usually communicates this, as would different types of books and magazines and travel souvenirs) and even about your conscientiousness, emotional stability, degree of extroversion, and agreeableness. Not surprisingly, bedrooms prove more revealing of personality than offices (Gosling, Ko, Mannarelli, & Morris, 2002).

## Touch Communication

The study of **touch communication**, technically referred to as **haptics**, suggests that touch is perhaps the most primitive form of communication (Montagu, 1971). Developmentally, touch is probably the first sense to be used. Even in the womb the child is stimulated by touch. Soon after birth the child is fondled, caressed, patted, and stroked. In turn, the child explores its world through touch. In a short time the child learns to communicate many different meanings through touch.

### The Meanings of Touch

Touch communicates a wide range of messages (Jones & Yarbrough, 1985). Here are five major types of messages that will illustrate this great variety.

■ Touch communicates positive feelings; for example, support, appreciation, inclusion, sexual interest or intent, composure, immediacy, affection,

trust, similarity and quality, and informality (Jones & Yarbrough, 1985; Burgoon, 1991). Touch also stimulates self-disclosure (Rabinowitz, 1991).

■ Touch often communicates your intention to play, either affectionately or aggressively.

■ Touch may control the behaviors, attitudes, or feelings of other people. To obtain compliance, for example, you touch a person to communicate "move over," "hurry," "stay here," or "do it." You might also touch a person to gain his or her attention, as if to say "look at me" or "look over here." In some situations touching can even amount to a kind of **nonverbal dominance** behavior. Touch even seems to increase a waitperson's tips. Researchers found that people who were touched by a female waitperson on the hand or shoulder tipped more than those who weren't touched (Crusco & Wetzel, 1984; Stephen & Zweigenhaft, 1986).

■ Ritualistic touching centers on greetings and departures; examples are shaking hands to say "hello" or "good-bye," hugging, kissing, or putting your arm around another's shoulder when greeting or saying farewell.

■ Task-related touching is associated with the performance of some function, as when you remove a speck of dust from another person's coat, help someone out of a car, or check someone's forehead for fever.

### Touch Avoidance

Much as you have a need and desire to touch and be touched, you also have a tendency to avoid touch from certain people or in certain circumstances (Andersen & Leibowitz, 1978). You may wish to examine your own **touch avoidance** tendency by taking the self-test on the following page.

# TEST YOURSELF

## Do You Avoid Touch?

This test is composed of 18 statements concerning how you feel about touching other people and being touched. Please indicate the degree to which each statement applies to you according to the following scale: 1 = strongly agree; 2 = agree; 3 = undecided; 4 = disagree; and 5 = strongly disagree.

_____ 1. A hug from a same-sex friend is a true sign of friendship.

_____ 2. Opposite-sex friends enjoy it when I touch them.

_____ 3. I often put my arm around friends of the same sex.

_____ 4. When I see two friends of the same sex hugging, it revolts me.

_____ 5. I like it when members of the opposite sex touch me.

_____ 6. People shouldn't be so uptight about touching persons of the same sex.

_____ 7. I think it is vulgar when members of the opposite sex touch me.

_____ 8. When a member of the opposite sex touches me, I find it unpleasant.

_____ 9. I wish I were free to show emotions by touching members of the same sex.

_____ 10. I'd enjoy giving a massage to an opposite-sex friend.

_____ 11. I enjoy kissing a person of the same sex.

_____ 12. I like to touch friends that are the same sex as I am.

_____ 13. Touching a friend of the same sex does not make me uncomfortable.

_____ 14. I find it enjoyable when my date and I embrace.

_____ 15. I enjoy getting a back rub from a member of the opposite sex.

_____ 16. I dislike kissing relatives of the same sex.

_____ 17. Intimate touching with members of the opposite sex is pleasurable.

_____ 18. I find it difficult to be touched by a member of my own sex.

**HOW DID YOU DO?** To score your touch avoidance questionnaire:

1. Reverse your scores for items 4, 7, 8, 16, and 18. Use these reversed scores in all future calculations.

2. To obtain your same-sex touch avoidance score (the extent to which you avoid touching members of your sex), total the scores for items 1, 3, 4, 6, 9, 11, 12, 13, 16, and 18.

3. To obtain your opposite-sex touch avoidance score (the extent to which you avoid touching members of the opposite sex), total the scores for items 2, 5, 7, 8, 10, 14, 15, and 17.

4. To obtain your total touch avoidance score, add the subtotals from steps 2 and 3.

The higher the score, the higher the touch avoidance—that is, the greater your tendency to avoid touch. In studies by Andersen and Leibowitz (1978), who constructed this test, average opposite-sex touch avoidance scores were 12.9 for males and 14.85 for females. Average same-sex touch avoidance scores were 26.43 for males and 21.70 for females. How do your scores compare with those of the college students in Andersen and Leibowitz's study? Is your touch avoidance likely to be higher when you are interacting with persons who are culturally different from you? Can you identify types of people and types of situations in which your touch avoidance would be especially high? Especially low?

**WHAT WILL YOU DO?** Are you satisfied with your score? Would you like to change your touch avoidance tendencies? What might you do about them?

Source: From "The Development and Nature of the Construct Touch Avoidance" by Andersen et al., _Journal of Nonverbal Behavior_, 3(2) 89–106. With kind permission from Springer Science and Business Media.

Researchers using the self-test presented here have found several interesting connections between touch avoidance and other factors (Andersen & Liebowitz, 1978). For example, touch avoidance is positively related to communication apprehension. If you have a strong fear of oral communication, then you probably also have strong touch avoidance tendencies. Touch avoidance is also high in those who self-disclose less.

Both touch and self-disclosure are intimate forms of communication. People who are reluctant to get close to another person by self-disclosing also seem reluctant to get close by touching.

Older people avoid touch with opposite-sex persons more than younger people do. As people get older they're touched less by members of the opposite sex; this decreased frequency of touching may lead them to avoid touching.

Not surprisingly, touch also varies with your relationship stage. In the early stages of a relationship, you touch little; in intermediate stages (involvement and intimacy), you touch a great deal; and at stable or deteriorating stages, you again touch little (Guerrero & Andersen, 1991, 1994).

## Paralanguage: The Vocal Channel

**Paralanguage** is the vocal but nonverbal dimension of speech. It has to do not with what you say but with how you say it. A traditional exercise students use to increase their ability to express different emotions, feelings, and attitudes is to repeat a sentence while accenting or stressing different words. One popular sentence is, "Is this the face that launched a thousand ships?" Significant differences in meaning are easily communicated depending on where the speaker places the stress. Consider the following variations:

- Is *this* the face that launched a thousand ships?
- Is this the *face* that launched a thousand ships?
- Is this the face that *launched* a thousand ships?
- Is this the face that launched a *thousand ships*?

Each sentence communicates something different; in fact, each asks a different question, even though the words are exactly the same. All that distinguishes the sentences is stress, one aspect of paralanguage. In addition to stress and **pitch** (highness or lowness), paralanguage includes such **voice qualities** as **rate** (speed), **volume** (loudness), rhythm, and pauses or hesitations as well as the vocalizations you make in crying, whispering, moaning, belching, yawning, and yelling (Trager, 1958, 1961; Argyle, 1988). A variation in any of these features communicates. When you speak quickly, for example, you communicate something different from when you speak slowly. Even though the words may be the same, if the speed (or volume, rhythm, or pitch) differs, the meanings people receive will also differ. The Building Communication Skills exercise, "Expressing Praise and Criticism," explores the different meanings that variations in paralanguage (and other nonverbal signals) can communicate.

### Judgments about People

Paralanguage cues are often used as a basis for judgments about people; for example, evaluations of their emotional state or even their personality. A listener can accurately judge the emotional state of a speaker from vocal expression alone if both speaker and listener speak the same language. Paralanguage cues are not so accurate when used to communicate emotions to those who speak a different language (Albas, McCluskey, & Albas, 1976). Also, some emotions are easier to identify than others; it's easy to distinguish between hate and sympathy but more difficult to distinguish between fear and anxiety. And, of course, listeners vary in their

---

**Building Communication Skills** Expressing Praise and Criticism

Consider how nonverbal messages can communicate praise and criticism by reading each of the following statements, first to communicate praise and second, criticism. In the second and third columns, record the nonverbal signals you used to help you communicate these differences in meaning between praise and criticism.

| Message | Nonverbal cues to communicate praise | Nonverbal cues to communicate criticism |
| --- | --- | --- |
| You lost weight. | | |
| You look happy. | | |
| You're an expert. | | |
| Your parents are something else. | | |

*You cannot speak a sentence without using nonverbal signals, and these signals influence the meaning the receiver gets. Acquiring the skills of nonverbal communication will help you communicate your meanings more effectively whether in interpersonal, small group, or public speaking.*

ability to decode, and speakers in their ability to encode emotions (Scherer, 1986).

### Judgments about Communication Effectiveness

In one-way communication (when one person is doing all or most of the speaking and the other person is doing all or most of the listening), those who talk fast (about 50 percent faster than normal) are more persuasive (MacLachlan, 1979). People agree more with a fast speaker than with a slow speaker and find the fast speaker more intelligent and objective.

When we look at comprehension, rapid speech shows an interesting effect. When the speaking rate is increased by 50 percent, the comprehension level drops by only 5 percent. When the rate is doubled, the comprehension level drops only 10 percent. These 5 and 10 percent losses are more than offset by the increased speed; thus, the faster rates are much more efficient in communicating information. If speeds are more than twice the rate of normal speech, however, comprehension begins to fall dramatically.

Do exercise caution in applying this research to all forms of communication (MacLachlan, 1979). For example, if you increase your rate to increase efficiency, you may create an impression so unnatural that others will focus on your speed instead of your meaning.

## Silence

Like words and gestures, **silence**, too, communicates important meanings and serves important functions (Johannesen, 1974; Jaworski, 1993). Silence allows the speaker *time to think*, time to formulate and organize his or her verbal communications. Before messages of intense conflict, as well as before those confessing un-dying love, there's often silence. Again, silence seems to prepare the receiver for the importance of these future messages.

Some people use silence as a *weapon* to hurt others. We often speak of giving someone "the silent treatment." After a conflict, for example, one or both individuals may remain silent as a kind of punishment. Silence used to hurt others may also take the form of refusing to acknowledge the presence of another person, as in disconfirmation (see Unit 5); here silence is a dramatic demonstration of the total indifference one person feels toward the other.

Sometimes silence is used as a *"response to personal anxiety,"* shyness, or threats. You may feel anx-

ious or shy among new people and prefer to remain silent. By remaining silent you preclude the chance of rejection. Only when you break your silence and make an attempt to communicate with another person do you risk rejection.

Silence may be used to *prevent communication* of certain messages. In conflict situations silence is sometimes used to prevent certain topics from surfacing and to prevent one or both parties from saying things they may later regret. In such situations silence often allows us time to cool off before expressing hatred, severe criticism, or personal attacks—which, as we know, are irreversible.

Like the eyes, face, and hands, silence can also be used to *communicate emotional responses* (Ehrenhaus, 1988). Sometimes silence communicates a determination to be uncooperative or defiant; by refusing to engage in verbal communication, you defy the authority or the legitimacy of the other person's position. Silence is often used to communicate annoyance, particularly when accompanied by a pouting expression, arms crossed in front of the chest, and nostrils flared. Silence may express affection or love, especially when coupled with long and longing gazes into each other's eyes.

Of course, you may also use silence when you simply have *nothing to say*, when nothing occurs to you, or when you don't want to say anything. James Russell Lowell expressed this best: "Blessed are they who have nothing to say, and who cannot be persuaded to say it." Silence may also be used to avoid responsibility for any wrongdoing (Beach, 1990–91).

## Time Communication

The study of **temporal communication**, known technically as **chronemics**, concerns the use of time—how you organize it, react to it, and communicate messages through it (Bruneau, 1985, 1990). Consider, for example, your **psychological time** orientation; the emphasis you place on the past, present, and future. In a past orientation, you have special reverence for the past. You relive old times and regard old methods as the best. You see events as circular and recurring, so the wisdom of yesterday is applicable also to today and tomorrow. In a present orientation, however, you live in the present: for now, not tomorrow. In a future orientation, you look toward and live for the future. You save today, work hard in college, and deny yourself luxuries because you're preparing for the future. Before reading more about time, take the following self-test.

# TEST YOURSELF

## What Time Do You Have?

For each statement, indicate whether the statement is true (T) or false (F) in relation to your general attitude and behavior. (A few statements are purposely repeated to facilitate scoring and analysis of your responses.)

_____ 1. Meeting tomorrow's deadlines and doing other necessary work comes before tonight's partying.

_____ 2. I meet my obligations to friends and authorities on time.

_____ 3. I complete projects on time by making steady progress.

_____ 4. I am able to resist temptations when I know there is work to be done.

_____ 5. I keep working at a difficult, uninteresting task if it will help me get ahead.

_____ 6. If things don't get done on time, I don't worry about it.

_____ 7. I think that it's useless to plan too far ahead, because things hardly ever come out the way you planned anyway.

_____ 8. I try to live one day at a time.

_____ 9. I live to make better what is rather than to be concerned about what will be.

_____ 10. It seems to me that it doesn't make sense to worry about the future, since fate determines that whatever will be, will be.

_____ 11. I believe that getting together with friends to party is one of life's important pleasures.

_____ 12. I do things impulsively, making decisions on the spur of the moment.

_____ 13. I take risks to put excitement in my life.

_____ 14. I get drunk at parties.

_____ 15. It's fun to gamble.

_____ 16. Thinking about the future is pleasant to me.

_____ 17. When I want to achieve something, I set sub-goals and consider specific means for reaching those goals.

_____ 18. It seems to me that my career path is pretty well laid out.

_____ 19. It upsets me to be late for appointments.

_____ 20. I meet my obligations to friends and authorities on time.

_____ 21. I get irritated at people who keep me waiting when we've agreed to meet at a given time.

_____ 22. It makes sense to invest a substantial part of my income in insurance premiums.

_____ 23. I believe that "A stitch in time saves nine."

_____ 24. I believe that "A bird in the hand is worth two in the bush."

_____ 25. I believe it is important to save for a rainy day.

_____ 26. I believe a person's day should be planned each morning.

_____ 27. I make lists of things I must do.

_____ 28. When I want to achieve something, I set sub-goals and consider specific means for reaching those goals.

_____ 29. I believe that "A stitch in time saves nine."

**HOW DID YOU DO?** This time test measures seven different factors. If you selected true (T) for all or most of the statements within any given factor, you are probably high on that factor. If you selected false (F) for all or most of the statements within any given factor, you are probably low on that factor.

The first factor, measured by items 1–5, is a future, work motivation, perseverance orientation. These people have a strong work ethic and are committed to completing a task despite difficulties and temptations. The second factor (items 6–10) is a present, fatalistic, worry-free orientation. High scorers on this factor live one day at a time, not necessarily to enjoy the day but to avoid planning for the next day or anxiety about the future.

The third factor (items 11–15) is a present, pleasure-seeking, partying orientation. These people enjoy the present, take risks, and engage in a variety of impulsive actions. The fourth factor (items 16–18) is a future, goal-seeking, planning orientation. These people derive special pleasure from planning and achieving a variety of goals.

The fifth factor (items 19–21) is a time-sensitivity orientation. People who score high are especially sensitive to time and its role in social obligations. The sixth factor (items 22–25) is a future, practical action orientation. These people do what they have to do—take practical actions—to achieve the future they want.

The seventh factor (items 26–29) is a future, somewhat obsessive daily planning orientation. High scorers on this factor make daily "to do" lists and devote great attention to specific details.

**WHAT WILL YOU DO?** Now that you have some idea of how you treat time, consider how these attitudes and behaviors work for you. For example, will your time orientations help you achieve your social and professional goals? If not, what might you do about changing these attitudes and behaviors?

Source: From "Time in Perspective" by Alexander Gonzalez and Philip G. Zimbardo in _Psychology Today_, V. 19, pp. 20–26. Reprinted with permission of _Psychology Today_ magazine, Copyright © 1985.

# REFLECTIONS
## ON ETHICS

## Silence

Remaining silent is at times your right. For example, you have the right to remain silent so as not to incriminate yourself. You have a right to protect your privacy —to withhold information that has no bearing on the matter at hand. And thus, your previous relationship history, affectional orientation, or religion is usually irrelevant to your ability to function in a job, and thus may be kept private in most job-related situations. On the other hand, these issues may be relevant when, for example, you're about to enter a more intimate phase of a relationship—then there may be an obligation to reveal information about yourself that could have been kept hidden at earlier relationship stages.

At other times, however, you have an obligation *not* to remain silent; and in fact in some cases it may be unlawful to say nothing. For example, you do not have the right to remain silent and to refuse to reveal information about crimes you've seen others commit. You have

a legal obligation to report such crimes and in some cases even suspicions of crime. Psychiatrists, clergy, and lawyers—fortunately or unfortunately—are often exempt from this requirement to reveal information about criminal activities when the information had been gained through privileged communication with clients.

### Ethical Choice Point

*On your way to work, you witness a father verbally abusing his three-year-old child. You worry that he might psychologically harm the child, and your first impulse is to speak up and tell this man that verbal abuse can have lasting effects on the child and often leads to physical abuse. At the same time, you don't want to interfere with his right to speak to his child, and you certainly don't want to make him angrier. What is your ethical obligation in this case? What would you do in this situation?*

---

The time orientation you develop depends largely on your socioeconomic class and your personal experiences (Gonzalez & Zimbardo, 1985). For example, parents with unskilled and semiskilled occupations are likely to teach their children a present-orientated fatalism and a belief that enjoying yourself is more important than planning for the future. Parents who are teachers, managers, and in other professions, teach their children the importance of planning and preparing for the future, along with strategies for success.

Different **cultural time** perspectives also account for much intercultural misunderstanding, as different cultures often teach their members drastically different time orientations. For example, members of some Latin cultures would rather be late for an appointment than end a conversation abruptly or before it has come to a natural end. So the Latin may see lateness as a result of politeness. But others may see this as impolite to the person with whom he or she had the appointment (Hall & Hall, 1987).

## Smell Communication

Smell communication, or **olfactory communication**, is extremely important in a wide variety of situations and is now big business. For example, there's some evidence (though clearly not very conclusive evidence) that the smell of lemon contributes to a perception of health, the smells of lavender and eu-

calyptus increase alertness, and the smell of rose oil reduces blood pressure. Findings such as these have contributed to the growth of aromatherapy and to a new profession of aromatherapists (Furlow, 1996). Because humans possess "denser skin concentrations of scent glands than almost any other mammal," it has been argued that it only remains for us to discover how we use scent to communicate a wide variety of messages (Furlow, 1996, p. 41). Research also finds that smells can influence your body's chemistry, which in turn influences your emotional state. For example, the smell of chocolate results in the reduction of theta brain waves, which produces a sense of relaxation and a reduced level of attention (Martin, 1998).

Here are some of the most important messages scent seems to communicate.

- *Attraction messages.* Humans use perfumes, colognes, after-shave lotions, powders, and the like to enhance their attractiveness to others and to themselves. After all, you also smell yourself. When the smells are pleasant, you feel better about yourself. Women, research finds, prefer the scent of men who bear a close genetic similarity to themselves; this finding may account in part for our attraction to people much like ourselves (Ober, Weitkamp, Cox, Dytch, Kostyu, & Elias, 1997; Wade, 2002). And although we often think of women as the primary users of perfumes and scents, increasingly men are using them as well—not only the cologne and aftershave lotions they have long used but also, more recently, body sprays, which have become big business with a market estimated at $180 million (Dell, 2005).

- *Taste messages.* Without smell, taste would be severely impaired. For example, without smell it would be extremely difficult to taste the difference between a raw potato and an apple. Street vendors selling hot dogs, sausages, and similar foods are aided greatly by the smells, which stimulate the appetites of passersby.

- *Memory messages.* Smell is a powerful memory aid; you often recall situations from months and even years ago when you encounter a similar smell.

- *Identification messages.* Smell is often used to create an image or an identity for a product. Advertisers and manufacturers spend millions of dollars each year creating scents for cleaning products and toothpastes, for example, which have nothing to do with their cleaning power. There's also evidence that we can identify specific significant others by smell. For example, young children were able to identify the T-shirts of their brothers and sisters solely on the basis of smell (Porter & Moore, 1981).

## CULTURE AND NONVERBAL COMMUNICATION

This chapter has already noted a few cultural and gender differences in nonverbal communication. The importance of culture in certain areas of nonverbal communication, however, has become the focus of sustained research. Here we consider just a sampling of research on gesture, facial expression, eye communication, colors, touch, silence, and time.

### Culture and Gesture

There is much variation in gestures and their meanings among different cultures (Axtell, 1993). Consider a few common gestures that you might use even without thinking, but that could easily get you into trouble if you used them in another culture (also, take a look at Figure 6.1):

- Folding your arms over your chest would be considered defiant and disrespectful in Fiji.
- Waving your hand would be insulting in Nigeria and Greece.
- Gesturing with the thumb up would be rude in Australia.
- Tapping your two index fingers together would be considered an invitation to sleep together in Egypt.

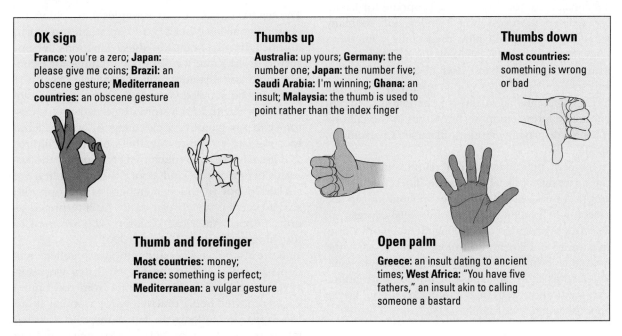

**OK sign**

**France:** you're a zero; **Japan:** please give me coins; **Brazil:** an obscene gesture; **Mediterranean countries:** an obscene gesture

**Thumbs up**

**Australia:** up yours; **Germany:** the number one; **Japan:** the number five; **Saudi Arabia:** I'm winning; **Ghana:** an insult; **Malaysia:** the thumb is used to point rather than the index finger

**Thumbs down**

**Most countries:** something is wrong or bad

**Thumb and forefinger**

**Most countries:** money; **France:** something is perfect; **Mediterranean:** a vulgar gesture

**Open palm**

**Greece:** an insult dating to ancient times; **West Africa:** "You have five fathers," an insult akin to calling someone a bastard

**FIGURE 6.1   Some Cultural Meanings of Gestures**

Cultural differences in the meanings of nonverbal gestures are often significant. The over-the-head clasped hands that signify victory to an American may signify friendship to a Russian. To an American, holding up two fingers to make a V signifies victory or peace. To certain South Americans, however, it is an obscene gesture that corresponds to the American's extended middle finger. This figure highlights some additional nonverbal differences. Can you identify others?

- Pointing with your index finger would be impolite in many Middle Eastern countries.

- Bowing to a lesser degree than your host would be considered a statement of your superiority in Japan.

- Inserting your thumb between your index and middle finger in a clenched fist would be viewed as a wish that evil fall on the person in some African countries.

- Resting your feet on a table or chair would be insulting and disrespectful in some Middle Eastern cultures.

## Culture and Facial Expression

The wide variations in facial communication that we observe in different cultures seem to reflect different attitudes about what reactions are permissible in public rather than differences in the way humans show emotions. For example, Japanese and American students watched a film of a surgical operation (Ekman, 1985). The students were videotaped both in an interview situation about the film and alone while watching the film. When alone the students showed very similar reactions; in the interview, however, the American students displayed facial expressions indicating displeasure, whereas the Japanese students did not show any great emotion. Similarly, it's considered "forward" or inappropriate for Japanese women to reveal broad smiles, and so many Japanese women will hide their smile, sometimes with their hands (Ma, 1996). Women in the United States, on the other hand, have no such restrictions and so are more likely to smile openly. Thus, the difference may not be in the way people in different cultures express emotions but rather in the cultural rules for displaying emotions in public (Matsumoto, 1991).

Similarly, people in different cultures may decode the meanings of facial expression differently. For example, American and Japanese students judged the meaning of a smiling and a neutral facial expression. The Americans rated the smiling face as more attractive, more intelligent, and more sociable than the neutral face. In contrast, the Japanese rated the smiling face as more sociable but not as more attractive—and they rated the neutral face as more intelligent (Matsumoto & Kudoh, 1993).

## Culture and Eye Communication

Not surprisingly, eye messages vary with both culture and gender. Americans, for example, consider direct eye contact an expression of honesty and forthrightness, but the Japanese often view this as a lack of respect. A Japanese person will glance at the other person's face rarely, and then only for very short periods (Axtell, 1990). Interpreting another's eye contact messages with your own cultural rules is a risky undertaking; eye movements that you may interpret as insulting may have been intended to show respect.

Women make eye contact more and maintain it longer (both in speaking and in listening) than men. This holds true whether women are interacting with other women or with men. This difference in eye behavior may result from women's greater tendency to display their emotions (Wood, 1994). When women interact with other women, they display affiliative and supportive eye contact, whereas when men interact with other men, they avert their gaze (Gamble & Gamble, 2003).

## Culture and Colors

Colors vary greatly in their meanings from one culture to another. Some of these cultural differences are summed up in Table 6.3; but before looking at the table, think about the meanings given to such colors as red, green, black, white, blue, yellow, and purple in your own culture or cultures.

## Culture and Touch

The several functions and examples of touching discussed so far have been based on studies in North America; in other cultures these functions are not served in the same way. In some cultures, for example, some task-related touching is viewed negatively and is to be avoided. Among Koreans, it is considered disrespectful for a store owner to touch a customer in, say, handing back change; it is considered too intimate a gesture. Members of other cultures that are used to such touching may consider the Korean's behavior cold and aloof. Muslim children are socialized not to touch members of the opposite sex, a practice which can easily be interpreted as unfriendly by American children who are used to touching each other (Dresser, 1996).

For example, in one study on touch, college students in Japan and in the United States were surveyed (Barnlund, 1989). Students from the United States reported being touched twice as much as did the Japanese students. In Japan there is a strong taboo against touching between strangers, and the Japanese are therefore especially careful to maintain sufficient distance.

Some cultures—including many in southern Europe and the Middle East—are contact cultures; others are noncontact cultures, such as those of north-

## Table 6.3 Cultural Meanings and Color

This table, constructed from research reported by various culture watchers, illustrates only some of the different meanings that colors may communicate and especially how they are viewed in different cultures (Dreyfuss, 1971; Hoft, 1995; Dresser, 1996; Singh & Pereira, 2005). As you read this table consider the meanings you give to these colors and where your meanings came from.

| Color | Cultural Meanings and Comments |
|---|---|
| Red | In China red signifies prosperity and rebirth and is used for festive and joyous occasions; in France and the United Kingdom it indicates masculinity, in many African countries blasphemy or death, and in Japan anger and danger. Red ink, especially among Korean Buddhists, is used only to write a person's name at the time of death or on the anniversary of the person's death; this can create problems when American teachers use red ink to mark homework. |
| Green | In the United States green signifies capitalism, go ahead, and envy; in Ireland patriotism; among some Native Americans femininity; to the Egyptians fertility and strength; and to the Japanese youth and energy. |
| Black | In Thailand black signifies old age, in parts of Malaysia courage, and in much of Europe death. |
| White | In Thailand white signifies purity, in many Muslim and Hindu cultures purity and peace, and in Japan and other Asian countries death and mourning. |
| Blue | In Iran blue signifies something negative, in Ghana joy; among the Cherokee it signifies defeat, for the Egyptian virtue and truth, and for the Greek national pride. |
| Yellow | In China yellow signifies wealth and authority; in the United States caution, cowardice, and support for troops; in Egypt happiness and prosperity; and in many countries throughout the world femininity. |
| Purple | In Latin America purple signifies death, in Europe royalty, in Egypt virtue and faith, in Japan grace and nobility, in China barbarism, and in the United States nobility and bravery. |

ern Europe and Japan. Members of contact cultures maintain close distances, touch one another in conversation, face one another more directly, and maintain longer and more focused eye contact. Members of noncontact cultures maintain greater distance in their interactions, touch one another rarely (if at all), avoid facing one another directly, and maintain much less direct eye contact. As a result, southern Europeans may perceive northern Europeans and Japanese as cold, distant, and uninvolved. Southern Europeans may in turn be perceived as pushy, aggressive, and inappropriately intimate.

## Culture, Paralanguage, and Silence

Cultural differences also need to be taken into consideration is evaluating the results of the studies on speech rate, as different cultures view speech rate differently. For example, in one study Korean male speakers who spoke rapidly were given unfavorable credibility ratings, as opposed to the results obtained by Americans who spoke rapidly (Lee & Boster, 1992). Researchers have suggested that in individualistic societies a rapid-rate speaker is seen as more competent than a slow-rate speaker, whereas in collectivist cultures a speaker who uses a slower rate is judged as more competent.

Similarly, all cultures do not view silence as functioning in the same way (Vainiomaki, 2004). In the United States, for example, silence is often interpreted negatively. At a business meeting or even in an informal social group, the silent member may be seen as not listening, having nothing interesting to add, not understanding the issues, being insensitive, or being too self-absorbed to focus on the messages of others. Other cultures, however, view silence more positively. In many situations in Japan, for example, silence is a response that is considered more appropriate than speech (Haga, 1988).

The traditional Apache, to take another example, regard silence very differently than do European Americans (Basso, 1972). Among the Apache, mutual friends do not feel the need to introduce strangers who may be working in the same area or on the same project. The strangers may remain silent for several days. This period enables them to observe and to form judgments about each other. Once this assessment is made, the individuals talk. When courting, especially during the initial stages, the Apache remain silent for hours; if they do talk, they generally talk very little. Only after a couple has been dating for several months will they have lengthy conversations. These periods of silence are generally attributed to shyness or self-consciousness; but the use of silence is explicitly taught to Apache women, who are especially discouraged from engaging in long discussions with their dates. Silence during courtship is a sign of modesty to many Apache.

## Culture and Time

People in different cultures view time very differently. Here are three aspects of time and some cultural differences: the social clock, formal and informal time, and monochronism versus polychronism.

### The Social Clock

Your culture maintains an implicit "schedule" for the right time to do a variety of important things; for example, the right time to start dating, to finish college, to buy your own home, or to have a child. This unspoken timetable provides you with a **social clock**, a schedule that tells you if you're keeping pace with your peers, are ahead of them, or are falling behind (Neugarten, 1979). On the basis of this social clock, which you learned as you grew up, you evaluate your own social and professional development. If you're in synch with the rest of your peers—for example, if you started dating at the "appropriate" age or if you're finishing college at the "appropriate" age—then you'll feel well adjusted, competent, and a part of the group. If you're late, you'll probably experience feelings of dissatisfaction. And although in some cultures the social clock is becoming more flexible and more tolerant of deviations from the conventional timetable, it still exerts pressure to keep pace with your peers (Peterson, 1996).

### Formal and Informal Time

Days are astronomically determined by the earth's rotation on its axis, months by the moon's movement around the earth, and years by the earth's rotation around the sun. But the rest of our time divisions are cultural (largely religious) in origin.

In the United States and in most of the world, formal time divisions include seconds, minutes, hours, days, weeks, months, and years. Some cultures, however, may use phases of the moon or the seasons to delineate their most important time periods. Other formal time units exist, too. For example, in the United States, if your college is on the semester system, your courses are divided into 50- or 75-minute periods that meet two or three times a week for 14-week periods. Eight semesters of 15 or 16 periods per week equal a college education. As these examples illustrate, formal time units are arbitrary. The culture establishes them for convenience.

**Informal time** terms are more hazy and subject to interpretation—terms such as "forever," "immediately," "soon," "right away," or "as soon as possible." This type of time creates the most communication problems, because the terms have different meanings for different people.

Attitudes toward both formal and informal time vary from one culture to another. One study, for example, measured the accuracy of clocks in six cultures—those of Japan, Indonesia, Italy, England, Taiwan, and the United States. Japan had the most accurate and Indonesia had the least accurate clocks. The researchers also measured the speed at which people in these six cultures walked, and results showed that the Japanese walked the fastest, the Indonesians the slowest (LeVine & Bartlett, 1984).

---

### Table 6.4 Monochronic and Polychronic Time

As you read down this table, based on Hall and Hall (1987), note the potential for miscommunication that these differences might create when M-time and P-time people interact. Have any of these differences ever created interpersonal misunderstandings for you?

| The Monochronic-Time Person | The Polychronic-Time Person |
| --- | --- |
| does one thing at a time | does several things at once |
| treats time schedules and plans very seriously; feels they may be broken only for the most serious of reasons | treats time schedules and plans as useful (not sacred); feels they may be broken for a variety of causes |
| considers the job the most important part of life, ahead of even family | considers the family and interpersonal relationships more important than the job |
| considers privacy extremely important; seldom borrows or lends to others; works independently | is actively involved with others; works in the presence of and with lots of people at the same time |

## Monochronism and Polychronism

Another important distinction is that between **monochronic** and **polychronic time orientations** (Hall, 1959, 1976, 1987). Monochronic people or cultures—such as those of the United States, Germany, Scandinavia, and Switzerland—generally schedule one thing at a time. In these cultures time is compartmentalized and there is a time for everything. Polychronic people or cultures, on the other hand—groups such as Latin Americans, Mediterranean people, and Arabs—tend to schedule more than one thing at the same time. Eating, conducting business with several different people, and taking care of family matters may all be conducted simultaneously. No culture is entirely monochronic or polychronic; rather, these are general tendencies that are found across a large part of the culture. Some cultures combine both time orientations; in Japan and in some American groups, for example, both orientations are found. Table 6.4 on page 146 identifies some of the distinctions between these two time orientations.

## SUMMARY: NONVERBAL MESSAGES

In this unit we explored nonverbal communication—communication without words. We considered body movements, facial and eye movements, spatial and territorial communication, artifactual communication, touch communication, paralanguage, silence, time communication, and smell communication. Finally, we looked at cultural variations in many types of nonverbal communication.

1. Nonverbal messages may accent or emphasize a part of a verbal message; complement or add nuances of meaning not communicated by a verbal message; contradict verbal messages (for example, when you cross your fingers or wink to indicate that you're lying); regulate, control, or show a wish to control the flow of verbal messages; repeat or restate a verbal message; or substitute for or take the place of verbal messages.

2. Nonverbal messages serve important communications functions: They help us form and manage impressions, form and define relationships, structure conversation and social interaction, influence others, and express emotions.

3. The five categories of body movements are emblems (nonverbal behaviors that directly translate words or phrases); illustrators (nonverbal behaviors that accompany and literally "illustrate" verbal messages); affect displays (nonverbal movements that communicate emotional meaning); regulators (nonverbal movements that coordinate, monitor, maintain, or control the speaking of another individual); and adaptors (nonverbal behaviors that are emitted without conscious awareness and that usually serve some kind of need, as in scratching an itch).

4. Facial movements may communicate a variety of emotions. The most frequently studied are happiness, surprise, fear, anger, sadness, disgust, and contempt. Facial management techniques enable you to control the extent to which you reveal the emotions you feel.

5. The facial feedback hypothesis claims that facial display of an emotion can lead to physiological and psychological changes.

6. Through eye contact you may seek feedback, signal others to speak, indicate the nature of a relationship, or compensate for increased physical distance. Eye avoidance may help you avoid prying or may signal a lack of interest.

7. Pupil enlargement shows a person's level of interest and positive emotional arousal.

8. Proxemics is the study of the communicative functions of space and spatial relationships. Four major proxemic distances are (1) intimate distance, ranging from actual touching to 18 inches; (2) personal distance, ranging from 18 inches to 4 feet; (3) social distance, ranging from 4 to 12 feet; and (4) public distance, ranging from 12 to more than 25 feet.

9. Your treatment of space is influenced by such factors as status, culture, context, subject matter, gender, age, and positive or negative evaluation of the other person.

10. Territoriality has to do with your possessive reaction to an area of space or to particular objects.

11. Artifactual communication consists of messages conveyed through human-made articles; for example, communication through color, clothing and body adornment, and space decoration.

12. The study of haptics indicates that touch may convey a variety of meanings, the most important being positive affect, playfulness, control, ritual, and task-relatedness. Touch avoidance is the desire to avoid touching and being touched by others.

13. Paralanguage involves the vocal but nonverbal dimensions of speech. It includes rate, pitch, volume, rhythm, and vocal quality as well as pauses and hesitations. Paralanguage helps us make judgments about people, their emotions, and their believability.

14. Silence may communicate a variety of meanings, from messages aimed at hurting another (the silent treatment) to deep emotional responses.

15. The study of time communication (chronemics) explores the messages communicated by our treatment of time.

16. Smell can communicate messages of attraction, taste, memory, and identification.

17. Among the cultural differences that researchers have focused on are facial expressions and displays, eye communication, the meanings of color, the appropriateness and uses of touch, the uses of silence, and the ways in which different cultures treat time.

# KEY TERMS IN NONVERBAL MESSAGES

adaptors (p. **127**)
affect displays (p. **127**)
alter-adaptors (p. **127**)
artifactual communication (p. **134**)
attractiveness (p. **128**)
boundary marker (p. **134**)
central marker (p. **134**)
chronemics (p. **140**)
civil inattention (p. **131**)
color communication (p. **135**)
cultural time (p. **142**)
earmarker (p. **134**)
emblems (p. **127**)
expectancy violations theory (p. **134**)

facial feedback hypothesis (p. **130**)
facial management techniques (p. **129**)
haptics (p. **137**)
home field advantage (p. **133**)
illustrators (p. **127**)
informal time (p. **146**)
intimate distance (p. **132**)
kinesics (p. **127**)
markers (p. **134**)
monochronic time orientation (p. **147**)
nonverbal communication (p. **124**)
nonverbal dominance (p. **137**)

object-adaptors (p. **127**)
olfactory communication (p. **142**)
paralanguage (p. **139**)
personal distance (p. **132**)
pitch (p. **139**)
polychronic time orientation (p. **147**)
primary territories (p. **133**)
proxemic distances (p. **132**)
proxemics (p. **132**)
psychological time (p. **140**)
public distance (p. **132**)
public territories (p. **133**)
pupillometrics (p. **131**)
rate (p. **139**)
regulators (p. **127**)

secondary territories (p. **133**)
self-adaptors (p. **127**)
silence (p. **140**)
social clock (p. **146**)
social distance (p. **132**)
spatial distance (p. **132**)
status (p. **133**)
temporal communication (p. **140**)
territoriality (p. **133**)
touch avoidance (p. **137**)
touch communication (p. **137**)
visual dominance (p. **130**)
voice qualities (p. **139**)
volume (p. **139**)

# THINKING CRITICALLY ABOUT NONVERBAL MESSAGES

1. **Physical Appearance.** On a 10-point scale, with 1 indicating "not at all important" and 10 indicating "extremely important," how important is body appearance to your own romantic interest in another person? Do the men and women you know conform to the stereotypes of males being more concerned with physical appearance and females more concerned with personality?

2. **Status and Invasion.** One signal of status is an the unwritten "law" granting the right of invasion. Higher-status individuals have more of a right to invade the territory of others than vice versa. The boss, for example, can invade the territory of junior executives by barging into their offices, but the reverse would be unacceptable. In what ways do you notice this "right" of territorial invasion in your workplace?

3. **Blaming the Victim.** A popular defense tactic in criminal trials for sex crimes against women, gay men, and lesbians is to blame the victim by implying that the way the victim was dressed provoked the attack. Currently, New York and Florida are the only states that prohibit defense attorneys from referring to the way a sex-crime victim was dressed at the time of the attack (*New York Times*, July 30, 1994, p. 22). What do you think of this?

If you don't live in New York or Florida, have there been proposals in your state to similarly limit this popular defense tactic?

4. **Gender and Nonverbal Communication.** Here is a brief summary of findings from research on gender differences in nonverbal expression (Burgoon, Buller, & Woodall, 1996; Eakins & Eakins, 1978; Pearson, West, & Turner, 1995; Arliss, 1991; Shannon, 1987): (1) Women smile more than men; (2) women stand closer to one another than do men and are generally approached more closely than men; (3) both men and women, when speaking, look at men more than at women; (4) women both touch and are touched more than men; (5) men extend their bodies, taking up greater areas of space, more than women. What problems might these differences create when men and women communicate with each other?

5. **Liking Cues.** What nonverbal cues should you look for in judging whether someone likes you? List cues in the order of their importance, beginning with 1 for the cue that is of most value in making your judgment. Do you really need two lists? One for judging a woman's liking and one for a man's?

## LogOn! MyCommunicationLab

WWW.MYCOMMUNICATIONLAB.COM

Several exercises and self-tests will help you better understand how nonverbal communication works and will give you opportunities to practice the skills of nonverbal communication: Facial Expressions, Eye Contact, Interpersonal Interactions and Space, Artifacts and Culture: The Case of Gifts, Communicating Vocally but Nonverbally, Communicating Emotions Nonverbally, Recognizing Verbal and Nonverbal Message Functions, Coloring Meanings, Deciphering Paralanguage Cues, Do You Avoid Touch? Also take the monochronic and polychronic time test and explore the activities on the human face, the human voice, and spatial communication. Recognizing Facial Expressions of Emotions is an interesting and instructive simulation.

An interesting blog dealing with nonverbal communication is available at www.geocities .com/marvin_hecht/nonverbal.html (accessed June 3, 2006).

# Part 2

## Interpersonal, Small Group, and Organizational Communication

### UNIT 7 Interpersonal Communication: Conversation

## MAJOR TOPICS

**The Conversation Process**

**Conversational Skills**

## Special Features

 Communicating Support: Gust A. Yep, 164

 How Flexible Are You in Communication?, 166

 Theories of Media Influence, 159

 Gossip, 154

 The Development of Interpersonal Communication, 152

 Opening Lines, 155

 Giving Feedback and Feedforward, 157

 Formulating Excuses, 162

Talking with another person seems so simple and so natural that most people are surprised to learn that the conversational process actually follows a complex set of rules and customs. In this unit we dissect this process and explain how it operates and the kinds of problems that can be created when these rules and customs are broken.

**In this unit you'll learn about:**
- how the process of conversation works.
- how you can become a more satisfying and more effective conversationalist.

**You'll learn to:**
- engage in conversation that is satisfying and mutually productive.
- apply the skills of interpersonal communication to a wide variety of situations.

Conversation is the essence of interpersonal communication. These two concepts are so closely related that some communication researchers think of the terms *conversation* and *interpersonal communication* as synonyms, as meaning essentially the same thing. Most researchers and theorists would claim that communication exists on a continuum such as that depicted in Figure 7.1 and that interpersonal communication occupies some significant portion of the right side of this continuum. Exactly where impersonal ends and interpersonal begins is a matter of disagreement. (One excellent attempt to pin down the characteristics of interpersonal communication is presented in the Understanding Theory and Research box on page 152.) This unit will first look at the process of conversation, then examine 12 important conversational skills.

## THE CONVERSATION PROCESS

**Conversation** occurs when two or three people exchange messages—whether face-to-face, over the telephone, through apartment walls, or over the Internet. In face-to-face interaction the messages exchanged are both verbal and nonverbal. In e-mail today most messages are basically words. But with the addition of emoticons and the popularity of digital video cameras and voice software, e-mail messages are increasingly blending the verbal with the nonverbal in much the same way as face-to-face conversation.

When reading about the process of conversation, therefore, keep in mind the wide range of channels through which conversation can take place—face-to-face as well as via the Internet, phones, and other

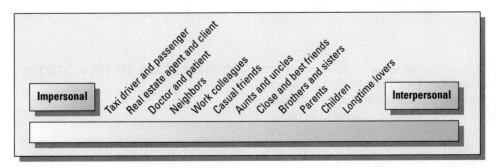

**FIGURE 7.1   An Interpersonal Continuum**

Here is one possible interpersonal continuum. Other people would position the relationships differently. You may want to try constructing an interpersonal continuum of your own relationships.

*Theory* *and* *Research*

**UNDERSTANDING**

## The Development of Interpersonal Communication

You can view communication as a continuum that has impersonal message at one end and personal or intimate communication at the other (somewhat like that presented in Figure 7.1 on p. 151). Interpersonal communication occupies a part of the continuum toward the more personal and intimate end and is distinguished from impersonal communication by three factors: (1) psychologically based predictions, (2) explanatory knowledge, and (3) personally established rules (Miller, 1978).

### Predictions Are Based on Psychological Data

In impersonal encounters, you respond to another person on the basis of sociological data—the classes or groups to which the person belongs. For example, a student responds to a particular college professor the way students respond to college professors generally. Similarly, the professor responds to the student the way professors respond to students generally. As the relationship becomes more personal, however, both professor and student begin to respond to each other not just as members of their groups but as individuals. They respond (to some degree) on the basis of psychological data, that is, on the basis of the ways the individual differs from the members of his or her group.

### Knowledge of Each Other Is Explanatory

In interpersonal interactions, you base your communications on explanatory knowledge of each other. When you know a particular person, you can predict how that person will act in a variety of situations. But as you get to know the person better, you can predict not only how the person will act, but also why the person behaves as he or she does; you can explain the behavior. For example, in an impersonal relationship the professor may be able to predict Pat's behavior and know that Pat will be late to class each Friday. But in an interpersonal situation, the professor can also offer explanations for the behavior, giving reasons for Pat's lateness.

### Rules of Interaction Are Personally Established

Society sets up rules for interaction in impersonal situations. As noted in the example of the student and professor, however, the social rules of interaction set up by the culture lose importance as the relationship becomes more personal. In the place of these social rules, the individuals set up personal rules. When individuals establish their own rules for interacting with each other rather than using the rules set down by the society, the situation becomes increasingly interpersonal.

### Working with Theories and Research

*Try applying these three factors to your own experiences in interpersonal relationships. Do you experience the kind of progression identified here?*

---

technologies—and the similarities and differences among them. Also, remember that like all communication, conversation also entails ethical responsibilities. One such ethical issue, gossip, is discussed in the accompanying Reflections on Ethics box on page 154.

Similarly, realize that not everyone speaks with the fluency and ease that many textbooks often assume. Speech and language disorders, for example, can seriously disrupt the conversation process if some elementary guidelines aren't followed. Table 7.1 offers suggestions for overcoming such difficulties.

## Conversation in Five Stages

Figure 7.2 on page 154 provides a model of the process of conversation and divides the process into five main stages: (1) opening, (2) feedforward, (3) business, (4) feedback, and (5) closing. Examining each stage will give you an overview of what goes on when two people talk.

### Opening

The first step is to open the conversation, usually with some kind of greeting. Greetings can be verbal or nonverbal and are usually both (Krivonos & Knapp, 1975; Knapp & Vangelisti, 2000). Verbal greetings include, for example, verbal salutes ("Hi," "Hello"); initiation of the topic ("The reason I called..."); making reference to the other ("Hey, Joe, what's up?"); and personal inquiries ("What's new?" "How are you doing?"). Nonverbal greetings include waving, smiling, shaking hands, and winking. Usually you greet another person both verbally and nonverbally: You smile when you say "Hello."

In normal conversation, your greeting is reciprocated with a greeting from the other person that is similar in degree of formality or informality and in intensity. When it isn't—when the other person turns away or responds coldly to your friendly "Good morning"—you know that something is wrong. Openings are also generally consistent in tone with the main part of the conversation; a cheery "How ya doing today, big guy?" is not normally followed by news of a family death. This, however, is distinctly cultural; in Finland, for example, the "How are you?" opening is interpreted as a genuine request for information and not simply as a "Hello" (Halmari, 1995). In e-mail, the opening is the header and the announcement from your ISP of "You've got mail" or "Mail truck."

A somewhat different type of opening is the infamous "opening line," a topic covered in the accompanying Understanding Theory and Research box on page 155.

In opening a conversation, consider two general guidelines. First, be positive. Lead off with something positive rather than something negative. Say, for example, "I really enjoy coming here" instead of "Don't you just hate this place?" Second, don't be too revealing; don't self-disclose too early in an interaction. If you do, you risk making the other person feel uncomfortable.

## Feedforward

At the second step there's usually some kind of feedforward. Here you give the other person a general idea of what the conversation will focus on: "I've got to tell you about Jack," "Did you hear what happened in class yesterday?" or "We need to talk about our vacation plans." Feedforward also may identify the tone of the conversation ("I'm really depressed and need to talk with you") or the time required ("This will just take a minute") (Frentz, 1976; Reardon, 1987); or you may use it to preface the conversation to ensure that your message will be

---

## Table 7.1  Communication Tips

**Between People with and without Speech and Language Disorders**

Speech and language disorders vary widely and include fluency problems such as stuttering; indistinct articulation; and difficulty in finding the right word, or aphasia. Communication between people with and without speech and language disorders can be facilitated by means of a few simple guidelines.

If you're the person without a speech or language disorder:

1. *Avoid finishing the person's sentences.* Although you may think you're helping the person who stutters or has word-finding difficulty, finishing sentences is not recommended. It may communicate the impression that you're impatient and don't want to spend the extra time necessary to interact effectively.

2. *Avoid giving directions to the person with a speech disorder.* Saying "slow down" or "relax" will often prove insulting and will make further communication more difficult.

3. *Maintain eye contact.* Show interest and at the same time avoid showing any signs of impatience or embarrassment.

4. *Ask for clarification as needed.* If you don't understand what the person said, ask him or her to repeat it. Don't pretend that you understand when you don't.

5. *Don't treat people who have language problems like children.* A person with aphasia, say, who has difficulty with names or nouns generally, is in no way childlike.

If you're the person with a speech or language disorder:

1. *Let the other person know what your special needs are.* For example, if you stutter, you might tell others that you have difficulty with certain sounds and so they need to be patient.

2. *Demonstrate your own comfort.* Show that you have a positive attitude toward the interpersonal situation. If you appear comfortable and positive, others will also.

These suggestions were drawn from a variety of sources: www.nsastuter.org, www.aphasia.org/NAAcommun.html, and www.conniedugan.com/tips.html (all accessed October 23, 2004).

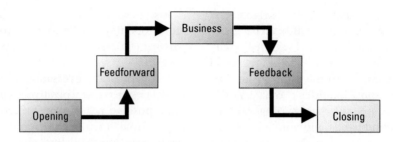

**FIGURE 7.2** **The Process of Conversation**

This model of the stages of conversation is best seen as a way of looking at conversation and not as defining unvarying stages that all conversations follow. As you read about conversation, consider how accurately you think this model reflects the progression of your last conversation.

understood and will not reflect negatively on you (see Unit 1).

In e-mail the title serves as feedforward; it gives the reader some idea of what to expect in the e-mail. Conveniently, this allows for quick deletion of spam and a concentrated focus on e-mail titled "sad news" or "family problem."

Here are a few suggestions for giving effective feedforward.

- Use feedforward to estimate the receptivity of the other person to what you're going to say. For example, before asking for a date, you'd probably use feedforward to test the waters and to see if you're likely to get a yes. You might ask if the other person enjoys going out to dinner or if he or she is dating anyone seriously. Before asking a friend for a loan, you'd probably feedforward your needy condition and say something like "I'm

# REFLECTIONS ON ETHICS

## Gossip

There can be no doubt that we spend a great deal of time gossiping. In fact, gossip seems universal among all cultures (Laing, 1993), and among some groups gossip is a commonly accepted ritual (Hall, 1993).

**Gossip** involves making social evaluations about a person who is not present during the conversation; it generally occurs when two people talk about a third party (Eder & Enke, 1991).

In the organization, gossip has particularly important consequences and in many instances has been shown to lead to firings, lawsuits, and damaged careers. And because of the speed and ease with which members of an organization can communicate with each other (instant messaging, e-mail, and blogs, for example) gossip can spread quickly and broadly (Armour, 2007).

People often gossip in order to get some kind of reward; for example, to hear more gossip, gain social status or control, have fun, cement social bonds, or make social comparisons (Rosnow, 1977; Miller & Wilcox, 1986; Leaper & Holliday, 1995).

Gossiping, however, often leads others to see you more negatively—regardless of whether your gossip is positive or negative or whether you're sharing this gossip with strangers or with friends (Turner, Mazur, Wendel, & Winslow, 2003).

In addition to its negative impact on the gossiper, gossiping often has ethical implications. In many instances gossiping would be considered unethical; for example, when you use it to unfairly hurt another person, when you know it's not true, when no one has the right to such personal information, or when you are breaking a promise of secrecy.

### Ethical Choice Point

*You and your longtime friend Pat are now working in the same company and are competing for the position of sales manager. You know that Pat's résumé contains many lies, claiming, for example, a long history of experience. And it is this claimed experience that is likely to land Pat the position over you. Pat's lying hasn't bothered you before, but now it's likely to work against your own promotion. You wonder if it would be ethical to let it be known, through informal gossip channels, that Pat doesn't really have all the experience claimed. What are your ethical obligations—to yourself, to your family, to your company? What would you do?*

### Theory and Research — UNDERSTANDING

## Opening Lines

How do you strike up a conversation with someone you're meeting for the first time? How have people tried to open conversations with you? Researchers investigating this question found three basic types of opening lines (Kleinke, 1986).

- *Cute-flippant openers* are humorous, indirect, and ambiguous as to whether or not the person opening the conversation really wants an extended encounter. Examples: "Is that really your hair?" "Bet I can outdrink you."

- *Innocuous openers* are highly ambiguous as to whether these are simple comments that might be made to just anyone or whether they're in fact openers designed to initiate an extended encounter. Examples: "What do you think of the band?" "Could you show me how to work this machine?"

- *Direct openers* demonstrate clearly the speaker's interest in meeting the other person. Examples: "I feel a little embarrassed about this, but I'd like to meet you." "Would you like to have a drink after dinner?"

Studies indicate that the opening lines most preferred by both men and women are generally those that are direct or innocuous. Least preferred by both men and women are opening lines that are cute–flippant; women, however, dislike these openers more than men (Kleinke & Dean, 1990).

### Working with Theories and Research

*Do you find support for these conclusions from your own experience? For example, do you find significant gender differences in preferences? What openers do you yourself find most effective? What types do you dislike?*

---

really strapped for cash and need to get my hands on $200 to pay my car loan" and wait for the other person to say (you hope), "Can I help?"

- Use feedforward that's consistent with your subsequent message. If your main message is one of bad news, then your feedforward needs to be serious to help to prepare the other person for this bad news. You might, for example, say something like "I need to tell you something you're not going to want to hear. Let's sit down."

- The more important or complex the message, the more important and more extensive your feedforward needs to be. For example, in public speaking, in which the message is relatively long, the speaker is advised to give fairly extensive feedforward in the form of what is called an orientation or preview (see Unit 15). At the start of a business meeting, the leader may give feedforward in the form of an agenda or meeting schedule.

### Business

The third step is the "business," the substance or focus of the conversation. This is obviously the longest part of the conversation, and it is the reason for both the opening and the feedforward. *Business* is a good term

to use for this stage, because it emphasizes that most conversations—whether face-to-face, on the phone, or via e-mail—are goal directed. You converse to fulfill one or several of the general purposes of interpersonal communication: to learn, relate, influence, play, or help (Unit 1). The term is also sufficiently general to incorporate all kinds of interactions, whether face-to-face or via computer-mediated communication such as e-mail, blogs, social network chat rooms, or cell phone. In e-mail you can easily supplement your message by attaching hotlinks to websites and to word, sound, and video files, as well as to other e-mails. Although you can also distribute supplementary materials in face-to-face conversation, it's not as common as it is in e-mail communication.

The business of a conversation is conducted through an exchange of speaker and listener roles. Usually, brief (rather than long) speaking turns characterize the most satisfying conversations. Here you talk about Jack, what happened in class, or your vacation plans.

Another important difference between e-mail and face-to-face communication is that in normal face-to-face communication there is no permanent record of the conversation; the record exists only in the memories of those who are present. In e-mail, in contrast, there is a permanent record of the interaction, a record that can easily be sent to third parties. In large organizations employees' e-mails are stored on hard disk or on backup tapes and may be retrieved from archives long thought destroyed. For this reason, using e-mail requires caution.

## Feedback

The fourth step in conversation is the reverse of the second. In feedback (see Unit 1), you reflect back on the conversation to signal that as far as you're concerned, the business is completed: "So, you may want to send Jack a get-well card," "Wasn't that the craziest class you ever heard of?" or "I'll call for reservations while you shop for what we need."

Of course, the other person may not agree that the business is completed and may therefore counter with, for example, "But what hospital is he in?" When this happens, you normally go back a step and continue the business.

Each feedback opportunity, then, presents you with choices along at least the five dimensions introduced in Unit 1: positive–negative, person focused–message focused, immediate–delayed, low-monitored–high-monitored, and supportive–critical. To use feedback effectively, you need to make educated choices along these dimensions. Realize that these categories are not exclusive, however. Feedback does not have to be either critical or supportive; it can be both. For example, in teaching someone how to become a more effective interviewer, you might critically evaluate a practice interview, but you might also express support for the effort. Similarly, you might respond to a friend's question immediately and then after a day or two elaborate on your response. Because each situation is unique, it's difficult to offer specific suggestions for making your feedback more effective. But, with some adjustments for the specifics of the situation, the following guides might prove helpful:

- Focus on the behavior or the message rather than the motives behind the message or behavior. Say, for example, "This letter has too many errors and needs to be redone" rather than "You're not concentrating" or "You don't care enough about these letters to do them correctly."

- If your feedback is largely negative, try to begin with something positive. There are always positives if you look hard enough. Your listener will find the negatives much easier to take after hearing some positives.

- Select an appropriate time and place. When feedback is negative, be especially careful to do this in private and when there is sufficient time to discuss the problems in full.

- Ask for feedback on your feedback; for example, say "Does this make sense?" or "Do you understand what I'm asking?"

The other half of the feedback equation is the person receiving the feedback (Robbins & Hunsaker, 2006). When you are the recipient of feedback, be sure to:

- Show your interest in the feedback. This is vital information that will help you improve whatever you're doing. Encourage the feedback giver.

- Be open to hearing this feedback. Don't argue; don't be defensive.

- Ask questions. Not all feedback is easy to understand; when you don't understand, ask for clarification (nondefensively, of course).

- Check your perceptions. Do you understand the feedback? Paraphrase the feedback you've just received to make sure you both understand it: "You want the mail delivered before nine a.m. to all executives, and this takes precedence over all other jobs."

The accompanying Building Communication Skills box ("Giving Feedback and Feedforward") provides an opportunity for you to practice the skills of feedback and feedforward.

## Closing

The fifth and last step, the opposite of the first step, is the closing, the good-bye (Knapp, Hart, Friedrich, & Shulman, 1973; Knapp & Vangelisti, 2000). Like the opening, the closing may be verbal or nonverbal but is usually a combination of both. Most obviously, the closing signals the end of accessibility. Just as the opening signaled access, the closing signals the end of access. The closing usually also signals some degree of supportiveness; for example, you express your pleasure in interacting, as in "Well, it was good talking with you." The closing may also summarize the interaction.

In e-mail the closing is similar to that in face-to-face conversation but has the added capability of including a "signature," perhaps along with a favorite quotation or saying or a phone number through which you can be reached.

Closing a conversation is almost as difficult as opening a conversation. It's frequently an awkward and uncomfortable part of interpersonal interaction. Here are a few **leave-taking cues** you might consider for closing a conversation.

- Reflect back on the conversation and briefly summarize it so as to bring it to a close. For example, "I'm glad I ran into you and found out what happened at that union meeting. I'll probably be seeing you at the meetings."

## Building Communication Skills  Giving Feedback and Feedforward

**Feedback.**  For any one or two of the following situations, (a) indicate the kind of feedback that you would consider appropriate (positive or negative? person-focused or message-focused? immediate or delayed? low-monitoring or high-monitoring? supportive or critical?), and (b) write one or two sentences in which you express feedback that has the qualities you identified in (a).

1. A neighbor—whom you like but don't have romantic feelings for—asks you for a date.
2. A colleague at work persists in talking explicitly about sex despite your frequent objections.
3. A homeless person smiles at you on the street and asks for some change.

**Feedforward.**  In each of the following situations, you may want to preface your main message with feedforward. For any one or two of the following situations, (a) identify the specific purpose you hope to achieve with your feedforward, and (b) write a brief feedforward message that helps you achieve the purpose you identified in (a).

1. You see an attractive person in one of your classes and would like to get to know the person a bit more, with the possible objective of a date.
2. You just saw the posted grades for the midterm; your close friend failed, but you did extremely well. In the cafeteria you meet your friend, who asks, "How'd I do on the midterm?"
3. You have a reputation for proposing outlandish ideas in the midst of otherwise formal and boring discussions. This time, however, you want to offer a proposal that you fear will seem to be one of your standard outlandish notions but is actually an idea that you think could work. You want to assure your group that this idea is worthy of their serious attention.

*Feedforward and feedback are essential communication skills; often they are the parts of your message remembered best.*

---

- State the desire to end the conversation directly and to get on with other things. For example, "I'd like to continue talking but I really have to run. I'll see you around."
- Refer to future interaction. For example, "E-mail me after you've had a chance to read the report," or "Why don't we get together next week sometime and continue this discussion?"
- Ask for closure. For example, "Have I explained what you wanted to know?"
- State that you enjoyed the interaction. For example, "I really enjoyed talking with you."

With any of these closings, it should be clear to the other person that you're attempting to end the conversation. Obviously, you'll have to use more direct methods with those who don't take these subtle hints—those who don't realize that both persons are responsible for bringing the conversation to a satisfying close.

Closing a conversation in e-mail follows the same principles as closing a face-to-face conversation. But exactly when you end an e-mail exchange is often unclear, partly because the absence of nonverbal cues creates ambiguity. For example, if you ask someone a question and the other person answers, do you then e-mail again and say, "Thanks"? If so, should the other person e-mail you back and say, "It was my pleasure"? And, if so, should you then e-mail back again and say, "I appreciate your willingness to answer my questions"? And, if so, should the other person then respond with something like "No problem"?

On the one hand, you don't want to prolong the interaction more than necessary; on the other hand, you don't want to appear impolite. So how do you signal (politely) that the e-mail exchanges should stop? Here are a few suggestions (Cohen, 2002):

- Include in your e-mail the notation NRN (no reply necessary).
- If you're replying with information the other person requested, end your message with something like "I hope this helps."

- Title or head your message FYI (for your information), indicating that your message is intended merely to keep someone in the loop.

- When you make a request for information, end your message with "Thank you in advance."

## Maintaining Conversations

The defining feature of conversation is that the roles of speaker and listener are exchanged throughout the interaction. You accomplish this exchange, or **conversational management**, by using a wide variety of verbal and nonverbal cues to signal **conversational turns**—the changing (or maintaining) of the speaker or listener role during the conversation.

The majority of today's e-mail lacks this frequent exchange of roles between sender and receiver; the exchanges take place with hours, days, or even weeks intervening between the sending and the responding. Such feedback lacks the immediacy that is common in face-to-face conversation—though, again, with video and voice capabilities, this distinction may fade.

For people with no hearing or vision impairments, turn-taking cues include both audio and visual signals. Among blind speakers the turn taking is governed in larger part by audio signals and often touch. Among deaf speakers turn-taking signals are largely visual and may also involve touch (Coates & Sutton-Spence, 2001).

Combining the insights of a variety of communication researchers (Burgoon, Buller, & Woodall, 1996; Duncan, 1972; Pearson & Spitzberg, 1990), we can look at conversational turns in terms of speaker cues and listener cues.

### Speaker Cues

Speakers regulate the conversation through two major types of cues: turn-maintaining cues and turn-yielding cues. Using these cues effectively not only ensures communication efficiency but also increases likability (Place & Becker, 1991; Heap, 1992). The ways of using the conversational turns identified here have been derived largely from studies conducted in the United States. Each culture appears to define the types and appropriateness of turns differently (e.g., Iizuka, 1993). In polychronic cultures, for example, people will often disregard the turn-taking rules used in monochronic cultures. The effect is that to monochronic people—who carefully follow these rules—polychronic people may appear rude as they interrupt and overlap conversations (Lee, 1984; Grossin, 1987). In some cultures (largely individualist), the conversational turn is more often passed to one person; in other cultures (largely collectivist) the turn is more often passed to several individuals (Ng, Loong, He, Liu, & Weatherall, 2000).

**Turn-Maintaining Cues.** Turn-maintaining cues are designed to enable a person to maintain the role of speaker and can take a variety of forms (Burgoon, Buller, & Woodall, 1996; Duncan, 1972):

- audibly inhaling breath to show that the speaker has more to say
- continuing a gesture or series of gestures to show that the thought is not yet complete
- avoiding eye contact with the listener so as not to indicate that the speaking turn is being passed along
- sustaining the intonation pattern to indicate that more will be said
- vocalizing pauses ("er," "umm") to prevent the listener from speaking and to show that the speaker is still talking

In most cases we expect the speaker to maintain relatively brief speaking turns and to turn over the speaking role to the listener willingly (when so signaled by the listener). People who don't follow those unwritten rules are likely to be evaluated negatively.

**Turn-Yielding Cues.** Turn-yielding cues tell the listener that the speaker is finished and wishes to exchange the role of speaker for the role of listener. They tell the listener (and sometimes they're addressed to a specific listener rather than to just any listener) to take over the role of speaker. For example, at the end of a statement you may add some cue such as "okay?" or "right?" which asks one of the listeners to assume the role of speaker. You can also indicate that you've finished speaking by dropping your intonation or by pausing at length (Wenner-strom & Siegel, 2003), by making direct eye contact with a listener, by asking some question, or by nodding in the direction of a particular listener.

### Listener Cues

As a listener, you can regulate the conversation by using three types of cues: turn-requesting cues, turn-denying cues, and backchanneling cues.

**Turn-Requesting Cues.** Turn-requesting cues let the speaker know that you would like to say something and take a turn as speaker. Sometimes you can do this simply by saying, "I'd like to say something," but often it's done more subtly through some vocalized "er" or "um" that tells the speaker that you would now like to speak. The request to speak is also often made with facial and mouth gestures. Frequently a listener will indicate a desire to speak by opening his or her eyes and mouth wide as if to say something, by beginning to gesture with a hand, or by leaning forward.

**Turn-Denying Cues.** You can use turn-denying cues to indicate your reluctance to assume the role of speaker; for example, by intoning a slurred "I

## MEDIA WATCH

## THEORIES OF MEDIA INFLUENCE

Media messages have effects on readers, listeners, and viewers. Some messages influence in obvious ways; for example, the advertisements on television or on the Internet and the editorials in newspapers. Other media messages influence indirectly; for example, the dramas and sitcoms that influence your view of family, of work and workplace relationships, and of friendship and love.

An early theory, called the *one-step theory*, argued that the influence of the media was direct and immediate; it occurred in one step—from the media to you. You read a newspaper or watched television and were persuaded by what they said (Schramm & Porter, 1982). As an audience member, you were viewed as relatively passive, as a target that could hardly resist being influenced.

A more sophisticated explanation visualizes media influence as a two-step process: First, the media influence opinion leaders (step 1); second,

these opinion leaders influence the rest of the people (step 2). A more current and complicated approach, the multistep theory, claims that media interact with interpersonal channels. So, for example, the media may influence you on a specific issue; then perhaps you chat online with others who may strengthen or weaken the original media influence. Then you may read more on the topic and perhaps talk in class about it. Influence here is seen as a result of a combination of all the messages you receive, both from the media and from interpersonal (face-to-face and online) encounters.

### Increasing Media Literacy

*Can you identify specific ways in which the media have influenced you? For example, have media messages influenced your buying habits, your view of relationships, or your attitudes toward the opposite sex? What theory seems to best explain how the media influence you?*

don't know" or by giving some brief grunt that signals you have nothing to say. Often people accomplish turn denying by avoiding eye contact with the speaker (who wishes them now to take on the role of speaker) or by engaging in some behavior that is incompatible with speaking—for example, coughing or blowing their nose.

**Backchanneling Cues.** People use backchanneling cues to communicate various types of information back to the speaker without assuming the role of the speaker. As discussed in Unit 4, you can send a variety of messages with backchanneling cues (Burgoon, Buller, & Woodall, 1996; Pearson & Spitzberg, 1990). You can indicate your agreement or disagreement with the speaker through smiles or frowns, gestures of approval or disapproval, brief comments such as "right" or "never," or a vocalization such as "uh-huh."

You can also indicate your degree of involvement or boredom with the speaker. Attentive posture, forward leaning, and focused eye contact will tell the speaker that you're involved in the conversation—and an inattentive posture, backward leaning, and avoidance of eye contact will communicate your lack of involvement.

Giving the speaker pacing cues helps regulate the speed of speech. You can, for example, ask the speaker to slow down by raising your hand near your ear and leaning forward, or to speed up by continuously nodding your head. You can also do this

verbally by simply asking the speaker to slow down ("Slow down, I want to make sure I'm getting all this"). Similarly, you can tell the speaker to speed up by saying something like "and—?" or "go on, go on."

A request for clarification is still another function of backchanneling cues. A puzzled facial expression, perhaps coupled with a forward lean, will probably tell most speakers that you want some clarification. Similarly, you can ask for clarification by interjecting some interrogative: "Who?" "When?" "Where?"

Some of these backchanneling cues are actually interruptions. These interruptions, however, are generally confirming rather than disconfirming. They tell the speaker that you are listening and are involved (Kennedy & Camden, 1988).

Figure 7.3 on page 160, diagrams the various turn-taking cues and shows how they correspond to the conversational wants of speaker and listener.

## Conversational Problems: Two Strategies

Two conversational strategies that may prove helpful at various times are the disclaimer and the excuse. Let's look first at the disclaimer.

### The Disclaimer

Suppose you fear that your listeners may think that what you're about to say is inappropriate in the present context or that they may rush to judge you

**Conversational Wants**

| | To speak | To listen |
|---|---|---|
| **Speaker** | 1<br>Turn-maintaining cues | 2<br>Turn-yielding cues |
| **Listener** | 3<br>Turn-requesting cues | 4<br>Turn-denying cues |

**FIGURE 7.3** Turn-Taking and Conversational Wants

Quadrant 1 represents the speaker who wants to speak (continue to speak) and uses turn-maintaining cues; quadrant 2, the speaker who wants to listen and uses turn-yielding cues; quadrant 3, the listener who wants to speak and uses turn-requesting cues; and quadrant 4, the listener who wants to listen (continue listening) and uses turn-denying cues. Backchanneling cues would appear in quadrant 4, because they are cues that listeners use while they continue to listen.

without hearing your full account. In these cases, as you'll recall from Unit 1, you may use some form of disclaimer, a statement that aims to ensure that your message will be understood and will not reflect negatively on you.

Think about your own use of disclaimers as you read about these five types (Hewitt & Stokes, 1975; McLaughlin, 1984):

- *Hedging* helps you to separate yourself from the message so that if your listeners reject your message, they won't reject you (for example, "I may be wrong here, but . . ." or "I didn't read the entire book, but it seems that . . .").

- *Credentialing* argues that you should not be disqualified for saying what you're about to say (for example, "Don't get me wrong, I'm not homophobic . . .").

- *Sin licenses* ask listeners for permission to deviate in some way from some normally accepted convention (for example, "I know this may not be the place to discuss business, but . . .").

- *Cognitive disclaimers* help you make the case that you're in full possession of your faculties (for example, "I know you'll think I'm crazy, but let me explain the logic of the case").

- *Appeals for the suspension of judgment* ask listeners to hear you out before making a judgment (for example, "Don't hang up on me until you hear my side of the story").

Disclaimers do work in some situations. For example, disclaimers are generally effective when you think you might offend listeners by telling a joke ("I don't usually like these types of jokes, but . . ."). In one study, 11-year-old children were read a story about someone whose actions created negative effects. Some children heard the story with a disclaimer, and others heard the same story without the disclaimer. When the children were asked to indicate how the person should be punished, those who heard the story with the disclaimer recommended significantly lower punishments (Bennett, 1990).

Disclaimers also can get you into trouble, however. For example, to inappropriately preface remarks with "I'm no liar" may well lead listeners to think that perhaps you are a liar. And if you use too many disclaimers, you may be perceived as someone who doesn't have any strong convictions or who wants to avoid responsibility for just about everything. This seems especially true of hedges.

In responding to statements containing disclaimers, it's often necessary to respond both to the disclaimer and to the statement. By doing so, you let the speaker know that you heard the disclaimer and that you aren't going to view this communication negatively. Appropriate responses might be: "I know you're no sexist, but I don't agree that . . ." or "Well, perhaps we should discuss the money now even if it doesn't seem right."

## The Excuse

In Unit 1 we examined the concept of irreversibility —the fact that once something is communicated, it cannot be uncommunicated. In part because of this fact, we need at times to defend or justify messages that may be perceived negatively. Perhaps the most common method for doing so is the excuse (Fraser, 2000). Excuses pervade all forms of communication and behavior. Although this discussion emphasizes their role in conversation, recognize that excuses occur in all forms of communication—interpersonal, group, public, and mass.

You learn early in life that when you do something that will be perceived negatively, an excuse is needed to justify your poor performance. The need for an excuse usually follows from three conditions (Snyder, 1984):

- You say something.

- Your statement is viewed negatively; you desire to disassociate yourself from it.

- Someone hears the message or the results of the message. The "witness" may be an outsider (for example, a boss, a friend, or a colleague) but also could be yourself—you're a witness to your own messages.

## CHATTING FOR FREE

A casual friend, who has a cell phone with free unlimited long distance calling, now calls you several times a week just to chat about nothing you're really interested in. You don't want to offend this person or kill the friendship (weak as it is) but you don't want to spend a few hours a week on the phone.

*WHAT DO YOU SAY?*
*Through what channel?*

More formally, Snyder (1984; Snyder, Higgins, & Stucky, 1983) defines **excuses** as "explanations or actions that lessen the negative implications of an actor's performance, thereby maintaining a positive image for oneself and others."

Excuses seem especially in order when we say or are accused of saying something that runs counter to what is expected, sanctioned, or considered "right" by the people involved or by society in general. The excuse, ideally, lessens the negative impact of the message.

Three kinds of excuses can be identified (Snyder, 1984; Snyder, Higgins, & Stucky, 1983).

- In the *I didn't do it* type, you claim not to have done the behavior of which you're accused: "I didn't say that." "I wasn't even near the place when it happened."

- In the *It wasn't so bad* type, you claim that the behavior was not really so bad, certainly not as bad as others may at first think: "I only copied one answer."

- In the *Yes, but* type, you claim that extenuating circumstances accounted for the behavior: "It was the liquor talking." "I really tried to help him; I didn't mean to hurt his feelings."

**Some Motives for Excuse Making.** The major motive for excuse making seems to be to maintain our self-esteem, to project a positive image to ourselves and to others. Excuses are also offered to reduce the stress that may be created by a bad performance. We feel that if we can offer an excuse—especially a good one that is accepted by those around us—it will lessen the negative reaction and the subsequent stress that accompanies a poor performance.

Anticipatory excuses enable you to take risks and engage in behavior that may be unsuccessful: "My throat's a bit sore, but I'll give the speech a try." The excuse is designed to lessen the criticism should you fail to deliver an acceptable speech.

Excuses also enable us to maintain effective interpersonal relationships even after some negative interaction. For example, after criticizing a friend's behavior and observing the negative reaction to our criticism, we might offer an excuse such as "Please forgive me; I'm really exhausted. I'm just not thinking straight." Excuses enable us to place our messages—even our possible failures—in a more favorable light.

**Good and Bad Excuses.** To most people, the most important question is what makes a good excuse and what makes a bad excuse (Snyder, 1984; Slade, 1995; Schlenker, Pontari, & Christopher, 2001). How can you make good excuses and thus get out of problems, and how can you avoid bad excuses that only make matters worse?

- Good excuse-makers use excuses in moderation; bad excuse-makers rely on excuses too often. Similarly, unnecessary excuses (which are often disguised attempts to ingratiate yourself) rarely create a positive impression (Levesque, 1995).

- Good excuse-makers avoid using excuses in the presence of those who know what really happened; bad excuse-makers make excuses even in these inopportune situations.

- Good excuse-makers avoid blaming others, especially those they work with; bad excuse-makers blame even their work colleagues.

- In a similar way, good excuse-makers don't attribute their failure to others or to the organization; bad excuse-makers do.

- Good excuse-makers acknowledge their own responsibility for the failure by noting that they did something wrong; bad excuse-makers refuse to accept any responsibility for their failure.

The best excuses contain five elements (Slade, 1995; Coleman, 2002).

1. You demonstrate that you really understand the problem and that your partner's feelings are legitimate and justified. Avoid minimizing the issue or your partner's feelings ("It was only $100; you're overreacting" or "I was only two hours late").

---

## Building Communication Skills — Formulating Excuses

Although excuses are not always appropriate, they are often helpful in lessening possible negative effects of your mishap. For any one of the situations listed below, try formulating an appropriate excuse, incorporating the five elements of a good excuse outlined on pages 161–162.

- Because of some e-mail glitch, all of the students in your communication class receive a personal letter you sent to a friend in which you admit to having homophobic feelings. As you enter class, you hear a group of students discussing your letter, looking very annoyed. You don't want to be disliked or have people think of you as a bigot.

- Your boss accuses you of making lots of personal long-distance phone calls from work, a practice that's explicitly forbidden, but which you violate because everyone else does. You need to stay in the good graces of your supervisor, who will soon make recommendations for promotions.

- Your relationship partner catches you in a lie; you weren't at work (as you said you were) but with a former relationship partner. You want to preserve your current relationship and avoid arguments over this now and in the future.

*You can't reverse errors or eliminate their negative impact with excuses, but you can use excuses to help repair—to some extent—any conversational or relationship damage.*

---

2. **You acknowledge your responsibility.** Avoid qualifying your responsibility ("I'm sorry *if* I did anything wrong") or expressing a lack of sincerity ("OK, I'm sorry; it's obviously my fault—*again*").

3. **You acknowledge your own displeasure at what you did;** make it clear that you're not happy with yourself for having done what you did.

4. **You request forgiveness for what you did;** be specific.

5. **You make it clear that this will never happen again.**

The worst excuses are the "I didn't do it" type, because they fail to acknowledge responsibility and offer no assurance that this failure will not happen again.

Table 7.2 provides examples of how the five elements of good excuses may be used in excuses in romantic and in business situations. The accompanying Building Communication Skills box, "Formulating Excuses," provides an opportunity for you to practice your own excuse-making skills.

## CONVERSATIONAL SKILLS

Skill in conversation depends on your ability to make adjustments along several dimensions. Recall from Unit 4 that listening effectiveness depends on your ability to make adjustments between, for

---

## Table 7.2  Excuses in Romantic and Workplace Relationships

Here are the five intended messages that effective apologies should convey, along with some specific examples. As you read this table, visualize a specific situation in which you recently made an excuse. Could what you said (or should have said) have been organized into this five-step structure?

| Intended Message | In Romantic Relationships | At Work |
|---|---|---|
| 1. I see | I should have asked you first; you have a right to be angry. | I understand that we lost the client because of this. |
| 2. I did it | I was totally responsible. | I should have acted differently. |
| 3. I'm sorry | I'm sorry that I didn't ask you first. | I'm sorry I didn't familiarize myself with the client's objections to our last offer. |
| 4. Forgive me | Forgive me? | I'd really like another chance. |
| 5. I'll do better | I'll never lend anyone money without first discussing it with you. | This will never happen again. |

example, empathic and objective listening. In a similar way, your effectiveness in conversation depends on your ability to make adjustments along specific skill dimensions. Here we discuss an even dozen such skills: dialogue, mindfulness, flexibility, cultural sensitivity, metacommunication, openness, empathy, positiveness, immediacy, interaction management, expressiveness, and other-orientation (Greene & Burleson, 2003; Apitzberg & Hecht, 1984; Rubin, 1985).

## Dialogue

Often the term *dialogue* is used as a synonym for *conversation*. But dialogue is more than simple conversation; it's conversation in which there is genuine two-way interaction (Buber, 1958; Yau-fair Ho, Chan, Peng, & Ng, 2001; McNamee & Gergen, 1999). It's useful to distinguish the ideal dialogic communicator from the opposite, the totally monologic communicator.

In true **dialogue** each person is both speaker and listener, sender and receiver. In this type of conversation there is deep concern for the other person and for the relationship between the two. The objective of dialogue is mutual understanding, supportiveness, and empathy. There is respect for the other person, not because of what this person can do or give but simply because this person is a human being and therefore deserves to be treated honestly and sincerely.

**Monologue** is the opposite; it's communication in which one person speaks and the other listens—there's no real interaction between participants. The monologic communicator is focused only on his or her own goals and has no real concern for the listener's feelings or attitudes; this speaker is interested in the other person only insofar as that person can serve his or her purposes.

### Increasing Dialogue

To increase dialogue and decrease monologic tendencies, try the following:

- *Demonstrate respect for the other person.* Allow that person the right to make his or her own choices without coercion, without the threat of punishment, without fear or social pressure. A dialogic communicator believes that other people can make decisions that are right for them and implicitly or explicitly lets them know that whatever choices they make, they will still be respected as individuals.

- *Avoid negative criticism* ("I didn't like that explanation") and negative judgments ("You're not a very good listener, are you?"). Instead, practice using positive criticism ("I liked those first two

**EXPRESSING THANKS**

Because of family problems, you fell behind in your rent and were threatened with eviction. Your next-door neighbor and friend bailed you out by paying the overdue rent. You want to express your deep appreciation.

WHAT DO YOU SAY?
*Through what channel*

explanations best; they were really well reasoned").

- *Keep the channels of communication open* by displaying a willingness to listen. Let the other person know that you are listening by giving cues (nonverbal nods, brief verbal expressions of agreement, paraphrasing) that tell the speaker you're listening. When in doubt about something that was said, ask for clarification, ask for that person's point of view, and thus signal a real interest in the other person and in what that person is saying.

- *Avoid manipulating the conversation* to try to get the person to say something positive about you or to force the other person to think, believe, or behave in any particular way.

## Mindfulness

**Mindfulness** is a state of awareness in which you're conscious of your reasons for thinking or behaving; its opposite, mindlessness, is a lack of conscious awareness of what or how you're thinking (Langer, 1989). To apply interpersonal skills effectively, become mindful of the unique communication situation you're in, your available communication options, and the reasons why one option is likely to be better than the others (Langer, 1989; Elmes & Gemmill, 1990; Burgoon, Berger, & Waldron, 2000).

### Increasing Mindfulness

To increase mindfulness, try the following suggestions (Langer, 1989).

# ASK THE RESEARCHER

## Dialoguing

*Our 14-year-old son has just told us that he's gay, but he doesn't seem to want to talk about it beyond his recent announcement. We want to help him be whoever he is, comfortably and securely. How can we best accomplish this with our talk? Can you give us any guidelines as to what we might say or what we shouldn't say?*

I applaud you for creating an open environment and nurturing a trusting relationship that allowed him to disclose. Before you offer help, pay attention to your own attitudes and feelings. Homophobic attitudes and beliefs are often deeply buried, and they can be expressed subtly in your tone of voice, facial expressions, posture, questions you ask, assumptions you make. To start a conversation about his recent announcement, I encourage you to acknowledge his disclosure, remind him that he is loved, and explore his feelings by listening actively. You can do this by showing interest, maintaining a feeling of closeness, using positive and encouraging feedback, and avoiding judgments and unsolicited opinions and solutions. Invite him to tell you how you can be most supportive, and let him know that you are open to talk whenever he wishes to do so. Honor his life journey by giving him the time and space to explore his sexuality in his own way.

For further information: Yep, G. A. (2002). From homophobia and heterosexism to heteronormativity: Toward the development of a model of queer interventions in the university classroom. *Journal of Lesbian Studies, 6*, 163–176. And Yep, G. A., Lovaas, K. E., & Elia, J. P. (Eds.). (2003). *Queer theory and communication: From disciplining queers to queering the discipline(s)*. New York: Harrington Park Press.

**Gust A. Yep** (Ph.D., University of Southern California) is a professor of communication studies and human sexuality studies at San Francisco State University, where he teaches courses and conducts research in culture, gender, sexuality, and communication. Dr. Yep was the San Francisco State University nominee for the Carnegie Foundation "U.S. Professors of the Year" award (1999) and the recipient of the National Communication Association Randy Majors Memorial Award for Outstanding Gay and Lesbian Scholarship in Communication (2006).

- *Create and recreate categories*. Learn to see objects, events, and especially people as belonging to a wide variety of categories. For example, try to see each person in your life in a variety of roles—as child, parent, employee, neighbor, friend, financial contributor, and so on. Avoid storing in memory an image of any person with only one specific label; if you do, you'll find it difficult to recategorize the person later.

- *Be open to new information and points of view*, even when these contradict your most firmly held beliefs. New information can help you challenge long-held but now inappropriate beliefs and attitudes about, for example, gender, race, or religion. Be willing to see your own and others' behaviors from the viewpoints of people very different from yourself.

- *Beware of relying too heavily on first impressions* (Chanowitz & Langer, 1981; Langer, 1989). Treat first impressions as tentative, as hypotheses that need further investigation. Be prepared to revise, reject, or accept these initial impressions.

## Flexibility

**Flexibility** is the ability to adjust communication strategies on the basis of the unique situation. One flexibility assessment scale asks you to consider how true you believe certain statements are; for example, "People should be frank and spontaneous in conversation" or "When angry, a person should say nothing rather than say something he or she will be sorry for later." The "preferred" answer to all such questions is "sometimes true," underscoring the importance of flexibility in all interpersonal situations (Hart, Carlson, & Eadie, 1980). For a more extensive test of flexibility, take the self-test on page 166, which will help you learn about your own flexibility.

### Increasing Flexibility

Here are a few ways to cultivate flexibility.

- *Realize that no two situations or people are exactly alike*. Ask yourself what is different about this situation or person, and take differences into consideration as you decide what to say and how to say it.

■ *Realize that communication always takes place in a context* (Unit 1). Ask yourself what is unique about this specific context and how this uniqueness should influence your messages.

■ *Realize that everything is in a state of flux.* The way you communicated last month may have been effective, but that doesn't necessarily mean it will be effective today or tomorrow. Realize, too, that major changes in people's lives (such as the loss of a job or a fatal illness) will influence what are and what are not appropriate messages.

■ *Realize that every situation offers you different options* for communicating. Think about these options and try to predict the effects each option might have.

## Cultural Sensitivity

Cultural sensitivity, as this book has often emphasized, is an attitude and way of behaving in which you're aware of and acknowledge cultural differences; it's crucial not only on the global level (in efforts for world peace and economic growth) but also for effective interpersonal communication as well as for general personal success (Franklin & Mizell, 1995). Without cultural sensitivity there can be no effective interpersonal communication between people who are different from each other in gender or race or nationality or affectional orientation. So be mindful of the cultural differences between yourself and the other person. Remember that the techniques of interpersonal communication that work well with European Americans may not work well with Asian Americans; what proves effective in Japan may not succeed in Mexico. The close physical distance that is normal in Arab cultures may prove too familiar or too intrusive in much of the United States and northern Europe. The empathy that most Americans welcome may be uncomfortable for the average Korean (Yun, 1976).

### Increasing Cultural Sensitivity

Here are a few guidelines to follow for achieving greater cultural sensitivity.

■ *Prepare yourself.* Read about and listen carefully for culturally influenced behaviors.

■ *Recognize and face your own fears* of acting inappropriately with members of different cultures.

■ *Recognize differences*: differences between yourself and people of other cultures, among members of the culturally different group, and in meaning (words rarely mean the same thing to members of different cultures).

■ *Become conscious of the cultural rules and customs of others.* Resist the temptation to assume that what works in your culture will necessarily work in others.

## Metacommunication

Metacommunication, as we saw in Unit 1, is communication that refers to other communications; it's communication about communication. Both verbal and nonverbal messages can be metacommunicational. Verbally, you can say, for example, "Do you understand what I'm trying to say?" Nonverbally, you can hug someone you're consoling.

Interpersonal effectiveness often hinges on the ability to metacommunicate. For example, in conflict situations it's often helpful to talk about the way you fight. In romantic relationships, it's often helpful to talk about what each of you means by "steady" or "really caring." On the job, it's often necessary to talk about the way orders are delegated or the way criticism should be expressed.

### Increasing Metacommunication

Here are a few suggestions for increasing your metacommunicational effectiveness.

■ *Explain your feelings* along with your thoughts. Often people communicate only the thinking part of their message, with the result that listeners aren't able to appreciate the other parts of their meaning.

■ *Give clear feedforward* to help the other person get a general picture of the messages that will follow.

■ *Paraphrase.* Paraphrase your own complex messages so as to make your meaning extra clear. Similarly, check on your understanding of another's message by paraphrasing what you think the other person means, then asking if that's what the person meant.

■ *Use metacommunication to talk about communication patterns* between yourself and another person. Say, for example, "I'd like to talk about the way you talk about me to our friends" or "I think we should talk about the way we talk about sex."

## Openness

**Openness** has to do with your willingness to self-disclose—to reveal information about yourself that you might normally keep hidden—provided that such disclosure is appropriate (as discussed in Unit 3). Openness also involves your willingness to listen openly and react honestly to the messages of others.

### Increasing Openness

Consider these few ideas.

■ *Self-disclose when appropriate.* Be mindful about your self-disclosures, remembering that there are both benefits and dangers to this form of intimate communication.

# TEST YOURSELF

## How Flexible Are You in Communication?

Here are some situations that illustrate how people sometimes act when communicating with others. The first part of each situation asks you to imagine that you are in the situation; then a course of action is identified, and you are asked to determine how much your own behavior would be like the action described in the scenario. If it is exactly like you, mark a 5; if it is a lot like you, 4; if it is somewhat like you, 3; if it is not much like you, 2; and if it is not at all like you, 1.

Imagine

_____ 1. Last week, as you were discussing your strained finances with your family, family members came up with several possible solutions. Even though you had already decided on one solution. you decided to spend more time considering all the possibilities before making a final decision.

_____ 2. You were invited to a Halloween party, and, assuming it was a costume party, you dressed as a pumpkin. When you arrived at the party and found everyone else dressed in formal attire, you laughed and joked about the misunderstanding, and decided to stay and enjoy the party.

_____ 3. You have always enjoyed being with your friend Chris, but do not enjoy Chris's habit of always interrupting you. The last time you met, every time Chris interrupted you, you then interrupted Chris to teach Chris a lesson.

_____ 4. Your daily schedule is very structured and your calendar is full of appointments and commitments. When asked to make a change in your schedule, you replied that changes are impossible before even considering the change.

_____ 5. You went to a party where more than 50 people attended. You had a good time, but spent most of the evening talking to one close friend rather than meeting new people.

_____ 6. When discussing a personal problem with a group of friends, you noticed that many different solutions were offered. Although several of the solutions seemed feasible, you already had your opinion and did not listen to any of the alternative solutions.

_____ 7. You and a friend planned a fun evening and you were dressed and ready ahead of time. You found that you are unable to do anything else until your friend arrived.

_____ 8. When you found your seat at the ball game, you realized you did not know anyone sitting nearby. However, you introduced yourself to the people sitting next to you and attempted to strike up a conversation.

_____ 9. You had lunch with your friend Chris, and Chris told you about a too-personal family problem. You quickly finished your lunch and stated that you had to leave because you had a lot to do that afternoon.

_____ 10. You were involved in a discussion about international politics with a group of acquaintances and you assumed that the members of the group were as knowledgeable as you on the topic; but, as the discussion progressed, you learned that most of the group knew little about the subject. Instead of explaining your point of view, you decided to withdraw from the discussion.

_____ 11. You and a group of friends got into a discussion about gun control and, after a while, it became obvious that your opinions differed greatly from those of the rest of the group. You explained your position once again, but you agreed to respect the group's opinion also.

_____ 12. You were asked to speak to a group you belong to, so you worked hard preparing a 30-minute presentation; but at the meeting, the organizer asked you to lead a question-and-answer session instead of giving your presentation. You agreed, and answered the group's questions as candidly and fully as possible.

_____ 13. You were offered a managerial position in which every day you would face new tasks and challenges and a changing day-to-day routine. You decided to accept this position instead of one that has a stable daily routine.

_____ 14. You were asked to give a speech at a Chamber of Commerce breakfast. Because you did not know anyone at the breakfast and would feel uncomfortable not knowing anyone in the audience, you declined the invitation.

**HOW DID YOU DO?**   To compute your score:

1. Reverse the scoring for items 4, 5, 6, 7, 9, 10, and 14. That is, for each of these questions, substitute as follows:
   a. If you answered 5, reverse it to 1.
   b. If you answered 4, reverse it to 2.
   c. If you answered 3, keep it as 3.
   d. If you answered 2, reverse it to 4.
   e. If you answered 1, reverse it to 5.

2. Add the scores for all 14 items. Be sure that you use the reversed scores for items 4, 5, 6, 7, 9, 10, and 14. Use your original scores for items 1, 2, 3, 8, 11, 12, and 13.

In general, you can interpret your score as follows:
- 65–70 = much more flexible than average
- 57–64 = more flexible than average
- 44–56 = about average
- 37–43 = less flexible than average
- 14–36 = much less flexible than average

**WHAT WILL YOU DO?**   Are you satisfied with your level of flexibility? What might you do to cultivate flexibility in general and communication flexibility in particular?

Source: From "Development of a Communication Flexibility Measure" by Matthew M. Martin and Rebecca B. Rubin in *The Southern Communication Journal*, V. 59, Winter 1994, pp. 171–178. Reprinted by permission of the Southern States Communication Association.

■ *Respond to those with whom you're interacting* with spontaneity and with appropriate honesty, but also with an awareness of what you're saying and what the possible outcomes of your messages might be.

■ *Own your own feelings and thoughts.* Take responsibility for what you say. Use **I-messages** instead of **you-messages**. Instead of saying, "You make me feel stupid when you don't ask my opinion," own your feelings and say, for example, "I feel stupid when you ask everyone else what they think but don't ask me." When you own your feelings and thoughts—when you use I-messages— you say, in effect, "This is how *I* feel," "This is how *I* see the situation," and "This is what *I* think." When you use I-messages, you make it explicit that your feelings result from the interaction between what is going on outside your skin (what others say, for example) and what is going on inside your skin (your preconceptions, attitudes, and prejudices, for example).

## Empathy

Empathy, which we explored in Unit 4, is an ability to feel what another person feels from that person's point of view without losing your own identity. When you empathize, you feel another's feelings in a somewhat similar way; you understand emotionally what another person is experiencing. (To sympathize, in contrast, is to feel *for* the person—to feel sorry or happy for the person, for example.)

### Increasing Empathy

Here are a few suggestions to help you communicate empathy effectively (Authier & Gustafson, 1982).

■ *Avoid evaluating, judging, or criticizing* the other person's behaviors. Make it clear that you are not evaluating or judging but trying to understand.

■ *Focus your concentration.* Maintain eye contact, an attentive posture, and physical closeness. Express your involvement through appropriate facial expressions and gestures.

■ *Reflect back to the speaker* the feelings that you think are being expressed so as to check the accuracy of your perceptions and to show your commitment to understanding the speaker. For example, you might make tentative statements such as "You seem really angry with your father" or "I hear some doubt in your voice."

■ *When appropriate, use your own self-disclosures* to communicate your understanding. Be careful, however, that you don't get so caught up in your own disclosures that you refocus the discussion on yourself.

**EXPRESSING SYMPATHY**

One of your colleague's father just died; you don't know this person well, nor do you know what kind of relationship there was with the father. Yet, you feel you want to express some sympathy.

*WHAT DO YOU SAY?*
*Through what channel?*

## Positiveness

**Positiveness** in interpersonal communication involves the use of positive rather than negative messages. For example, instead of the negative "I wish you wouldn't ignore my opinions," consider the value of the positive alternative: "I feel good when you ask my opinions." Instead of the negative "You look horrible in stripes," consider the value of the positive: "I think you look great in solid colors." Interestingly enough, accumulating research suggests that positiveness in attitude is physically beneficial, making us less susceptible to illness (Goode, 2003).

### Increasing Positiveness

Here are just a few suggestions for communicating positiveness. This may be a bit easier for women than for men, because women generally are more apt to express positiveness in their evaluations in both face-to-face and computer-mediated communication (Adrianson, 2001).

■ *Look for and compliment the positive* in the person or in the person's work. Compliment specifics; overly general compliments ("Your project was interesting") are rarely as effective as those that are specific and concrete ("Your proposal will mean a great financial saving").

■ *Express satisfaction* in interpersonal communication by, for example, using facial expressions, maintaining a reasonably but appropriately close distance, focusing eye contact, and avoiding glancing away from the other person for long periods of time.

**SAYING THE RIGHT THING**

Your roommate just made the dean's list and as a reward received a new BMW from a rich uncle. Your roommate is ecstatic and in listening to her tell you about it, you want to demonstrate empathy. But you're really annoyed that some people just seem to get everything.

WHAT DO YOU SAY?

- *Recognize cultural differences* when expressing positiveness (Dresser, 1996; Chen, 1992). For example, in the United States it's considered appropriate for a supervisor to compliment a worker for doing an exceptional job. But in other cultures (collectivist cultures, for example) such praise would be considered inappropriate, because it singles out one individual and separates that person from the group.

## Immediacy

**Immediacy** is a quality of interpersonal effectiveness that creates a sense of togetherness, of oneness between speaker and listener. When you communicate immediacy you show interest and attention; you convey your liking for and attraction to the other person. People respond more favorably to communication that is immediate than to communication that is not. For example, students of instructors who communicated immediacy felt that the instruction was better and the course more valuable than students of instructors who did not communicate immediacy (Moore, Masterson, Christophel, & Shea, 1996; Witt & Wheeless, 2001). Students and teachers liked each other largely on the basis of immediacy (Wilson & Taylor, 2001; Baringer & McCroskey, 2000).

### Increasing Immediacy

Here are a few suggestions for communicating immediacy.

- *Express psychological closeness and openness* by, for example, maintaining physical closeness and arranging your body to exclude third parties. Maintain appropriate eye contact, limit looking around at others, smile, and express your interest in the other person.
- *Use the other person's name*; for example, say, "Joe, what do you think?" instead of "What do you think?"
- *Focus on the other person's remarks.* Make the speaker know that you heard and understood what was said, and give the speaker appropriate verbal and nonverbal feedback.
- *Be culturally sensitive when expressing immediacy.* In the United States most people see immediacy behaviors as friendly and appropriate. In other cultures, however, people may view the same immediacy behaviors as overly familiar—as presuming a close relationship when only an acquaintanceship exists (Axtell, 1993).

## Interaction Management

**Interaction management** skills are the techniques and strategies by which you regulate and carry on an interpersonal interaction. Effective interaction management results in an interaction that's satisfying to both parties. Neither person feels ignored or on stage; each contributes to and benefits from the interpersonal exchange.

### Increasing Interaction Management

In a sense, this entire text is devoted to the effective management of interpersonal interactions. However, here are a few specific suggestions for managing conversations.

- *Maintain conversational turns,* passing the opportunity to speak back and forth through appropriate eye movements, vocal expressions, and body and facial gestures.
- *Keep the conversation fluent,* avoiding long and awkward pauses. For example, it's been found that patients are less satisfied with their interaction with their doctor when the silences between their comments and the doctor's responses are overly long (Rowland-Morin & Carroll, 1990).
- *Communicate with consistent verbal and nonverbal messages*—messages that harmonize and reinforce one another. Avoid sending contradictory signals—for example, a resentful look combined with a verbal expression of thanks.

## Expressiveness

**Expressiveness** is the skill of communicating genuine involvement; it includes abilities such as taking responsibility for your thoughts and feelings, encouraging expressiveness or openness in others, and providing appropriate feedback.

## Increasing Expressiveness

Here are a few suggestions for communicating expressiveness.

- *Use appropriate variations* in vocal rate, pitch, volume, and rhythm to convey involvement and interest. Use appropriate variations in verbal language, too; avoid clichés and trite expressions, which can signal a lack of originality and personal involvement.
- *Use appropriate gestures*, especially gestures that focus on the other person rather than yourself. For example, maintain eye contact and lean toward the person; at the same time, avoid making self-touching gestures or directing your eyes to others in the room.
- *Be culturally aware when communicating expressiveness*. Some cultures (Italian and Greek, for example) encourage expressiveness and teach children to be expressive. Other cultures (Japanese and Thai, for example) encourage a more reserved response style (Matsumoto, 1996). Some cultures (Arab and many Asian cultures, for example) consider expressiveness by women in business settings to be generally inappropriate (Lustig & Koester, 2006; Axtell, 1993; Hall & Hall, 1987).
- *Give verbal and nonverbal feedback* to show that you're listening. Such feedback—called "conversational pitchback" by one researcher—promotes relationship satisfaction (Ross, 1995).

## Other-Orientation

**Other-orientation** is the ability to adapt your messages to the other person. It involves communicating attentiveness and interest in the other person and in what the person says.

## Increasing Other-Orientation

You'll recognize the following behaviors in those with whom you enjoy talking.

- *Show consideration and respect*—for example, ask if it's all right to dump your troubles on someone before doing so, or ask if your phone call comes at a good time before launching into your conversation.
- *Acknowledge the other person's feelings as legitimate*. Comments such as "You're right" or "That's interesting" or "I can understand why you're so angry; I would be, too" help focus the interaction on the other person and assure the person that you're listening. At the same time, grant the other person permission to express (or to not express) her or his feelings. A simple statement such as "I know how difficult it is to talk about feelings" opens up the topic of feelings and gives the person permission to pursue such a discussion or to say nothing.
- *Acknowledge the presence and the importance of the other person.* Ask the other person for suggestions and opinions. Similarly, ask for clarification as appropriate. This will ensure that you understand what the other person is saying from that person's point of view.
- *Focus your messages on the other person.* Verbally, use open-ended questions to involve the other person in the interaction (as opposed to questions that merely ask for a yes or no answer) and make statements that directly address the person. Nonverbally, use focused eye contact and appropriate facial expressions; smile, nod, and lean toward the other person.

## SUMMARY: INTERPERSONAL COMMUNICATION: CONVERSATION

In this unit, we examined the conversation process from opening to closing; conversational problems and their prevention and repair; and 12 key principles of conversational effectiveness.

1. Conversation consists of five general stages: opening, feedforward, business, feedback, and closing.

2. Conversations can be initiated in various ways, for example, with self, other, relational, and context references.

3. The closing of a conversation may be achieved through a variety of methods. For example, you may reflect back on the conversation, as in summarizing; directly state your desire to end the conversation; refer to future interaction; ask for closure; and/or state your pleasure in the interaction.

4. The business of conversation is maintained by the passing of speaking and listening turns; turn-maintaining

and turn-yielding cues are used by the speaker, and turn-requesting, turn-denying, and backchanneling cues are used by the listener.

5. One way to avert potential conversational problems is through the disclaimer, a statement that helps ensure that your message will be understood and will not reflect negatively on you.

6. Another way to repair a conversational problem is with the excuse, a statement designed to lessen the negative impact of a speaker's messages.

7. Twelve skills of conversational effectiveness include dialogue, mindfulness, flexibility, cultural sensitivity (as appropriate), metacommunication, openness, empathy, positiveness, immediacy, interaction management, expressiveness, and other-orientation.

## KEY TERMS IN INTERPERSONAL COMMUNICATION: CONVERSATION

conversation (p. **151**)

conversational management (p. **158**)

conversational turns (p. **158**)

dialogue (p. **163**)

excuse (p. **161**)

expressiveness (p. **168**)

flexibility (p. **164**)

gossip (p. **154**)

I-messages (p. **167**)

immediacy (p. **168**)

interaction management (p. **169**)

leave-taking cues (p. **156**)

mindfulness (p. **163**)

monologue (p. **163**)

openness (p. **165**)

other-orientation (p. **169**)

positiveness (p. **168**)

you-messages (p. **167**)

## THINKING CRITICALLY ABOUT INTERPERSONAL COMMUNICATION: CONVERSATION

1. **The Negatives of Empathy.** Although empathy is almost universally considered positive, there is some evidence to show that it has a negative side. For example, people are most empathic with those who are similar—racially and ethnically as well as in appearance and social status. The more empathy we feel toward our own group, the less empathy—possibly even the more hostility—we feel toward other groups. The same empathy that increases our understanding of our own group decreases our understanding of other groups. So while empathy may encourage group cohesiveness and identification, it can also create dividing lines between "us" and "them" (Angier, 1995b). Have you ever witnessed these negative effects of empathy?

2. **Disclaimers.** Try collecting and analyzing examples of disclaimers from your interpersonal interactions as well as from the media. For example, what type of disclaimer is being used? Why is it being used? Is the disclaimer appropriate? What other kinds of disclaimers could have been used more effectively?

3. **Conversational Etiquette.** Another way of looking at conversational rule violations is as breaches of etiquette. When you fail to follow the rules of etiquette, you're often breaking a conversational rule. A variety of websites focus on etiquette in different communication situations. For the etiquette of online conversation, see www.internetiquette.org/; for Web etiquette, see www.w3.org/Provider/Style/Etiquette.html; and for

cell phone etiquette, see www.cell-phone-etiquette.com/index.htm. Visit one or more of these websites and record any rules you find particularly applicable to interpersonal communication and conversation.

4. **Conversational Taboos.** Not surprisingly, each culture has its own conversational taboos—topics that should be avoided, especially by visitors from other cultures. A few examples: In Norway avoid talk of salaries and social status; in Spain avoid discussing family, religion, or jobs, and don't make negative comments on bullfighting; in Egypt avoid talk of Middle Eastern politics; in Japan avoid talking about World War II; in the Philippines avoid talk of politics, religion, corruption, and foreign aid; in Mexico avoid talking about the Mexican-American war and illegal aliens; in the Caribbean avoid discussing race, local politics, and religion (Axtell, 1993). Do you consider some topics taboo? In particular, are there topics that you do not want members of other cultures to talk about? Why?

5. **Interruptions.** In an analysis of 43 published studies on interruptions and gender differences, men interrupted significantly more than women (Anderson, 1998). Among the reasons offered to explain why men interrupt more is men's desire to shift the focus to their areas of competence (and away from their areas of incompetence) and to maintain power and control. Do you find that your own experience supports these findings on gender differences in interrupting? Based on your experiences, how would you explain the reasons for interrupting?

## LOGON! MYCOMMUNICATIONLAB

### WWW.MYCOMMUNICATIONLAB.COM

Visit MCL and take the self-tests that measure how satisfying you find a conversation and how apprehensive you are in conversations. Also try the exercises Analyzing a Conversation, Giving and Taking Directions, Gender and the Topics of Conversation, and Responding Effectively in Conversation.

Take a look at the Interpersonal Communication website maintained by Allyn & Bacon: www.abacon.com/commstudies/interpersonal/interpersonal.html. The site covers topics like relationship development, relationship patterns, and interpersonal conflict and offers additional points of view and perspectives.

# UNIT 8  Interpersonal Relationship Stages and Theories

## MAJOR TOPICS

**Relationship Stages**
**Relationship Theories**

## Special Features

Much of your life focuses on relationships: friends, lovers, and family relations probably occupy an enormous part of your day-to-day thoughts and experiences.

**In this unit you'll learn about:**
- the ways in which relationships develop, the stages they go through.
- the theories that attempt to account for our relationship decisions and choices.

**You'll learn to:**
- communicate in ways appropriate to your relationship stage.
- assess your own relationship behavior and make adjustments as needed.

A good way to begin the study of interpersonal relationships is to examine your own relationships (past, present, or those you look forward to) by taking the following self-test, "What Do Your Relationships Do for You?" It highlights the advantages and the disadvantages that relationships serve.

# TEST **YOURSELF**

## What Do Your Relationships Do for You?

Focus on your own relationships in general (friendship, romantic, family, and work); or focus on one particular relationship (say, your life partner or your child or your best friend); or focus on one type of relationship (say, friendships), and respond to the following by indicating the extent to which your relationship(s) serve each of these functions. Use a 10-point scale on which 1 indicates that your relationship(s) never serves this function, 10 indicates that your relationship(s) always serves this function, and the numbers in between indicate levels between these extremes.

_____ **1.** My relationships help to lessen my loneliness.

_____ **2.** My relationships put uncomfortable pressure on me to expose my vulnerabilities.

_____ **3.** My relationships help me to secure stimulation (intellectual, physical, and emotional).

_____ **4.** My relationships increase my obligations.

_____ **5.** My relationships help me gain in self-knowledge and in self-esteem.

_____ **6.** My relationships prevent me from developing other relationships.

_____ **7.** My relationships help enhance my physical and emotional health.

_____ **8.** My relationships scare me because they may be difficult to dissolve.

_____ **9.** My relationships maximize my pleasures and minimize my pains.

_____ **10.** My relationships hurt me.

**HOW DID YOU DO?** The numbers from 1 to 10 that you used to respond to each statement should give you some idea of how strongly your relationships serve these advantages. The odd-numbered statements (1, 3, 5, 7, and 9) express what most people would consider advantages of interpersonal relationships:

(1) One of the major benefits of relationships is that they help to lessen loneliness (Rokach, 1998; Rokach & Brock, 1995). They make you feel that someone cares, that someone likes you, that someone will protect you, that someone ultimately will love you. (3) As plants are heliotropic and orient themselves to light, humans are stimulotropic and orient themselves to sources of stimulation (Davis, 1973). Human contact is one of the best ways to secure this stimulation—intellectual, physical, and emotional. Even an imagined relationship seems better than none, one type of which is covered in the Media Watch box on "Parasocial Relationships" on page 175.

(5) Through contact with others you learn about yourself and see yourself from different perspectives and in different roles, as a child or parent, as a coworker, as a manager, as a best friend. Healthy interpersonal relationships help enhance self-esteem and self-worth. Simply having a friend or romantic partner (at least most of the time) makes you feel desirable and worthy.

(7) Research consistently shows that interpersonal relationships contribute significantly to physical and emotional health (Rosen, 1998; Goleman, 1995; Rosengren, 1993; Pennebacker, 1991) and to personal happiness (Berscheid & Reis, 1998). Without close interpersonal relationships you're more likely to become depressed, and this depression, in turn, contributes significantly to physical illness. Isolation, in fact, contributes as much to mortality as high blood pressure, high cholesterol, obesity, smoking, or lack of physical exercise (Goleman 1995).

(9) The most general function served by interpersonal relationships, and the function that encompasses all the

others, is that of maximizing pleasure and minimizing pain. Your good friends, for example, will make you feel even better about your good fortune and less hurt when you're confronted with hardships.

The even-numbered statements (2, 4, 6, 8, and 10) express what most people consider disadvantages of interpersonal relationships:

(2) Close relationships put pressure on you to reveal yourself and to expose your vulnerabilities. While this is generally worthwhile in the context of a supporting and caring relationship, it may backfire if the relationship deteriorates and these weaknesses are used against you.

(4) Close relationships increase your obligations to other people, sometimes to a great extent. Your time is no longer entirely your own. And although you enter relationships to spend more time with these special people, you also incur time (and perhaps financial) obligations with which you may not be happy.

(6) Close relationships can lead you to abandon other relationships. Sometimes the other relationship involves someone you like but your partner can't stand. More often, however, it's simply a matter of time and energy; relationships take a lot of both and you have less to give to these other and less intimate relationships.

(8) The closer your relationship, the more emotionally difficult it is to dissolve, a feeling which may be uncomfortable for some people. If the relationship is deteriorating, you may feel distress or depression. In some cultures, for example, religious pressures may prevent married couples from separating. And if lots of money is involved, dissolving a relationship can often mean giving up the fortune you've spent your life accumulating.

(10) And, of course, your partner may break your heart. Your partner may leave you—against all your pleading and promises. Your hurt will be in proportion to how much you care and need your partner. If you care a great deal, you're likely to experience great hurt; if you care less, the hurt will be less—it's one of life's little ironies.

**WHAT WILL YOU DO?** One way to use this self-test is to consider how you might lessen the disadvantages of your interpersonal relationships; at least those disadvantages that you find are always or almost always present in your relationships. Consider, for example, if your own behaviors are contributing to the disadvantages. Do you bury yourself in one or two relationships and discourage the development of others? At the same time, consider how you can maximize the advantages that your relationships currently serve.

To complement this discussion of the disadvantages of interpersonal relationships, we'll look also at what has come to be called the "dark side of interpersonal relationships" in the next unit.

## RELATIONSHIP STAGES

It's useful to look at interpersonal relationships as created and constructed by the individuals involved. That is, in any interpersonal relationship—say between Pat and Chris—there are actually several relationships: (1) the relationship that Pat sees, (2) the relationship as Chris sees it, (3) the relationship that Pat wants and is striving for, (4) the relationship that Chris wants. And of course there are the many relationships that friends and relatives see and that they reflect back in their communications; for example, the relationship that Pat's mother (who dislikes Chris) sees and reflects in her communication with Pat and Chris is very likely to influence Pat and Chris in some ways. And then there's the relationship that a dispassionate researcher/observer would see. Looked at in this way, there are many interpersonal relationships in any interpersonal relationship.

This is not to say that there is no *real* relationship; it's just to say that there are many real relationships. And because there are these differently constructed relationships, people often disagree about a wide variety of issues and evaluate the relationship very differently. Regularly on *The Jerry Springer Show* and *Maury*, you see couples who see their relationship very differently. The first guest thinks all is going well until the second guest comes on and explodes—often identifying long-held dissatisfactions and behaviors that shock the partner.

The quality that makes a relationship interpersonal is **interdependency**; that is, the actions of one person have an impact on the other; one person's actions have consequences for the other person. The actions of a stranger (for example, actions such as working overtime or flirting with a coworker) will have no impact on you; you and the proverbial stranger are independent—your actions have no effect on each other. If, however, you were in an interpersonal relationship and your partner worked overtime or flirted with a coworker, it would affect you and the relationship in some way.

The six-stage model shown in Figure 8.1 on page 174 describes the significant stages you may go through as you try to achieve your relationship goals. As a general description of relationship development (and sometimes dissolution), the stages seem standard: They apply to all relationships, whether friendship or love, whether face-to-face or computer-mediated. The six stages are contact, involvement, intimacy, deterioration, repair, and dissolution. Each stage can be divided into an initial and a final phase.

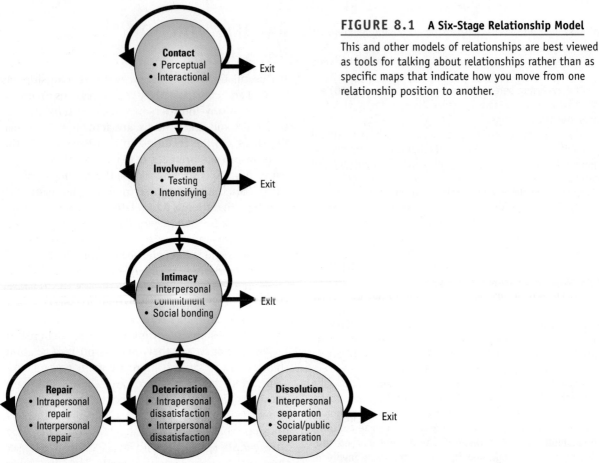

**FIGURE 8.1** **A Six-Stage Relationship Model**

This and other models of relationships are best viewed as tools for talking about relationships rather than as specific maps that indicate how you move from one relationship position to another.

As important as the stages themselves is the movement from stage to stage, depicted in Figure 8.1 by the different types of arrows. The exit arrows show that each stage offers the opportunity to exit the relationship: After saying hello, you can say good-bye and exit. The vertical or movement arrows going to the next stage and back again represent the fact that you can move either to a more intense stage (say, from involvement to intimacy) or to a less intense stage (say, from intimacy to deterioration). The self-reflexive arrows—the arrows that return to the beginning of the same level or stage—signify that any relationship may become stabilized at any point. You may, for example, remain at the contact stage without getting any further involved, a situation that exists among residents of many large apartment complexes.

Movement from one stage to another depends largely on your relationship communication skills—the skills you deploy to initiate and open a relationship, to present yourself as likable, to express affection, and to self-disclose appropriately—and in fact all the interpersonal skills you've been acquiring throughout this course (Dindia & Timmerman, 2003). Recognize that these skills will prove relevant in both face-to-face and in computer-mediated rela-

tionships; though the specific ways in which you express empathy, for example, will vary depending on you're expressing it with only written cues or with facial, vocal, and body as well as verbal cues.

Because relationships differ so widely, it's best to think of any relationship model as a tool for talking about relationships, rather than as a specific map that indicates how you move from one relationship position to another. This six-stage model is certainly not the only way you can look at relationships. Tables 8.1 (on page 175) and 8.2 (on page 176) depict models of different types.

## Contact

At the **contact** stage, there is first *perceptual contact*—you see what the person looks like, you hear what the person sounds like, you may even smell the person. From this, you get a physical picture: gender, approximate age, height, and so on. If this is an online relationship, this initial perception relies on a different set of cues. Depending on your expectations for this relationship, you might develop a visual image based on the written messages exchanged; or, if you have audio and video capabilities,

## MEDIA WATCH
# PARASOCIAL RELATIONSHIPS

**Parasocial relationships** are relationships that viewers perceive themselves to have with media personalities (Rubin & McHugh, 1987; Giles, 2001). Some viewers develop these relationships with real media personalities—Katie Couric, Regis Philbin, Oprah Winfrey, or Dr. Phil, for example. As a result they may watch these people faithfully and communicate with them in their own imaginations. In other cases these relationships are with fictional characters—an investigator on *CSI*, a lawyer on *Law and Order*, or a doctor on a soap opera. In fact, actors who portray doctors frequently get mail asking for medical advice. And soap opera stars who are about to be "killed" frequently get warning letters from their parasocial relationship fans. Obviously, however, most people don't go quite this far.

Parasocial relationships develop from an initial attraction based on the character's social and task roles, then progress to a perceived relationship and finally to a sense that this relationship is important (Rubin & McHugh, 1987). The more you can predict the behavior of a character, the more likely you are to develop a parasocial relationship with that character (Perse & Rubin, 1989). In addition, the chat sessions that celebrities hold on the Internet help to foster the illusion of a real interpersonal relationship. And the screen savers of television performers make it difficult not to think of them in relationship terms when they face you every time you leave your computer idle for a few minutes.

As might be expected, research indicates that these parasocial relationships are most important to those who spend a great deal of time with the media, who have few interpersonal relationships, and who are generally anxious (Rubin, Perse, & Powell, 1985; Cole & Leets, 1999).

## Increasing Media Literacy

*In what ways do the media encourage parasocial relationships between viewers on the one hand and television and film characters on the other? In what ways does the culture encourage such relationships? All things considered, what do you think about parasocial relationships?*

## Table 8.1 Knapp's Model of Relationship Stages

Try comparing the 6-stage model presented in Figure 8.1 (p. 174) with mark Knapp's 10-stage model, shown here. You'll find it helpful to read Knapp's more complete explanation of this model (see Knapp & Vangelisti, 2005). The first five stages of Knapp's model describe the processes of coming together and moving toward greater connection and intimacy.

- *Initiation* is the stage at which you first perceive and interact with the other person. Here you try to present yourself in a positive light and to open the channels of communication.
- *Experimenting* involves trying to learn about the other person.
- *Intensifying* involves interacting on a more personal and intimate level; your speech becomes more informal, and you use lots of terms that have meaning only for the two of you.
- *Integrating* consists of a fusion of the two individuals, a stage when mutual opinions and attitudes are cultivated.
- *Bonding* has to do with the social naming of the relationship; for example, as marriage or domestic partnership or exclusive partnership.

The next five stages describe the stages of coming apart and moving away from intimacy.

- *Differentiating* is the process by which the individuals begin to think of themselves as different and distinct from each other.
- *Circumscribing* involves restricting communication, perhaps to topics that are safe and will not cause conflict.
- *Stagnating* is the stage of inactive communication; when you do communicate it's with difficulty and awkwardness.
- *Avoiding* involves active physical separation and the absence of face-to-face interaction.
- *Terminating* involves the breaking of the bonds that once held the relationship together.

Source: Adapted from Mark L. Knapp and Anita L. Vangelisti, *Interpersonal Communication and Human Relationships* (5th ed.). (Boston: Allyn & Bacon, 2005), p. 35. Published by Allyn & Bacon, Boston, MA. Copyright © by Pearson Education. Adapted by permission of the publisher.

### "CLARIFYING" YOUR RELATIONSHIP RÉSUMÉ

Although you've been mostly honest in your two-month Internet relationship, you have padded your relationship résumé—lopped off a few years and pounds and made your temporary job seem like the executive fast-track. You need to come clean. WHAT DO YOU SAY? *Through what channel?*

on the sound of the person's voice, facial features, the way the person moves, and so on. From these cues you develop a physical picture.

After this perception, there is usually *interactional contact*. Here the interaction is superficial and impersonal. This is the stage of "Hello, my name is Joe"—the stage at which you exchange basic information that needs to come before any more intense involvement. This interactional contact may also be nonverbal, as in, for example, exchanging smiles, concentrating your focus on one person, or decreasing the physical distance between the two of you.

## Table 8.2 Online Relationship Stages

This table represents one attempt to identify the stages that people go through in Internet relationships. As you read down the table, consider how accurately this represents what you know of online relationships. How would you describe the way Internet relationships develop?

| Stage | Behavior |
|---|---|
| 1. Curiosity | You explore and search for individuals through chat rooms and other online sources. |
| 2. Investigation | You find out information about an individual. |
| 3. Testing | You introduce various topics, looking for common ground. |
| 4. Increasing frequency of contact | You increase the breadth and depth of your relationship. |
| 5. Anticipation | You anticipate face-to-face interaction and wonder what that will bring. |
| 6. Fantasy integration | You create a fantasy of what the person looks like and how the person behaves. |
| 7. Face-to-face meeting | You meet face-to-face, and reality and fantasy meet. |
| 8. Reconfiguration | You adjust the fantasy to the reality; you may decide to end the relationship or to pursue it more vigorously. |
| 9. Already separated | If you decide to maintain the relationship, you explore ways you can increase the depth and breadth of communication to compensate for the long-distance relationship. |
| 10. Long-term relationship | You negotiate the new relationship, whether it will be maintained in its online form or in a new face-to-face form. |

Source: This table is adapted from Leonard J. Shedletsky and Joan E. Aitken, *Human Communication on the Internet* (Boston: Allyn & Bacon, 2004), p. 159. Published by Allyn & Bacon, Boston, MA. Copyright © by Pearson Education. Reprinted by permission of the publisher.

This is the stage at which you initiate interaction ("May I join you?") and engage in invitational communication ("May I buy you a drink?"). The invitational messages in computer-mediated communication may involve moving to a face-to-face meeting. According to some researchers, it's at this contact stage—within the first four minutes of initial interaction—that you decide if you want to pursue the relationship or not (Zunin & Zunin, 1972).

Physical appearance is especially important in the initial development of attraction, because it's the characteristic most readily available to sensory inspection. Yet through both verbal and nonverbal behaviors, qualities such as friendliness, warmth, openness, and dynamism are also revealed at the contact stage.

Not surprisingly, people make contact through various means. Table 8.3 provides the results of one survey on the major places at which couples (all of whom were Internet users) met.

## Involvement

At the **involvement** stage a sense of mutuality, of being connected, develops. During this stage you experiment and try to learn more about the other person. At the initial phase of involvement, a kind of preliminary *testing* goes on. You want to see if your initial judgment—made perhaps at the contact stage—proves reasonable. So you may ask questions: "Where do you work?" "What are you majoring in?"

If you're committed to getting to know the person even better, you continue your involvement by *intensifying* your interaction. In this process you

**DISCOVERING PERSONAL INFORMATION**

You're becoming romantically involved with someone at work but before this relationship goes any further, you want to know about this person's HIV status and safe-sex practices. At the same time, you don't want to create a rift in the relationship.

WHAT DO YOU SAY?
*Through what channel?*

not only try to get to know the other person better, but also begin to reveal yourself. It's at this stage that you begin to share your feelings and your emotions. If this is to be a romantic relationship, you might date. If it's to be a friendship, you might share in activities related to mutual interests—go to the movies or to some sports event together.

And throughout the relationship process—but especially during the involvement and early stages of intimacy, partners continue testing each other.

## Table 8.3 Where People Meet

Here are the major places at which couples say they met.

| Where? | How Many? |
| --- | --- |
| Work or school | 38% |
| Through friends and family | 34% |
| At a night club, bar, or social gathering | 13% |
| Through the Internet | 3% |
| At a religious institution | 2% |
| In the same neighborhood | 1% |
| At a recreational facility | 1% |
| On a blind date or through a dating service | 1% |

Source: Data for this table come from the Pew Internet & American Life Project (Rainie & Madden, 2006).

Each person tests the other—each tries to find out how the other feels about the relationship. For example, you might ask your partner directly how he or she feels; or you might disclose your own feelings on the assumption that your partner will also self-disclose; or you might joke about a shared future together, touch more intimately, or hint that you're serious about the relationship; or you might question mutual friends as to your partner's feelings (Bell & Buerkel-Rothfuss, 1990; Baxter & Wilmot, 1984).

## Intimacy

One way to define **intimacy** is as a feeling that you can be honest and open when talking about yourself, that you can express thoughts and feelings you wouldn't reveal in other relationships (Mackey, Diemer, & O'Brien, 2000). At the intimacy stage, you commit yourself still further to the other person and, in fact, establish a kind of relationship in which this individual becomes your best or closest friend, lover, or companion. Your communication becomes more personalized, more synchronized, and easier (Gudykunst, Nishida, & Chua, 1987). Usually the intimacy stage divides itself quite neatly into two phases: an *interpersonal commitment* phase, in which you commit yourselves to each other in a kind of private way, and a *social bonding* phase, in which the commitment is made public—revealed perhaps to family and friends, perhaps to the public at large through a formal ceremony. Here the two of you become a unit, a pair.

# ASK THE RESEARCHER

## Topic Avoidance

*Recently I've started dating seriously, and I want to know if there are certain topics that are best avoided in romantic relationships. And while I'm at it, are there topics friends should avoid? Any suggestions?*

Every disclosure comes with risk. In the worst-case scenarios, disclosure begets violent reactions. However, a recent study showed that people's responses to negative disclosures were consistently better than people thought they would be.

Avoidance of certain topics (for example, past relational partners, future of the relationship) can sometimes help relationships. But we also know that the strongest relationships are those in which there is relatively limited avoidance. A perfect example is friendships. A lot of friendships, especially ones with potential for romance, never develop into closer relationships because of people's tendency to avoid talking about the most important issue—the relationship. So, less avoidance is generally better, but it serves little purpose to discuss issues that you know will incite conflict.

Of course, avoiding disclosure of issues that would clearly be of interest to your partner (for example, infidelity) or your friend (for example, theft) is a different ball game and almost never advised. The key issue in those cases is how to best disclose an issue, not whether to do so.

For further information: Petronio, S. (Ed). (2000). *Balancing the secrets of private disclosures*. Mahwah, NJ: Erlbaum. Also Greene, K., Derlega, V. J., Yep, G. A., & Petronio, S. (2003). *Privacy and disclosure of HIV in interpersonal relationships: A sourcebook for researchers and practitioners*. Mahwah, NJ: Erlbaum. And Afifi, T. D., Caughlin, J., & Afifi, W. A. (in press). The darkside of avoidance and secrets in interpersonal relationships: Reasons to question the ideology of openness. In B. Spitzberg and B. Cupach (Eds.), *The darkside of interpersonal relationships*. Mahwah, NJ: Lawrence Erlbaum.

**Walid A. Afifi** (Ph.D., University of Arizona) is an associate professor of communication at the University of California, Santa Barbara, where he teaches courses in interpersonal and relational communication and conducts research in information seeking, topic avoidance, and health communication (w-afifi@comm.ucsb.edu).

## Building Communication Skills    Talking Cherishing

Cherishing behaviors are an especially insightful way to affirm another person and to increase favor exchange, a concept that comes from the work of William Lederer (1984). **Cherishing behaviors** are those small gestures you enjoy receiving from your partner (a smile, a wink, a squeeze, a kiss, a phone call). Prepare a list of 10 cherishing behaviors that you would like to receive from your real or imagined relationship partner. Identify cherishing behaviors that are:

a. specific and positive—nothing overly general or negative

b. focused on the present and future rather than on issues about which the partners have argued in the past

c. capable of being performed daily

d. easily executed—nothing you really have to go out of your way to accomplish

In an actual relationship each partner would prepare a list, then the partners would exchange lists. Ideally, each partner would then perform the cherishing behaviors the other had chosen during their normal activities. In time, these behaviors should become a normal part of your interaction, which is exactly what you'd hope to achieve.

*Lists of cherishing behaviors will also give you insight into your own relationship needs and the kind of communicating partner you want.*

In addition, in the intimacy stage you increase your display of **affiliative cues** (signs that show you love the other person), including head nods, gestures, and forward leaning. You give **Duchenne smiles**, smiles that are beyond voluntary control and that signal genuine joy (Gonzaga, Keltner, Londahi, & Smith, 2001). These Duchenne smiles give you crow's-feet around the eyes, raise up your cheeks, and puff up the lower eyelids (Lemonick, 2005).

Commitment may take many forms; it may be an engagement or a marriage, a commitment to help the person or to be with the person, or a commitment to reveal your deepest secrets. It may consist of living together or agreeing to become lovers. Or it may consist of becoming a romantic pair either in face-to-face or in online relationships. The type of commitment varies with the relationship and with the individuals. The important characteristic is that the commitment made is a special one; it's a commitment that you do not make lightly or to everyone. Each of us reserves this level of intimacy for very few people at any given time—sometimes just one person; sometimes two, three, or perhaps four. In computer-mediated communication, there is the potential for a much greater number of intimates.

One important characteristic of intimacy is that we talk more affectionately, more lovingly, more

deeply. The accompanying Building Communication Skills box explores a particular type of intimacy talk, cherishing.

## Deterioration

Although many relationships remain at the intimacy stage, some enter the stage of **relationship deterioration**—the stage that sees the weakening of bonds between the parties and that represents the downside of the relationship progression. Relationships deteriorate for many reasons. When the reasons for coming together are no longer present or change drastically, relationships may deteriorate. Thus, for example, when your relationship no longer lessens your loneliness or provides stimulation or self-knowledge, or when it fails to increase your self-esteem or maximize pleasures and minimize pains, it may be in the process of deteriorating. Among the other reasons for deterioration are third-party relationships, sexual dissatisfaction, dissatisfaction with work, or financial difficulties (Blumstein & Schwartz, 1983).

The first phase of deterioration is usually *intrapersonal dissatisfaction.* You begin to feel that this relationship may not be as important as you had previously thought. You may experience personal dissatisfaction with everyday interactions, and begin to view the future together negatively. If this

## Theory and Research   Relationship Commitment

**UNDERSTANDING**

An important factor influencing the course of relationship deterioration (as well as relationship maintenance) is the degree of commitment the individuals have toward each other and toward the relationship. Three types of commitment are often distinguished and can be identified from your answers to the following questions (Johnson, 1973, 1982, 1991; Knapp & Taylor, 1995; Kurdek, 1995):

- Do I want to stay in this relationship? Do I have a desire to keep this relationship going?
- Do I have a moral obligation to stay in this relationship?
- Do I have to stay in this relationship? Is it a necessity for me to stay in this relationship?

All relationships are held together, in part, by desire, obligation, or necessity, or by some combination of these elements. The strength of the relationship, including its resistance to possible deterioration, is related to the degree of commitment. When a relationship shows signs of deterioration and yet there's a strong commitment to preserving it, the individuals may well surmount the obstacles and reverse the process. In contrast, when commitment is weak and the individuals doubt that there are good reasons for staying together, the relationship deteriorates faster and more intensely.

### Working with Theories and Research

*Has commitment or the lack of it (from either or both of you) ever influenced the progression of one of your relationships? What happened?*

---

dissatisfaction continues or grows, you may pass to the second phase, *interpersonal deterioration*, in which you discuss these dissatisfactions with your partner.

During the process of deterioration, communication patterns change drastically. These altered patterns are in part a response to the deterioration; you communicate as you do because of the way you feel your relationship is deteriorating. However, the way you communicate (or fail to communicate) also influences the fate of your relationship. During the deterioration stage you may, for example, increase withdrawal, communicate less, respond to computer messages more briefly and with greater delays, and self-disclose less.

The accompanying Understanding Theory and Research box examines relationship commitment, which greatly influences the course of relationship deterioration.

## Repair

The first phase of the **relationship repair** stage is *intrapersonal repair*, in which you analyze what went wrong and consider ways of solving your

relational difficulties. At this stage, you may consider changing your behaviors or perhaps changing your expectations of your partner. You may also weigh the rewards of your relationship as it is now against the rewards you could anticipate if your relationship ended.

If you decide that you want to repair your relationship, you may discuss this with your partner at the *interpersonal repair* level. Here you may talk about the problems in the relationship, the corrections you would want to see, and perhaps what you would be willing to do and what you would want the other person to do. This is the stage of negotiating new agreements, new behaviors. You and your partner may try to solve your problems yourselves, seek the advice of friends or family, or perhaps enter professional counseling.

You can look at the strategies for repairing a relationship in terms of the following six suggestions—which conveniently spell out the word REPAIR, a useful reminder that repair is not a one-step but a multistep process: Recognize the problem, Engage in productive conflict resolution, Pose possible solutions, Affirm each other, Integrate solutions into normal behavior, and Risk.

- *Recognize* the problem. What, in concrete terms, is wrong with your present relationship? What changes would be needed to make it better—again, in specific terms? Create a picture of your relationship as you would want it to be and compare that picture to the way the relationship looks now.

- *Engage* in productive conflict resolution. Interpersonal conflict is an inevitable part of relationship life. It's not so much the conflict that causes relationship difficulties as the way in which the conflict is approached (as we'll see in Unit 12). If it's confronted through productive strategies, the conflict may be resolved, and the relationship may actually emerge stronger and healthier. If, however, unproductive and destructive strategies are used, the relationship may well deteriorate further.

- *Pose* possible solutions. Ideally, each person will ask, "What can we do to resolve the difficulty that will allow both of us to get what we want?"

- *Affirm* each other. For example, happily married couples engage in greater positive behavior exchange; that is, they communicate more agreement, approval, and positive affect than do unhappily married couples (Dindia & Fitzpatrick, 1985).

- *Integrate* solutions into your life—make the solutions a part of your normal behavior.

- *Risk* giving favors without any certainty of reciprocity. Risk rejection by making the first move to make up or say you're sorry. Be willing to change, to adapt, to take on new tasks and responsibilities.

## Dissolution

The **dissolution** stage, in both friendship and romance, is the cutting of the bonds tying you together. At first it usually takes the form of *interpersonal separation*, in which you may not see each other anymore or may not return messages. If you live together,

---

**B u i l d i n g   C o m m u n i c a t i o n   s k i l l s**   Repairing Relationships

Whether expert or novice, each of us tries to repair relationships—not only our own but also those of others. Here are three situations that call for repair. Can you use what you've read about here (as well as your own experiences, readings, observations, and so on) to come up with some reasonable repair advice? What specific suggestions would you offer to each of the people in these situations?

1. *Friends and colleagues*: Mike and Jim, friends for 20 years, have had a falling out over the fact that Mike supported another person for promotion over Jim. Jim is resentful and feels that Mike should have helped him; Mike feels that his first obligation was to the company and that he chose the person he believed would do the best job. Mike feels that if Jim resents him and can't understand or appreciate his motives, then he no longer cares to be friends. Assuming that both Mike and Jim want the friendship to continue or will do so at some later time, what do you suggest that Mike and Jim do?

2. *Coming out*: Tom, a junior in college, recently came out as gay to his family. Contrary to his every expectation, they went ballistic. His parents want him out of the house, and his two brothers refuse to talk with him. Assuming that all parties will be sorry at some later time if the relationship is not repaired, what would you suggest that each of the individuals do?

3. *Betraying a confidence*: Pat and Chris have been best friends since elementary school. Even now, in their twenties, they speak every day and rely on each other for emotional support. Recently Pat betrayed a confidence and told several mutual friends that Chris had been having emotional problems and had been considering suicide. Chris found out and no longer wants to maintain the friendship. Assuming that the friendship is more good than bad and that both parties will regret it if they don't patch up the friendship, what do you suggest that Pat and Chris do?

you may move into separate apartments and begin to lead lives apart from each other. If this relationship is a marriage, you may seek a legal separation. If this separation period proves workable and if the original relationship is not repaired, you may enter the phase of *social or public separation*. In marriage, this phase corresponds to divorce. Avoidance of each other and a return to being "single" are among the primary identifiable features of dissolution. In some cases, however, the former partners change the definition of their relationship; for example, ex-lovers become friends, or ex-friends become "just" business partners.

The final, "good-bye," phase of dissolution is the point at which you become an ex-lover or ex-friend. In some cases this is a stage of relief and relaxation; finally, it's over. In other cases this is a stage of anxiety and frustration, of guilt and regret, of resentment over time ill spent and now lost. In more materialistic terms, the good-bye phase is the stage when property is divided and when legal battles may ensue over who should get what.

No matter how friendly the breakup, dissolution is likely to bring some emotional difficulty. Here are some suggestions for dealing with this:

- *Break the loneliness–depression cycle.* Avoid sad passivity, a state in which you feel sorry for yourself, sit alone, and perhaps cry. Instead, try to engage in active solitude (exercise, write, study, play computer games) and seek distraction (do things to put loneliness out of your mind; for example, take a long drive or shop). The most effective way to deal with loneliness is through social action, especially through helping people in need.

- *Take time out.* Take some time for yourself. Renew your relationship with yourself. Get to know yourself as a unique individual, standing alone now but fully capable of entering a meaningful relationship in the future.

- *Bolster self-esteem.* Positive and successful experiences are most helpful in building self-esteem. As in dealing with loneliness, helping others is one of the best ways to raise your own self-esteem.

- *Seek the support of others.* Avail yourself of your friends and family for support; it's an effective antidote to the discomfort and unhappiness that occurs when a relationship ends.

- *Avoid repeating negative patterns.* Ask, at the start of a new relationship, if you're entering a relationship modeled on the previous one. If the answer is yes, be especially careful that you do not repeat the problems. At the same time, avoid becoming a prophet of doom. Do not see in every new relationship vestiges of the old. Use past relationships and experiences as guides, not filters.

# RELATIONSHIP THEORIES

Many theories offer insight into why and how we develop and dissolve our relationships. Here we'll examine six relationship theories: theories focusing on attraction, relationship rules, relationship dialectics, social penetration, social exchange, and equity. Two theories that address online relationships are highlighted in the accompanying Understanding Theory and Research box on page 185.

## Attraction Theory

**Attraction theory** holds that people form relationships on the basis of **attraction.** You are no doubt drawn, or attracted, to some people and not to others. In a similar way, some people are attracted to you and some are not. If you're like most people, then you're attracted to others on the basis of four major factors:

### Similarity

If you could construct your mate, according to the **similarity** principle, it's likely that your mate would look, act, and think very much like you (Burleson, Samter, & Luccetti, 1992; Burleson, Kunkel, & Birch, 1994). Generally, people like those who are similar to them in nationality, race, abilities, physical characteristics, intelligence, and attitudes (Pornpitakpan, 2003).

Research also finds that you're more likely to help someone who is similar in race, attitude, and general appearance. Even the same first name is significant. For example, when an e-mail (asking receivers to fill out surveys of their food habits) identified the sender as having the same name as the receiver, there was a greater willingness to comply with the request (Gueguen, 2003). Sometimes people are attracted to their opposites, in a pattern called **complementarity**; for example, a dominant person might be attracted to someone who is more submissive. Generally, however, people prefer those who are similar.

### Proximity

If you look around at people you find attractive, you will probably find that they are the people who live or work close to you. People who become friends are the people who have the greatest opportunity to interact with each other. **Proximity**, or physical closeness, is most important in the early stages of interaction—for example, during the first days of school (in class or in dormitories). It decreases in importance, though always remaining significant, as the opportunity to interact with more distant others increases.

## Theory and Research  UNDERSTANDING  Online Relationship Theories

Here are two theories of online relationships that raise issues that are unique to online communication and that the other theories do not address.

■ *Social presence theory* argues that the "bandwidth" (the number of message cues exchanged) of communication influences the degree to which the communication is personal or impersonal (Walther & Parks, 2002; Wood & Smith, 2005). When lots of cues are exchanged (especially nonverbal cues), as in face-to-face communication, you feel great social presence—the whole person is there for you to communicate with and exchange messages with. When the bandwidth is smaller (as in e-mail or chat communication), then the communication is largely impersonal. So, for example, personal communication is easier to achieve in face-to-face situations (where tone of voice, facial expressions, eye contact and similar nonverbal cues come into play) than in computer-mediated communication, which essentially contains only written cues.

It's more difficult, the theory goes, to communicate supportiveness, warmth, and friendliness in text-based chat or e-mail exchanges because of the smaller bandwidth. Of course, as noted elsewhere, as video and audio components become more widely used this bandwidth will increase.

■ *Social information processing* (SIP) theory argues, contrary to social presence theory, that whether you're communicating face-to-face or online, you can communicate the same degree of personal involvement and develop similar close relationships (Walther, 1992; Walther & Parks, 2002). The idea behind this theory is that communicators are clever people: Given whatever channel they have available to send and receive messages, they will make adjustments to communicate what they want and to develop the relationships they want. It is true that when the time span studied is limited—as it is in much of the research—it is probably easier to communicate and develop relationships in face-to-face interaction than in online situations. But SIP theory argues that when the interaction occurs over an extended time period, as it often does in ongoing chat groups and in repeated e-mail exchanges, then the communication and the relationships can be as personal as those you develop in face-to-face situations.

### Working with Theories and Research

*How would you compare the level of closeness that you can communicate in face-to-face and in online situations? Do you feel it's more difficult (even impossible) to communicate, say, support, warmth, and friendship in online communication than in face-to-face communication?*

## Reinforcement

Not surprisingly, you're attracted to people who give rewards or **reinforcements**, which can range from a simple compliment to an expensive cruise. You're also attracted to people you reward (Jecker & Landy, 1969; Aronson, Wilson, & Akert, 1999). That is, you come to like people for whom you do favors; for example, you've probably increased your liking for persons after buying them an expensive present or going out of your way to do them a special favor. In these situations you justify your behavior by believing that the person was worth your efforts; otherwise, you'd have to admit to spending effort on people who might not deserve it.

## Physical Attractiveness and Personality

It's easily appreciated that people like physically attractive people more than they like physically unattractive people. What isn't so obvious is that we also feel a greater sense of familiarity with more attractive people than with less attractive people; that is, we're more likely to think we've met a person before if that person is attractive (Monin, 2003). Also, although culture influences what people think is physical attractiveness and what isn't, some research indicates that there are certain facial features that seem to be thought attractive in all cultures—a kind of universal attractiveness (Brody, 1994). Additionally, you probably tend to like people who have a pleasant rather than an unpleasant personality (although people will differ on what is and what is not an agreeable personality).

## Relationship Rules Theory

You can gain an interesting perspective on interpersonal relationships by looking at them in terms of the rules that govern them (Shimanoff, 1980). The general assumption of **rules theory** is that relationships—friendship and love in particular—are held together by adherence to certain rules. When those rules are broken, relationships may deteriorate and even dissolve.

Relationship rules theory helps us clarify several aspects of relationships. First, these rules help identify successful versus destructive relationship behavior. In addition, these rules help pinpoint more specifically why relationships break up and how they may be repaired. Further, if we know what the rules are, we will be better able to master the social skills involved in relationship development and maintenance. And because these rules vary from one culture to another, it is important to identify those unique to each culture so that intercultural relationships may be more effectively developed and maintained.

### Friendship Rules

One approach to friendship argues that friendships are maintained by rules (Argyle & Henderson, 1984; Argyle, 1986). When these rules are followed, the friendship is strong and mutually satisfying. When these rules are broken, the friendship suffers and may die. For example, the rules for keeping a friendship include such behaviors as standing up for your friend in his or her absence, sharing information and feelings about successes, demonstrating emotional support for a friend, trusting and offering to help a friend in need, and trying to make a friend happy when you're together. On the other hand, a friendship is likely to be in trouble when one or both friends are intolerant of the other's friends, discuss confidences with third parties, fail to demonstrate positive support, nag, and/or fail to trust or confide in the other. The strategy for maintaining a friendship, then, depends on your knowing the rules and having the ability to apply the appropriate interpersonal skills (Trower, 1981; Blieszner & Adams, 1992).

### Romantic Rules

Other research has identified the rules that romantic relationships establish and follow. These rules, of course, will vary considerably from one culture to another. For example, the different attitudes toward permissiveness and sexual relations with which Chinese and American college students view dating influence the romantic rules each group will establish and live by (Tang & Zuo, 2000). Leslie Baxter (1986) has identified eight major romantic rules. Baxter argues that these rules keep the relationship together—or, when broken, lead to deterioration and eventually dissolution. The general form for each rule, as Baxter phrases it, is, "If parties are in a close relationship, they should . . .":

1. acknowledge each other's individual identities and lives beyond the relationship;
2. express similar attitudes, beliefs, values, and interests;
3. enhance each other's self-worth and self-esteem;
4. be open, genuine, and authentic with each other;
5. remain loyal and faithful to each other;
6. have substantial shared time together;
7. reap rewards commensurate with their investments relative to the other party; and
8. experience a mysterious and inexplicable "magic" in each other's presence.

### Family Rules

Family communication research points to the importance of rules in defining and maintaining the family (Galvin, Bylund, & Brommel, 2007). Family rules concern three main interpersonal communication issues (Satir, 1983):

- What can you talk about? Can you talk about the family finances? Grandpa's drinking? Your sister's lifestyle?

- How can you talk about something? Can you joke about your brother's disability? Can you address directly questions of family history or family skeletons?

- To whom can you talk? Can you talk openly to extended family members such as cousins and aunts and uncles? Can you talk to close neighbors about family health issues?

All families teach rules for communication. Some of these are explicit, such as "Never contradict the family in front of outsiders" or "Never talk finances with outsiders." Other rules are unspoken; you deduce them as you learn the communication style of your family. For example, if financial issues are always discussed in secret and in hushed tones, then you can infer that you shouldn't tell other more distant family members or neighbors about family finances.

Like the rules governing relationships between friends and lovers, family rules tell you which behaviors will be rewarded (and therefore what you should do) and which will be punished (and therefore what you should not do). Family rules also provide a kind of structure that defines the family as a cohesive unit and that distinguishes it from other similar families.

Not surprisingly, the rules a family develops are greatly influenced by the culture. Although there are many similarities among families throughout the world, there are also differences (Georgas et al., 2001). For example, members of collectivist cultures are more likely to shield family information from outsiders as a way of protecting the family than are members of individualist cultures. As already noted, this tendency to protect the family can create serious problems in cases of wife abuse. Many women will not report spousal abuse, because they feel they must protect the family image and must not let others know that things aren't perfect at home (Dresser, 1996, 2005).

Family communication theorists argue that rules should be flexible so that special circumstances can be accommodated; there are situations that necessitate changing the family dinner time, vacation plans, or savings goals (Noller & Fitzpatrick, 1993). Rules should also be negotiable so that all members can participate in their modification and feel a part of family government.

## Relationship Dialectics Theory

**Relationship dialectics theory** argues that people in a relationship experience dynamic tensions between pairs of opposing motives or desires. Research generally finds three such pairs of opposites (Baxter, 1988, 1990; Baxter & Simon, 1993; Rawlins, 1989, 1992):

- The tension between *closeness and openness* has to do with the conflict between the desire to be in a closed, exclusive relationship and the wish to be in a relationship that is open to different people. You like the exclusiveness of your pairing, and yet you want also to relate to a larger group.

- The tension between *autonomy and connection* involves the desire to remain an autonomous, independent individual and the wish to connect intimately to another person and to a relationship.

This tension, by the way, is a popular theme in women's magazines, which teach readers to want both autonomy and connection (Prusank, Duran, & DeLillo, 1993).

- The tension between *novelty and predictability* centers on the competing desires for newness, different experiences, and adventure on the one hand and for sameness, stability, and predictability on the other. You're comfortable with being able to predict what will happen, and yet you also want newness, difference, novelty.

The closedness-openness tension occurs most during the early stages of relationship development. The autonomy-connection and novelty-predictability tensions occur more often as the relationship progresses. Each individual in a relationship may experience a somewhat different set of desires. For example, one person may want exclusivity above all, whereas that person's partner may want greater openness. Sometimes a happy combination can be negotiated; at other times these differences are irreconcilable, with the result that the couple becomes dissatisfied with their relationship or dissolves it.

Perhaps the major implication of relationship dialectics theory is that these tensions will influence a wide variety of behaviors. For example, the person who finds the primary relationship excessively predictable may seek novelty elsewhere, perhaps with a vacation to exotic places, perhaps with a different partner. The person who finds the primary relationship too connected (even suffocating) may need physical and psychological space to meet his or her autonomy needs. As you can appreciate, meeting your partner's needs—while also meeting your own needs—is one of the major relationship challenges you'll face.

## Social Penetration Theory

**Social penetration theory** is a theory not of why relationships develop but of what happens when they do develop; it describes relationships in terms of the number of topics that people talk about and their degree of "personalness" (Altman & Taylor, 1973). The **breadth** of a relationship has to do with the number of topics you and your partner talk about. The **depth** of the relationship involves the degree to which you penetrate the inner personality—the core—of the other individual. We can represent an individual as a circle and divide that circle into various parts, as in Figure 8.2 on page 186. This figure illustrates different models of social penetration. Each circle in the figure contains eight topic areas to depict breadth (identified as A through H) and five levels of intimacy

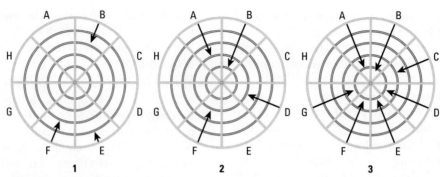

**FIGURE 8.2** **Models of Social Penetration**

Can you visualize your own relationships in terms of these varying levels of depth and breadth?
What can you do to increase both depth and breadth? What can you do to decrease both depth and breadth?

to depict depth (represented by the concentric circles). Note that in Circle 1, only three topic areas are penetrated. Of these, one is penetrated only to the first level and two to the second. In this type of interaction, three topic areas are discussed, and only at rather superficial levels. This is the type of relationship you might have with an acquaintance. Circle 2 represents a more intense relationship, one that has greater breadth and depth; more topics are discussed and to deeper levels of penetration. This is the type of relationship you might have with a friend. Circle 3 represents a still more intense relationship. Here there is considerable breadth (seven of the eight areas are penetrated) and depth (most of the areas are penetrated to the deepest levels). This is the type of relationship you might have with a lover or a parent.

When a relationship begins to deteriorate, the breadth and depth will, in many ways, reverse themselves, in a process called **depenetration**. For example, while ending a relationship, you might cut out certain topics from your interpersonal communications. At the same time, you might discuss the remaining topics in less depth. In some instances of relational deterioration, however, both the breadth and the depth of interaction increase. For example, when a couple breaks up and each is finally free from an oppressive relationship, the partners may—after some time—begin to discuss problems and feelings they would never have discussed when they were together. In fact, they may become extremely close friends and come to like each other more than when they were together. In these cases the breadth and depth of their relationship may increase rather than decrease (Baxter, 1983).

## Social Exchange Theory

**Social exchange theory** claims that you develop relationships that will enable you to maximize your profits (Chadwick-Jones, 1976; Gergen, Greenberg,

& Willis, 1980; Thibaut & Kelley, 1986)—a theory based on an economic model of profits and losses. The theory begins with the following equation: Profits = Rewards − Costs.

■ *Rewards* are anything that you would incur costs to obtain. Research has identified six types of rewards in a love relationship: money, status, love, information, goods, and services (Baron & Byrne, 1984). For example, to get the reward of money, you might have to work rather than play. To earn the status of an A in an interpersonal communication course, you might have to write a term paper or study more than you want to.

■ *Costs* are things that you normally try to avoid, that you consider unpleasant or difficult. Examples might include working overtime; washing dishes and ironing clothes; watching your partner's favorite television show, which you find boring; or doing favors for those you dislike.

■ *Profit* is what results when the rewards exceed the costs.

Using this basic economic model, social exchange theory claims that you seek to develop the friendships and romantic relationships that will give you the greatest profits, that is, relationships in which the rewards are greater than the costs.

When you enter a relationship, you have in mind a **comparison level**—a general idea of the kinds of rewards and profits that you feel you ought to get out of such a relationship. This comparison level consists of your realistic expectations concerning what you feel you deserve from this relationship. For example, a study of married couples found that most people expect high levels of trust, mutual respect, love, and commitment. Couples' expectations are significantly lower for time spent together, privacy, sexual activity, and communication (Sabatelli & Pearce, 1986). When the rewards that you get equal or surpass your comparison level, you feel satisfied with your relationship.

However, you also have a comparison level for alternatives. That is, you compare the profits that you get from your current relationship with the profits you think you could get from alternative relationships. Thus, if you see that the profits from your present relationship are below the profits that you could get from an alternative relationship, you may decide to leave your current relationship and enter a new, more profitable relationship.

## Equity Theory

**Equity theory** uses the ideas of social exchange, but goes a step farther and claims that you develop and maintain relationships in which the ratio of your rewards relative to your costs is approximately equal to your partner's (Walster, Walster, & Berscheid, 1978; Messick & Cook, 1983). For example, if you and a friend start a business—you put up two-thirds of the money and your friend puts up one-third—equity would demand that you get two-thirds of the profits and your friend gets one-third. An *equitable relationship*, then, is simply one in which each party derives rewards that are proportional to their costs. If you contribute more toward the relationship than your partner, then equity requires that you should get greater rewards. If you both work equally hard, then equity demands that you should both get approximately equal rewards. Conversely, inequity will exist in a relationship if you pay more of the costs (for example, if you do more of the unpleasant tasks) but your partner enjoys more of the rewards. Inequity will also exist if you and your partner work equally hard but one of you gets more of the rewards.

Much research supports this idea that people want equity in their interpersonal relationships (Ueleke et al., 1983). The general idea behind the theory is that if you are underbenefited (you get less than you put in), you'll be angry and dissatisfied.

---

# REFLECTIONS ON ETHICS

## Relationship Ethics

Ethics is a significant part of meaningful relationship communication. Relationships built and maintained on lies are not likely to survive in the long run. But there is more to relationship ethics than the injunction not to lie. For a beginning perspective, the ethical issues and guidelines that operate within a friendship, romantic, family, or workplace relationship can be reviewed with the acronym ETHICS—Empathy (Cheney & Tompkins, 1987), Talk rather than force, Honesty (Krebs, 1990), Interaction management, Confidentiality, and Supportiveness (Johannesen, 2001). As you read these guidelines, think about whether you and your relationship partners follow them.

> *Empathy*: People in a relationship have an ethical obligation to try to understand what others are feeling and thinking from their point of view. This is especially important when relationship members from different cultures communicate.
>
> *Talk*: Decisions in a relationship should be arrived at by talk, not by force—by persuasion rather than coercion.
>
> *Honesty*: Relationship communication should be honest and truthful.
>
> *Interaction management*: Relationship communication should be satisfying and comfortable and is the responsibility of all individuals.

> *Confidentiality*: People in a relationship have a right to expect that what they say in confidence will not be made public or even whispered about.
>
> *Supportiveness*: A supportive and cooperative climate should characterize interpersonal interactions in a relationship.

### Ethical Choice Point

*You're managing a work team of three colleagues charged with redesigning the company website. The problem is that Jack doesn't do any work and misses most of the meetings. You spoke with him about it, and he confided that he's going through a divorce and can't concentrate. You feel sorry for Jack and have been carrying him for the last few months, but you now realize that you'll never be able to bring the project in on time if you don't replace Jack. In addition, you really don't want to get a negative appraisal because of Jack; in fact, you were counting on the raise that this project was going to get you. What are your ethical obligations in this situation—to yourself? to the other team members? to your employer? What would you do?*

## ACHIEVING EQUITY

After thinking about equity, you realize that you put a lot more effort into the relationship; you pay significantly more of the costs than your partner. You want this imbalance corrected but at the same time don't want to create problems or destroy the relationship.

*WHAT DO YOU SAY?*
*Through what channel?*

If, on the other hand, you are overbenefited (you get more than you put in), you'll feel guilty. Some research, however, has questioned this rather neat but intuitively unsatisfying assumption and finds that the overbenefited person is often quite happy and contented; guilt from getting more than you deserve seems easily forgotten (Noller & Fitzpatrick, 1993).

Equity theory puts into clear focus the sources of the relational dissatisfaction we all hear about every day. For example, in a relationship both partners may have full-time jobs, but one partner may also be expected to do the major share of the household chores. Thus, although both may be deriving equal rewards—they have equally good cars, they live in the same three-bedroom house, and so on—one partner is paying more of the costs. According to equity theory, this partner will be dissatisfied because of this lack of equity.

Equity theory claims that you will develop, be satisfied with, and maintain relationships that are equitable. You will not develop, will be dissatisfied with, and will terminate relationships that are inequitable. The greater the inequity, the greater the dissatisfaction and the greater the likelihood that the relationship will end.

Though each relationship is unique, relationships for many people possess similar characteristics, and it is these general patterns that these theories tried to explain. Taken together, the theories actually explain a great deal about why you develop relationships, the way relationships work, the ways you seek to maintain relationships, and the reasons why some relationships are satisfying and others are not. With this awareness, you'll be in a better position to regulate and manage your own friendship, romantic, and family relationships, the topic of the next unit.

## SUMMARY: INTERPERSONAL RELATIONSHIP STAGES AND THEORIES

In this unit we looked at interpersonal relationships: some of the reasons we enter relationships, relationship stages, and the theories that try to explain what happens in an interpersonal relationship.

1. Interpersonal relationships may be characterized as those that are based on psychological data, involve explanatory knowledge, and rely on personally established rules.

2. Interpersonal relationships have both advantages and disadvantages. Among the advantages are that these relationships stimulate you, help you learn about yourself, and generally enhance your self-esteem. Among

the disadvantages are that they force you to expose your vulnerabilities, make great demands on your time, and often cause you to abandon other relationships.

3. Most relationships involve various stages. Recognize at least these: contact, involvement, intimacy, deterioration, repair, and dissolution.

4. In contact there is first perceptual contact and then interaction.

5. Involvement includes a testing phase (will this be a suitable relationship?) and an intensifying of the interaction; often a sense of mutuality, of connectedness, begins.

6. In intimacy there is an interpersonal commitment, and perhaps a social bonding, in which the commitment is made public.

7. Some relationships deteriorate, proceeding through a period of intrapersonal dissatisfaction to interpersonal deterioration.

8. Along the process, repair may be initiated. Intrapersonal repair generally comes first (should I change my behavior?); it may be followed by interpersonal repair, in which you and your partner discuss your problems and seek remedies.

9. If repair fails, the relationship may dissolve, moving first to interpersonal separation and later, perhaps, to public or social separation.

10. Theories that focus on attraction, relationship rules, social penetration, social exchange, and relationship equity offer five explanations for what happens when you develop, maintain, and dissolve interpersonal relationships.

11. Attraction depends on four factors: similarity (especially attitudinal), proximity (physical closeness), reinforcement, and attractiveness (physical attractiveness and personality).

12. The relationship rules approach views relationships as held together by adherence to an agreed-on set of rules.

13. Social penetration theory describes relationships in terms of breadth and depth: respectively, the number of topics partners talk about and the degree of personalness with which the partners pursue topics.

14. Social exchange theory holds that we develop relationships that yield the greatest profits. We seek relationships in which our rewards exceed our costs, and we are more likely to dissolve relationships when costs exceed rewards.

15. Equity theory claims that we develop and maintain relationships in which each partner's rewards are distributed in proportion to his or her costs. When our share of the rewards is less than would be demanded by equity, we are likely to experience dissatisfaction and to exit the relationship.

## KEY TERMS IN INTERPERSONAL RELATIONSHIP STAGES AND THEORIES

affiliative cues (p. **179**)

attraction (p. **182**)

attraction theory (p. **182**)

breadth (p. **185**)

cherishing behaviors (p. **179**)

comparison level (p. **186**)

complementarity (p. **182**)

contact (p. **174**)

depenetration (p. **186**)

depth (p. **185**)

dissolution (p. **181**)

Duchenne smiles (p. **179**)

equity theory (p. **187**)

interdependency (p. **173**)

intimacy (p. **178**)

involvement (p. **177**)

parasocial relationships (p. **175**)

proximity (p. **182**)

reinforcements (p. **183**)

relationship deterioration (p. **179**)

relationship dialectics theory (p. **185**)

relationship repair (p. **180**)

rules theory (p. **184**)

similarity (p. **182**)

social exchange theory (p. **186**)

social penetration theory (p. **185**)

## THINKING CRITICALLY ABOUT INTERPERSONAL RELATIONSHIP STAGES AND THEORIES

1. **Positive Behaviors.** One way to improve communication during difficult times is to ask your partner for positive behaviors rather than to try to stop negative behaviors. How might you use this suggestion to replace the following statements? (1) "I hate it when you ignore me at business functions." (2) "I can't stand going to these cheap restaurants; when are you going to start spending a few bucks?" (3) "Stop being so negative; you criticize everything and everyone."

2. **Sexual Relationships.** As noted earlier, different cultures look at relationships very differently. How do your own cultural beliefs and values influence what you consider an appropriate and an inappropriate relationship?

Do your cultural beliefs and values influence what you consider appropriate relationship behavior? In what ways do your cultural beliefs and values influence what you actually do as a relationship partner (as friend, lover, or family member)?

3. **Turning Points.** Throughout the life of a relationship, there exist "turning points"—jumps or leaps that project you from one relationship level to another. Do men and women see turning points in the same way? For example, what turning points are most important to women? Which are most important to men?

4. **Flirting Online.** One research study found that women flirt online by stressing their physical attributes, whereas

men flirt by focusing on their socioeconomic status (Whitty, 2003). Do you observe flirting on the Internet? If so, how would you describe the way men and women flirt?

5. **Internet Courage.** Anonymity often leads people to feel more courageous, enabling them to say or do things they would not say or do if their identity was known (Barrett, 2006). It may be argued that when communicating in chat rooms, where you can conceal your true identity, you're likely to be more assertive, take more chances, and risk possible failure than you would in face-to-face situations. Do you display "Internet courage"? Do others you know display "Internet courage"?

## LogOn! MyCommunicationLab

WWW.MYCOMMUNICATIONLAB.COM

Visit MCL for a variety of materials relevant to this unit, including self-tests (on beliefs about relationships, the type of relationship you prefer, and relationship commitment) as well as several exercises and discussions: Making Relationship Predictions, Relationship Theories and Relationship Movement, Analyzing Stage Talk, Interpersonal Relationships in Songs and Cards, Relationship Repair from Advice Columnists, and Mate Preferences.

# UNIT 9 Friends, Lovers, and Families

## MAJOR TOPICS

**Friendship**
**Romantic Relationships**

**Families**
**The Dark Side of Interpersonal Relationships**

## Special Features

Now that you have a firm understanding of the ways in which relationships work, let's look at the varied types of relationships in more detail and examine the influence of culture and technology on these relationships.

**In this unit, you'll learn about:**
- the types and functions of friendship, love, and family relationships.
- the ways in which culture and technology impact on relationships of all types.
- the "dark side" of relationships.

**You'll learn to:**
- interact in interpersonal relationships in ways that are appropriate to the type of relationship.
- take greater control of what influences your relationship life.
- deal with relationship violence in productive ways.

Interpersonal relationships come in a variety of forms. Although the romantic relationship perhaps comes to mind most quickly, interpersonal relationships exist between friends, between mentors and protégés, between family members, and between work colleagues, to mention a few examples. Building on the discussion of the stages and theories of relationships in Unit 8, this unit will consider three major types of relationships (friendship, romantic, and family) and then look at the dark side of relationships.

## FRIENDSHIP

Friendship has engaged the attention and imagination of poets, novelists, and artists of all kinds. In television, our most influential mass medium, friendships have become almost as important as romantic pairings. Friendship now engages the attention of a range of interpersonal communication researchers. Throughout your life you'll meet many people, but out of this wide array you'll develop relatively few relationships you would call friendships. Yet despite the low number of friendships you may form, their importance is great.

**Friendship** is an interpersonal relationship between two persons that is mutually productive and characterized by mutual positive regard. Let's take a closer look at the components of this definition:

- *Friendship is an interpersonal relationship.* This means that communication interactions must have taken place between the people. Further, the interpersonal relationship involves a "personalistic focus" (Wright 1978, 1984). Friends react to each other as complete persons; as unique, genuine, and irreplaceable individuals.

- *Friendships must be mutually productive.* This qualifier emphasizes that, by definition, they cannot be destructive to either of the involved parties. Once destructiveness enters into a rela-

tionship, it can no longer be characterized as a friendship. Unlike almost all other types of relationships, friendship must enhance the potential of each person and can only be productive.

- *Friendships are characterized by mutual positive regard.* You like your friend and your friend likes you. Liking people is essential if we are to call them friends. Three major characteristics of friends—trust, emotional support, and sharing of interests (Blieszner & Adams 1992)—testify to this positive regard.

The closer friends are, the more interdependent they become; that is, when friends are especially close, the actions of one will impact more significantly on the other than they would if the friends were just casual acquaintances. At the same time, however, the closer friends are, the more independent they are of, for example, the attitudes and behaviors of others. Also, they're less influenced by the societal rules that govern more casual relationships (as explained in the box on "The Development of Interpersonal Communication" in Unit 7, page 152). Close friends are likely to make up their own rules for interacting with each other; they decide what they will talk about and when, what they can say to each other without offending and what they can't, when and for what reasons they can call each other, and so on.

In North America, friendships clearly are a matter of choice; you choose—within limits—who your friends will be. The density of the cities and the ease of communication and relocation makes friendships voluntary, a matter of choice. But in many parts of the world—in small villages miles away from urban centers, for example, where people are born, live, and die without venturing much beyond their home community—relationships aren't voluntary. In these cases, you simply form relationships with those in your village. Here you don't have the luxury of selecting certain people to interact with and others to ignore. You

## ASK THE RESEARCHER

### Increasing Popularity

*Quite honestly, I'm not very popular with my peers, but I really want to be. Any suggestions that can help?*

When we say someone is "popular," what we probably mean is that he or she is a likable person and therefore included in activities. Being liked, valued, and included as a friend or companion in various activities satisfies a social need that scholars refer to as our "positive face wants." How do we achieve this goal?

**Self-Reflection:** Make an honest assessment of how you appear to others.

- Do you express appreciation for other people by talking about topics of interest to them?
- Do your nonverbal responses make other people comfortable?
- Are you aware of and willing to respond to the conversational goals of others, or more interested in your own agenda?

**Social Action:** Invest the effort it takes to develop relationships.

- Be aware that small talk is not small—it shows that you are interesting and interested in the other person.
- Show positive emotions when interacting with others—smiles signal that you are approachable and likable.
- Initiate plans and activities. Don't always wait to be asked.

For more information: Metts, S., & Grohskopf, E. (2003). Impression management: Goals, strategies, and skills. In J. O. Greene & B. R. Burleson (Eds.), *Handbook of communication and social interaction skills*. Mahwah, NJ: Erlbaum. Also Metts, S., & Mikucki, S. (2007). The emotional landscape of romantic relationship initiation. In S. Sprecher, A. Wenzel, & J. Harvey (Eds.), *The handbook of relationship initiation*. Mahwah, NJ: Erlbaum.

**Sandra Metts** (Ph.D., University of Iowa) is a professor in the School of Communication at Illinois State University.

must interact with and form relationships with members of the community simply because these people are the only ones you come into contact with on a regular basis (Moghaddam, Taylor, and Wright 1993).

## Friendship Types

Not all friendships are the same. But how do they differ? One way of answering this question is by distinguishing among the three major types of friendship: friendships of reciprocity, receptivity, and association (Reisman, 1979, 1981).

The **friendship of reciprocity** is the ideal type, characterized by loyalty, self-sacrifice, mutual affection, and generosity. A friendship of reciprocity is based on equality: Each individual shares equally in giving and receiving the benefits and rewards of the relationship.

In the **friendship of receptivity**, in contrast, there is an imbalance in giving and receiving; one person is the primary giver and one the primary receiver. This imbalance, however, is a positive factor, because each person gains something from the relationship. The different needs of both the person who receives and the person who gives affection are satisfied. This is the friendship that may develop between a teacher and a student or between a doctor and a patient. In fact, a difference in status is essential for the friendship of receptivity to develop.

The **friendship of association** is a transitory one. It might be described as a friendly relationship rather than a true friendship. Associative friendships are the kind we often have with classmates, neighbors, or coworkers. There is no great loyalty, no great trust, no great giving or receiving. The association is cordial, but not intense.

Another answer to the question of how friendships differ can be deduced if we examine the needs that friends serve. On the basis of our experiences or our predictions, we select as friends those who will help to satisfy our basic growth needs. Selecting friends on the basis of need satisfaction is similar to choosing a marriage partner, an employee, or any person who may be in a position to satisfy our needs. Thus, for example, if you need to be the center of attention or to be popular, you might select friends who allow and even encourage you to be the center of attention or who tell you, verbally and nonverbally, that you're popular.

As your needs change, the qualities you look for in friendships also change. In many instances, old friends are dropped from your close circle to be replaced by new friends who better serve these new needs. One way to look at the needs that friendships serve is to look at the values or rewards that you seek to gain through your friendships (Wright 1978, 1984). Consider the values you look for in a friend. Do you look for values such as these?

1. *Utility* (someone who may have special talents, skills, or resources that will help you achieve your specific goals and needs)? For example, might you become friends with someone who is particularly bright because such a person might assist you in getting better grades, in solving problems, or in getting a better job?
2. *Affirmation* (someone who will affirm your personal value and help you to recognize your attributes)? For example, might you develop a friendship with someone who would help you see more clearly your leadership abilities, your athletic prowess, or sense of humor?
3. *Ego support* (someone who behaves in a supportive, encouraging, and helpful manner)? For example, would you seek friendships with people who would help you view yourself as worthy and competent?
4. *Stimulation* (someone who introduces you to new ideas and new ways of seeing the world and helps you to expand your worldview)? For example, would you form friendships with those who might bring you into contact with previously unfamiliar people, issues, religions, cultures, and experiences?
5. *Security* (someone who does nothing to hurt you or to emphasize or call attention to your inadequacies or weaknesses)? For example, would you select a friend because you'd not have to worry about him or her betraying you or making negative comments about you?

# Friendship and Communication

Friendships develop over time in stages. At one end of the friendship continuum are strangers, or two persons who have just met, and at the other end are intimate friends. What happens between these two extremes?

As you progress from the initial contact stage to intimate friendship, the depth and breadth of communications increase (see Unit 8). You talk about issues that are closer and closer to your inner core. Similarly, the number of communication topics increases as your friendship becomes closer. As depth and breadth increase, so does the satisfaction you derive from the friendship. This increase in depth and breadth can and does occur in all forms of communication—face-to-face as well as online. It's interesting to note that research has found that friendship was the primary goal for Internet communication among college students. More than 60 percent of online users successfully found online friends, and about 50 percent felt more comfortable meeting someone online than in person (Knox, Daniels, Sturdivant, & Zusman, 2001). In another study 36 percent indicated that they had established an online friendship compared to 22 percent who had established an online romance (Nice & Katzev, 1998).

In the discussion of relationship dialectics theory in Unit 8, we saw that in each person there is a dynamic tension between, for example, the need for autonomy and the need for connection—the desire to be an individual but also to be connected to another person. Friendships also are defined by dynamic tensions (Rawlins, 1983). One tension is between our impulse to be open and to reveal personal thoughts and feelings on the one hand, and the impulse to protect ourself by not revealing personal information to the other. Also, there is the tension between being open and candid with our friend and being discreet. These contradictory impulses make it clear that friendships don't follow a straight path of always increasing, for example, openness or candor. This is not to say that openness and candor don't increase as you progress from initial to casual to close friendships; they do. But the pattern does not follow a straight line; throughout the friendship development process, there are tensions that periodically restrict openness and candor.

Similarly, there are regressions that may temporarily pull the friendship back to a less intimate stage. Friendships stabilize at a level that is, ideally at least, comfortable to both persons; some friendships will remain casual and others will remain close. Keep in mind that although this discussion presents friendship in stages, the progression is not always a straight line to ever-increasing intimacy.

With these qualifications in mind, we can discuss three stages of friendship development and the role of communication in these stages. The assumption made here is that as the friendship progresses from initial contact and acquaintanceship through casual friendship to close and intimate friendship, the level of effective interpersonal communication increases. However, keep in mind that close relationships are not necessarily the preferred type or that they're better than casual or temporary relationships. We need all types.

## Initial Contact and Acquaintanceship

The first stage of friendship development is obviously an initial meeting of some kind. This does not mean that what has happened prior to the encounter is unimportant—quite the contrary. In fact, your prior history of friendships, your personal needs, and your readiness for friendship development are extremely important in determining whether the relationship will develop.

At the initial stage, you're guarded rather than open or expressive, lest you reveal aspects of yourself that might be viewed negatively. Because you don't yet know the other person, your ability to empathize with or to orient yourself significantly to the other is limited, and the relationship—at this stage, at least—is probably viewed as too temporary to be worth the effort. Because the other person is not well known to you, supportiveness, positiveness, and equality would all be difficult to manifest in any meaningful sense. The characteristics demonstrated are probably more the result of politeness than any genuine expression of positive regard.

At this stage there is little genuine immediacy; the two individuals see themselves as separate and distinct, rather than as a unit. The confidence that is demonstrated is probably more a function of the individual personalities than of the relationship. Because the relationship is so new and because the people don't know each other very well, the interaction is often characterized by awkwardness—for example, by overlong pauses, uncertainty over topics to be discussed, and ineffective exchanges of speaker and listener roles.

## Casual Friendship

In this second stage, there is a **dyadic consciousness**, a clear sense of "we-ness," of togetherness; communication demonstrates a sense of immediacy. At this stage you participate in activities as a unit rather than as separate individuals. A casual friend is one we would go with to the movies, sit with in the cafeteria or in class, or ride home with from school.

### PROJECTING AN IMAGE

You're interviewing for a job and want to be perceived as likeable and friendly but also serious and conscientious.
WHAT DO YOU SAY?
*What do you definitely not say?*

At this casual-friendship stage, you start to express yourself openly and become interested in the other person's disclosures. You begin to own your feelings and thoughts and respond in an open and honest way to the person's communications. Because you're beginning to understand this person, you empathize and demonstrate significant other-orientation. You also demonstrate supportiveness and develop a genuinely positive attitude toward both the other person and mutual communication situations. As you learn this person's needs and wants, you can stroke more effectively.

There is an ease at this stage, a coordination in the interaction between you and the other person. You communicate with confidence, maintain appropriate eye contact and flexibility in body posture and gesturing, and use few adaptors signaling discomfort.

## Close and Intimate Friendship

At the stage of close and intimate friendship, there is an intensification of the casual friendship; you and your friend see yourselves more as an exclusive unit, and each of you derives greater benefits (for example, emotional support) from intimate friendship than from casual friendship (Hays, 1989).

Because you know each other well (for example, you know one another's values, opinions, attitudes), your uncertainty about each other has been significantly reduced—you're able to predict each other's behaviors with considerable accuracy. This knowledge makes possible significant interaction management. Similarly, you can read your friend's nonverbal signals more accurately and can use these signals as guides to your interactions—avoiding certain topics at certain times or offering consolation on the basis of facial expressions. At this stage, you exchange significant messages of affection, messages that express fondness, liking, loving, and caring for the other person. Openness and expressiveness are more clearly in evidence.

You become more other-oriented and willing to make significant sacrifices for your friend. You'll go far out of your way for the benefit of this friend, and the friend does the same for you. You empathize and exchange perspectives a great deal more, and you expect in return that your friend will also empathize with you. With a genuinely positive feeling for this individual, your supportiveness and positive stroking become spontaneous. Because you see yourselves as an exclusive unit, equality and immediacy are in clear evidence. You view this friend as one who is important in your life; as a result, conflicts—inevitable in all close relationships—become important to work out and resolve through compromise and empathic understanding rather than through, for example, refusal to negotiate or a show of force.

You're willing to respond openly, confidently, and expressively to this person and to own your feelings and thoughts. Your supportiveness and positiveness are genuine expressions of the closeness you feel for this person. Each person in an intimate friendship is truly equal; each can initiate and each can respond; each can be active and each can be passive; each speaks and each listens.

# Friendships, Culture, Gender, and Technology

Your friendships and the way you look at friendships will be influenced by your culture and your gender. Let's look first at culture.

## Culture and Friendships

In the United States, you can be friends with someone yet never really be expected to go much out of your way for this person. Many Middle Easterners, Asians, and Latin Americans would consider going significantly out of their way an essential ingredient in friendship; if you're not willing to sacrifice for your friend, then this person is really not your friend (Dresser, 1996).

Generally, friendships are closer in collectivist cultures than in individualist cultures (see Unit 2). In their emphasis on the group and on cooperation, collectivist cultures foster the development of close friendship bonds. Members of a collectivist culture are expected to help others in the group. When you help or do things for someone else, you increase your own attraction to this person (recall the discussion in Unit 8 on attraction and reinforcement), and this is certainly a good start for a friendship. And of course, the collectivist culture continues to reward these close associations.

Members of individualist cultures, on the other hand, are expected to look out for Number One, themselves. Consequently, they're more likely to compete and to try to do better than each other—conditions that don't support, generally at least, the development of friendships.

As noted in Unit 2, these characterizations are extremes; most people have both collectivist and individualist values but have them to different degrees, and that is what we are talking about here—differences in degree of collectivist and individualist orientation.

## Gender and Friendships

Gender influences who becomes your friend and the way you look at friendships. Perhaps the best-documented finding—already noted in Unit 3's discussion of self-disclosure—is that women self-disclose more than men do (e.g., Dolgin, Meyer, & Schwartz, 1991). This difference holds throughout male and female friendships. Male friends self-disclose less often and with less intimate details than female friends do. Some research has argued that men generally don't view intimacy as a necessary quality of their friendships (Hart, 1990).

Women engage in significantly more affectional behaviors with their friends than do males; this difference may account for the greater difficulty men experience in beginning and maintaining close friendships (Hays, 1989). Women engage in more casual communication; they also share greater intimacy and more confidences with their friends than do men. Communication, in all its forms and functions, seems a much more important dimension of women's friendships.

When women and men were asked to evaluate their friendships, women rated their same-sex friendships higher in general quality, intimacy, enjoyment, and nurturance than did men (Sapadin, 1988). Men, in contrast, rated their opposite-sex friendships higher in quality, enjoyment, and nurturance than did women. Both men and women rated their opposite-sex friendships similarly in intimacy. These differences may be due, in part, to our society's suspicion of male friendships; as a result, a man may be reluctant to admit to having close relationship bonds with another man.

Men's friendships are often built around shared activities—attending a ball game, playing cards, working on a project at the office. Women's friendships, on the other hand, are built more around a sharing of feelings, support, and "personalism." Similarity in status, in willingness to protect one's friend in uncomfortable situations, in academic major, and even in proficiency in playing the game Password were significantly related to the relationship closeness of male–male friends but not of female–female or female–male friends (Griffin & Sparks, 1990). Perhaps similarity is a criterion for male friendships but not for female or mixed-sex friendships.

The ways in which men and women develop and maintain their friendships will undoubtedly change considerably—as will all gender-related variables. Perhaps there will be a further differentiation or perhaps an increase in similarities. In the meantime, given the present state of research in gender differences, we need to be careful not to exaggerate and to treat small differences as if they were highly significant. We need to avoid stereotypes and the stress on opposites to the neglect of the huge number of similarities between men and women (Wright, 1988; Deaux & LaFrance, 1998).

## Technology and Friendships

Perhaps even more obvious than culture is the influence of technology on interpersonal relationships. Clearly, online interpersonal relationships are on the increase. The number of Internet users is rapidly increasing, and commercial websites devoted to helping people meet other people are proliferating, making it especially easy to develop online relationships. The daytime television talk shows frequently focus on computer-mediated relationships, especially bringing together individuals who have established a relationship online but who have never met. As mentioned earlier, many people are turning to the Internet to find a friend or romantic partner. And, as you probably know, college students are making the most of sites such as Facebook.com and MySpace.com to meet other students on their own or other campuses.

As early as the mid-1990s, research on Internet use found that almost two-thirds of newsgroup users had formed new acquaintances, friendships, or other personal relationships with someone they met on the Net. Almost one-third said that they communicated with their partner at least three or four times a week; more than half communicated on a weekly basis (Parks & Floyd, 1996).

As relationships develop on the Internet, **network convergence** occurs; that is, as a relationship between two people develops, they begin to share their network of other communicators with each other (Parks, 1995; Parks & Floyd, 1996). This, of course, is similar to relationships formed through face-to-face contact. Online work groups also are on the increase and have been found to be more task oriented and more efficient than face-to-face groups (Lantz, 2001). Online groups also provide a sense of belonging that may once have been thought possible only through face-to-face interactions (Silverman, 2001).

## MEDIA WATCH

# INTERPERSONAL RELATIONSHIPS AND THE MEDIA

Far from merely reflecting society, the media put forth their own beliefs and values about relationships (friendship, romantic, and family) and influence our thinking about what makes for appropriate and inappropriate relationship behavior. Consider your own beliefs about what constitutes a good friend, what an ideal romantic partner would be like, and what makes for a happy and productive family. Very likely many of these ideas came from the media; you were taught by television, film, books and magazines, and other media about all sorts of relationships. Perhaps the best way to appreciate this impact is to analyze a specific media example for its implicit or explicit statements about interpersonal relationships.

### Increasing Media Literacy

*Select a television sitcom or drama, a film, or a novel that deals with interpersonal relationships and analyze it for at least the following: (1) What does your selection say about relationships generally? Does it make some relationships seem better than others? Are some relationships denigrated? (2) What does it say about men and women? (3) What relationship characteristics are valued? Which are devaluated? (4) What role does communication play in the relationships depicted? Are specific principles of communication advocated or discouraged? (5) If an alien who knew nothing about relationships among Earthlings were to view or read your selection and nothing else, what would this alien "learn" about interpersonal relationships?*

# ROMANTIC RELATIONSHIPS

Of all the qualities of interpersonal relationships, none seems as important as love. "We are all born for love," noted famed British Prime Minister Benjamin Disraeli; "It is the principle of existence and its only end." It's also an interpersonal relationship developed, maintained, and sometimes destroyed through communication.

## Love Types

As a preface to this discussion of the types of love, you may wish to respond to the self-test "What Kind of Lover Are You?"

# TEST YOURSELF

### What Kind of Lover Are You?

Respond to each of the following statements with T for true (if you believe the statement to be a generally accurate representation of your attitudes about love) or F for false (if you believe the statement does not adequately represent your attitudes about love).

_____ **1.** My lover and I have the right physical "chemistry" between us.

_____ **2.** I feel that my lover and I were meant for each other.

_____ **3.** My lover and I really understand each other.

_____ **4.** I believe that what my lover doesn't know about me won't hurt him or her.

_____ **5.** My lover would get upset if he or she knew of some of the things I've done with other people.

_____ **6.** When my lover gets too dependent on me, I want to back off a little.

_____ **7.** I expect to always be friends with my lover.

_____ **8.** Our love is really a deep friendship, not a mysterious, mystical emotion.

_____ **9.** Our love relationship is the most satisfying because it developed from a good friendship.

_____ **10.** In choosing my lover, I believed it was best to love someone with a similar background.

_____ **11.** An important factor in choosing a partner is whether or not he or she would be a good parent.

_____ **12.** One consideration in choosing my lover was how he or she would reflect on my career.

_____ **13.** Sometimes I get so excited about being in love with my lover that I can't sleep.

_____ **14.** When my lover doesn't pay attention to me, I feel sick all over.

_____ **15.** I cannot relax if I suspect that my lover is with someone else.

_____ **16.** I would rather suffer myself than let my lover suffer.

_____ **17.** When my lover gets angry with me, I still love him or her fully and unconditionally.

_____ **18.** I would endure all things for the sake of my lover.

**HOW DID YOU DO?** This scale, from Hendrick and Hendrick (1990), is based on the work of Lee (1976), as is the discussion of the six types of love that follows. The statements refer to the six types of love that we discuss below: eros, ludus, storge, pragma, mania, and agape. "True" answers represent your agreement and "false" answers represent your disagreement with the type of love to which the statements refer. Statements 1–3 are characteristic of the eros lover. If you answered "true" to these statements, you have a strong eros component to your love style; if you answered "false," you have a weak eros component. Statements 4–6 refer to ludus love, 7–9 refer to storge love, 10–12 to pragma love, 13–15 to manic love, and 16–18 to agapic love.

**WHAT WILL YOU DO?** Are there things you can do to become more aware of the different love styles and to become a more well-rounded lover? How might you go about incorporating the qualities of effective interpersonal communication—for example, being more flexible, more respectful, and more other-oriented—to become a more responsive, more exciting, more playful love partner?

Although there are many theories about love, the theory that has captured the attention of interpersonal researchers is the conceptualization featured in the above self-test, which claims there is not one but six types of love (Lee, 1976). View the descriptions of the six types as broad characterizations that are generally but not always true.

- **Eros: Beauty and sexuality.** The erotic lover focuses on beauty and physical attractiveness, sometimes to the exclusion of qualities you might consider more important and more lasting. The erotic lover has an idealized image of beauty that is unattainable in reality. Consequently, the erotic lover often feels unfulfilled. Not surprisingly, erotic lovers are particularly sensitive to physical imperfections in the ones they love.

- **Ludus Entertainment and excitement.** Ludus love is experienced as a game, as fun. The better the lover can play the game, the greater the enjoyment. Love is not to be taken too seriously; emotions are to be held in check lest they get out of hand and make trouble; passions never rise to the point where they get out of control. A ludic lover is self-controlled, always aware of the need to manage love rather than allow it to be in control. Perhaps because of this need to control love, some researchers have proposed that ludic love tendencies may reveal tendencies toward sexual aggression (Sarwer, Kalichman, Johnson, Early, et al., 1993). Not surprisingly, the ludic lover retains a partner only as long as the partner is interesting and amusing. When interest fades, it's time to change partners. Perhaps because love is a game, sexual fidelity is of little importance. In fact, recent research shows that people who score high on ludic love are more likely to engage in "extradyadic" dating and sex than those who score low on ludus (Wiederman & Hurd, 1999).

- *Storge: Peaceful and slow.* Storge love lacks passion and intensity. Storgic lovers don't set out to find lovers but to establish a companionable relationship with someone they know and with whom they can share interests and activities. Storgic love is a gradual process of unfolding thoughts and feelings; the changes seem to come so slowly and so gradually that it's often difficult to define exactly where the relationship is at any point in time. Sex in storgic relationships comes late, and when it comes, it assumes no great importance.

- *Pragma: Practical and traditional.* The pragma lover is practical and seeks a relationship that will work. Pragma lovers want compatibility and a relationship in which their important needs and desires will be satisfied. They're concerned with the social qualifications of a potential mate even more than with personal qualities; family and background are extremely important to the pragma lover, who relies not so much on feelings as on logic. The pragma lover views love as a useful relationship, one that makes the rest of life easier. So the pragma lover asks such questions as "Will this person earn a good living?" "Can this person cook?" "Will this person help me advance in my career?" Pragma lovers' relationships rarely deteriorate. This is partly because pragma lovers choose their mates carefully and emphasize similarities. Another reason is that they have realistic romantic expectations.

- *Mania: Elation and depression.* Mania is characterized by extreme highs and extreme lows. The manic lover loves intensely and at the same time

## Theory and Research   Intimacy and Risk
*Understanding*

To some people, relational intimacy seems extremely risky. To others, intimacy involves only low risk. Consider your own view of relationship risk by responding to the following questions.

- Is it dangerous to get really close to people?
- Are you afraid to get really close to someone because you might get hurt?
- Do you find it difficult to trust other people?
- Do you believe that the most important thing to consider in a relationship is whether you might get hurt?

People who answer *yes* to these and similar questions see intimacy as involving considerable risk (Pilkington & Richardson, 1988). Such people have fewer close friends, are less likely to have romantic relationships, have less trust in others, have lower levels of dating assertiveness, have lower self-esteem, are more possessive and jealous, and are generally less sociable and extroverted than those who see intimacy as involving little risk (Pilkington & Woods, 1999).

Risk in online relationships involves many of the same issues as in face-to-face relationships. For example, in both kinds of relationships you risk losing face and damaging your self-esteem so there's also likely to be considerable similarity between both types of relationships.

### Working with Theories and Research
*How would you describe your willingness to take relationship risks? What exactly are you willing to risk in establishing a relationship? What exactly are you unwilling to risk?*

intensely worries about the loss of the love. This fear often prevents the manic lover from deriving as much pleasure as possible from the relationship. With little provocation, the manic lover may experience extreme jealousy. Manic love is obsessive; the manic lover has to possess the beloved completely. In return, the manic lover wishes to be possessed, to be loved intensely. The manic lover's poor self-image seems capable of being improved only by love; self-worth comes from being loved rather than from any sense of inner satisfaction. Because love is so important, danger signs in a relationship are often ignored; the manic lover believes that if there is love, then nothing else matters.

■ *Agape: Compassionate and Selfless.* Agape is a compassionate, egoless, self-giving love. The agapic lover loves even people with whom he or she has no close ties. This lover loves the stranger on the road even though they will probably never meet again. Agape is a spiritual love, offered without concern for personal reward or gain. This lover loves without expecting that the love will be reciprocated. Jesus, Buddha, and Gandhi preached this unqualified love, agape (Lee, 1976). In one sense, agape is more a philosophical kind of love than a love that most people have the strength to achieve. Not surprisingly, people who believe in *yuan*, a Chinese concept which comes from the Buddhist belief in predestiny, are more likely to favor agapic (and pragmatic) love and less likely to favor erotic love (Goodwin & Findlay, 1997).

Each of these varieties of love can combine with others to form new and different patterns (for example, manic and ludic or storge and pragma). These six, however, identify the major types of love, and illustrate the complexity of any love relationship. The six styles should also make it clear that different people want different things, that each person seeks satisfaction in a unique way. The love that may seem lifeless or crazy or boring to you may be ideal for someone else. At the same time, another person may see these very same negative qualities in the love you're seeking.

Also keep in mind that love changes. A relationship that began as pragma may develop into ludus or eros. A relationship that began as erotic may develop into mania or storge. One approach sees this as a developmental process having three major stages (Duck 1986):

■ First stage: Initial attraction: eros, mania, and ludus

■ Second stage: Storge (as the relationship develops)

■ Third stage: Pragma (as relationship bonds develop)

## Love and Communication

How do you communicate when you're in love? What do you say? What do you do nonverbally? According to research, you exaggerate your beloved's virtues and minimize his or her faults. You share emotions and experiences and speak tenderly, with an extra degree of courtesy, to each other; "please," "thank you," and similar polite expressions abound. You frequently use "personalized communication." This type of communication includes secrets you keep from other people and messages that have meaning only within your specific relationship (Knapp, Ellis, & Williams, 1980). You also create and use personal idioms (and pet names)—words, phrases, and gestures that carry meaning only for the particular relationship and that say you have a special language that signifies your special bond (Hopper, Knapp, & Scott 1981). When outsiders try to use personal idioms—as they sometimes do—the expressions seem inappropriate, at times even an invasion of privacy.

You engage in significant self-disclosure. There is more confirmation and less disconfirmation among lovers than among either nonlovers or those who are going through romantic breakups. You're also highly aware of what is and is not appropriate to the one you love. You know how to reward, but also how to punish, each other. In short, you know what to do to obtain the reaction you want.

Among your most often used means for communicating love are telling the person face-to-face or by telephone (in one survey 79 percent indicated they did it this way), expressing supportiveness, and talking things out and cooperating (Marston, Hecht, & Robers, 1987).

Nonverbally, you also communicate your love. Prolonged and focused eye contact is perhaps the clearest nonverbal indicator of love. So important is eye contact that its avoidance almost always triggers a "what's wrong?" response. You also have longer periods of silence than you do with friends (Guerrero, 1997).

You grow more aware not only of your loved one but also of your own physical self. Your muscle tone is heightened, for example. When you're in love, you engage in preening gestures, especially immediately prior to meeting your lover, and you position your body attractively—stomach pulled in, shoulders square, legs arranged in appropriate masculine or feminine positions. Your speech may even have a somewhat different vocal quality. There is some evidence to show that sexual excitement enlarges the nasal membranes, which introduces a certain nasal quality into the voice (Davis, 1973).

You eliminate socially taboo adaptors, at least in the presence of the loved one. You would curtail,

# REFLECTIONS ON ETHICS

## Your Obligation to Reveal Yourself

At some point in any close relationship, an ethical issue arises as to your obligation to reveal information about yourself. After all, people in a close relationship have considerable impact on each other (recall, as we noted earlier, that people in an interpersonal relationship are *inter*dependent), so you may have an obligation to reveal certain things about yourself. Conversely, you may feel that the other person—because he or she is so close to you—has an ethical obligation to reveal certain information to you.

### Ethical Choice Point

*At what point—if any—do you feel you have an ethical obligation to reveal each of the 10 items of*

| Romantic Partner | Close Friend |
| --- | --- |
| _____ | _____ |
| _____ | _____ |
| _____ | _____ |
| _____ | _____ |
| _____ | _____ |
| _____ | _____ |
| _____ | _____ |
| _____ | _____ |
| _____ | _____ |
| _____ | _____ |

*information listed here? Record your answers for romantic relationships in the first column and for close friendship relationships in the second column. Use numbers from 1 to 10 to indicate at what point you would feel your partner or friend has a right to know this information about you by visualizing a relationship as existing on a continuum on which 1 = initial contact and 10 = extreme intimacy. If you feel you would never have the obligation to reveal this information, use 0. As you respond to these items, consider what gives one person the right to know personal information about another person.*

*At what point do you have an ethical obligation to reveal:*

1. Age
2. Family genetic history
3. HIV status
4. Sexual experiences
5. Salary/net financial worth
6. Affectional orientation
7. Race and nationality
8. Religious beliefs
9. Past criminal activities
10. Political attitudes and beliefs

for example, scratching your head, picking your teeth, cleaning your ears, and passing gas. Interestingly enough, these adaptors often return after the lovers have achieved a permanent relationship.

You touch more frequently and more intimately (Guerrero, 1997). You also use more "tie signs," nonverbal gestures that show that you're together, such as holding hands, walking with arms entwined, kissing, and the like. You may even dress alike. The styles of clothes and even the colors selected by lovers are more similar than those worn by nonlovers.

## Love, Culture, Gender, and Technology

Like friendship, love is heavily influenced by culture and by gender (Dion & Dion, 1996). Let's consider

first some of the cultural influences on the way you look at love and perhaps on the love you're seeking or maintaining.

## Culture and Love

Although most of the research on love styles has been done in the United States, some research has been conducted in other cultures (Bierhoff & Klein, 1991). Here is a small sampling of the research findings—just enough to illustrate that culture is an important factor in love. Asians have been found to be more friendship oriented in their love style than are Europeans (Dion & Dion, 1993b). Members of individualist cultures (for example, Europeans) are likely to place greater emphasis on romantic love and on individual fulfillment. Members of collectivist cultures are likely to spread their love over a large network of relatives (Dion & Dion, 1993a).

One study finds a love style among Mexicans characterized as calm, compassionate, and deliberate (Leon, Philbrick, Parra, Escobedo, et al., 1994). In comparisons between loves styles in the United States and France, it was found that subjects from the United States scored higher on storge and mania than the French; in contrast, the French scored higher on agape (Murstein, Merighi, & Vyse, 1991). Caucasian women, when compared to African American women, scored higher on mania, whereas African American women scored higher on agape. Caucasian and African American men, however, scored very similarly; no statistically significant differences have been found (Morrow, Clark, & Brock, 1995).

## Gender and Love

Gender also influences love. In the United States, the differences between men and women in love are considered great. In poetry, novels, and the mass media, women and men are depicted as acting very differently when falling in love, being in love, and ending a love relationship. As Lord Byron put it in *Don Juan*, "Man's love is of man's life a thing apart,/'Tis woman's whole existence." Women are portrayed as emotional, men as logical. Women are supposed to love intensely; men are supposed to love with detachment.

Despite such differences, women and men seem to experience love to a similar degree, and research continues to find great similairites between men's and women's conceptions of love (Rubin, 1973; Fehr & Broughton, 2001). However, women indicate greater love than men do for their same-sex friends. This may reflect a real difference between the sexes, or it may be a function of the greater social restrictions on men. A man is not supposed to admit his love for another man, but women are permitted greater freedom to communicate their love for other women.

Men and women also differ in the types of love they prefer (Hendrick, Hendrick, Foote, & Slapion-Foote, 1984). For example, on one version of the love self-test presented earlier, men have been found to score higher on erotic and ludic love, whereas women score higher on manic, pragmatic, and storgic love. No difference has been found for agapic love.

Women have their first romantic experiences earlier than men. The median age of first infatuation for females is 13 and for males 13.6; the median age for first time in love for females is 17.1 and for males 17.6 (Kirkpatrick & Caplow, 1945; Hendrick, Hendrick, Foote, & Slapion-Foote, 1984).

In much research, men are found to place more emphasis on romance than women. For example, when college students were asked the question "If a man (woman) had all the other qualities you desired, would you marry this person if you were not in love with him (her)?" approximately two-thirds of the men responded no, which seems to indicate that a high percentage were concerned with love and romance. However, less than one-third of the women responded no (LeVine, Sato, Hashimoto, & Verma, 1994). Further, when men and women were surveyed concerning their view on love—whether it's basically realistic or basically romantic—it was found that married women had a more realistic (less romantic) conception of love than did married men (Knapp & Vangelisti, 2005).

Additional research also supports the view that men are more romantic. For example, "Men are more likely than women to believe in love at first sight, in love as the basis for marriage and for overcoming obstacles, and to believe that their partner and relationship will be perfect" (Sprecher & Metts, 1989). This difference seems to increase as the romantic relationship develops: Men become more romantic and women less romantic (Fengler, 1974).

## ENDING THE RELATIONSHIP

You want to break up your 8-month romantic relationship and still remain friends.

WHAT DO YOU SAY?
*Through what channel?*

## Theory and Research · Love Styles and Personality

In reading about the six love styles, you may have felt that certain personality types would be likely to favor one type of love over another. Consider your own assumptions about which personality characteristics would go with which love style (eros, ludus, storge, pragma, mania, and agape), then consider this list of the personality descriptions that research finds people assign to each love style (Taraban & Hendrick, 1995):

1. inconsiderate, secretive, dishonest, selfish, and dangerous
2. honest, loyal, mature, caring, loving, and understanding
3. jealous, possessive, obsessed, emotional, and dependent
4. sexual, exciting, loving, happy, and optimistic
5. committed, giving, caring, self-sacrificing, and loving
6. family-oriented, planning, careful, hard-working, and concerned

Very likely you perceived these personality factors in the same way as did the participants in research from which this list was drawn: 1 = ludus, 2 = storge, 3 = mania, 4 = eros, 5 = agape, and 6 = pragma. Do note, of course, that these results do not imply that ludus lovers *are* necessarily inconsiderate, secretive, and dishonest. They merely mean that people in general (and perhaps you in particular) *think* of ludus lovers as inconsiderate, secretive, and dishonest.

### Working with Theories and Research

*How would you go about furthering this research on love styles and personality? What type of research might you undertake to increase our understanding of the relationship of personality and love style?*

One further gender difference may be noted, and that is differences between men and women in breaking up a relationship (Blumstein & Schwartz, 1983; cf. Janus & Janus, 1993). Popular myth would have us believe that love affairs often break up as a result of the man's outside affair. But the research does not support this. When surveyed as to the reason for breaking up, only 15 percent of the men indicated that it was their interest in another person, whereas 32 percent of the women noted this as a cause of the breakup. These findings are consistent with their partners' perceptions as well: 30 percent of the men (but only 15 percent of the women) noted that their partner's interest in another person was the reason for the breakup.

In their reactions to broken romantic affairs, women and men exhibit similarities and differences. For example, the tendency for women and men to recall only pleasant memories and to revisit places with past associations was about equal. However, men engaged in more dreaming about the lost partner and in more daydreaming generally as a reaction to the breakup than did women.

At least one research study shows that romanticism seems to increase on the basis of the amount of choice you have in selecting a partner. In countries where there is much choice, as in the United States and Europe, romanticism is high; in countries where there is less choice, as in India and parts of Africa, romanticism is lower (Medora, Larson, Hortacsu, & Dave, 2002). Internet dating provides greater choice than do face-to-face interactions, so it may be argued that romanticism will be higher in Internet than in face-to-face interactions.

### Technology and Love

Perhaps even more important than culture and gender is the influence of technology on romantic relationships. In face-to-face relationships, you perceive the other person through nonverbal cues—you see the person's eyes, face, body—and you form these perceptions immediately. In online relationships of just a few years ago, physical attractiveness was signaled exclusively through words and self-descriptions (Levine, 2000). Under such circumstances, as you can appreciate, the face-to-face encounter strongly favored those who were physically attractive, whereas the online encounter favored those who were verbally adept at self-presentation and did not disadvantage less-attractive individuals. Today, with photos, videos, and voice a part of many online dating and social networking sites, this distinction is fading—though probably not entirely erased. Certainly the face-to-face encounter still provides more nonverbal cues about the physical person.

Women, it seems, are more likely to form relationships on the Internet than men. In a study some years ago, about 72 percent of women and 55 percent of men had formed personal relationships online (Parks & Floyd, 1996). Not surprisingly, those who communicated more frequently formed more relationships.

There are many advantages to establishing romantic relationships online. For example, online relationships are safe in terms of avoiding the potential for physical violence or sexually transmitted diseases. Unlike relationships established in face-to-face encounters, in which physical appearance tends to outweigh personality, Internet communication reveals your inner qualities first. Rapport and mutual self-disclosure become more important than physical attractiveness in promoting intimacy (Cooper & Sportolari, 1997). And, contrary to some popular opinions, online relationships rely just as heavily on the ideals of trust, honesty, and commitment as do face-to-face relationships (Whitty & Gavin, 2001). Friendship and romantic interaction on the Internet are a natural boon to shut-ins and extremely shy people, for whom traditional ways of meeting someone are often difficult. Computer talk is empowering for those who have been disfigured or who have certain disabilities for whom face-to-face interactions are often superficial and often end with withdrawal (Lea & Spears, 1995; Bull & Rumsey, 1988). By eliminating the physical cues, computer talk equalizes the interaction and doesn't put the disfigured person, for example, at an immediate disadvantage in a society where physical attractiveness is so highly valued. On the Internet you're free to reveal as much or as little about your physical self as you wish, when you wish.

Another obvious advantage is that the number of people you can reach is so vast that it's relatively easy to find someone who matches what you're looking for. The situation is like finding a book that covers just what you need from a library of millions of volumes rather than from a collection holding only several thousand.

Of course, there are also disadvantages. For one thing, and depending on the software you're using, you may not be able to see the person. And even if photos are exchanged, how certain can you be that the photos are of the person or that they were taken recently? In addition, you may not be able to hear the person's voice, and this too hinders you as you seek to develop a total picture of the other person.

### REFUSING A GIFT POSITIVELY

You're becoming friendly with a coworker who you think you might like to date. Without any warning, your coworker gives you a bouquet of flowers and asks you to a very expensive dinner. You think this is too much, too soon. You don't want to allow the relationship to progress this quickly and yet you don't want to ruin it either.

WHAT DO YOU SAY?
*Through what channel?*

Online, people can present a false self with little chance of detection; minors may present themselves as adults, and adults may present themselves as children in order to conduct illicit and illegal sexual communications and, perhaps, meetings. Similarly, people can present themselves as poor when they're rich, as mature when they're immature, as serious and committed when they're just enjoying the online experience. Although people can also misrepresent themselves in face-to-face relationships, the fact that it's easier to do online probably accounts for greater frequency of misrepresentation in computer relationships (Cornwell & Lundgren, 2001).

Another potential disadvantage—though some might argue it is actually an advantage—is that computer interactions may become all-consuming and may substitute for face-to-face interpersonal relationships.

## Building Communication *Skills* Till This Do Us Part

This exercise is designed to stimulate you to examine the factors that might lead you to dissolve a romantic relationship. Here are listed a number of factors that might lead someone to end a romantic relationship. For each factor identify the likelihood that you would dissolve romantic relationships of various types, using a 10-point scale on which 10 = "would definitely dissolve the relationship" and 1 = "would definitely not dissolve the relationship," with the numbers 2 through 9 representing intermediate levels. Use 5 for "don't know what I'd do."

| Factor | Budding romantic relationship of 1 or 2 weeks | Steady dating for the last few months | Romantic relationship of about a year | Committed romantic relationship of 5 or more years |
|---|---|---|---|---|
| 1. Person lies frequently about insignificant and significant issues | | | | |
| 2. Person abuses you emotionally or physically | | | | |
| 3. Person is sexually unfaithful | | | | |
| 4. Person has an addiction to gambling, alcohol, or drugs | | | | |
| 5. Person is close to relatives and friends you dislike | | | | |
| 6. Person has a serious illness that will require lots of your time, energy, and financial resources | | | | |
| 7. Person lacks ambition and doesn't want to do anything of significance | | | | |
| 8. Person has a commitment phobia and seems unwilling to increase the intimacy of the relationship | | | | |
| 9. Person has very different religious beliefs from you | | | | |
| 10. Person embarrasses you because of bad manners, poor grammar, and inappropriate dress | | | | |
| 11. Person has really poor hygiene habits | | | | |
| 12. Person spends 4 to 5 hours a day talking in chat rooms | | | | |

*These are just a few factors that might cause difficulties in varied relationships. Part of relationship competence is to recognize behaviors that are likely to cause problems and to work on eliminating these from your own communication patterns or at least to deal effectively with their consequences.*

## FAMILIES

Today you hear a great deal about "family," as if there were one kind of **family**. Actually, there are many types of families.

## Types of Families

The "traditional" family of a husband, a wife, and one or more children is now just one of many family types. And in fact, as shown in Table 9.1, which provides some statistics on the American family as constituted in 1970 and in 2002, families headed by married couples have decreased in the United States from about 87 percent to about 76 percent of households.

Another type of family consists of people living together in an exclusive relationship who are not married. For the most part these cohabitants live much like married couples; there is an exclusive sexual commitment; there may be children; there are shared financial responsibilities, shared time, and shared space. As you can see from Table 9.1, although the number of families headed by married couples is decreasing, cohabiting (nonmarried couples) are increasing.

Also increasing are single-parent families. Some such families result from the death of a spouse or from a divorce. But increasingly, single people are opting to have children and to form families. As the table indicates, the number of single-parent families doubled over the 32 years recorded.

### Table 9.1 The Changing Face of Family

Here are a few statistics on the nature of the American family for 1970 and 2002, as reported by the *New York Times Almanac 2005* and *The World Almanac and Book of Facts 2005,* along with some possible trends these figures indicate. What other trends do you see occurring in the family?

| Family Characteristic | 1970 | 2002 | Trends |
|---|---|---|---|
| Number of members in average family | 3.58 | 3.21 | Reflects the tendency toward smaller families |
| Families without children | 44.1% | 52% | Reflects the growing number of families opting to not have children |
| Families headed by married couples | 86.8% | 76.3% | Reflects the growing trend for heterosexual couples to live as a family without marriage, for singles to have children, and for gay men and lesbians to form families |
| Females as heads of households | 10.7% | 17.7% | Reflects the growing trend of women having children without marriage as well as the increase in divorce and separation |
| Married-couple families | 86.8% | 76.3% | Reflects the growing number of couples who form families without being married |
| Single-parent families | 13% | 27.8% | Reflects the growing trend for women (especially) to maintain families without a partner |
| Households headed by never-married women with children | 248,000 | 4.3 million | Reflects the growing trend for women to have children and maintain a family without marriage |
| Children living with only one parent | 12% | 23% | Reflects the growing divorce rate and the increased number of children born to unwed mothers |
| Children between 25 and 34 living at home with parents | 8% (11.9 million) | 9.3% (19.2 million) | Reflects the increased economic difficulty of establishing a home and perhaps the increased divorce rate and later dates for marriage (especially true for men) |

The gay male or lesbian couple who live together as "domestic partners" or are married are yet another kind of family. Many of these couples have children, whether from previous heterosexual unions, through artificial insemination, or by adoption. Although accurate statistics are difficult to secure, gay and lesbian couples seem also to be increasing. In the early 1980s, a major study of couples concluded: " 'Couplehood', either as a reality or as an aspiration, is as strong among gay people as it is among heterosexuals" (Blumstein & Schwartz, 1983). More recent studies continue to support this conclusion (Fitzpatrick, Jandt, Myrick, & Edgar, 1994; Kurdek, 2003, 2004; Gottman, 2004).

Another way of categorizing family types sees the partners as "traditionals," "independents," or "separates" (Fitzpatrick, 1983, 1988, 1991; Noller & Fitzpatrick, 1993). Let's look more closely at this typology:

- **Traditional couples** share a basic belief system and philosophy of life. They see themselves as a blending of two persons into a single couple rather than as two separate individuals. They're interdependent and believe that an individual's independence must be sacrificed for the good of the relationship. Traditionals believe in mutual sharing and do little separately. This couple holds to the traditional sex roles, and there are seldom any role conflicts. There are few power struggles and few conflicts, because each person knows and adheres to a specified role within the relationship. In their communications traditionals are highly responsive to each other. Traditionals lean toward each other, smile, talk a lot, interrupt each other, and finish each other's sentences.

- **Independent couples** stress their individuality. The relationship is important but never more important than each person's individual identity. Although independents spend a great deal of time together, they don't ritualize it, for example, with schedules. Each individual spends time with outside friends. Independents see themselves as relatively androgynous, as individuals who combine the traditionally feminine and the traditionally masculine roles and qualities. The communication between independents is responsive. They engage in conflict openly and without fear. Their disclosures are quite extensive and include high-risk and negative disclosures that are typically absent among traditionals.

- **Separate couples** live together but view their relationship more as a matter of convenience than a result of their mutual love or closeness. They seem to have little desire to be together and, in fact, usually are together only at ritual functions, such as mealtime or holiday get-togethers. It's important to these separates that each has his or her own physical as well as psychological space. Separates

share little; each seems to prefer to go his or her own way. Separates hold relatively traditional values and beliefs about sex roles, and each person tries to follow the behaviors normally assigned to each role. What best characterizes this type, however, is that each person sees himself or herself as a separate individual and not as a part of a "we."

In addition to these three pure types, there are also combinations. For example, in the separate-traditional couple one individual is a separate and one a traditional. Another common pattern is the traditional–independent, in which one individual follows the traditional view of relationships and one emphasizes autonomy and independence.

## Family Characteristics

Despite this diversity, all families have some characteristics in common; for example, defined roles, recognition of responsibilities, shared history and future, and shared living space.

### Defined Roles

Family members have relatively defined roles that each person is expected to play in relation to the other and to the relationship as a whole. Each has acquired the rules of the culture and social group; each knows approximately what his or her obligations, duties, privileges, and responsibilities are. The partners' roles might include those of wage earner, cook, house-cleaner, child caregiver, social secretary, home decorator, plumber, carpenter, food shopper, money manager, nurturer, philosopher, comedian, organizer, and so on. At times the roles may be shared, but even then it's often assumed that one person has *primary* responsibility for certain tasks and the other person for others.

### Recognition of Responsibilities

Family members recognize their responsibilities to one another; for example, responsibilities to help others financially; to offer comfort when family members are distressed; to take pleasure in family members' pleasures, to feel their pain, to raise their spirits. Each person in a couple also has a temporal obligation to reserve some large block of time for the other. Time sharing seems important to all relationships, although each family may define it a bit differently.

### Shared History and Future

Family members have a history that is at least partly shared by other members, and the prospect is that they will share the future together as well. This history has enabled the members to get to know one another, to understand one another a little better, and ideally to like and even love one another. And, in most cases, family members view the relationship as persisting into the future.

## Shared Living Space

Most families in the United States share their living space, although an increasing number of couples retain their original apartments or houses and may spend substantial time apart. These relationships, it should be stressed, are not necessarily less satisfying. After a thorough review of the research, one researcher concluded that "there is little, if any, decrease in relationship satisfaction, intimacy, and commitment as long as lovers are able to reunite with some frequency (approximately once a month)" (Rohlfing, 1995, pp. 182–183). In some cultures, in fact, men and women don't share the same living space; the women may live with the children while the men live together in a communal arrangement (Harris & Johnson, 2007).

## Families and Communication

One helpful way to understand families and primary relationships—a **primary relationship** is a relationship between two people that the partners see as their most important interpersonal relationship—is to look at the communication patterns that dominate the relationship. Four general communication patterns are identified here; each interpersonal relationship may then be viewed as a variation on one of these basic patterns.

### Equality

The *equality* pattern probably exists more in theory than in practice, but it's a good starting point for looking at communication in primary relationships. It exists more among same-sex couples than opposite-sex couples, however (Huston & Schwartz, 1995). In the equality pattern, each person shares equally in the communication transactions; the roles played by each are equal. Thus, each person is accorded a similar degree of credibility; each is equally open to the ideas, opinions, and beliefs of the other; each engages in self-disclosure on a more or less equal basis. The communication is open, honest, direct, and free of the power plays that characterize so many other interpersonal relationships. There is no leader or follower, no opinion giver or opinion seeker; rather, both parties play these roles equally. Because of this basic equality, the communication exchanges themselves, over a substantial period, are equal. For example, the number of questions asked, the depth and frequency of self-disclosures, and the nonverbal behaviors of touching and eye gaze would all be about the same for both people.

Both parties share equally in decision-making processes—in the insignificant choices, such as which movie to attend, as well as in the significant decisions, such as where to send the child to school, whether to attend religious services, and what house to buy. Conflicts in equality relationships may occur with some frequency, but they're not seen as threatening to the individuals or to the relationship. They're viewed, rather, as exchanges of ideas, opinions, and values. These conflicts are about content rather than being relational in nature (Unit 12), and the couple has few power struggles within the relationship domain.

Equal relationships are also equitable. According to equity theory, family or relationship satisfaction will be highest when there is equity, when the rewards are distributed in proportion to the costs each partner pays into the relationship (Unit 8). Dissatisfaction over inequities can lead to a "balancing of the scales" reaction. For example, an under-benefited partner may seek outside affairs as a way to get more relationship benefits—more love, more consideration, more support (Walster, Walster, & Traupmann, 1978; Noller & Fitzpatrick, 1993).

### Balanced Split

In the *balanced split* pattern, an equality relationship is maintained, but each person has authority over different domains. Each person is seen as an expert or a decision maker in different areas. For example, in the traditional nuclear family, the husband maintains high credibility in business matters and perhaps in politics. The wife maintains high credibility in such matters as child care and cooking. These gender roles are breaking down in many cultures, although they still define lots of families throughout the world (Hatfield & Rapson, 1996).

Conflict is generally viewed as nonthreatening by these individuals because each has specified areas of expertise. Consequently, the outcome of the conflict is almost predetermined.

### Unbalanced Split

In the *unbalanced split* relationship, one person dominates; one person is seen as an expert in more than half the areas of mutual communication. In many unions this expertise takes the form of control. Thus, in the unbalanced split, one person is more or less regularly in control of the relationship. In some cases this person is the more intelligent or more knowledgeable, but in many cases he or she is the more physically attractive or the higher wage earner. The less attractive or lower-income partner compensates by giving in to the other person, allowing the other to win the arguments or to have his or her way in decision making.

The person in control makes more assertions, tells the other person what should or will be done, gives opinions freely, plays power games to maintain control, and seldom asks for opinions in return. The noncontrolling person, conversely, asks questions, seeks opinions, and looks to the other for decision-making leadership.

## Building Communication Skills — Using Affinity-Seeking Strategies

Here are a few affinity-seeking strategies that people use to make others like them, to draw people closer to them (Bell & Daly, 1984). As you read and think about such strategies, try composing at least one message that would help you communicate the desired qualities. Be sure to coordinate both verbal and nonverbal messages.

**Affinity-Seeking Strategies**

*Altruism:* Be of help to the other person.

*Assumption of equality:* Present yourself as socially equal to the other.

*Comfortable self:* Present yourself as comfortable and relaxed with the other.

*Conversational rule-keeping:* Follow the cultural rules for polite, cooperative conversation.

*Dynamism:* Appear active, enthusiastic, and dynamic.

*Self-concept confirmation:* Show respect for the other person and help the person feel positive about himself or herself.

*All communication involves such strategies; practicing with these strategies will help increase your arsenal of ways to best achieve one of your most important interpersonal purposes.*

## Monopoly

In a *monopoly* relationship, one person is seen as the authority. This person lectures rather than communicates. Rarely does this person ask questions to seek advice, and he or she always reserves the right to have the final say. In this type of couple, the arguments are few, because both individuals already know who is boss and who will win the argument should one arise. When the authority is challenged, there are arguments and bitter conflicts.

The controlling person tells the partner what is and what is not to be. The controlling person talks more frequently and goes off the topic of conversation more than does the noncontrolling partner (Palmer, 1989). The noncontrolling person looks to the other to give permission, to voice opinion leadership, and to make decisions, almost as a child looks to an all-knowing, all-powerful parent.

## Families, Culture, Gender, and Technology

As with friendship and love, families too vary from one culture to another, are viewed differently by men and women, and are influenced by technology.

## Culture, Gender, and Families

In U.S. society it is assumed, in discussions of relationship development such as the model presented in this text, that you voluntarily choose your relationship partners. You consciously choose to pursue certain relationships and not others. In some cultures, however, your romantic partner is chosen for you by your parents. In some cases your husband or wife is chosen to unite two families or to bring some financial advantage to your family or village. An arrangement such as this may have been entered into by your parents when you were an infant or even before you were born. In most cultures, of course, there's pressure to marry the "right" person and to be friends with certain people and not others.

Similarly, U.S. researchers study and textbook authors write about dissolving relationships and how to survive relationship breakups. It's assumed that you have the right to exit an undesirable relationship. But in some cultures you cannot simply dissolve a relationship once it's formed or once there are children. In the practice of Roman Catholicism, once people are validly married, they're always married and cannot dissolve that relationship. More important in such cultures may be such issues as "How do you maintain a relationship that has problems?" "What can you do to survive in this unpleasant relationship?" or "How can you repair a troubled relationship?" (Moghaddam, Taylor, & Wright, 1993).

Further, your culture will influence the difficulty that you go through when relationships do break up. For example, married persons whose religion forbids divorce and remarriage will experience religious disapproval and condemnation as well as the same economic and social difficulties everyone else goes through. In India women experience greater difficulty than men in divorce because of their economic dependence on men, the cultural beliefs about women, and the patriarchal order of the family (Amato, 1994). And it was only as recently as 2002 that the first wife in Jordan was granted a divorce. Before that date only men had been granted divorces (*New York Times*, May 15, 2002, p. A6).

Culture also seems to influence the kind of love people want. For example, when compared to their Chinese counterparts, American men scored higher on ludic and agapic love and lower on erotic and pragma love. American men are also less likely to view emotional satisfaction as crucial to relationship maintenance (Sprecher & Toro-Morn, 2004).

Culture influences heterosexual relationships by assigning different roles to men and women. In the United States men and women are supposed to be equal—at least that is the stated ideal. As a result, both men and women can initiate relationships, and both can dissolve them. Both men and women are expected to derive satisfaction from their interpersonal relationships; and when that satisfaction isn't present, either person may seek to exit the relationship. In Iran, on the other hand, only the man has the right to dissolve a marriage without giving reasons.

Gay and lesbian relationships are accepted in some cultures and condemned in others. In some areas of the United States, "domestic partnerships" may be registered, and these grant gay men, lesbians, and (in some cases) unmarried heterosexuals rights that were formerly reserved only for married couples, such as health insurance benefits and the right to make decisions when one member is incapacitated. In Belgium, the Netherlands, Spain, South Africa, and Canada same-sex couples can marry; and in Norway, Sweden, and Denmark, same-sex relationship partners have the same rights as married partners. As of this writing, only one U.S. state—Massachusetts—has issued marriage licenses to same-sex couples. And, as mentioned in the discussion of heterosexism in Unit 5, in many countries same-sex couples would be considered criminals and could face severe punishment; in some cultures they could even face death.

## Technology and Families

You know from your own family interactions that technology has greatly changed the communication among family members. Cell phones enable parents and children to keep in close touch in case of emergencies or just to chat. College students today stay in closer touch with their parents than did earlier generations, in part because of the cell phone but also through e-mail and instant messaging. On the other hand, some people—in some cases parents, in most cases children—become so absorbed with their online community that they have little time for their biological family members. In some cases (in South Korea, for example), Internet use seems to be contributing further to the already significant generational conflict between children and parents (Rhee & Kim, 2004).

Research on young people (ages 10–17) finds that for both girls and boys, those who form close online relationships are more likely to have low levels of communication with their parents and to be more "highly troubled" than those who don't form such close online relationships (Wolak, Mitchell, & Finkelhor, 2003).

# THE DARK SIDE OF INTERPERSONAL RELATIONSHIPS

In any interpersonal interaction, there is the potential not only for productive and meaningful communication but also for unproductive and destructive communication. This "dark side" is perhaps most obvious in the various forms of relationship violence. Before reading about this important but often neglected topic, take the self-test on page 211.

## What Is Relationship Violence?

Three types of **relationship violence** may be distinguished: verbal or emotional abuse, physical abuse, sexual abuse (Rice, 2007). **Verbal** or **emotional abuse** involves humiliating, isolating, criticizing, and stalking as well as economic abuse such as controlling the finances or preventing the partner from working. Some research shows that people who use verbal or emotional abuse are more likely to escalate to physical abuse (Rancer & Avtgis, 2006). **Physical abuse** involves threats of violence as well as pushing, hitting, slapping, kicking, choking, throwing things at the partner, and breaking things. **Sexual abuse** involves touching that is unwanted, accusations of sexual infidelity without reason, forced sex, and referring to the partner with abusive sexual terms.

A great deal of research has centered on trying to identify the warning signs of relationship violence. Here, for example, are a few signs compiled by the State University of New York at Buffalo, which you might want to use to start thinking about your own relationship or those that you know of (http://ub-counseling.buffalo.edu/warnings/shtml, accessed February 1, 2006). You should be concerned if your partner:

- belittles, insults, or ignores you
- controls pieces of your life; for example, the way you dress or who you can be friends with
- gets jealous without reason
- can't handle sexual frustrations without anger
- is so angry or threatening that you've changed your life so as not to provoke additional anger

## TEST YOURSELF

### Is Violence a Part of Your Relationship?

Based on your present relationship or on one you know, respond to the following questions with Yes if you do see yourself in the question or No if you do not see yourself here.

_____ **1.** Do you fear your partner's anger?

_____ **2.** Does your partner ever threaten you?

_____ **3.** Has your partner ever verbally abused you?

_____ **4.** Has your partner ever forced you to do something you didn't want to do?

_____ **5.** Has your partner ever hit (slapped, kicked, pushed) you?

_____ **6.** Has your partner isolated you from your friends or relatives?

**HOW DID YOU DO?** These six items are all signs of a violent partner and a violent relationship. You might also want to change the questions around a bit and ask yourself if your partner would answer Yes to any of these questions about you.

**WHAT WILL YOU DO?** If any of these questions describes your relationship, you may wish to seek professional help. Discussing these questions with your partner, which might seem the logical first step, may well create additional problems and perhaps incite violence. So you're better off discussing this with a school counselor or some other professional. At the same time, if any of these apply to you—if you are prone to relationship violence—do likewise: Seek professional help.

Source: These questions were drawn from a variety of sources, including SUNY at Buffalo Counseling Services (http://ub-counseling.buffalo.edu/warnings.shtml, accessed February 1, 2006), the American College of Obstetricians and Gynecologists, Women's Heath Care Physicians (www.acog .org/departments/dept_notice.cfm?recno=17&bulletin=198, accessed February 1, 2006), and the University of Texas at Austin, the Counseling and Mental Health Center (www .utexas.edu/student/cmhc/booklets/relatvio/relaviol.html, accessed February 1, 2006).

## The Effects of Violence

As you may expect, there are a variety of consequences to relationship violence: psychological injuries, physical injuries, and economic "injuries" (www.cdc.gov/ncic/factsheets/ipvfacts.htm, accessed May 7, 2007):

■ Even when physical injuries are relatively minor, the *psychological injuries* caused by relationship

violence may be major. Psychological difficulties may include, for example, depression, anxiety, fear of intimacy, and of course low self-esteem.

■ Most obviously, when there is relationship violence, there are often *physical injuries*. Physical injuries may range from scratches and bruises to broken bones, knife wounds, and damage to the central nervous system.

■ Consider the *economic injuries*, the cost to society of relationship violence. It's been estimated that this problem costs the United States approximately $6.2 billion for physical assaults and almost $500 million for rape annually. Relationship violence also results in lost days of work. The Centers for Disease Control has estimated that relationship violence costs the equivalent of 32,000 full-time jobs in lost work each year. Additional economic costs are incurred when relationship violence prevents women from maintaining jobs or continuing their education.

## The Alternatives to Relationship Violence

Here are some of the ways in which a nonviolent relationship differs from a violent relationship (www .utexas.edu/student/cmhc/booklets/relavio/relaviol .html, accessed February 1, 2006):

■ Instead of emotional abuse, there is fairness; you look for mutually fair resolutions to conflicts.

■ Instead of control and isolation, there is communication that makes each partner feel safe and comfortable expressing himself or herself.

■ Instead of intimidation, there is mutual respect, affirmation, and valuing of opinions.

■ Instead of economic abuse, there is cooperation; the partners make financial decisions together.

■ Instead of threats, there is accountability—each person accepts responsibility for his or her own behavior.

■ Instead of one partner's exercising power over the other, there is a fair distribution of responsibilities.

■ Instead of sexual abuse, there is trust and respect for what each person wants and doesn't want.

## Dealing with Relationship Violence

In addition to seeking professional help (and of course the help of friends and family where appropriate), here are several additional suggestions for you to consider, whether you're a victim or a perpetrator (www.utexas.edu/student/cmhc/booklets/relavio/ relaviol.html, accessed February 1, 2006):

If your partner has been violent:

- Realize that you're not alone.

- Realize you're not at fault. You did not deserve to be a victim of violence.

- Plan for your safety. Violence, if it occurred once, is likely to occur again.

- Know your resources—the phone numbers you need to contact help, the locations of money and a spare set of keys.

If you are the violent partner:

- Realize that you too are not alone.

- Know that you can change.

- Own your own behaviors; take responsibility.

Relationship violence is not inevitable, yet it's important to know that there is the potential for violence in all relationships. Knowing the difference between productive and destructive relationships seems the best way to make sure that your own relationships are as you want them to be.

## SUMMARY: FRIENDS, LOVERS, AND FAMILIES

1. Friendship is an interpersonal relationship between two persons that is mutually productive and characterized by mutual positive regard.

2. The types of friendships are: (1) reciprocity, characterized by loyalty, self-sacrifice, mutual affection, and generosity; (2) receptivity, characterized by a comfortable and positive imbalance in the giving and receiving of rewards, in which each person's needs are satisfied by the exchange; and (3) association, a transitory relationship, more like a friendly relationship than a true friendship.

3. Friendships serve a variety of needs and give us a variety of rewards, among which are utility, affirmation, ego support, stimulation, and security.

4. Friendships, their development, and the expectations you have for them are greatly influenced by culture and gender as well as by technology.

5. Love is a feeling that may be characterized by passion and caring and by intimacy, passion, and commitment.

6. Six types of love have been distinguished by research: (1) Eros love focuses on beauty and sexuality, sometimes to the exclusion of other qualities. (2) Ludus love is seen as a game and focuses on entertainment and excitement. (3) Storge love is a kind of companionship, peaceful and slow. (4) Pragma love is practical and traditional. (5) Mania love is obsessive and possessive, characterized by elation and depression. (6) Agape love is compassionate, selfless, and altruistic.

7. Verbal and nonverbal messages echo the intimacy of a love relationship. With increased intimacy, you share more, speak in a more personalized style, engage in prolonged eye contact, and touch each other more often.

8. The kind of love you look for and the place it occupies in your life will be influenced by your culture and your gender and by the opportunities afforded by computer-mediated communication.

9. Among the characteristics of families are (1) defined roles—members understand the roles each of them serves; (2) recognition of responsibilities—members realize that each person has certain responsibilities to the relationship; (3) shared history and future—members have an interactional past and an anticipated future together; and (4) shared living space—generally, members live together.

10. Among the family types, (1) traditionals see themselves as a blending of two people into a single couple; (2) independents see themselves as primarily separate individuals, an individuality that is more important than the relationship or the connection between the individuals; and (3) separates see their relationship as a matter of convenience rather than of mutual love or connection.

11. Communication patterns in families include (1) equality—in which each person shares equally in the communication transactions and decision making; (2) balanced split—each person has authority over different but relatively equal domains; (3) unbalanced split—one person maintains authority and decision-making power over a wider range of issues than the other; and (4) monopoly—one person dominates and controls the relationship and the decisions made.

12. Families and the attitudes toward them vary from one culture to another and are being heavily influenced by the new computer-mediated communication.

13. There is also a dark side to interpersonal relationships, most obvious in relationship violence. Verbal or emotional abuse, physical abuse, and sexual abuse are the major types of relationship violence. Relationship violence may result in psychological, physical, and economic injuries.

## KEY TERMS IN FRIENDS, LOVERS, AND FAMILIES

agape love (p. **200**)
dyadic consciousness (p. **195**)
emotional abuse (p. **210**)
eros love (p. **198**)
family (p. **206**)
friendship (p. **192**)

friendship of association (p. **193**)
friendship of receptivity (p. **193**)
friendship of reciprocity (p. **193**)
independent couples (p. **207**)

ludus love (p. **198**)
mania love (p. **199**)
network convergence (p. **197**)
physical abuse (p. **210**)
pragma love (p. **199**)
primary relationship (p. **208**)

relationship violence (p. **210**)
separate couples (p. **207**)
sexual abuse (p. **210**)
storage love (p. **199**)
traditional couples (p. **207**)

## THINKING CRITICALLY ABOUT FRIENDS, LOVERS, AND FAMILIES

1. **Matching Hypothesis.** The *matching hypothesis* claims that people date and mate people who are very similar to themselves in physical attractiveness (Walster & Walster, 1978). When this does not happen—when a very attractive person dates someone of average attractiveness—there may be "compensating factors," factors that the less attractive person possesses that compensate or make up for being less physically attractive. What evidence can you find to support or contradict this theory? How would you go about testing this theory?

2. **Romantic Love.** When researchers asked college students to identify the features that characterize romantic love, the five qualities most frequently noted were trust, sexual attraction, acceptance and tolerance, spending time together, and sharing thoughts and secrets (Regan, Kocan, & Whitlock, 1998). How would you characterize love? Would men and women characterize love similarly? Would heterosexuals and homosexuals characterize love similarly?

3. **Family Characteristics.** How would you describe your own family in terms of (1) the defined roles, recognition of responsibilities, shared history and future, and shared living space, and (2) the most often used communication pattern (equality, balanced split, unbalanced split, or monopoly)?

4. **Virtual Infidelity.** Online infidelity is a relatively new problem with which couples must cope. Generally such infidelity is seen as a consequence of a failure in communication between the couple (Young, Griffin-Shelley, Cooper, O'Mara, & Buchanan, 2000). How would you describe online infidelity? What warning signs would lead you to suspect that your partner may be engaging in a secretive online relationship?

5. **Safety Precautions.** One study suggests that people who make friends online take safety precautions such as protecting anonymity and talking on the phone before meeting face-to-face (McCown, Fischer, Page, & Homant, 2001). What safety precautions do you take in online relationships?

## LOGON! MYCOMMUNICATIONLAB

### WWW.MYCOMMUNICATIONLAB.COM

Visit MyCommunicationLab for a variety of exercises relevant to this unit, including The Needs Friendships Serve, Other Views of Love, A POSITIVE Communication Approach to Relationship Effectiveness, Getting Someone to Like You, and The Television Relationship. Also, you'll find an interesting self-test of romanticism. Also watch the video Friends and analyze the friendship portrayed in terms of the concepts discussed in this unit.

# UNIT 10  Small Group Communication

## MAJOR TOPICS

**Small Groups**

**Idea-Generation Groups**

**Personal Growth Groups**

**Information-Sharing Groups**

**Problem-Solving Groups**

## Special Features

A great deal of your social and professional life will revolve around your participation in groups—groups for developing ideas, increasing self-awareness, learning, and solving problems. Understanding the nature and functions of small groups and learning to use these groups effectively and efficiently will help you throughout your social and professional career.

**In this unit, you'll learn about:**
- the nature and types of small groups.
- the stages and formats of small groups.
- the structure and functions of idea-generation, personal growth, information-sharing, and problem-solving groups.

**You'll learn to:**
- use small groups to achieve a variety of personal, social, and professional goals.
- participate effectively in a variety of small groups.

## SMALL GROUPS

A **group** is (1) a collection of individuals who (2) are connected to one another by some common purpose, (3) are interdependent, (4) have some degree of organization among them, and (5) see themselves as a group. For small groups in particular, each of these characteristics needs to be explained a bit further.

- *Collection of Individuals.* A **small group** is, first, a collection of individuals few enough in number so that all members may communicate with relative ease as both senders and receivers. Generally, a small group consists of approximately 3 to 12 people. The important point to keep in mind is that each member should be able to function as both source and receiver with relative ease. If the group gets much larger than 12, this becomes difficult.

- *Common Purpose.* Second, the members of a group must be connected to one another through some common purpose. People on a bus normally do not constitute a group, because they're not working at some common purpose. But if the bus gets stuck in a ditch, the riders may quickly become a group and work together to get the bus back on the road. This does not mean that all members must have exactly the same purpose in being part of the group. But generally there must be some similarity in the individuals' reasons for interacting.

- *Interdependence.* Third, in a small group, members are interdependent, meaning that the behavior of one member is significant for and has an impact on all other members. When one member attacks or supports the ideas of another member, that behavior influences the other members and the group as a whole. When one member proposes a great idea, that behavior has an effect on all group members.

- *Organizing Rules.* Fourth, members of small groups must be connected by some organizing rules or structure. At times the structure is rigid—as in groups operating under parliamentary procedure, in which each comment must follow prescribed rules. At other times, as in a social gathering, the structure is very loose. Yet in both instances there's some organization and some structure: Two people don't speak at the same time, comments or questions by one member are responded to by others rather than ignored, and so on.

- *Self-Perception as a Group.* Fifth, members of small groups feel they are, in fact, members of this larger whole. This doesn't mean that individuality is ignored or that members do not see themselves as individuals; it simply means that each member thinks, feels, and acts as a part of the group. The more members see themselves as part of the group, the greater the group cohesion (or sense of "groupness"); the more they see themselves as individuals, separate from the group, the less the group cohesion. Members in high-cohesive groups are usually more satisfied and more productive than members of low-cohesive groups.

## Basic Types of Groups

A good way to begin the study of small group communication is to look at the various types of groups in which we all participate: relationship and task groups and reference and membership groups.

### Relationship and Task Groups

You can look at groups as serving two broad and overlapping purposes: social or relationship purposes on the one hand and work or task purposes on the other. Social or relationship groups are what sociologists call **primary groups**. These are the groups in which you participate early in life and include, for example, your immediate family, your group of friends at school, and perhaps your neighbors. Usually these groups serve your relationship needs for affiliation, affirmation, and affection. Some of these groups, like family, are extremely long lasting; some, like friends at college, may last only a year or two. It is largely through participating in primary groups and through your strong identification with other group members that you develop your self-concept.

Task groups, which sociologists call **secondary groups**, are groups formed to accomplish something. Some task groups are put together to solve a specific problem; for example, a committee of college professors might be formed to hire a new faculty member, select a textbook, or serve on a graduate student's dissertation committee. Once the specific task is accomplished, the group is dissolved. Other task groups have more long-range concerns; for example, a committee to oversee diversity in the workplace, to monitor fairness in advertising, or to rate feature films may be an ongoing, permanent group.

Unlike relationship groups, which are informal and in which the reward of participation consists simply of being together, task groups are more formal, and the reward of participation comes from accomplishing the specific task. Another interesting difference between relationship and task groups is that in relationship groups each member is irreplaceable and unique. In task groups, in contrast, each member plays a role but can be replaced by a similarly competent individual. For example, in a group formed to develop a core curriculum for undergraduates, the professor representing the sciences could easily be replaced by another science professor and the group would remain essentially the same.

Relationship and task functions often overlap. In fact, it would be difficult to find a group in which these two functions were not combined in some way at some times. The coworkers who bowl together or the two chemistry professors who begin dating are clear examples of how functions can overlap. Not surprisingly, when groups normally devoted to one function start serving another function, they often encounter difficulties. For example, the much-in-love couple who are effective at home may find their relationship under stress when they open a business together.

### Reference and Membership Groups

A **reference group** is a group from which you derive your values and norms of behavior. It is a group you use as a standard and against which you compare yourself; in other words, you judge your successes and failures in comparison with the outcomes of other members of reference groups. Reference groups may be primary or secondary. For example, early in life you may compare yourself with and measure your successes against those of your siblings or cousins (primary groups); later you may look to classmates or coworkers (generally secondary groups) as reference groups.

A **membership group** is a group you participate in but do not use as a guide or to measure yourself. Reference and membership groups are often the same. For the most part you participate in the groups whose values you share, and, at the same time, you acquire the values of the groups in which you participate. In some cases, however, reference and membership groups may differ. For example, if you are a student in medical school, you are not yet a member of the "doctor group," but you certainly will have learned the group's norms and values. As such, you probably emulate doctors in your preparation to be an MD and would likely view the "doctor group" as your reference group.

## Small Group Stages

The small group develops in much the same way that a conversation develops. As in conversation, there are five **small group stages**: (1) opening, (2) feedforward, (3) business, (4) feedback, and (5) closing.

A small group's *opening stage* is usually a getting-acquainted time in which members introduce themselves and engage in social small talk, or phatic communication (recall Unit 1). After this preliminary get-together, there's usually *a feedforward stage* in which members make some attempt to identify what needs to be done, who will do it, and so on. In formal business groups, the meeting agenda (which is a perfect example of feedforward) may be reviewed and the tasks of the group identified. In informal social groups, the feedforward may consist simply of introducing a topic of conversation or talking about what the group's members should do.

The *business stage* is the actual work on the tasks—the problem solving, the sharing of information, or whatever else the group needs to do. At the *feedback stage*, the group may reflect on what it has done and perhaps on what remains to be done. Some groups may even evaluate their performance at this stage. At the *closing stage*, the group members again return to their focus on individuals and will perhaps exchange closing comments—"Good seeing you again," and the like.

These stages are rarely distinct from one another. Rather, they blend into one another. For example, the opening stage is not completely finished before the feedforward begins. Rather, as the opening comments are completed, the group begins to introduce feedforward; as the feedforward begins to end, the business starts.

## Small Group Formats

Small groups serve their functions in a variety of formats. Among the most popular **small group formats** for relatively formal functions are the round table, the panel, the symposium, and the symposium–forum (Figure 10.1).

### The Round Table

In the **round table** format, group members arrange themselves in a circular or semicircular pattern. They share the information or solve the problem without any set pattern of who speaks when. Group interaction is informal, and members contribute as they see fit. A leader or moderator may be present; he or she may, for example, try to keep the discussion on the topic or encourage more reticent members to speak up.

### The Panel

In the **panel**, group members are "experts" but participate informally and without any set pattern of who speaks when, as in a round table. The difference is that there's an audience whose members may interject comments or ask questions. Many talk shows, such as the Jerry Springer and Oprah Winfrey shows, use this format.

A variation is the two-panel format, with an expert panel and a lay panel. The lay panel discusses the topic but may turn to the expert panel members when in need of technical information, additional data, or direction.

### The Symposium

In the **symposium**, each member delivers a prepared presentation much like a public speech. All speeches are addressed to different aspects of a single topic. A symposium leader introduces the speakers, provides transitions from one speaker to another, and may provide periodic summaries.

### The Symposium–Forum

The symposium–forum consists of two parts: a symposium, with prepared speeches, and a **forum**, with questions from the audience and responses by the speakers. The leader introduces the speakers and moderates the question-and-answer session.

## Small Groups Online

Small groups use a wide variety of channels. Often, of course, they take place face-to-face; this is the channel that probably comes to mind when you think of group interaction. But today much small group interaction also takes place online, where groups serve both relationship or social purposes on the one hand and business and professional purposes on the other. **Virtual groups** are groups that rarely meet face-to-face but instead carry on their work through computer-mediated communication (Roebuck, 2001; Kelly, 2006). As you know, more and more work groups are virtual groups; members may work in their offices that are separated geographically or they may work from home.

The advantages of such virtual teams, of course, is that the members may communicate with one another without the expenses of traveling or of establishing office space for meetings. Another advantage is that members may be drawn from an ever-widening pool of competent workers spanning the entire globe. Members from India, Germany, and the United States can communicate in virtual groups just as easily as can members from New York, Connecticut, and New Jersey. An organization need not restrict its membership to those who live close by.

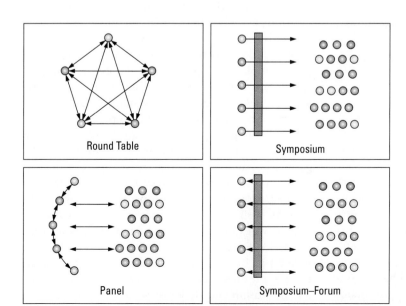

Round Table

Symposium

Panel

Symposium–Forum

**FIGURE 10.1  Small Group Formats**

These four formats are general patterns that may describe a wide variety of groups. Within each type there will naturally be considerable variation. For example, in the symposium–forum there's no set pattern for how much time will be spent on the symposium part and how much time will be spent on the forum part. Similarly, combinations may be used. Thus, for example, group members may each present a position paper (basically a symposium) and then participate in a round table discussion.

As technology becomes more sophisticated and less expensive, virtual teams will become even more prevalent and more productive.

Of course, there are also disadvantages. Members may not feel as connected to the organization when they're not "at the office," and much of the interpersonal interaction that is so vital to many undertaking may be missing.

Two major types of online groups may be noted here: the mailing list group and the chat group. In conjunction with the following discussions, take a look at the "Credo for Free and Responsible Use of Electronic Communication Networks" at www .natcom.org. It's one attempt by a national communication association to articulate some of the ethical issues in electronic group communication.

### Mailing List Groups

**Mailing list groups** are groups of people interested in particular topics who communicate with one another through e-mail. Generally, you subscribe to a list and communicate with all other members by addressing your mail to the group e-mail address. Any message you send to this address will be sent to all members who subscribe to the list at the same time; there are no asides to the person sitting next to you (as in face-to-face groups). Several websites provide extensive lists of listservs or mailing group lists; for example, L-Soft at www.isolft.com/lists/ listref.html and Cool List at www.coollist.com. A list of frequently asked questions and mailing list addresses can be found at www.intuitive.com/social-faq .html. Of course you could also go to one of the search engines and search for mailing lists.

Communication through mailing lists does not take place in real time. It's like regular e-mail; you may send your message today, but it may not be read until next week and you may not get an answer for another week. Much of the spontaneity created by real-time communication is lost. For example, you may be very enthusiastic about a topic when you send your e-mail but may practically forget about it by the time someone responds.

### Chat Groups

**Chat groups** have proliferated across the Internet. These groups enable members to communicate with one another in real time and are now extremely popular. Social networking websites such as MySpace (www.myspace.com) and Facebook (www.facebook .com) are especially popular among college students.

Unlike mailing lists, chat groups let communication take place in real time; you see and in many cases hear a member's message as it's being sent, with virtually no delay. As in mailing lists and face-to-face conversation, the purposes of chat groups vary from communication that simply maintains connection with others (what many would call "idle chatter" or phatic communication) to extremely significant interchanges of ideas.

Communication in a chat group resembles the conversation you would observe at a large party. The total number of guests divide up into small groups varying from two on up, and members of each subgroup discuss their own topic or their own aspect of a general topic. For example, in a group about food, 10 people may be discussing food calories, 8 people may be discussing restaurant food preparation, and 2 people may be discussing the basic food groups, all on this one channel. So although you may be communicating in one primary group (say, dealing with restaurant food), you also have your eye trained to pick up something particularly interesting in another group, much as you do at a party. Like mailing lists, chat groups have the great advantage that they enable you to communicate with people you would never meet or interact with otherwise. Because such groups are international, they provide excellent exposure to other cultures, other ideas, and other ways of communicating.

## Small Group Culture

Small groups, especially those of long standing, develop their own culture. Especially relevant to understanding this cultural dimension of small groups are the group norms and the high or low context with which the group operates. Let's look at each in turn.

### Small Group Norms

In much the same way as a society establishes norms—rules for acceptable and unacceptable social behavior concerning everything from cell phone etiquette to child discipline or relationship fidelity—small groups establish group norms. **Group norms** are rules or standards of behavior identifying which behaviors are considered appropriate (for example, being willing to take on added tasks or directing conflict toward issues rather than toward people) and which are considered inappropriate (for example, coming in late or not contributing actively). Sometimes these rules for appropriate behavior are *explicit*; they're clearly stated in a company contract or policy, such as "All members must attend department meetings." Sometimes the rules are *implicit*: "Members should be well groomed." Regardless of whether norms are spelled out or not, they're powerful regulators of members' behaviors.

Small group norms may apply to individual members as well as to the group as a whole and, of course, will differ from one society to another (Axtell, 1993). For example, in the United States men and women in business are expected to interact when making business decisions as well as when socializing. In Muslim and Buddhist societies, however, reli-

## GROUP NORMS

Your manager wastes the first twenty minutes of just about every meeting at work with talk of his weekend or his personal life. You could really put this time to much better use.

*WHAT DO YOU SAY?*
*To whom? Through what channel?*

gious restrictions prevent mixed-gender groups. In groups in some societies, including those of the United States, Bangladesh, Australia, Germany, Finland, and Hong Kong, punctuality for business meetings is very important. But in Morocco, Italy, Brazil, Zambia, Ireland, and Panama, time is less highly regarded; being late is no great insult and is even expected. In the United States and in much of Asia and Europe, meetings are typically held between two parties at a time. In many Persian Gulf states, however, the business executive is likely to conduct meetings with several different people—sometimes dealing with totally different issues—at the same time. In this situation you have to expect to share what in the United States would be "your time" with these other parties. In the United States very little interpersonal touching goes on during business meetings; in Arab countries, however, touching (for example, hand holding) is common and is a gesture of friendship.

Norms that regulate a particular group member's behavior, called **role** expectations, identify what each person in an organization is expected to do; for example, Pat is great at formatting and editing and so should play the role of secretary.

You're more likely to accept the norms of your group's culture when you feel your group membership is important and want to continue your membership in the group. You're also more likely to accept these norms when your group is cohesive. **Cohesiveness** means that you and the other members are closely connected, are attracted to one another, and depend on one another to meet your needs. Lastly, you're more apt to accept these norms if you'd be punished by negative reactions or exclusion from the group for violating them (Napier & Gershenfeld, 1992).

## High- and Low-Context Cultures

A cultural distinction introduced in Unit 2 has special relevance to small group communication (and to public speaking, which is considered in Units 14–19): the distinction between high- and low-context cultures. A high-context culture, you'll recall, is a culture in which much of the information in communication is in the context or in the person rather than explicitly coded in the verbal messages. In a high-context culture people have lots of information in common, so it does not have to be made explicit. A low-context culture, on the other hand, is a culture in which most of the information in communication is explicitly stated in the verbal messages. In a low-context culture people do not assume they share certain information and so make all crucial details explicit.

As you might expect, group members in high-context cultures spend a lot of time getting to know one another before engaging in any important transactions. Because of this prior personal knowledge, a great deal of information is shared and therefore does not have to be explicitly stated in the group's deliberations. Members of low-context cultures, on the other hand, spend less time getting to know one another and therefore do not have that shared knowledge. As a result everything has to be stated explicitly during the group's discussions. When this simple difference is not taken into account, misunderstandings can easily result. For example, the directness and explicitness characteristic of the low-context culture may prove insulting, insensitive, or unnecessary to members of a high-context culture. Conversely, to members of a low-context culture, someone from a high-context culture may appear vague, underhanded, even dishonest in his or her reluctance to be explicit or to engage in communication that a low-context culture would consider open and direct.

Members of high-context cultures also are reluctant to question the judgments of their superiors. So, for example, if a group leader or manager in a high-context culture proposes something that is obviously in error, group members may be reluctant to express disagreement or to correct the error (Gross, Turner, & Cederholm, 1987).

## Power in the Small Group

Power permeates all small groups and all relationships. It influences what you do, when, and with whom. It influences the employment you seek and the employment you get. It influences the friends you choose and don't choose and those who choose you and those who don't. It influences your romantic and family relationships—their success, failure, and level of satisfaction or dissatisfaction.

**Power** is what enables one person (the one with power) to control the behaviors of others. Thus, if A has power over B and C, then A, by virtue of this power and through the exercise of this power (or the threat of exercising it), can control the behaviors of B and C. Differences in individuals' amounts and types of power influence who makes important decisions, who will prevail in an argument, and who will control the finances.

Although all relationships involve power, they differ in the types of power that the people use and to which they respond. The self-test on page 221 will help you identify the six major types of power.

The six types of power covered in the self-test are (1) legitimate, (2) referent, (3) reward, (4) coercive, (5) expert, and (6) information or persuasion power (French & Raven, 1968; Raven, Centers, & Rodrigues, 1975). You have **legitimate power** (self-test statement 1) over another person when this person believes you have a right by virtue of your position (for example, you're the appointed group leader) to influence or control his or her behavior. Legitimate power usually comes from the leadership roles people occupy. Teachers are often seen to have legitimate power, and this is doubly true for religious teachers. Parents are seen as having legitimate power over their children. Employers, judges, managers, doctors, and police officers are others who may hold legitimate power.

# REFLECTIONS ON ETHICS

## Telling Secrets

In groups of close friends, among family members, or in standing workplace committees, people often exchange secrets with the explicit or only implied assumption that these secrets will not be revealed to outsiders. Revealing or not revealing such secrets often has ethical implications.

In *Secrets* (1983) ethicist Sissela Bok identifies three types of situations in which she argues it would be *unethical* to reveal the secrets of another person. These conditions aren't always easy to identify in any given instance, but they do provide excellent starting points for asking whether or not it's ethical to reveal what we know about another person. And, of course, for any situation, there may be legitimate exceptions.

- It's unethical *to reveal information that you have promised to keep secret.*
- It's unethical *to say things about another person when you know the information to be false.*
- It's unethical *to invade the privacy to which everyone has a right*—to reveal information that no one else has a right to know.

In other situations, however, you may actually have *an obligation* to reveal a secret. For example, Bok (1983) argues that you have an obligation to reveal a secret when keeping the information hidden will do more harm than good. For example, if a teenager confided in you that he or she intended to commit suicide, you'd have an ethical obligation to say something.

### Ethical Choice Point

*How would you handle the following situations? (1) An instructor who supervises your study group confides that she is a confirmed racist and proud of it. (2) A 16-year-old member of the wilderness group you're leading confides that she's having unprotected sex with her supervisor at work, a married man. (3) A community religious leader confides that he's skimming a portion of the members' contributions to fund his retirement.*

# TEST YOURSELF

## How Powerful Are You?

For each statement, indicate which of the following descriptions is most appropriate, using the following scale: 1 = true of 20 percent or fewer of the people I know; 2 = true of about 21 to 40 percent of the people I know; 3 = true of about 41 to 60 percent of the people I know; 4 = true of about 61 to 80 percent of the people I know; and 5 = true of 81 percent or more of the people I know.

_____ **1.** My position is such that I often have to tell others what to do. For example, a mother's position demands that she tell her children what to do, a manager's position demands that he or she tell employees what to do, and so on.

_____ **2.** People wish to be like me or identified with me. For example, high school football players may admire the former professional football player who is now their coach and want to be like him.

_____ **3.** People see me as having the ability to give them what they want. For example, employers have the ability to give their employees increased pay, longer vacations, or improved working conditions.

_____ **4.** People see me as having the ability to administer punishment or to withhold things they want. For example, employers have the ability to reduce voluntary overtime, shorten vacation time, or fail to improve working conditions.

_____ **5.** Other people realize that I have expertise in certain areas of knowledge. For example, a doctor has expertise in medicine and so others turn to the doctor to tell them what to do. Someone knowledgeable about computers similarly possesses expertise.

_____ **6.** Other people realize that I possess the communication ability to present an argument logically and persuasively.

**HOW DID YOU DO?** These statements refer to the six major types of power, as described in the text following this self-test. Low scores (1s and 2s) indicate your belief that you possess little of these particular types of power, and high scores (4s and 5s) indicate your belief that you possess a great deal of these particular types of power.

**WHAT WILL YOU DO?** How satisfied are you with your level of power? If you're not satisfied, what might you do about it? A good starting place, of course, is to learn the skills of communication—interpersonal, small group, and public speaking—discussed in this text. Consider the kinds of communication patterns that would help you communicate power and exert influence in group situations.

## GROUP PRESSURE

Everyone at your new job pads their expense accounts. You don't want to go along with this but, if you don't, everyone else will be found out. You don't want to make waves and yet you don't want to do something unethical.

*WHAT DO YOU SAY?*
*To whom? Through what channel?*

You have **referent power** (statement 2) over another person when that person wishes to be like you or identified with you. For example, an older brother may have referent power over a younger brother because the younger sibling wants to be like his older brother. Your referent power over another person increases when you're well liked and well respected, when you're seen as attractive and prestigious, when you're of the same gender, and when you have attitudes and experiences similar to those of the other person. This is why role models are so important: By definition, role models (sports figures are probably the best examples) possess referent power and exert great influence on those looking up to them.

You have **reward power** (statement 3) over a person if you have the ability to give that person rewards—either material (money, promotions, jewelry) or social (love, friendship, respect). Reward power increases attractiveness; we like those who have the power to reward us and who do in fact give us rewards.

## Theory and Research    Group Power

### UNDERSTANDING

Recall (from Unit 2) that high-power-distance cultures are those in which power is concentrated in the hands of a few and there's a great difference between the power held by these people and the power held by the ordinary citizen; in contrast, in low-power-distance cultures power is more evenly distributed throughout the citizenry (Hofstede, 1997). Groups also may be viewed in terms of high and low power distance. In high-power-distance groups, the leader is far more powerful than the members. In low-power-distance groups, leaders and members differ much less in their power.

Of the groups in which you'll participate—as a member or as a leader—some will be high in power distance and others will be low. The skill is to recognize which is which, to follow the rules generally, and to break the rules only after you've thought through the consequences. For example, in low-power-distance groups, you're expected to confront a group leader (or friend or supervisor) assertively; acting assertively denotes a general feeling of equality (Borden, 1991). In high-power-distance groups, direct confrontation and assertiveness toward the leader (or toward any person in authority, such as a teacher or doctor) may be viewed negatively (Westwood, Tang, & Kirkbride, 1992; also see Bochner & Hesketh, 1994).

### Working with Theories and Research

*Visit one of the online databases to which you have access—for example, Research Navigator at* www.researchnavigator.com—*and search the communication and sociology databases for "power." What types of questions engage the attention of researchers?*

Conversely, you have **coercive power** (statement 4) if you have the ability to remove rewards or to administer **punishments**. Usually, the two kinds of power go hand in hand; if you have reward power, you also have coercive power. For example, parents may grant as well as deny privileges to their children.

You possess **expert power** (statement 5) if group members regard you as having expertise or knowledge—whether or not you truly possess such expertise. Expert power increases when you are seen as being unbiased and having nothing to gain personally from influencing others. It decreases if you are seen as biased and as having something to gain from securing the compliance of others.

You have **information power**, or persuasion power (statement 6), if you're seen as someone who can communicate logically and persuasively. Generally, persuasion power is attributed to people who are seen as having significant information and the ability to use that information in presenting a well-reasoned argument.

Now that the general nature of the small group is clear, let's look at several of the more important types of small groups you'll encounter: idea-generation groups, personal growth groups, information-sharing groups, and problem-solving groups.

## IDEA-GENERATION GROUPS

**Idea-generation groups** are small groups that exist solely to generate ideas and often follow a formula called brainstorming (Osborn, 1957; Beebe & Masterson, 2006; DeVito, 1996). **Brainstorming** is a technique for bombarding a problem and generating as many ideas as possible. This technique involves two stages. The first is the brainstorming period proper; the second is the evaluation period.

The procedures are simple. A problem is selected that is amenable to many possible solutions or ideas. Group members are informed of the problem to be brainstormed before the actual session so that they can think about the topic. When the group meets, each person contributes as many ideas as he or she can think of. All ideas are recorded either in writing or on tape. During this idea-generating session, four general rules are followed.

■ *Brainstorm Rule 1: Don't Criticize.* In a brainstorming session all ideas are recorded. They're not evaluated, nor are they even discussed. Any negative criticism—whether verbal or nonverbal—is itself criticized by the leader or the members. This is a good general rule to follow in all creative thinking: Allow your idea time to develop before you look for problems with it. At the same time, don't praise the ideas either. All evaluations should be suspended during the brainstorming session.

- *Brainstorm Rule 2: Strive for Quantity.* Linus Pauling, Nobel Prize winner for chemistry in 1954 and for peace in 1962, once said, "The best way to have a good idea is to have lots of ideas." This second rule of brainstorming embodies this concept. If you need an idea, you're more likely to find it in a group of many than in a group of few. Thus, in brainstorming, the more ideas the better.

- *Brainstorm Rule 3: Combine and Extend Ideas.* Although you may not criticize a particular idea, you're encouraged to extend it or combine it in some way. The value of a particular idea may be the way it stimulates someone to combine or extend it. Even if your modification seems minor or obvious, say it. Don't censor yourself.

- *Brainstorm Rule 4: Develop the Wildest Ideas Possible.* The wilder the idea, the better. It's easier to tone an idea down than to build it up. A wild idea can easily be tempered, but it's not so easy to elaborate on a simple or conservative idea.

Sometimes a brainstorming session may break down, with members failing to contribute new ideas. At this point the moderator may prod the members with statements such as the following:

- Let's try to get a few more ideas before we close this session.

- Can we piggyback any other ideas or add extensions on the suggestion to . . .

- Here's what we have so far. As I read the list of contributed suggestions, additional ideas may come to mind.

## BRAINSTORMING

You're in charge of a brainstorming group to generate ideas for improving the company website. On the basis of past experiences, you anticipate that a few of the members will just sit there, afraid to offer any suggestions. You need to combat this.

WHAT DO YOU SAY?
*To whom?*

- Here's an aspect we haven't focused on. Does this stimulate any ideas?

After all the ideas are generated—a period lasting no longer than 15 or 20 minutes—the group evaluates the entire list of ideas, using the critical thinking skills developed throughout this text. The ideas that are unworkable are thrown out; those that show promise are retained and evaluated. During this stage negative criticism is allowed.

---

## Building Communication Skills   Combating Idea Killers

Think about how you can be on guard against negative criticism and how you can respond to "idea killers" or "killer messages." Some expressions, such as those listed below, aim to stop an idea from being developed—to kill it in its tracks before it can even get off the ground. As you read down the list of these commonly heard killer messages, formulate at least one response you might give if someone used one of these on you or if you yourself used it to censor your own creative thinking.

1. It'll never work.
2. No one would vote for it.
3. It's too complex.
4. It's too simple.
5. It would take too long.

6. It's too expensive.
7. It's not logical.
8. What we have is good enough.
9. It just doesn't fit us.
10. It's impossible.

*Creativity needs a great deal of freedom to develop; try not to stifle it by allowing ideas to be put down before you have a chance to examine them carefully.*

---

### Building Communication Skills  Listening to New Ideas

A useful skill for listening to new ideas is PIP'N, a technique that derives from Carl Rogers's (1970) emphasis on paraphrasing as a means for ensuring understanding and Edward deBono's (1976) PMI (*plus*, *minus*, and *interesting*) technique. PIP'N involves four steps:

*P = Paraphrase.* State in your own words what you think the other person is saying. This will ensure that you and the person proposing the idea are talking about the same thing. Your paraphrase also will provide the other person with the opportunity to elaborate or clarify his or her ideas.

*I = Interesting.* State something interesting that you find in the idea. Say why you think this idea might be interesting to you, to others, to the organization.

*P = Positive.* Say something positive about the idea. What is good about it? How might it solve a problem or make a situation better?

*N = Negative.* State any negatives that you think the idea might entail. Might it prove expensive? Difficult to implement? Is it directed at insignificant issues?

Try using PIP'N the next time you hear about a new idea; say, in conversation or in a small group. For practice, try PIP'N on the PIP'N technique itself: (1) Paraphrase the PIP'N technique; (2) say why the technique is interesting; (3) say something positive about it; and (4) say something negative about it.

*It's often easier to analyze an idea when you follow specific steps; in this way there's less likelihood that you'll omit some crucial element in the process.*

---

## PERSONAL GROWTH GROUPS

Some **personal growth groups**, sometimes referred to as support groups, aim to help members cope with particular difficulties—such as drug addiction, not being assertive enough, having an alcoholic parent, being an ex-convict, or having a hyperactive child or a promiscuous spouse. Other groups are more clearly therapeutic and are designed to change significant aspects of an individual's personality or behavior. Still other groups are devoted to making healthy individuals function even more effectively.

Personal growth groups vary widely in the procedures they follow, so it's not possible to provide a standard pattern that all such groups follow (as is the case with brainstorming or with problem-solving groups, discussed later in this chapter). But let's look briefly at three well-known types of personal growth groups: the encounter group, the assertiveness training group, and the consciousness-raising group.

### The Encounter Group

**Encounter groups**, also known as "sensitivity groups" or "T [Training]-groups," for example, constitute a form of psychotherapy; these groups try to facilitate members' personal growth and foster their ability to deal effectively with other people (Rogers, 1970; Hirsch, Kett, & Trefil, 2002). One of the encounter group's assumptions is that the members will be more effective, both psychologically and interpersonally, if they get to know and like themselves better. Consequently, members are encouraged to look at themselves and their relationships honestly and in depth and to react to others in the group openly and honestly. Members are encouraged to express their inner thoughts, fears, and doubts in the encounter group, in which interactions are always characterized by total acceptance and support.

### The Assertiveness Training Group

The **assertiveness training group** aims to increase the willingness of its members to stand up for their rights and to act more assertively in a wide variety of situations (Adler, 1977; Bishop, 2006). Distinctions are made between being assertive (which is good and effective); being nonassertive (which is ineffective, because your own wants and needs are unlikely to be met); and being aggressive (which also is ineffective, because it contributes to escalating the conflict and causing resentment). The group aims to increase the assertiveness skills of its members, who are likely to be people who feel they are not assertive enough. The skill of assertiveness is covered in more detail in the discussion of conflict in Unit 12.

### The Consciousness-Raising Group

The **consciousness-raising group** aims to help people cope with the problems society confronts them with. The members of a consciousness-raising group

## MEDIA WATCH

### THE THIRD-PERSON EFFECT

The *third-person effect* concept is a theory of media influence claiming that people routinely believe they are influenced less by the media than their peers are. So, according to this theory, you tend to believe that your friends, neighbors, and coworkers are influenced more by the media than you are; you believe yourself to be the most resistant to media influence. A variety of studies conducted on college students have supported this idea (Davison, 1983). Whether the topic was political advertising, rap music, or pornography, students felt they were less susceptible to media influence than were their peers (Hoffner et al., 2001). This belief, research finds, is especially strong when the media message is a negative or socially unacceptable one; for example, people think that messages of violence, racism, or sexism influence them much less than their peers. The effect is weakened but still present when the message is a more acceptable one (for example, public service announcements).

#### Increasing Media Literacy

*Visit one of the online databases to which you have access and search the communication and psychology databases for "third-person effect." What can you add to the brief discussion presented here? You also might wish to try testing out this theory. For example, survey 10 or 20 people and ask them how influenced they feel they are by, say, media violence or racism. Then ask them if their friends and relatives are influenced by such media messages more than they are. Then conduct the same type of two-step survey with a more socially acceptable message, such as a media campaign on the value of education or the importance of proper diet. On the basis of your research, what can you add to this discussion?*

all have one characteristic in common (for example, they may all be women, unwed mothers, gay fathers, or recently unemployed executives). It's this commonality that leads the members to join together and help one another. In the consciousness-raising group the assumption is that similar people are best equipped to assist one another's personal growth. The procedures generally followed are simple: A topic is selected, and each member speaks on the topic as it relates to the general group topic. For example, if the group consists of unwed mothers, then whatever the topic (taxes, children, school, prejudice), the members address it in the context of the group's focus on unwed motherhood. No interruptions are allowed. After each member has finished, the other group members may ask questions of clarification. The feedback from other members is to be totally supportive. After the last member has spoken, a general discussion follows. This procedure is designed to help raise members' consciousness by giving them an opportunity to formulate and verbalize their thoughts on a particular topic, hear how others feel and think about the same topic, and formulate and answer questions of clarification.

## INFORMATION-SHARING GROUPS

The purpose of **information-sharing groups** is to enable members to acquire new information or skills through a sharing of knowledge. In most information-sharing groups, all members have something to teach and something to learn. In some, however, the interaction takes place because some members have information and some don't.

## Educational or Learning Groups

In *educational or learning groups*, the members pool their knowledge to the benefit of all, as in the popular law and medical student learning groups. Members may follow a variety of discussion patterns. For example, a historical topic might be developed chronologically, with the discussion progressing from the past into the present and perhaps predicting the future. Issues in developmental psychology, such as physical maturity or language development in the child, also might be discussed chronologically. Some topics lend themselves to spatial development. For example, study of the development of the United States might take either a spatial pattern, going from east to west, or a chronological pattern, going from 1776 to the present. Other suitable patterns, depending on the nature of the topic and the needs of the discussants, might be developed in terms of causes and effects, problems and solutions, or structures and functions.

Perhaps the most popular is the topical pattern. A group might discuss the challenges of raising a hyperactive child by itemizing and discussing each of the major problems. The structure of a corporation might also be considered in terms of its major divisions. As can be appreciated, topical approaches may be further systematized; for instance, a learning group might rank the problems of hyperactivity in

# THE RESEARCHER

## Team Problems

*My professor placed us in teams to work on a project for the whole semester. Our group is having problems with several members' dominating the team, especially when we need to make a "team decision." These people just assume we all accept their decisions because we don't say anything different. We want to say something, but if we are going to work with them all semester, we don't want to get them mad at us or hurt their feelings. What can we do to survive this team experience and still get our voices heard?*

Teams and small groups all have their own personalities. Your team is made up of individuals! It is common for some members to dominate or talk all the time—perhaps even to argue for arguing's sake. You can use idea-generating techniques to enable all members to have a voice in the decisions being made by your team. Your team needs to try out the nominal group technique described in this unit. It enables all members to participate by writing and presenting their ideas one at a time in a round-robin fashion. The technique even has a rank-ordering procedure to let the team members understand how important each suggestion was to the majority of its members. Try it! I think it will work for your team. Sometimes talking can be hazardous to a team's health. The technique will enable all members to participate whether they like to talk or not. It also takes the personality out of decision suggestions.

For further information: Moore, C. M. (1994). *Group techniques for idea building* (2nd ed.). Thousand Oaks, CA: Sage. Also Gorden, W. I., Nagel, E. L., Myers, S. A., and Barbato, C. A. (1996). *The team trainer: Winning tools and tactics for successful workouts*. Chicago, IL: Irwin.

**Carole A. Barbato** (Ph.D., Kent State University) is a professor of communication studies and graduate faculty member at Kent State. She teaches classes in public speaking and in small group and interpersonal communication. Her research interests include small group communication, communication motives, and communication and aging. Carole (cbarbato@kent.edu) has provided team training to numerous organizations and small businesses.

---

terms of their importance or complexity or might order the major structures of the corporation in terms of decision-making power.

## Focus Groups

A different type of learning group is the **focus group**, a small group assembled for a kind of in-depth interview. The aim here is to discover what people think about an issue or product; for example, what do men between 18 and 25 think of the new aftershave lotion and its packaging? What do young executives earning more than $100,000 think about buying a foreign luxury car?

In the focus group, a leader tries to discover the beliefs, attitudes, thoughts, and feelings that members have so as to help an organization make decisions on changing the scent or redesigning the packaging or constructing advertisements for luxury cars. It is the leader's task to prod members to analyze their thoughts and feelings on a deeper level

and to use the thoughts of one member to stimulate the thoughts of others.

Generally, approximately 12 people are assembled. The leader explains the process, the time limits, and the general goal of the group—let's say, for example, to discover why these 12 individuals requested information on the XYZ health plan but purchased a plan from another company. The idea, of course, is that these 12 people are representing a wider population. The leader, who is usually a professional focus group facilitator rather than a member of the client organization itself, asks a variety of questions such as: How did you hear about the XYZ health plan? What other health plans did you consider before making your actual purchase? What influenced you to buy the plan you eventually bought? Were any other people influential in helping you make your decision? Through the exploration of these and similar questions, the facilitator and the relevant members of the client organization (who may be seated behind a one-way mirror, watching the discussion) may put together a more effective health plan or more effective advertising strategies.

# PROBLEM-SOLVING GROUPS

A **problem-solving group** is a collection of individuals who meet to solve a problem or to reach a decision. In one sense this is the most exacting kind of group to participate in. It requires not only a knowledge of small group communication techniques, but also a thorough knowledge of the particular problem. And it usually demands faithful adherence to a somewhat rigid set of rules. We'll look at this group first in terms of the classic and still popular problem-solving approach, whereby we identify the steps to go through in solving a problem. In the context of this sequence, we'll consider the major decision-making methods. Finally, we'll survey some types of groups that are popular in organizations today: the nominal group, the Delphi method, quality circles, and improvement groups.

## The Problem-Solving Sequence

The approach developed by philosopher John Dewey (1910), the **problem-solving sequence**, is probably the technique used most often. The six steps of the sequence (see Figure 10.2 on page 228) are designed to make problem solving more efficient and effective: (1) Define and analyze the problem, (2) establish criteria, (3) identify possible solutions, (4) evaluate solutions, (5) select the best solution(s), and (6) test the selected solution(s).

### Define and Analyze the Problem

In many instances the nature of the problem is clearly specified. For example, a group of designers might discuss how to package a new soap product. In other instances, however, the problem may be vague, and it may remain for the group to define it in concrete

terms. Thus, for example, the general problem may be that your company is losing money, and the solution that needs to be found is a way to make the company profitable. But such a broad and general topic is difficult to tackle in a single problem-solving discussion, so it may be helpful to specify the problem in more specific and limited terms. Perhaps this hypothetical problem will need to be dealt with in a series of problem-solving discussions on "How to reduce waste," "How to increase market visibility," and/or "How to attract bright college graduates to join the firm."

Define the problem as an open-ended question ("How can we improve the company website?") rather than as a statement ("The company website needs to be improved") or a yes/no question ("Does the website need improvement?"). The open-ended question allows greater freedom of exploration.

Appropriate questions for most problems revolve around the following issues:

- *Duration*: How long has the problem existed? Is it likely to continue in the future? What is the predicted course of the problem? For example, will it grow or lessen in impact?

- *Causes*: What are the major causes of the problem? How certain can we be that these are the actual causes?

- *Effects*: What are the effects of the problem? How significant are they? Who is affected by this problem? How significantly are they affected? Is this problem causing other problems? How important are these other problems?

### Establish Criteria for Evaluating Solutions

Before any solutions are proposed, you need to decide how to evaluate them. At this stage you identify the standards or criteria that you'll use in evaluating solutions or in selecting one solution over another. Generally, two types of criteria need to be consid-

## CRITICAL THINKING

You're on a team charged with designing the packaging for a new shampoo and you want to use the six critical thinking hats technique to evaluate the proposed solutions.

WHAT DO YOU SAY (FOR EACH HAT)?

**FIGURE 10.2** **Steps in Problem-Solving Discussion**

Although most small group theorists would advise you to follow the problem-solving pattern as presented here, others would alter it somewhat. For example, the pattern here advises you first to define the problem and then to establish criteria for identifying possible solutions. You would then keep these criteria in mind as you generated possible solutions (step 3). Another school of thought, however, would advise you to generate solutions first and to consider how they will be evaluated only after these solutions are proposed (Brilhart & Galanes, 1992). The advantage of this second approach is that you may generate more creative solutions if you're not restricted by standards of evaluation. The disadvantage is that you may spend a great deal of time generating impractical solutions that would never meet the standards you'll eventually propose.

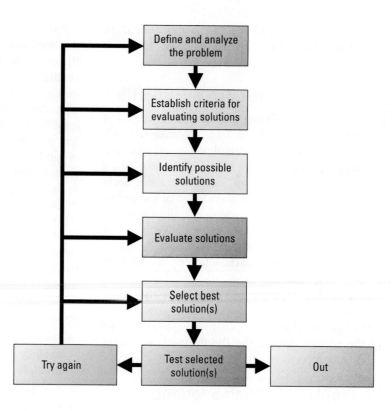

ered. First, there are the practical criteria. For example, you might decide that solutions to the website problem must not increase the budget, must lead to a higher volume of business, must be constructed in-house, must load almost immediately, and so on. Second, there are the value criteria. These are more difficult to identify. These might include, for example, requirements that the website reflect the culture of the company or that it represent the company's commitment to multiculturalism.

### Identify Possible Solutions

At this stage identify as many solutions as possible. Focus on quantity rather than quality. Brainstorming may be particularly useful at this point (see the earlier discussion of idea-generation groups). Solutions to the website problem might include incorporating reviews of publications by company members, reviews of restaurants in the area, recruitment guidelines, and new employment opportunities within the company.

### Evaluate Solutions

After all the solutions have been proposed, you go back and evaluate each according to the criteria you have established. For example, to what extent does incorporating reviews of area restaurants meet the evaluation criteria? Will it increase the budget? Each potential solution should be matched against the criteria.

An especially insightful technique for evaluating solutions (or gaining a different perspective on a problem) was offered by **critical thinking** pioneer

Edward deBono (1987). DeBono's **critical thinking hats technique** involves thinking with six different "hats" and, in doing so, subjecting an issue to a six-part analysis.

- The *fact hat* focuses attention on the data—the facts and figures that bear on the problem. For example: What are the relevant data on the website? How much does it cost to establish and maintain a website? How much advertising revenue can we get?

- The *feeling hat* focuses attention on your feelings, emotions, and intuitions concerning the problem. How do we feel about the website and about making major changes?

- The *negative argument hat* asks that you become the devil's advocate. Why might this proposed solution fail? What is the worst-case scenario?

- The *positive benefits hat* asks that you look at the upside. What opportunities will a new format open up? What benefits will this website provide for employees? What would be the best thing that could happen?

- The *creative new idea hat* focuses attention on new ways of looking at the problem and can be easily combined with the techniques of brainstorming discussed earlier in this unit. In what other ways can we look at this problem? How can the website provide a service to the community?

- The *control of thinking hat* helps you analyze what you have done and are doing. It asks that you reflect on your own thinking processes and synthesize the results of your thinking. Have we adequately defined the problem? Are we focusing too much on insignificant issues? Have we given enough attention to possible negative effects?

## Select the Best Solution(s)

At this stage the best solution or solutions are selected and put into operation. For instance, in the company website example, if "reviews of area restaurants" and "listings of new positions" best met the evaluation criteria, the group might then incorporate these two new items in the redesign of the website.

Groups may use different decision-making methods in deciding, for example, which criteria to use or which solutions to accept. Generally, groups use one of three methods: decision by authority, majority rule, or consensus.

**Decision by Authority.** In decision by authority, members voice their feelings and opinions, but the leader, boss, or CEO makes the final decision. This is surely an efficient method; it gets things done quickly, and the amount of discussion can be limited as desired. Another advantage is that experienced and informed members (for example, those who have been with the company longest) will probably exert a greater influence on the final decision. The great disadvantage is that group members may not feel the need to contribute their insights and may become distanced from the power within the group or organization. Another disadvantage is that this method may lead members to tell the decision maker what they feel she or he wants to hear, a condition that can easily lead to groupthink (Unit 11).

**Decision by Majority Rule.** With this method the group members agree to abide by the majority decision and may vote on various issues as the group works toward solving its problem. Majority rule is efficient, as there's usually the option of calling for a vote when the majority is in agreement. One disadvantage of this method is that it can lead to factioning, in which various minorities align against the majority. The method may also lead to limiting discussion once a majority has agreed and a vote is called.

**Decision by Consensus.** In some situations *consensus* means unanimous agreement; for example, a criminal jury must reach a unanimous decision to convict or acquit a defendant. In most business groups, however, consensus means that members agree that they can live with the solution; they agree that they can do whatever the solution requires (Kelly, 1994). Consensus is especially important when the group wants each member to be satisfied with and committed to the decision and the decision-making process as a whole (DeStephen & Hirokawa, 1988; Beebe & Masterson, 2006). The consensus method obviously takes the longest, and it

---

**Theory and Research** — **Group Polarization**

**UNDERSTANDING**

Groups frequently make more extreme decisions than individuals—a tendency known as *group polarization* (Brauer, Judd, & Gliner, 1995; Friedkin, 1999; Bullock, et al., 2002). For example, a group will take greater risks if the individual members are already willing to take risks (a condition known as the "risky shift phenomenon"), or will become more cautious if the members are already cautious. What seems to happen is that as a group member you estimate how others in the group feel about risk taking. If you judge the group as one of high risk takers, you're likely to become more willing to take risks than you were before the group interaction. Similarly, if you judge the group members as cautious and as low risk takers, you'll become even more cautious than you were before the interaction. In other words—and not surprisingly—your own attitudes toward risk will be heavily influenced by the attitudes you think the group possesses, and you're likely to change your attitudes to more closely match those of the group.

### Working with Theories and Research

*Have you ever observed group polarization? What happened? What implications does this theory have for, say, gang members, professors joining a new faculty, or investment analysts?*

can lead to a great deal of wasted time if members wish to prolong the discussion process needlessly or selfishly.

## Test Selected Solution(s)

After solutions are put into operation, test their effectiveness. The group might, for example, poll employees about the website changes, examine the number of hits, or analyze the advertising revenue.

If the solutions you have adopted prove ineffective, you will need to go back to one of the previous stages and repeat part of the process. Often this takes the form of selecting other solutions to test. But it may also involve going further back—to, for example, a reanalysis of the problem, an identification of other solutions, or a restatement of evaluation criteria.

# Problem-Solving Groups at Work

The problem-solving sequence discussed here is used widely in business in a variety of different types of groups. Let's examine three group approaches popular in business that rely largely on the problem-solving techniques just discussed: the nominal group technique, the Delphi method, and quality circles.

As you read these discussions, realize that the available technology will dictate some of the ways in which these groups operate. If all the members have is a chalkboard, then much will be recorded on the board. If all members have laptops connected to the company website, then much of the record keeping will go onto the website and at the same time into each laptop.

## The Nominal Group Technique

The **nominal group** technique is a method of problem solving that uses limited discussion and confidential voting to obtain a group decision. It's especially helpful when some members may be reluctant to voice their opinions in a regular problem-solving group or when the issue is controversial or sensitive. With this technique, each member contributes equally and each contribution is treated equally. Another advantage of the nominal group process is that it can be accomplished in a relatively short period of time. The nominal group approach can be divided into seven steps (Kelly, 1994):

1. The problem is defined and clarified for all members.
2. Each member writes down (without discussion or consultation with others) his or her ideas on or possible solutions to the problem.

3. Each member—in sequence—states one idea from his or her list, which is recorded on a board or flip chart so everyone can see it. This process is repeated until all suggestions are stated and recorded. Duplicates are then eliminated. Group agreement is secured before overlapping ideas are combined.
4. Each suggestion is clarified (without debate). Ideally, each suggestion is given equal time.
5. Each member rank-orders the suggestions in writing.
6. The rankings of the members are combined to get a group ranking, which is then written on the board.
7. Clarification, discussion, and possible reordering may follow.
8. The highest-ranking solution may then be selected to be tested, or perhaps several high-ranking solutions may be put into operation.

## The Delphi Method

In the **Delphi method** a group of "experts" is established, but there's no interaction among them; instead, they communicate by repeatedly responding to questionnaires (Tersine & Riggs, 1980; Kelly, 1994). The Delphi method is especially useful when you want to involve people who are geographically distant from one another, when you want all members to become part of the solution and to uphold it, or when you want to minimize the effects of dominant members or even of peer pressure. The method is best explained as a series of steps (Kelly, 1994):

1. The problem is defined (for example, "We need to improve intradepartmental communication"). What each member is expected to do is specified (for example, each member should contribute five ideas on this specific question).
2. Each member then anonymously contributes five ideas in writing. This step used to be completed through questionnaires sent through traditional mail but now is more frequently done through e-mail, which greatly increases the speed with which this entire process can be accomplished.
3. The ideas of all members are combined, written up, and distributed to all members.
4. Members then select the three or four best ideas from this composite list and submit these.
5. From these responses another list is produced and distributed to all members.
6. Members then select the one or two best ideas from the new list and submit these.

7. From these responses another list is produced and distributed to all members. The process may be repeated any number of times, but usually three rounds are sufficient for achieving a fair degree of agreement.

8. The "final" solutions are identified and are communicated to all members.

## Quality Circles

A **quality circle** is a group of workers (usually about 6 to 12) whose task it is to investigate and make recommendations for improving the quality of some organizational function. The members are drawn from the workers whose area is being studied; for example, if the problem were how to improve advertising on the Internet, then the quality circle membership would be drawn from the advertising and technology departments. The basic assumption is that people who work on similar tasks will be better able to improve their departments or jobs by pooling their insights and working through problems they share.

Generally, the motivation for establishing quality circles is economic; the company's aim is to improve profitability. Another related goal is to improve worker morale: Because quality circles involve workers in decision making, workers may feel empowered and see themselves as more essential to the organization (Gorden & Nevins, 1993).

Quality circle members investigate problems using any method they feel might be helpful; for example, they may form face-to-face problem-solving groups or use nominal groups or Delphi methods. The group then reports its findings and its suggestions to those who can implement the proposals.

## SUMMARY: SMALL GROUP COMMUNICATION

This unit introduced the nature of the small group and discussed four major types of groups and their functions.

1. A small group is a collection of individuals who are connected to one another by some common purpose, are interdependent, have some degree of organization among them, and see themselves as a group.

2. Relationship groups (primary groups) generally serve relationship needs for affiliation, affirmation, and affection and include family and friendship networks. Task groups (secondary groups) are formed to accomplish something, often work related, and may then be disbanded.

3. Reference groups are groups from which you derive your values and norms of behavior; membership groups are groups in which you participate but whose values you don't necessarily adopt.

4. Small groups make use of four major formats: the round table, the panel, the symposium, and the symposium–forum.

5. Online groups, such as mailing lists and chat groups, serve both relationship and professional purposes.

6. Most small groups develop norms or rules that operate much like cultural norms, identifying what is considered appropriate behavior for the group members.

7. Power operates in all groups. Six types of power may be identified: legitimate, referent, reward, coercive, expert, and information or persuasion.

8. The idea-generation or brainstorming group attempts to generate as many ideas as possible.

9. The personal growth group helps members to deal with personal problems and to function more effectively. Popular types of personal growth groups are the encounter group, the assertiveness training group, and the consciousness-raising group.

10. Information-sharing groups attempt to enable members to acquire new information or skill through a mutual sharing of knowledge or insight. In educational or learning groups, the members pool their knowledge to the benefit of all. The focus group aims to discover what people think about an issue or product through a kind of in-depth group interview.

11. The problem-solving group attempts to solve a particular problem, or at least to reach a decision that may cause the problem to solve itself.

12. The six steps in the problem-solving sequence are: Define and analyze the problem; establish criteria for evaluating solutions; identify possible solutions; evaluate solutions; select best solution(s); and test solution(s).

13. The six critical thinking hats technique is especially useful in analyzing problems and evaluating solutions. This technique consists of focusing on different aspects of the issue: facts, feelings, negative arguments, positive benefits, creative or new ways of viewing problems, and control of thinking processes.

14. Decision-making methods include decision by authority, decision by majority rule, and decision by consensus.

15. Small group approaches that are widely used in business today include the nominal group, the Delphi method, and quality circles.

## KEY TERMS IN SMALL GROUP COMMUNICATION

| | | | |
|---|---|---|---|
| assertiveness training group (p. **224**) | expert power (p. **222**) | nominal group (p. **230**) | referent power (p. **221**) |
| brainstorming (p. **222**) | focus group (p. **226**) | panel (p. **217**) | reward power (p. **221**) |
| chat groups (p. **218**) | forum (p. **217**) | personal growth groups (p. **224**) | role (p. **219**) |
| coercive power (p. **222**) | group (p. **215**) | power (p. **220**) | round table (p. **217**) |
| cohesiveness (p. **219**) | group norms (p. **218**) | primary groups (p. **216**) | secondary groups (p. **216**) |
| consciousness-raising group (p. **224**) | idea-generation group (p. **222**) | problem-solving group (p. **227**) | small group (p. **215**) |
| critical thinking (p. **228**) | information power (p. **222**) | problem-solving sequence (p. **227**) | small group formats (p. **217**) |
| critical thinking hats technique (p. **228**) | information-sharing groups (p. **225**) | punishment (p. **222**) | small group stages (p. **216**) |
| Delphi method (p. **230**) | legitimate power (p. **220**) | quality circle (p. **231**) | symposium (p. **217**) |
| encounter group (p. **224**) | mailing list group (p. **218**) | reference group (p. **216**) | virtual groups (p. **217**) |
| | membership group (p. **216**) | | |

## THINKING CRITICALLY ABOUT SMALL GROUP COMMUNICATION

1. **Small Group Creativity.** Studies find that persons high in communication apprehension are generally less effective in idea-generation groups than those who are low in apprehension (Jablin, 1981; Comadena, 1984; Cragan & Wright, 1990). Why do you think this is so?

2. **Group Norms.** What norms govern your class in human communication? What norms govern your family? Your place of work? Do you have any difficulty with these norms?

3. **Chat Groups.** In research on chat groups, it was found that people were more likely to comment on a participant's message when that message was negative than when it was positive (Rollman, Krug, & Parente, 2000). Do you find this to be true? If so, why do you think this occurs?

4. **Developing Criteria.** What type of criteria would an advertising agency use in evaluating a campaign to sell soap? A university, in evaluating a new multicultural curriculum? Parents, in evaluating a preschool for their children?

5. **Uses and Gratifications.** One study identified seven gratifications you derive from online communication: being in a virtual community, seeking information, aesthetic experience, financial compensation, diversion, personal status, and maintaining relationships (Song, LaRose, Eastin, & Lin, 2004). How would you describe the gratifications you receive from online groups?

## LogOn! MyCommunicationLab
### WWW.MYCOMMUNICATIONLAB.COM

Visit MCL for a variety of video clips on small group communication and for a variety of exercises and study aids. Watch the video Team Project Conflict and analyze the conflict in terms of the principles discussed in this unit. Also, try the web activity Technology and Groups. Another website devoted to small group communication, maintained by the publisher of this book, provides a wealth of additional insights into why people join groups, types of groups, decision making, roles in groups, and mediated groups: www.abacon.com/commstudies/groups/group.html.

While you're online and in connection with brainstorming, take a look at the Creativity Web at http://members/optusnet.com.au/~charles57/creative/index2.html for a wealth of links to all aspects of creativity—quotations, affirmations, humor, discussions of the brain and the creative process, and more.

# UNIT 11  Members and Leaders

## MAJOR TOPICS

Members in Small Group Communication
Leaders in Small Group Communication
Membership, Leadership, and Culture

## Special Features

Throughout your life, you'll participate in a wide variety of groups—as a member of a work group, as a part of a social or neighborhood group, or as a player on a team. Probably you'll also lead some of these social or work groups, and your leadership responsibilities are likely to increase as you rise in the group hierarchy.

**In this unit, you'll learn about:**
- the kinds of roles members play in groups.
- the types and styles of leadership.

**You'll learn to:**
- participate more effectively as a group member.
- lead a wide variety of groups effectively and efficiently.

## MEMBERS IN SMALL GROUP COMMUNICATION

You can view membership in small group communication situations from a variety of perspectives—in terms of the roles that members serve, the types of contributions they make, and the principles for more effective participation.

## Member Roles

Before reading about the roles of members in small groups, take the following self-test, which encourages you to look at your own small group membership behavior.

## TEST YOURSELF

### What Kind of Group Member Are You?

For each statement below, respond with T for true if the statement is often true of your group behavior or F for false if the statement generally does not apply to your group behavior.

_____ **1.** I present new ideas and suggest new strategies.

_____ **2.** I ask for facts and opinions.

_____ **3.** I stimulate the group.

_____ **4.** I give examples and try to look for positive solutions.

_____ **5.** I positively reinforce group members.

_____ **6.** I try to reconcile differences.

_____ **7.** I go along with the other members.

_____ **8.** I offer compromises as ways of resolving conflict.

_____ **9.** I express negative evaluation of the actions and feelings of the group members.

_____ **10.** I try to run the group.

_____ **11.** I express personal perspectives and feelings.

_____ **12.** I express confusion or deprecate myself.

**HOW DID YOU DO?** As you'll see as you read further, these behaviors are characteristic of the three general types of group member roles. The first four statements refer to your taking on group task roles, and the next four refer to your taking on group building and maintenance roles. Both of these types of roles are productive. The final four refer to your taking an individual rather than a group focus; these are the behaviors that often work against the group's achieving its goals.

**WHAT WILL YOU DO?** As you read the following sections on member roles, try to relate these roles to your own behavior or to group behavior you've witnessed. Then ask yourself what worked and what didn't work. What roles were productive, and what roles were unproductive?

As mentioned in the preceding self-test, group member roles fall into three general classes—group task roles, group building and maintenance roles, and individual roles—a classification introduced in early research (Benne & Sheats, 1948) and still widely used today (Lumsden & Lumsden, 1996; Beebe & Masterson, 2006). These roles are, of course, frequently served by leaders as well.

## Group Task Roles

**Group task roles** are those that help the group focus more specifically on achieving its goals. In serving any of these roles, you act not as an isolated individual but rather as a part of the larger whole. The needs and goals of the group dictate the task roles you serve. As an effective group member you would serve several of these functions.

Some people, however, lock into a few specific roles. For example, one person may almost always seek the opinions of others; another may concentrate on elaborating details; still another, on evaluating suggestions. Usually this kind of single focus is counterproductive. It's usually better for group task roles to be spread more evenly so that each member may serve many roles. The 12 specific group task roles include:

- The *initiator-contributor* presents new ideas or new perspectives on old ideas, suggests new goals, or proposes new procedures or organizational strategies.
- The *information seeker* asks for facts and opinions and seeks clarification of the issues being discussed.
- The *opinion seeker* tries to discover the values underlying the group's task.
- The *information giver* presents facts and opinions to the group members.
- The *opinion giver* presents values and opinions and tries to spell out what the values of the group should be.
- The *elaborator* gives examples and tries to work out possible solutions, trying to build on what others have said.
- The *coordinator* spells out relationships among ideas and suggested solutions and coordinates the activities of the different members.
- The *orienter* summarizes what has been said and addresses the direction the group is taking.
- The *evaluator-critic* evaluates the group's decisions, questions the logic or practicality of the suggestions, and thus provides the group with both positive and negative feedback.
- The *energizer* stimulates the group to greater activity.
- The *procedural technician* takes care of various mechanical duties such as distributing group materials and arranging seating.
- The *recorder* writes down the group's activities, suggestions, and decisions; he or she serves as the memory of the group.

## Group Building and Maintenance Roles

Most groups focus not only on the task to be performed but also on interpersonal relationships among members. If the group is to function effectively, and if members are to be both satisfied and productive, these relationships must be nourished. When these needs are not met, group members may become irritable when the group process gets bogged down, may engage in frequent conflicts, or may find the small group process as a whole unsatisfying. The group and its members need the same kind of support that individuals need. The **group building and maintenance roles** serve this general function. Group building and maintenance functions are broken down into seven specific roles:

- The *encourager* supplies members with positive reinforcement in the form of social approval or praise for their ideas.
- The *harmonizer* mediates differences among group members.
- The *compromiser* offers compromises as a way to resolve conflicts between his or her ideas and those of others.
- The *gatekeeper-expediter* keeps the channels of communication open by reinforcing the efforts of others.
- The *standard setter* proposes standards for the functioning of the group or for its solutions.
- The *group observer and commentator* keeps a record of the proceedings and uses this in the group's evaluation of itself.
- The *follower* goes along with the members of the group, passively accepts the ideas of others, and functions more as an audience than as an active member.

## Individual Roles

The group task and group building and maintenance roles just considered are productive roles; they aid the group in achieving its goals. **Individual roles**, on the other hand, are counterproductive; they hinder the group's productivity and member satisfaction, largely because they focus on serving individual rather than group needs. As you read about these eight specific types, consider what you'd say to each of them if you were a member or a leader of the group and wanted to deal with this dysfunctional role playing but, at the same time, didn't want to alienate the individual or the group.

- The *aggressor* expresses negative evaluation of the actions or feelings of the group members; he or she attacks the group or the problem being considered.
- The *blocker* provides negative feedback, is disagreeable, and opposes other members or suggestions regardless of their merit.
- The *recognition seeker* tries to focus attention on himself or herself rather than on the task at hand, boasting about his or her own accomplishments.

- The *self-confessor* expresses his or her own feelings and personal perspectives rather than focusing on the group.
- The *playboy/playgirl* jokes around without any regard for the group process.
- The *dominator* tries to run the group or the group members by pulling rank, flattering members of the group, or acting the role of the boss.
- The *help seeker* expresses insecurity or confusion or deprecates himself or herself and thus tries to gain sympathy from the other members.
- The *special interest pleader* disregards the goals of the group and pleads the case of some special group.

As you might expect, your tendency to play group versus individual roles will be influenced by your culture—and especially by your individualist or collectivist orientation, as discussed in Unit 2, and your power orientation, as discussed in Unit 10.

## Interaction Process Analysis

Another way of looking at the contributions group members make is through **interaction process analysis** (IPA), developed by Robert Bales (1950). In this system you analyze the contributions of members under four general categories: (1) social-emotional positive contributions, (2) social-emotional negative contributions, (3) attempted answers, and (4) questions. Each of these four areas contains three subdivisions, yielding a total of 12 categories into which you can classify group members' contributions (Table 11.1). Note that the categories under social-emotional positive are the natural opposites of those under social-emotional negative, and those under attempted answers are the natural opposites of those under questions. You may want to try out Bales's IPA system by listening to a small group discussion or a televised situation comedy or drama and recording the interactions using Table 11.1.

Both the three-part member role classification and the IPA categories are useful for analyzing the contributions members make in small group situations. When you look at member contributions through these systems, you can see, for example, if one member is locked into a particular role or if the group process is breaking down because too many people are serving individual rather than group goals or because social-emotional negative comments dominate the discussion. You should also be in a better position to offer improvement suggestions for individual members based on this analysis.

## Member Participation

For another perspective on group membership, let's consider the recommendations for effective participation in small group communication. Look at these

### Table 11.1 Interaction Process Analysis Form

The names of participants appear in the top spaces, as shown by the examples here. In the column under each participant's name, you place a slash mark for each contribution in each of the 12 categories.

|  |  | Joe | Judy | Liz | Mike | Peg |
|---|---|---|---|---|---|---|
| Social–Emotional Positive Contributions | Shows solidarity |  |  |  |  |  |
|  | Shows tension release |  |  |  |  |  |
|  | Shows agreement |  |  |  |  |  |
| Social–Emotional Negative Contributions | Shows disagreement |  |  |  |  |  |
|  | Shows tension |  |  |  |  |  |
|  | Shows antagonism |  |  |  |  |  |
| Attempted Answers | Gives suggestions |  |  |  |  |  |
|  | Gives opinions |  |  |  |  |  |
|  | Gives information |  |  |  |  |  |
| Questions | Asks for suggestions |  |  |  |  |  |
|  | Asks for opinions |  |  |  |  |  |
|  | Asks for information |  |  |  |  |  |

## INDIVIDUAL ROLES

In a group of workers you're leading, one member consistently plays the role of blocker, objecting to everything anyone says. Another member plays the role of self-confessor, revealing feelings no one wants to hear. You need to lessen these comments if your group is to succeed.

WHAT DO YOU SAY?
*To whom? Through what channel?*

suggestions as an elaboration and extension of the characteristics of effective conversation enumerated in Unit 7.

### Be Group or Team Oriented

In the small group you're a member of a team, a larger whole. As a group your task is to pool your talents, knowledge, and insights so as to arrive at a better solution than any one person could have developed. This call for group orientation is not to be taken as a suggestion that members abandon their individuality or give up their personal values or beliefs for the sake of the group, however. Individuality with a group orientation is what is advocated here.

### Center Conflict on Issues

It's particularly important in the small group to center conflict on issues rather than on personalities. When you disagree, make it clear that your disagreement is with the solution suggested or with the ideas expressed, not with the person who expressed them. Similarly, when someone disagrees with what you say, don't take it as a personal attack. Instead, view this as an opportunity to discuss issues from an alternative point of view.

### Be Critically Open-Minded

Because the most effective and creative solutions often emerge from a combination of ideas, approach small group situations with flexibility; come to the group with ideas and information but without firmly formulated conclusions. Advance any solutions or conclusions tentatively rather than with certainty.

Be willing to alter your suggestions and revise them in light of the discussion.

### Ensure Understanding

Make sure that your ideas are understood by all participants. If something is worth saying, it's worth saying clearly. When in doubt, ask: "Is that clear?" "Did I explain that clearly?" Make sure, too, that you understand fully the contributions of other members, especially before you take issue with them. In fact, as explained in Unit 10, it's often wise to preface any extended disagreement with some kind of paraphrase to give the other person the opportunity to clarify, deny, or otherwise alter what was said. For example, you might say, "As I understand it, you want to exclude freshmen from playing on the football team. Is that correct? I disagree with that idea and I'd like to explain why I think that would be a mistake."

### Beware of Groupthink

**Groupthink** is a way of thinking that people use when agreement among members has become excessively important. Groupthink is most likely to occur when there is high stress, when like-minded individuals are isolated from others, and when there is an especially strong and opinionated leader. Overemphasis on agreement among members tends to shut out realistic and logical analysis of a problem or of possible alternatives (Janis, 1983; Mullen, Tara, Salas, & Driskell, 1994). The term *groupthink* itself is meant to signal a "deterioration of mental efficiency, reality testing, and moral judgment that results from in-group pressures" (Janis, 1983, p. 9).

The following symptoms should help you recognize groupthink in groups you observe or participate in (Janis, 1983; Schafer & Crichlow, 1996; Richmond, McCroskey, & McCroskey, 2005):

- *Illusion of invulnerability.* Group members think the group and its members are invulnerable, that they are virtually beyond being harmed.

- *Avoidance.* Members create rationalizations to avoid dealing with warnings or threats.

- *Assumption of morality.* Members believe their group is moral and, often, that any opposition is immoral.

- *Intolerance of differences of opinion.* Those opposed to the group are perceived in simplistic, stereotyped ways, and group pressure is applied to any member who expresses doubts or questions the group's arguments or proposals.

- *Self-censorship.* Members censor their own doubts.

- *Assumption of unanimity.* Group members believe that all members are in unanimous agreement, whether this is stated or not. This belief is encouraged, of course, by members censoring their own doubts and not allowing differences of opinion to be discussed.

- *Gatekeeping.* Group members emerge whose function it is to guard the information that gets to other members, especially when it may create diversity of opinion.

- *Peer pressure.* Groupthinkers pressure others to go along with the group and not to express any disagreement.

Here are three suggestions for combating groupthink.

1. When too-simple solutions are offered to problems, try to illustrate (with specific examples, if possible) for the group members how the complexity of the problem is not going to yield to the solutions offered.

2. When you feel that members are not expressing their doubts about the group or its decisions, encourage members to voice disagreement. Ask members to play devil's advocate, to test the adequacy of the solution. Or, if members resist, do it yourself. Similarly, if you feel there is unexpressed disagreement, ask specifically if anyone disagrees. If you still get no response, it may be helpful to ask everyone to write his or her comments anonymously, then read them aloud to the group.

3. To combat the group pressure toward agreement, reward members who do voice disagreement or doubt. Say, for example, "That's a good argument; we need to hear more about the potential problems of this proposal. Does anyone else see any problems?"

# LEADERS IN SMALL GROUP COMMUNICATION

**Leadership** is defined in two very different ways in research and theory:

- Leadership is the process of influencing the thoughts, feelings, and behaviors of group members and establishing the direction that others follow; leadership and influence are parts of the same skill.

- Leadership is the process of empowering others; the leader is the person who helps others to maximize their potential and to take control of their lives.

### ASSERTING YOURSELF IN A GROUP

In your casual conversations with friends as well as at work meetings, people consistently ignore your cues that you want to say something. And when you do manage to say something, no one reacts. You're determined to change this situation.

WHAT DO YOU SAY?
*To whom? Through what channel?*

**Building Communication Skills** Combating Groupthink

Develop specific messages you might use as a member or a leader of a group in which you see the signs of groupthink noted on the left and you wish to use the combat tactic noted in the center column.

| Suspected problem | Combat tactic | Messages to accomplish your combat goal |
| --- | --- | --- |
| Group members assume there's unanimous agreement. | Ask for a poll of opinion; survey the group members. | _____ |
| Members are not expressing their doubts about the group or its decisions. | Encourage members to voice disagreement, or ask if anyone disagrees. | _____ |
| There's lots of group pressure toward agreement. | Reward members who voice disagreement, or voice it yourself. | _____ |

*Groupthink prevents creativity and logical analysis; watch out for it and try to reduce its influence whenever you can.*

These two definitions are not mutually exclusive; in fact, most effective leaders do both; they influence and they empower. As you read the remaining discussion of leadership, keep these two definitions in mind and see leadership as embodying both power and empowerment.

In many small groups one person serves as leader. In other groups leadership may be shared by several persons.

In some cases a person may be appointed the leader or may serve as leader because of her or his position within the company or hierarchy. In other cases the leader may emerge as the group proceeds in fulfilling its functions or may be elected leader by the group members. Two significant factors exert considerable influence on who emerges as group leader. One is the extent of active participation: The person who talks the most is more likely to emerge as leader (Mullen, Salas, & Driskell, 1989; Shaw & Gouran, 1990). The second factor is effective listening: Members who listen effectively will emerge as leaders more often than those who don't (Johnson & Bechler, 1998; Bechler & Johnson, 1995).

The **emergent leader** performs the duties of leadership, though not asked or expected to, and gradually becomes recognized by the members as the group's leader. And because this person has now proved herself or himself an effective leader, it's not surprising that this emergent leader often becomes the designated leader for future groups.

The role of the leader or leaders is vital to the well-being and effectiveness of the group. Even in leaderless groups in which all members are equal, leadership functions must still be served.

## Myths about Leadership

As with many important concepts, beliefs about leadership have grown. Some of these beliefs are erroneous and need to be recognized as such. Here are just three myths about leadership offered by—and here paraphrased from—small group theorists (Bennis & Nanus, 2003):

- *Myth: The skills of leadership are rare.* Actually, all of us have the potential for leadership; and, of course, there are millions of leaders throughout the world who are serving a variety of functions in government, business, education, and countless other fields.

- *Myth: Leaders are born.* Actually, the major leadership skills can be learned by just about everyone. No specific genetic endowment is necessary. We all can improve our leadership abilities.

- *Myth: Leaders are all charismatic.* Actually, only some leaders are. According to one survey of leaders (Bennis & Nanus, 2003, p. 208): "Our leaders were all 'too human'; they were short and tall, articulate and inarticulate, dressed for success and dressed for failure, and there was virtually nothing in terms of physical appearance, personality, or style that set them apart from their followers."

# ASK THE RESEARCHER

## Becoming a Leader

*I'm going to start a new job—a great position at a large investment firm. I'm very focused on rising in the organization (yes, I want status and money), and I want to know what I can do to establish myself as someone who has leadership potential. Are there any communication skills that are absolutely essential and that I should concentrate on?*

There are a number of things you can do to establish yourself as having leadership potential. First and foremost, demonstrate task-relevant expertise. Don't be a know-it-all, but do share accurate information and insightful interpretations of complex data when you have the opportunity to do so. If you don't know the answer to a question, say so, but show initiative by offering to find the answer for the person who posed the question. Then be sure to follow up with a correct, detailed response in a timely way.

Second, demonstrate relational competence. Always be civil and pleasant to your colleagues, regardless of the circumstances. Don't engage in political squabbles with your peers, but do work to maintain productive lines of communication between conflicted persons or groups.

Finally, let your word be your bond. Credibility is your most precious possession. Always be authentic in your dealings with others. If you want to be a leader, your colleagues must trust you.

For further information: Frey, L. R., & Barge, J. K. (1997). *Managing group life: Communicating in decision-making groups.* Boston: Houghton Mifflin. Also Hawkins, K. W., & Fillion, B. (1999). Perceived communication skill needs for work groups. *Communication Research Reports, 16,* 167–174.

**Katherine Hawkins** (Ph.D., University of Texas) is a professor of communication studies at Clemson University. She teaches courses in communication theory and research methods. She also serves as department chair and is a past president of the Southern States Communication Association.

## Approaches to Leadership

Not surprisingly, leadership has been the focus of considerable attention from theorists and researchers, who have used numerous approaches to understand this particular communication behavior. Before reading about these approaches, you may wish to take the self-test below to examine yourself as a leader.

## TEST YOURSELF

### What Kind of Leader Are You?

This self-test is designed to stimulate you to think about yourself in the role of leader. Respond to the following statements in terms of how you perceive yourself and how you think others perceive you, using a 10-point scale ranging from 10 (extremely true) to 1 (extremely false).

| Others see me as | I see myself as | Perceptions |
|---|---|---|
| _____ 1. | _____ 1. | Generally popular with group members |
| _____ 2. | _____ 2. | Knowledgeable about the topics and subjects discussed |
| _____ 3. | _____ 3. | Dependable |
| _____ 4. | _____ 4. | Effective in establishing group goals |
| _____ 5. | _____ 5. | Competent in giving directions |
| _____ 6. | _____ 6. | Capable of energizing group members |
| _____ 7. | _____ 7. | Charismatic (dynamic, engaging, powerful) |

| | | | |
|---|---|---|---|
| _____ 8. | _____ | **8.** | Empowering of group members |
| _____ 9. | _____ | **9.** | Moral and honest |
| _____ 10. | _____ | **10.** | Skilled in balancing the concerns of getting the task done and satisfying the group members' personal needs |
| _____ 11. | _____ | **11.** | Flexible in adjusting leadership style on the basis of the unique situation |
| _____ 12. | _____ | **12.** | Able to delegate responsibility |

**HOW DID YOU DO?** This test was designed to encourage you to look at yourself in terms of the four approaches to leadership that will be discussed in the following text. Phrases 1–3 refer to the traits approach to leadership, which defines a leader as a person who possesses certain qualities. Phrases 4–6 refer to the functional approach, which defines a leader as a person who performs certain functions. Phrases 7–9 refer to the transformational approach, which defines a leader as a person who inspires the group members to become the best they can be. Phrases 10–12 refer to the situational approach, which defines a leader as someone who can adjust his or her style to balance the needs of the specific situation.
To compute your scores:

1. Add your scores for statements 1–3: _____.
   This will give you an idea of how you and others see you in terms of the leadership qualities identified by the _traits approach_.

2. Add your scores for statements 4–6: _____.
   This will give you an idea of how you and others see you in relation to the varied leadership functions considered in the _functional approach_.

3. Add your scores for statements 7–9: _____.
   This will give you an idea of how you and others see you as a _transformational leader_.

4. Add your scores for statements 10–12: _____.
   This will give you an idea of how you and others see you as a _situational leader_.

**WHAT WILL YOU DO?** As you read the remainder of this unit and the rest of the book, try to identify specific skills and competencies you might learn that would enable you to increase your scores on all four approaches to leadership. Also, try searching the Web for information on "leadership" as well as, say, "business leadership" and "political leaders."

## Traits Approach

The **traits approach to leadership** argues that leaders must possess certain qualities if they're to function effectively. Some of the traits found to be associated with leadership are intelligence, dominance, honesty, foresight, altruism, popularity, sociability, cooperativeness, knowledge, and dependability (Hackman & Johnson, 1991). The problem with the traits approach is that the specific qualities called for will vary with the situation, with the members, and with the culture in which the leader functions. Thus, for example, the leader's knowledge and personality are generally significant factors; but for some groups a knowledge of financial issues and a serious personality might be effective, whereas for other groups a knowledge of design and a more humorous personality might be effective.

## Functional Approach

The **functional approach to leadership** focuses on what the leader should do in a given situation. We have already considered some of these functions in the discussion of group membership, which identified group roles. Other functions found to be associated with leadership are setting group goals, giving direction to group members, and summarizing the group's progress (Schultz, 1996). Still other functions are identified in the section entitled "Functions of Leadership," later in this unit.

## Transformational Approach

In the **transformational approach to leadership** the leader elevates the group's members, enabling them not only to accomplish the group task but also to emerge as more empowered individuals (Li & Shi, 2003). At the center of the transformational approach is the concept of charisma, that quality of an individual that makes us believe in or want to follow him or her. Gandhi, Martin Luther King Jr., and John F. Kennedy may be cited as examples of transformational leaders. These leaders were seen as role models of what they asked of their members, were perceived as extremely competent and able leaders, and articulated moral goals (Northouse, 1997). We'll return to this concept of charisma in the discussion of credibility in Unit 18.

## Situational Approach

The **situational approach to leadership** focuses on the two major responsibilities of the leader—accomplishing the task at hand and ensuring the satisfaction of the members—and recognizes that the leader's style must vary on the basis of the

## SITUATIONAL LEADERSHIP

You're in an advanced Internet design team whose leader uses a telling style, creating resentment among members. You've been elected to clue the leader into appropriate and inappropriate styles.

WHAT DO YOU SAY?
*Through what channels?*

specific situation. Just as you adjust your interpersonal style in conversation or your motivational appeals in public speaking on the basis of the particular situation, so you must adjust your leadership style. Leadership effectiveness, then, depends on combining the concerns for task and people according to the specifics of the situation. Some situations will call for high concentration on task issues but will need little in the way of people encouragement. For example, a group of scientists working on AIDS research would probably need a leader primarily to provide them with the needed information to accomplish their task. They would be self-motivating and would probably need little in the way of social and emotional encouragement. On the other hand, a group of recovering alcoholics might require leadership that stressed the social and emotional needs of the members.

An interesting extension of the situational approach portrays four basic leadership styles, as illustrated in Figure 11.1 (Hersey, Blanchard, & Johnson, 2001). This model claims that groups differ in their degree of readiness. A group that contains members who are knowledgeable, experienced, and demonstrating that skill at a sustained and acceptable level have a high degree of readiness. Because of that readiness, group members are able to set realistic and attainable goals. Continued success and supportive behavior from others tends to build confidence which leads to higher levels of readiness where group members are willing to appropriately take responsibility for their decisions. A group this high in readiness is characterized by members who are both willing and able to perform the task in question. This is a critical point. A group or individual's readiness varies with the task; an individual may be

### FIGURE 11.1 A Model of Situational Leadership

This figure depicts four different styles of leadership that differ in the degree to which they are supportive (relationship oriented) or directive (task oriented). Are there any leadership styles with which you're uncomfortable? What skills can you acquire to help you feel more comfortable and competent with these styles?

Source: "Model of Situational Leadership" by Paul Hersey and Kenneth Blanchard in *Management of Organizational Behavior*, p. 277. Copyright © 2006. Reprinted with permission of the Center for Leadership Studies, Inc. Escondido, CA 92025. All rights reserved.

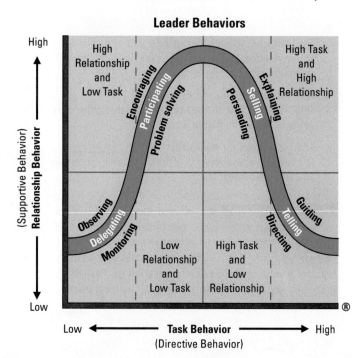

skilled at, and more than happy to engage in, discussions about food and exercise, but less than amenable when it comes to talking about their finances.

Effective leadership, then, depends on the leader's assessment of the group's ability and willingness to do the task. To complicate matters even more, the readiness of the group will also change as the group develops or regresses over time—so the style of leadership will have to change in response to the changes in the group. The Situational Leadership Model identifies four different leadership styles that provide the highest probability of successfully and effectively influencing the behaviors of others based on their level of readiness for a specific task:

- The **telling style** of leadership is appropriate for a group that lacks knowledge of the issues involved and needs the direct guidance of the telling leader, the leader who tells the members what they should do. The telling style focuses almost exclusively on the task; this leader offers little if any relationship support.

- The **selling style** is appropriate for a group that is trying hard but still lacks the needed skills or information to accomplish their task. The selling style is a persuasive strategy; it is high in both directiveness and in relationship support. Here the leader seeks to gain the group members' psychological support (to get them to "buy into" the ideas) and so does lots of explaining. At the same time, however, this leader provides direct guidance for what the group should do.

- The **participating style** is appropriate for groups that know what to do but may not be so willing to do it. This leader, therefore, relies heavily on communicating, facilitating, and encouraging group members. This leader participates in the group's problem solving but, because group members already know what to do, provides little direction.

- The **delegating style** is appropriate for groups that know what to do and are eager to do it. Here the leader need not provide extensive direction or relationship support but instead monitors and observes.

**Theory and Research** **Styles of Leadership**

**UNDERSTANDING**

Small group communication researchers distinguish three basic types of group leaders: *laissez-faire, democratic,* and *authoritarian* (Bennis & Nanus, 1985; Hackman & Johnson, 1991).

The **laissez-faire leader** takes no initiative in directing or suggesting alternative courses of action. Rather, this leader allows the group to develop and progress on its own, even allowing it to make its own mistakes. The laissez-faire leader answers questions and provides information only when specifically asked. During the group interaction, this leader neither compliments nor criticizes the group's members or their progress. Generally, this type of leadership results in a satisfied but inefficient group.

The **democratic leader** provides direction but allows the group to develop and progress the way its members wish. This leader encourages group members to determine their own goals and procedures and works to stimulate the self-direction and self-actualization of group members. Unlike the laissez-faire leader, the democratic leader does contribute suggestions and does comment on member and group performance. Generally, this form of leadership results in both satisfaction and efficiency.

The **authoritarian leader**, the opposite of the laissez-faire leader, determines group policies and makes decisions without consulting or securing agreement from the members. This leader discourages member-to-member communication but encourages communication from member to leader. The authoritarian leader is concerned with getting the group to accept his or her decisions rather than making its own. If the authoritarian leader is competent, the group may be highly efficient, but its members are likely to be less personally satisfied.

### Working with Theories and Research

*Which leadership style—say, in a work situation with colleagues—are you likely to feel most comfortable using? Most comfortable working with as a group member?*

## MEDIA WATCH
### GATEKEEPING

The concept of "gatekeeping," introduced by Kurt Lewin in his *Human Relations* (1947), has to do with both *the process* by which a message passes through various gates and *the people or groups*, or gatekeepers, that allow the message to pass.

As you were growing up, your parents—your first gatekeepers—gave you certain information and withheld other information. For example, depending on the culture in which you were raised, you may have been told about Santa Claus and the tooth fairy but not about cancer or mutual funds. When you went to school, your teachers served a similar gatekeeping function. They taught you about certain historical events, for example, but not others. Textbook authors also serve as gatekeepers (Robinson, 1993). Editors of newspapers and magazines; television producers, writers, and advertisers; and those who regulate and monitor Internet messages are all gatekeepers: They allow certain information to come through and other information to be filtered out (Lewis 1995; Bodon, Powell, & Hickson, 1999).

Often the media gatekeeps to increase profits, as when they emphasize (open the gates for) stories of celebrities, violence, and sex—because these sell—and deemphasize (close the gates on) minority issues, classical drama, or antireligious statements. At times they may gatekeep because of legal restrictions.

So, when you hear a news broadcast, read an article, or listen to a commentator, ask yourself if you're seeing or hearing an incomplete or unrealistic picture. Ask yourself, what might not have passed through the gate?

### Increasing Media Literacy

*How do one, two, or three of the following people function as gatekeepers in relation to your ability to acquire information: the editor of your local or college newspaper, Oprah Winfrey, your romantic partner (past or present), the president of the United States, network news shows, or the advertising department of a large corporation?*

As you can tell from these descriptions, the leader exerts more control with immature groups (telling and selling) and less control with mature groups (participating and delegating). As groups become more mature, members assume greater responsibility and control and leaders' control diminishes.

## Functions of Leadership

In relatively formal small group situations, as when politicians plan a strategy, advertisers discuss a campaign, or teachers consider educational methods, the leader has several specific functions. These functions—a mixture of task and people functions—are not the exclusive property of the leader. Nevertheless, when there's a specific leader, he or she is expected to perform them.

As you read these functions, keep in mind that an effective leader needs not only knowledge of the topic of the discussion but also communication competence—the ability to effectively use the group process as well as to use mindfulness, flexibility, and cultural sensitivity plus the more specific skills of openness, empathy, positiveness, immediacy,

interaction management, expressiveness, and other-orientation that we discussed in Unit 7.

Still another skill the leader needs is the ability to manage any group conflict that might arise. Unit 12 will examine group conflict along with interpersonal and relationship conflict.

### Prediscussion Functions

It often falls to the leader to provide members with necessary materials prior to the meeting. Prediscussion functions may include, for example, arranging a convenient meeting time and place; informing members of the purposes and goals of the meeting; providing them with materials they should read or view; and recommending that they come to the meeting with, for example, general ideas or specific proposals.

Similarly, groups form gradually and need to be eased into meaningful discussion. Diverse members should not be expected to sit down and discuss a problem without becoming familiar with one another. Put more generally, the leader is responsible for any preparations and preliminaries necessary to ensure an orderly and productive group experience.

## Activating the Group Agenda

Most groups have an agenda. An **agenda** is simply a list of the tasks the group wishes to complete. It's an itemized listing of what the group should devote its attention to. In some cases the supervisor or consultant or CEO prepares the agenda and simply presents it to the group; the group is then expected to follow the agenda item by item. In other cases the group will develop its own agenda, usually as its first or second order of business.

Generally, the more formal the group, the more important the agenda becomes. In informal groups the agenda may simply consist of general ideas in the minds of the members (for example, "We'll review the class assignment and then make plans for the weekend"). In formal business groups the agenda will be much more detailed and explicit. Some agendas specify not only the items that must be covered but also the order in which they should be covered and even the amount of time that should be devoted to each item.

## Promoting Group Interaction

Many groups need some prodding to interact. Perhaps the group is newly formed and the members feel a bit uneasy with one another. One of the leader's functions is to stimulate the members to interact. A leader also serves this function when members act as individuals rather than as a group. In this instance the leader needs to focus the members on their *group* task.

## Maintaining Effective Interaction

Suppose that you are leading a group and have successfully stimulated group interaction, but now the discussion begins to drag. Your job is to prod the group to maintain effective interaction: "Do we have any additional comments on the proposal to eliminate required courses?" "What do those of you who are members of the college curriculum committee think about the English Department's proposal to restructure required courses?" "Does anyone want to make any additional comments on eliminating the minor area of concentration?" As the leader, you must strive to ensure that all members have an opportunity to express themselves.

## Empowering Group Members

An important function in at least some leadership styles (though not limited to leadership) is to empower others—to help other group members (but also your relational partner, coworkers, employees, other students, or siblings) to gain increased power over themselves and their environment. Some ways to empower others include the following:

- Raise the person's self-esteem. Compliment, reinforce. Resist faultfinding; it doesn't benefit anyone and in fact disempowers.

- Share skills as well as decision-making power and authority.

- Be constructively critical. Be willing to offer your perspective, to lend an ear to an intern's first proposal, for example. Be willing to react honestly to suggestions from all group members and not just those in high positions.

- Encourage growth in all forms: academic, relational, and professional, among others. The growth and empowerment of the other person enhances your own growth and power.

### LEADER GUIDANCE

Members of your group are not participating equally. Of the five members, two monopolize the discussion while three say as little as possible. You want greater participation from the silent ones and less from the monopolizers.

WHAT DO YOU SAY?
*To whom?*

## Building Communication Skills    Empowering Others

As Bennis and Nanus (2003, p. 209) argue, "leadership is not so much the exercise of power itself as the empowerment of others." For each situation below, indicate what you might say to help empower the other person(s), using such strategies as (a) raising the other person's self-esteem; (b) listening actively and supportively; (c) being open, positive, and empathic; and (d) avoiding verbal aggressiveness or any unfair conflict strategies.

1. Your partner is having lots of difficulties—recently he lost his job, received poor grades in a night class, and started gaining a lot of weight. At the same time, you're doing extremely well. You want to give your partner back his confidence. What do you say?

2. You're managing four college interns who are redesigning your company's website, three men and one woman. The men are extremely supportive of one another and regularly contribute ideas. Although equally competent, the woman doesn't contribute; she seems to lack confidence. But the objective of this redesign is to increase the number of female visitors, so you really need her input and want to empower her. What do you say?

3. You're a third-grade teacher. Most of the students are from the same ethnic–religious group; three, however, are from a very different group. The problem is that these three have not been included in the social groupings of the students; they're considered outsiders. As a result these children stumble when they have to read in front of the class and make a lot of mistakes at the chalkboard (though they consistently do well in private). You want to empower these students. What do you say?

*Empowering others, far from reducing your own power, actually increases it.*

### Keeping Members on Track

Many individuals are egocentric and will pursue only their own interests and concerns, even in a group setting. Your task as the leader is to keep all members reasonably on track. Here are a few ways you might accomplish this:

- Ask questions that focus on the specific topic at hand, especially of those who seem to be wandering off in other directions.

- Interject internal summaries in which you briefly identify what has been accomplished and what the group needs to move on to next.

- Consider setting a formal agenda and sticking to it.

- Focus your own attention on the topics at hand; your example will influence the behavior of the other members.

### Ensuring Member Satisfaction

Group members have different psychological needs and wants; in fact, many people enter groups primarily to satisfy these personal concerns. Even though a group may, for example, deal with political issues, the members may have come together for reasons that are more psychological than political. If a group is to be effective, it must meet not only the surface purposes of the group but also the underlying or interpersonal purposes that motivated many of the members to come together in the first place.

Depending on the specific people involved, special adjustments may have to be made to accommodate group members with disabilities. You can easily adapt to group situations the principles identified in the special tables in Units 1, 2, 4, and 7 that deal with communication between people with and without disabilities.

### Encouraging Ongoing Evaluation

Most groups could profit from improving their techniques. If any group is to improve, it must focus on itself. Along with trying to accomplish some objective task, it must try to solve its own internal problems as well: issues such as personal conflicts, the failure of members to meet on time, or the tendency of some members to come unprepared. As the leader, try to identify any such difficulties and encourage and help the group to analyze and resolve them.

## Managing Conflict

When there is small group conflict—whether openly expressed or hidden in subtle nonverbal cues—the leader needs to address it. The conflict management techniques that are useful in small groups are the same techniques that are useful in an interpersonal interaction. The nature of interpersonal and small group conflict and the ways to effectively manage it are covered in Unit 12.

## Postdiscussion Functions

Just as the leader is responsible for prediscussion functions, the leader also is responsible for postdiscussion functions. Such functions might include summarizing the group's discussion, organizing future meetings, or presenting the group's decisions to

some other group. All in all, the leader is responsible for doing whatever needs to be done to ensure that the group's experience is productive.

## MEMBERSHIP, LEADERSHIP, AND CULTURE

Most research on and theories about small group communication, membership, and leadership have emerged from universities in the United States and reflect U.S. culture. For example, in the United States—and in individualist cultures generally—each group member is important. But in collectivist cultures the individual is less important; it's the *group* that is the significant entity. In Japan, for example, group researchers find that "individual fulfillment of self is attained through finding and maintaining one's place within the group" (Cathcart & Cathcart, 1985, p. 191). In the United States, in contrast, individual fulfillment of self is attained by the individual and through his or her own efforts, not by the group.

---

# REFLECTIONS
## ON ETHICS

## The Leader's Ethical Responsibilities

In addition to mastering the skills of effective and efficient leadership, the leader needs also to consider the ethical issues involved in leading a group or an organization. Since the leader is often a chair, CHAIR seems an appropriate acronym to help identify at least some of the characeristics of the ethical leader:

> ***Concern for the welfare of their members.*** Leaders who are more concerned with their own personal interests, rather than with the group task or the interpersonal needs of the members, would clearly be acting unethically.

> ***Honesty.*** Leaders should be honest with the group members by, for example, revealing any hidden agendas and presenting information fairly.

> ***Accountability.*** Leaders should take responsibility for their actions and decisions, admit making mistakes, and take corrective action when necessary.

***Integrity.*** Leaders have integrity; they take the high road. They don't lie or deceive. And they avoid any actions that might violate the basic rights of others.

***Responsiveness.*** The leader must be responsive to all members of the group or the organization.

### Ethical Choice Point

*You're leading a discussion among a group of high school freshmen whom you're mentoring. The topic turns to marijuana, and the students ask you directly if you smoke pot. The truth is that on occasion you do—but it's a very controlled use, and you feel that it would only destroy your credibility and lead the students to experiment with or continue smoking pot if they knew you did (something you do not want to do). At the same time, you wonder if you can ethically lie to them and tell them that you do not smoke. What is your ethical obligation in this situation? What would you do?*

## SMALL GROUP CONFLICTS

You're leading a group of graduate and undergraduate students, charged with evaluating the core curriculum. The problem is that neither the graduate students nor the undergraduates want to listen fairly to each other.

WHAT DO YOU SAY?
*To whom? Through what channel?*

It's often thought that because group membership and group identity are so important in collectivist cultures, it's the group that makes important decisions. Actually, this does not seem to be the case. In fact, a study of 48 (highly collectivist) Japanese organizations found that participating in decision-making groups did not give the members decision-making power. Group members were encouraged to contribute ideas, but the decision-making power was reserved for the CEO or for managers higher up the organizational ladder (Brennan, 1991).

The discussion of member roles earlier in this unit devoted an entire category to individual roles: roles adopted by individuals to satisfy individual

---

### Theory and Research · UNDERSTANDING · Attila's Theory of Leadership

From a totally different perspective, consider these leadership qualities, paraphrased from Wes Roberts's *Leadership Secrets of Attila the Hun* (1987), a study of the warrior who united many of the nomadic tribes in first-century Asia.

- *Empathy:* Leaders must develop an appreciation for and an understanding of other cultures and the values of their group members.

- *Courage:* Leaders should be fearless and should have the courage to complete their assignments; they must not complain about obstacles or be discouraged by adversity.

- *Dependability:* Leaders must be dependable in carrying out their responsibilities; leaders must also be willing to depend on their group members to accomplish matters they themselves can't oversee.

- *Credibility:* Leaders must be seen as believable by both friends and enemies; they must possess the integrity and intelligence needed to secure and communicate accurate information.

- *Stewardship:* Leaders must be caretakers of their group members' interests and well-being; they must guide and reward subordinates.

#### Working with Theories and Research

*Of these five qualities, which do you see as being the most important to you in your personal and social life? In your business and professional life?*

rather than group goals. In other cultures (notably collectivist cultures) these roles probably would not even be mentioned—simply because they wouldn't be acted out often enough to deserve such extended discussion. For example, in many collectivist cultures the group orientation is too pervasive for individuals to violate it by acting as the blocker, the recognition seeker, or the dominator.

In a similar way, each culture's belief system influences group members' behavior. For example, members of many Asian cultures, influenced by Confucian principles, believe that "the protruding nail gets pounded down" and are therefore not likely to voice disagreement with the majority of the group. Americans, on the other hand, influenced by the belief that "the squeaky wheel gets the grease," are more likely to voice disagreement or to act differently from other group members in order to get what they want.

Also, each culture has its own rules of preferred and expected leadership style. In the United States the general and expected style for a group leader is democratic. Our political leaders are elected by a democratic process; similarly, boards of directors are elected by the shareholders of a corporation. In other situations, of course, leaders are chosen by those in authority. The directors choose the president of a company, and the president will normally decide who will supervise and who will be supervised within the organization. Even in this situation, however, we expect the supervisor to behave democratically—to listen to the ideas of employees, to take their views into consideration when decisions are to be made, to keep them informed of corporate developments, and generally to respect their interests. Also, we expect that leaders will be changed fairly regularly, much as we elect a president every four years and company directors each year.

The important point to realize is that your membership and leadership styles are influenced by the culture in which you were raised. Consequently, when in a group with members of different cultures, consider the differences in both membership and leadership styles that individuals bring with them. For example, a member who plays individual roles may be tolerated in many groups in the United States and in some cases may even be thought amusing and different. That same member playing the same roles in a group with a more collectivist orientation is likely to be evaluated much more negatively. Multicultural groups may find it helpful to discuss members' views of group membership and leadership and what constitutes comfortable interaction for them.

## SUMMARY: MEMBERS AND LEADERS

This unit examined the roles of members and leaders of small groups and the principles that govern effective small group interaction.

1. A popular classification of small group member roles divides them into group task roles, group building and maintenance roles, and individual roles.

2. Twelve group task roles are: initiator–contributor, information seeker, opinion seeker, information giver, opinion giver, elaborator, coordinator, orienter, evaluator–critic, energizer, procedural technician, and recorder.

3. Seven group building and maintenance roles are: encourager, harmonizer, compromiser, gatekeeper–expediter, standard setter, group observer and commentator, and follower.

4. Eight individual roles are: aggressor, blocker, recognition seeker, self-confessor, playboy/playgirl, dominator, help seeker, and special interest pleader.

5. Interaction process analysis categorizes group members' contributions into four areas: social–emotional positive contributions, social–emotional negative contributions, attempted answers, and questions.

6. Member participation should be group oriented, should center conflict on issues, should be critically open-minded, and should ensure understanding.

7. Groupthink is a way of thinking that develops when concurrence seeking in a cohesive group overrides realistic appraisal of alternative courses of action.

8. Among the major myths about leadership are that leaders are rare, that leaders are born, and that all leaders are charismatic.

9. The traits approach to leadership focuses on personal characteristics that contribute to leadership; the functional approach centers on what the leader does (the functions the leader serves); and the transformational approach focuses on the leader's empowerment of the group members.

10. In the situational theory of leadership, leadership is seen as concerned with both accomplishing the task and serving the interpersonal needs of the members.

The degree to which either concern is emphasized should depend on the specific group and the unique situation.

11. An extension of this situational approach to leadership identifies four leadership styles: the telling style, the selling style, the participating style, and the delegating style. The appropriate style to use depends on the group's level of task and relationship maturity.

12. Among the leader's functions are to activate the group agenda, activate group interaction, maintain

effective interaction, empower group members, keep members on track, ensure member satisfaction, encourage ongoing evaluation and improvement, and wrap up the discussion (with summaries or notices of future meetings, for example). In addition, the leader is responsible for appropriate pre- and post-discussion functions.

13. The culture in which people are raised will greatly influence the ways in which members and leaders interact in small groups.

## KEY TERMS IN MEMBERS AND LEADERS

agenda (p. 245)
authoritarian leader (p. 243)
delegating style (p. 243)
democratic leader (p. 243)
emergent leader (p. 239)

functional approach to leadership (p. 241)
group building and maintenance roles (p. 235)
group task roles (p. 234)
groupthink (p. 237)

individual roles (p. 235)
interaction process analysis (p. 236)
laissez-faire leader (p. 243)
leadership (p. 238)
participating style (p. 243)
selling style (p. 243)

situational approach to leadership (p. 241)
telling style (p. 243)
traits approach to leadership (p. 241)
transformational approach to leadership (p. 241)

## THINKING CRITICALLY ABOUT MEMBERS AND LEADERS

1. **Group Roles in Interpersonal Relationships.** Can you identify roles that you habitually serve in certain groups? Do you serve these roles in your friendship, love, and family relationships as well?

2. **Groupthink.** Have you ever been in a group when groupthink was operating? If so, what were its symptoms? What effect did groupthink have on the process and conclusions of the group?

3. **Leadership Style.** How would you characterize the leadership style of one of your local politicians, religious leaders, college instructors, or talk show hosts? How would you characterize your own leadership style? For example, are you usually more concerned with people or with tasks? Are you more likely to be a laissez-faire, democratic, or authoritarian leader?

4. **The Emergent Leader.** It's been found that the group member with the highest rate of participation is the person most likely to be chosen leader (Mullen, Salas, & Driskell, 1989). Do you find this to be true of the groups in which you have participated? Why do you suppose this relationship exists?

5. **Gender Differences.** Do you find that women and men respond similarly to the different leadership styles? Do women and men exercise the different leadership styles with equal facility, or are women more comfortable and more competent in certain leadership styles and men more comfortable and competent in other styles?

## LOGON! MYCOMMUNICATIONLAB
### WWW.MYCOMMUNICATIONLAB.COM

Visit MCL and take the self-tests on the kind of leader you are and on your Machiavellian tendencies. Also explore the videos depicting leadership styles and try the Web activity on groupthink. In addition, visit the Small Group Communication website at **www.abacon.com/commstudies/groups/group.html** for discussions of groupthink, leadership, and group conflict.

# UNIT 12 Interpersonal and Small Group Conflict

## MAJOR TOPICS

**Interpersonal and Small Group Conflict**
**Types of Conflict**
**Conflict Management Strategies**

## Special Features

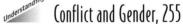

No matter how effective a communicator you are, you'll still experience conflict and disagreements in interpersonal relationships and in the social and work groups of which you are a part. At some point you are bound to find yourself in conflict with another person or even with an entire group. Because conflict is an inevitable part of interpersonal and group life, it's essential to learn how it works, how it can go wrong, and what you can do to resolve conflicts effectively.

**In this unit, you'll learn about:**
- the nature of conflict.
- the types of conflict.
- the strategies that people use to manage conflict.

**You'll learn to:**
- approach conflict positively and realistically.
- engage in interpersonal and group conflict using productive conflict management strategies.

## INTERPERSONAL AND SMALL GROUP CONFLICT

Pat wants to go to the movies with Chris; Chris wants to stay home. Pat's insisting on going to the movies interferes with Chris's staying home, and Chris's determination to stay home interferes with Pat's going to the movies. Carl is a member of a work team and wants to convince the group to change advertising agencies; other members don't want any change. Each person in these scenarios has goals that interfere with someone else's desired goals.

Interpersonal and small group conflicts may concern goals to be pursued (for example, parents get upset that their child wants to become an actor instead of a doctor); the allocation of resources such as money or time (for example, group members differ on how to spend the advertising dollar); decisions to be made (for example, some people want a holiday party and others want a cash bonus); or behaviors that are considered appropriate or desirable by one person but inappropriate or undesirable by the other (for example, two people disagree over whether one of them was flirting or drinking or not working at full speed).

As these examples illustrate, interpersonal and small group **conflict** occurs (Hocker & Wilmot, 1985; Folger, Poole, & Stutman, 1997) when people:

- are interdependent; what one person does has an effect on the other person.
- perceive their goals to be incompatible; if one person's goal is achieved, the other's cannot be (for example, if one person wants to buy a new car and the other person wants to save the money for a house).
- see each other as interfering with the attainment of their own goals.

## Myths about Conflict

One of the problems many people have in dealing with conflict is that they may be operating on the basis of false assumptions about what conflict is and what it means. Think about your own assumptions about interpersonal and small group conflict, which were probably derived from the communications you witnessed in your family and in your social interactions. For example, do you think the following are true or false?

- Conflict is best avoided.
- If two people are in a relationship conflict, it means they have a bad relationship.
- Conflict damages an interpersonal relationship or small group.
- Conflict is bad because it reveals our negative selves—our pettiness, our need to be in control, our unreasonable expectations.

Simple answers are usually wrong. In this case, each of the four assumptions above may be true or may be false. It depends. In and of itself, conflict is neither good nor bad. Conflict is a part of every interpersonal relationship—of relationships between parents and children, brothers and sisters, friends, lovers, coworkers. If it isn't, then the interaction is probably dull, irrelevant, or insignificant. Conflict seems inevitable.

It's not so much conflict that creates problems as the way in which you approach and deal with the conflict. Some ways of approaching conflict can resolve difficulties and actually improve a relationship. Other ways can hurt the relationship; they can destroy self-esteem, create bitterness, and foster suspicion. Your task, therefore, is not to try to create relationships or groups that will be free of conflict but rather to learn appropriate and productive ways of managing conflict.

## Theory *and* Research — UNDERSTANDING — Conflict Issues

Think about your own interpersonal conflicts, and particularly about the issues you fight over. What exactly do you fight about? Here are the results of two studies that investigated what couples fight about. One study focused on heterosexual couples and identified the four conditions that most often led up to a couple's "first big fight" (Siegert & Stamp, 1994): uncertainty over commitment, jealousy, violation of expectations, and personality differences.

Another study asked what heterosexual, gay, and lesbian couples argued about most and found that all three types of couples were amazingly similar in their conflict issues. All three types argued primarily about these six issues (Kurdek, 1994):

- *Intimacy* issues such as affection and sex
- *Power* issues such as excessive demands or possessiveness, lack of equality in the relationship, friends, and leisure time
- *Personal flaws* issues such as drinking or smoking, personal grooming, and driving style
- *Personal distance* issues such as frequently being absent and school or job commitments
- *Social issues* such as politics, friendships, parents, and personal values
- *Distrust issues* such as previous lovers and lying

### Working with Theories and Research

*Log on to an online database (for example, Research Navigator at* www.researchnavigator.com*) and search the New York Times archives for recent articles dealing with world conflict. How much of the conflict in the world can be interpreted in communication terms?*

Similarly, it's not the conflict (the disagreement itself) that will reveal your negative side but the fight strategies you use. Thus, if you attack other people, use force, or use personal rejection or manipulation, you will reveal your negative side. But in fighting you can also reveal your positive self—your willingness to listen to opposing points of view, your readiness to change unpleasant behaviors, your willingness to accept imperfection in others.

## The Context of Conflict

Conflict, like any form of communication, takes place in a context that is physical, sociopsychological, temporal, and—perhaps most important—cultural.

### The Physical, Sociopsychological, and Temporal Contexts

The *physical context*—for example, whether you engage in conflict privately or publicly, alone or in front of children or relatives—will influence the way the conflict is conducted as well as the effects that this conflict will have.

The *sociopsychological context* also will influence the conflict. If the atmosphere is one of equality, for example, the conflict is likely to progress very differently than it would in an atmosphere of inequality. A friendly or a hostile context will exert different influences on the conflict.

The *temporal context* will likewise prove important to understand. A conflict that follows a series of similar conflicts will be seen differently than a conflict that follows a series of enjoyable experiences and an absence of conflict. A conflict immediately after a hard day of work will engender feelings different from a conflict after an enjoyable dinner.

### The Cultural Context

Culture influences not only the issues that people fight about, but also what is considered appropriate and inappropriate in terms of dealing with conflict. Researchers have found, for example, that cohabiting 18-year-olds are more likely to experience conflict with their parents about their living style if they live in the United States than if they live in Sweden, where cohabitation is much more accepted. Similarly, male infidelity is more likely to cause conflict between American spouses than in southern European couples. Students from the United States are more likely to engage in conflict with another U.S. student than with someone from another culture. Chinese students, on the other hand, are more likely to engage in a conflict with a non-Chinese student than with another Chinese (Leung, 1988).

The types of conflicts that arise depend on the cultural orientation of the individuals involved. For example, in collectivist cultures, such as those of Ecuador, Indonesia, and Korea, conflicts are more likely to center on violations of collective or group norms and values. Disagreeing in public or proving a colleague wrong in front of others and causing this person to lose face (and violate important cultural norms) is likely to create conflict. Conversely, in individualist cultures, such as those of the United States, Canada, and western Europe, conflicts are more likely to occur when people violate individual norms; for example, if bonuses are not distributed according to merit (Ting-Toomey, 1985).

Americans and Japanese differ in their view of the aim or purpose of conflict. The Japanese (a collectivist culture) tend to see conflicts and conflict resolution in terms of compromise; each side gains something and each side gives up something. Americans (an individualist culture), on the other hand, often see conflict in terms of winning; it's an "I win, you lose" approach (Gelfand, et al., 2001). Also, different cultures seem to teach their members different views of conflict strategies (Tardiff, 2001). For example, in Japan it's especially important that you not embarrass the person with whom you are in conflict, especially if the disagreement occurs when others are present. This face-saving principle prohibits the use of such strategies as personal rejection or verbal aggressiveness. In another example, many Middle Eastern and Pacific rim cultures discourage women from direct and forceful expressions; rather, these societies expect more agreeable and submissive postures on the part of women. Also, in general, members of collectivist cultures tend to avoid conflict more than members of individualist cultures (Dsilva & Whyte, 1998; Haar & Krabe, 1999; Cai & Fink, 2002).

Even within a given general culture, more specific cultures differ from one another in their methods of conflict management. African American men and women and European American men and women, for example, engage in conflict in very different ways (Kochman, 1981). The issues that cause conflict and aggravate conflict, the conflict strategies that are expected and accepted, and the entire attitude toward conflict vary from one group to the other (Collier, 1991; Hecht, Jackson, & Ribeau, 2003).

The cultural norms of organizations also influence the types of conflicts that occur and the ways people may deal with them. Some work environments, for example, would not tolerate the expression of disagreement with high-level management; others might welcome it. In individualist cultures there is greater tolerance for conflict, even when it involves different levels of an organizational hierarchy. In collectivist cultures, there's less tolerance. And, not surprisingly, the culture influences how the conflict will be resolved. For example, managers in the United States (an individualist culture) deal with workplace conflict by seeking to integrate the demands of the different sides; managers in China (a collectivist culture) are more likely to call on higher management to make decisions—or not to resolve the conflict at all (Tinsley & Brett, 2001).

## The Negatives and Positives of Conflict

The kind of conflict we are considering here is conflict among or between "connected" individuals, whether in a primary relationship or in a small group. Such conflict occurs frequently between lovers, best friends, siblings, and parent and child; it also occurs within the extended family as well as in workplaces or on sports teams. Such conflict is all the more difficult because, unlike many other conflict situations, interpersonal and small group disagreements often involve people you care for, like, even love. At the very least, these are people with whom you're going to have to interact—so even if there were no other reason, you might as well make conflict as pleasant and productive as you can. There are both negative and positive aspects or dimensions to conflict; let's look at each of these.

### Some Negatives of Conflict

Conflict often leads to increased negative regard for the opponent; when this opponent is someone you love or work with on a daily basis, it can create serious problems for the relationship. One reason is that many conflicts involve unfair fighting methods that aim largely to hurt the other person. When one person hurts the other, increased negative feelings are inevitable; even the strongest relationship has limits.

Conflict frequently leads to a depletion of energy better spent on other areas. This is especially true in the small group context; days and even weeks of 10 or 12 people's time can be wasted on conflicts instead of being devoted to solving the problem at hand.

At times, conflict leads you to close yourself off from the other people involved. In an intimate rela-

## Theory and Research

# UNDERSTANDING   Conflict and Gender

Not surprisingly, there are significant gender differences in interpersonal conflict. For example, men are more apt to withdraw from a conflict situation than are women. It's been argued that this may be due to the fact that men become more psychologically and physiologically aroused during conflict (and retain this heightened level of arousal much longer) than do women and so may try to distance themselves and withdraw from the conflict to prevent further arousal (Gottman & Carrere, 1994; Canary, Cupach, & Messman, 1995; Goleman, 1995). Women, on the other hand, want to get closer to the conflict; they want to talk about it and resolve it. Even adolescents reveal these differences; in a study of boys and girls aged 11 to 17, boys withdrew more than girls (Lindeman, Harakka, & Keltikangas-Jarvinen, 1997; Heasley, Babbitt, & Burbach, 1995).

Other research finds that women are more emotional and men are more logical when they argue (Schaap, Buunk, & Kerkstra, 1988; Canary, Cupach, & Messman, 1995). Women have been defined as conflict "feelers" and men as conflict "thinkers" (Sorenson, Hawkins, & Sorenson, 1995). Another difference is that women are more apt to reveal their negative feelings than are men (Schaap, Buunk, & Kerkstra, 1988; Canary, Cupach, & Messman, 1995).

It should be noted, however, that much research fails to support the gender "differences" in conflict style that cartoons, situation comedies, and films portray so readily and so clearly. For example, numerous studies of both college students and men and women in business found no significant differences in the ways men and women engage in conflict (Wilkins & Andersen, 1991; Canary & Hause, 1993; Gottman & Levenson, 1999).

### Working with Theories and Research

*Log on to an online database and search the communication, psychology, and sociology databases for research on gender and conflict. What can you add to the discussion presented here?*

---

tionship, for example, you may hide your true self on the theory that it would not be to your advantage to reveal your weaknesses to your "enemy." But at the same time, closing yourself off may also prevent meaningful communication from taking place. One possible consequence is that one or both parties may seek intimacy elsewhere. This often leads to further conflict, mutual hurt, and resentment—all of which can add heavily to the costs carried by the relationship. As these costs increase, exchanging rewards may become difficult, perhaps impossible. The result is a situation in which the costs increase and the rewards decrease—a situation that often results in relationship deterioration and eventual dissolution.

## Some Positives of Conflict

The major value of interpersonal and small group conflict is that it forces you to examine a problem and work toward a potential solution. If people use productive conflict strategies, the relationship or group may well emerge from the encounter stronger, healthier, and more satisfying than before.

Conflict enables each of you to state what you want and—if the conflict is resolved effectively—perhaps to get it. In fact, a better understanding of each other's feelings has been found to be one of the main results of the "first big fight" (Siegert & Stamp, 1994).

Conflict also prevents hostilities and resentments from festering. Suppose you're annoyed at your partner for e-mailing colleagues from work for two hours instead of giving that time to you. If you say nothing, your annoyance and resentment are likely to grow. Further, by saying nothing you implicitly approve of the e-mailing and so make it more likely that such behavior will be repeated. In contrast, through conflict and its resolution you can stop resentment from increasing. In the process you each can let your own needs be known—for example, that you need lots of attention when you come home from work and that your partner needs to review and get closure on the day's work. If you both can appreciate the legitimacy of each other's needs, then solutions may be easily identified. Perhaps the e-mailing can be done after your attention needs are met, or perhaps you can delay your need for attention until your partner gets closure about work. Or perhaps you can learn to provide for your partner's closure needs—and in doing so also get the attention you need.

Consider, too, that when you try to resolve conflict within an interpersonal or small group situation, you're saying in effect that the relationship or group is worth the effort; otherwise you'd walk away from such a conflict. Although there may be exceptions—as when you engage in conflict to save face or to gratify some ego need—usually confronting a conflict indicates concern, commitment, and a desire to improve the relationship or group.

## TYPES OF CONFLICT

Conflict can occur in many situations and may be of varied types. Especially important to understand are the differences between (1) content and relationship conflicts, (2) online and workplace conflicts, and (3) the various conflict styles that individuals have.

### Content and Relationship Conflicts

Using concepts developed in Unit 1, we may distinguish between content conflict and relationship conflict. **Content conflicts** center on objects, events, and persons in the world that are usually, though not always, external to the parties involved in the conflict. These include the millions of issues that you argue and fight about every day—the value of a particular movie, what to watch on television, the fairness of the last examination or job promotion, the way to spend your savings.

**Relationship conflicts** are equally numerous and include such conflict situations as a younger brother who does not obey his older brother, group members who all want the final say in what the group decides, and the mother and daughter who each want to have the final word concerning the daughter's lifestyle. Here the conflicts are concerned not so much with some external object as with the relationships between the individuals—with such issues as who is in charge, how equal the partners in a primary relationship are, the importance of each group member, or who has the right to set down rules of behavior.

Content conflicts are usually *manifest*; that is, they're clearly observable and identifiable. Relationship conflicts are often *latent*; they tend to be hidden and much more difficult to identify. Thus, a conflict over where you should vacation may on the surface, or manifest, level center on the advantages and disadvantages of Mexico versus Hawaii. On a relationship and often latent level, however, the conflict may be about who has the greater right to select the place to vacation, who should win the argument, who is the decision maker in the relationship, and so on.

### Online and Workplace Conflicts

Two special conflict situations should be noted. The first is online conflict. Just as you can experience disagreement in face-to-face communication, you can experience conflict online; but there are a few conflict situations that are unique to online communication, and we'll look at them here. The second is conflict in the workplace or formal group—in any group that consists of a leader and various members of the organization.

### CONFRONTING A PROBLEM

Your neighbor never puts out the garbage in time for pickup and so the garbage—often broken into by stray animals—remains until the next pickup. You're fed up with the rodents the garbage draws, the smell, and the horrible appearance. You're determined to stop this problem and yet not have your next door neighbor hate you.

WHAT DO YOU SAY?
*To whom? Through what channel?*

## Online Conflicts

Sending commercial messages to those who didn't request them often creates conflict. Junk mail is junk mail; but on the Internet, junk mail slows down the entire Internet system, as well as the individual who has to sit through the downloading of unwanted messages. In many cases (when you access your e-mail from an Internet café, for example), you have to pay for the time it takes to download junk mail.

Spamming often causes conflict. *Spamming* is sending someone unsolicited mail, repeatedly sending the same mail, or posting the same message on lots of bulletin boards, even when the message is irrelevant to the focus of the group. One of the very practical reasons spamming is frowned upon is that it generally costs people money. And even if the e-mail is free, it takes up valuable time and energy to read something you didn't want in the first place. Another reason, of course, is that spam clogs the system, slowing it down for everyone.

*Flaming*, especially common in newsgroups, is sending messages that personally attack another user. Flaming frequently leads to flame wars, in which everyone in the group gets into the act and attacks other users. Generally, flaming and flame wars prevent us from achieving our goals and so are counterproductive.

## Workplace and Formal Group Conflicts

Unlike conflicts that might occur in an informal group of friends or in a family, which are more similar to interpersonal encounters, disagreements in the workplace group present a specific set of issues.

In formal groups it's often the leader's responsibility to manage conflict. Small group communication researchers distinguish between procedural and people conflicts and offer a wide variety of conflict management strategies (Patton, Giffin, & Patton, 1989; Folger, Poole, & Stutman, 1997; Kindler, 1996).

*Procedural conflicts* involve disagreements over who is in charge (who is the leader or who should be the leader), what the agenda or task of the group should be, and how the group should conduct its business. The best way to deal with procedural problems is to prevent them from occurring in the first place by establishing early in the group's interaction who is to serve as leader and what the agenda should be. If procedural problems arise after these agreements are reached, the leader or members can refer the conflicting participants to the group's earlier decisions. When members oppose or become dissatisfied with these early decisions, however, they may become negative or antagonistic and cease to participate in the discussion. If this happens (or if members want to change procedures), a brief discussion on the procedures can be held. The important point is to deal with procedural conflicts as procedural conflicts and not allow them to escalate into something else.

*People conflicts* can occur when one member dominates the group, when several members battle for control, or when some members refuse to participate. The leader should try to secure the commitment of all members and to convince them that the progress of the group depends on everyone's contributions. At times, it may be necessary to concentrate on people needs—on the importance of satisfying members' needs for group approval, for periodic rewards, or for encouragement. People conflicts also can develop in the course of debate if members attack people rather than ideas. The leader needs to ensure that attacks and disagreements are clearly focused on ideas, not people. If a personal attack does get started, the leader should step in to refocus the discussion to the idea and away from the person.

The conflict management strategies presented later in this unit are applicable to the workplace or formal group situation. In addition, here are four principles that have special relevance to conflict in this type of group (Kindler, 1996):

- *Preserve the dignity and respect of all members.* Assume, for example, that each person's disagreement is legitimate and stems from a genuine concern for the good of the group. Therefore, treat disagreements kindly; even if someone attacks you personally, it's generally wise not to respond in kind but to redirect the criticism to the issue at hand.

- *Listen empathically.* See the perspectives of the other members; try to feel what they're feeling without making any critical judgments. Try to ask yourself why others see the situation differently from the way you see it.

- *Seek out and emphasize common ground.* Even in the midst of disagreement, there are areas of common interest, common beliefs, and common aims. Find these and build on them.

- *Value diversity and differences.* Creative solutions often emerge from conflicting perspectives. So don't gloss over differences; instead, explore them for the valuable information they can give you.

## Conflict Styles

Figure 12.1 illustrates an approach to conflict that identifies five basic styles or ways of engaging in conflict and is especially helpful in relation to interpersonal and small group conflicts (Blake & Mouton, 1984). The five-styles model, plotted along the dimensions of "concern for oneself" and "concern for the other person," provides considerable insight into the ways people engage in conflict and some of the advantages and disadvantages of each approach. As you read through these styles, try to identify the conflict style you generally use as well as the styles of those with whom you have close relationships.

### Competing

The competitive style reflects great concern for your own needs and desires and little for those of others. As long as your needs are met, the conflict has been dealt with successfully. In conflict motivated by competitiveness, you'd be likely to be verbally aggressive while blaming the other person. This style represents an *I win, you lose* philosophy.

### Avoiding

The avoider fails to address his or her own or the other's needs or desires. This person avoids any real communication about the problem, changes the topic when the problem comes up, and generally withdraws from the scene both psychologically and physically. As you can appreciate, this style does little to resolve any conflicts and may be viewed as an *I lose, you lose* philosophy.

### Accommodating

In accommodating you sacrifice your own needs for the needs of the other person. Your major purpose is to maintain harmony and peace in the relationship or group. This style may help you achieve the immediate goal of maintaining peace and perhaps may satisfy the other person; but it does little to meet your own needs, which are unlikely to go away. This style represents an *I lose, you win* philosophy.

### Collaborating

In collaborating you focus on both your own and the other person's needs. This style, often considered the ideal, takes time and a willingness to communicate, and especially a readiness to listen to the perspectives and needs of the other person. Ideally, this style of conflict resolution results in each person's needs being satisfied, an *I win, you win* situation.

### Compromising

The compromising style  in the middle; there is some concern for  needs and some concern for the other  the kind of strategy

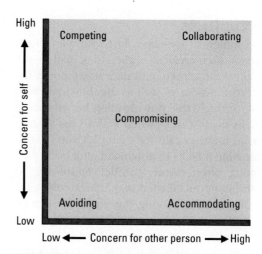

**FIGURE 12.1  Five Conflict Styles**

This figure is adapted from Blake and Mouton's (1984) approach to managerial leadership and conflict. Try to locate your usual conflict style on this grid. How well does this style work for you?

Source: An adaptation of The Managerial Grid®, Blake and Mouton's approach to managerial and leadership styles from *The Managerial Grid III*, 3rd Ed. by Blake & Mouton, p. 12. Permission granted by Grid International Inc., copyright owners.

you might refer to as "meeting each other halfway," "horse trading," or "give and take." Compromising is likely to help you maintain peace but to involve some dissatisfaction over the inevitable losses that have to be endured. It results in an *I win and lose and you win and lose* outcome.

## CONFLICT MANAGEMENT STRATEGIES

In managing conflict, you can choose from a variety of strategies, which this section will describe. Before getting to the specific conflict management strategies, however, we need to consider some preliminaries.

### Preliminaries to Conflict Management Skills

You're more likely to select appropriate strategies if you prepare for and follow up the conflict appropriately, understand the influences on your choice of conflict strategies, and apply the stages of conflict management.

### Before the Conflict

Try to fight in private—within the relationship or within the group. When you air your conflicts in front of others, you create a wide variety of other problems. You may not be willing to be totally honest when third parties are present; you may feel you

## Building Communication Skills  Managing Conflicts Early

This exercise helps you look at your own way of dealing with conflict starters—something someone says that signals to you that this is the start of an interpersonal conflict. For each situation, (a) write an *un*productive response (a response that is likely to cause the conflict to escalate); (b) write a productive response (a response that will likely lessen the potential conflict); and (c) in one sentence explain the major difference that you see between the productive and the unproductive responses.

1. You're late again. You're always late. Your lateness is so inconsiderate!

2. I just can't bear another weekend of sitting home watching cartoon shows with the kids.

3. Well, there goes another anniversary that you forgot.

4. You think I'm fat, don't you?

5. You never want to do what I want. We always have to do what you want.

*Impending conflicts are often signaled at a stage when they can be confronted and relatively easily resolved. If they aren't caught early, they may escalate and prove a lot more difficult to resolve later.*

have to save face and therefore must win the fight at all costs. This may lead you to use strategies aimed at winning the argument rather than strategies aimed at resolving the conflict. Also, of course, you run the risk of embarrassing or upsetting others, which will cause resentment and hostility.

Be sure everyone is ready to fight. Although conflicts arise at the most inopportune times, you can choose the time when you will try to resolve them. The moment when your partner comes home after a hard day of work may not be the right time for a confrontation. When a group is completing the company's most important project on a deadline, it may not be the wisest time to raise minor conflict issues. In general, make sure that all individuals are relatively free of other problems and ready to deal with the conflict at hand.

Know what you're fighting about. Sometimes people in a relationship or in a close-knit group become so hurt and angry that they lash out at the other person just to vent their own frustration. The "content" of the conflict is merely an excuse to express anger. Any attempt at resolving such a "problem" will of course be doomed to failure, because the problem addressed is not what really gave rise to the conflict. Instead, it may be underlying hostility, anger, and frustration that need to be dealt with.

At other times, people argue about general and abstract issues that are poorly specified; for example, a friend's or colleague's lack of consideration or failure to accept responsibility. Only when you de-

fine your differences in specific terms can you begin to understand them and thus resolve them.

Fight about problems that can be solved. Fighting about past behaviors or about family members or situations over which you have no control solves nothing; instead, it creates additional difficulties. Any attempt at resolution is doomed, because by their nature such problems can't be solved. Often such conflicts are concealed attempts at expressing frustration or dissatisfaction.

Consider what beliefs you hold that may need to be reexamined. Unrealistic beliefs are often at the heart of interpersonal and group conflicts. Such beliefs include ideas like "If my partner really cared, he or she would do what I ask," "If people really cared about the success of the group, they'd devote 100 percent of their time to the project," or "People don't listen to what I have to say."

### After the Conflict

After the conflict is resolved, there's still work to be done. Often, after one conflict is supposedly settled, another conflict will emerge—because, for example, one person may feel harmed and may feel the need to retaliate and take revenge in order to restore self-worth (Kim & Smith, 1993). So it's especially important that the conflict be resolved in such a way that it does not generate other, perhaps more significant, conflicts.

Learn from the conflict and from the process you went through in trying to resolve it. For example, can you identify the fight strategies that aggravated the situation? Do some people need a cooling-off period? Do you need extra space when upset? Can you identify when minor issues are going to escalate into major arguments? Does avoidance make matters worse? What issues are particularly disturbing and likely to cause difficulties? Can these be avoided?

Keep the conflict in perspective. Be careful not to blow it out of proportion—to define your relationship or your social or work group in terms of the conflict. Also, avoid the tendency to see disagreement as inevitably leading to major blowups. Conflicts in most interpersonal and group situations actually occupy a very small percentage of real time, even though in recollection they often loom extremely large.

Negative feelings frequently arise after a conflict, most often because unfair fight strategies were used—strategies such as personal rejection, manipulation, or force. Resolve to avoid such unfair tactics in the future, but at the same time let go of guilt and blame for yourself and others. If you think it would help, discuss these feelings with your partner, your group members, or even a therapist.

Increase the exchange of rewards and cherishing behaviors to demonstrate your positive feelings and to show that you're over the conflict. It's a good way of saying you want the relationship or the group to survive and to flourish.

## Influences on Your Choice of Conflict Strategies

A variety of factors will influence the strategies you choose to manage your interpersonal conflicts (Koerner & Fitzpatrick, 2002):

- the goals to be achieved
- your emotional state
- your cognitive assessment of the situation
- your personality and communication competence
- your family history

Understanding these factors may help you select more appropriate and more effective strategies to manage conflict with success (Weitzman & Weitzman, 2000; Weitzman, 2001; Neff & Harter, 2002).

The *goals* (short-term and long-term) you wish to achieve will influence what strategies seem appropriate to you. If you just want to enjoy the moment, you might want to simply "give in" and ignore the difficulty. On the other hand, if you want to build a long-term relationship, you might want to fully analyze the cause of the problem and look for strategies that will enable both parties to win.

Your *emotional state* will influence your strategies; you're not likely to select the same strategies when you're sorry as when you're angry. When sorry, you're likely to use conciliatory strategies designed to make peace; but when you're angry, you're more likely to use strategies that attack the other person.

Your *cognitive assessment* of the situation will exert powerful influence on your selection of strategies. For example, your attitudes and beliefs about what is fair and equitable will influence your readiness to acknowledge the fairness in the other person's position. Your own assessment of who (if anyone) is the cause of the problem also will influence your conflict style. You may also assess the likely effects of your various strategies. For example, what do you risk if you fight with your boss by using blame or personal rejection? As a parent, do you risk alienating your teenager if you use force?

Your *personality and communication competence* will influence the way you engage in conflict. For example, if you're shy and unassertive, you may want to avoid conflict rather than fighting actively. If you're extroverted and have a strong desire to state your position, you may be more likely to fight actively and to argue forcefully.

Your *family history* influences the strategies you use, the topics you choose to fight about, and perhaps your tendencies to obsess or forget about interpersonal conflicts. People often imitate their parents; if your parents argued about money or gave each other the silent treatment when conflict arose, you may repeat these patterns yourself.

## The Stages of Conflict Management

Earlier (Unit 10, pages 227–231) we looked at the stages of problem solving in small group communication. If you make the assumption that a conflict is a problem to be resolved, then the steps you go through in managing interpersonal and small group conflict will (generally at least) follow the problem-solving stages. In brief review, you'll recall that these:

- Define and analyze the problem—just what is causing the conflict?
- Establish criteria for evaluating solutions—what will a productive resolution look like?
- Identify possible solutions—what changes will help resolve or manage the conflict?
- Evaluate solutions—which solutions seem to best meet the criteria already identified and thus go furthest in managing the conflict?
- Select the best solution—what solution seems to satisfy all sides the most?
- Test the selected solution—how does the relationship do under this new solution?

With these preliminary guidelines in mind, let's turn now to several different conflict strategies, both productive and unproductive.

---

B̲u̲i̲l̲d̲i̲n̲g̲ ̲C̲o̲m̲m̲u̲n̲i̲c̲a̲t̲i̲o̲n̲  *Skills*  Finding Win–Win Solutions

As this section explains, win-win conflict strategies are preferable to win-lose approaches, at least when the conflict is interpersonal. Often, however, people fail even to consider what possible win-win solutions might exist. To get into the habit of looking for these types of solutions, try generating as many win-win solutions as possible (that you feel the individuals could reasonably accept) for the following scenarios. Give yourself two minutes for each case. If possible, share your win-win solutions with other individuals or groups; also, consider ways in which you might incorporate win-win strategies into your own conflict management behavior.

1. Pat and Chris plan to take a two-week vacation in August. Pat wants to go to the shore and relax by the water. Chris wants to go the mountains and go hiking and camping.

2. Pat recently got a totally unexpected $3,000 bonus. Pat wants to buy a new computer and printer for the home office; Chris wants to take a much-needed vacation.

3. Philip has recently come out as gay to his parents. He wants them to accept him and his life (which includes a committed relationship with another man). His parents want him to seek religious counseling for help in changing his orientation.

*Win-win solutions exist for most but probably not all conflict situations. Whether you find them or not, it's generally worth looking for them.*

---

## Win–Lose and Win–Win Strategies

If you look at interpersonal and small group conflict in terms of winning and losing, you'll see that there are four potential outcomes: (1) A wins, B loses; (2) A loses, B wins; (3) A loses, B loses; and (4) A wins, B wins.

In managing conflict you have a choice and can seek to achieve any one of those combinations of winning and losing. You can look for solutions in which one person or one side wins (usually you or your side) and the other person or other side loses: **win–lose solutions**. Or you can look for solutions in which both you and the other person or side win: **win–win solutions**.

Obviously, win-win solutions are the most desirable. Perhaps the most important reason is that win-win solutions lead to mutual satisfaction and prevent the resentment that win-lose solutions often engender. Looking for and developing win-win solutions makes the next conflict less unpleasant; the participants can more easily view conflict as "solving a problem" rather than as "fighting." Still another advantage is that win-win solutions promote mutual face-saving: Both parties can feel good about themselves. Also, people are more likely to abide by the decisions reached in a win-win conflict than they are in win-lose or lose-lose situations. For all these reasons, win-win solutions are worth seeking whenever possible.

Take an interpersonal example: Let's say that I want to spend our money on a new car (my old one is unreliable) and you want to spend it on a vacation (you're exhausted and feel the need for a rest). Through our conflict and its resolution, ideally we learn what each of us really wants. We may then be able to figure out a way for each of us to get what we want. I might accept a good used car and you might accept a less expensive vacation. Or we might buy a used car and take an inexpensive road trip. Each of these win-win solutions will satisfy both of us; each of us wins, each of us gets what we wanted.

## Avoidance and Active Fighting

One nonproductive conflict strategy is **avoidance**. Avoidance may involve actual physical flight: You may leave the scene (walk out of the apartment or meeting room). Or you may simply psychologically tune out all incoming arguments or problems. In the United States men are more likely to use avoidance than women (Markman, Silvern, Clements, & Kraft-Hanak, 1993; Oggins, Veroff, & Leber, 1993), often additionally denying that anything is wrong (Hafer-kamp, 1991-92).

**Nonnegotiation** is a special type of avoidance. Here you refuse to discuss the conflict or to listen to the other person's argument. At times, nonnegotiation takes the form of hammering away at your point

## AVOIDING CONFLICT

Your work team members all seem to have the same conflict style: avoidance. When alternatives are discussed or there is some kind of disagreement, they refuse to argue for one or the other or even to participate in the discussion. You need spirited discussion and honest debate if your team is going to come up with appropriate solutions.

WHAT DO YOU SAY?
*To whom? Through what channel?*

of view until the other person gives in, a method referred to as steamrolling.

Instead of avoiding the issues, take an active role in your conflicts. Don't close your ears (or mind) or walk out during an argument. This does not mean that taking time out to cool off is not a useful first strategy. Sometimes it is. In an e-mail conflict, for example, a cooling-off period is an easy-to-use and often effective strategy. By delaying your response until you've had time to think things out more logically and calmly, you'll be better able to respond constructively and to address possible ways to resolve the conflict and get the relationship back to a less hostile stage.

To take an active role, involve yourself on both sides of the communication exchange. That is, participate actively as a speaker–listener; voice your own feelings and listen carefully to the voicing of your opponent's feelings. Be willing to communicate as both sender and receiver—to say what is on your mind and to listen to what the other person is saying.

Another part of active fighting involves taking responsibility for your thoughts and feelings. For example, when you disagree with your partner or with other group members, say, "I disagree with . . ." or "I don't like it when you . . ." Avoid statements that deny your responsibility, as in, "Everybody thinks you're wrong about . . ." or "Even the photography department thinks we shouldn't. . . ."

## Force and Talk

When confronted with conflict, many people prefer not to deal with the issues but rather to force their position on the other person. **Force** may be emotional or physical. In either case, it is an unproductive strategy: The issues are avoided and the person

who "wins" is merely the combatant who exerts the most force. This is the technique used by warring nations, children, and even some normally sensible and mature adults. It seems also to be the technique of some persons who are dissatisfied with the power they perceive themselves to have in a relationship, as research shows that perpetrators of violence against both men and women often are motivated to gain control or to defend their own image (Ronfeldt, Kimerling, & Arias, 1998; Felson, 2002).

The use of force is surely one of the most serious problems confronting relationships today, although many approach it as if it were a minor—or even humorous—issue. Researchers found that more than 50 percent of both single and married couples reported that they had experienced physical violence in their relationship. If we add symbolic violence (for example, threatening to hit the other person or throwing something), the percentages are above 60 percent for singles and above 70 percent for marrieds (Marshall & Rose, 1987). In a study of divorced couples, 70 percent reported at least one episode of violence in their premarital, marital, or postmarital relationship. Violence during marriage was higher than for pre- or postmarital relationships (Olday & Wesley, 1990). In another study, 47 percent of a sample of 410 college students reported some experience with violence in a dating relationship (Deal & Wampler, 1986). In most cases the violence was reciprocal—each person in the relationship used violence. In cases in which only one person was violent, the research results were conflicting. For example, in cases in which only one partner was violent, the aggressor was significantly more often the female partner (Deal & Wampler, 1986). Earlier research found similar gender differences (for example, Cate et al., 1982). Other research, however, has tended to confirm the widespread view that men are more likely to use force than women (DeTurck, 1987). Still other research shows that both men and women are likely to use violence but that women are more likely to be injured (Frieze, 2000).

Findings such as these point to problems well beyond the prevalence of unproductive conflict strategies that we want to identify and avoid. They demonstrate the existence of underlying pathologies that we are discovering are a lot more common than were thought previously, when issues like these were never mentioned in college textbooks or lectures. Awareness, of course, is only a first step in understanding and eventually combating such problems.

The only real alternative to force is talk. Instead of using force, you need to talk and listen. The qualities of empathy, openness, and positiveness (see Unit 7), for example, are suitable starting points.

## Blame and Empathy

Conflict is rarely caused by a single, clearly identifiable problem or by only one of the parties. Usually, conflict occurs because of a wide variety of factors, and all concerned play a role. Any attempt to single out one person for **blame** is sure to be unproductive. Even so, a frequently used fight strategy is to blame another person. Consider, for example, the couple who fight over their child's getting into trouble with the police. Instead of dealing with the conflict itself, the parents may blame each other for the child's troubles. Such blaming, of course, does nothing to resolve the problem or to help the child.

Often, when you blame someone, you attribute motives to the person, a process often referred to as "mind reading." Thus, if the person forgot your birthday and this disturbs you, tackle the actual behavior—the forgetting of the birthday. Try not to presuppose motives: "Well, it's obvious you just don't care about me. If you really cared, you could never have forgotten my birthday!"

Empathy is an excellent alternative to blame. Try to feel what the other person is feeling and to see the situation as the other person does. Try to see the situation as punctuated by the other person, and think about how this differs from your own punctuation.

### VIOLENCE AND THE MEDIA

Most research on media violence has focused on television and, to a lesser extent, on films. But increasingly researchers are examining video games, music, and Internet entertainment for their violent content and potential influence on children. For example, a study of Nintendo and Sega Genesis video games showed that approximately 80 percent of the games included aggression or violence as an essential part of the strategy (Dietz, 1998).

Generally, research finds that media violence can contribute to a variety of effects (Rodman, 2001; Bok, 1998):

- The viewing of violence can teach young people how to be violent; it can teach them the techniques of violence.

- Media violence often gives people (and children especially) role models to emulate (Derne, 1999).

- Because media violence is so prevalent, it can desensitize people to real-life violence around them, which often is not as extreme as they regularly see on television and in the movies.

Media violence can make viewers afraid of becoming victims of violence. The extent to which watching media violence contributes to actual viewer violence, however, has not been determined. In its latest study, unfortunately already more than 20 years old, the National Institute of Mental Health (1982) reported that heavy viewing of violence is related to aggressive behavior and that the greater the viewing of violence, the more likely the person is to be aggressive. But there are probably other factors that lead some people to watch violent films, and these factors may well contribute—in large or small part—to aggressive behavior. Family and social factors, developmental and affective disorders, substance abuse, experience with crime, and the motivation to watch violence, for example, interact with exposure to media violence to produce violent behavior (Withecomb, 1997; Haridakis & Rubin, 2003).

### Increasing Media Literacy

*How do you feel about violence in the media? If you're unhappy with the current state of media violence, what would you like to see changed? How might you go about effecting these changes?*

Demonstrate empathic understanding. Once you have empathically understood the feelings of the other person or group members, validate those feelings as appropriate. If your partner is hurt or angry and you feel that such feelings are legitimate and justified (from the other person's point of view), say so; say, "You have a right to be angry; I shouldn't have said what I did. I'm sorry. But I still don't want to go on vacation with your college roommate." In expressing validation you're not necessarily expressing agreement on the point at issue; you're merely stating that your partner's feelings are legitimate and that you recognize them as such.

## Gunnysacking and Present Focus

A *gunnysack* is a large bag, usually made of burlap. The unproductive conflict strategy known as **gunnysacking** is the practice of storing up grievances so as to unload them at another time (Bach & Wyden, 1968). The occasion for unloading may be relatively minor (or so it might seem at first); for example, you come home late without calling, or you fail to fulfill your assigned task before a meeting at work. Instead of addressing the immediate problem, the gunnysacker unloads all past grievances. The birthday you forgot, the times you were absent from meetings, the hotel reservations you forgot to make. As you probably know from experience, gunnysacking begets gunnysacking. When one person gunnysacks, the other person gunnysacks. The result is that both sides dump their stored-up grievances on each other. Frequently, the trigger problem never gets addressed. Instead, resentment and hostility escalate.

Focus your conflict on the here and now rather than on issues that occurred two months ago. Similarly, focus your conflict on the person with whom you're fighting, not on the person's mother, child, or friends.

## Manipulation and Spontaneity

**Manipulation** involves an avoidance of open conflict. The manipulative individual tries to divert conflict by being especially charming (disarming, actually). The manipulator gets the other individual into a receptive and noncombative frame of mind, then presents his or her demands to a weakened opponent. The manipulator relies on our tendency to give in to people who are especially nice to us.

Instead of manipulating, try expressing your feelings with **spontaneity** and honesty. Remember that in conflict situations there's no need to plan a strategy to win a war. The objective is not to win but to increase mutual understanding and to reach a decision that both parties can accept.

## Personal Rejection and Acceptance

A person practicing **personal rejection** withholds approval and affection from his or her opponent in conflict, seeking to win the argument by getting the other person to break down in the face of this withdrawal. The individual acts cold and uncaring in an effort to demoralize the other person. In a group situation a person might practice rejection by not listening, not giving any positive feedback, or perhaps even giving negative feedback, making you think everything you're saying is gibberish. In withdrawing positive messages, the rejecting individual hopes to make the other person question his or her own self-worth. Once the other is demoralized and feels less than worthy, it's relatively easy for "rejectors" to get their way. They hold out the renewal of approval and affection as a reward for a resolution in their own favor.

Instead of rejection, express positive feelings for the other person and for the relationship or group. Throughout any conflict, harsh words will probably be exchanged, later to be regretted. The words cannot be unsaid or uncommunicated, but they can be partially offset by the expression of positive statements.

## Fighting below and above the Belt

Much like boxers in a ring, each of us has a "belt line." When you hit someone below the emotional belt line, a tactic called **beltlining,** you can inflict serious injury. When you hit above the belt, however, the person is able to absorb the blow. With most interpersonal relationships, especially those of long standing, we know where the belt line is. You know, for example, that to hit Pat with the inability to have children is to hit below the belt. You know that to hit Chris with the failure to get a permanent job is to hit below the belt. You know that to stress the number of years your colleague has been in the same position without a promotion is to hit below the belt. Hitting below the belt line causes everyone involved added problems. Keep blows to areas your opponent can absorb and handle.

Remember that the aim of interpersonal and small group conflict is not to win and have your opponent lose. Rather, it's to resolve a problem and strengthen the relationship or group. Keep this ultimate goal always in clear focus, especially when you're angry or hurt.

## Face-Detracting and Face-Enhancing Strategies

Another dimension of conflict strategies is that of *face orientation*. Face-detracting or face-attacking

## REFLECTIONS ON ETHICS

### Ethical Fighting

This unit emphasizes the differences between effective and ineffective conflict strategies. But every conflict strategy also has an ethical dimension. Consider just a few examples:

■ Does conflict avoidance have an ethical dimension? For example, is it unethical for one romantic partner to refuse to discuss issues of disagreement with the other?

■ Is it ever ethical to force someone to accept your position? Can you identify situation in which it would be appropriate for someone with greater physical strength to overpower another person to enforce his or her point of view?

■ Is it ever ethical to use face-detracting strategies? Are face-detracting strategies inherently unethical, or might it be appropriate to use them in certain situations? Can you identify such situations?

■ What are the ethical implications of verbal aggressiveness? Why might it be argued that argumentativeness is more ethical than verbal aggressiveness?

### Ethical Choice Point

*At your high-powered and highly stressful job you sometimes use coke with your colleagues. This happens several times a month. You don't use drugs of any kind at any other times. Your partner—who you know hates drugs and despises people who use any recreational drug—asks you if you take drugs. Because your use is so limited, but mostly because you know that admitting it will cause a huge conflict in a relationship that's already having difficulties, you wonder if you can ethically lie about this. What is your ethical obligation in this situation? What would you say?*

---

strategies involve treating the other person as incompetent or untrustworthy, as unable or bad (Donohue, 1992). Such attacks can vary from mildly embarrassing to severely damaging to the other person's ego or reputation (Imahori & Cupach, 1994). When such attacks become extreme, they may be similar to verbal aggressiveness—another unproductive tactic that we'll consider shortly. Protecting our image (or face), especially in the midst of conflict, is important to everyone, but especially important to members of the collectivist cultures of Asia (Zane & Yeh, 2002).

Face-enhancing techniques, in contrast, help the other person maintain a positive image—an image as competent and trustworthy, able and good. There's some evidence to show that even when, say, you get what you want in a bargaining situation, it is wise to help the other person retain positive face. This makes it less likely that future conflicts will arise (Donohue, 1992).

Not surprisingly, people are more likely to make a greater effort to support their opponent's "face" if they like the opponent than if they don't (Meyer, 1994). So be especially careful to avoid "fighting words"—words that are sure to escalate the conflict rather than to help resolve it. Words like *stupid*, *liar*, and *bitch*, as well as words like *always* and *never* (as in "you always" or "you never"), invariably create additional problems. In contrast, confirming the other person's definition of self, avoiding attack

and blame, and using excuses and apologies as appropriate are some generally useful face-positive strategies.

## Nonassertive and Assertive Strategies

Nonassertiveness can be unproductive, because it involves the failure to express your thoughts and feelings in certain or all communication situations. Nonassertive people often fail to assert their rights. In many instances these people do what others tell them to do—parents, employers, and the like—without questioning. They operate with a "you win, I lose" philosophy, giving others what they want without concern for themselves (Lloyd, 2001). Nonassertive people often ask permission from others to do what is their perfect right. They are often anxious in social situations and their self-esteem is likely to be low.

**Assertiveness** means acting in your own best interests *without* denying or infringing on the rights of others. Not surprisingly, assertiveness can be especially helpful in conflict situations (Fodor & Collier, 2001). Assertive people operate with an "I win, you win" philosophy; they assume that both parties can gain something from conflict. Assertive people speak their minds and welcome others' doing likewise. Assertive people also tend to be more positive and generally score higher on measures of hopefulness than nonassertive individuals (Velting, 1999).

There are wide cultural differences in assertiveness. For example, individualist cultures are more likely to value assertiveness than are collectivist cultures. That is, cultures that stress competition, individual success, and independence also will admire assertiveness; cultures that stress cooperation, group success, and the interdependence of all members will value assertiveness much less. American students, for example, are found to be significantly more assertive than Japanese or Korean students (Thompson, Klopf, & Ishii, 1991; Thompson & Klopf, 1991). Thus, in conflict situations assertiveness may prove an effective strategy in one culture but may create problems in another culture.

Here are a few suggestions to help you communicate more assertively:

- *Describe the problem; don't evaluate or judge it:* "We both want what's right for the kids, but we haven't gotten together to discuss the problems." Be sure to use I-messages and to avoid messages that accuse or blame the other person.

- *State how this problem affects you:* "I'm worrying about this during the day and it's affecting my job."

- *Propose solutions that are workable and that allow the person to save face:* "Let's make some time tomorrow to discuss how we want to handle things."

- *Confirm understanding:* "Would that be okay? Say, about eight?"

## Aggressiveness and Argumentativeness

An especially interesting perspective on conflict has emerged from researchers' work on verbal aggressiveness and argumentativeness (Infante, 1988; Rancer, 1998; Wigley, 1998). Understanding these two concepts will help you understand some of the reasons why things go wrong and some of the ways in which you can use conflict to actually improve your relationships.

### Verbal Aggressiveness

**Verbal aggressiveness** is an unproductive conflict strategy in which one person tries to win an argument by inflicting psychological pain, by attacking the other person's self-concept. The technique relies on many of the other unproductive conflict strategies we've already considered. It's a type of disconfirmation in that it seeks to discredit the individual's view of self (see Unit 5). To explore this tendency further, take the following self-test of verbal aggressiveness.

## TEST YOURSELF

### How Verbally Aggressive Are You?

This scale measures how people try to obtain compliance from others. For each statement, indicate the extent to which you feel it's true for you in your attempts to influence others. Use the following scale: 5 = strongly agree, 4 = agree, 3 = undecided, 2 = disagree, and 1 = strongly disagree.

_____ 1. If individuals I am trying to influence really deserve it, I attack their character.

_____ 2. When individuals are very stubborn, I use insults to soften their stubbornness.

_____ 3. When people behave in ways that are in very poor taste, I insult them in order to shock them into proper behavior.

_____ 4. When people simply will not budge on a matter of importance, I lose my temper and say rather strong things to them.

_____ 5. When individuals insult me, I get a lot of pleasure out of really telling them off.

_____ 6. I like poking fun at people who do things that are stupid in order to stimulate their intelligence.

_____ 7. When people do things that are mean or cruel, I attack their character in order to help correct their behavior.

_____ 8. When nothing seems to work in trying to influence others, I yell and scream in order to get some movement from them.

_____ 9. When I am unable to refute others' positions, I try to make them feel defensive in order to weaken their positions.

_____ 10. When people refuse to do a task I know is important without good reason, I tell them they are unreasonable.

**HOW DID YOU DO?** To compute your verbal aggressiveness score, simply add up your responses. A total score of 30 would indicate the neutral point, not especially aggressive but not especially confirming of the other either. If you scored about 35, you would be considered moderately aggressive; and if you scored 40 or more, you'd be considered very aggressive. If you scored below the neutral point, you'd be considered less verbally aggressive and more confirming when interacting with others. In looking over your responses, take special note of the behaviors identified in the 10 statements, all of which indicate a tendency to act verbally aggressive. Note any inappropriate behaviors that you're especially prone to commit.

**WHAT WILL YOU DO?** Because verbal aggressiveness is likely to seriously reduce communication effectiveness, you probably want to reduce your tendencies to respond aggressively. Review the times when you acted verbally aggressive toward another person. What effect did such actions have on your subsequent interaction? What effect did they have on your relationship with the other person? What alternative ways of getting your point across might you have used? Might these have proved more effective? Perhaps the most general suggestion for reducing verbal aggressiveness is to increase your argumentativeness, as will be discussed below.

Source: From a 20-item scale developed by Infante and Wigley (1986) and factor analyzed by Beatty, Rudd, and Valencic (1999). Also see Dominic Infante & C. J. Wigley, "Verbal Aggressiveness," *Communication Monographs, 53,* 1986; Michael J. Beatty, Jill E. Rudd, & Kristin Marie Valencic, "A Re-evaluation of the Verbal Aggressiveness Scale: One Factor or Two?" *Communication Research Reports, 16,* 10–17, 1999; and T. R. Levine, M. J. Beatty, S. Limon, M. A. Hamilton, R. Buck, & R. M. Chory-Assad, "The Dimensionality of the Verbal Aggressiveness Scale," *Communication Monographs, 71,* 245–268, September 2004. Copyright © 1986 by the National Communication Association. Reprinted by permission of the publisher and authors.

# ASK THE RESEARCHER

## Verbal Aggressiveness

*My boyfriend is really sweet, and I know he really loves me. But at times, he's verbally aggressive. Sometimes he gets really angry (like when I do something wrong) and says really hurtful things. He's asked me to move in with him, and I'm not sure what to do. Any ideas?*

Can a sweet guy be hurtful? Some people attack so often, they become less sensitive to their hurtfulness. Tell him what made you feel badly. If he was more aware of his unfriendly language, maybe he'd curtail it.

When you "do something wrong," he gets angry. Is his behavior justified? Most people believe justified aggression is okay (like shooting back!) but that aggression without justification is bad. Maybe you said something "well-intended" to him that made him feel attacked. Maybe your words served as a Verbal Trigger Event, a catalyst to a verbal "shooting back." He might think he's justified, even though it's just misplaced defensiveness.

Is aggression ever justified? Here's a simple test: If his boss made the "mistake," would he react the same way? I'll bet he wouldn't! Assertiveness, constructive arguing, and, sometimes, silence are nice alternatives.

Remember, words can't hurt you, only people can hurt you. Should you move in? Harry Connick Jr. sings, never "build a house in a hurricane."

For further information: Venable, K. V., & Martin, M. M. (1997). Argumentativeness and verbal aggressiveness in dating relationships. *Journal of Social Behavior and Personality, 12*(4), 955–964. Also Rancer, A. S., & Avtgis, T. A. (2006). *Argumentative and aggressive communication: Theory, research, and application*, pp. 87–108. Thousand Oaks, CA: Sage.

**Charles J. Wigley III** (Ph.D., Kent State University; J.D., University of Akron) is a professor of communication at Canisius College and teaches research methods and training and development (wigley@canisius.edu). An experienced defense attorney, he studies the role of communication in jury selection.

## Argumentativeness

Contrary to popular usage, argumentativeness is a quality to be cultivated rather than avoided. The term **argumentativeness** in this context refers to your willingness to argue for a point of view, your tendency to speak your mind on significant issues. It's the mode of dealing with disagreements that is the preferred alternative to verbal aggressiveness (Infante & Rancer, 1995). Assess your own degree of argumentativeness by taking the self-test below.

# TEST YOURSELF

## How Argumentative Are You?

This questionnaire contains statements about controversial issues. Indicate how often each statement is true for you personally according to the following scale: 1 = almost never true, 2 = rarely true, 3 = occasionally true, 4 = often true, and 5 = almost always true.

_____ 1. While in an argument, I worry that the person I am arguing with will form a negative impression of me.

_____ 2. Arguing over controversial issues improves my intelligence.

_____ 3. I enjoy avoiding arguments.

_____ 4. I am energetic and enthusiastic when I argue.

_____ 5. Once I finish an argument, I promise myself that I will not get into another.

_____ 6. Arguing with a person creates more problems for me than it solves.

_____ 7. I have a pleasant, good feeling when I win a point in an argument.

_____ 8. When I finish arguing with someone, I feel nervous and upset.

_____ 9. I enjoy a good argument over a controversial issue.

_____ 10. I get an unpleasant feeling when I realize I am about to get into an argument.

_____ 11. I enjoy defending my point of view on an issue.

_____ 12. I am happy when I keep an argument from happening.

_____ 13. I do not like to miss the opportunity to argue a controversial issue.

_____ 14. I prefer being with people who rarely disagree with me.

_____ 15. I consider an argument an exciting intellectual challenge.

_____ 16. I find myself unable to think of effective points during an argument.

_____ 17. I feel refreshed and satisfied after an argument on a controversial issue.

_____ 18. I have the ability to do well in an argument.

_____ 19. I try to avoid getting into arguments.

_____ 20. I feel excitement when I expect that a conversation I am in is leading to an argument.

**HOW DID YOU DO?** To compute your score follow these steps:

1. Add your scores on items 2, 4, 7, 9, 11, 13, 15, 17, 18, and 20.

2. Add 60 to the sum obtained in step 1.

3. Add your scores on items 1, 3, 5, 6, 8, 10, 12, 14, 16, and 19.

4. Subtract the total obtained in step 3 from the total obtained in step 2.

Your score will range between a low of 20 to a high of 100. Scores between 73 and 100 indicate high argumentativeness; scores between 56 and 72 indicate moderate argumentativeness; and scores between 20 and 55 indicate low argumentativeness.

**WHAT WILL YOU DO?** The researchers who developed this test note that both high and low argumentatives may experience communication difficulties. The high argumentative, for example, may argue needlessly, too often, and too forcefully. The low argumentative, on the other hand, may avoid taking a stand even when it seems necessary. Persons scoring somewhere in the middle are probably the more interpersonally skilled and adaptable, arguing when it is necessary but avoiding arguments that are needless and repetitive. Does your experience support this observation? What specific actions might you take to improve your level of argumentativeness?

Source: From Dominic Infante and Andrew Rancer, "A Conceptualization and Measure of Argumentativeness," _Journal of Personality Assessment, 46_ (1982), 72–80. Copyright © 1982 Lawrence Erlbaum Associates, Inc. Reprinted by permission of Lawrence Erlbaum Associates, Inc., and the authors.

### Differences between Argumentativeness and Verbal Aggressiveness.

As you can appreciate, there are numerous differences between argumentativeness and verbal aggressiveness. Here are just a few (Infante & Rancer, 1996; Rancer & Atvgis, 2006):

| Argumentativeness | Verbal Aggressiveness |
|---|---|
| Is *constructive;* the outcomes are positive in a variety of communication situations (interpersonal, group, organizational, family, and intercultural). | Is destructive; the outcomes are negative in a variety of communication situations (interpersonal, group, organizational, family, and intercultural). |
| Leads to relationship *satisfaction*. | Leads to relationship dissatisfaction, not surprising for a strategy that aims to attack another's self-concept. |
| May prevent *relationship violence*, especially in domestic relationships. | May lead to relationship violence. |
| Enhances *organizational life*; for example, subordinates prefer supervisors who encourage argumentativeness. | Damages organizational life and demoralizes workers on varied levels. |
| Enhances *parent-child communication* and enables parents to gain greater compliance. | Prevents meaningful parent-child communication and makes corporal punishment more likely. |
| Increases the user's *credibility*; argumentatives are seen as trustworthy, committed, and dynamic. | Decreases the user's credibility, in part because it's seen as a tactic to discredit the person rather than address the argument. |
| Argumentativeness increases the user's *power of persuasion* in varied communication contexts; argumentatives are more likely to be seen as leaders. | Decreases the user's power of persuasion. |

### TALKING AGGRESSIVELY

Your partner is becoming more and more verbally aggressive and you're having trouble with this new communication pattern. Regardless of what the conflict is about, your self-concept is attacked. You've had enough and you want to stop this kind of attack.

WHAT DO YOU SAY?
*Through what channel?*

### Strategies for Becoming More Argumentative.

Here are some suggestions for developing argumentativeness—and for preventing it from degenerating into aggressiveness (Infante, 1988).

- Treat disagreements as objectively as possible; avoid assuming that because someone takes issue with your position or your interpretation, they're attacking you as a person.

- Center your arguments on issues rather than personalities. Avoid attacking a person (rather than the person's arguments), even if this would give you a tactical advantage—it will probably backfire at some later time and make your relationship or group participation more difficult.

- Reaffirm the other person's sense of competence; compliment the other person as appropriate.

- Allow the other person to state her or his position fully before you respond; avoid interrupting.

- Stress equality, and stress the similarities that you have with the other person or persons; stress your areas of agreement before attacking the disagreements.

- Express interest in the other person's position, attitude, and point of view.

- Avoid getting overemotional; using an overly loud voice or interjecting vulgar expressions will prove offensive and eventually ineffective.

- Allow people to save face; never humiliate another person.

# SUMMARY: INTERPERSONAL AND SMALL GROUP CONFLICT

This unit has explored interpersonal and small group conflict: the types of conflicts that occur, the don'ts and dos of conflict management, and what to do before and after the conflict.

1. Relationship and small group conflict occurs among people who are connected but who have opposing goals that interfere with others' desired goals. Conflicts may occur face-to-face or on the Internet, through e-mail, in newsgroups, and in other contexts.

2. Interpersonal conflicts may yield both positive and/or negative results.

3. Content conflicts center on objects, events, and persons in the world that are usually, though not always, external to the parties involved.

4. Relationship conflicts are concerned not so much with some external object as with relationships between individuals—with such issues as who is in charge, how equal the partners are in a primary relationship, or who has the right to set down rules of behavior.

5. In preparation for conflict, try to fight in private and when all are ready to fight. Have a clear idea of what you want to fight about, and be specific; fight about things that can be solved; and reexamine beliefs that may be unrealistic. Consider, too, the value of following a standard sequence of steps in dealing with the conflict.

6. After the conflict, assess what you've learned, keep the conflict in perspective, let go of negative feelings, and increase positiveness.

7. Among the conflict styles are competing, avoiding, accommodating, collaborating, and compromising.

8. Unproductive and productive conflict strategies include: win–lose and win–win approaches, avoidance and fighting actively, force and talk, blame and empathy, gunnysacking and present focus, manipulation and spontaneity, personal rejection and acceptance, fighting below and above the belt, face-detracting and face-enhancing tactics, nonassertive and assertive approaches, and fighting aggressively and argumentatively.

9. To cultivate constructive argumentativeness, treat disagreements objectively and avoid attacking the other person, reaffirm the other's sense of competence, avoid interrupting, stress equality and similarities, express interest in the other's position, avoid presenting your arguments too emotionally, and allow the other to save face.

# KEY TERMS IN INTERPERSONAL AND SMALL GROUP CONFLICT

argumentativeness (p. **268**)
assertiveness (p. **265**)
avoidance (p. **261**)
beltlining (p. **264**)
blame (p. **263**)

conflict (p. **252**)
content conflict (p. **256**)
force (p. **262**)
gunnysacking (p. **264**)
manipulation (p. **264**)

nonnegotiation (p. **261**)
personal rejection (p. **264**)
relationship conflict (p. **256**)
spontaneity (p. **264**)

verbal aggressiveness (p. **266**)
win–lose solution (p. **261**)
win–win solution (p. **261**)

# THINKING CRITICALLY ABOUT INTERPERSONAL AND SMALL GROUP CONFLICT

1. **Gender Differences.** Why do you think men are more likely to withdraw from conflict than women? For example, what arguments can you present for or against any of these reasons (Noller, 1993): Because men have difficulty dealing with conflict? Because the culture has taught men to avoid it? Because withdrawal is an expression of power?

2. **Culture and Conflict.** What does your own culture teach about conflict and its management? What strategies does it prohibit? Are some strategies prohibited in conflicts with certain people (say, your parents) but not in conflicts with others (say, your friends)? Does your culture prescribe certain ways of dealing with conflict? Does it have different expectations for men and for women? To what degree have you internalized these teachings? What effect do these teachings have on your actual conflict behaviors?

3. **Conflict Style.** How would you describe your conflict style in your own close relationships in terms of the competing/avoiding/accommodating/collaborating/compromising model?

4. **E-mail and Interpersonal Conflict.** In what ways do you find that e-mail can escalate interpersonal conflict? In what ways might e-mail help resolve conflict?

5. **Positiveness.** One study found that, at least in general, people are more positive in dealing with conflict in face-to-face situations than in computer-mediated communication (Zornoza, Ripoll, & Peiró, 2002). Do you find this to be true? If so, why do you think it's true?

## LogOn! MyCommunicationLab
### WWW.MYCOMMUNICATIONLAB.COM

Visit MCL and take the self-test to measure your own assertiveness. Try also working with the exercises and reading the additional discussions: Managing Power Plays, Assertiveness, The Influence of Culture on Conflict: An Example, Analyzing a Conflict Episode and How Do You Fight? Like a Man? Like a Woman? Explore the video on conflict among prom planners and listen to the brief discussions on Domestic Violence against Men and The Reunion. Also take a look at the Small Group Communication website at www.abacon.com/commstudies/groups and read about conflict in groups.

# UNIT 13 Human Communication in the Workplace: Organizational Communication

## MAJOR TOPICS

**Organizations**
**Organizational Messages**
**Organizational Relationships**

## Special Features

 Practical Principles: Pam Shockley-Zalabak, 274

Are You X, Y, or Z?, 280

 Advertising and
Public Relations, 279

The Five C's of Organizational
Ethics, 286

*Understanding* Approaches to Organizations, 276

*Understanding* Peter and Dilbert, 278

*Skills* Workplace Analysis, 285

*Skills* Dealing with Organizational
Complaints, 287

Your success at your job, regardless of what that job is, will depend heavily on your mastery of the theories and skills of communication discussed throughout this text and course. This unit looks specifically at communication in the workplace, a popular area of communication called organizational communication.

**In this unit you'll learn about:**
- the nature and types of organizations.
- the characteristics of organizations.
- the types of organizational messages and relationships.

**And you'll learn to:**
- communicate more effectively in the organizational context.
- advance your own status and personal satisfaction within the organization.

This unit ranges widely through the organization, considering the nature of the organization, the varied forms of organizational messages, and organizational relationships.

# ORGANIZATIONS

Here we look at the importance of the organization, the nature of the organization, and the major characteristics of organizations.

## The Importance of Organizations and Organizational Communication

Why study organizational communication? Organizations and organizational communication are important for many reasons (Persell, 1990).

- Perhaps the most obvious reason is that the vast majority of jobs are in organizations. You are more than likely to work and earn a living within the structure of an organization of some kind than to work for yourself; fewer and fewer people work for themselves. Organizations employ people, give health and pension benefits, provide work space, and so on.

- A second reason is that organizations are becoming larger and more complex; mergers and acquisitions are frequent events in the corporate world. And with this increase in size comes an increase in complexity. If you are to function effectively within an organization, it's crucial that you understand how organizations work.

- A third reason is that organizations exert major influence over public policy—they are, for example, among the largest contributors to political candidates—and thus over just about everyone.

When you visualize an organization, the one activity that comes to mind most quickly is communication. Chester Barnard (1938/2005) one of the great organizational theorists, noted that "organizations are almost entirely determined by communication techniques." Communication is what keeps an organization running. It is through communication that most of the work of an organization gets done. We have moved from a society of organizations concerned with manufacturing to a society of organization specializing in information transfer, in moving information from one place to another.

## What Is an Organization?

An **organization** may be defined as (1) an organized (2) group of people (3) who work together (4) to achieve compatible goals.

(1) The word *organized* in this definition refers to the fact that all organizations are structured in some way. Some are rigidly structured; each person's role and position within the hierarchy is clearly defined. You know exactly where you stand. Other organizations are more loosely structured; roles may

# ASK THE RESEARCHER

## Practical Principles

*The principles of communication are interesting, but—and forgive me
for seeming so mercenary—can they help me get a job, get promoted,
or otherwise help me earn a living?*

The principles of communication can be directly related to career success. Interviewing skills help us describe our competencies to a prospective employer and seek information about employment opportunities. Today's organization needs individuals with strong interpersonal skills who can work in diverse groups and situations. Problem-solving and decision-making skills, team and group communication expertise, presentation capabilities, conflict management competencies, and the ability to do organizational communication analysis all are related to job and career advancement. Studies in the United States and internationally have described both human and technological communication as the key to excellence in the twenty-first century. Numerous employer surveys have found that accurately processing large volumes of information within companies, although necessary, is not sufficient for excellence; organizations need employees who take personal responsibility for building relationships that contribute to trust, quality communication, innovation, and change.

For further information: Shockley-Zalabak, P. (2004). *Fundamentals of organizational communication* (6th ed.). Boston: Allyn & Bacon.

**Pam Shockley-Zalabak** (Ph.D., University of Colorado) is a professor of communication and chancellor at the University of Colorado at Colorado Springs. She conducts research on organizational trust and teaches organizational communication classes.

be interchanged, and a person's status and function within the organization may be less clear. Figure 13.1 depicts a representative organizational chart of a publishing company, which shows the hierarchical structure of an organization and how the varied functions of the organization are related and coordinated. The organizational chart is a kind of road map for message travel; it visualizes the routes that messages—at least the formal kind—generally take. The chart also, of course, visualizes the power structure and identifies who is in charge of whom and where the decision-making power lies.

Within any organization there are both formal and informal structures that are much like channels of communication. For example, in a college there is a formal academic structure, with the president at the top, the provost at the next level, deans at the next, department chairs at the next, and faculty next. These structures identify the formal channels of communication—the president communicates to the provost, who communicates to the deans, and so on down the line. There are also informal structures throughout the university, and in many cases these

cross hierarchical lines. These might include, for example, the three computer science professors who play Dungeons and Dragons together or the public relations professor and the dean of arts who attend AA meetings together.

(2) *A group of people:* The number of individuals varies greatly from one organization to another—from three or four members working in close contact to thousands of members working in a variety of different cultures throughout the world. The workers are organized or structured in some way.

(3) *Working together:* Each person's job is related and connected to the jobs of others within the organization. Even when members are separated geographically—as is true in many of today's organizations—the job of one person is connected in some way with the job of the other persons in the organization.

(4) *Achieving compatible goals:* The goals that each person works for are not necessarily the same, but they are compatible. For example, one person may work to earn money (the objective we think of most readily when we think of why someone works), but another may work to learn the

business (as in the case of interns or apprentices), to be close to someone he or she loves, or even to satisfy conditions of parole. Yet these varied goals do not contradict each other. Regardless of the specific motivation, each person's job contributes to the goal of the organization—which, most often, is to earn a profit. Nonprofit organizations may aim to distribute food to the homeless, aid the sick, or educate students. Yet, as you know from just the example of colleges as organizations, a very large part of a nonprofit's time and energy is directed at raising money.

## Characteristics of Organizations

To understand organizations on a somewhat deeper level, we need to look at some of the major characteristics of all organizations: Organizations have rules and regulations, rely on a division of labor, use systems of rewards and consequences, and have their own cultures.

### Rules and Regulations

Like all large groups, organizations have rules and regulations. Some of these are written down in company policy—what is required for promotion, salary schedules, vacation leave, health benefits, the use of office equipment, using the office e-mail system, and so on. Written rules, as you can imagine,

**VIOLATING ORGANIZATIONAL NORMS**

In an animated discussion with an influential colleague you criticize one of the managers who, you discover later, is one of the most loved workers in the organization—no one talks negatively about this person (except you, as it turns out). You need to smooth this over with your colleague.

WHAT DO YOU SAY?
*To whom? Through what channel?*

help to reduce uncertainty and ambiguity. Some of the rules are unwritten but are known by the workers nevertheless. These are the "rules" against, say, sexual harassment or romantic relationships among

**FIGURE 13.1** **Hierachy of an organization**

Organizations differ widely in the number of hierarchical levels they maintain. *Tall organizations* are those with many levels between the CEO and the trainee; *flat organizations* are those with few hierarchical levels. How would you describe the organization of your college? The U.S. government? The organization you work for?

## Theory and Research    Approaches to Organizations

### UNDERSTANDING

Organizations may be viewed from several different theoretical perspectives, each of which will give you different insights into what an organization is and how organizational communication may be understood. Four approaches are particularly significant: the scientific, the behavioral, the systems, and the cultural.

*The scientific approach* focuses on the science of increasing productivity, which studies the physical demands of the job in relation to the physiological capabilities of the workers. Time and motion studies—designed to enable the organization to reduce the time and motions it takes to complete a specific task and thus to increase productivity and profit—are most characteristic of this approach. The scientific approach emphasizes communication as the giving of orders, from management down to the workers.

*The behavioral approach*—also called the humanistic, organic, or human relations approach—holds that increased worker satisfaction will result in increased productivity. This approach acknowledges the importance of informal social groups within the organization and gives special consideration to the interpersonal communication within the subgroups of these organizations.

*The systems approach* combines the scientific and the behavioral approaches and views an organization as a system in which all parts interact and in which each part influences every other part. Communication, in this approach, is what holds the organization together and effectively coordinates the various parts of the organization.

*The cultural approach* views the organization as a culture or society with, for example, rules, norms, values, and heroes. This approach views the workers and the organization itself as having similar values and goals. Teamwork, pride in work and in accomplishment, commitment to high standards and to the organization, honesty, and a willingness to change in order to grow despite difficulties from competition characterize the effective organization in this view (Uris, 1986).

### Working with Theories and Research

*What type of organizational approach characterized the work environments you've experienced? What do you see as the advantages and disadvantages of each approach to organizations?*

coworkers and "rules" promoting punctuality and appropriate dress. Increasingly, organizations are in fact writing these unwritten rules into policy statements in an attempt to avoid lawsuits. Still, unwritten rules are generally less certain and more ambiguous than are the written rules.

### Division of Labor

Organizations, especially large ones, have a clear *division of labor*; workers are increasingly specialized. When you call for computer assistance, for example, the response system asks you a series of questions—what platform do you use, what edition of the operating system are you using, the nature of your problem (whether it's Internet related or has to do with accessing software programs), and so on—in order to direct your question to a specialist in your specific problem. Workers are responsible for limited ar-

eas within a company; the accountant is not responsible for the cafeteria menu, and the cooks are not responsible for getting paychecks to members.

### Systems of Rewards and Consequences

Organizations rely largely on a system of rewards and punishments. If you do the job expected of you and do it well, you'll be rewarded with bonuses, pay raises, a corner office, a better parking space, or a promotion, for example. If you don't do your job, you're likely to be punished; you'll be denied the bonus or promotion and may even be fired. The power to reward and punish is always controlled by those above you. Ideally, whether you're rewarded or punished will depend on your performance, though in reality it often depends on how much those above you like you (see Table 13.1).

## Table 13.1 **How to Be Liked at Work**

Whether in a job interview, in the early days on a new job, or in meeting new colleagues, first impressions are especially important—because they're so long lasting and so powerful in influencing future impressions and interactions (Parsons, Liden, & Bauer, 2001; Flocker, 2006; Grobart, 2007). Here are a few guidelines that will help you make a good first impression and should increase your likeability on the job.

| Strategy | Comments |
|---|---|
| Look the Part | Dress appropriately; even "casual Fridays" have dress codes, and these include body jewelry and tattoos. Any drastic deviation from the standard dress for your position is likely to be perceived negatively and may communicate that you don't fit in. |
| Be Positive | Both verbally and nonverbally, express positive attitudes toward the organization, the job, and your colleagues. Avoid negative talk and sarcasm (even in your humor); it's often perceived as an attack on others. |
| Be Culturally Sensitive | Avoid stereotyping and talk that might be considered racist, heterosexist, ageist, or sexist. You're sure to offend someone with any of these -isms. Discover what the organization's cultural rules and norms are, and avoid violating them. |
| Be Respectful and Friendly | Be respectful of other people; for example, be respectful of other people's time or personal quirks. At the same time, be open and friendly; be available and helpful as appropriate. Be cooperative; share rather than monopolize. |
| Be Interested | Focus attention on the other person. Verbally, express interest in who the person is and what he or she says and does. Nonverbally, maintain eye contact, a pleasant facial expression, an open posture, and relatively close proximity. Be a good listener; good listeners are invariably among the most popular people anywhere, and the workplace is no exception. |

*What types of first impressions do you usually make? Are you pleased with these first impressions? How might you go about improving these early impressions?*

## Organizational Culture

Each organization has its own *culture* and, like any cultural group, has its own rituals, norms, and rules for communicating. These **cultural rules**—whether in an interview situation or in a friendly conversation—delineate appropriate and inappropriate verbal and nonverbal behavior, specify rewards (or punishments for breaking the rules), and tell you what will help you get the job and what won't. For example, the general advice given throughout this text is to emphasize your positive qualities, to highlight your abilities, and to minimize any negative characteristics or failings. But in some organizations—especially in collectivist cultures such as those of China, Korea, and Japan—workers are expected to show modesty (Copeland & Griggs, 1985). If you stress your own competencies too much, you may be seen as arrogant, brash, and unfit to work in an organization where teamwork and cooperation are emphasized.

In collectivist organizational cultures, great deference is to be shown to managers, who represent the company. If you don't treat managers with respect, you may appear to be disrespecting the entire company. In contrast, in the individualist cultures that prevail in many U.S. companies, too much deference may

make you appear unassertive, unsure of yourself, and unqualified to assume a position of authority. Not surprisingly, research finds that Japanese managers emphasize cooperation and exert influence through appeals to personal motives. American managers, however, emphasize individualism and exert influence through the control of rewards and punishments (Hirokawa & Miyahara, 1986; Hirokawa & Wagner, 2004).

When you join an organization, you learn the rules and norms of a culture different from, say, the college culture from which you came or the culture of another organization for which you worked previously. Put differently, and in terms of the concepts discussed in Unit 2, you become acculturated, much as you would if you moved to a foreign country.

When the new organizational culture is similar to the culture from which you come, acculturation is simple and easy. For workers who move from GM's Buick division to its Pontiac division, the process is likely to be smooth; both divisions are likely to be governed by an overall General Motors culture. Moving from IBM to Google, however, might be more difficult, because the corporate cultures are very different. The same is true, to perhaps an even

## Theory and Research — UNDERSTANDING — Peter and Dilbert

Two interesting "principles" will give you an idea of how some critics of the organization view organizational practices.

The *Peter Principle*, developed by college professor Lawrence J. Peter, states that "in a hierarchy every employee tends to rise to his [or her] level of incompetence" (Peter & Hull, 1969). The principle applies to all levels of the organization. For example, a publishing house may reward a great salesperson (for being a great salesperson) by promoting him or her to, say, editor. If the person proves a good editor, he or she will again be removed from a job he or she does extremely well and will be promoted to another job. The person will keep moving up in the hierarchy until he or she no longer performs well and so no longer deserves to be rewarded with another promotion. You see this regularly in education; the great teacher becomes dean (a position that requires a totally different set of skills). The great teacher may make a lousy dean and so will not advance further to, say, president. Put in terms of the Peter Principle, this person has now risen to his or her level of incompetence.

Because this is a system used by many corporations, the Peter Principle became a way of describing the illogic of organizational hierarchy and of organizations' methods of promoting and rewarding workers. The principle is clearly stated in an exaggerated form, but there seems enough truth to it to keep it a very lively organizational topic.

A somewhat similar principle is the *Dilbert Principle*, articulated by satirist Scott Adams (1997) who also writes the popular *Dilbert* comic strip: Organizations promote the most incompetent workers to managerial positions where they'll be able to do the least damage. All organizations have these people—workers who have served the company for many years but are now incompetent. Rather than have these people go to other organizations (and reveal trade secrets perhaps), the organization holds on to them, pays them a salary, but doesn't expect them to do much.

### Working with Theories and Research

*What evidence can you find that would support or refute either of these principles?*

---

greater extent, when you move from an organization in one country to an organization in another country, a situation that more and more workers are experiencing throughout the world. In such a move, you would have to be acculturated both to the country's culture and to the organization's culture.

As you can appreciate, it's essential to learn the organization's culture to know what the rules of the game are—and especially to learn the rules of organizational communication and to understand what kinds of messages will get you rewarded and what will get you punished.

## ORGANIZATIONAL MESSAGES

As defined in Unit 1, the term *organizational communication* refers to the process of sending and receiving verbal and nonverbal messages that convey meaning and that occur within an organizational context. The meaning of *organizational communication* is thus limited to messages occurring *within* the organization's formal and informal groups. Communication from the organization to the public would be part of advertising and public relations. These forms of communication are covered briefly in the accompanying Media Watch box.

As an organization becomes larger and more complex, so do the members' communications. In a three-person organization, communication is relatively simple; but in a multinational organization of thousands, communication becomes highly complex.

Your organizational communication—as sender and as receiver—will be greatly influenced by the way in which you view the organization and the workers within that organization. To help you explore some of your own attitudes and beliefs, take the self-test on page 280.

## MEDIA WATCH

## ADVERTISING AND PUBLIC RELATIONS

*You can tell the ideals of a nation by its advertisements.*

—*Norman Douglas*

*Small groups of people can, and do, make the rest of us think what they please about a given subject.*

—*Edward Bernays*

Organizations use advertising and public relations to communicate with their customers and other publics. *Advertising* is a communication strategy designed to persuade listeners, readers, or viewers to do something—usually to buy a product. *Public relations* is a communication strategy designed to convey information so as to establish positive relationships between a corporation, agency, or other group and the public (Folkerts & Lacy, 2001; Rodman 2001).

**Advertising** informs you in a variety of ways by:

■ making you aware of a particular product or service, a function that's especially important with new products. Advertising also informs you about the product and its ingredients, features, or uses.

■ telling you where to buy the product, its cost, and other details.

■ correcting erroneous claims made in previous ads. For example, Listerine was required to advertise that it doesn't kill germs that cause colds—as had been previously advertised.

Of course, the real business of advertising is persuasion. An advertiser seeks to persuade you by:

■ establishing a favorable image of its product—making you think a certain way about the product, or associate a positive feeling with it, so that you will want to buy the product. Advertising also may try to associate a product with negative feelings. The American Cancer Society's advertisements against smoking regularly attack the glamorous image of smoking by showing pictures of wrinkled and sick smokers.

■ convincing you of the superiority of the advertiser's product and the inferiority of the competition. This comparative advertising pits one product against another.

■ getting you to buy the product. Whether it's a product or a service, the advertiser wants to get you to the point where you'll go the store, make the phone call, or type in your credit card number and complete the sale.

**Public relations** practitioners engage in a wide variety of activities to accomplish their purposes:

■ *Lobbying* to influence government officials or agencies to fund a proposal, support a nominee, or vote for or against an upcoming bill.

■ *Raising funds* for college, political candidates, charities, or public broadcasting stations.

■ *Controlling crises.* The work of PR practitioners often involves efforts to repair potentially damaged images, whether in regard to defective or problematic products—cars, dietary supplements, or drugs—or in regard to an organization's financial problems.

■ *Influencing public opinion*, to get voters to support a political candidate or initiative or to change their attitudes on a variety of issues—abortion, campaign financing, gay rights, and a host of other issues you read about daily.

■ *Establishing good relationships* between, say, a community and a company that wants to erect a mall in the neighborhood, between a community and its police department, or between a company and the general public. Microsoft's donations to public education and to health organizations, and the numerous companies that support AIDS and cancer research, literacy programs, college scholarships, and safe driving are good examples.

### Increasing Media Literacy

*Keep a log for one day of all the advertising and public relations efforts with which you come into contact. Be prepared—it's going to be a very extensive log. In what ways did these advertisements and public relations acts influence you? How would you describe the techniques practitioners use to achieve their purposes?*

# TEST YOURSELF

## Are You X, Y, or Z?

Respond to each of the following statements with T for true if you believe the statement is generally or usually true, or with F for false if you believe the statement is generally or usually false:

The average worker:

_____ 1. Must be persuaded, even motivated by fear, to do work.

_____ 2. Has little real ambition and will avoid work is possible.

_____ 3. Wants to be directed as a way of avoiding responsibility.

_____ 4. Will accept and even seek responsibility.

_____ 5. Will direct himself or herself to achieve organizational objectives.

_____ 6. Is capable and willing to learn new tasks.

_____ 7. Focuses on the entire organization rather than just his or her own department.

_____ 8. Favors group decision making and responsibility.

_____ 9. Seeks to expand career opportunities within the organization.

**HOW DID YOU DO?** These statements refer to theories of management that have been labeled X, Y, and Z (McGregor, 1980; 2005). Statements 1, 2, and 3 would be believed by a Theory X manager, who holds that the worker is unmotivated and really does not want to work. Statements 4, 5, and 6 would be believed by a Theory Y manager, who holds that the worker is in fact motivated, responsible, and eager to work. Statements 7, 8, and 9 would be believed by a Theory Z manager, who holds that the worker focuses on the entire organization rather than on just his or her own area and wants to advance within the organization (Ouchi, 1981).

**WHAT WILL YOU DO?** The important principle to derive from this brief excursion into management beliefs is that your beliefs about other workers will influence the way you communicate and interact with other workers. If, for example, you believe that the average worker doesn't really want to work, you may respond to workers as if this belief were true—and, in an example of the self-fulfilling prophecy, may actually influence workers to act as if they do not want to work. If you believe that the worker is motivated and wants to assume responsibility, you'll communicate with workers in ways that assume this is true and, in turn, may influence workers to motivate themselves and assume responsibility.

# Formal and Informal Communication

Organizational communication may be both formal and informal. **Formal communication** consists of messages that are sanctioned by the organization itself and are organizationally focused. They deal with the workings of the organization, with productivity, and with the various jobs done by the employees. Most often they follow the organizational chart. **Informal communication** consists of messages that are socially sanctioned. They are oriented not to the conduct of the business but to the individual members and their relationship to the organization. These informal communications may include gossip about what is going on in the company, what changes are being considered, the status of a promised raise or holiday bonus, and so on.

## Formal Organizational Communication

Upward, Downward, and Lateral Formal communication may be looked at in terms of its direction, whether upward, downward, or lateral. I'll explain each in turn and offer some suggestions for improving these organizational messages.

**Upward Communication.** **Upward communication** consists of messages sent from the lower levels of a hierarchy to the upper levels—for example, line worker to manager, or faculty member to dean. This type of communication usually is concerned with job-related activities and problems; ideas for change and suggestions for improvement; and feelings about the organization, work, other workers, or similar issues.

Upward communication is vital to the growth of any organization. It provides management with feedback on worker morale and possible sources of dissatisfaction and offers leaders the opportunity to acquire new ideas from workers. At the same time, it gives subordinates a sense of belonging to and being a part of the organization. Among the guidelines for improving upward communication are, for managers:

- Set up a nonthreatening system for upward communication that is acceptable to the cultural norms of the workforce, for example, a suggestion box or periodic meetings. Realize that from a worker's point of view, upward communication involves risk.

- Be open to hearing worker comments, and eliminate unnecessary gatekeepers that prevent important messages from traveling up the organizational hierarchy (Callan, 1993).

- Be willing to listen to workers' messages even when they're critical.

## COMPLAINING

One of your managers is favoring a person he's secretly dating and giving you all the unpleasant tasks and his date all the pleasant ones.

WHAT DO YOU SAY?
*To whom? Through what channel?*

And for employees:

- Be especially careful to avoid messages that may be perceived as disconfirming fellow workers.

- Avoid sending too many messages and contributing to information overload. Too many messages may also make it difficult for managers to distinguish the really important from the routine.

- Beware of sending messages that may be ambiguous or that may contradict previous messages. Usually, it's better to err on the side of excess explanation.

## Downward Communication. **Downward communication** consists of messages sent from the higher levels to the lower levels of the hierarchy; for example, messages sent by managers to workers or by deans to faculty members. Common forms of downward communication include orders; expla-

nations of procedures, goals, and changes; and appraisals of workers. Among the guidelines for effective downward communication are:

- Use a vocabulary known to the workers. Keep technical jargon to a minimum, especially with workers who are not native speakers of the managers' language.

- Provide workers with sufficient information for them to function effectively, but avoid information overload.

- When criticizing, be especially careful not to damage the image or face of those singled out.

## Lateral Communication. **Lateral communication** refers to messages between equals—manager to manager, worker to worker. Such messages may move within the same subdivision or department of the organization or across divisions. Lateral communication, for example, is the kind of communication that takes place between two history professors at Illinois State University, between a psychologist at Ohio State and a communicologist at Kent State, or between a bond trader and an equities trader at a brokerage house.

Lateral communication facilitates the sharing of insights, methods, and problems. It helps the organization to avoid some problems and to solve others. Lateral communication also builds morale and worker satisfaction. Good relationships and meaningful communication between workers are among the main sources of worker satisfaction. More generally, lateral communication serves the purpose of coordinating the various activities of the organization and enabling the various divisions to pool insights and expertise.

Among the guidelines for improving lateral communication are these:

- Recognize that your own specialty has a technical jargon that others outside your specialty might not know. Clarify when and as needed.

- See the entire organizational picture, and recognize the importance of all areas. Seeing one's own area as important and all others as unimportant does little to foster meaningful communication.

- Balance the needs of an organization that relies on cooperation and yet rewards competition. In most cases it seems that cooperation can be increased without doing any individual damage.

## Informal Organizational Communication: The Grapevine

As noted earlier, informal organizational messages may concern just about any topic germane to workers and the organization. These messages are called grapevine messages because they follow twisting routes reminiscent of grapevines.

**Grapevine** messages don't follow any of the formal, hierarchical lines of communication established in an organization; rather, they seem to have a life of their own. Grapevine messages, like the formal organizational messages, concern job-related issues that you want to discuss in a more interpersonal setting; for example, organizational issues that have not yet been made public, the *real* relationship among the regional managers, or possible changes that are being considered but not yet finalized. Not surprisingly, the grapevine also grows as the size of the organization increases. In fact, large organizations often have several grapevines: The grapevine among interns is not the same as the grapevine used by upper management, and the student grapevine is not the same as the faculty grapevine. Sometimes, of course, they overlap; interns and management or students and faculty may exchange grapevine messages with each other.

The grapevine is most likely to be used when (Crampton, Hodge, & Mishra, 1998):

- the issues are considered important to the workers (the more important the topic, the more likely the grapevine will focus on it);

- there is ambiguity or uncertainty about what an organization is going to do (a lack of clarity encourages grapevine communication); and/or

- the situation is perceived as threatening or insecure and anxiety may be running high (in such circumstances grapevine messages will be rampant).

One research study notes that workers spend between 65 and 70 percent of their time on the grapevine during a crisis. And even in noncrisis times, workers spend 10 to 15 percent of their time on the grapevine (Smith, 1996). As you can imagine, listening to grapevine messages will therefore give you insight into what workers consider important, what needs added clarification, and what issues make workers anxious.

The grapevine is surprisingly accurate, with estimates of accuracy ranging from 75 to 95 percent. Workers hear about organizational matters first through the grapevine about 75 percent of the time. And, perhaps equally important, workers believe the grapevine to be accurate—at times, even more accurate than management's formal messages (Davis, 1980; Hellweg, 1992; Smith, 1996).

Here are a few useful suggestions for dealing with the inevitable office grapevine:

- Understand the variety of purposes the grapevine serves. Its speed and general accuracy make it an ideal medium to carry many of the social communications that so effectively bind workers together. So listen carefully; it will give you an insider's view of the organization and will help you understand those with whom you work.

- Treat grapevine information as tentative, as possibly not necessarily true. Although grapevine information is generally accurate, it's often incomplete and ambiguous; it may also contain crucial distortions.

- Repeat only what you know or strongly believe to be true, and indicate your own level of belief in your grapevine messages; for example, "I heard we're all getting a nice bonus, but it may be just wishful thinking from the mailroom staff."

- Tap into the grapevine. Whether you're a worker or a member of management, it's important to hear grapevine information. It may clue you into events that will affect your future with the organization, and it will help you network with others in the organization.

- Always assume that what you say in grapevine communication will be repeated to others (Smith, 1996; Hilton, 2000). So be mindful of your organizational communications; the potentially offensive joke that you e-mail a colleague can easily be forwarded to the very people who may take offense.

## Communication Channels in Organizations

Organizations use the same communication channels that everyone else uses. The major difference—depending on an organization's finances—is that usually the organization's methods are at the cutting edge of technology and make use of the most sophisticated equipment available. The organization makes use of all the forms of communication discussed in this text. Face-to-face interpersonal communication, small group meetings, and public presentations are all used in today's organizations. But organizations also make use of instant messaging, blogs, interactive websites, and video conferencing, for example.

All communication channels are potentially useful; the channels used in any given situation are chosen on the basis of what's best for the specific task being addressed. If editors want to solicit the opinions of authors who are widely scattered throughout the world on an issue, then e-mail will probably work most efficiently. Face-to-face meetings would be prohibitively expensive and would probably not be any more effective than e-mail. When short messages need to be sent and quick responses are needed, then instant messaging seems the logical option. When a CEO wants to present a reorganization plan to top-level management, a face-to-face public presentation may serve best.

## Communication Networks

Organizations use a variety of different **communication networks**—configurations of channels through which messages pass from one person to another. The five types of networks shown in Figure 13.2 are among the most commonly used organizational communication patterns. These networks are defined by the exchange of messages, which may be transmitted face-to-face or via telephone, e-mail, intranet, teleconferencing, informal memos, or formal reports.

- In the *circle*, members may communicate with the two members on either side. The circle has no leader; all members have exactly the same authority or power to influence the group.
- In the *wheel*, all messages must go through the central position or leader. Members may not communicate directly with each other.
- In the *Y*, the messages pass mainly to the third person from the bottom and to a lesser extent to the person second from the bottom.
- In the *chain*, messages may be sent only to the person next to you. In this pattern there are some power differences; the middle positions receive more messages than the end positions.
- In the *all-channel* or *star pattern*, each member may communicate with any other member, allowing for the greatest member participation. All members, as in the circle, have the same power to influence others.

## Information Overload and Isolation

One of the greatest barriers to organizational efficiency is **information overload**—a condition in which a worker has to deal with an excessive amount of information. Information overload is created not only by the vast number of messages that a worker receives but also by the ambiguity and complexity that often characterize such messages. To-

gether, these factors make it extremely difficult for workers to process and respond to the messages that come across their desk. As you can easily appreciate, advances in information technology have made it easier to send more and more information in less and less time, increasing the likelihood of greater and greater overload.

Information is now generated at such a rapid rate that it's impossible to keep up with all that's relevant to your job. Invariably, you must select only certain information to attend to. The junk mail and spam that seems to grow every day is a perfect example. Today the American worker is exposed to more information in one year than a person living in 1900 was in his or her entire life. Technology has made it easy (perhaps too easy) to create and disseminate information on the Web, on blogs, and through mailing lists; and there seems every reason to expect this trend to increase.

One of the problems with information overload is that it absorbs an enormous amount of time for workers at all levels of an organization. The more messages you have to deal with, the less time you have for those messages or tasks that are central to your functions. Research finds, for example, that when you're overloaded, you're more likely to respond to simpler messages and to generate simpler messages, which may not always be appropriate (Jones, Ravid, & Rafaeli, 2004). Similarly, errors become more likely under conditions of information overload, simply because you cannot devote the needed time to any one item.

Other communication problems include the risk that you will lower your normally high standards of precision or assign responsibility for responding to messages to subordinates or interns who may not have the knowledge and background to respond as appropriately as you might. Or you may seek to escape the overload by not accessing information—for example, by not reading your e-mails, ignoring memos, or not responding to phone messages (Timm & DeTienne, 1995).

Information overload has even been linked to health problems in more than one-third of managers

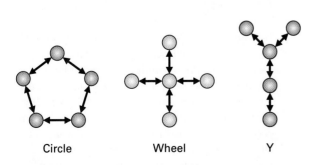

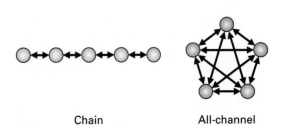

Circle          Wheel          Y                    Chain          All-channel

**FIGURE 13.2    Five Network Structures**

- Get rid of extra copies. When you receive multiple copies of an item, get rid of all but the one (if any) that you need.
- Periodically take inventory of the messages you receive regularly and, where appropriate, eliminate one or more sources of unnecessary messages.

At the other extreme is **message isolation**, the situation that exists when a worker is given little or no information. Such isolation may occur when formal messages are not sent to certain people or when some people are excluded from informal gossip and grapevine messages.

Message isolation also may occur when workers are at remote locations or work at home; when a worker has an unpleasant personality or is difficult to work with; or when someone is isolated because of prejudice toward his or her race, gender, or affectional orientation.

Message isolation makes it difficult for the individual to do the job assigned, deprives the organization of potentially useful input from the individual, and generally creates an unhappy and unmotivated worker.

## Organizational Message Competence

Throughout this text the important of message competence has been stressed; here is a brief list of these skills with specific application to the workplace.

1. Listen actively, empathically, critically, and in depth. Especially when new to an organization, it's through listening that you'll learn the rules for organizational success.
2. Apologize when you make an error, following the suggestions offered in Unit 7, pages 161–162. No one is expected to be right all the time, so when you are the cause of a problem or do make a significant error, be ready to apologize effectively.
3. Avoid contributing to information overload or information isolation. You don't have to copy everyone with every e-mail; you don't have to e-mail everyone in the listserv when you really want to address only one person. Follow the rules of netiquette.
4. Use the grapevine. Ignoring the grapevine will prevent you from learning what is happening beyond your purview and what may happen in the future and enable you to prepare.
5. Demonstrate the communication skills of leadership. Be prepared to lead a group successfully and to give an effective public presentation. And be able to do this with the latest and most appropriate technology. At the same time, be prepared to be a small group participant and an audience member.

## DEALING WITH MESSAGE ISOLATION

One of the workers you're supervising has been isolated, largely because the individual has been extremely negative and doesn't socialize with others in the organization. You need this person to participate more actively in day-to-day operations.

WHAT DO YOU SAY?

(Lee, 2000). "Technostress" is a new term that denotes the anxiety and stress resulting from a feeling of being controlled by the overwhelming amount of information and from the inability to manage the information in the time available.

Several suggestions should help you deal with information overload (Uris, 1986; Timm & DeTienne, 1995):

- Think before passing on messages. Not all messages must be passed on; not everyone needs to know everything.
- Use the messages as they come to you; record the relevant information and then throw them out or delete them. Similarly, throw out or delete materials that contain information that can be easily located elsewhere.
- Organize your messages. Create folders to help you store and retrieve the information you need quickly.

**Building Communication Skills**   Workplace Analysis

Much as you would analyze an audience so as to tailor your messages to them (as will be detailed in Unit 14), you can analyze a workplace to reduce your uncertainty (Berger & Bradac, 1982). In this way you'll be better able to fit your messages to the organization, the hierarchy, and your coworkers. Here are five kinds of information you might focus on in your workplace analysis; for each, create an example of how this specific knowledge might help a worker new to the organization.

- *Cultural norms:* All organizations have rules for interacting, beliefs about their mission, and values that they seek to cultivate. Discover what these are.

- *Communication pathways:* Organizations have specific pathways that they expect communication to follow; for example, interns do not send messages directly to the CEO of a large corporation but may address them to other interns or to those who are supervising the internship program.

- *Grapevine:* In most organizations, grapevines flourish; tap into the grapevine to learn about your workplace. The grapevine often will clue you in to what is going on in the organization and will provide the very information that you need to interact effectively with a wide variety of individuals.

- *Power:* All members of organizations exercise power over those who work for them. Seek to understand who has power and what types of power are used. Ultimately, you'll want to learn how to acquire such power yourself and to empower others.

- *Reward system:* All organizations exercise control through a system of rewards (promotions, raises, bonuses, choice offices, and the like) and punishments (termination, no bonuses, undesirable offices, and the like). Seek to discover the behaviors that are rewarded and those that are punished as well as who controls the reward system.

*Success in an organization will depend greatly on how well you understand the organization and especially its communication patterns.*

6. Avoid the various -isms discussed in Unit 5, pages 109–113. Speech that is racist, heterosexist, ageist, or sexist will invariably offend someone, and you don't need that kind of hostility.

7. Help manage conflict; don't aggravate it, as some do, to stir up excitement. To the organization conflict is not excitement, it's a headache.

8. Use power effectively. Learn the power structure of the organization and understand your current and your future role in that structure. Use verbal and nonverbal messages that communicate power, and avoid those that signal a lack of power.

9. Understand the communication flow. Understand the channels that various messages are expected to go through and how you can make the available patterns work best for you.

10. Treat all your messages as if they were being graded by your instructor.

## ORGANIZATIONAL RELATIONSHIPS

Within any organization there are interpersonal relationships. Understanding these relationships will further your understanding of organizations and organizational competence. Here we look at sexual harassment, romance in the workplace, mentoring, and networking.

### Sexual Harassment

No discussion of communication in the workplace can omit a discussion of **sexual harassment**, one of organizations' major problems today. In conjunction with this section, take a look at some of the many websites devoted to this topic. Perhaps the first visit should be to the government website at **www.eeoc.gov/facts/fs-sex.html**. There you'll find

# REFLECTIONS ON ETHICS

## The Five C's of Organizational Ethics

Considering the importance of ethics in organizations and the frequent ethics violations that appear in the news, there is surprisingly little of substance written on the ethical guides an organization and workers should follow. Here, then, is an attempt to identify at least some of the principles an ethical organization should follow.

- *Clear policies and expectations.* Management has an obligation to set forth clear and unambiguous policies concerning organizational matters; people have a right to know what is expected of them.

- *Comfortable work environment,* free of harassment and bullying. No one should have to endure harassment or intimidation.

- *Channels for communication,* open and well known and listened to. Everyone has a right to

hear what is relevant to their position and to be listened to.

- *Cooperation* for the betterment of both management and workers. Each person has a right to expect that cooperation will yield benefits to the organization and to the workers.

- *Commitment* to contracts, verbal agreements, and job descriptions. People have a right to expect promises to be kept.

### Ethical Choice Point

*At your workplace management seems to condone sexual harassment; at least they do nothing to stop it. You've witnessed both* quid pro quo *and* hostile environment *sexual harassment toward women and gay men and lesbians. What is your ethical obligation in this situation? What would you do?*

the laws and the statistics on sexual harassment. Many universities also maintain websites devoted to this topic; one particularly good site is that of the University of North Carolina at Greensboro, http://library/uncg.edu/depts/docs/us/harassment.asp.

In one survey, conducted by the American Association of University Women, one in four college students said they had experienced unwanted sexual contact (unwillingly being touched or grabbed or having someone brush up against them). One out of 6 of those surveyed in this study reported receiving sexually suggestive photos, messages, or websites. And 1 out of 20 reported being asked for sexual favors in return for a recommendation, notes from class, or a better grade. Thirty-five percent of the women and 16 percent of the men reported that the experience lowered their self-confidence (*New York Times,* January 25, 2006, p. B7). Government statistics indicate that in 2006 there were 23,034 charges of sexual harassment filed with the Equal Employment Opportunity Commission (EEOC) (www.eeoc.gov/facts/fs-sex.html, accessed March 27, 2007).

There are two general categories of workplace sexual harassment: quid pro quo (a Latin term that literally means "something for something") harassment and the creation of a hostile environment.

In **quid pro quo harassment**, employment opportunities (as in hiring and promotion) may be made dependent on the granting of sexual favors. Quid pro quo harassment also can include threats of reprisals or

of various negative consequences that would result from a person's failure to grant such sexual favors.

**Hostile environment harassment** is a much broader category and includes all sexual behaviors (verbal and nonverbal) that make a worker uncomfortable. For example, putting sexually explicit pictures on the office bulletin board, using sexually explicit screen savers, telling sexual jokes and stories, and using sexual and demeaning language or gestures all constitute hostile environment harassment.

How can you avoid sexual harassment behaviors? You can avoid conveying messages that might be considered sexual harassment by following these suggestions (Bravo & Cassedy, 1992; Geffner, Braverman, Galasso, & Marsh, 2004). First, begin with the assumption that others at work are not interested in your sexual advances, sexual stories and jokes, or sexual gestures. Second, listen and watch for negative reactions to any sex-related discussion. Use the suggestions and techniques discussed throughout this book (such as perception checking and critical listening) to become aware of such reactions. When in doubt, find out; ask questions, for example. Third, avoid saying or doing anything you think your parent, partner, or child would find offensive in the behavior of someone with whom she or he worked.

What can you do about sexual harassment? If you think you're being sexually harassed, consider these suggestions (Petrocelli & Repa, 1992; Bravo & Cassedy, 1992; Rubenstein, 1993; Marshall, 2005):

1. Talk to the harasser. Tell this person, assertively, that you do not welcome the behavior and that you find it offensive. If this doesn't solve the problem, then consider the next suggestion.
2. Collect evidence—perhaps get corroboration from others who have experienced similar harassment and/or keep a log of the offensive behaviors.
3. Use the channels established by the organization to deal with such grievances. If this doesn't stop the harassment, consider going further.
4. File a complaint with an organization or governmental agency, or perhaps take legal action.
5. Don't blame yourself. Like many who are abused, you may tend to blame yourself, feeling that you are responsible for being harassed. You aren't; however, you may need to secure emotional support from friends or perhaps from trained professionals.

## Romance in the Workplace

Opinions vary widely concerning workplace romances. On the positive side, the work environment seems a perfect place to meet a potential partner. By virtue of the fact that you're working in the same office, you're probably both interested in the same field, have similar training and ambitions, and spend considerable time together—all factors that foster the development of a successful interpersonal relationship. In one survey, 59 percent of the people felt that office romances were nothing to worry about; 23 percent said they had had affairs within office walls; and 19 percent said they had dated a subordinate (Flocker, 2006).

If you're romantically attracted to another worker, it can make going to work, working together, and even working added hours more enjoyable. If the relationship is mutually satisfying, you're likely to develop empathy for each other and to act in ways that are supportive, cooperative, friendly, and beneficial to the organization.

On the negative side, even if a workplace relationship is good for the lovers themselves, it may not necessarily be good for other workers. They may see the lovers as a team that has to be confronted as a pair and may feel that they can't criticize one partner without incurring the wrath of the other. Such relationships may also cause problems for management—for example, when a promotion is to be made or when relocation decisions are necessary.

Of course, if an office romance goes bad, or if it's one-sided, it can be stressful for the individuals involved to see each other regularly and perhaps to work together. Also, other workers may feel they have to take sides, being supportive of one partner and critical of the other. This can easily cause friction throughout the organization.

---

**Building Communication Skills** | **Dealing with Organizational Complaints**

Assume that you're the leader of a work team consisting of members from each of the major departments in your company. For any one of the complaints listed below, explain what you would say and the objectives you'd hope to achieve. In framing your responses follow these guidelines: (a) Let the other person know that you're open to complaints and that you do view complaints as essential sources of information; (b) show that you're following the suggestions for effective listening discussed in Unit 4, such as listening supportively and with empathy; (c) show that you understand both the thoughts and the feelings that go with the complaint; and (d) ask the other person what he or she would like you to do about the complaint.

1. You're calling these meetings much too often and much too early to suit us. We'd like fewer meetings scheduled for later in the day.

2. That's not fair. Why do I always have to take the minutes of these meetings? Can't we have a real secretary here?

3. There's a good reason why I don't contribute to the discussion. I don't contribute because no one listens to what I say.

*Complaints are vital sources of information; they help an organization grow and improve.*

Management is necessarily concerned with the potential that office romances gone bad can lead to charges of sexual harassment. This concern has prompted some organizations to consider "love contracts"—agreements between management and workers as to what constitutes appropriate and inappropriate romantic behavior in the workplace (Pierce & Aquinis, 2001; Schaefer & Tudor, 2001).

## Mentoring

In a **mentoring** relationship, an experienced individual (mentor) helps to train a less-experienced person who is sometimes referred to as a mentee or, more often, a protégé (Ragins & Kram, 2007). An accomplished teacher, for example, might mentor a newly arrived or novice teacher. The mentor guides the new person through the ropes, teaches the strategies and techniques for success, and otherwise communicates his or her knowledge and experience to the newcomer.

Mentoring usually involves a one-on-one relationship between an expert and a novice—a relationship that is supportive and trusting. There's a mutual and open sharing of information and thoughts about the job. The relationship enables the novice to try out new skills under the guidance of an expert, to ask questions, and to obtain the feedback so necessary in learning complex skills.

In a study of middle-level managers, those who had mentors and participated in mentoring relationships were found to earn more frequent promotions and higher salaries than those who didn't (Scandura, 1992). And the mentoring relationship is one of the three primary paths to career achievement among African American men and women (Bridges, 1996). It's also interesting to note that similarity in race or gender between mentor and protégé doesn't seem to influence the mentoring experience (Barr, 2000).

At the same time that a mentor helps a novice, the mentor benefits from clarifying his or her thoughts, from seeing the job from the perspective of a newcomer, and from considering and formulating answers to a variety of questions. Much the way a teacher learns from teaching and from his or her students, a mentor learns from mentoring and from his or her protégés.

## Networking

**Networking** is more than a technique for securing a job. It is a broad process of enlisting the aid of other people to help you solve a problem or to offer insights that bear on your problem—for example, on how to publish your manuscript, where to go for low-cost auto insurance, how to find an apartment, or how to empty your e-mail cache (Heenehan,

1997). Here are a few principles for effective networking, which have special application to the workplace but which you'll find useful generally.

- Start your networking with people you already know. You'll probably discover that you know a great number of people with specialized knowledge who can be of assistance (Rector & Neiva, 1996). You can also network with people who know the people you know. Thus, you may contact a friend's friend to find out if the firm where he or she works is hiring. Or you may contact people with whom you have no connection. Perhaps you've read something the person wrote or heard the person's name raised in connection with an area in which you're interested, and you want to get more information. With e-mail addresses so readily available, it's now quite common to e-mail individuals who have particular expertise and ask your questions. Newsgroups and chat rooms are other obvious networking avenues.

- Try to establish relationships that are mutually beneficial. If you can provide others with helpful information, it's more likely that they'll provide helpful information for you. In this way you establish a mutually satisfying and productive network.

- Create folders, files, and directories of potentially useful sources that you can contact. For example, if you're a freelance artist, you might develop a list of persons in positions to offer you work or who might lead you to others who could offer work, such as authors, editors, art directors, administrative assistants, or people in advertising.

- Be proactive; initiate contacts rather than waiting for them to come to you. If you're also willing to help others, there's nothing wrong in asking these same people to help you. If you're respectful of your contacts' time and expertise, it's likely that they will respond favorably to your networking attempts. Following up your requests with thank-you notes will help you establish networks that can be ongoing relationships.

- Consider the possible value of the variety of web-based organizations devoted to enabling you to network with others. For example, visit www .linked.com, www.ryze.com, www.ecademy.com, www.soflow.com, and www.xing.com.

## Organizational Relationship Competence

The importance of relationship competence has been a keynote of this text. Here is a list of some relationship competence skills that are particularly applicable to the workplace.

1. Be a mentor and a network giver as well as a protégé and network seeker. From a purely practical point of view, those you mentor or help are likely to reward you in various ways.

2. Be supportive of your coworkers; avoid being either overly critical or unconcerned with their specific jobs.

3. Exercise caution in the development of office romances, and understand your company's policies regarding such relationships. At the same time, be careful of getting in the middle of the office romances of others.

4. Self-disclose selectively. Be especially careful with disclosures that may be negative or may be too intimate for the relationship you have with your colleagues.

5. Avoid bringing your relationship problems into work with you. Unless you have a very close friend at work or a company counselor you can go to with problems, it's best not to mix at-home and at-work relationship issues. Clearly, this separation of work and relationships is not always possible and not always the best solution; each situation is unique, so it's important to think about the pros and cons of such relationship mixing.

6. Learn the cultural rules of the organization, and unless there's an outstanding reason, don't break them. And don't denigrate them; many consider these rules and norms valuable and personally meaningful and will be offended by any negative attitudes. Further, when appropriate, display **value congruence**, your own agreement with the values of the organization (Shockley-Zalabak, 2004).

7. Stress the positive; negative people are disliked generally, and in organizations they are especially problematic because the negativity they spread diminishes worker satisfaction and productivity. So, be friendly, helpful, and generally positive.

## SUMMARY: HUMAN COMMUNICATION IN THE WORKPLACE

This unit looked at organization communication and defined the nature of the organization, described some of the major organizational messages, and looked at some of the important relationships in organizations.

1. An organization may be defined as (1) an organized (2) group of people (3) who work together (4) to achieve compatible goals.

2. Within any organization, there are both formal and informal structures that are much like channels of communication. These structures define the communication patterns of the organization.

3. All organizations have rules and regulations, rely on a division of labor, use systems of rewards and punishments to motivate workers, and have their own cultures.

4. Organizational communication is the process of sending and receiving verbal and nonverbal messages that convey meaning and that occur within an organizational context.

5. Formal communications are those that are sanctioned by the organization itself and are organizationally focused. They deal with the workings of the organization, with productivity, and with the various jobs served by the employees. Most often they follow the organizational chart.

6. Informal messages are socially sanctioned. They are oriented more to the individual members and their relationship to the organization.

7. Organizational networks are the configurations of channels through which messages pass from one person to another.

8. In any hierarchical organization, communication flows upward, downward, and across, or laterally.

9. *Upward communication* consists of messages sent from the lower levels of a hierarchy to the upper levels—for example, from line worker to manager or from faculty member to dean.

10. *Downward communication* consists of messages sent from the higher levels to the lower levels of the hierarchy; for example, messages sent by managers to workers or by deans to faculty members.

11. *Lateral communication* refers to messages between equals—manager to manager, worker to worker. Such messages may move within the same subdivision or department of the organization or across divisions.

12. Grapevine messages, unlike formal messages, don't follow any of the formal lines of communication established in an organization; rather, they seem to have a life of their own.

13. The term *information overload* refers to the excessive amount of information that workers have to deal with, the lack of clarity in many messages, and the increasing complexity of messages. Information isolation is the opposite and refers to the situation in which certain workers receive little or no information or when some people are excluded from the informal gossip and grapevine messages.

14. Sexual harassment is the sending of unwanted sexual messages. Two general categories of workplace sexual harassment are quid pro quo (Latin term for "something for something") harassment and the creation of a hostile environment.

15. Opinions vary widely concerning workplace romances. On the positive side, the work environment seems a perfect place to meet a potential partner. On the negative side, even if a workplace relationship is good for the lovers themselves, it may not necessarily be good for other workers. More important, perhaps, is that organizations often have very strict rules against office romance.

16. In a mentoring relationship, an experienced individual (mentor) helps to train a less-experienced person (mentee or protégé).

17. Networking is a broad process of enlisting the aid of other people to help you solve a problem or offer insights that bear on your problem—for example, on how to publish your manuscript, where to go for low-cost auto insurance, how to find an apartment, or how to empty your e-mail cache.

# **K**EY **T**ERMS IN HUMAN COMMUNICATION IN THE WORKPLACE

communication networks (p. **283**)
cultural rules (p. **277**)
downward communication (p. **281**)
formal communication (p. **280**)

grapevine (p. **282**)
hostile environment harassment (p. **286**)
informal communication (p. **280**)
information overload (p. **283**)

lateral communication (p. **281**)
mentoring (p. **288**)
message isolation (p. **284**)
networking (p. **288**)
organization (p. **273**)

quid pro quo harassment (p. **286**)
sexual harassment (p. **285**)
upward communication (p. **280**)
value congruence (p. **289**)

# **T**HINKING **C**RITICALLY ABOUT HUMAN COMMUNICATION IN THE WORKPLACE

1. **Facilitating Upward and Downward Communication.** You've been assigned the task of creating a system that will facilitate both upward and downward communication. Explain the system you'll use and the communication principles it is designed to incorporate.

2. **Organizational Behaviors.** How would you describe the communication behaviors of the following organizational members:
   a. The person who is determined to rise to the top in the shortest time possible
   b. The person who just wants to have fun
   c. The person who wants to meet relationship partners

3. **Networking.** Develop a network list of people who might help you get a job in your chosen profession.

4. **Romance on the Job.** You've just taken a position at a new firm and you find that your manager is romantically interested in you. You decide to do a cost-benefit analysis. List all the costs (potential problems and disadvantages) and the benefits (potential advantages) of pursuing this relationship.

5. **Organizational Hierarchies.** Some theorists believe that computer-mediated communication will eventually eliminate the hierarchical structure of organizations, largely because CMC "encourages wider participation, greater candor, and an emphasis on merit over status" (Kollock & Smith, 1996, p. 109). What evidence can you find to support or refute this claim?

# **L**OG**O**N! MYCOMMUNICATIONLAB

### WWW.MYCOMMUNICATIONLAB.COM

Visit MCL for a variety of materials relevant to organizational communication. See, for example, the videos The Interns, Job Promotion, Virtual Miscommunication, and Professional Appearance. Also see the PRPSA, the scale to measure apprehension, particularly the subscale on meetings.

Revisit the small group communication website (www.abacon.com/commstudies/groups) and review any of the material there that you haven't accessed earlier and that will prove relevant to the study of workplace communication.

# UNIT 14 Public Speaking Topics, Audiences, and Research

## MAJOR TOPICS

Introducing Public Speaking

Apprehension in Public Speaking

Step 1: Select Your Topic and Purpose

Step 2: Analyze Your Audience

Step 3: Research Your Topic

## Special Features

As you move up the hierarchy in your personal and professional lives, you'll find an ever greater need for public speaking. At the same time, learning the skills of public speaking will enable you to reap important benefits both now and in the future.

**In this unit you'll learn about:**
- the nature of public speaking.
- the very normal nervousness that most people feel.
- the first three steps for preparing a public speech.

**And you'll learn to:**
- manage your own anxiety and not let it prevent you from developing and presenting effective speeches.
- select an appropriate speech topic and purpose.
- analyze and adapt to your audiences.
- research your topic.

Public speaking is one of the essential skills people need to function effectively in today's society. The higher you move in any chain of command—say, from intern, to junior analyst, to manager, to CEO—the more important public speaking becomes. This text explains these essential skills, the skills you'll need to prepare and present effective public speeches. As you'll see throughout this and the next five units, these skills will also prove useful to you in a variety of other situations as well.

## INTRODUCING PUBLIC SPEAKING

Although public speaking principles were probably developed soon after our species began to talk, it was in ancient Greece and Rome that our Western tradition of public speaking got its start. This Greco-Roman tradition has been enriched by the experiments, surveys, field studies, and historical studies that have been done since classical times and that continue to be done today.

Aristotle's *Rhetoric*, written some 2,300 years ago in ancient Greece, was one of the earliest systematic studies of public speaking. It was in this work that the three kinds of persuasive appeals—*logos* (or logical proof), *pathos* (emotional appeals), and *ethos* (appeals based on the character of the speaker)—were introduced. This three-part division is still followed today; Unit 18 discusses these in more detail.

Roman rhetoricians added to the work of the Greeks. Quintilian, who taught in Rome during the first century, built an entire educational system—from childhood through adulthood—based on the development of the effective and responsible orator. Over the following 2,000 years, the study of public speaking continued to grow and develop.

Contemporary public speaking—the kind discussed in this text—builds on this classical heritage but also incorporates insights from the humanities, the social and behavioral sciences, and computer science and information technology. Likewise, perspectives from different cultures are being integrated into our present study of public speaking. Table 14.1 shows some of the contributors to contemporary public speaking and illustrates the wide research and theory base from which the principles of this discipline are drawn.

## The Benefits of Public Speaking

Here are just a few of the benefits you'll derive from this section of the text and from your course work in public speaking.

### Improve Your Personal and Social Abilities

Public speaking provides training in a variety of personal and social competencies. For example, you'll learn to manage your fear of communication situations, develop greater self-confidence and self-presentation skills, enhance your own personal and interpersonal power and influence, and regulate and adapt your listening to the specific situation.

### Improve Your Academic and Career Skills

As you learn public speaking, you'll also learn a wide variety of academic and career skills, many of which are largely communication skills (as you can tell from reading the employment ads, especially for middle management positions in just about every field you can name). For example, you will learn to:

- conduct research efficiently and effectively, using the latest and the best techniques available.

## Table 14.1 Growth and Development of Public Speaking

| Academic Roots | Contributions to Contemporary Public Speaking |
|---|---|
| Classical rhetoric | Emphasis on substance; ethical responsibilities of the speaker; use of a combination of logical, ethical, and emotional appeals; the strategies of organization |
| Literary and rhetorical criticism | Approaches to and standards for evaluation; insights into style and language |
| Philosophy | Emphasis on the logical validity of arguments; continuing contribution to ethics |
| Public address | Insights into how famous speakers dealt with varied purposes and audiences to achieve desired effects |
| Psychology | How language is made easier to understand and remember; principles of attitude and behavior change; emphasis on speech effects |
| General semantics | Emphasis on using language to describe reality accurately; techniques for avoiding common thinking errors that faulty language usage creates |
| Communication theory | Insights on information transmission; the importance of viewing the whole of the communication act; the understanding of such concepts as feedback, noise, channel, and message |
| Computer science and information technology | The virtual audience; design, outlining, and presentation software; search tools for research; easily accessed databases |
| Interpersonal communication | Transactionalism; emphasis on mutual influence of speaker and audience. |
| Sociology | Data on audiences' attitudes, values, opinions, and beliefs and how these influence exposure to and responses to messages |
| Anthropology | Insights into the attitudes, beliefs, and values of different cultures and how these influence communication in general and public speaking in particular |

- critically analyze and evaluate arguments and evidence from any and all sources.

- understand human motivation and make effective use of your insights in persuasive encounters.

- develop an effective communication style (whether for conversation or for that important job interview) that you feel comfortable with.

- give and respond appropriately to criticism so as to increase your insight into your own strengths and weaknesses.

- communicate your competence, character, and charisma to make yourself believable.

## Improve Your Public Speaking Abilities

Speakers aren't born; they're made. Through instruction, exposure to different speeches, experience with diverse audiences, feedback on your own speeches, and individual learning experiences, you can become an effective speaker. Regardless of your present level of competence, you can improve through proper training.

At the end of your public speaking training, you'll be a more competent, confident, and effective public speaker. You'll also be a more effective listener—more open yet more critical, more empathic yet more discriminating. And you'll emerge a more competent and discerning critic of public communication. You'll learn to organize and explain complex concepts and processes clearly and effectively to a wide variety of listeners. You'll learn to support an argument with all the available means of persuasion and to present a persuasive appeal to audiences of varied types.

As a leader (and in many ways you can look at this course as training in leadership skills), you'll need the skills of effective communication to help preserve a free and open society. As a speaker who wants your message understood and accepted, as a listener who needs to evaluate and critically analyze ideas and arguments before making decisions, and as a critic who needs to evaluate and judge the thousands of public communications you hear every day, you will draw on the public speaking skills you'll learn here.

## Beliefs about Public Speaking

A good way to begin your study of public speaking is to examine your own beliefs about public speaking and public speakers. Compare some common beliefs with the research and theory that bear on these beliefs:

*Belief:* Good public speakers are born, not made.

*Research finds* that effective public speaking is actually a learned skill. Although some people are born brighter or more extroverted—which will certainly help in public speaking—all people can improve their abilities and become more effective public speakers.

*Belief:* The more speeches you give, the better you'll become at it.

*Research finds* that this is true only if you practice effective skills. If you practice bad habits, you're more likely to grow less effective than to become more effective; consequently, it's important to learn and follow the principles of effectiveness.

*Belief:* You'll never be a good public speaker if you're nervous giving speeches.

*Research finds* that most speakers are nervous; managing, not eliminating, the fear will enable you to become effective regardless of your current level of anxiety. In fact, your fear may actually encourage you to prepare more thoroughly and to practice more often, which will contribute to more effective speaking.

## MEDIA WATCH

### THE DIFFUSION OF INNOVATIONS

Mass media audiences are even more diverse and varied than public speaking audiences. One of the most interesting theories to illustrate this diversity is the theory of the *diffusion of innovations*, which focuses on the ways in which mass communications influence people to adopt something new or different. *Diffusion* refers to the spread of new information or innovation through society. The innovation may be of any type—soft contact lenses, laptop computers, PDAs, PowerPoint software for public speaking. In this theory the word *adoption* refers to people's positive reactions to and use of the innovation. Research distinguishes five types of adopters:

- The *innovators* are the first to adopt the innovation. They are not necessarily the originators of the new idea, but they're the ones who take the innovation to the point that others become aware of it.

- The early adopters, sometimes called the "influentials," legitimize the idea and make it acceptable to large numbers of people.

- The early majority follows the influentials and further legitimates the innovation.

- The late majority adopts the innovation after about half the population has adopted it.

- The laggards are the last group to adopt the innovation and may take the lead from any of the preceding groups.

One last group, the *diehards*, never adopt the innovation. These include accountants who continue to do tax returns without the aid of tax-preparation software and lawyers and doctors who don't avail themselves of computerized databases.

### Increasing Media Literacy

*Where would you position yourself on this diffusion of innovation curve? In what ways do the media influence you to adopt innovations? Which media are most influential with you? With your friends?*

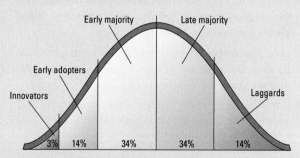

**The Five Types of Adopters**

Source: Reprinted with permission of The Free Press, a Division of Simon & Schuster, Inc., from The Diffusion of Inventions, Fourth Edition, by Everett M. Rogers. Copyright © 1995 by Everett M. Rogers, Copyright © 1962, 1971, 1983 by The Free Press.

*Belief:* It's best to memorize your speech, especially if you're fearful.

*Research finds* that memorizing your speech is one of the worst things you can do; there are easier ways to deal with fear.

*Belief:* The skills of public speaking are similar throughout the world.

*Research finds* that they are not; the techniques of public speaking are culture specific. In other words, what proves effective with an Asian audience may not work with audiences in the United States or in Latin America, and vice versa.

## A Definition of Public Speaking

In *public speaking*, as defined in Unit 1, a speaker presents a relatively continuous message to a relatively large audience in a unique context (see Figure 14.1). Like all forms of communication, public speaking is transactional (Watzlawick, Beavin, & Jackson 1967; Watzlawick 1978): Each element in the public speaking process depends on and interacts with all other elements. For example, the way in which you organize a speech will depend on such factors as the speech topic, the specific audience, the purpose you hope to achieve, and a host of other variables—all of which are explained in the remainder of this unit and in the units to follow.

Especially important is the mutual interaction and influence between speaker and listeners. True, when you give a speech, you do most of the speaking and the listeners do most of the listening. How-

ever, the listeners also send messages in the form of feedback—for example, applause, bored looks, nods of agreement or disagreement, and attentive glances. The audience also influences how you'll prepare and present your speech. It influences your arguments, your language, your method of organization, and, in fact, every choice you make. You would not, for example, present the same speech on saving money to high school students as you would to senior citizens.

## APPREHENSION IN PUBLIC SPEAKING

Being fearful of giving a public speech is perfectly normal. Everyone experiences some degree of fear in the relatively formal public speaking situation. After all, in public speaking you're the sole focus of attention, and you are usually being evaluated for your performance.

Although you may at first view apprehension as harmful, it's not necessarily so. In fact, apprehension can work for you. Fear can energize you. It may motivate you to work a little harder to produce a speech that will be better than it might have been. Further, the audience cannot see the apprehension that you may be experiencing. Even though you may think that the audience can hear your heart beat faster and faster, they can't. They can't see your knees tremble. They can't sense your dry throat—at least not most of the time.

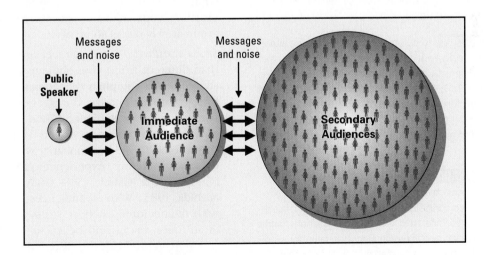

**FIGURE 14.1    Process and Elements of Public Speaking**

This diagram is designed to illustrate the interplay of elements in the public speaking process and to emphasize that there are a variety of audiences of public speaking: (1) the immediate audience—the audience that hears the speaker as he or she is speaking, whether in person, on television, on the Internet, or even via cell phone—and (2) the additional audiences that get the material second hand; for example, people who read the speech, read about the speech, or hear from those who heard the speech, from those who heard about the speech from immediate audience members, or from those who heard about the speech from those who heard about the speech.

Before beginning the actual speech preparation process, let's look first at fear of public speaking, or what is now called **communication apprehension**. People experience apprehension in all forms of communication (as illustrated throughout this text), but public speaking apprehension is the most common (Richmond & McCroskey, 1998; Daly, McCroskey, Ayres, Hopf, & Ayres, 1997). Take the following apprehension test to measure your own fear of speaking in public.

# TEST YOURSELF

## How Apprehensive Are You in Public Speaking?

This questionnaire consists of six statements concerning your feelings about public speaking. Indicate the degree to which each statement applies to you, using the following scale: 1 = strongly agree; 2 = agree; 3 = are undecided; 4 = disagree; 5 = strongly disagree. There are no right or wrong answers. Don't be concerned that some of the statements are similar to others. Work quickly; just record your immediate response.

____ **1.** I have no fear of giving a speech.

____ **2.** Certain parts of my body feel very tense and rigid while giving a speech.

____ **3.** I feel relaxed while giving a speech.

____ **4.** My thoughts become confused and jumbled when I am giving a speech.

____ **5.** I face the prospect of giving a speech with confidence.

____ **6.** While giving a speech, I get so nervous that I forget facts I really know.

**HOW DID YOU DO?** To obtain your public speaking apprehension score, begin with the number 18 (selected so that you won't wind up with negative numbers) and add to it the scores for items 1, 3, and 5. Then, from this total, subtract the scores from items 2, 4, and 6. A score above 18 shows some degree of apprehension. Most people score above 18, so if you scored relatively high, you're among the vast majority of people.

**WHAT WILL YOU DO?** As you read the suggestions for reducing apprehension in the text that follows, consider what you can do to incorporate these into your own public speaking experiences. Consider too how these suggestions might be useful in reducing apprehension more generally; for example, in social situations and in small groups and meetings.

Source: From James C. McCroskey, *An Introduction to Rhetorical Communication* (9th ed.). Published by Allyn & Bacon, Boston, MA. Copyright © 2006 by Pearson Education. Adapted by permission of the publisher.

# Reducing Your Apprehension

The following suggestions will help you overcome communication apprehension in public speaking as well as in small group and interpersonal communication situations (Beatty, 1988; Richmond & McCroskey, 1998).

- *Gain experience:* New and different situations such as public speaking are likely to make you anxious, so try to reduce their newness and differentness. The best way to do this is to get as much public speaking experience as you can. With experience, your initial fears and anxieties will give way to feelings of control, comfort, and pleasure. Try also to familiarize yourself with the public speaking context. For example, try to rehearse in the room in which you will give your speech.

- *Think positively:* When you see yourself as inferior—when, for example, you feel that others are better speakers or that they know more than you do—anxiety increases. Therefore, think positive thoughts and build your confidence through preparation. At the same time, maintain realistic expectations for yourself. Fear increases when you feel that you can't meet your own or your audience's expectations (Ayres, 1986).

- *See public speaking as conversation:* When you are the center of attention (as you are in public speaking), you feel especially conspicuous, and this often increases anxiety. It may help to think of public speaking as another type of conversation (some theorists call it "enlarged conversation"). Or, if you're comfortable talking in small groups, visualize your audience as an enlarged small group; it may dispel some of the anxiety you feel.

- *Stress similarity:* When you feel similar to (rather than different from) your audience, your anxiety should lessen (Stephan & Stephan, 1992). Therefore, try to emphasize the likenesses between yourself and your audience. When cultural differences exist between you and your audience, you're likely to feel less similarity with your listeners and therefore experience greater anxiety (Gudykunst & Nishida, 1984; Gudykunst, Yang, & Nishida, 1985). With all audiences, but especially with multicultural listeners, stress commonalities in attitudes, values, and beliefs; it will make you feel more at one with your listeners.

- *Prepare and practice thoroughly:* Much of the fear you experience is a fear of failure. Practice and preparation will lessen the possibility of failure and the accompanying apprehension. Because apprehension is greatest at the beginning of the speech, try memorizing the first few sentences of

## Theory and Research   Performance Visualization

### UNDERSTANDING

The theory of **performance visualization** argues that you can reduce the outward signs of apprehension and the negative thinking that often creates anxiety through a few simple techniques (Ayres & Hopf, 1992, 1993; Ayres, Hopf, & Ayres, 1994).

First, develop a positive attitude and a positive self-perception. Visualize yourself in the role of the effective public speaker. Visualize yourself walking to the front of the room—fully and totally confident, fully in control of the situation. The audience pays rapt attention to your talk and bursts into wild applause as you finish. Throughout this visualization, avoid all negative thoughts. As you visualize yourself as this effective speaker, take note of how you walk, look at your listeners, handle your notes, and respond to questions; especially, think about how you feel about the public speaking experience.

Second, model your performance on that of an especially effective speaker. View a particularly competent public speaker on video, for example, and make a mental "movie" of it. As you review the actual video and mental movie, shift yourself into the role of speaker; become this speaker.

### Working with Theories and Research

*Try performance visualization as you rehearse for your next speech. Did it help reduce your apprehension?*

---

your speech. If there are complicated facts or figures, be sure to write these out; plan to read them so as to remove your worries of forgetting them.

- *Move about and breathe deeply:* Physical activity—large bodily movements as well as small movements of the hands, face, and head—lessens apprehension. Using a presentation aid, for example, will temporarily divert attention from you and will allow you to get rid of your excess energy. Also, try breathing deeply a few times before getting up to speak. Your body will relax, and this will help you overcome your initial fear of walking to the front of the room.

- *Avoid chemicals as tension relievers:* Unless prescribed by a physician, chemical means for reducing apprehension are not a good idea. Tranquilizers, marijuana, or artificial stimulants are likely to create problems rather than reduce them. They're likely to impair your ability to remember the parts of your speech, to accurately read audience feedback, and to regulate the timing of your speech. And, of course, alcohol does nothing to reduce public speaking apprehension (Himle, Abelson, & Haghightgou, 1999).

With the nature of public speaking and its benefits in mind and with an understanding of communication apprehension and some ways for managing it, we can look at the essential steps for preparing an

**APPREHENSION MANAGEMENT**

This is your first experience with public speaking and you're very nervous. You're afraid you'll forget your speech or stumble somehow so you're wondering if it would be a good idea to alert your audience to your nervousness.

WHAT DO YOU SAY?

---

**Theory and Research**  **UNDERSTANDING**  Systematic Desensitization

The theory of **systematic desensitization** holds that you can reduce fear through a process of gradually adapting to lesser and then successively greater versions of the thing you fear. This technique has been used to deal with many kinds of fear, including public speaking fears (Wolpe 1957; Goss, Thompson, & Olds, 1978; Richmond & Mc-Croskey, 1998). In the case of public speaking, the general idea of systematic desensitization is to create a hierarchy of behaviors leading up to the desired but feared behavior. One specific hierarchy might look like this:

5.  Giving a speech in class

4.  Introducing another speaker to the class

3.  Speaking in a group in front of the class

2.  Answering a question in class

1.  Asking a question in class

You begin at the bottom of this hierarchy and rehearse behavior number 1 mentally over a period of days until you can clearly visualize asking a question in class without any uncomfortable anxiety. Once you can accomplish this, move to the second level. Here you visualize a somewhat more threatening behavior: answering a question. Once you can do this, move to the third level, and so on until you get to the desired behavior.

---

**Working with Theories and Research**

*Create a hierarchy for dealing with communication apprehension. Use small steps to help you get from one step to the next more easily.*

---

effective public speech (Figure 14.2): (1) Select your topic and purpose; (2) analyze your audience; (3) research your topic; (4) develop your thesis and main points; (5) support your main points; (6) organize your speech materials; (7) construct your conclusion, introduction, and transitions; (8) outline your speech; (9) word your speech; and (10) rehearse and deliver your speech. The first three of these steps are discussed in this unit; the remaining seven are discussed in the next two units.

## STEP 1: SELECT YOUR TOPIC AND PURPOSE

Your first step in preparing to give a speech is to select your topic and purpose.

### Your Topic

As you begin to think about public speaking, and especially about your own speech, perhaps the first question you have is "What do I speak about?"—that is,

what **topic** would be appropriate? The answer to this question will change as your life situation changes; in the years ahead you'll most likely speak on topics that grow out of your job or your social or political activities. In the classroom, however, where your objective is to learn the skills of public speaking, there are literally thousands of subjects to talk about. Nevertheless, the question remains: "What do I speak about?" To answer this question, focus on three related questions: "What makes a good topic?" "How do I find such a topic?" and "How do I focus or limit my topic?"

### A Good Public Speaking Topic

A good public speaking topic is one that deals with matters of substance, is appropriate to you and the audience, and is culturally sensitive. These three characteristics suggest some guidelines for selecting a good topic. Let's consider each briefly.

**Substantive.** The most important criterion of a good topic is that it be *substantive*—that it deal with matters of substance. Select a topic that is important enough to merit the time and attention of a group of intelligent people. Ask yourself: Would this topic engage the attention of my classmates? Would a reputable newspaper cover such a topic? Would students find this topic relevant to their social or professional lives?

**Appropriate.** Select a topic that is *appropriate to you as the speaker*. For example, if you're male, it probably isn't a good idea to give a speech on the stages of childbirth. On the other hand, if you're female and have just given birth, this might be a good topic. If you've never been incarcerated, then a speech on what life is like in prison is probably not going to ring true to your audience. If you're known to be a big spender, then giving a speech on how to eke by on $3 a day is not likely to be well received by your listeners. The best way to look at this criterion is to ask if— given what the audience already knows about you and what you'll tell them during your speech—your listeners will see you as a knowledgeable and believable spokesperson on this topic. If the answer is yes, then you have a topic appropriate to you as a speaker. If the answer is no, then it will probably be useful to continue your search for an appropriate topic. (The next section will focus on this issue.)

Also, select a topic that is *appropriate to your audience in terms of their interests and needs*. Giving a speech to students in your class on the need to have a computer would be inappropriate, simply because they already know the importance of

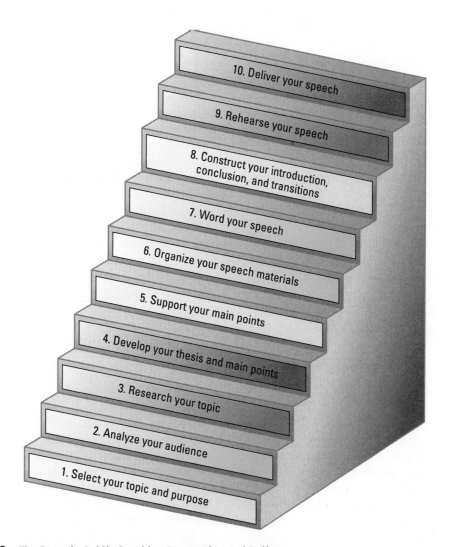

10. Deliver your speech

9. Rehearse your speech

8. Construct your introduction, conclusion, and transitions

7. Word your speech

6. Organize your speech materials

5. Support your main points

4. Develop your thesis and main points

3. Research your topic

2. Analyze your audience

1. Select your topic and purpose

**FIGURE 14.2  The Steps in Public Speaking Preparation and Delivery**

Speakers differ in the order in which they follow these steps. Some speakers, for example, prefer to begin with audience analysis; they ask themselves what the audience is interested in and then select the topic and purpose. Some speakers prefer to identify their main points before conducting extensive research, whereas others prefer to allow the points to emerge from the research. The order presented here will prove useful to most speakers for most situations, but you can vary the order to serve your purposes. As long as you cover all steps, you should be in good shape.

# ASK THE RESEARCHER

## Nervousness

*I'm nervous giving speeches, and I feel this comes through to the audience and I'm not as effective as I'd like to be. What can I do to help reduce and manage my apprehension? Is there anything I can do to hide the symptoms of nervousness from the audience?*

Feeling anxious and nervous prior to a presentation is normal. Try these ideas before a presentation:

1. Know your subject matter better than the audience.
2. Dress and look like a competent communicator.
3. Spend time in the room in which you are to give the presentation and practice.
4. Relax and reassure yourself that you have the knowledge and skills to give a successful presentation.
5. Review videos of previous students who have given presentations.
6. Think positive thoughts, not negative ones, and attempt to relax.

During the presentation, look at a positive person first. Looking at this one positive person can lower your nervousness. Next, look at other members of the audience. Scan the audience on a regular basis, avoiding negative persons (e.g., the person who is asleep or yawning). Practice your nonverbal immediacy skills.

Remember that immediacy behaviors on your part will generate a positive audience response and can generate an easy rapport with your audience.

For further information: Richmond, V. P., & McCroskey, J. C. (1998). *Communication: Apprehension, avoidance, and effectiveness* (5th ed.). Boston: Allyn & Bacon. And Mottet, T., Richmond, V. P., & McCroskey, J. C. (2005). *Instructional communication: Rhetorical and relational perspectives*. Boston: Allyn & Bacon. Or go to www .virginiapeckrichmondphd.com or www.jamescmccroskey.com.

**Virginia Peck Richmond** (Ph.D., University of Nebraska) is a professor and chair of the department of Communication Studies at the University of Alabama, Birmingham, where she teaches and conducts research in the areas of instructional communication, nonverbal communication, and organizational communication.

the computer. But that same topic might be quite appropriate if given at a senior center where most of the members did not own computers. Giving a speech advocating a specific religious belief might well prove insulting to members of the audience who didn't share your religious beliefs. Yet that same speech might be very well received by members of a particular religious congregation. Always look to your audience when thinking about a topic, and try to gauge their reaction to it. After all, your audience is giving you their time and attention; selecting a topic that is responsive to their needs and interests seems only fair.

**Culturally Sensitive.** A good topic is *culturally sensitive*, so select a topic that will not offend members of other cultures (who may even be in your audience). At the same time, recognize that we live in a time when a person's level of cultural sensitivity is taken as a sign of education and sophistication, qualities that can only help a speaker.

To take one example, in many Arab, Asian, and African cultures, discussing sex in an audience of both men and women would be considered obscene and offensive. In Scandinavian cultures, on the other hand, sex is expected to be discussed openly and without embarrassment or discomfort. Here are some addi-

## TOPIC APPROPRIATENESS

Stephen, a 20-year-old student, gave a speech on flower arranging—a topic so unexpected that members of the audience giggled and avoided eye contact with the speaker throughout the speech. You're called upon to offer a critique of the speech.

WHAT DO YOU SAY?

tional examples of topics that intercultural experts recommend that visiting Americans avoid. These **taboo** topics change with the times, however, so what is true today may not be true tomorrow (Axtell, 1993; Allan & Burridge, 2006):

- In the Caribbean, avoid discussions of race, local politics, and religion.
- In Colombia, avoid politics and the criticism of bullfighting.
- In Egypt, avoid Middle Eastern politics.
- In Japan, avoid discussion of World War II.
- In Mexico, avoid talking about the Mexican-American War and illegal aliens.
- In the Philippines, avoid discussing politics, religion, corruption, or foreign aid.
- In South Korea, don't talk about internal politics or voice criticism of the government, socialism, or communism.
- In Spain, avoid discussions of family, religion, or jobs, and refrain from making negative comments on bullfighting.

## Finding Topics

Here are five ways to find topics: *yourself, brainstorming, surveys, news items,* and *topic lists.*

**Yourself.** Perhaps your first step in thinking about appropriate speech topics is to look at yourself. What are you interested in? What engages your time and interest? If you were in a bookstore, what book topics would encourage you to flip through a book? What titles of magazine articles would entice you to thumb through a magazine? In short, think about your own interests; they may be similar to your audience's.

As you consider your interests, also consider your own unique experiences. Have you been a part of well-known events or lived in different places? Do you have special talents? Are you knowledgeable about odd or different topics? What are your hobbies? If you're a philatelist, a speech on unique stamps or the value of stamps or the way in which stamps are printed might prove interesting. If you're a spelunker, perhaps a speech on caves—how they form and what they mean to the ecology—might prove interesting.

If you plan a speech on a topic that you're interested in and want to learn more about, you'll enjoy and profit from the entire experience a great deal more. The research that you do for your speech, for example, will be more meaningful; the facts you uncover will be more interesting. At the same time, your enthusiasm for your topic is likely to make your delivery more exciting, less anxiety provoking, and more engaging to the audience. All around, you win by selecting a topic in which you're especially interested or to which you have a special connection.

**Brainstorming.** Another useful method for finding a topic is *brainstorming* (see Unit 10), a technique designed to enable you to generate lots of topics in a relatively short time (DeVito, 1996; Osborn, 1957). To apply brainstorming to your public speaking "problem"—namely, "What will I talk about?"—you first record any and all ideas that occur to you. Allow your mind to free-associate. Don't censor yourself;

instead, allow your ideas to flow as freely as possible. Record all your thoughts, regardless of how silly or inappropriate they may seem. Write them down or record them on tape. Try to generate as many ideas as possible. The more ideas you think of, the better your chances of finding a suitable topic in your list. After you've generated a sizable list—it should take you no longer than five minutes—read over the list or replay the tape. Do any of the topics on your list suggest other topics? If so, write these down as well. Can you combine or extend your ideas? Which ideas seem workable?

**Surveys.** Look at some of the national and regional *surveys* concerning what people think is important—polls that identify the significant issues, the urgent problems. Survey data are now easier than ever to get, because many of the larger poll results are available on the Internet. For example, the Gallup Organization maintains a website at http://www.gallup.com that includes national and international surveys on political, social, consumer, and other issues speakers often talk about. The Polling Report website also will prove useful; it provides a wealth of polling data on issues such as political science, business, journalism, health, and social science (www.pollingreport.com). Other sources are search directories, such as Hotbot or Yahoo!, where you can examine the major directory topics and any subdivisions of those you'd care to pursue—a process that's explained later in this unit. Many search engines and browsers provide lists of "hot topics," which are often useful starting points. These topics are exactly the topics that people are talking about and therefore often make excellent speech topics.

Or you can conduct a survey yourself. Roam through the nonfiction section of your bookstore (online, if you prefer—for example, at Amazon, www.amazon.com; Barnes & Noble, www.bn.com; or Borders, www.borders.com) and you'll quickly develop a list of the topics book buyers consider important. A glance at your newspaper's best-seller list will give you an even quicker overview.

**News Items.** Other useful starting points are *news items* in newspapers and newsmagazines. Here you'll find the important international and domestic issues, the financial issues, and the social issues all conveniently packaged in one place. The editorial page and the letters to the editor also are useful indicators of what people are concerned about.

Newsmagazines such as *Time* and *Newsweek* and financial magazines such as *Forbes*, *Money*, and *Fortune* (in print or online) will provide a wealth of suggestions. Similarly, news shows such as *20/20*, *60 Minutes*, and *Meet the Press* and even the ubiquitous talk shows (and their corresponding websites) often identify the very issues that people are concerned with and on which there are conflicting points of view.

**Topic Lists.** One of the easiest ways to examine and select a potential topic is to look at some of the *topic lists* that are available. For example, The Dictionary of Topics (available at www.myspeechlab.com) lists hundreds of appropriate topics for informative and persuasive speeches. It's simply a dictionary-like listing of subjects, within which each topic is broken down into several subtopics. These subtopics should begin to suggest potential subjects for your informative and persuasive speeches. A small sample of this dictionary is presented in Table 14.2. There are also useful topic lists that have been compiled by various communication and English instructors. For example, the University of Hawaii maintains a website, Topic Selection Helper, which lists hundreds of topics (www.hawaii.edu/mauispeech/html/infotopichelp.html). Similarly, Cincinnati State Technical and Community College has lists for informative and persuasive speeches at http://faculty.cinstate.cc.oh.us/gesellsc/publicspeaking/topics.html.

Some websites contain topic generators where you can repeatedly press a button and view a wide variety of topics. For example, WritingFix (www.writingfix.com) helps you with topics for writing (which can often, though not always, be adapted for public speaking). And McMaster eBusiness Research Center (http://merc.mcmaster.ca/mclaren/ebiztopics.html) maintains a topic generator for business topics.

There is another class of websites that will sell you speeches and term papers for a fee, and in searching for topics you're likely to run across these sites. Avoid these websites. Many colleges now have software to identify plagiarism, so it's easy to get caught; and considering that the consequences are often severe, it's not worth going there. Finally, using such sites and services will keep you from learning critical skills that you'll need in your professional life.

## Limiting Topics

Many beginning speakers make the error of trying to cover a huge topic in too short a period of time. The inevitable result is that such speakers cannot cover anything in depth; they touch on everything superficially. To be suitable for a public speech, a topic must be limited in scope; it must be narrowed down so as to fit the time restrictions and yet permit some depth of coverage.

Another reason to narrow your topic is that it will help you focus your collection of research materials.

## Table 14.2  The Dictionary of Topics

This table presents just a few general topics to illustrate how you can use existing lists as ideas for speech topics. Lists like these will stimulate you to think of subjects dealing with topics you're interested in but may not have thought of as appropriate to a public speech. Each topic is broken down into several subtopics that should stimulate you to see these as potential ideas for your informative and persuasive speeches. Just a small sampling of topics is presented here; a much more extensive "dictionary of topics" may be found at **www.mycommunicationlab.com**.

*Abortion* arguments for and against; techniques of; religious dimension; legal views; differing views of

*Academic freedom* nature of; censorship; teachers' role in curriculum development; and government; and research; restrictions on

*Acupuncture* nature of; development of; current practices in; effectiveness of; dangers of

*Adoption* agencies for; procedures; difficulties in; illegal; concealment of biological parents; search for birth parents

*Advertising* techniques; expenditures; ethical; unethical; subliminal; leading agencies; history of; slogans

*Age* ageism; aging processes; aid to the aged; discrimination against the aged; treatment of the aged; different cultural views of aging; sex differences

*Aggression* aggressive behavior in animals; in humans; as innate; as learned; and territoriality

*Agriculture* science of; history of; in ancient societies; technology of; theories of

*Alcoholism* nature of; Alcoholics Anonymous; Al-Anon; abstinence; among the young; treatment of

*Amnesty* in draft evasion; in criminal law; and pardons; in Civil War; in Vietnam War; conditions of

*Animals* experimentation; intelligence of; aggression in; ethology; and communication

If your topic is too broad, you'll be forced to review a lot more research material than you're going to need. If you narrow your topic, you can search for research materials more efficiently. Here are three methods for narrowing and limiting your topic: *topoi*, *tree diagrams*, and *search directories*.

**Topoi, the System of Topics.** Topoi, the system of topics, is a technique that originated with the classical rhetorics of ancient Greece and Rome but today is used more widely as a stimulus to creative thinking (DeVito, 1996). Using this method of **topoi**, you ask yourself a series of questions about your general subject. The process will help you see divisions of your general topic on which you might want to focus. Table 14.3 on page 304 provides an example; the column on the left contains seven general questions (Who? What? Why? When? Where? How? and So?) and a series of subquestions (which will vary depending on your topic). The right column illustrates how some of the questions on the left might suggest specific aspects of the general subject of "homelessness."

**Tree Diagrams.** **Tree diagrams** help you to divide your topic repeatedly into its constituent parts. Starting with the general topic, you divide it into its parts. Then you take one of these parts and divide it into its

parts. You continue with this dividing process until the topic seems manageable—until you believe you can reasonably cover it in some depth in the time allotted.

For example, suppose you begin with the topic of mass communication and choose television programs as the first general subtopic. Television programs, without some limitation, would take a lifetime to cover adequately. So you might divide this topic into such subtopics as comedy, children's programs, educational programs, news, movies, reality programs, soap operas, game shows, and sports. You might then take one of these topics, say comedy, and divide it into subtopics. Perhaps you might consider it on a time basis and divide television comedy into its significant time periods: pre-1960, 1961–1999, 2000 to the present. Or you might focus on situation comedies. Here you might examine a topic such as women in situation comedies, race relations in situation comedies, or family relationships in situation comedies. The resulting topic is at least beginning to look manageable. Figure 14.3 on page 305 illustrates a tree diagram, showing another way of subdividing the general topic of television programs.

**Search Directories.** A more technologically sophisticated way of both selecting and limiting your topic is to let a **search directory** do some of the

## Table 14.3 Topoi: The System of Topics

These questions should enable you to use general topics to generate more specific ideas for your speeches. Try this system on any one of the topics listed in the Dictionary of Topics at www.mycommunicationlab.com. You'll be amazed at how many topics you'll be able to find. Your problem will quickly change from "What can I speak on?" to "Which one of these should I speak on?" Here's an example on the topic of homelessness.

| General Questions | Subject-Specific Questions |
| --- | --- |
| *Who?* Who is he or she? Who is responsible? To whom was it done? | Who are the homeless? Who is the typical homeless person? Who is responsible for the increase in homelessness? Who cares for the homeless? |
| *What?* What is it? What effects does it have? What is it like? What is it different from? What are some examples? | What does it mean to be homeless? What does homelessness do to the people themselves? What does homelessness do to the society in general? What does homelessness mean to you and me? |
| *Why?* Why is there homelessness? Why does it happen? Why does it not happen? | Why are there so many homeless people? Why did this happen? Why does it happen in the larger cities more than in smaller towns? Why is it more prevalent in some countries than in others? |
| *When?* When did it happen? When will it occur? When will it end? | When did homelessness become so prevalent? When does it occur in the life of a person? |
| *Where?* Where did it come from? Where is it going? Where is it now? | Where is homelessness most prevalent? Where is there an absence of homelessness? |
| *How?* How does it work? How is it used? How do you do it? How do you operate it? How is it organized? | How does someone become homeless? How can we help the homeless? How can we prevent others from becoming homeless? |
| *So?* What does it mean? What is important about it? Why should I be concerned with this? Who cares? | Why is homelessness such an important social problem? Why must we be concerned with homelessness? How does all this affect me? |

work for you. A search directory is a nested list of topics. You go from the general to the specific by selecting a topic, then a subdivision of that topic, then a subdivision of that subdivision. Eventually you'll be directed to relatively specific areas and websites that will suggest topics that may be suitable for a classroom speech.

## Your Purpose

The *purpose* of your speech is the goal you want to achieve; it identifies the effect that you want your speech to have on your audience. In constructing your speech you'll first identify your general purpose and then your specific purpose.

### General Purposes

Since you're now in a course in learning public speaking skills, your general purpose will likely be chosen for you. In this way, the classroom is like the real world. The situation, the audience you'll address, the nature of your job will dictate your general purpose; that is, whether your speech is to be informative or persuasive. If you're a lawyer giving a closing at a trial, you're speech must be persuasive. If you're an engineer explaining blueprints to clients, your speech must be informative. If you're a college professor, your speeches will be largely informative; if you're a politician, they will be mostly persuasive.

To inform and to persuade are the two general purposes of most public speeches. Another purpose is to serve some special occasion function—to toast, to bid farewell, to present an award. Special occasion speeches are in many ways combinations of informative and persuasive purposes.

In the **informative speech** (for example, a speech composed to inform your audience about a career seminar), you seek to create understanding: to clarify, to enlighten, to correct misunderstandings, to demonstrate how something works. In this type of speech, you'll rely most heavily on materials that amplify—examples, illustrations, definitions, testimony, visual aids, and the like.

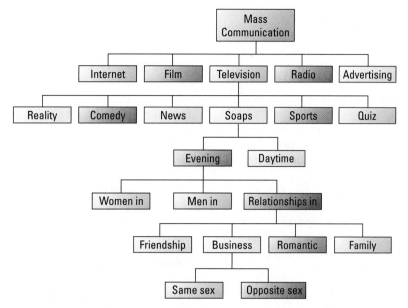

**FIGURE 14.3   A Tree Diagram for Limiting Speech Topics**

How would you draw a tree diagram for limiting topics beginning with such general subjects as immigration, education, sports, transportation, or politics? An alternative method for limiting topics with the "fishbone diagram" may be found at **www.mycommunicationlab.com**.

In the **persuasive speech** (for example, a speech aimed at persuading your audience to vote in the next election), you try to influence attitudes or behaviors; you seek to strengthen or change existing attitudes or to get the audience to take some action. In this type of speech, you'll rely heavily on ma-

terials that offer proof—on evidence, argument, and psychological appeals, for example.

In the **special occasion speech**, which contains elements of information and persuasion, you might, for example, introduce another speaker or a group of speakers, present a tribute, try to secure the good-

---

# Building Communication Skills   Limiting a Topic

Here are some overly general speech topics. Limit each of these topics to a subtopic that would be reasonable for a 5- to 10-minute speech.

1. Dangerous sports
2. Race relations
3. Parole
4. Censorship on the Internet
5. Ecological problems
6. Problems faced by college students
7. Morality
8. Health and fitness
9. Ethical issues in politics
10. Urban violence

*As a general rule, focus on depth rather than breadth; avoid trying to cover too much in short speeches.*

will of the listeners, toast your friends' anniversary, or "just" entertain your listeners.

## Specific Purposes

Once you have chosen your general purpose, develop your **specific purpose** by identifying more precisely what you aim to accomplish. For example, in an informative speech, your specific purpose will identify the information you want to convey to your audience. Here are a few examples on the topic of stem cell research:

General purpose: To inform.

Specific purposes: To inform my audience of the differences between embryonic and adult stem cell research.

To inform my audience of two areas of stem cell research progress.

To inform my audience of the current federal regulations for funding stem cell research.

You may find it helpful to view your specific informative purposes in behavioral terms, identifying how you want the audience to demonstrate what they've learned from your speech. Here are a few examples:

- After listening to my speech, listeners should be able to describe the procedures for systematic desensitization.

- After listening to my speech, listeners should be able to define the three major differences between communism and capitalism.

- After listening to my speech, listeners should be able to demonstrate the five steps of active listening.

In a persuasive speech, your specific purpose identifies what you want your audience to believe, to think, or perhaps to do. Here are a few examples:

General purpose: To persuade.

Specific purposes: To persuade listeners to use systematic desensitization to reduce their apprehension.

To persuade listeners to believe that capitalism is superior to communism.

To persuade listeners to use active listening more often.

As you formulate your specific purposes, follow these five guidelines: Use an infinitive phrase; focus your purpose on your audience; limit it to one idea; limit it to what you can reasonably expect to achieve; and use specific terms.

**Use an Infinitive Phrase.** Begin the statement of each specific purpose with your general purpose (to inform, to persuade) and then elaborate on your general purpose. For example:

- To inform my audience of the new registration procedures.

- To persuade my audience to contribute a book for the library fund-raiser.

- To introduce the main speaker of the day to my audience.

**Focus on the Audience.** Right now, your audience is your public speaking class, and it may at first seem unnecessary to include reference to them in each specific purpose statement. Actually, however, including the words "my audience" is crucial, because it keeps you focused on the people you want to inform or persuade; it's a reminder that everything you do in your speech needs to be directed by the purpose you want to achieve with this specific audience. Your speech purpose must be relevant to your audience. And in your career in years to come, you'll probably address a variety of different audiences; you need to keep each unique and distinct audience clearly in focus.

**Limit Your Specific Purpose to One Idea.** Try not to accomplish too much in too short a time. For example, consider the following statement of a specific purpose:

To persuade my audience of the prevalence of date rape in our community and that they should attend the dating seminars offered on campus.

This statement contains two specific purposes: (1) informing my audience of the prevalence of date rape in our community and (2) persuading my audience to attend the dating seminars offered on campus. This speaker needs to limit the specific purpose statement by selecting one specific purpose or the other. As you construct your specific purpose statement, beware of the word *and*—it's often a sign that your statement contains more than one specific purpose.

**Limit Your Specific Purpose to What Is Reasonable.** Limit your specific purposes to what you can reasonably develop and achieve in the allotted time. Specific purposes that are too broad are useless. Note how broad and overly general are such purposes as *To inform my audience about clothing design* or *To persuade my audience to improve their health*. You couldn't hope to cover such topics in one speech. It would be much more reasonable to have such purposes as *To inform my audience of the importance of color in clothing design* or *To persuade my audience to exercise three times a week.*

**Use Specific Terms.** Phrase your specific purposes with specific terms. The more precise your specific purpose statement, the more effectively it will guide you in the remaining steps of preparing your speech. Notice that the purposes used as examples of covering too much are also overly general and very unspecific ("clothing design" can mean hundreds of things, as can "improve your health"). Instead of the overly general *To persuade my audience to help the homeless,* consider the more specific *To persuade my audience to donate a few hours a month to make phone calls for the Homeless Coalition.*

# STEP 2: ANALYZE YOUR AUDIENCE

The characteristic that seems best to define an audience is common purpose: A public speaking **audience** is a group of individuals gathered together to hear a speech. If you're to be a successful speaker, then you must know your audience. This knowledge will help you in selecting your topic; phrasing your purpose; establishing a relationship between yourself and your audience; and choosing examples, illustrations, and logical and emotional appeals.

Your first step in **audience analysis** is to construct an audience profile in which you analyze audience members' sociological or demographic characteristics. These characteristics help you estimate the attitudes, beliefs, and values of your audience. If you want to effect changes in these attitudes, beliefs, and values, you have to know what they are.

## Attitudes, Beliefs, and Values

An **attitude** is a tendency to act for or against a person, object, or position. If you have a positive attitude toward the death penalty, you're likely to argue or act in favor of the death penalty (for example, vote for a candidate who supports the death penalty). If you have a negative attitude toward the death penalty, then you're likely to argue or act against it. Attitudes toward the death penalty will influence how favorably or unfavorably listeners will respond to a speaker who supports or denounces capital punishment.

A **belief** is the confidence or conviction you have in the truth of some proposition. For example, you may believe that there is an afterlife, that education is the best way to rise from poverty, that democracy is the best form of government, or that all people are born equal. If your listeners believe that the death penalty is a deterrent to crime, for example, then they will be more likely to favor arguments for (and speakers who support) the death penalty than will listeners who don't believe in the connection between the death penalty and deterrence.

The term **value** refers to your perception of the worth or goodness (or worthlessness or badness) of some concept or idea. For example, you probably attribute positive values to financial success, education, and contributing to the common welfare. At the same time, you probably place negative values on chemical weapons, corrupt politicians, and selling drugs to children. Because the values an audience holds will influence how it responds to ideas related to those values, it's essential that you learn the values of your specific audience. For example, if the people in your audience place a high positive value on child welfare, then they are likely to vote for legislation that protects children or allocates money for breakfasts and lunches in school—and they might consider signing a petition, volunteering their time, or donating their money to advance the welfare of children. If you find that your audience places a negative value on big business, you may want to reconsider using the testimony of corporate leaders or the statistics compiled by corporations.

## Analyzing the Sociology of the Audience

In analyzing an audience, be careful not to assume that people covered by the same label are necessarily all alike. As soon as you begin to think about a sociological characteristic in terms of an expressed or implied "all," consider the possibility that you may be stereotyping. Don't assume that all women or all older people or all highly educated people think or believe the same things. They don't.

Nevertheless, there are characteristics that seem to be more common among one group than another, and it is these characteristics that you want to explore in your sociological analysis of your audience. Let's look at four major sociological or demographic variables: (1) cultural factors, (2) age, (3) gender, and (4) religion and religiousness.

### Cultural Factors

Cultural factors such as nationality, race, and cultural identity are crucial in audience analysis. Largely because of different training and experiences, the interests, values, and goals of various cultural groups will differ. Further, cultural factors will influence each of the remaining sociological factors; for example, attitudes toward age and gender will differ greatly from one culture to another. Perhaps the primary

---

**Building Communication Skills** — Using Cultural Beliefs as Assumptions

Evaluate each of the cultural beliefs listed below in terms of how effective each would be if used as a basic assumption by a speaker addressing your public speaking class. Use the following scale:

A = The audience would accept this assumption and would welcome a speaker with this point of view.

B = Some audience members would listen receptively and others wouldn't.

C = The audience would reject this assumption and would not welcome a speaker with this point of view.

1. A return to religious values is the best hope for the world.

2. The welfare of our country must come first, even before our own individual interests.

3. Sex outside of marriage is wrong and sinful.

4. Winning is all important; it's not how you play the game, it's whether or not you win that matters.

*There are probably few topics that the audience has not been culturally influenced about. So don't neglect cultural analysis regardless of your specific topic or audience.*

---

question to ask is "Are the cultural beliefs and values of the audience relevant to your topic and purpose?" That is, might the cultural background(s) of your audience members influence the way they see your topic? If so, find out what these beliefs and values are and take these into consideration as you build your speech.

## Age

Different age groups have different attitudes and beliefs, largely because they have had different experiences in different contexts. Take these differences into consideration in preparing your speeches. For example, let's say that you're an investment counselor and you want to persuade your listeners to invest their money to increase their earnings. Your speech to an audience of retired people (say in their 60s) would be very different from an address to an audience of young executives (say in their 30s). In considering the age of your audience, ask yourself if the age groups differ in goals, interests, and day-to-day concerns that may be related to your topic and purpose. Graduating from college, achieving corporate success, raising a family, and saving for retirement are concerns that differ greatly from one age group to another.

## Gender

Gender is one of the most difficult audience variables to analyze. In recent decades rapid social changes have made it difficult to pin down the effects of gender. As you analyze your audience in

terms of gender, ask yourself if men and women differ in the values they consider important insofar as these values are related to your topic and purpose. For example, traditionally, men have been found to place greater importance on theoretical, economic, and political values. Traditionally, women have been found to place greater importance on aesthetic, social, and religious values. In framing appeals and in selecting examples, take into account the values your audience members consider most important.

Ask too if your topic will be seen as more interesting by one gender or the other. Will men and women have different attitudes toward the topic? Men and women do not, for example, respond in the same way to such topics as abortion, rape, and equal pay for equal work. Select your topics and supporting materials in light of the gender of your audience members.

## Religion and Religiousness

The religion and religiousness of your audience often will influence their responses to your speech. Religion permeates all topics and all issues. On a most obvious level, such issues as attitudes toward birth control, abortion, and divorce are often connected to religion. Similarly, people's views on premarital sex, marriage, child rearing, money, cohabitation, responsibilities toward parents, and thousands of other issues are frequently influenced by religion. Religion also influences many people's ideas concerning such topics as obedience to authority; responsibility to government; and the usefulness of such qualities as honesty, guilt, and happiness.

## UNFAVORABLE AUDIENCE

From their initial reactions you immediately see that your audience is totally against your thesis and are tuning you out.

WHAT DO YOU SAY?

Ask yourself if your topic or purpose might be seen as an attack on the religious beliefs of any segment of your audience. If so, then you might want to make adjustments—not necessarily to abandon your purpose, but to rephrase your arguments or incorporate different evidence.

In analyzing the religiousness of your audience, also consider whether members identify themselves as being a part of a secular or a sacred culture. Secular cultures are those in which religion does not dominate the attitudes and views of the people or greatly influence political or educational decisions (Hofstede, 1997; Dodd, 1995). Liberal Protestant cultures such as those of the Scandinavian countries would be clearly secular. Sacred cultures, on the other hand, are those in which religion and religious beliefs and values dominate everything a person does and influence politics, education, and just about every topic or issue imaginable. Islamic cultures would be traditional examples of sacred cultures. Technically, the United States would be a secular culture (the Constitution, for example, expressly separates church and state); but in some areas of the country, religion exerts a powerful influence on schools (from prayers to condom distribution to sex education) and in politics (from the selection of political leaders to concern for social welfare to gay rights legislation).

## Analyzing the Psychology of the Audience

In addition to looking at the sociological characteristics of audience members, it's often useful to consider their psychological characteristics—particularly their willingness to listen to you, their favorableness to your purpose, and their background knowledge.

## How Willing Is Your Audience?

Your immediate concern in a public speaking class, of course, is with audience willingness on the part of your fellow students. Do they come to hear your speech because they have to, or do they come because they're interested in what you'll say? If they're a willing group, then you have few problems. And even if they're an unwilling group, all is not lost; you just have to work a little harder in preparing your speech. The unwilling audience demands special and delicate handling. Here are a few suggestions to help change your listeners from unwilling to willing:

- Secure their interest and attention as early in your speech as possible, and reinforce their interest throughout the speech by using little-known facts, quotations, startling statistics, examples, narratives, audiovisual aids, and the like.

- Reward the audience for their attendance and attention. Let the audience know you're aware they're making a sacrifice in coming to hear you speak. Tell them you appreciate it.

- Relate your topic and supporting materials directly to your audience's needs and wants. Show the audience how they can—for example—save time, make money, solve important problems, or become more popular.

## How Favorable Is Your Audience?

Audiences vary in the degree to which their ideas and attitudes will be favorable or unfavorable toward you, your topic, or your point of view. You may wish to examine your ability to predict audience favor toward various topics or beliefs by taking the following self-test.

# TEST YOURSELF

## How Well Do You Know Your Audience?

Here are some statements of beliefs that members of your class may agree or disagree with—and which you might want to use as basic theses (propositions) in your in-class speeches. Try predicting how favorable or unfavorable you think your class members would be to each of these beliefs. Use a 10-point scale ranging from 1 (extremely unfavorable) through 5 (relatively neutral) to 10 (extremely favorable).

_____ 1. The welfare of the family must come first, even before your own.

_____ 2. Sex outside of marriage is wrong and sinful.

_____ 3. In a heterosexual relationship, a wife should submit graciously to the leadership of her husband.

_____ 4. Individual states should be allowed to fly the Confederate flag if they wish.

_____ 5. Intercultural relationships are OK in business but should be discouraged when it comes to intimate or romantic relationships; generally, the different ethnic groups should be kept "pure."

_____ 6. Money is good; the quest for financial success is a perfectly respectable (even noble) one.

_____ 7. Immigration into the United States should be curtailed, at least until current immigrants are assimilated.

_____ 8. Parents who prevent their children from receiving the latest scientific cures because of a belief in faith healing should be prosecuted.

_____ 9. Same-sex marriage should be legalized.

_____ 10. Medicinal marijuana should be readily available.

_____ 11. Physician-assisted suicide should be legalized.

_____ 12. Male and female prostitution should be legalized and taxed like any other job that produces income.

**HOW DID YOU DO?** After you've indicated your predictions, discuss these with the class as a whole. How accurate were you in guessing your audience's beliefs?

**WHAT WILL YOU DO?** Practice adapting a thesis to both the favorable and the unfavorable audience. Select a thesis (one of those listed in this self-test or one of your own) toward which your audience would be highly favorable, and indicate how you'd adapt your speech to them. Then try the more difficult task: Select a thesis toward which your audience would be highly unfavorable, and indicate how you'd adapt to them.

If you conclude that your audience will be unfavorable to your chosen topic or viewpoint, the following suggestions should help:

- Clear up any possible misapprehensions that may be causing disagreement. For example, if they believe that the new parking regulations are the first step to higher parking fees, but that isn't true, mention it. Say, quite directly, "I understand that some people believe that these new regulations will lead to higher parking fees, but they won't; in fact, they will save money."

- Build on commonalities; stress what you and the audience share as people, as interested citizens, as fellow students. When audience members see similarity or common ground between themselves and you, they become more favorable to both you and your speech.

- Organize your speech inductively. Try to build your speech from areas of agreement, through areas of slight disagreement, up to the major differences between the audience's attitudes and your position. Once areas of agreement are established, it's easier to bring up differences.

- Strive for small gains. Don't try, in a five-minute speech, to convince a pro-life group to contribute money for a new abortion clinic or to persuade a pro-choice group to vote against liberalizing abortion laws. Be content to get the audience to listen fairly and to see some validity in your position.

- Acknowledge the differences explicitly. If it's clear to the audience that they and you are at opposite ends of an issue, you might want to acknowledge this fact and use it as a takeoff point to stress what you both agree on. You might say, for example, "I know that our differences on this issue are great, but what I also know is that we have the same ultimate goal."

## How Knowledgeable Is Your Audience?

Listeners differ greatly in the knowledge they have. Some listeners will be quite knowledgeable about a given topic; others will be almost totally ignorant. Mixed audiences are the most difficult to address. Treat audiences that lack knowledge of your topic very carefully. Never confuse a lack of audience knowledge with a lack of ability to understand.

- Don't talk down to your audience. No one wants to listen to a speaker putting them down.

- Don't confuse a lack of knowledge with a lack of intelligence. An audience may have no knowledge of your topic but be quite capable of following a clearly presented, logically developed argument. Try especially hard to use concrete examples, audiovisual aids, and simple language. Fill in background details as required. Avoid jargon and other specialized terminology that may not be clear to someone new to the subject.

- Let the audience know that you're aware of their knowledge and expertise. Try to do this as early in the speech as possible. Emphasize that what you have to say will be relevant and valuable. Tell them that you'll be presenting recent developments or new approaches. In short, let them know that they will not be wasting their time listening to your speech.

- Emphasize your credibility, especially your competence in this general subject area.

## Analyzing and Adapting during the Speech

In addition to analyzing your audience and making adaptations in your speech *before* delivering your speech, devote attention to analysis and adaptation *during* the speech. Although this during-the-speech analysis is especially important when you know little of your audience or find yourself facing a very different audience than you expected, it is always crucial to public speaking success. Here are a few suggestions:

### Focus on Listeners as Message Senders

As you're speaking, look at your listeners. Remember that just as you're sending messages to your audience, they're also sending messages to you. Pay attention to these messages; and on the basis of what they tell you, make whatever adjustments are necessary.

You can make a wide variety of adjustments to each type of audience response. For example, if your audience shows signs of boredom, increase your volume, move closer to them, or tell them that what you're going to say will be of value to them. If your audience shows signs of disagreement or hostility, stress a similarity you have with them. If your audience looks puzzled or confused, pause a moment and rephrase your ideas, provide necessary definitions, or insert an internal summary. If your audience seems impatient, say, for example, "my last argument . . ." instead of your originally planned "my third argument . . ."

### Ask "What If" Questions

As you prepare your speech, it's helpful to ask "what if" questions. These will help you make any necessary on-the-spot adjustments and adaptations. For example, let's say you have been told that you're to explain the opportunities available to the nontradi-

tional student at your college. You've been told that your audience will consist mainly of working women in their 30s and 40s who are just beginning college. As you prepare your speech with this audience in mind, ask yourself "what if" questions. For example:

- What if the audience has a large number of men?

- What if the audience consists of women much older than 40?

- What if the audience members also come with their spouses or their children?

Keeping such questions in mind will force you to consider alternatives as you prepare your speech. Then you'll have ideas readily available if you face a new or different audience.

### Address Audience Responses Directly

Another way of dealing with audience responses is to confront them directly. To those who are giving disagreement feedback, for example, you could say something like:

> You may disagree with this position, but all I ask is that you hear me out and see if this new way of doing things will not simplify your accounting procedures.

Or, to those who seem puzzled, you might say:

> I know this plan may seem confusing, but bear with me; it will become clear in a moment.

Or, to those who seem impatient, you might respond:

> I know this has been a long day, but give me just a few more minutes and you'll be able to save hours recording your accounts.

By responding to your listeners' reactions and feedback, you acknowledge your audience's priorities. You let them know that you hear them, that you're with them, and that you're responding to their very real needs.

## STEP 3: RESEARCH YOUR TOPIC

Throughout the process of preparing your public speeches, you'll need to find information to use as source material in your speech. This means doing research. Through research you'll find examples, illustrations, and definitions to help you inform your listeners; testimony, statistics, and arguments to support your major ideas; personal anecdotes, quotations, and stories to help you bring your topics to life.

Research, however, also serves another important function: It helps you persuade your listeners, because it makes you appear more believable. For example, if your listeners feel you've examined lots of research, they'll be more apt to see you as competent and knowledgeable and therefore more apt to believe what you say. And of course, presenting the research is itself convincing. When you present research to your listeners, you give them the very reasons they need to draw conclusions or decide on a course of action.

In this section we'll consider research in some depth: (1) general principles, (2) taking research notes, (3) the major sources of information, (4) evaluating research, (5) integrating research into your speech, (6) citing research sources, and lastly the dreaded topic of plagiarism.

## General Research Principles

Here are a few principles to help you research your speeches more effectively and more efficiently.

### Examine What You Know

Begin your search by examining what you already know. For example, write down relevant books, articles, or websites that you're familiar with or people who might know something about the topic. Also consider what you know from your own personal experiences and observations. In this way you can attack the problem systematically and not waste effort or time.

### Begin with a General Overview

Continue your search by getting an authoritative but general overview of the topic. An encyclopedia article, book chapter, or magazine article in print or online will serve this purpose well. This general overview will help you see the topic as a whole and understand how its various parts fit together.

### Consult Increasingly Specific Sources

Follow up the general overview with increasingly more detailed and specialized sources. Fortunately, many of the general articles contain references or links to direct this next stage of your search for more specific information.

## Research Time Management

Because a great deal of your time—in this course and in numerous others—will be spent on research, learn to use your research time efficiently. Here are a few suggestions:

- *Multitask.* Combine your research tasks and do them simultaneously. For example, when going to the library or logging on to the Internet, have more than one task in mind. If you know the topics of your next few speeches, or if you're writing a sociology paper on a related topic, do the research for both at the same time.

- *Watch detours.* When you are searching the Net, it's easy to get lured into taking long detours. These are often excellent learning experiences and are not necessarily detrimental. For purposes of time management, however, it will help if you keep your purpose clearly in mind—even to the point of writing it down—as you surf the Net or lurk among the chat groups.

- *Access your library from home.* If possible, access your college library's online catalog of books from home; it will save you time if you can go to the library with your searches already completed. If your library subscribes to full text databases that can be accessed from your home computer (ProQuest and Lexis-Nexis are popular examples), you may be able to do all your research from the comfort of your home.

- *Consult your librarian.* One useful but often overlooked research resources is your librarian. Librarians are experts in the very researching issues that may be giving you trouble. They'll be able to help you access biographical material, indexes of current articles, materials in specialized collections at other libraries, and a wide variety of computerized databases.

## Research Notes

The more accurate your research notes are, the less time you'll waste going back to sources to check on a date or a spelling. Accurate records also will prevent you from going to sources you've already consulted but may have forgotten about. The following suggestions may prove helpful to you as you take notes during the research process.

### Create Folders

If you want to collect your material on paper, loose-leaf notebooks or simple manila folders work well to keep everything relating to a speech or article in the same place. If you want to file your material electronically, create a general folder and subfolders as you need them. This will work especially well if you can scan into your folder material you find in print. In this notebook or folder, you can consolidate the sources consulted, quotations, ideas, arguments,

# REFLECTIONS ON ETHICS

## Plagiarism

The term **plagiarism** refers to passing off the work (ideas, words, illustrations) of others as our own. It is not the act of using another's ideas—we all do that. Plagiarism is using another's ideas without acknowledging that they are the ideas of this other person; it is presenting the ideas as if they were ours.

Plagiarism exists on a continuum, ranging from appropriating an entire term paper or speech written by someone else to using a quotation or research finding without citing the author.

Plagiarism also includes situations in which, for example, a student gets help from a friend without acknowledging this assistance. In some cultures—especially in collectivist cultures (cultures that emphasize the group and mutual cooperation) such as those of Korea, Japan, and China—teamwork is strongly encouraged. Students are taught to help other students with their work. But in the United States and in many other individualist cultures (cultures that emphasize individuality and competitiveness), teamwork without acknowledgment is considered plagiarism.

In U.S. institutions of higher education, plagiarism is a serious violation of the rules of academic honesty and carries serious penalties, sometimes even expulsion. And it's interesting to note that instructors are mobilizing and educating themselves in the techniques for detecting plagiarism. Further, as with all crimes, ignorance of the rules is not an acceptable defense against charges of plagiarism. This last point is especially important because a good deal of plagiarism is committed through a lack of information as to what does and what does not constitute plagiarism. Here are just a few reasons why plagiarism is wrong.

### Why Plagiarism Is Unacceptable

Plagiarism is unacceptable for a variety of reasons:

- Plagiarism is a violation of another's intellectual property rights. Much as it would be wrong to take another person's watch without permission, it's wrong to take another person's ideas without acknowledging that you did it.

- You're in college to develop your own ideas and ways of expressing them; plagiarism defeats this fundamental purpose.

- Evaluations (everything from grades in school to promotions in the workplace) assume that what you present as your work is in fact your work.

### Avoiding Plagiarism

Let's start with the easy part. You do not have to—and should not—cite sources for common knowledge: information that is readily available in numerous sources and is not likely to be disputed. For example, the population of Thailand, the amendments to the U.S. Constitution, the actions of the United Nations, or the way the heart pumps blood are all common knowledge, and you would not cite an almanac or political science text from which you got this information. On the other hand, if you were talking about the attitudes of people from Thailand or the reasons constitutional amendments were adopted, then you'd need to cite your sources, because this information is not common knowledge and may well be disputed.

For information that is not common knowledge, you need to acknowledge your source. Here are a few rules that will help you avoid even the suggestion of plagiarism:

1. Acknowledge the source of any ideas you present that are not your own. If you learned of an idea in your history course, then cite the history instructor or history textbook. If you read an idea in an article, then cite the article.

2. Acknowledge the words of another. It's obvious what to do when you're quoting another person exactly; you need to cite the person you're quoting. You should also cite others even when you paraphrase their words, because you are still using others' ideas; but when paraphrases need to be credited may not always be so clear. To help with this question, some of the plagiarism websites established by different universities include exercises and extended examples; see, for example, Indiana University's site at **www.indiana.edu/&sim;uts/ wts/plagiarism.html** or Purdue University's at **http://owl.english.purdue.edu/handouts/ print/reseach/r-plagiar.html**. The same is true when you use the organizational structure of another person; just say, for example, "I'm following the line of reasoning proposed by Andrew Rancer in his comparison of aggression and argument."

3. Acknowledge help from others. If your roommate gave you examples or ideas or helped you style your speech, acknowledge the help.

### Ethical Choice Point

*While listening to an impressive speech in your class, you recognize that you've read this exact same material in an obscure online publication. You're annoyed that this student has not done the work that everyone else has done and yet will probably earn a high grade. However, you wonder if you want to or should take on being the ethical conscience of your class. What is your ethical obligation in this case? What would you do?*

suggested references, preliminary outlines, and material you've printed or downloaded.

### Key Your Notes

Notes are most effective when they're keyed to specific topics. For example, let's say that your speech is to be on animal experimentation. Your notebook or major folder might be titled *Animal Experimentation*. The notebook divisions or subfolders might then be labeled "Basic Information" (statistics on animal experimentation, people to contact, organizations involved in this issue), "Arguments for Animal Experimentation," and "Arguments against Animal Experimentation." Taking notes with reference to your preliminary outline will help focus your research and will remind you of those topics for which you need more information. It will also help you keep the information logically organized.

### Take Complete Notes

Make sure your notes are complete (and legible). If you have to err, then err on the side of too much detail. You can always cut the quotation or select one example out of the three at a later time. As you take notes, be sure to identify the source of the material—so that you can find that reference again should you need it, and so that you can reference it in your speech outline. When you use material from a Web source, be sure to print out or save to folder the Web page, noting the URL and the date you accessed this site. This way you'll be able to cite a source even if the Web page disappears, a not unlikely possibility.

The resources available to you today are rich and varied. A brief survey follows.

## Libraries and Bookstores

Libraries, the major depositories of stored information, have evolved from a concentration on print sources to their current focus on computerized databases. Starting your research at the library (and with the librarian's assistance) is probably a wise move.

Here are a few online libraries that you'll find especially helpful.

- Quick Study, the University of Minnesota's Library Research Guide (http://tutorial.lib.umn.edu), will help you learn how to find the materials you need and will answer lots of questions you probably have about research.

- For a list of library catalogs that will help you find the location of the material you need, try www.libdex.com/. By clicking on "library-type index"

you'll get a list of categories of libraries; for example, government or medical or religious.

- The largest library in the United States is the Library of Congress, which houses millions of books, maps, multimedia, and manuscripts. Time spent at this library (begin with www.loc.gov) will be well invested. The home page will guide you to a wealth of information.

- Maintained by the National Archives and Records Administration, the presidential libraries may be accessed at www.archives.gov/.

- The Virtual Library is a collection of links to 14 subject areas; for example, agriculture, business and economics, computing, communication and media, and education. Visit this at www.vlib.org.

- If you're not satisfied with your own college library, visit the libraries of some of the large state universities, such as the University of Pennsylvania (www.library.upenn.edu/cgi-bin/res/sr.cgi) or the University of Illinois (http://gateway.library.uiuc.edu).

- The Internet Public Library (www.ipl.org) is actually not a library; it's a collection of links to a wide variety of materials. But it will function much like the reference desk at any of the world's best libraries.

Also visit some of the online bookstores, such as Amazon (www.amazon.com), Barnes & Noble (www.bn.com), or Borders (www.Borders.com) and their brick-and-mortar counterparts. In addition, other useful sites include: http://aaupnet.org/ (the Association of American University Presses) and http://www.cs.cmu.edu/Web/People/spok/banned-books.html (contains links to texts of books that have been banned in the United States and elsewhere). Some online bookstores now enable you to search some of their books for specific topics and read a paragraph or so on each topic reference.

Of course, you'll also go to a brick-and-mortar library, because it houses materials that are not on the Net and/or that you want to access in print. Because each library functions somewhat differently, your best bet in learning about a specific library—such as your own college library—is to talk with your librarian about what the library has available, what kinds of training or tours it offers, and how materials are most easily accessed.

## Interviewing for Information

One research activity that you'll often find helpful is interviewing people who have special information that you might use in your speech. For example, you might want to interview a veterinarian for informa-

## ASKING A FAVOR

You're preparing a speech on the architectural ideas for rebuilding Ground Zero and you want to ask some of the famous architects a few questions so you can integrate their most recent thoughts (and interject a more personalized note) into your speech.

WHAT DO YOU SAY?
*In what channel?*

tion on proper diet for household pets, a meteorologist for information on living through a hurricane, or average people for information on their opinions on politics, religion, or any of a wide variety of topics. In these informational interviews, a great part of your effectiveness will hinge on your ability to listen actively, for total meaning, with empathy, with an open mind, and ethically, all of which are covered in this chapter. Here are a few additional suggestions to help you use interviewing to find needed information.

- *Select the person you wish to interview.* You might, for example, look through your college catalog for an instructor teaching a course that involves your topic. Or visit newsgroups and look for people who have posted articles on your topic. If you want to contact a book author, you can always write to the author in care of the publisher or editor (listed on the copyright page), though many authors are now including their e-mail addresses. You often can find the address and phone number of a professional person in the *Encyclopedia of Associations*, or you can write to the person via the association's website. Newsgroup and listserv writers are of course the easiest to contact, as their e-mail addresses are included with their posts. To find an expert, try *The Yearbook of Experts, Authorities, and Spokespersons* or any of a variety of websites, such as www.experts.com or http://uscnews3.usc.edu/experts/.

- *Secure an appointment.* Phone the person or send an e-mail requesting an interview. State the purpose of your request and say that you hope to conduct a brief interview by phone or that you'd like to send a series of questions by e-mail.

- *Develop your questions.* Generally, ask questions that provide the interviewee with room to dis-

cuss the issues you want to raise. Fore example, asking, "Do you have formal training in the area of family therapy?" may elicit a simple yes or no, which will not be very informative. On the other hand, asking, "Can you tell me something of your background in this field?" is open-ended, allowing the interviewee to talk in some detail. Ask questions phrased in a neutral manner. Try not to lead the interviewee to give the answers you want.

- *Establish rapport with the interviewee.* Open the in-person, telephone, e-mail, or chat-group interview by thanking the person for making the time available and again stating your purpose. You might say something like: "I really appreciate your making time for this interview. As I mentioned, I'm preparing a speech on XYZ, and your experience in this area will help a great deal."

- *Ask for permission to tape or print the interview.* It's a good idea to keep an accurate record of the interview, so ask permission to tape the interview if it's in person or by telephone. Taping will eliminate your worry about taking notes and having to ask the interviewee to slow down or repeat. It will also provide you with a much more accurate record of the interview than will handwritten notes. But always ask permission first. Similarly, if the interview is by e-mail or via chat group and you want to quote the interviewee's responses, ask permission first. An agreement to be interviewed does not include permission to print or distribute the interview or even parts of it.

- *Close with an expression of appreciation, and follow up with a thank-you note.* Thank the person for making the time available for the interview and for being informative, cooperative, helpful, and so forth. Follow up the interview with a note of thanks. Or perhaps you might send the person you interviewed a copy of your speech (e-mail would work well here), again with a note of thanks.

## Primary and Secondary Sources

As a researcher, be sure to distinguish between primary and secondary source material, whether your materials come from print or online. **Primary sources** include, for example, an original research study reported in an academic journal, a corporation's annual report, or an eyewitness report of an accident. With primary sources there is nothing (or very little) standing between the event (say, an accident) and the reporting of it (the eyewitness testimony). **Secondary sources** include, for example, a summary of research appearing in a popular magazine, a television news report on a corporation's earnings, or a report by someone who talked to someone who witnessed an accident. With secondary sources someone stands between the actual event and the report; for example, a science reporter reads the scientist's monograph (primary source), then writes up a summary for the popular press (secondary source).

As a listener and speaker you'll hear and use both types of source material. Yet there are important differences that you should keep in mind. Above all, secondary source material is less reliable than primary source material, because it is a step removed from the actual facts or events. The writer of secondary material may have forgotten important parts, may be biased and so may have slanted the reporting to reflect his or her attitudes, or may have distorted the material because he or she misunderstood the data.

On the other hand, the writer may have been able to express complicated scientific data in simple language—often making it easier for a nonscientist to understand than the original report. In any case, when using or listening to secondary sources, examine the information for any particular spin the writer may be giving the material. If possible, check the primary source material itself to see if anything was left out or if the conclusions are really warranted on the basis of the primary evidence.

## General Reference Works

General reference works are excellent starting points for researching your topic. One of the best general reference works is the standard encyclopedia. Any good encyclopedia will give you a general overview of your subject and suggestions for additional reading. The most comprehensive and the most prestigious is the *Encyclopaedia Britannica*,

available in print, on CD-ROM, and online. A variety of other encyclopedias also are available in print, on CD-ROM, or online. The best way to search for these is to visit Freeality.com (www.freeality.com//encyclop.htm) and search through the available general and specific encyclopedias.

Perhaps the most widely known online encyclopedia, and a resource that you'll find extremely useful, is Wikipedia (www.wikipedia.com). This encyclopedia is a bit different from those mentioned above. The articles in Wikipedia—some brief and some extremely long and detailed—are written by people who are not necessarily experts. Therefore, although many of the articles are reviewed, updated, and corrected periodically, Wikipedia doesn't have the authority of the more traditional encyclopedias. Some universities have even banned the use of this source because of some inaccuracies, so you may want to check on the acceptance of referencing such work. If you do use Wikipedia, you'll need to check its facts and statistics—most of which you'll find easy to do because of the extensive hotlinks written into each article and the list of additional sources provided for most articles.

## News Sources

Often you'll want to read reports on scientific breakthroughs, political speeches, congressional actions, obituaries, financial news, international developments, United Nations actions, or any of a host of other topics. Or you may wish to locate the date of a particular event and learn something about what else was going on in the world at that particular time. For this type of information, you may want to consult one or more of the many *news sources* available. Especially relevant are newspaper indexes, newspaper and newsmagazine websites, news wire services, and broadcast news networks.

- *Newspaper indexes.* One way to start a newspaper search is to consult one of the newspaper indexes, such as those at www.all-links.com/newscentral, www.newspapers.com, www.newslink.org/menu .html, and www.newspaperlinks.com. At sites like these you'll find hot links to thousands of national and local newspapers.

- *Newspaper and newsmagazine websites.* Most newspapers and magazines maintain their own websites from which you can access current and past issues. Here are a few to get you started: www.latimes.com/ (*Los Angeles Times*), www .usatoday.com/ (*USA Today*), www.wsj.com (Wall Street Journal), www.nytimes.com (the *New York Times*), and www.washingtonpost .com (the *Washington Post*).

- *News wire services.* Four wire services should prove helpful. The Associated Press can be accessed at www.ap.org/, Reuters at www.reuters.com/, United Press International at www.upi.com, and PR Newswire at www.prnewswire.com/.

- *News networks online.* All of the television news stations maintain extremely useful websites. Here are some of the most useful: Access CNN at www.cnn.com/, ESPN at http://espn.sportszone.com/, ABC News at www.abcnews.com/newsflash, CBS News at www.cbs.com/news/, or MSNBC News at www.msnbc.com/news.

You'll find it helpful to compare the news available on one of the major newspapers' websites (for example, the *Washington Post* site or the *New York Times* site) with the news presented by a wire service such as the Associated Press (www.ap.org) or Reuters (www.reuters.com). Which seems the more reliable? The more complete? The more impartial?

## Biographical Material

As a speaker you'll often need information about particular individuals. For example, in using the testimony of experts in various fields, it's helpful to stress their qualifications, which you can easily learn about from even brief biographies. Or you may want to look up authors of books or articles to find out something about their education, their training, or their other writings. Or you may wish to discover if there have been critical evaluations of their work—such as, say, book reviews or articles about them or their writings. Knowing something about your sources enables you to more effectively evaluate their competence, convey their credibility to the audience, and answer audience questions about them.

One of the most enjoyable and useful biography sites is maintained by The Biography Channel (www.biography.com) and contains biographies of some 25,000 individuals from all walks of life. Another great source is the Biography and Genealogy Master Index, which indexes several hundred biographical sources. Online versions of this are maintained by a variety of colleges; one of the best is Arizona State University Libraries (www.asu.edu/lib/resources/db/biogr.htm). This master index will send you to numerous specialized works.

Other excellent general resources include the Biography Almanac available at Infoplease (www.infoplease.com), which lists some 30,000 biographies; the University of Michigan's Internet Public Library (http://ipl.sils.umich.edu), which contains a great list of biography websites; and the Biograph-ical Dictionary (http://s9.com/biography), which covers some 28,000 men and women.

## The Government

Governmental bodies and agencies throughout the United States (at the federal, state, and municipal levels) publish an enormous amount of information that you're sure to find useful in speeches on almost any topic. One excellent starting point is Google's government search (www.usgov.google.com). This engine covers all websites in the *.gov* domain. The amount of information you'll find, however, may at first be daunting. For example, if you search for "publications," you find more than 4 million websites; for "education," more than 11 million; and for "health," more than 24 million. You'll definitely need to limit your search. One way to do this is of course to include additional terms (for example, health + drugs + teenagers) or to use phrases in quotations ("teenage drug use").

Another way is to visit one or more of the 13 relevant departments of the federal government (these are the Departments of Agriculture, Commerce, Defense, Education, Energy, Health and Human Services, Housing and Urban Development, Interior, Justice, Labor, State, Treasury, and Transportation). All issue reports, pamphlets, books, and assorted documents dealing with their various concerns. Here are a few of the topics on which some of the departments have information that you'll find useful in researching your speeches.

- Department of the Treasury (www.ustreas.gov): taxes, property auctions, savings, economy, financial markets, international business, and money management.

- Department of Housing and Urban Development (www.hud.gov): home buying, selling, renting, and owning; fair housing; foreclosures; consumer information; FHA refunds; homelessness; and information for tenants, landlords, farm workers, senior citizens, and victims of discrimination.

- Department of Defense (www.defenselink.mil/): news releases, speech texts, military pay and benefits, casualty reports.

- Department of Justice (www.usdoj.gov): drugs and drug enforcement; Patriot Act information; trafficking in persons; inmate locator; Americans with Disabilities Act; sentencing statistics; and information from the Bureau of Alcohol, Tobacco, Firearms, and Explosives.

- Department of Health and Human Services (www.hhs.gov): aging, AIDS, disease, safety issues, food and drug information, disaster and emergency

## The Public Speaking Sample Assistant

# A Speech of Introduction

Throughout these six public speaking units, you'll find Public Speaking Sample Assistant boxes. These boxes present complete speeches or outlines with annotations; they will help you to see the public speech as a whole and to ask critical questions about structure, support, language, and numerous other public speaking factors we consider in these units.

One of the first speeches you may be called upon to make is the speech in which you introduce yourself or (as illustrated in this particular speech) some other person. This speech also will let you see a public speech as a whole and will give you reference points for examining each of the 10 steps for preparing and delivering a public speech.

### Introduction

It's a real pleasure to introduce Joe Robinson to you. I want to tell you a little about Joe's background, his present situation, and his plans for the future.

In this introduction, the speaker accomplishes several interrelated purposes: to place the speech in a positive context, to explain the purpose of the speech and orient the audience, to tell them what the speech will cover and that it will follow a time pattern—beginning with the past, moving to the present, and then ending with the proposed future. What other types of opening statements might be appropriate? In what other ways might you organize a speech of introduction?

### Transition

Let's look first at Joe's past.

This transitional statement alerts listeners that the speaker is moving from the introduction to the first major part of what is called the "body" of the speech.

### Body, first main point (the past)

Joe comes to us from Arizona, where he lived and worked on a small ranch with his father and grandparents—mostly working with dairy cows. Working on a farm gave Joe a deep love and appreciation for animals that he carries with him today and into his future plans.

Joe's mother died when he was three years old, and so he lived with his father most of his life. When his father, an air force lieutenant, was transferred to Stewart Air Force Base here in the Hudson Valley, Joe thought it would be a great opportunity to join his father and continue his education.

Joe also wanted to stay with his father to make sure he eats right, doesn't get involved with the wrong crowd, and meets the right woman to settle down with.

The speaker here gives us information about Joe's past that makes us see him as a unique individual. We also learn something pretty significant about Joe, namely that his mother died when he was very young. The speaker continues here to answer one of the questions that audience members probably have; namely, why this somewhat older person is in this class and in this college. If this were a longer speech, what else might the speaker cover here? What else would you want to know about Joe's past?

Here the speaker shows that Joe has a sense of humor in his identifying why he wanted to stay with his father, the very same things that a father would say about a son. Can you make this more humorous?

### Transition

So Joe and his father journeyed from the dairy farm in Arizona to the Hudson Valley.

Here's simple transition, alerting the audience that the speaker is moving from the first main point (the past) to the second (the present). In what other ways might you state such a transition?

### Second main point (the present)

Right now, with the money he saved while working on the ranch and with the help of a part-time job, Joe's here with us at Hudson Valley Community College.

Like many of us, Joe is a little apprehensive about college and worries that it's going to be a difficult and very different experience, especially at 28. Although an avid reader—mysteries and biographies are his favorites—Joe hasn't really studied, taken an exam, or written a term

Here the speaker shifts to the present and gives Joe a very human dimension by identifying his fears and concerns about being in college and taking this course and his concern for animals. The speaker also explains some commonalities between Joe and the rest of the audience (for example, being apprehensive in a public speaking class is something shared by nearly everyone). Some textbook writers would suggest that telling an audience that a speaker has apprehension about speaking is a bad idea. What do you think of its disclosure here?

## The Public Speaking Sample Assistant

## A Speech of Introduction *(Continued)*

paper since high school, some 10 years ago. So he's a bit anxious, but at the same time he's looking forward to the changes and the challenges of college life.

And, again, like many of us, Joe's a bit apprehensive about taking a public speaking course.

Joe is currently working for a local animal shelter. He was especially drawn to this particular shelter because of their no-kill policy; lots of shelters will kill the animals they can't find adopted homes for, but this one sticks by its firm no-kill policy.

**Transition**

But it's not the past or the present that Joe focuses on, it's the future.

This transition tells listeners that the speaker has finished talking about the past and present and is now moving on to the future.

**Third main point (the future)**

Joe is planning to complete his AB degree here at Hudson Valley Community and then to move on to the State University of New Paltz, where he intends to major in communication with a focus on public relations.

His ideal job would be to work for an animal rights organization. He wants to help make people aware of the ways in which they can advance animal rights and stop so much of the cruelty to animals common throughout the world.

From the present, the speaker moves to the future and identifies Joe's educational plans. This is the one thing that everyone has in common and something that most in the class would want to know. The speaker also covers Joe's career plans: again, something the audience is likely to be interested in. In this the speaker also reveals important aspects of Joe's interests and belief system—his concern for animals and his dedication to building his career around this abiding interest. What kinds of information might this speech of introduction give you about the attitudes and beliefs of its listeners?

**Transition, internal summary**

Joe's traveled an interesting road from a dairy farm in Arizona to the Hudson Valley, and the path to New Paltz and public relations should be just as interesting.

This transition (a kind of internal summary) tells you that the speaker has completed the three-part discussion (past, present, and future) and offers a basic summary of what has been discussed.

**Conclusion**

Having talked with him for the last few days, I'm sure he'll do well—he has lots of ideas, is determined to succeed, is open to new experiences, and enjoys interacting with people. I'd say that gives this interesting dairy farmer from Arizona a pretty good start as a student in this class, as a student at Hudson Valley Community, and as a soon-to-be public relations specialist.

In this concluding comment the speaker appropriately expresses a positive attitude toward Joe and summarizes some of Joe's positive qualities. These qualities are then tied to the past–present–future organization of the speech. Although the speaker doesn't say "thank you"—which can get trite when 20 speakers in succession say this—it's clear that this is the end of the speech from the last sentence, which brings Joe into his future profession. How effective do you think this conclusion is? What other types of conclusions might the speaker have used?

protection, families and children, disabilities, homelessness, and immigration.

- Department of Education (www.ed.gov): teaching resources in science, math, history, and language arts; innovations in education; reports on performance and accountability, "no child left behind," at-risk and gifted students, the Pell grant program, and religious expression in the schools.

- Deparment of Labor (www.dol.gov): pensions, unemployment, wages, insurance, and just about any other topic even remotely related to labor.

At each of these departments, you'll be able to find statistics appropriate to the topics covered, but an easier way is to log on to FedStats (www.fedstats .gov). Here you'll find statistics from more than 100 federal agencies, including statistical profiles of each

### CORRECTING ERRORS

In your speech you say that over 70 percent of the students favored banning alcohol. Toward the end of the speech, you realize that you mixed up the figures (only 30 percent favored banning alcohol). During the question-and-answer period no one asks about the figures.

WHAT DO YOU SAY?

state, county, and city as well as statistics on crime, population, economics, mortality, and energy, along with comparisons with other countries.

## Databases

A database is simply an organized collection of information. Today there are a wide variety of research database packages available from an increasing number of vendors. These databases contain resources that you most likely will not be able to find on the Web without paying a fee. ProQuest, EBSCO, Info-Trac, WilsonWeb, and Search Premier are some of the names you'll probably run across in your exploration of databases. All of these vendors package databases in different ways. Your college library has no doubt purchased certain of these packages and makes them available to students and faculty for access from home or from the library without charge.

Some databases focus on specific areas; for example, history (America: History and Life, Historical Abstracts), health (Medline, Health Source), or communication (Communication & Mass Media Complete, Sage: Communication Studies Collection). Some databases are combinations of a variety of specific databases and contain a variety of publications from the major disciplines. Some databases focus on scholarly

articles published in professional journals by academic researchers and scientists. Other databases focus on popular articles in magazines and newspapers. There is almost surely to be a database on just about any topic you'll want to research.

## Integrating and Citing Research

Even the best and most extensive research would count for little if you didn't integrate it into your speech. By integrating and acknowledging your sources of information in your speech, you'll give fair credit to those whose ideas and research findings you're using, and you'll lessen the risk that anything you say can be intepreted as plagiarism (see page 313). At the same time, you'll help establish your own reputation as a responsible researcher and thus increase your own credibility. Here are a few suggestions for integrating your research into your speech (additional suggestions are presented in Table 14.4, pages 322–323).

### Mention the Sources in Your Speech

Cite at least the author; if appropriate, cite the publication and the date. Check out some of the speeches reprinted in this book and any of the many public speaking sites on the Internet, and note how the speakers integrate their sources in their talks. In your written preparation outline, give the complete bibliographical reference.

Here is an example of how you might cite your source:

> My discussion of the causes of anorexia nervosa is based on the work of Dr. Peter Rowan of the Priory Hospital in London. In an article titled "Introducing Anorexia Nervosa," which I last accessed on October 5, 2007, Rowan notes that "this is a disorder of many causes that come together." It's these causes that I want to cover in this talk.

Although it's possible to overdo oral source citations—to give more information than listeners really need—there are even greater dangers in leaving out potentially useful source information. Because your speeches in this course are learning experiences, it will be better to err on the side of being more rather than less complete.

### Avoid Unnecessary Lead-In Expressions

Comments such as "I have a quote here" or "I want to quote an example" serve no persuasive purpose. Let the audience know that you're quoting by pausing before the quote, taking a step forward, or—to read an extended quotation—referring to your notes. If you want to state more directly that this is a quotation, you might do it this way:

Recently, Mary Kay Ash put this in perspective: "A woman can no more duplicate the male style of leadership than an American businessman can exactly reproduce the Japanese style."

In addition to the oral citation, you'll most likely want to include a listing of your references in your preparation outline. In citing references, first find out what style manual is used in your class or at your school. Generally, it will be a style manual developed by the American Psychological Association (APA), the Modern Language Association (MLA), or the University of Chicago (*The Chicago Manual of Style*). Different colleges and even different departments within a given school often rely on different formats for citing research, which, quite frankly, makes a tedious process even worse.

Fortunately, a variety of websites provide guides to the information you'll need to cite any reference in your speech. For example, Purdue University offers an excellent site that covers APA and MLA style formats and provides examples for citing books, articles, newspaper articles, websites, e-mail, online postings, electronic databases, and more (http://owl.english .purdue.edu/handouts/research). Another excellent website is Capital Community College's Guide for Writing Research Papers (http://ccc.commnet.edu/ apa/apa_index.htm). Guidelines for using *The Chicago Manual of Style* may be found at Ohio State's website (www.lib.ohio-state.edu/). This site provides guidance for citing all types of print and electronic sources. Another valuable source is the *Columbia Guide to Online Style* (www.columbia .edu/cu/cup/cgos/idx_basic.html), which provides detailed instructions and examples for citing e-mail, listserv, and newsgroup communications and even software programs and video games.

## Evaluating Internet Resources

As you research your topic, keep in mind that anyone can "publish" on the Internet, making it essential that you subject everything you find on the Net to critical analysis. An article on the Internet can be written by world-renowned scientists or by elementary school students; by fair and objective reporters or by people who would spin the issues to serve their own political, religious, or social purposes. It's not always easy to tell which is which. Here are a few questions to ask in evaluating Internet resources (or in evaluating information from print sources, from interpersonal interaction, or from the media):

- *Is the author qualified?* Does the author have the necessary credentials? For example, does the author have sufficient background in science or medicine to write authoritatively on health issues? Do

an Internet search using the biography sites already discussed, or simply enter the author's name in your favorite search engine and check on the author's expertise.

- *Is the information current?* When was the information published? When were the sources cited in the article written? Generally, the more recent the material, the more useful it will be. With some topics—for example, unemployment statistics; developments in AIDS research; tuition costs; stem cell research; or attitudes toward the Iraq war, same-sex marriage, or organized religion—the currency of the information is crucial to its usefulness, simply because these things change so rapidly. Other topics—for example, historical or literary topics—may well rely on information that was written even hundreds of years ago. Even here, however, new understanding frequently sheds light on events that happened in the far distant past.

- *Is the information fair?* Does the author of the material present the information objectively, or is there a bias favoring one position? Some websites, although seemingly objective on the surface, are actually organs of political, religious, or social organizations, so it's often useful to go to the home page and look for information on the nature of the organization sponsoring the website. Reviewing a range of research in the area will help you see how other experts view the issue. It will also enable you to see if this author's view of the situation takes into consideration all sides of the issue and if these sides are represented fairly.

- *Is the information sufficient to substantiate your claim?* The opinion of one dietitian is insufficient to support the usefulness of a particular diet; statistics on tuition increases at five elite private colleges are insufficient to illustrate national trends in tuition costs. Generally, the broader your conclusion, the greater the information you'll need to meet the requirements for sufficiency. If you want to claim the usefulness of a diet for all people, then you're going to need a great deal of information from different populations—men and women, old and young, healthy and sickly, and so on.

- *Is the information accurate?* Determining accuracy is not easy, but the more you learn about your topic, the more able you'll be to judge accuracy. Is the information primary or secondary? If it's secondary information, you may be able to locate the primary information (often provided as a hot link in the Internet article or in a reference at the end of a printed text). Check to see if the information is consistent with information found in other sources and if the recognized authorities in the field accept this information.

## Table 14.4 The Oral Citation

Here are a few examples and notes on citing your sources in your speech. The written citations would be included at the end of your preparation outline in a list of references. Additional help is available on Research Navigator (**www.mycommunicationlab.com**), which provides guidance for citing sources in reference lists and bibliographies using all major style manuals; the American Psychological Association (APA) style is used here.

| Source to Be Cited and Written Citation | Oral Citation | Tips for Success |
|---|---|---|
| **Book** | | |
| Brownell, J. (2006). *Listening: Attitudes, principles, and skills* (3rd ed.). Boston: Allyn & Bacon. | Judi Brownell, an authority on listening and a professor at Cornell University, in *Listening: Attitudes, Principles, and Skills*, argues that listening is . . . | Try to establish the importance of the book or the author to add weight to your argument. |
| **Magazine Article** | | |
| Cloud, J. (2007, February 5). Yep, they're gay. *Time*, 169 (6), 54. | A February 2007 article in *Time* magazine notes, and here I'm quoting the author, John Cloud, "Zoologists have known for many years that homosexuality isn't uncommon among animals." | If the magazine is well known, as is *Time*, it's sufficient to name the magazine. If it were less well known, then you might establish its credibility for your listeners by noting, for example, its reputation for fairness, its longevity, its well-known authors. |
| **Newspaper Article** | | |
| Whitlock, C. (2007, March 12). Terrorists proving harder to profile. Retrieved March 12, 2007, from www.washingtonpost.com, p. A1. If a letter to the editor or an editorial, then insert [Letter to the Editor] or [Editorial] after the article title. | A news report dated March 12, 2007, in the online *Washington Post*, one of the world's great newspapers, reports that . . . | It sometimes helps to establish the credibility of the newspaper—some are more reputable than others. And always include reference to the date of the article. You should also indicate whether it was a regular news item or a letter to the editor or an editorial. |
| **Encyclopedia** | | |
| Feminism (2007). In *Encyclopaedia Britannica*. Retrieved March 12, 2007, from Encyclopedia Britannica Online: http://www.britannica.com/search?query=feminism&CT=. | The online version of the *Encyclopaedia Britannica*, accessed March 7, 2007, defines feminism as "the belief in the social, economic, and political equality of the sexes." | It isn't necessary to say "www.britannica.com." Your audience will know how to access the encyclopedia—especially if they're in this course. |
| **Research Study** | | |
| Andrejevic, M. (2006). The discipline of watching: Detection, risk, and lateral surveillance. *Critical Studies in Media Communication, 23* (December), 391–407. | In the December 2006 issue of *Critical Studies in Media Communication*, one of the official journals of the National Communication Association, a research study conducted by Mark Andrejevic found that . . . | In citing a research study, make it clear that what you're reporting is from the primary source and not from a popular magazine's summary of the research (that is, a secondary source) |
| **Website** | | |
| New developments (2008, March 22). Retrieved May 14, 2008, from www.texas.gov. If an author is identified, then: Smith, C. (2008, March 17). The truth. Retrieved April 5, 2008, from www.hhhsmith.org. | The official State of Texas website, which you can access at www.texas.gov, contains the full text of the speeches on this issue; they all are in favor of . . . | Like blogs, websites vary in accuracy and credibility. Some are designed to sell a product or service, so their information may be suspect. (It also may be quite accurate, of course.) Government (.gov domain), educational (.edu domain), and organizational (.org domain) websites are usually more reliable and are more likely to be believed by an educated audience. |

### Blog

Sullivan, A. (2007, January 28). The Webb factor. Retrieved January 30, 2007, from http:time.blogs.com/daily_dish.

Andrew Sullivan, the author of *The Conservative Soul*, in an article posted on January 28, 2007, to his blog *The Daily Dish*—one of the most widely read blogs on the Internet—had this to say about Webb . . .

Anyone can maintain a blog. If the blog is used for more than examples or illustrations, you need to establish the authority of the blogger and the date of the post you're citing.

### Chat Room Conversation

Seabiscuit. (2008, May 4). Happiness. Retrieved June 8, 2008, from www.myheart.com.

One important insight on this issue was posted this week in a chat room by Seabiscuit.

Chat room conversation can give you good examples or ideas. Even if the conversation is no longer available, you need to credit the writer and indicate where you got the idea.

### News Broadcast

Charlie Rose. (2008, May 4). Interview with C. A. Smith, broadcast on PBS.

In August of this year, Charlie Rose interviewed Smith on *The Nation* on PBS, and Smith agreed that . . .

It's helpful to name the network (rather than just saying "a television news show said . . .") as well as the specific news show, the person being interviewed and perhaps the interviewer. By naming all these, you create a clearer picture in the minds of your listeners and at the same time ensure accuracy.

### Personal Interview

Because personal interviews are not retrievable, they are not included in the references list.

In an e-mail interview I conducted in September of this year with James Wilder, the sheriff of Forest County, Wilder wrote that . . .

State how the interview was conducted—in person, by telephone, or through e-mail—and when it took place. Again, the currency of the date is more important than the specific date, so it's fine to say either "September of this year" or, for example, "September 22."

### Classroom Lecture

Smith, R. (2007, September 16). History of American Public Address at Queens College, City University of New York.

In a lecture last week in History of American Public Address, Professor Russel Smith noted that . . .

Citations to classroom lectures should include the professor's name, the course, and the approximate time the comment was made.

### Statistics

Hurricane Information. (2006, June 7). Retrieved January 29, 2007, from www.FedStats.gov.hurricane2.html

FedStats—the U.S. federal government's online statistics website, which I accessed on Wednesday—provides sobering statistics on the devastation of Katrina and Rita.

Stress the authority of the source that collected the statistics (.gov sites are more reliable than .com sites) and the recency of the statistics. Providing information on when you accessed the website will further help you establish the statistics' currency.

Major textbook and trade book publishers go to enormous effort to ensure the accuracy of what appears in print or on their websites, so the information they provide is generally reliable. Some publishers, however, are arms of special interest groups with specific agendas. If this is the case with one of the sources you have selected, try to balance this publisher's perspective with information that represents other views of the issue. If an article appears in a journal sponsored by a major academic organization such as the American Psychological Association or the National Communication Association, you can be pretty sure that experts in the field have carefully reviewed the article before publication. Again, if an article appears in a well-respected major newspaper like the *New York Times*, the *Washington Post*, or the *Wall Street Journal*, or in any of the major newsmagazines or news networks (or online on their websites), you can be pretty sure that the information is accurate. Do realize that these claims of accuracy are generalizations and that errors do occur. Both academic journals and newspapers have printed fraudulent articles, though these instances are rare.

# SUMMARY: PUBLIC SPEAKING TOPICS, AUDIENCES, AND RESEARCH

This unit introduced the nature of public speaking and covered selecting and limiting the topic and purpose, analyzing and adapting to your audience, and researching your speech.

1. Public speaking also provides training to improve your personal and social competencies, academic and career skills, and general communication abilities.

2. Apprehension in public speaking is normal and can be managed by reversing the factors that cause anxiety, practicing performance visualization, and systematically desensitizing yourself.

3. The preparation of a public speech involves 10 steps: (1) select the topic and purpose; (2) analyze the audience; (3) research the topic; (4) formulate the thesis and identify the main points; (5) support the main points; (6) organize the speech materials; (7) construct the conclusion, introduction, and transitions; (8) outline the speech; (9) word the speech; and (10) rehearse and deliver the speech. The first three of these steps were discussed in this unit; the remaining seven are discussed in the next two units.

4. Speech topics should deal with significant issues that interest the audience. Subjects and purposes should be limited in scope.

5. In analyzing an audience, consider the audience members' attitudes, beliefs, and values.

6. In analyzing the audience, also consider age, gender, cultural factors, religion and religiousness, the occasion, and the specific context.

7. Also analyze and adapt to your audience's willingness to hear your speech, how favorable the audience is to your point of view, and the knowledge that your audience has of your topic.

8. Research the topic, beginning with general sources and gradually exploring more specific and specialized sources.

9. Useful sources of information include libraries, interviews, scholarly articles, popular publications, reference works, news media, biographical material, government publications, electronic databases, and more.

10. Integrate research into your speech by mentioning the sources, providing smooth transitions, and avoiding useless expressions such as "I have a quote."

11. Avoid plagiarism by clearly acknowledging the source of any words or ideas you use that are not your own.

12. Critically evaluate your research by asking if the research is current, if it is fair and unbiased, and if the evidence is sufficient and accurate.

# KEY TERMS IN PUBLIC SPEAKING TOPICS, AUDIENCES, AND RESEARCH

attitude (p. **307**)
audience (p. **307**)
audience analysis (p. **307**)
belief (p. **307**)
communication
  apprehension (p. **296**)
general purpose (p. **304**)

informative speech (p. **304**)
performance visualization
  (p. **297**)
persuasive speech (p. **305**)
plagiarism (p. **313**)
primary sources (p. **316**)
search directory (p. **303**)

secondary sources (p. **316**)
special occasion speech
  (p. **305**)
specific purpose (p. **306**)
systematic desensitization
  (p. **298**)
taboo (p. **301**)

topic (p. **298**)
topoi (p. **303**)
tree diagrams (p. **303**)
value (p. **307**)

# THINKING CRITICALLY ABOUT SPEAKING TOPICS, AUDIENCES, AND RESEARCH

1. **Listservs and newsgroups.** Using L-soft's Catalist of listserv lists (**www.lsoft.com/lists/listref.html**), explore the listservs that deal with topics related to your next speech. How many can you find? Using Google (**http://groups.google.com/**), investigate the available newsgroups dealing with topics related to your next speech. Try to find at least three.

2. **Winning over the unwilling.** Jack is scheduled to give a speech on careers in computer technology to a group of high school students who have been forced to go to a

Saturday "career day" and to attend at least three of the speeches. The audience is definitely an unwilling group. What advice can you give Jack to help him deal with this type of audience?

3. **Biographical information.** Jill wants to give a speech on television talk shows and wants to include biographical information on some of the talk show hosts. What sources might Jill go to in order to get authoritative and current information on these hosts? What sources might she go to in order to get "fan" type information?

What advice would you give Jill for distinguishing the two types of sources and information?

4. **Two-minute speeches.** Prepare and deliver a two-minute speech in which you do one of the following:
   - evaluate the topics of recent talk shows against the criteria for a worthwhile and appropriate topic
   - explain the cultural factors operating in this class that need to be taken into consideration by the speaker selecting a topic and purpose
   - explain a particularly strong belief that you hold
   - describe members of your class in terms of how willing, favorable, and knowledgeable you believe them to be about any specific topic or speaker
   - describe the audience of a popular magazine or television show or movie

   - explain the value of one reference book, website, database, listserv, or newsgroup for research in public speaking

5. **Accessing the Internet.** According to one survey, approximately 23 percent of Internet users in the United States (about 30 million people) accessed the Internet from a place other than home or office. The leading places were school (27 percent), a friend's or neighbor's house (26 percent), and libraries (26 percent) (Use of the Internet in Places other than Home or Work: A PIP Data Memo, **www.pewinternet.org/ PPF/r/115/report_ display.asp**, dated March 3, 2004, accessed February 10, 2005). Where do you use the Internet, and does the location make a difference in your Internet activities?

# LogOn! MyCommunicationLab
## WWW.MYCOMMUNICATIONLAB.COM

Visit MCL for a variety of useful resources. For this unit it contains two self-tests on satisfaction with public speaking and knowledge of research; discussions titled Historical Roots of Public Speaking, Growth and Development of Public Speaking, Apprehension, Developing Confidence in Public Speaking, and The Dictionary of Topics (suitable for your classroom speeches); and the exercises Analyzing and Adapting to Your Audience during the Speech, Seeking Audience Information, and Fishbone Diagram for Limiting Topics.

Several useful speeches and speech excerpts are available. Select one of the student speeches and examine it in terms of the topic, intended audience, and research, as discussed in this unit. Also visit **www.ablongman/pubspeak**. Examine the material under the Access, Research, and Analyze tabs; it will provide another perspective on the discussion presented in this unit.

# UNIT 15 Supporting and Organizing Your Speech

## MAJOR TOPICS

**Step 4: Formulate Your Thesis and Main Points**

**Step 5: Support Your Main Points**

**Step 6: Organize Your Speech**

**Step 7: Construct Your Introduction, Conclusion, and Transitions**

## Special Features

 The Motivated Sequence:
Bruce E. Gronbeck, 347

Product Placement, 330

 Communicating in Cyberspace, 348

Here the discussion of public speaking continues.

**In this unit you'll learn about:**
- the main idea or thesis of the speech and its main points.
- the nature of support.
- the organizational patterns, introductions, and conclusions for speeches of all types.

**And you'll learn to:**
- formulate a clear thesis statement.
- support your ideas with interesting and persuasive materials (examples, testimony, statistics).
- organize your thoughts so that your speech is easy to follow and maintains your audience's interest and attention.

## STEP 4: FORMULATE YOUR THESIS AND MAIN POINTS

Your **thesis** is your main assertion; it's what you want the audience to absorb from your speech. The thesis of the *Rocky* movies is that the underdog can win; the thesis of the Martin Luther King Jr. "I Have a Dream" speech is that true equality must be granted to African Americans and to all people. From your thesis you'll be able to derive your main points, the major ideas that you will explore in order to prove or support your thesis.

### Your Thesis

In an informative speech, the thesis statement focuses on what you want your audience to learn. For example, a thesis for an informative speech on jealousy might be: "There are two main theories of jealousy." In a persuasive speech, your thesis is what you want your audience to believe as a result of your speech. For example, a thesis for a persuasive speech against using animals for experimentation might be: "Animal experimentation should be banned." Notice that in informative speeches the thesis is relatively neutral and objective. In persuasive speeches, however, the thesis statement puts forth a point of view, an opinion; it's an arguable, debatable proposition.

Be sure to limit the thesis statement to one central idea. A statement such as "Animal experimentation should be banned, and companies engaging in it should be prosecuted" contains not one but two basic ideas.

Word your thesis as a simple declarative sentence: "Animal experimentation should be banned." This will help you focus your thinking, your collection of materials, and your organizational tasks.

Use the thesis statement to help you generate your main points. Each thesis contains within it an essential question, and it is this question that allows you to explore and subdivide the thesis. Your objective is to find this question and ask it of your thesis. For example, let's say your thesis is: "The Hart bill provides needed services for senior citizens." Stated in this form, the thesis suggests the obvious question "What are they?" The answers to this question suggest the main points of your speech; for example, health care, food, shelter, and recreational services. These four areas then become the four main points of your speech.

Use the thesis to help focus the audience's attention on your central idea. In some cases you may wish to state your thesis early in your speech. In other cases, such as situations in which your audience may be hostile to your thesis, it may be wise to give your evidence first and gradually move the audience into a more positive frame of mind before stating your thesis. Here are a few guidelines to help you make the right decision about when to introduce your thesis:

- In an informative speech, state your thesis early and state it clearly and directly.

- In a persuasive speech before a neutral or positive audience, state your thesis explicitly and early in your speech.

- In a persuasive speech before an audience that is hostile to your position, delay revealing your thesis until you've moved your listeners closer to your point of view.

- Recognize that there are cultural differences in the way a thesis should be stated. In some Asian cultures, for example, making a point too directly or asking directly for audience compliance may be considered rude or insulting.

Here, for example, is how student Stephanie Cagniart of the University of Texas at Austin expressed her thesis, along with a clear preview of the main points she would cover in her speech:

> The commerce clause is being used by the federal government to dictate social issues—from gun control to same-sex marriage—in a way that threatens our individual liberties and undermines states' rights. So let's first, examine why the commerce clause has broadened; second, explore this abuse's dangers; and finally, investigate how we can scale back what the October 20, 2005, *Wanderer* magazine calls "the clause that ate the Constitution."

## Main Points

If your speech were a play, the main points would be its acts. Let's look at how you can select and word your main points and how you can logically arrange them.

As we discussed earlier, you can develop your main points by asking strategic questions. To see how this works in detail, imagine that you are giving a speech on the values of a college education to a group of high school students. Your thesis is: "A college education is valuable." You then ask, "Why is it valuable?" From this question you generate your main points. Your first step might be to brainstorm this question and generate as many answers as possible without evaluating them. You might come up with answers such as the following:

1. It helps you get a good job.
2. It increases your earning potential.
3. It gives you greater job mobility.
4. It helps you secure more creative work.
5. It helps you appreciate the arts more fully.
6. It helps you understand an extremely complex world.
7. It helps you understand different cultures.
8. It allows you to avoid taking a regular job for a few years.
9. It helps you meet lots of people and make new friends.
10. It helps you increase your personal effectiveness.

---

**Theory and Research** / **UNDERSTANDING** Primacy and Recency

Let's say that you have three points that you intend to arrange in topical order. How will you determine which to put first? The theory and research on primacy and recency offer help. As explained in Unit 3, the rule of primacy tells you that what an audience hears first will be remembered best and will have the greatest effect. The rule of recency tells you that what the audience hears last (or most recently) will be remembered best and will have the greatest effect. Research findings on these seemingly incompatible "rules" offer a few useful general suggestions.

- The middle is remembered least and has the least general effect. Thus, if you have a speech with three points, put the weakest one in the middle.

- If your listeners are favorable or neutral, lead with your strongest point. In this way you'll strengthen the conviction of those who are already favorable and you'll get the neutrals on your side early.

- If your audience is hostile or holds very different views than you, put your most powerful argument last and work up to it gradually—assuming, that is, that you can count on the listeners' staying with you until the end.

  Research on memory tells us that the audience will remember very little of what you say in a speech. Therefore, repeat your main assertions—whether you put them first or last in your speech—in your conclusion.

### Working with Theories and Research

*Examine your previous speech or the speech you're currently working on in terms of the order of the main points. What insights does primacy–recency theory give you for ordering your main points?*

---

## Building Communication Skills Generating Main Points

Try generating two or three main points (suitable for an informative or persuasive speech) from any one of the following thesis statements by asking strategic questions of each. Try following the general format illustrated in the text in the example of the values of a college education.

1. Property owned by religious organizations should be taxed.
2. Adoption agencies should be required to reveal the names of birth parents to all children when they reach 18 years of age.
3. The growing of tobacco should be declared illegal.
4. Medicinal marijuana should be legalized.
5. Gay men and lesbians should be granted full equality in the military.

*The more main points you generate, the more likely you'll find ones that will be especially appropriate for your thesis and audience.*

---

There are, of course, many other possibilities—but for purposes of illustration, these 10 possible main points will suffice. But not all 10 are equally valuable or relevant to your audience, so you should look over the list to see how to make it shorter and more meaningful. Try these suggestions:

- Eliminate those points that seem least important to your thesis. On this basis you might want to eliminate number 8, as this seems least consistent with your intended emphasis on the positive values of college.

- Combine those points that have a common focus. Notice, for example, that the first four points all center on the value of college in terms of jobs. You might, therefore, consider grouping these four items into one proposition: A college education helps you get a good job. This main point and its elaboration might look like this in your speech outline:

  **I.** A college education helps you get a good job.
  **A.** College graduates earn higher salaries.
  **B.** College graduates enter more creative jobs.
  **C.** College graduates have greater job mobility.

  Note that A, B, and C all relate to aspects or subdivisions of a "good job."

- Select the points that are most relevant or interesting to your audience. You might decide that high school students would be interested in increasing personal effectiveness, so you might select point 10 for inclusion as a second main point.

- In general, limit the number of main points. For your class speeches, which will generally range from 5 to 15 minutes, use two, three, or four major ideas. Too many main points will result in a speech that is confusing, contains too much information and too little amplification, and proves difficult for listeners to remember.

- Word each of your main points in the same (parallel) style. When outlining, phrase points labeled with Roman numerals in a similar (parallel) style. Likewise, phrase points labeled with capital letters and subordinate to the same Roman numeral (for example, A, B, and C under point I or A, B, and C under point II) in a similar style. In item 2 above, parallel style was used in the example on college education and getting a good job. This parallel styling helps the audience follow and remember your speech.

- Develop your main points so they are separate and discrete; don't allow them to overlap one another. Each section labeled with a Roman numeral should be a separate entity.

## STEP 5: SUPPORT YOUR MAIN POINTS

Now that you've identified your main points—and having learned in Unit 14 how to search for information—you can devote attention to your next step: supporting your main points. Supporting materials (such as examples, statistics, and presentation aids) are essential to the public speaker: They give life to the main points; they help maintain attention; and they contribute to your purpose, whether that is to inform or to persuade. Presenting examples of homelessness, for instance, helps you show your listeners what homelessness is, how it happens, and how it affects people. Presenting statistics on the new health insurance plans helps your listeners understand why they should make certain decisions and not make others. Showing slides of your main points will help your listeners remember the most important parts of your speech.

Among the most important sources of support are examples, narratives, analogies, definitions, testimony, statistics, and presentation aids, all of which this section will cover in depth.

## Examples

**Examples** are specific instances that are explained in varying degrees of detail. Examples are useful when you wish to make an abstract concept or idea con-crete. It's easier for an audience to understand what you mean by, say, "love" or "friendship" if you provide a specific example along with your definition.

In using examples, keep in mind that their function is to make your ideas vivid and easily understood. Examples are useful for explaining a concept; they're not ends in themselves. Make them only as long as necessary to ensure that your purpose is achieved.

Also, use only enough examples to make your point. Make sure that the examples are sufficient to re-create your meaning in the minds of your listeners, but be careful not to use so many that the audience loses the very point you are making.

Show the audience exactly how your example relates to the assertion or concept you are explaining. Here, for example, former New York mayor Rudolph Giuliani, in his address to the United Nations after the World Trade Center attack of September 11, 2001, gave relevant examples to support his point that we are a land of immigrants and must continue to be so (www.nyc.gov/html/rwg/html/96/united .html, accessed September 17, 2007).

### MEDIA WATCH

## PRODUCT PLACEMENT

*Let advertisers spend the same amount of money improving their product that they do on advertising, and they wouldn't have to advertise it.*

—*Will Rogers*

James Bond's Aston Martin and E.T.'s Reese's Pieces were early examples of **product placement**—the insertion of brand-name products in movies. Today, the practice of product placement for a fee is becoming increasingly popular throughout all media. The reason is that it means big money to the media producers and effective advertising for the product. For example, *Tomorrow Never Dies*, one of the Bond movies, earned $34 million for placing in the movie such products as BMW, Omega watches, Heineken beer, Avis rental cars, and Bollinger champagne (Rodman, 2001).

In 2005 *The Contender*, a reality boxing show on NBC, had 7,502 product placements (including the presence of the product and/or its mention), from Gatorade to a Toyota truck: more placements than any other show. In 2004 the total number of product placements in television was 81,739; in 2005 it rose to 107,839 (*New York Times*, March 20, 2006, p. C3). In televised sports, products are advertised not only during commercial breaks but on billboards, in the names of the stadiums, or on the players' sneakers.

It's estimated that in 2005 magazines will have earned some $160.9 million and newspapers approximately $65 million for product placements—for advertising products without telling readers that these were in fact advertisements designed to sell the products (Lamb, 2005).

The use of product placement in news shows has created the most debate. For example, *Good Morning America* broadcast one of its shows from a Norwegian Cruise Line ship. Although no fees were paid for the product placement, the Cruise Line reportedly did pay for the airfare, room, and board for 300 contest winners on a cruise to the West Indies (Schiller, 2006). And the *New York Times* has already agreed to allow "watermark" ads to appear behind news and editorial articles (Mandese, 2006).

### Increasing Media Literacy

*Product placements will surely increase over the coming years and will invade all media forms. When you see a product in a movie or television show, keep in mind that advertisers paid heavily for its being there.*

New York City was built by immigrants and it will remain the greatest city in the world as long as we continue to renew ourselves with and benefit from the energizing spirit from new people coming here to create a better future for themselves and their families. Come to Flushing, Queens, where immigrants from many lands have created a vibrant, vital commercial and residential community. Their children challenge and astonish us in our public school classrooms every day. Similarly, you can see growing and dynamic immigrant communities in every borough of our city: Russians in Brighton Beach, West Indians in Crown Heights, Dominicans in Washington Heights, the new wave of Irish in the Bronx, and Koreans in Willow Brook on Staten Island.

## Narratives

**Narratives**, or stories, are often useful as supporting materials in a speech. Narratives give the audience what it wants: a good story. They help you maintain your audience's attention, because listeners automatically perk up when a story is told. Narratives allow you to bring an abstract concept down to specifics. Following Clella Jaffe (1998), we can distinguish three types of narrative: explanatory, exemplary, and persuasive.

- *Explanatory narratives* explain the way things are. The biblical book of Genesis, for example, explains the development of the world from a particular religious viewpoint. An eyewitness report might explain the events leading up to an accident.

- *Exemplary narratives* provide examples of excellence (or its opposite)—examples to follow or admire (or to avoid following). The stories of the lives of saints and martyrs are exemplary narratives, as are the Horatio Alger success stories. Similarly, many motivational speakers often include exemplary narratives in their speeches and will tell stories of what they were like when they were out of shape or on drugs or deep in debt.

- *Persuasive narratives* try to strengthen or change beliefs and attitudes. When Sally Struthers tells us of the plight of starving children, she's using a persuasive narrative. The parables in religious writings are persuasive in urging listeners to lead life in a particular way.

Keep your narratives relatively short and few in number. In most cases, one or possibly two narratives should be sufficient in a short 5- to 15-minute speech. Make explicit the connection between your story and the point you are making. If the people in the audience don't get this connection, you lose not only the effectiveness of the story but also their attention (as they try to figure out why you told that story).

## Analogies

**Analogies** are comparisons that are often extremely useful in making your ideas clear and vivid to your audience. Analogies may be of two types: figurative and literal.

### Figurative Analogies

Figurative analogies compare items from different classes—for example, the flexibility afforded by a car with the freedom of a bird, a college degree with a passport to success, playing baseball with running a corporation. Figurative analogies are useful for illustrating possible similarities; they provide vivid examples that are easily remembered.

### Literal Analogies

Literal analogies compare items from the same class, such as two cars or two cities. For example, in a literal analogy you might argue (1) that two companies are similar—both are multinational, multibillion-dollar pharmaceutical companies, both have advertising budgets in the hundreds of millions of dollars, and so on; and (2) that therefore the advertising techniques that worked for one company will work for the other.

In evaluating your literal analogies, ask yourself two questions:

- Are the cases compared (the companies in this case) alike in essential respects? Or do the two cases differ from each other in ways that might weaken the comparison? For example, do they differ in the location of their headquarters? Do the two companies differ in the types of drugs they manufacture? Do the companies differ in their pricing of drugs?

- Do the differences make a difference? Obviously, not all differences are significant. Very likely a difference in the headquarters location is not a difference that will bear on the type of advertising that will prove effective. On the other hand, differences in the types of drugs they sell or in pricing may well prove significant. These differences may have an impact on the type of advertising that will prove most effective; advertising techniques used to sell over-the-counter painkillers like aspirin may not prove effective in selling drugs for cancer or diabetes patients.

### USING DEFINITIONS

You want to define vegan and vegetarian and distinguish between them using a variety of types of definitions.

WHAT DO YOU SAY?

## Definitions

A **definition** is a statement of the meaning of a term or concept; it explains what something is. Use definitions when you wish to explain difficult or unfamiliar concepts or when you wish to make a concept more vivid or forceful.

As you can appreciate, definitions are often helpful when you are explaining a concept that the audience may be unfamiliar with or may have misconceptions about. If the purpose of the definition is to clarify, then it must do just that. This would be too obvious to mention if not for the fact that many speakers, perhaps for want of something to say, define terms that don't need extended definitions. Some speakers use definitions that don't clarify and that, in fact, complicate an already complex concept. Make sure your definitions define only what needs defining.

As you think of terms to define, or after you've selected your term, take a look at the OneLook Dictionary Search website at www.onelook.com. This website will enable you to search a wide variety of dictionaries at the same time. There are, of course, many other useful online dictionaries; search for "dictionary," "definitions," or "thesaurus" and you'll find a wealth of material for speeches of definition.

Here are some of the most important approaches you might use to define a term.

## Definition by Etymology

One way to define a term is to trace its *etymology*—its historical or linguistic development. In defining the word *communication*, for example, you might note that it comes from the Latin *communis*, meaning "common"; in "communicating" you seek to establish a commonness, a sameness, a similarity with another individual. And *woman* comes from the Anglo-Saxon *wifman*, which meant literally a "wife man," with the word *man* applied to both sexes. Through phonetic change *wifman* became *woman*. Most large dictionaries and, of course, etymological dictionaries will help you find useful etymological definitions.

Or you might define a term by noting not its linguistic etymology, but how it came to mean what it now means. For example, you might note that the word *spam*, meaning junk messages on the Net, comes from a *Monty Python* television skit in which every item on the menu contained the product Spam. And much as the diner was forced to get Spam, so the Net surfer gets spam—even when he or she wants something else.

## Definition by Authority

You can often clarify a term by explaining how a particular *authority* views it. You might, for example, define lateral thinking by authority and say that Edward deBono, who developed the concept of lateral thinking, has noted that "lateral thinking involves moving sideways to look at things in a different way. Instead of fixing on one particular approach and then working forward from that, the lateral thinker tries to find other approaches" (deBono, 1973). Or you might use the authority of cynic and satirist Ambrose Bierce and define love as nothing but "a temporary insanity curable by marriage" and friendship as "a ship big enough to carry two in fair weather, but only one in foul."

## Definition by Negation

You also might define a term by noting what the term is not; that is, define it by *negation*. "A wife," you might say, "isn't a cook, a cleaning person, a babysitter, a seamstress, a sex partner. A wife is . . ." or "A teacher isn't someone who tells you what you should know but rather one who . . ."

Here Michael Marien (1992) defines futurists first negatively and then positively:

> Futurists do not use crystal balls. Indeed, they're generally loath to make firm predictions of what will happen. Rather, they make forecasts of what is probable, sketch scenarios of what is possible,

and/or point to desirable futures—what is preferable and what strategies we should pursue to get there.

### Definition by Direct Symbolization

You also might define a term by *direct symbolization*—by showing the actual thing or a picture or model of it. For example, a sales representative explaining a new computer keyboard would use an actual keyboard in the speech. Similarly, a speech on magazine layout or types of fabrics would include actual layout pages and fabric samples.

## Testimony

The term **testimony** refers to the opinions of experts or the accounts of witnesses. Testimony helps to amplify your speech by adding a note of authority to your arguments. For example, you might want to use the testimony of a noted economist to support your predictions about inflation, or the testimony of someone who spent two years in a maximum-security prison to discourage young people from committing crimes.

When you cite testimony, stress first the competence of the person, whether that person is an expert or a witness. For example, citing the predictions of a world-famous economist of whom your audience has never heard will mean little unless you first explain the person's competence. You might say something like "This prediction comes from the world's leading economist, who has successfully predicted all major financial trends over the past 20 years." Now the audience will be prepared to lend credence to what this person says.

Second, stress the unbiased nature of the testimony. If the audience perceives the testimony to be biased—whether or not it really is—it will have little effect. You want to check out any possible biases in a witness so that you can present accurate information. But you also want to make the audience see that the testimony is in fact unbiased.

Third, stress the recency of the testimony. If an audience has no way of knowing when the statement was made, it has no way of knowing how true this statement is today.

## Statistics

Let's say you want to show that significant numbers of people are now getting their news from the Internet, that the cost of filmmaking has skyrocketed over the last 20 years, or that women buy significantly more books and magazines than men. To communicate these types of information, you'd use

**statistics**—summary numbers that help you communicate the important characteristics of an otherwise complex set of numbers. Statistics help the audience see, for example, the percentage of people getting their news from the Internet, the average cost of films in 2007 versus previous years, or the difference between male and female book and magazine purchases. Excellent aids for using and interpreting statistics may be found at http://nilesonline.com/stats/. This site will assist you in understanding and evaluating research results and in using statistics in your own speeches. Some general guidelines for employing statistics:

- *Make the statistics clear to your audience.* Remember, they'll hear the figures only once. Round off figures so they are easy to understand and retain.

- *Make the statistics meaningful.* When you are using statistics, it's often helpful to remind the audience of what the statistic itself means. For example, if you say, "The median price of a co-op apartment in San Francisco is $875,000," remind the audience that this means the middle price—that half the prices are above $875,000 and half are below. Also, present numbers so that the audience can appreciate the meaning you want to convey. To say, for example, that the Sears Tower in Chicago is 1,559 feet tall doesn't help your hearers visualize its height. So consider saying something like "The Sears Tower is 1,559 feet tall. Just how tall is 1,559 feet? Well, it's as tall as the length of more than five football fields. It's as tall as 260 six-foot people standing on each other's heads."

- *Connect the statistics with your point.* Make explicit the connection between the statistics and what they show. A statement, for example, that college professors make an average of $85,000 per year needs to be related specifically to the proposition that teachers' salaries should be raised—or lowered, depending on your point of view.

- *Use statistics in moderation.* Most listeners' capacity for numerical data presented in a speech is limited, so in most cases statistics should be used sparingly.

- *Visually (and verbally) reinforce the statistics.* Numbers are difficult to grasp and remember when they are presented without some kind of visual reinforcement, so it's often helpful to complement your oral presentation of statistics with some type of presentation aid—perhaps a graph or a chart.

Here is a good example of how U.S. Senator Barack Obama (Illinois) used statistics in his speech to the

2006 Global Summit on AIDS and the Church (http://obama.senate.gov, accessed January 14, 2007):

> You know, AIDS is a story often told by numbers. Forty million infected with HIV. Nearly 4.5 million this year alone. Twelve million orphans in Africa. Eight thousand deaths and 6,000 new infections every single day. In some places, 90 percent of those with HIV do not know they have it. And we just learned that AIDS is set to become the third leading cause of death worldwide in the coming years. These are staggering, these numbers, and they help us understand the magnitude of this pandemic.

## Presentation Aids

When you're planning a speech, consider using some kind of **presentation aid**—a visual or auditory means for clarifying ideas. Ask yourself how you can represent visually (or via audio) what you want your audience to remember. How can you reinforce your ideas with additional media? If you want your audience to grasp increases in the sales tax, consider showing them a graph of rising sales taxes over the last 10 years. If you want them to see that Brand A is superior to Brand X, consider showing them a comparison chart identifying the superior qualities of Brand A.

### Types of Presentation Aids

Among the presentation aids you have available are the actual object, models of the object, graphs, word charts, maps, people, photographs and illustrations, and tapes and CDs.

As a general rule (to which there are many exceptions), the best presentation aid is *the object itself*; bring it with you if you can. Notice that infomercials sell their product not only by talking about it but also by showing it to potential buyers. You see what George Foreman's Lean Mean Grilling Machine looks like and how it works. You see the jewelry, the clothing, and the new mop from a wide variety of angles and in varied settings. If you want to explain some tangible thing and you can show it to your audience, do so.

**Models**—replicas of actual objects—are useful for a variety of purposes. For example, if you wanted to explain complex structures such as the hearing or vocal mechanism, the brain, or the structure of DNA, you would almost have to use a model. You may remember from science classes that these models (and the pictures of them in the textbooks) make a lot more sense than verbal explanations alone. Models help to clarify relative size and position and how each part interacts with each other part. Large models can be used to help listeners visualize objects that are too small (or unavailable) to appreciate otherwise. In other cases, small models of large objects—objects that are too large to bring to your speech—are helpful. For example, in a speech on stretching exercises, one student used a 14-inch wooden artist's model.

*Graphs* are useful for showing differences over time, for showing how a whole is divided into parts, and for showing different amounts or sizes. Figure 15.1 shows different types of graphs that can be drawn freehand or generated with the graphics capabilities of any word-processing or presentation software.

*Word charts* (which can also contain numbers and even graphics) are useful for lots of different types of information. For example, you might use a word chart to identify the key points that you cover in one of your propositions or in your entire speech—in the order in which you cover them, of course. Slide 4 in the Public Speaking Sample Assistant box on page 340 is a good example of a simple word chart listing the major topics discussed in the speech. Or you could use word charts to identify the steps in a process; for example, to summarize the steps in programming a VCR, dealing with sexual harassment, or installing a new computer program. Another use of charts is for presenting information you want your audience to write down. Emergency phone numbers, addresses to write to, or titles of recommended books and websites are examples of the type of information that listeners will welcome in written form.

*Maps* are useful for illustrating a wide variety of concepts. If you want to show the locations of cities, lakes, rivers, or mountain ranges, maps will obviously prove useful as presentation aids. Maps are also helpful for illustrating population densities, immigration patterns, varied economic conditions, the spread of diseases, and hundreds of other issues you may wish to develop in your speeches. For example, in a talk on natural resources, one speaker used maps to illustrate the locations of large reserves of oil, gas, and precious metals. Another speaker used maps to illustrate concentrations of wealth; still another used maps to show worldwide differences in mortality rates.

You also can use maps to illustrate numerical differences. For example, you might use a map to show the wide variation in literacy rates throughout the world. You could color the countries with 90 to 100 percent literacy red, the countries with 80 to 89 percent literacy green, and so on. When you use maps in this way, it's often helpful to complement them with charts or graphs that, for example, give the specific literacy rates for the specific countries on which you want to concentrate.

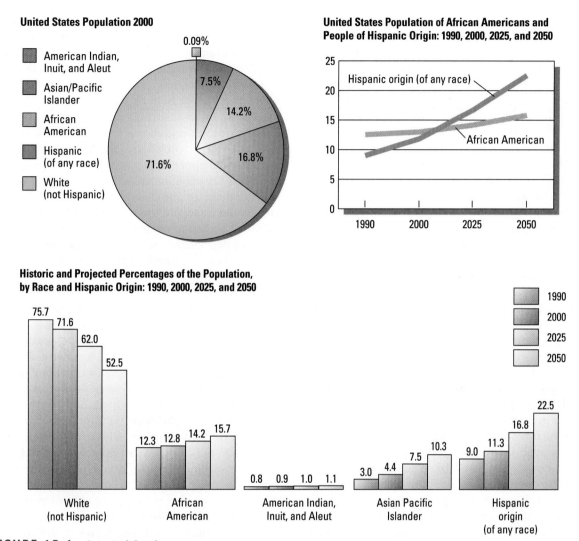

**FIGURE 15.1   Assorted Graphs**

Notice that each of the graphs serves a somewhat different purpose. The *pie chart* is especially useful if you want to show how some whole is divided into its parts and the relative sizes of the parts. From the pie chart you can easily see the relative percentages of the different groups in the U.S. population. Pie charts are especially helpful when you have three to five values to illustrate; any more than five creates a pie that is difficult to read at a glance. The *line graph* shows how comparisons can be visualized with a very simple illustration. Notice that the graph is especially clear because it focuses on only 2 groups. Had it focused on 8 or 10 groups, it would have been difficult for an audience to understand. The *bar graph* presents the same information as the pie chart but for four different time periods. You might have used four pie charts—with each pie representing a different year—but comparisons would not have been as easy for an audience to make.

*People* can also function effectively as "presentation aids." For example, if you wanted to demonstrate the muscles of the body, you might use a bodybuilder. If you wanted to discuss different voice patterns, skin complexions, or hairstyles, you might use people as your aids. Aside from the obvious assistance they provide in demonstrating their muscles or voice qualities, people help to secure and maintain the attention and interest of the audience.

And don't overlook yourself as a (kind of) presentation aid. For example, if you are giving a speech on boxing strategies, exercise techniques, or sitting and standing postures that can lead to backaches, consider demonstrating them yourself. As an added plus, going through these demonstrations is likely to reduce your apprehension and make you more relaxed.

*Photographs and illustrations* are useful aids for a variety of purposes. Speeches on types of trees, styles of art or architecture, or types of exercise machines would profit greatly from a few well-chosen photographs or illustrations. If you want to show these but don't have the opportunity to put them onto slides, you may try simply holding them up as you refer to them. There are many hazards involved in using this type of aid, however, so pictures are recommended only with reservations. If the image is large enough for all members of the audience to see clearly (say, poster size); if it clearly illustrates what you want to illustrate; and if it's mounted on cardboard, then use it. Otherwise, don't.

Do not pass pictures around the room. This only draws attention away from what you are saying: Listeners will look for the pictures before the pictures circulate to them, will wonder what the pictures contain, and meanwhile will miss a great deal of your speech.

*Tapes, CDs*, and *DVDs* can be useful for many types of speeches as well. For a speech on advertising, for example, actual samples of commercials as played on radio or television would go a long way in helping the audience see exactly what you are talking about. These aids also provide variety by breaking up the oral presentation.

## The Media of Presentation Aids

Once you've decided on the type of presentation aid you'll use, you need to decide on the medium you'll use to present it. The decisions you make concerning which types of media to use should be based on the message you want to communicate and on the audience to whom you'll be speaking.

Some presentation media are low tech—for example, chalkboards, transparencies, and flip charts. These media are generally more effective in smaller, more informal situations, and especially for presentations that arise without prior notice, for which you simply don't have the time to prepare high-tech resources. Low-tech devices are also useful for highly interactive sessions; for example, the flip chart is still one of the best ways to record group members' contributions.

More high-tech media such as slides and videotapes are generally more effective with larger, more formal groups, in which you do most of the talking and the audience does most of the listening. High-tech materials also may be your only choice if the material you have to communicate is extremely complex or if the norms of your organization simply require that you use high-tech presentation formats.

The *chalkboard* or *whiteboard* is the easiest to use, but not necessarily the most effective. All classrooms have such boards, and you have seen them used by teachers with greater or lesser effect; in some way, you've had "experience" with them. Boards may be used effectively to present key terms or important definitions or even to outline the general structure of your speech. But don't use these boards if you can present the same information with a prepared chart or model. It takes too long to write out anything substantial. If you do write on a board, be careful not to turn your back to the audience. In this brief time you can easily lose their attention.

*Chartboards* (large pieces of semiflexible cardboard that can be held up for an audience to read, placed on an easel or bulletin board, or taped to a chalkboard) are useful when you have just one or two relatively simple charts that you want to display during your speech. If you want to display your charts for several minutes, be sure you have a way of holding them up. For example, bring masking tape if you intend to secure them to the wall, or enlist the aid of an audience member to hold them up. Use a light-colored board; white generally works best. Write in black; it provides the best contrast and is the easiest for people to read.

*Flip charts*, charts on large pads of paper (usually about 24 by 24 inches) mounted on a stand, can be used to record many types of information, which you reveal by flipping the pages as you deliver your speech. For example, if you were to discuss the various departments in an organization, you might have the key points relating to each department on a separate page of your flip chart. As you discussed the advertising department, you would show the advertising department chart. When you moved on to discuss the personnel department, you would flip to the chart dealing with personnel. You may find this device useful if you have a large number of word charts that you want to have easy control over. Make sure that the flip chart is positioned so that everyone in the audience can see it clearly and that the folding legs are positioned securely so it doesn't collapse when you flip the first page. Make sure you write large enough so that the people in the back can read your material without straining their eyes.

Flip charts also are especially useful for recording ideas at small group meetings. Unlike the chalkboard, the flip chart enables you to retain a written record of the meeting; should you need to, you can easily review the group's contributions.

*Slides and transparency projections* are helpful for showing a series of visuals that may be of very different types; for example, photographs, illustrations, charts, or tables. The slides can easily be created with many popular computer programs (see "Computer-Assisted Presentations" on page 339). To produce actual 35mm slides, you'll need considerable lead time; be sure to build this into your preparation time.

If you don't have access to a slide projector or don't have the time needed to construct slides, consider somewhat less sophisticated transparencies. You can create your visual in any of the word-processing or spreadsheet programs you normally use and probably can find a printer that will enable you to print transparencies. Another alternative is to use a copier that will produce transparencies.

An advantage of transparencies is that you can write on the transparencies (and on slides in computer presentations, as we discuss later) while you're speaking. You can circle important items, underline key terms, and draw lines connecting different terms.

When using any presentation aid, but especially with slides and transparencies, make sure that you have the proper equipment; for example, a projector, a table, a working outlet nearby, control over the lighting in the room, and whatever else you'll need to have the audience see your projections clearly.

*Videos* may serve a variety of purposes in public speaking. Basically, you have two options. First, you can tape a scene from a film or television show with your VCR and show it at the appropriate time in your speech. Thus, for example, you might record examples of sexism in television sitcoms, violence on television talk shows, or types of transitions used in feature films and show these excerpts during your speech. As you can see, however, this type of video takes a great deal of time and preparation, so if you are going to use such excerpts you must plan well in advance.

Second, you can create your own video with a video camera. One student created a video of ethnic store signs to illustrate the "interculturalization" of the city. With the help (and agreement to be recorded) of a few friends, another student created a three-minute video of religious holidays as celebrated by members of different religions and carefully coordinated each segment with her discussion of the relevant holiday.

In using videos, do make sure that they don't occupy too much of your speaking time; after all, your main objective is to learn the principles of public speaking.

*Handouts*, or printed materials that you distribute to members of the audience, are especially helpful in explaining complex material and also in providing listeners with a permanent record of some aspect of your speech. Handouts are also useful for presenting information that you want your audience to refer to throughout the speech. Handouts encourage listeners to take notes, especially if you leave enough white space or even provide a specific place for notes—and this keeps your listeners actively involved in your presentation. Handouts also reward the audience by giving them something for their attendance and attention. A variety of handouts can be easily prepared with many of the computer presentation packages that we'll consider in the last section of this unit.

You can distribute handouts at the beginning of, during, or after your speech; but realize that whichever system you use has both pros and cons. If you distribute materials before or during your speech, you run the risk of your listeners' reading the handout and not concentrating on your speech. On the other hand, if the listeners are getting the information you want to communicate—even if primarily from the handout—that isn't too bad. And, in a way, handouts allow listeners to process the information at their own pace.

You can encourage your audience to listen to you when you want them to, and to look at the handout when you want them to, by simply telling them: "Look at the graph at the top of page two of the handout; it summarizes recent census figures on immigration" or "We'll get back to the handout in a minute; now, however, I want to direct your attention to this next slide [or the second argument]."

If you distribute your handouts at the end of the speech, they will obviously not interfere with your presentation—but they may not be read at all. After all, listeners might reason, they heard the speech; why bother going through the handout? To counteract this very natural tendency, you might include additional material in the handout and mention this to your audience, saying something like "This handout contains all the slides shown here and three additional slides that provide economic data for Thailand, Cambodia, and Vietnam, which I didn't have time to cover. When you look at the data, you'll see that they mirror exactly the data provided in my talk on the other countries." When you provide additional information on your handout, it's more likely that it will get looked at and thus provide the reinforcement you want.

## Preparing Presentation Aids

In preparing presentation aids, make sure that they add clarity to your speech, that they're appealing to the listeners, and that they're culturally sensitive. *Clarity* is the most important consideration, and you can achieve it by following these simple guidelines:

1. Use colors that will make your message instantly clear; light colors on dark backgrounds or dark colors on light backgrounds provide the best contrast and seem to work best for most purposes. Be cautious about using yellow, which is often difficult to see, especially if there's glare from the sun.
2. Use direct phrases (not complete sentences); use bullets to highlight your points or your support (see the slides in the Public Speaking Sample Assistant box on pages 340–341). Just as you phrase your main points in parallel style whenever possible, try to phrase your bullets in parallel style, usually by using the same part of speech (for example, all nouns or all infinitive phrases). And make sure that the meaning or relevance of any graphic is immediately clear. If it isn't, explain it.

3. Use the aid to highlight a few essential points; don't clutter it with too much information. A maximum of four bullets on a slide or chart, for example, are as much information as you should include.
4. Use typefaces that can be read easily from all parts of the room. For a chart of typefaces available with most word-processing programs and suggestions for their use, see Table 15.1.
5. Give the slide or chart or transparency a title—a general heading—to further guide your listeners' attention and focus.

Create presentation aids so that they're *appealing* to your audience. Presentation aids should be attractive enough to engage the attention of the audience, but not so attractive that they're distracting.

An almost nude body draped across a car may be effective in selling underwear, but it will probably detract if your objective is to explain the profit-and-loss statement of General Motors.

Make sure your presentation aids are *culturally sensitive* and can be easily interpreted by people from other cultures. Just as your words will be interpreted within a cultural framework, so too will the symbols and colors you use in your aids. For example, when speaking to international audiences, you need to use universal symbols or explain those that are not universal. Be careful that your icons don't reveal an ethnocentric bias: Using the American dollar sign to symbolize "wealth" might be quite logical in your public speaking class, but it could be interpreted as ethnocentric if used with an audience of international visitors.

## Table 15.1   Some Typefaces

You have an enormous number of typefaces to choose from. Generally, select typefaces that are easy to read and that are consistent in tone with the message of your speech.

| Typeface | Comments |
| --- | --- |
| Palatino<br>Century Schoolbook<br>Garamond<br>Times | Serif typefaces retain some of the cursive strokes found in handwriting. The cursive stroke is illustrated especially in the *m* and *n*, which begin with a slight upsweep. Serif styles are easy to read and useful for blocks of text. |
| **Helvetica**<br>Bauhous<br>Avant Garde<br>Futura | Sans-serif typefaces (a style that is more bold and doesn't include the serif or upsweep) are useful for titles and headings but make reading long text difficult. |
| **Serif Gothic Black**<br>**STENCIL**<br>**Gill Sans Ultra Bold** | These extremely bold typefaces are tempting to use; but, as you can see, they're not easy to read. They're most appropriate for short titles. |
| Akzidenz Grotesk<br>BETON COMPRESSED BOLD<br>Franklin Gothic | These compressed typefaces are useful when you have to fit a lot of text into a small space. They are, however, difficult to read and so should generally be avoided (or at least used sparingly) in slides. It would be better to use an easier-to-read typeface and spread out the text over additional slides. |
| CASTELLAR<br>ROSEWOOD<br>JAZZ<br>ASHLEY INLINE<br>Linotext | Decorative styles like these, although difficult to read for extended text, make great headings or titles. Be careful, however, that the originality of your typefaces doesn't steal attention away from your message. |
| Mistral<br>Brush Script<br>Freestyle Script<br>Pepita | Script typefaces are interesting and will give your presentation a personal look, as if you wrote it longhand. But they'll be difficult to read. If you're going to read the slides aloud word for word, then typefaces that are a bit more difficult to read may still be used with considerable effect. |

# Using Presentation Aids

Keep the following guidelines clearly in mind when using presentation aids.

- Know your aids intimately. Be sure you know in what order they are to be presented and how you plan to introduce them. Know exactly what goes where and when.

- Test the aids before using them. When testing the presentation aids ahead of time, be certain that they can be seen easily from all parts of the room.

- Rehearse your speech with the presentation aids incorporated into the presentation. Practice your actual movements with the aids you'll use. If you're going to use a chart, how will you use it? Will it stand by itself? Can you tape it somewhere? Do you have tape with you?

- Integrate your aids seamlessly into your speech. Just as a verbal example should flow naturally into the text and seem an integral part of the speech, so should the presentation aid. It should appear not as an afterthought but as an essential part of the speech.

- Don't talk to your aid. Both you and the aid should be focused on the audience. Know your aids so well that you can point to what you want without breaking eye contact with your audience. Or, at most, break audience eye contact for only a few seconds at a time.

- Use the aid when it's relevant: Show it when you want the audience to concentrate on it, then remove it. If you don't remove it, the audience's attention may remain focused on the visual when you want them to focus on your next point.

## Computer-Assisted Presentations

There are a variety of presentation software packages available: PowerPoint, Corel Presentations, and Lotus Freelance are among the most popular and are very similar in what they do and how they do it. The Public Speaking Sample Assistant box on pages 340–341 illustrates what a set of slides might look like; the slides are built around a speech outline that we'll discuss in Unit 16 and were constructed in PowerPoint, though a similar slide show could be produced with most presentation software programs. Also, realize that you can easily import photographs and have slides of these inserted into your slide show; or you can add video clips. As you review the speech in the Public Speaking Sample Assistant box, try to visualize how you would use a slide show in presenting your next speech.

After you read the following material, which applies PowerPoint technology to public speaking, take one of the many available PowerPoint tutorials available online. A tutorial may be on your own computer or may be available somewhere on your campus. If not, visit one of the excellent tutorials from different colleges that are available to everyone; for example, visit Florida Gulf Coast University at www.fgcu.edu/support/office2000/ppt/, the University of Rhode Island at http://einstein.cs.uri.edu/tutorials/csc101/powerpoint/ppt.html, or Indiana–Purdue University at www.science.iupui.edu/SAC98/pp.htm. If you need more advanced training, try the University of Northern Iowa's advanced tutorial at www.uni.edu/plschool/index/profdev/briley/Advppt.html.

## Ways of Using Presentation Package Software.

Computer presentation software enables you to produce a variety of aids; the software will produce what you want. For example, you can construct slides on your computer, save them on a disk, and then have 35mm slides developed from the disk. To do this, you need access to a slide printer—or you can send your files out (you can do this via modem) to a lab specializing in converting electronic files into 35mm slides. There may be a slide printer at your school, so check there first. Similarly, your local office supply store or copy shop, such as Staples, OfficeMax, or Kinko's, may have exactly the services you need.

Or you can create your slides and then show them on your computer screen. If you are speaking to a very small group, it may be possible to have your listeners gather around your computer as you speak. With larger audiences, however, you'll need a computer projector or an LCD projection panel. Assuming that you have a properly equipped computer in the classroom, you can copy your entire presentation to a floppy disk and bring it with you on the day of the speech.

Computer presentation software also enables you to print out a variety of handouts:

- the slides shown during your speech, as well as additional slides that you may not have time to include in the speech but that you nevertheless want your listeners to look at when they read your handout (as in the Public Speaking Sample Assistant box on pages 340–341)

- the slides plus speaker's notes, the key points that you made as you showed each of the slides (see Figure 15.2, page 342)

- the slides plus places for listeners to write notes next to each of them (see Figure 15.3, page 343)

- an outline of your talk

- any combination of the above

Overhead transparencies also can be created from your computer slides. To make overheads on

**A Slide Show Speech**

This PowerPoint speech is intended to illustrate the general structure of a slide show speech and is derived from the speech in the Public Speaking Sample Assistant box on pages 359–361; you may find it helpful to look ahead to that speech to consider how you might improve this purposely sparse slide show. This PowerPoint presentation is available online at MyCommunicationLab. Copy it to your computer and try altering this basic outline as you learn more about PowerPoint or similar presentation software.

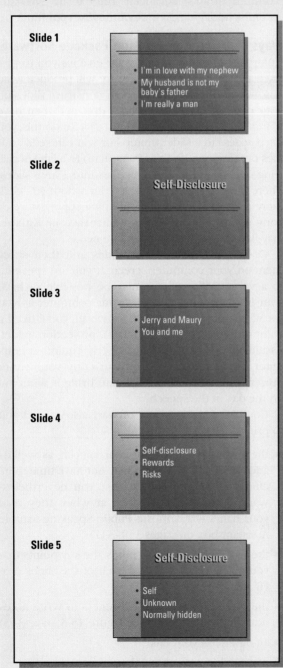

**Slide 1**

- I'm in love with my nephew
- My husband is not my baby's father
- I'm really a man

This first slide aims to gain attention with these provocative confessions. These three bullets would come up one at a time, with the speaker pausing for (with luck) some laughter. After you review the entire list of slides, try inserting graphics where you think they'd be appropriate.

**Slide 2**

Self-Disclosure

This second slide introduces the topic of the speech, self-disclosure.

**Slide 3**

- Jerry and Maury
- You and me

This slide recalls the popular confessions heard on the *Jerry Springer Show* and *Maury* but also relates the process of self-disclosure to the speaker and the audience, establishing an S-A-T connection.

**Slide 4**

- Self-disclosure
- Rewards
- Risks

This slide orients the audience by identifying the three main ideas to be discussed in the speech: the nature of self-disclosure, its rewards, and its risks. As with slide number 1, these three bullets should come up one at a time to give the speaker a chance to elaborate on each item and to give the audience a chance to digest the informatiion. Note that this slide show does not contain transitions; if you think they might help, insert transitions.

**Slide 5**

Self-Disclosure

- Self
- Unknown
- Normally hidden

This fifth slide focuses on the first major idea, the nature of self-disclosure as communication about the self, about something previously unknown, and about something that is normally kept hidden. Note here that very few words are used in the actual slide; the speaker will elaborate on each of these items in the actual speech. The words on the slide are best thought of as tags you want the audience to hang on to as you explain each point.

**Public Speaking Sample Assistant**

# A Speech of Introduction *(Continued)*

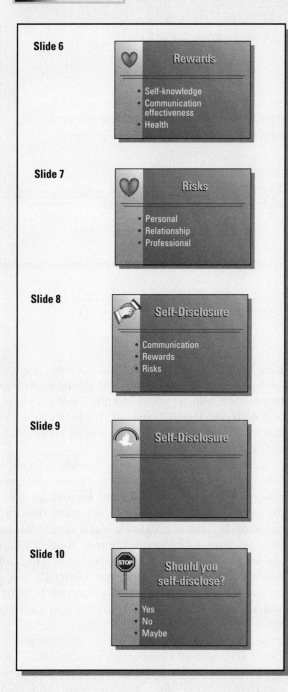

**Slide 6**

This sixth slide focuses on the second main idea: the rewards of self-disclosure. Those rewards include better self-knowledge, greater communication effectiveness, and improved health. Again, these "rewards" should come up on the screen one at a time, rather than all together.

**Slide 7**

This is the third main idea: the risks of self-disclosure (personal, relationship, and professional risks). What types of graphics might make this slide more interesting and yet not take attention away from the main ideas?

**Slide 8**

This slide begins the conclusion and summarizes the three main points of the speech: the nature of self-disclosure, the rewards, and the risks.

**Slide 9**

While this slide, which contains only the term "Self-Disclosure," is on screen, the speaker would likely motivate the audience to learn more about self-disclosure. Take a look at the speech from which this slide show was derived (pages 359–361) and create slides for the specific suggestions for learning more about self-disclosure.

**Slide 10**

This slide closes the speech by repeating the theme of the speech, namely that self-disclosure is both rewarding and risky and that the pros and cons need to be weighed in any decision to self-disclose.

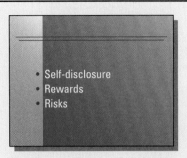

**FIGURE 15.2** **Slide with Speaker Notes**

This example is from slide number 4, the orientation, in the "Self-Disclosure" speech on page 340.

many printers and most copiers, simply substitute transparency paper for computer or copy paper. If you create your slides with a computer presentation package, you'll be able to produce professional-looking transparencies.

**Suggestions for Using Presentation Software.**
The templates and the suggestions of the program "wizards" will parallel the suggestions offered here. Nevertheless, it's important to understand the qualities of effective slides in case you want to make changes in the suggested formats or even want to start from scratch.

In developing your slides, strive for clarity and consistency. For example, choose typeface styles, sizes, and colors that clearly distinguish the main points from the supporting materials. At the same time, use a consistent combination of fonts, colors, backgrounds, and graphics throughout your slides to give your presentation unity.

Use color (of type and background) and graphics sparingly. Remember that clarity is your goal; you want your audience to remember your ideas and not just the fact that all your slides were red, white, and blue. Likewise, too many graphics will distract your audience's attention from your verbal message. Also, be sure to choose graphics that support your tone. If

your speech is on a serious topic, then the graphics (and photographs or illustrations) should contribute to this tone. Also, try to use graphics that are consistent with one another; generally, it's better to use all shadow figures or all stick figures or all Victorian images than to mix them.

Generally, put one complete thought on a slide. Don't try to put too many words on one slide; use a few words on each slide, and expand on these during your speech. Try not to use more than two levels of thought in a slide—a major statement and two to four subordinate phrases (bulleted) are about all you can put on one slide. Avoid using subheads of subheads of subheads. Generally, use a sans-serif type (more attention-getting) for headings and a serif type (easier to read) for text (refer to Table 15.1, page 338).

A good guideline to follow in designing your slides is to give all items in your outline that have the same-level heads (for example, all the Roman numeral heads) the same typeface, size, and color throughout your presentation. Similarly, use the same font for all the A, B, C subheads, and so on. This will help your listeners follow the organization of your speech. Notice that this principle is followed for the most part in the slides in the Public Speaking Sample Assistant box. The rule is broken in one case,

**FIGURE 15.3** Slides with Space for Listeners' Notes

however: The introduction and conclusion are set apart by being in a color and typeface different from the rest of the slides.

Consider using graphs, charts, and tables; you have a tremendous variety of graph and chart types (for example, pie and bar graphs and cumulative charts) and tables to choose from. If you are using presentation software that's part of a suite, then you'll find it especially easy to import files from your word processor or spreadsheet.

If there's a question-and-answer period following your speech, consider preparing a few extra slides to support responses to questions you anticipate being asked. Then, when someone asks you a predicted question, you can say: "I anticipated that someone might ask that question; it raises an important issue. The data I've been able to find are presented in this chart." You then show the slide and explain it more

fully. This is surely going the extra mile, but it can easily make your speech a real standout.

Use transitions wisely. Just as verbal transitions help you move from one part of your speech to another, presentational transitions help you move from one slide to the next with the desired effect—for example, blinds folding from left or right or top or bottom, or a quick fade.

Generally, consistency works best. Don't try to use too many different transitions in the same talk; it will detract attention from what you are saying. Generally, use the same transitions for all the slides in a single presentation. You might vary this a bit by, say, having the last slide introduced by a somewhat different transition; but any more variation is likely to work against the listeners' focusing on your message. In choosing transitions select one that's consistent with your speech purpose; don't use a frivolous black-and-yellow

## Theory and Research    Culture and Speech Organization

Members of low-context cultures (see Unit 2) are usually direct in their messages and appreciate directness in others. But directness may be unnecessary or even insulting to the high-context cultural member. Conversely, the indirectness of the high-context member may appear vague or even dishonest to a member of a low-context culture.

High-context cultures prefer indirectness. Speakers in Japan, to take one well-researched example, need to be careful lest they make their point too obvious or too direct and insult the audience. Speakers in Japan are expected to lead their listeners to the conclusion through example, illustration, and various other indirect means (Lustig & Koester, 2006). In contrast, in the United States (a low-context culture) speakers are encouraged to be explicit and direct—to tell the listeners, for example, exactly what the speaker wants them to do.

Another cultural difference influences how focused the speech ought to be. For example, in the United States, each main point of a speech or written composition should be developed by itself. Only when one point is fully developed and finalized does the speaker or writer move on to the next. Hindu culture, however, is less rigid and allows for many ideas being considered in the same paragraph of an essay or in the same part of a speech (Lustig & Koester, 2006).

### Working with Theories and Research

*As a listener, what type of organization do you prefer? For example, do you prefer a speaker who is direct or indirect? Do you prefer speakers who clearly separate the main points or who consider several points together?*

---

checkerboard transition in a speech on child abuse, for example.

Consider using sound effects with your transitions; but again, go easy. Overdoing it is sure to make your speech seem carelessly put together.

Build effects with bulleted items to focus your listeners' attention. For example, you can have each bulleted phrase fly from the top of the screen into its position; with the next mouse click, the next bullet flies into position. Or you can have your bullets slide in from right to left or from left to right, and so on.

In listing four or five bulleted items, consider the value of hiding or dimming the previous bullet as you introduce the next one. Making the previous bullet disappear or fade into a lighter color when the next bullet appears further enables you to focus your listeners' attention on exactly the point you're discussing. Do be careful that you allow the audience time to read each bullet; otherwise they'll be frustrated when it disappears.

Use the spell-checker. You don't want to show professional-looking slides with misspellings; it can ruin your credibility and seriously damage the impact of your speech.

## STEP 6: ORGANIZE YOUR SPEECH

When you organize your ideas, you derive a variety of benefits. First, organization will help you prepare the speech. For example, as you organize your speech you'll be able to see if you have adequately and fairly supported each of your main points and if you are devoting approximately equal time to each main idea. Organization also makes your speech easy to understand and remember. When you organize perhaps 30 pieces of specific information (such as statistics, statement of thesis, examples, illustrations, testimonials, transitions) into, say, three or four or five chunks, you're making it much easier for the audience to remember what you want them to remember. An added bonus here is that organization will also help you remember your speech. You'll be less likely to forget a carefully organized speech than you would a disorganized one. Organization will also contribute to your credibility. The audience is more likely to see the well-organized speaker as more competent, more knowledgeable, and more in control of the information in the speech.

Once you've identified the main points you wish to include in your speech, you need to devote attention to how you'll arrange these points in the **body**, or main part, of your speech. When you follow a clearly identified organizational pattern, your listeners will be able to see your speech as a whole and will be able to grasp the connections and relationships among your various pieces of information. Should they have a momentary lapse in attention—as they surely will at some point in just about every speech—you will be able to refocus their attention.

Consider each of the following organizational patterns in terms of the topics to which it's most applicable and the ways in which you can arrange your main points and supporting materials. The introduction, conclusion, and transitions are considered in depth under Step 7 in this unit. The mechanical aspects of outlining and additional guidance in preparing the outline are presented in Unit 16.

## Temporal Pattern

Organization on the basis of some temporal (time) relationship is a pattern listeners will find easy to follow. Generally, when you use a **temporal pattern**, you organize your speech into two, three, or four major parts, beginning with the past and working up to the present or the future—or beginning with the present or the future and working back to the past.

The temporal (sometimes called "chronological") pattern is especially appropriate for informative speeches in which you wish to describe events or processes that occur over time. It's also useful when you wish to tell a story, demonstrate how something works, or examine the steps involved in some process. The events leading up to the Civil War, the steps toward a college education, or the history of writing would all be appropriate for temporal patterning. A speech on the development of language in the child might be organized in a temporal pattern and could be broken down something like this:

    **I.** Babbling occurs around the 5th month.
    **II.** Lallation occurs around the 6th month.
    **III.** Echolalia occurs around the 9th month.
    **IV.** "Communication" occurs around the 12th month.

## Spatial Pattern

You can also organize your main points on the basis of space. The **spatial pattern** is especially useful when you wish to describe objects or places. Like the temporal pattern, it's an organizational pattern that listeners will find easy to follow as you progress—from top to bottom, from left to right, from inside to outside, or from east to west, for example. The structure of a place, an object, or even an animal is easily placed into a spatial pattern. You might describe the layout of a hospital, a school, or a skyscraper, or perhaps even the structure of a dinosaur, with a spatial pattern of organization. Here's an example of an outline describing the structure of the traditional textbook and using a spatial pattern:

    **I.** The front matter contains the preface and the table of contents.
    **II.** The text proper contains the chapters or units.
    **III.** The back matter contains the glossary, bibliography, and index.

## Topical Pattern

When your topic conveniently divides itself into subdivisions, each of which is clear and approximately equal in importance, the **topical pattern** is most useful. A speech on important cities of the world might be organized into a topical pattern, as might be speeches on problems facing the college graduate, great works of literature, the world's major religions, and the like. The topical pattern would be an obvious choice for organizing a speech on the powers of the government. The topic itself divides into three parts: legislative, executive, and judicial. A sample outline might look like this:

    **I.** The legislative branch is controlled by Congress.
    **II.** The executive branch is controlled by the president.
    **III.** The judicial branch is controlled by the courts.

## Problem–Solution Pattern

The **problem–solution pattern** is especially useful in persuasive speeches in which you want to convince the audience that a problem exists and that your solution would solve or lessen the problem. Let's say that you believe that jury awards for damages have gotten out of hand. You may want to persuade your audience, then, that jury awards for damages should be limited. A problem–solution pattern might be appropriate here. In the first part of your speech, you'd identify the problem(s) created by these large awards; in the second part, you'd propose the solution. A sample outline for such a speech might look something like this:

    **I.** Jury awards for damages are out of control. [the general problem]
      **A.** These awards increase insurance rates. [a specific problem]

**B.** These awards increase medical costs. [a second specific problem]
**C.** These awards place unfair burdens on business. [a third specific problem]
**II.** Jury awards need to be limited. [the general solution]
  **A.** Greater evidence should be required before a case can be brought to trial. [a specific solution]
  **B.** Part of the award should be turned over to the state. [a second specific solution]
  **C.** Realistic estimates of financial damage must be used. [a third specific solution]

Here, for example, is how one student, Ashley Hatcher of the University of Texas at Austin, organized her problem-solution speech on issues in military recruitment—an organization clearly revealed in her introduction:

> Because of this [which the speaker had already covered in the speech], we must first, delve into the problems of recruiter wrongdoings; next, examine the underlying causes as to why these travesties occur; and finally, develop solutions that will ensure that, as the Albuquerque *Tribute* of November 29, 2006, writes, we and those wielding weapons "are satisfied that they made the right decision for the right reasons at the right time."

As you can see from this example, a problem-solution speech often has an additional main point—sometimes an explanation of the development of the problem or a review of some historical background. Sometimes, as in the case of the above excerpt, the speaker provides added discussion of the problem by discussing the causes of the problems. In this speech the speaker has three main points: (1) the problems, (2) the causes of the problems, and (3) the solution.

## Cause–Effect/Effect–Cause Pattern

Similar to the problem-solution pattern is the cause-effect or effect-cause pattern. This pattern is useful in persuasive speeches in which you want to convince your audience of the causal connection existing between two events or elements. In the **cause–effect pattern** you divide the speech into two major sections: causes and effects. For example, a speech on the reasons for highway accidents or birth defects might lend itself to a cause-effect pattern. Here you might first consider, say, the causes of highway accidents or birth defects, then turn to some of the effects; for example, the number of deaths, the number of accidents, and so on.

Or suppose you wanted to demonstrate the causes for the increase in AIDS in your state. In this case you might use an **effect–caus pattern** that might look something like this:

**I.** AIDS is increasing. [general effect]
  **A.** AIDS is increasing among teenagers. [a specific effect]
  **B.** AIDS is increasing among IV drug users. [a second specific effect]
  **C.** AIDS is increasing among women. [a third specific effect]
**II.** Three factors contribute to this increase. [general causal statement]
  **A.** Teenagers are ignorant about how the HIV virus is transmitted. [a specific cause]
  **B.** IV drug users exchange contaminated needles. [a second specific cause]
  **C.** Women are not practicing safe sex. [a third specific cause]

As you can see from this example, this type of speech is often combined with the problem-solution type. For example, after identifying the causes, the speaker might then treat the causes as problems and offer solutions for each problem/cause (for example: education for teens, free needle exchange programs, and education on safer sex for men and women).

## The Motivated Sequence

The **motivated sequence** is an organizational pattern in which you arrange your information so as to motivate your audience to respond positively to your purpose (McKerrow, Gronbeck, Ehninger, & Monroe, 2000). In contrast to the previous organizational patterns, which provided ways of organizing the main ideas in the body of the speech, the motivated sequence is a pattern for organizing the entire speech. Here the speech (introduction, body, and conclusion) is divided into five parts or steps: (1) attention, (2) need, (3) satisfaction, (4) visualization, and (5) action.

1. The attention step makes the audience give you their undivided *attention*. If you execute this step effectively, your audience should be ready and eager to hear what you have to say. You can gain audience attention through a variety of means; examples include asking a question (rhetorical or actual) or making reference to audience members. These methods are presented in the "Introduction" discussion in the Step 7 section of this unit.

2. In the second part of your speech, you establish that a *need* exists for some kind of change. The audience should feel that something has to be learned or something has to be done because of this demonstrated need.

3. You satisfy the need by presenting the answer or the solution to the need you demonstrated in step 2 of the motivated sequence. On the

# ASK THE RESEARCHER

## The Motivated Sequence

*What's so special about the motivated sequence, and how can
I use it in preparing to speak on the job?*

Alan Monroe originally adapted the motivated sequence from 1920s sales workshops
he'd attended, when motivational psychology was all the rage. Since then, it's been
thought about more as a convenient organizational form, but one that still makes motivational appeals central to persuasion: Unless I can make you want to act, you won't. Since
the '20s, motivational psychology, thanks particularly to Professor David McClelland, has
gotten more sophisticated, for he groups motivational appeals into three clusters: (1)
affiliation (appeals to positive relationships with others), (2) achievement (appeals to
individual success), and (3) power (appeals to dominance or defense). McClelland's work
guides your selection of specific appeals for specific audiences, while the motivated
sequences provide an easy-to-use organizational pattern for any speech. Get decision-
makers' attention, convince them it's in their self-interest to listen, make your pitch,
depict the results vividly, and clinch the deal—that's it! It works!

For further information: visit www.ablongman.com/german15e. On motivational
psychology, see Hoyenga, K. B., & Hoyenga, H. (1984). *Motivational explanations of
behavior: Psychological and cognitive ideas.* Monterey, CA: Brooks/Cole.

**Bruce E. Gronbeck** (Ph.D., University of Iowa) is A. Craig Baird Distinguished Professor of Public
Address. As director of the University of Iowa Center for Media Studies and Political Culture, he
studies the impact of television and the Internet on political public address. Every four years, he
becomes one of the national experts on the Iowa caucuses, doing newspaper, radio, and television
interviews on presidential candidates' performances (bruce-gronbeck@uiowa.edu). Used with the
permission of Bruce Gronbeck.

basis of this *satisfaction* step, the audience
should now believe that what you are informing them about or persuading them to do will
satisfy the need.

4. *Visualization* intensifies the audience's feelings or beliefs. In this step you take the people
in the audience beyond the present time and
place and enable them to imagine the situation
as it would be if the need were satisfied as you
suggested in step 3. You might, for example,
demonstrate the benefits that people would
receive if your ideas were put into operation—
or perhaps demonstrate the negative effects
that people would suffer if your plan were not
put into operation.

5. Tell the audience what *action* they should take
to ensure that the need (step 2) is satisfied
(step 3) as visualized (step 4). Here you want to
move the audience in a particular direction—
for example, to contribute free time to read to
the blind. You can accomplish this step by stating what the audience members should do, using a variety of supporting materials and logical, emotional, and ethical appeals.

Unit 18 will discuss the use of the motivated sequence in persuasive speeches, and Table 18.1
(page 426) offers a useful summary of the essential
characteristics of this important organizational
strategy.

## Additional Organizational Patterns

The six patterns just considered are the most common and the most useful for organizing most public
speeches. But there are other patterns that might be
appropriate for different topics:

**Structure–Function.** The **structure–function
pattern** is well suited to informative speeches in
which you want to discuss how something is constructed (its structural aspects) and what it does (its
functional aspects). This pattern might be useful, for
example, in a speech to explain what an organization is and what it does, the parts of a university and
how they operate, or the sensory systems of the
body and their various functions. This pattern also
might be useful in a discussion of the nature of a living organism: its anatomy (that is, its structures) and
its physiology (that is, its functions).

**Comparison and Contrast.** Arranging your material in a **comparison-and-contrast pattern** is useful in informative speeches in which you want to analyze, for example, two different theories, proposals, departments, or products in terms of their similarities and differences. In this type of speech, you would be concerned not only with explaining each theory or proposal but also with clarifying how they're similar and how they're different.

**Pro and Con, Advantages and Disadvantages.** The **pro-and-con pattern**, sometimes called the advantages–disadvantages pattern, works well in informative speeches in which you want to explain objectively the advantages (pros) and the disadvantages (cons) of, say, a plan, method, or product.

**Claim and Proof.** The **claim-and-proof pattern** is especially appropriate in a persuasive speech in which you want to prove the truth or usefulness of a particular proposition. It's the pattern that you see frequently in trials: The prosecution claims that the defendant is guilty and that the proof is the varied evidence—for example, evidence that the defendant had a motive, the defendant had the opportunity, and the defendant had no alibi. In this pattern your speech would consist of two major parts. In the first part, you'd explain your claim (tuition must not be raised, library hours must be expanded, courses in

Caribbean studies must be instituted). In the second part, you'd offer your evidence or proof as to why, for example, tuition must not be raised.

**Multiple Definition.** The **multiple-definition pattern** is often helpful for explaining specific concepts: What is a born-again Christian? What is a scholar? What is multiculturalism? In this pattern each major heading consists of a different type of definition or way of looking at the concept. Earlier, this unit looked at a variety of definition types, and Unit 17 discusses Speeches of Definition as a major category of informative speeches.

**Who? What? Why? Where? When?** The **5W pattern** is the pattern of the journalist and is useful when you wish to report or explain an event such as a robbery, political coup, war, ceremony, or trial. In this pattern you'd have five major parts to the body of your speech, each dealing with the answers to one of these five questions.

**Fiction–Fact.** The **fiction–fact pattern** may be useful when you wish to clarify certain misconceptions that people have about various things. For example, if you were giving a speech on fiction and fact about flu viruses, you might use this pattern. You first would give the fiction (for example, you can get the flu from a flu shot, or antibiotics can help the

---

# REFLECTIONS ON ETHICS

## Communicating in Cyberspace

Because of the explosion in computer communication, the ethics of Internet communication (sometimes referred to as *nethics*) has become an important part of ethical communication. Of course, the same principles that govern ethical public speaking should also prevail when you communicate on the Internet. Here, however, are a few ethical principles with special relevance to computer communication. It is unethical to:

- Invade the privacy of others. Reading the files of another person or breaking into files that you're not authorized to read is unethical.

- Harm others or their property. Creating computer viruses; publishing instructions for making bombs; and creating websites that promote racism, heterosexism, ageism, or sexism are some examples of unethical computer use.

- Spread falsehoods. Lying on the Internet—about other people, the powers of medical or herbal

treatment, or yourself—is just as unethical as it is in other forms of communication.

- Plagiarize. Appropriating the work of another as your own—whether the original work appeared on the Internet or in a book or journal—is unethical.

- Steal passwords, PINs, or authorization codes that belong to others.

- Copy software programs that you haven't paid for.

### Ethical Choice Point

*As an experiment, you develop a computer virus that can destroy websites. Recently, you've come across a variety of websites that market child pornography. You wonder if you can ethically destroy these websites. Indeed, you wonder if not destroying them is actually more unethical than using your newly developed virus. What is your ethical obligation in this situation? What would you do?*

## INTRODUCTIONS

You're scheduled to give a speech on careers in computer technology to students who have been forced to attend this career day on Saturday. If you don't win over this unwilling audience in your introduction, you figure you're finished.

WHAT DO YOU SAY?

flu, or older people spread the flu most often) and then follow it with the fact (you can't get the flu from a flu shot; antibiotics are useful only against bacteria, not against viruses; children, rather than older people, spread the flu most often and most easily).

## STEP 7: CONSTRUCT YOUR INTRODUCTION, CONCLUSION, AND TRANSITIONS

Now that you have the body of your speech organized, devote your attention to the introduction, conclusion, and transitions that will hold the parts of your speech together.

## Introduction

Begin collecting suitable material for your introduction as you prepare the entire speech, but wait until all the other parts are completed before you put the introduction together. In this way, you'll be better able to determine which elements should be included and which should be eliminated.

Together with your general appearance and your nonverbal messages, the introduction gives your audience its first impression of you and your speech. Your introduction sets the tone for the rest of the speech; it tells your listeners what kind of a speech they'll hear.

Your **introduction** should serve three functions: It should (1) gain attention, (2) establish a speaker-audience-topic connection, and (3) orient the audience as to what is to follow. Let's look at each of these functions and at the ways you can serve these functions.

### Gain Attention

In your introduction, gain the attention of your audience and focus it on your speech topic. (Then, of course, maintain that attention throughout your speech.) You can secure attention in numerous ways; here are just a few of them.

- **Ask a question.** Questions are effective because they are a change from declarative statements and call for an active response from listeners.

- **Refer to audience members.** Talking about the audience makes them perk up and pay attention, because you are involving them directly in your talk.

- **Refer to recent happenings.** Citing a previous speech, recent event, or prominent person currently making news helps you gain attention, because the audience is familiar with this current event and will pay attention to see how you are going to connect it to your speech topic.

- **Use humor.** A clever (and appropriate) anecdote is often useful in holding attention.

- **Stress the importance of the topic.** People pay attention to what they feel is important to them and ignore what seems unimportant or irrelevant. If your topic focuses on the interests of the audience, you might begin by referring directly to the audience.

- **Use a presentation aid.** Presentation aids are valuable because they are new and different. They engage our senses and thus our attention.

- **Tell the audience to pay attention.** A simple, "I want you to listen to this frightening statistic," or "I want you to pay particularly close attention to . . . ," used once or twice in a speech, will help gain audience attention.

## AROUSING THE AUDIENCE

You notice that your audience doesn't seem to pay much attention to those who have spoken before you. And your speech topic, at least on first acquaintance, isn't one with a lot of audience appeal. You need to gain their attention early in your introduction.

WHAT DO YOU SAY?

- Use a quotation. Quotations are useful because the audience is likely to pay attention to the brief and clever remarks of someone they've heard of or read about. Do make sure, however, that the quotation relates directly to your topic.

- Cite a little-known fact or statistic. Little-known facts or statistics will help perk up an audience's attention. For example, headlines on unemployment statistics, crime in the schools, and political corruption sell newspapers because they gain attention.

- Use an illustration or dramatic story. Much as we are drawn to soap operas, so are we drawn to illustrations and stories about people. Here's a good example of using a dramatic illustration to gain attention; it was given by U.S. Senator (California) Dianne Feinstein (2006) in a speech on gang violence (http://feinstein.senate.gov/public/index):

> On September 24 of this year, Los Angeles experienced a new low. Three-year-old Kaitlyn Avila was shot point-blank by a gang member who mistakenly thought her father was a member of a rival gang. The gang member shot and wounded her father, then intentionally fired into little Kaitlyn's chest. This is the first time law enforcement officials remember a young child being "targeted" in a gang shooting.

## Establish a Speaker–Audience–Topic Relationship

In addition to gaining attention, your introduction should establish connections among yourself as the speaker, the audience members, and your topic. Try to answer your listeners' inevitable question: Why should we listen to you speak on this topic? You can establish an effective **speaker–audience–topic connection**, or S-A-T connection, in many different ways.

- Refer to others present. Not only will this help you to gain attention; it will also help you to establish a bond with the audience.

- Refer to the occasion. Often your speech will be connected directly with the occasion. By referring to the reason the audience has gathered, you can establish a connection between yourself, the audience, and the topic.

- Express your pleasure or interest in speaking.

- Establish your competence in the subject. Show the audience that you are really interested in and knowledgeable about the topic.

- Compliment the audience. Complimenting the audience is a commonly used technique to establish an S-A-T connection in much professional public speaking. In the classroom this technique may seem awkward and obvious, so it is probably best avoided here. But it's important to realize that in other settings paying the audience an honest and sincere compliment (though never overdoing it) will not only encourage your listeners to give you their attention, but also help make them feel a part of your speech. In some cultures—Japan and Korea are good examples—the speaker is expected to compliment the audience, the beauty of the country, or its culture. It's one of the essential parts of the introduction. In this example, musician Billy Joel compliments his audience, the graduating class of the Berklee College of Music, directly and honestly (www.berklee.edu/commencement/past/bjoel.html, accessed February 6, 2004):

> I am truly pleased that the road has twisted and turned its way up the East Coast to Boston. The Berklee College of Music represents the finest contemporary music school there is, and I am honored to be here with you this morning to celebrate.

- Express similarities with the audience. By stressing your own similarity with members of the audience, you create a relationship with them and become an "insider" instead of an "outsider."

## Orient the Audience

The introduction should orient the audience in some way as to what is to follow in the body of the speech. This **orientation** can take various forms.

You can preview for the audience what you are going to say, as in "Tonight I'm going to discuss nuclear waste"; give a detailed preview, perhaps outlining your major propositions; or identify your goal by, for example, stating your thesis.

Here Texas governor Rick Perry, in a speech to the Border Governors Conference on August 25, 2006 (www.governor.state.tx.us/divisions/press/speeches, accessed January 14, 2007), orients the audience by briefly identifying the three main points he will cover in his speech:

> In signing this declaration, we commit our resources and our resolve to making the border healthier, better educated, and more secure.

And here a student, Tapashya Ghosh of the University of Texas at Austin, similarly orients by identifying the main ideas to be covered, after explaining the nature and danger of the Stand Your Ground Law:

> To rectify this dangerous and unnecessary situation, it is imperative that we first study the problems of this law, next see how these laws came about, and finally explore solutions to change a situation that ABC News of May 24, 2006, calls the law that gives us the "right to commit murder."

# Conclusion

Your **conclusion** is especially important, because it's often the part of the speech that the audience remembers most clearly. It's your conclusion that in many cases determines what image of you is left in the minds of the audience. Devote special attention to this brief but crucial part of your speech. Let your conclusion serve three major functions: to (1) summarize, (2) motivate, and (3) provide closure.

## Summarize

The **summary** function is particularly important in an informative speech; it is less so in persuasive speeches or in speeches to entertain. You may summarize your speech in a variety of ways:

- Restate your thesis or purpose. In this type of brief summary, you restate the essential thrust of your speech, repeating your thesis or perhaps the goals you hoped to achieve.
- Restate the importance of the topic. Tell the audience again why your topic or thesis is so important.
- Restate your main points. That is, restate both your thesis and the major points you used to support it.

## Motivate

A second function of the conclusion—most appropriate in persuasive speeches—is to motivate the people in the audience to do what you want them to do. In your conclusion you have the opportunity to give the audience one final push in the direction you wish them to take. Whether it's to buy stock, vote a particular way, or change an attitude, you can use the conclusion for a final **motivation**, a final appeal. Here are two excellent ways to motivate:

- Ask for a specific response. Specify what you want the audience to do after listening to your speech.
- Provide directions for future action. Spell out, most often in general terms, the direction you wish the audience to take.

## Close

The third function of your conclusion is to provide **closure**. Often your summary will accomplish this, but in some instances it will prove insufficient. End your speech with a conclusion that is crisp and definite. Make the audience know that you have definitely and clearly ended. Some kind of wrap-up, some sort of final statement, is helpful in providing this feeling of closure. You may achieve closure through a variety of methods:

- Use a quotation. A quotation is often an effective means of providing closure.
- Refer to subsequent events. You may also achieve closure by referring to future events—events taking place either that day or soon afterwards.
- Refer back to the introduction. It's sometimes useful to connect your conclusion with your introduction.
- Pose a challenge or question. You may close your speech by leaving the audience with a provocative question to ponder or a challenge to consider. Or, you can pose a question and answer it by recapping your thesis and perhaps some of your major arguments or propositions.
- Thank the audience. Speakers frequently conclude their speeches by thanking the audience for their attention or for their invitation to address them.

Here, for example, a student, Nicole Kreisberg from the University of Texas at Austin, concludes her speech on alternative existence with a provocative thought that tells you the speech is over:

> And while the idea of living an alternative existence may seem a little absurd, as Kurt Vonnegut contends: So is real life.

# Transitions

**Transitions** are words, phrases, or sentences that connect the various parts of your speech. They provide the audience with guideposts that help them follow the development of your thoughts and arguments. Use transitions in at least the following places:

- between the introduction and the body of the speech
- between the body and the conclusion
- between the main points in the body of the speech

Here are the major transitional functions and some stylistic devices that you might use to serve these functions.

*To announce the start of a major proposition or piece of evidence:* First, . . ., A second argument . . ., A closely related problem . . ., If you want further evidence, look at . . ., Next . . ., Consider also. . ., An even more compelling argument . . ., My next point. . . .

*To signal that you're drawing a conclusion from previously given evidence and argument:* Thus, . . ., Therefore, . . ., So, as you can see . . ., It follows, then, that. . . .

*To alert the audience to your introduction of a qualification or exception:* But, . . ., However, also consider. . . .

*To remind listeners of what has just been said and of its connection with another issue that will now be considered:* In contrast to . . .; Consider also . . .; Not only . . . but also . . .; In addition to . . . we also need to look at . . .; Not only should we . . ., we should also. . . .

*To signal the part of your speech you're approaching:* By way of introduction . . .; In conclusion . . .; Now, let's discuss why we're here today . . .; So,

what's the solution? What should we do?

*To signal your organizational structure:* I'll first explain the problems with jury awards and then propose a workable solution.

*To summarize what you've already discussed.* Consider using a special kind of transition: the internal summary. It's a statement that usually summarizes some major subdivision of your speech. Incorporate several internal summaries into your speech—perhaps working them into the transitions connecting, say, the major parts of your speech. An internal summary that also serves as a transition might look something like this:

> Inadequate recreational facilities, poor schooling, and a lack of adequate role models seem to be the major problems facing our youngsters. Each of these, however, can be remedied and even eliminated. Here's what we can do.

This brief passage reminds listeners of what they've just heard and previews what they'll hear next. The clear connection in their minds will fill in any gaps that may have been created through inattention, noise, and the like.

You can enhance your transitions by pausing between your transition and the next part of your speech. This will help the audience realize that a new part of your speech is coming. You might also take a step forward or to the side after saying your transition. This will also help to reinforce the movement from one part of your speech to another.

---

**Building Communication** SKILLS | ## Constructing Conclusions and Introductions

Prepare a conclusion and an introduction to a hypothetical speech on one of the topics listed below, making sure that in your conclusion you (a) review the speech's main points and (b) provide closure, and that in your introduction you (a) gain attention and (b) orient the audience. Be prepared to explain the methods you used to accomplish each of these functions.

1. Proficiency in a foreign language should be required of all college graduates.

2. All killing of wild animals should be declared illegal.

3. Suicide and its assistance by qualified medical personnel should be legalized.

4. Gambling should be legalized by all states.

5. Maximum sentences should be imposed for hate crimes.

6. Alcoholic beverages should be banned from campus.

*Because the conclusion and introduction are often what listeners remember best, give these opening and closing remarks careful attention.*

# Pitfalls in Introductions, Conclusions, and Transitions

In addition to understanding the principles of effective pubic speaking, it often helps to become aware of common mistakes. Here, then, are some of the common mistakes you'll want to avoid.

### In your introduction:

- Don't apologize (generally). In the United States and western Europe, an apology may be seen as an excuse and so is to be avoided. In certain other cultures (those of Japan, China, and Korea are good examples), however, speakers are expected to begin with an apology. It's a way of complimenting the audience.

- Avoid promising something you won't deliver. The speaker who promises to tell you how to make a fortune in the stock market or how to be the most popular person on campus (and fails to deliver such insight) quickly loses credibility.

- Avoid gimmicks that gain attention but are irrelevant to the speech or inconsistent with your treatment of the topic. For example, slamming a book on the desk or telling a joke that bears no relation to your speech may accomplish the limited goal of gaining attention, but quickly the audience will see that they've been fooled, and they'll resent it.

- Don't introduce your speech with ineffective statements such as "I'm really nervous, but here goes" or "Before I begin my talk, I want to say . . . ." These statements will make your audience uncomfortable and will encourage them to focus on your delivery rather than on your message.

### In your conclusion:

- Don't introduce new material. Instead, use your conclusion to reinforce what you've already said and to summarize.

- Don't dilute your position. Avoid being critical of your own material or your presentation. Saying, for example, "The information I presented is probably dated, but it was all I could find" or "I hope I wasn't too nervous" will detract from the credibility you've tried to establish.

- Don't drag out your conclusion. End crisply.

### In your transitions:

- Avoid too many or too few transitions. Either extreme can cause problems. Use transitions to help your listeners, who will hear the speech only once, to understand the structure of your speech.

- Avoid transitions that are out of proportion to the speech parts they connect. If you want to connect the two main points of your speech, you need something more than just "and" or "the next point." In contrast, if you want to connect two brief examples, then a simple "another example occurs when . . ." will do.

## SUMMARY: SUPPORTING AND ORGANIZING YOUR SPEECH

This unit covered ways of supporting and organizing your main thoughts and introducing and concluding your speech.

1. Formulate the thesis of the speech. Develop your main points by asking relevant questions about this thesis.

2. Reinforce your main points with a variety of materials that support them. Suitable supporting materials include examples, narratives, analogies, definitions, testimony, statistics, and presentation aids as well as such devices as quotations, comparisons, statements of facts, and repetition and restatement.

3. Among the presentation aids you might consider are the actual object, models of the object, graphs, word charts, maps, people, photographs and illustrations, and tapes and CDs. These can be presented with a variety of media; for example, the chalkboard, chartboards, flip charts, slides and transparency projections, videotapes, and handouts. Presentation aids work best when they add clarity to your speech, are appealing to listeners, and are culturally sensitive.

4. Computer-assisted presentations such as PowerPoint, which have become extremely popular, allow you to communicate lots of information in an interesting format, to print handouts to coordinate with your speech, and to create an outline and speaker's notes for your speech.

5. Organize the speech materials into a clear, easily identifiable thought pattern. Suitable organizing principles include temporal, spatial, topical, problem–solution, cause–effect/effect–cause, motivated sequence, structure–function, comparison-and-contrast, pro-and-con, claim-and-proof, multiple-definition, and who-what-why-where-when (5W) patterns.

6. Introductions should gain attention, establish a speaker–audience–topic (S-A-T) connection, and orient the audience as to what is to follow.

7. Conclusions should summarize the main ideas, provide a final motivation, and provide a crisp closing to the speech.

8. Transitions and internal summaries help connect and integrate the parts of the speech; they also help the listeners to better remember the speech.

# KEY TERMS IN SUPPORTING AND ORGANIZING YOUR SPEECH

analogies (p. **331**)

body (p. **345**)

cause–effect pattern (p. **346**)

claim-and-proof pattern (p. **348**)

closure (p. **351**)

comparison-and-contrast pattern (p. **348**)

conclusion (p. **351**)

definition (p. **332**)

effect–cause pattern (p. **346**)

example (p. **330**)

fiction–fact pattern (p. **348**)

5W pattern (p. **348**)

introduction (p. **349**)

models (p. **334**)

motivated sequence (p. **346**)

motivation (p. **351**)

multiple-definition pattern (p. **348**)

narrative (p. **331**)

orientation (p. **350**)

presentation aid (p. **334**)

pro-and-con pattern (p. **348**)

problem–solution pattern (p. **345**)

product placement (p. **330**)

spatial pattern (p. **345**)

speaker–audience–topic connection (p. **350**)

statistics (p. **333**)

structure–function pattern (p. **347**)

summary (p. **351**)

temporal pattern (p. **345**)

testimony (p. **333**)

thesis (p. **327**)

topical pattern (p. **345**)

transitions (p. **351**)

# THINKING CRITICALLY ABOUT SUPPORTING AND ORGANIZING YOUR SPEECH

1. **Strategies of Arrangement.** What strategies of arrangement would you use if you were giving a pro-choice speech to a pro-life audience? What strategies would you use if you were giving a speech in favor of domestic partnership insurance to gay rights leaders?

2. **Vivid Support.** Jamie, a student at a community college in Texas, wants to give a speech on the cruelty of cockfighting. Most people in the predominantly Hispanic audience come from Mexico, where cockfighting is a legal and popular sport. Among the visuals Jamie is considering are extremely vivid photographs of cocks literally torn to shreds by their opponents, which have razor blades strapped to their feet. Would you advise Jamie to use these photographs if the listeners were, say, moderately in favor of cockfighting? What if they were moderately against cockfighting?

3. **Quotations.** Visit one of the websites for quotations; for example, try **www.bartleby.com** or **http://us .imdb.com/** (a database of quotations from films). Select a quotation suitable for use with the slide show

of the speech on self-disclosure in the Public Speaking Sample Assistant box on pages 340–341, and explain how you would use this on a slide.

4. **Presentation Aids.** Shana wants to illustrate the rise and fall in the prices of 12 stocks over the last 10 years to show that her investment club should sell 3 stocks and keep the other 9. This is the first time Shana will be using visual aids, and she needs advice on what aids best serve her purpose. What suggestions do you have for Shana?

5. Prepare and deliver a two-minute speech in which you do any one of the following:
   - Tell a personal story to illustrate a specific point.
   - Explain a print ad that relies on statistics, and show how the advertiser uses statistics to make a point.
   - Describe the events portrayed in a recently seen television program, using a temporal pattern.
   - Discuss a recent newspaper editorial or op-ed letter, using a problem–solution or cause–effect pattern.
   - Explain how television commercials get your attention.

# LOGON! MYCOMMUNICATIONLAB

## WWW.MYCOMMUNICATIONLAB.COM

Visit MCL for a self-test on culture-specific icons and discussions of evaluating testimony and arranging supporting materials. A video illustrates principles of PowerPoint presentations and presents techniques for public speaking. View the videos of Writing Position Papers, one of which uses visual aids and one of which doesn't. Which do you find most effective? Explore the material on statistics, transitions, connecting key ideas, and organization. Template outlines are available, as is a scrambled outline exercise. View one or more of the video speeches and consider how these speakers organized their speeches and what you might do differently.

# UNIT 16 Style and Delivery in Public Speaking

## MAJOR TOPICS

**Step 8: Outline Your Speech**

**Step 9: Word Your Speech**

**Step 10: Rehearse and Present Your Speech**

**Criticizing Speeches**

## Special Features

Here the last three steps in public speaking are discussed.

**In this unit, you'll learn about:**
- the kinds of outlines used in public speaking.
- language and how it influences us.
- ways that speakers use to rehearse and deliver their speeches.

**You'll learn to:**
- outline your speeches.
- use language to best achieve your purposes.
- rehearse your speech efficiently and deliver your speech with maximum impact.

## STEP 8: OUTLINE YOUR SPEECH

The **outline** is a blueprint for your speech; it lays out the elements of the speech and their relationship to one another. With this blueprint in front of you, you can see at a glance all the elements of organization—the functions of the introduction and conclusion, the transitions, the main points and their relationship to the thesis and purpose, and the adequacy of the supporting materials. And, like a blueprint for a building, the outline enables you to spot weaknesses that might otherwise go undetected.

Begin outlining when you first begin constructing your speech. In this way, you'll take the best advantage of one of the major functions of an outline—to tell you where change is needed. Change and alter the outline as necessary at every stage of the speech construction process.

Outlines may be extremely detailed or extremely general. But because you're now in a learning environment whose objective is to make you a more proficient public speaker, a detailed full-sentence outline will serve best. The more detail you put into the outline, the easier it will be for you to examine the parts of the speech for all the qualities and characteristics that make a speech effective.

### Constructing the Outline

After you've completed your research and mapped out an organizational plan for your speech, put this plan (this blueprint) on paper. Construct a "preparation outline" of your speech, using the following guidelines.

**Preface the Outline with Identifying Data.**
Before you begin the outline proper, identify the general and specific purposes as well as your thesis. This prefatory material should look something like this:

Title: What Media Do

General purpose: To inform.

Specific purpose: To inform my audience of four major functions of the mass media.

Thesis: The mass media serve four major functions.

These identifying notes are not part of your speech proper. They're not, for example, mentioned in your oral presentation. Rather, they're guides to the preparation of the speech and the outline. They're like road signs to keep you going in the right direction and to signal when you've gone off course. One additional bit of identifying data should preface the statements of purposes and thesis: the title of your speech.

**Outline the Introduction, Body, and Conclusion as Separate Units.** The introduction, body, and conclusion of the speech, although intimately connected, should be labeled separately and should be kept distinct in your outline. Like the preliminary identifying data, these labels are not spoken to the audience but are further guides to your preparation.

By keeping the introduction, body, and conclusion separate, you'll be able to see at a glance if they do in fact serve the functions you want them to serve. You'll be able to see where further amplification and support are needed. In short, you'll be able to see where there are problems and where repair is necessary.

At the same time, do make sure that you examine and see the speech as a whole—how the introduction leads to the body, and how the conclusion summarizes your propositions and brings your speech to a close.

**Insert Transitions.** Insert [using square brackets, like these] transitions between the introduction and the body, the body and the conclusion, the main points of the body, and wherever else you think they might be useful.

**Include a List of References.** Some instructors require that you include a list of references in your preparation outline. If this is requested, then do so at the end of the outline or on a separate page. Some instructors require that only sources cited in the speech be included in the list of references, whereas others require that the full list of sources consulted be provided (those mentioned in the speech as well as those not mentioned).

Your research and references will prove most effective with your audience if you carefully integrate them into the speech. It will count for little if you consulted the latest works by the greatest authorities but never mention this to your audience. So, when appropriate, weave into your speech the source material you've consulted. In your outline, refer to the source material by author's name, date, and page in parentheses and then provide the complete citation in your list of references.

---

**Theory and Research — UNDERSTANDING**   One-Sided versus Two-Sided Messages

When you're presenting persuasive arguments, should you devote all your time to your side of the case—or should you also mention the other side and show why that side is not acceptable? Originally studied during the 1940s, this question continues to engage the attention of researchers. Early studies found that one-sided presentations were more effective with less-educated audiences, whereas two-sided presentations were more effective with more-educated listeners. One-sided presentations also were more effective with people who were already in favor of the speaker's point of view, whereas two-sided presentations were more persuasive with those who were initially opposed to the speaker's position.

Whether you choose to use a one-sided or a two-sided persuasive approach will depend on your topic (are there two competing positions?), the time you have available (limited time may prevent you from covering both sides), your audience's existing attitude (if they already reject the other position, there may not be a need to include it), and perhaps other factors as well.

If you do decide to present both sides, here are a few points to consider:

1. Using a two-sided presentation generally helps establish your credibility; by mentioning the other side, you demonstrate your knowledge of the entire area and by implication tell the audience that you understand both positions.

2. In a two-sided presentation, be sure to demonstrate the superiority of your position and the reasons why the other position is not as good as yours (O'Keefe, 1999). If you merely mention the other position without pointing out its flaws, then you risk creating doubt in minds of your listeners about the superiority of your position.

3. If your audience is aware of an alternative position, then you need to demonstrate that you too are aware of it but that it's not as good as your position.

4. Demonstrate that you have analyzed the alternative position as carefully and thoroughly as the position you're supporting.

---

**Working with Theories and Research**

*Take a look at print, television, or Internet ads and identify a few ads that use a two-sided approach (Brand A is better than Brand X). What makes a two-sided advertisement effective?*

In your actual speech, a source citation might be phrased something like this:

According to John Naisbitt, author of the nation-wide best-seller *Megatrends*, the bellwether states are California, Florida, Washington, Colorado, and Connecticut.

Regardless of what specific sourcing system is required (find out before you prepare your outline), make certain to include all sources of information, not just written materials. Personal interviews, information derived from course lectures, and data learned from television should all be included in your list of references.

**Use a Consistent Set of Symbols.** The following is the standard, accepted sequence of symbols for outlining:

I.
  A.
    1.
      a.
        (1)
          (a)

Begin the introduction, the body, and the conclusion with Roman numeral I. Treat each of the three major parts as a complete unit.

**Use Visual Aspects to Reflect the Organizational Pattern.** Use proper and clear indentation. The outlining function of word-processing programs has many of these suggestions built into them.

Not this:

**I.** Television caters to the lowest possible intelligence.
**II.** Talk shows illustrate this.
**III.** *General Hospital*

This:

**I.** Television caters to the lowest possible intelligence.
  **A.** Talk shows illustrate this.
    1. *Montel*
    2. *Maury*
    3. *The Jerry Springer Show*
  **B.** Soap operas illustrate this.
    1. *As the World Turns*
    2. *General Hospital*
    3. *The Young and the Restless*

**Use One Discrete Idea per Symbol.** If your outline is to reflect the organizational pattern structur-

ing the various items of information, use just one discrete idea per symbol, and make sure each item does not overlap with any other item. Instead of the overlapping "Education might be improved if teachers were better trained and if students were better motivated," break this statement into two propositions: "I. Education would be improved if teachers were better trained" and "II. Education would be improved if students were better motivated."

**Use Complete Declarative Sentences.** Phrase your ideas in the outline in complete declarative sentences rather than as questions or as phrases. This will further assist you in examining the essential relationships. It's much easier, for example, to see if one item of information supports another if both are phrased in the declarative mode. If one is a question and one is a statement, this will be more difficult.

## Sample Outlines

Now that the principles of outlining are clear, let's look at some specific examples to illustrate how those principles are put into operation in specific outlines. We'll look first at preparation outlines with two different organizational patterns; then at a template outline, a kind of skeletal pattern for a speech; and finally at a delivery outline, the type of outline you might take with you when you deliver your speech.

### The Preparation Outline

Two **preparation outlines** are presented in the Public Speaking Sample Assistant boxes on pages 359–363. One uses a topical organizational pattern, perhaps the most common pattern among public speeches; the other uses the motivated sequence, an extremely popular pattern both for informative talks (see Unit 17) and for persuasive speeches (see Unit 18).

These full-sentence outlines are similar to the written materials you might prepare in constructing your own speeches. The side notes in the boxes are designed to clarify both the content and the format of full-sentence outlines.

### Template Outline

Another useful type of outline is the **template outline**. Much as a template in PowerPoint guides you to fill in certain information in particular places, the template outline serves a similar function; it ensures that you include all the relevant material in reasonable order. At the same time, it also helps you see your speech as a whole—perhaps with gaps that

**Public Speaking Sample Assistant**

# A Preparation Outline (Topical Organization)

### Self-Disclosure

**General purpose:** To inform.
**Specific purpose:** To inform my audience of the advantages and disadvantages of self-disclosing.
**Thesis:** Self-disclosure has advantages and disadvantages.

Generally, the title, thesis, and general and specific purposes of the speech are prefaced to the outline. When the outline is an assignment that is to be handed in, additional information may be requested.

## Introduction

Note the general format for the outline: the headings (introduction, body, and conclusion) are clearly labeled, and the sections are separated visually.

I. We've all heard them:

Notice that the introduction serves the three functions discussed in the text: it gains attention (by these extreme confessions); establishes an S-A-T connection (by noting that all of us, speaker and audience, have had this experience); and orients the audience (by identifying the three major ideas of the speech).

 A. I'm in love with my nephew.

Note how the indenting helps you to see clearly the relationship that one item bears to another. For example, in Introduction I, the outline format helps you to see that A, B, and C are explanations (amplification and support) for I.

 B. My husband is not my baby's father.
 C. I'm really a woman.

These brief statements are designed to get attention, perhaps a laugh or two, but also to introduce the nature of the topic.

II. We've all disclosed.
 A. Sometimes it was positive, sometimes negative, but always significant.
 B. Knowing the potential consequences will help us make better decisions.

Here the speaker seeks to establish a speaker-audience-topic connection.

III. We look at this important form of communication in three parts:
 A. First, we look at the nature of self-disclosure.
 B. Second, we look at the potential rewards.
 C. Third, we look at the potential risks.
 [Let's look first at the nature of this type of communication.]

Here the speaker orients the audience and explains the three parts of the speech. The use of guide phrases (first, second, third) helps the audience fix clearly in mind the major divisions of the speech.

This transition cues the audience that the speaker will consider the first of the major parts of the speech. Notice that transitions are inserted between all major parts of the speech. Although they may seem too numerous in this abbreviated outline, transitions will be appreciated by your listeners, because they will help them follow and understand your speech.

## Body

I. Self-disclosure is a form of communication (Petronio, 2000).
 A. S-D is about the self.
 1. It can be about what you did.
 2. It can be about what you think.

**Public Speaking Sample Assistant**

# A Preparation Outline (Topical Organization) *(Continued)*

**B.** S-D is new, previously unknown information.

**C.** S-D is normally about information usually kept hidden.

    **1.** It can be something about which you're ashamed.

    **2.** It can be something for which you'd be punished in some way.

[Knowing what self-disclosure is, we can now look at its potential rewards.]

**II.** Self-disclosure has three potential rewards.

    **A.** It gives us self-knowledge.

    **B.** It increases communication effectiveness (Schmidt & Cornelius, 1987).

    **C.** It improves physiological health (Sheese, Brown, & Graziano, 2004).

[Although these benefits are substantial, there are also risks.]

**III.** Self-disclosure has three potential risks.

    **A.** It can involve personal risks.

        **1.** This happened to a close friend.

        **2.** This also happened with well-known celebrities.

    **B.** It can involve relationship risks (Petronio, 2000).

        **1.** This happens on *Jerry Springer* five times a week.

        **2.** It also happened to me.

    **C.** It can involve professional risks (Korda, 1975; Fesko, 2001).

        **1.** This occurred recently at work.

        **2.** There are also lots of political examples.

[Let me summarize this brief excursion into self-disclosure.]

## Conclusion

**I.** Self disclosure is a type of communication.

    **A.** It's about the self, concerns something new, and concerns something that you usually keep hidden.

    **B.** Self-disclosure can lead to increased self-knowledge, better communication, and improved health.

This transition helps the audience see that the speaker is finished discussing what self-disclosure is and will now consider the potential rewards.

Notice the parallel structure throughout the outline. For example, note that II and III in the body are phrased in similar style. Although this may seem unnecessarily redundant, it will help your audience follow your speech more closely and will also help you in logically structuring your thoughts.

Note that the referencese are integrated throughout the preparation outline just as they would be in a term paper. In the actual speech, the speaker might say something like: "Communication theorist Sandra Petronio presents evidence to show that. . . ."

These examples would naturally be recounted in greater detail in the actual speech. One of the values of outlining these examples is that you'll be able to see at a glance how many you have and how much time you have available to devote to each of these examples. Examples, especially personal ones, have a way of growing beyond their importance to the speech.

Note that each statement in the outline is a complete sentence. You can easily convert this outline into a phrase or keyword outline for use in presentation (see Public Speaking Sample Assistant box, page 365). The full sentences, however, will help you see more clearly the relationships among items.

This first part of the conclusion summarizes the major parts of the speech. The longer the speech, the more extensive the summary should be.

# A Preparation Outline
## (Topical Organization) *(Continued)*

**C.** Self-disclosure can also create risks to your personal, relational, and professional lives.

**II.** Self-disclosure is not only an interesting type of communication; it's also vital.

  **A.** You may want to explore this further by simply typing "self-disclosure" in your favorite search engine.

  **B.** If you want a more scholarly presentation, take a look at Sandra Petronio's *Balancing the Secrets of Private Disclosures* in the library or online.

**III.** The bottom line, of course: Should you self-disclose?

  **A.** Yes.

  **B.** No.

  **C.** Maybe.

### References

Korda, M. (1975). *Power! How to get it, how to use it.* New York: Ballantine.

Petronio, S. (Ed.). (2000). *Balancing the secrets of private disclosures.* Mahwah, NJ: Erlbaum.

Schmidt, T. O., & Cornelius, R. R. (1987). Self-disclosure in everyday life. *Journal of Social and Personal Relationships, 4,* 365–373.

Sheese, B. E., Brown, E. L, & Graziano, W. G. (2004). Emotional expression in cyberspace: Searching for moderators of the Pennebaker disclosure effect via e-mail. *Health Psychology, 23* (September), 457–464.

Notice that the Introduction's III A, B, and C correspond to the Body's I, II, and III, and to the Conclusion's I A, B, and C. This pattern will help you emphasize the major ideas in your speech—first in the orientation, second in the body of the speech, and third in the conclusion's summary.

This step, in which the speaker motivates the listeners to continue learning about self-disclosure, is optional in informative speeches. In persuasive speeches, you'd use this step to encourage listeners to act on your purpose—to vote, to donate time, to give blood, and so on.

This step provides closure; it makes it clear that the speech is finished. It also serves to encourage reflection on the part of the audience as to their own self-disclosing communication.

This reference list includes just those sources that appear in the completed speech.

need to be filled or items that are discussed at too great a length. In some sense the template outline is mechanical (some might say too mechanical), but it's an extremely useful device for organizing a speech. As you become more familiar with the public speaking process, as with PowerPoint, you'll develop your speech, and your slides, without any template or wizard. As you review the template outline in the Public Speaking Sample Assistant box on page 364, the phrases printed in light ink will remind you of the functions of each outline item.

## The Phrase/Key-Word Presentation Outline

Now that you've constructed a preparation outline, perhaps using a template outline for guidance, you need to construct a presentation outline. Resist the temptation to use your preparation outline to deliver the speech. If you use your preparation outline, you'll tend to read from the outline instead of presenting a seemingly extemporaneous speech in which you attend to and respond to audience feedback. Instead, construct a brief

**Public Speaking Sample Assistant**

# A Preparation Outline
## (Motivated Sequence Organization)

This outline illustrates how you might construct an outline and a speech using the motivated sequence. This outline focuses on the establishment of a youth center as a means of combating juvenile crime. In a longer speech, if you wanted to persuade an audience to establish a youth center, you might include two or three issues and not limit yourself to the single issue of reducing juvenile crime.

As you will see, in the motivated sequence outline, the five steps identified in Unit 15 (attention, need, satisfaction, visualization, and action) take the place of the Introduction, Body, and Conclusion structure of many outlines discussed earlier and of the topical organization in the Public Speaking Sample Assistant box on pages 359–361.

## The Youth Center

**General purpose:** To persuade.
**Specific purpose:** To persuade my listeners to vote in favor of Proposition 14, which would establish a community youth center.
**Thesis:** A youth center will reduce juvenile crime.

I. If you could reduce juvenile crime by some 20 percent by just flipping a lever, would you do it?
   A. Thom's drugstore was broken into by teenagers.
   B. Loraine's video store windows were broken by teenagers.

Step 1: Attention
The speaker asks a question to gain attention and follows it with specific examples of juvenile crime that audience members have experienced. The question and the specific examples focus on one single issue: the need to reduce juvenile crime. If the speech were a broader and longer one and included other reasons for the youth center, then it would have been appropriate to preview them here as well.

II. Juvenile crime is on the rise.
   A. The overall number of crimes has increased.
      1. In 2002 there were 32 juvenile crimes.
      2. In 2004 there were 47 such crimes.
      3. In 2006 there were 63 such crimes.
   B. The number of serious crimes also has increased.
      1. In 2004 there were 30 misdemeanors and 2 felonies.
      2. In 2007 there were 35 misdemeanors and 28 felonies.

Step 2: Need
The speaker states directly and clearly the need and shows that a problem exists. The speaker then demonstrates that the rise in crime is significant both in absolute numbers and in the severity of the crimes. To help the listeners understand these figures, the speaker could display these figures on a chalkboard, on a prepared chart, or on PowerPoint slides. In a longer speech, other needs might also be identified in this step; for example, teenagers' needs for vocational and social skills.

III. A youth center will help reduce juvenile crime.
   A. Three of our neighboring towns reduced juvenile crime after establishing a youth center.
      1. In Marlboro there was a 20 percent decline in overall juvenile crime.
      2. In both Highland and Ellenville the number of serious crimes declined 25 percent.

Step 3: Satisfaction
In this step, the speaker shows the listeners that the proposal to establish a youth center offers great benefits and no significant drawbacks.
The speaker argues that the youth center will satisfy the need to reduce juvenile crime by showing statistics from neighboring towns. The speaker also preemptively answers any objections about increased taxes. If the speaker had reason to believe that listeners had other possible objections, these concerns too should be addressed in this step.

**Public Speaking Sample Assistant**

## A Preparation Outline (Motivated Sequence Organization) *(Continued)*

**B.** The youth center will not increase our tax burden.
  **1.** New York State grants will pay for most of the expenses.
  **2.** Local merchants have agreed to pay any remaining expenses.
**IV.** Juvenile crime will decrease as a result of the youth center.
  **A.** If we follow the example of our neighbors, our juvenile crime rates are likely to decrease by 20 to 25 percent.
  **B.** Thom's store would not have been broken into.
  **C.** Loraine's windows would not have been broken.
**V.** Vote yes on Proposition 14.
  **A.** In next week's election you'll be asked to vote on Proposition 14, establishing a youth center.
  **B.** Vote yes if you want to help reduce juvenile crime.
  **C.** Urge your family members, your friends, and your work colleagues also to vote yes.

Step 4: Visualization
Here the speaker visualizes what the town would be like if the youth center were established, using both the statistics developed earlier and the personal examples introduced in the beginning of the speech.

Step 5: Action
In this step the speaker asks the audience for a specific action—to vote in favor of the youth center—and urges listeners to influence others to do the same. The speaker also reiterates the main theme of the speech; namely, that the youth center will help reduce juvenile crime.

---

**presentation outline**: an outline that will assist rather than hinder your delivery of the speech. Here are some guidelines to follow in preparing this delivery outline.

- Be brief. Try to limit yourself to one side of one sheet of paper.

- Be clear. Be sure that you can see the outline while you're speaking. Use different colored inks, underlining, or whatever system will help you communicate your ideas.

- Be delivery minded. Include any guides to delivery that will help while you're speaking. Note in the outline when you'll use your presentation aid and when you'll remove it. A simple "show PA" or "remove PA" should suffice. You might also wish to note some speaking cues, such as "slow down" when reading a poetry excerpt, or perhaps a place where an extended pause might help.

- Rehearse with the presentation outline. In your rehearsals, use the delivery outline only. Remember, the objective is to make rehearsals as close to the real thing as possible.

The Public Speaking Sample Assistant box on page 365 shows a sample presentation outline constructed from the preparation outline on self-disclosure (on pages 359–361). Note that the outline is brief enough so that you'll be able to use it effectively without losing eye contact with the audience. It uses abbreviations (for example, S-D for self-disclosure) and phrases rather than complete sentences. And yet it's detailed enough to include all essential parts of your speech, including transitions. It contains delivery notes specifically tailored to your own needs, such as pause suggestions and guides to using visual aids. Note also that it's clearly divided into introduction, body, and conclusion and uses the same numbering system as the preparation outline.

## Public Speaking Sample Assistant

# A Template Outline

This template outline would be appropriate for a speech using a temporal, spatial, or topical organization pattern. Note that in this template outline there are three main points (I, II, and III in the body). These correspond to the III A, B, and C in the introduction (where you'd orient the audience) and to the A, B, and C in the conclusion (where you'd summarize your main points). Once again, the transitions are signaled by square brackets. As you review this outline, the phrases printed in light ink will remind you of the functions of each outline item. Additional template outlines are available at My-CommunicationLab (www.mycommunicationlab.com).

**Title:** [short, relevant, and attention-getting]
**General purpose:** your general aim (to inform, to persuade, to entertain)
**Specific purpose:** what you hope to achieve from this speech
**Thesis:** your main assertion: the core of your speech

### Introduction

I. gain attention
II. establish S-A-T connection
III. orient audience
  A. first main point; same as I in body
  B. second main point; same as II in body
  C. third main point; same as III in body
    connect the introduction to the
[**Transition:** body]

### Body

I. first main point
  A. support of I (the first main point)
  B. further support for I
    connect the first main point to
[**Transition:** the second]
II. second main point
  A. support for II (the second main point)
  B. further support for II
    connect the second main point
[**Transition:** to the third]
III. third main point
  A. support for III (the third main point)
  B. further support for III
    connect the third main point (or
[**Transition:** all main points) to the conclusion]

### Conclusion

I. summary
  A. first main point; same as I in body
  B. second main point; same as II in body
  C. third main point; same as III in body
II. motivation
III. closure

### References

Alphabetical list of sources cited

## STEP 9: WORD YOUR SPEECH

You're a successful public speaker when your listeners create in their minds the meanings you want them to create. You're successful when your listeners adopt the attitudes and behaviors you want them to adopt. The language choices you make—the words you select and the sentences you form—will greatly influence the meanings your listeners receive and, thus, how successful you are.

## Oral Style

**Oral style** is the quality of spoken language that differentiates it from written language. You do not speak as you write (Akinnaso, 1982). The words and sentences you use differ. The major reason for this difference is that you compose speech instantly. You select your words and construct your sentences as you think your thoughts. There's very little time between the thought and the utterance. When you

**Public Speaking Sample Assistant**

# A Phrase/Key-Word Presentation Outline

## Self-Disclosure

PAUSE!
LOOK OVER THE AUDIENCE!

### Introduction

  I. We've heard them:
   **A.** I'm in love with my nephew.
   **B.** My husband is not my baby's father.
   **C.** I'm really a woman.
 II. We've all S-D.
   **A.** Sometimes +, −, significant
   **B.** consequences = better decisions.
III. 3 parts: (WRITE ON BOARD)
   **A.** 1. nature of S-D
   **B.** 2. rewards
   **C.** 3. risks
[1st = type of communication.]
PAUSE, STEP FORWARD

### Body

  I. S-D: communication
   **A.** about self
   **B.** new
   **C.** hidden information
[Knowing what self-disclosure is, now rewards.]
 II. 3 rewards.
   **A.** self-knowledge
   **B.** communication effectiveness
   **C.** physiological health

[Benefits substantial, there are also risks.]
PAUSE!
**III.** 3 risks
   **A.** personal
   **B.** relationship
   **C.** professional
[Summarize: S-D]

### Conclusion

  I. S-D = communication.
   **A.** about self, new, and usually hidden
   **B.** rewards: increased self-knowledge, better communication, and improved health
   **C.** risks: personal, relational, and professional
 II. S-D, not only interesting, it's vital
   A. Explore further "S-D" on www
   B. Scholarly: Sandra Petronio's *Boundaries*.
III. Should you S-D?
   **A.** Yes
   **B.** No
   **C.** Maybe
PAUSE!
ANY QUESTIONS?

---

write, however, you compose your thoughts after considerable reflection. Even then you probably often rewrite and edit as you go along. Because of this, written language has a more formal tone. Spoken language is more informal, more colloquial.

Generally, spoken language consists of shorter, simpler, and more familiar words than does written language. Also, there's more qualification in speech than in writing. For example, when speaking you probably make greater use of such expressions as *although, however, perhaps*, and the like. When writing, you probably edit these out.

Spoken language has a greater number of self-reference terms (terms that refer to the speaker herself or himself): *I, me, our, us,* and *you.* Spoken language

also has a greater number of "allness" terms such as *all, none, every, always,* and *never.* When you write, you're probably more careful to edit out such allness terms, realizing that such terms often are not very descriptive of reality.

Spoken language has more pseudo-quantifying terms (for example, *many, much, very, lots*) and terms that include the speaker as part of the observation (for example, *It seems to me that* or *As I see it*). Further, speech contains more verbs and adverbs; writing contains more nouns and adjectives.

Spoken and written language not only *do* differ, they *should* differ. The main reason why spoken and written language should differ is that the listener hears speech only once; therefore, speech must be

# ASK THE RESEARCHER

## Making Myself Clear

*I notice that some people are very good at getting their ideas across clearly, while others are quite confusing. I'd like to know some things the clear speakers are doing that confusing speakers often fail to do.*

It's important to recognize that your listeners view your topic differently than you do. Your picture is clear, while theirs is blurry. So first, give listeners a general sense or overview of your topic. Tell them in general terms what you'll be discussing. Second, condense your topic to three or four main points—too many main points will only confuse an audience, especially if the topic is new to them.

Then, to truly make your topic clear and vivid to listeners, give examples, tell stories as illustrations, and use analogies, for example. Audiences like this, and it will enhance clarity, as long as listeners can see how these supporting materials relate to your topic. Third, begin with terms that are familiar to your audience before introducing terms or concepts that are new or unique to your topic. By the end of the speech, your audience's blurry sense of the topic will become clearer.

For further information: Chesebro, J. L. (2002). Teaching clearly. In J. L. Chesebro & J. C. McCroskey (Eds.), *Communication for teachers*. Boston: Allyn & Bacon. Also Civikly, J. M. (1992). Clarity: Teachers and students making sense of instruction. *Communication Education, 41*, 138-152. And Rowan, K. E. (2003). Informing and explaining skills: Theory and research on informative communication. In J. Green & B. Burleson (Eds.), *Handbook of communication and social interaction skills* (pp. 403-438). Mahwah, NJ: Erlbaum.

**Joseph Chesebro** (Ed.D., West Virginia University) is an assistant professor of communication at the State University of New York at Brockport. He teaches courses in interpersonal and organizational communication and conducts research on clear teaching and conversational sensitivity as an aspect of listening. He also plays drums.

---

instantly intelligible. The reader can reread an essay or look up an unfamiliar word; the reader can spend as much time as he or she wishes with the written page. The listener, in contrast, must move at the pace set by the speaker. The reader may reread a sentence or paragraph if there's a temporary attention lapse. The listener doesn't have this option.

## Choosing Words

Choose carefully the words you use in your public speeches. Choose words to achieve clarity, vividness, appropriateness, a personal style, and forcefulness. At the same time that you work to achieve these qualities, be careful to avoid the common fallacies of language (see Table 16.1).

### Clarity

**Clarity** in speaking style should be your primary goal. Here are some guidelines to help you make your speech clear.

**Be Economical.** Don't waste words. Notice the wasted words in such expressions as "at nine *a.m. in*

*the morning,*" "we *first* began the discussion," "I *myself personally,*" and "blue *in color.*" By withholding the italicized terms you eliminate unnecessary words and move closer to a more economical and clearer style.

**Use Specific Terms and Numbers.** As we get more and more specific, we get a clearer and more detailed picture. Be specific. Don't say "dog" when you want your listeners to picture a St. Bernard. Don't say "car" when you want them to picture a limousine. The same is true of numbers. Don't say "earned a good salary" if you mean "earned $90,000 a year." Don't say "taxes will go up" when you mean "taxes will increase 7 percent."

**Use Guide Phrases.** Use guide phrases to help listeners see that you're moving from one idea to another—phrases such as "now that we have seen how . . . , let us consider how . . . ," and "my next argument. . . ." Terms such as *first, second, and also, although,* and *however* will help your audience follow your line of thinking.

**Use Short, Familiar Terms.** Generally, favor the short word over the long one. Favor the familiar

## Table 16.1 **Fallacies of Language**

In listening to and critically evaluating speeches, look carefully for language fallacies—ways of using language that subvert instead of clarify truth and accuracy. In Unit 5's discussion of verbal messages, five such barriers to language accuracy were identified: polarization, fact–inference confusion, allness, static evaluation, and indiscrimination. Here are additional language fallacies, these focusing on words that mislead and give listeners the wrong impression. After you read these several fallacies, review some commercial websites for vitamins, clothing, books, music, or any such topic you're interested in and try to find examples of misleading language. It won't be difficult.

| Fallacy | Examples | Critical Response |
|---|---|---|
| *Weasel words* are words whose meanings are slippery and difficult to pin down (Hayakawa & Hayakawa, 1989). | The medicine that claims to "work better than Brand X" doesn't specify how much better or in what respect it performs better. "Better" is a weasel word, as are "help," "virtually," "as much as," "like" (as in "it will make you feel like new"), and "more economical." | Ask yourself: Exactly what is being claimed? For example, "What does 'may reduce cholesterol' mean? What exactly is being asserted?" |
| *Euphemisms* make the negative and unpleasant appear positive and appealing. Often this inflated language makes the mundane seem extraordinary, the common seem exotic. | Euphemisms are all around, as in calling the firing of 200 workers "downsizing" or "reallocation of resources" or trumpeting "the vacation of a lifetime" or "unsurpassed vistas." | Don't let words get in the way of accurate firsthand perception. The word is *not* the thing; words merely symbolize the thing (sometimes inaccurately). |
| *Jargon*, the specialized language of a professional class, becomes a problem when used with those who are not professionals in the field. | The specialized languages of communication, computer, and psychology professionals offer clear examples of jargon: terms such as *content and relationship messages*, *blogosphere*, and *attribution*. | Don't be intimidated by jargon; ask questions when you don't understand. |
| *Doublespeak* is language used to confuse rather than inform. | Doublespeak is evident when someone uses technical or little-known words that confuse people who don't know the meanings of these words without defining them. | As with jargon, don't allow words to intimidate you; when in doubt, find out. |
| *Gobbledygook* is overly complex language that overwhelms the listener instead of communicating meaning. | Big and relatively uncommon words and foreign terms (especially Latin or French) are examples of gobbledygook. | Don't confuse complex language with truth or accuracy; ask for simplification when appropriate. |

word over the unfamiliar word. Favor the more commonly used term over the rarely used term.

Here are a few examples:

| Poor Choices | Better Choices |
|---|---|
| *innocuous* | *harmless* |
| *elucidate* | *clarify* |
| *utilize* | *use* |
| *ascertain* | *find out* |
| *erstwhile* | *former* |
| *eschew* | *avoid* |
| *expenditure* | *cost or expense* |

**Carefully Assess Idioms.** Idioms are expressions that are unique to a specific language and whose meaning cannot be deduced from the individual words used. Expressions such as "kick the bucket," or "doesn't have a leg to stand on" are idioms: Either you know the meaning of the expression or you don't; you can't figure it out from only a knowledge of the individual words.

The positive side of idioms is that they give your speech a casual and informal air; they make your speech sound like a speech and not like a written essay. The negative side of idioms is that they create problems for listeners who are not native speakers of your language. Many non–native speakers will simply not understand the meaning of your idioms. This problem is especially important because audiences are becoming increasingly intercultural and because the number of idioms we use is extremely high.

**Distinguish between Commonly Confused Words.** Many words, because they sound alike or are used in similar situations, are commonly confused. Try the self-test below, which covers 10 of the most frequently confused words.

# TEST YOURSELF

## Can You Distinguish between Commonly Confused Words?

Underline the word in parentheses that you would use in each sentence.

_____ 1. She (accepted, excepted) the award and thanked everyone (accept, except) the producer.

_____ 2. The teacher (affected, effected) his students greatly and will now (affect, effect) an entirely new curriculum.

_____ 3. Are you deciding (between, among) red and green or (between, among) red, green, and blue?

_____ 4. I've scaled higher mountains than this, so I'm sure I (can, may) scale this one; I and a few others know the hidden path, but I (can, may) not reveal this.

_____ 5. The table was (cheap, inexpensive) but has great style; the chairs cost a fortune but look (cheap, inexpensive).

_____ 6. We (discover, invent) uncharted lands but (discover, invent) computer programs.

_____ 7. He was direct and (explicit, implicit) in his denial of the crime but was vague and only (explicit, implicit) concerning his whereabouts.

_____ 8. She (implied, inferred) that she'd seek a divorce; we can only (imply, infer) her reasons.

_____ 9. The wedding was (tasteful, tasty) and the food (tasteful, tasty).

_____ 10. The student seemed (disinterested, uninterested) in the lecture. The teacher was (disinterested, uninterested) in who received what grades.

**HOW DID YOU DO?** Here are the principles that govern correct usage: (1) Use *accept* to mean "receive" and *except* to mean with "the exclusion of." (2) Use *to affect* to mean "to have an effect on or to influence," and *to effect* to mean "to produce a result." (3) Use *between* when referring to two items and *among* when referring to more than two items. (4) Use *can* to refer to ability and *may* to refer to

permission. (5) Use *cheap* to refer to something that is inferior and *inexpensive* to something that costs little. (6) Use *discover* to refer to the act of finding something out or learning something previously unknown, but use *invent* to refer to the act of originating something new. (7) Use *explicit* to mean "directly stated" and *implicit* to indicate the act of expressing something without actually stating it. (8) Use *imply* to mean "state indirectly" and *infer* to mean "draw a conclusion." (9) Use *tasteful* to refer to good taste, but use *tasty* to refer to something that tastes good. (10) Use *uninterested* to indicate a lack of interest and use *disinterested* to mean "objective" or "unbiased."

**WHAT WILL YOU DO?** Your use of language can greatly enhance (or detract from) your persuasiveness. A word used incorrectly can lessen your credibility and general persuasiveness. Review your English handbook and identify other commonly confused words. Get into the habit of referring to a good dictionary whenever you have doubts about which word is preferred.

## Vividness

Select words to make your ideas vivid and to help your arguments come alive in the minds of your listeners. To achieve **vividness**, use active verbs, strong verbs, figures of speech, and imagery.

**Use Active Verbs.** Favor verbs that communicate activity rather than passivity. The verb *to be*, in all its forms—*is, are, was, were, will be*—is relatively inactive. Try using verbs of action instead. Rather than saying "The teacher was in the middle of the crowd," say "The teacher stood in the middle of the crowd." Instead of saying "The report was on the president's desk for three days," try "The report rested [or slept] on the president's desk for three days." Instead of saying "Management will be here tomorrow," consider "Management will descend on us tomorrow" or "Management jets in tomorrow."

**Use Strong Verbs.** The verb is the strongest part of your sentence. Choose verbs carefully, and choose them so they accomplish a lot. Instead of saying "He walked through the forest," consider such terms as *wandered, prowled, rambled,* or *roamed*. Consider whether one of these might not better suit your intended meaning. Consult a thesaurus for any verb you suspect might be weak.

**Use Figures of Speech.** Figures of speech help achieve vividness, in addition to making your speech more memorable and giving it a polished, well-crafted tone. **Figures of speech** are stylistic devices that have been a part of rhetoric since ancient times. Here are some of the major figures of speech; you may wish to incorporate a few of these into your next speech.

- *Alliteration* is the repetition of the same initial sound in two or more words, as in "fifty famous flavors" or the "cool, calculating leader."

- *Hyperbole* is the use of extreme exaggeration, as in "He cried like a faucet" or "I'm so hungry I could eat a whale."

- *Irony* is the use of a word or sentence whose literal meaning is the opposite of the message actually conveyed; for example, a teacher handing back failing examinations might say, "So pleased to see how many of you studied so hard."

- *Metaphor* compares two unlike things by stating that one thing "is" the other, as in "She's a lion when she wakes up" or "He's a real bulldozer."

- *Synecdoche* is the use of a part of an object to stand for the whole object, as in "All hands were on deck" (where "hands" stands for "sailor" or "crew member") or "green thumb" for "expert gardener."

- *Metonymy* is the substitution of a name for a title with which it's closely associated, as in "City Hall issued the following news release," in which "City Hall" stands for "the mayor" or "the city council."

- *Antithesis* is the presentation of contrary ideas in parallel form, as in "My loves are many, my enemies are few." Charles Dickens's opening words in *A Tale of Two Cities* are a famous antithesis: "It was the best of times; it was the worst of times."

- *Simile*, like metaphor, compares two unlike objects; but simile explicitly uses the words *like* or *as*; for example, "The manager is as gentle as an ox."

- *Personification* is the attribution of human characteristics to inanimate objects, as in "This room cries for activity" or "My car is tired and wants a drink."

- *Rhetorical questions* are questions used to make a statement or to produce a desired effect rather than to secure an answer, as in "Do you want to be popular?" "Do you want to get well?"

**Use Imagery.** Appeal to the senses, especially your listeners' visual, auditory, and tactile senses. Make your audience see, hear, and feel what you're talking about.

In describing people or objects, create word "pictures" or *visual imagery*. When appropriate, describe such visual qualities as height, weight, color, size, shape, length, and contour. Let your audience see the sweat pouring down the faces of the coal miners; let them see the short, overweight, cigar-smoking executive in his pin-striped suit.

Use *auditory imagery* to describe sounds; let your listeners hear the car's tires screeching, the wind whistling, the bells chiming, the angry professor roaring.

Use terms referring to temperature, texture, and touch to create *tactile imagery*. Let your listeners feel the cool water running over their bodies or the punch of the prizefighter; let them feel the smooth skin of the newborn baby.

## Appropriateness

Use language that is appropriate to you as the speaker—and that is appropriate to your audience, the occasion, and the speech topic. Here are some general guidelines to help you achieve **appropriateness**.

### Speak on the Appropriate Level of Formality.
The most effective public speaking style is less formal than the written essay, but more formal than conversation. One way to achieve an informal style is to use contractions. Say *don't* instead of *do not*, *I'll* instead of *I shall*, and *wouldn't* instead of *would not*. Contractions give a public speech the sound and rhythm of conversation, a quality that most listeners react to favorably. Also, use personal pronouns rather than impersonal expressions. Say "I found" instead of "It has been found," or "I will present three arguments" instead of "Three arguments will be presented."

**Avoid Unfamiliar Terms.** Avoid using terms the audience doesn't know. Avoid foreign and technical terms unless you're certain the audience is familiar with them. Similarly, avoid **jargon** (the technical vocabulary of a specialized field) unless you're sure the meanings are clear to your listeners. Some acronyms (such as NATO, UN, NOW, and CORE) are probably familiar to most audiences; many, however, are not. When you wish to use any specialized terms or abbreviations, explain their meaning fully to the audience.

**Avoid Slang.** **Slang** is language that is used by special groups but is generally considered impolite or not quite proper. *Webster's New World College Dictionary* defines *slang* as "highly informal speech that is outside conventional or standard usage and consists both of coined words and phrases and of new or extended meanings attached to established terms." Generally, it's best to avoid slang, which may offend or embarrass your audience. Although your listeners may use slang interpersonally, they probably don't want to hear it in a relatively formal situation such as public speaking. If you're in doubt about whether a word is considered slang, consult a dictionary; usually, dictionaries identify slang terms as "informal."

## MEDIA WATCH
## HATE SPEECH

*It is not only true that the language we use puts words in our mouths; it also puts notions in our heads.*

—*Wendell Johnson*

Hate speech is speech that is hostile, offensive, degrading, or intimidating to a particular group of people. Women, African Americans, Muslims, Jews, Asians, Hispanics, and gay men and lesbians are among the major targets in the United States.

Hate speech occurs in all forms of human communication; it occurs when people utter insults to someone passing by; when posters and fliers degrade specific groups; when radio talk shows denigrate members of certain groups; when computer games are reconfigured to target members of certain groups; or when websites insult, demean, and encourage hostility toward certain groups. Because the media reach so many people and are so powerful in influencing opinions, the issue of hate speech in the media takes on special importance (Ruscher, 2001).

One of the difficulties in attacking hate speech is that it's often difficult to draw a clear line between speech that is protected by the First Amendment right to freedom of expression but is simply at odds with the majority viewpoint and speech that is designed to denigrate members of certain groups and encourage hostility against them.

Some colleges are instituting hate speech codes—written statements of what constitutes hate speech as well as enumerations of the penalties for hate speech. Proponents of such codes argue that they teach students that hate speech is unacceptable, is harmful to all people (but especially to those who are the targets of such attacks), and may be curtailed in the same way as other undesirable acts (such as child pornography or rape). Opponents argue that such codes do not address the underlying prejudices and biases that give rise to hate speech and that the codes stifle free expression and may be used unfairly by the majority to silence minority opinion and dissent.

### Increasing Media Literacy

*Search for "hate speech" and "campus codes," or take a look at "The Price of Free Speech" at* www.scu.edu/ethics/publications/iie/v5n2/codes.html, *for a review of the arguments for and against hate speech codes. After reading about hate speech and hate codes, formulate your own position on campus codes for hate speech. With this position in mind, examine a few media in terms of their own policies regarding hate speech.*

---

**Avoid Ethnic Expressions (Generally).** Unit 5 discussed the dangers of using racist, heterosexist, ageist, or sexist terms; these can only insult the audience members themselves or people they know and care about. So avoid these terms at all costs. In addition, however, avoid ethnic expressions, at least generally. Ethnic expressions are words and phrases that are peculiar to a particular ethnic group. At times these expressions are known only by members of the ethnic group; at other times they may be known more widely but still recognized as ethnic expressions.

When you are speaking to a multicultural audience, it's generally best to avoid ethnic expressions unless they're integral to your speech and you explain them. Such expressions are often interpreted as exclusionist; they highlight the connection between the speaker and the members of that particular ethnic group and the lack of connection between the speaker and all others who are not members of that ethnic group. And, of course, ethnic expressions should never be used if you're not a member of the ethnic group.

If, on the other hand, you're speaking to people who all belong to one ethnic group and if you're also a member, then such expressions are fine. In fact, they may well prove effective; being part of the common language of speaker and audience, they can help you stress your own similarities with the audience.

### Personal Style

Audiences favor speakers who speak in a personal rather than an impersonal style, who speak with them rather than at them. You can achieve a more **personal style** by using personal pronouns, asking questions, and creating immediacy.

**Use Personal Pronouns.** Say *I*, *me*, *he*, *she*, and *you*. Avoid impersonal expressions such as *one* (as in "One is led to believe . . ."), *this speaker*, or *you, the listeners*. These expressions distance the audience and create barriers rather than bridges.

**Use Questions.** Ask the audience questions to involve them. In a small audience, you might even briefly entertain responses. In larger audiences, you might ask the question, pause to allow the audience time to consider their responses, and then move on. When you direct questions to your listeners, they feel a part of the public speaking transaction.

**Create Immediacy.** Immediacy, as discussed in Unit 7, is a connectedness, a relatedness with one's listeners. Immediacy is the opposite of disconnectedness and separation. Here are some suggestions for creating immediacy through language:

- Use personal examples.

- Use terms that include both you and the audience; for example, *we* and *our*.

- Address the audience directly; say *you* rather than *students*; say "You'll enjoy reading" instead of "Everyone will enjoy reading"; say "I want you to see" instead of "I want people to see."

- Use specific names of audience members when appropriate.

- Express concern for the audience members.

- Reinforce or compliment the audience.

- Refer directly to commonalities between you and the audience; for example, "We are all children of immigrants" or "We all want to see our team in the playoffs."

- Refer to shared experiences and goals; for example, "We all want, we all need, a more responsive PTA."

- Recognize audience feedback and refer to it in your speech. Say, for example, "I can see from your expressions that we're all anxious to get to our immediate problem."

## Forcefulness/Power

Forceful or powerful language will help you achieve your purpose, whether it be informative or persuasive. **Forcefulness** in language enables you to direct the audience's attention, thoughts, and feelings. To make your speech more forceful, eliminate weakeners, vary intensity, and avoid overused expressions.

**Eliminate Weakeners.** Delete **weakeners**, or phrases that weaken your sentences. Among the major weakeners are uncertainty expressions and weak modifiers. Uncertainty expressions such as "I'm not sure of this, but"; "Perhaps it might"; or "Maybe it works this way" communicate a lack of commitment and conviction and will make your audience wonder if you're worth listening to. Weak modifiers such as "It works pretty well," "It's kind of like," or "It may be the one we want" make you seem unsure and indefinite about what you're saying.

Cut out any unnecessary verbiage that reduces the impact of your meaning. Instead of saying "There are lots of things we can do to help," say "We can do lots of things to help." Instead of saying "I'm sorry to be so graphic, but Senator Bingsley's proposal . . . ," say "We need to be graphic. Senator Bingsley's proposal. . . ." Instead of saying, "It should be observed in this connection that, all things considered, money is not productive of happiness," say "Money doesn't bring happiness."

Here are a few additional suggestions—which, of course, are not limited in application to public speaking but relate as well to interpersonal and small group communication.

- Avoid hesitations ("I, er, want to say that, ah, this one is, er, the best, you know"); they make you sound unprepared and uncertain.

- Avoid using too many intensifiers ("Really, this was the greatest; it was truly phenomenal"); audiences will begin to doubt the speaker who goes overboard with the superlatives.

- Avoid tag questions ("I'll review the report now, okay?" "That is a great proposal, don't you think?"); they signal your need for approval and your own uncertainty and lack of conviction.

- Avoid self-critical statements ("I'm not very good at this," "This is my first speech"); they signal a lack of confidence and make public your sense of inadequacy.

- Avoid slang and vulgar expressions; they may signal low social class and hence little power.

Table 16.2 on page 372 identifies a variety of suggestions for nonverbal action that will also help you to communicate forcefulness and power.

**Vary Intensity as Appropriate.** Just as you can vary your voice in intensity, you can also phrase your ideas with different degrees of stylistic intensity. You can, for example, refer to an action as "failing to support our position" or as "stabbing us in the back"; you can say that a new proposal will "endanger our goals" or will "destroy us completely"; you can refer to a child's behavior as "playful," "creative," or "destructive." Vary your language to express different degrees of intensity—from mild through neutral to extremely intense.

**Avoid Bromides and Clichés.** Bromides are trite sayings that are worn out because of constant usage. A few examples:

- Honesty is the best policy.

- If I can't do it well, I won't do it at all.

- I don't understand modern art, but I know what I like.

## Table 16.2 **Powerful Bodily Action**

Here are some nonverbal behaviors that are likely to help you communicate power in public speaking (Lewis, 1989; Burgoon & Bacue, 2003; Burgoon & Hoobler, 2002; Guerrero, DeVito, & Hecht, 1999):

| Suggestions for Communicating Power with Bodily Action | Reasons |
| --- | --- |
| While speaking, avoid self-manipulations (playing with your hair or touching your face, for example); avoid leaning backward. | These signals communicate a lack of comfort and an ill-at-ease feeling and are likely to damage your persuasiveness. |
| Walk slowly and deliberately to and from the podium. | To appear hurried is to appear powerless, as if you were rushing to meet the expectations of those who have power over you. |
| Use facial expressions and gestures as appropriate. | These help you express your concern for the audience and for the interaction and help you communicate your comfort and control of the situation. |
| Use consistent packaging; be careful that your verbal and nonverbal messages do not contradict each other. | Inconsistency between verbal and nonverbal messages will be seen as uncertainty and a lack of conviction. |

When we hear these hackneyed statements, we recognize them as unoriginal and uninspired.

**Clichés** are phrases that have lost their novelty and part of their meaning through overuse. Clichés call attention to themselves because of their overuse. Here are some examples of clichés to avoid:

- in this day and age
- tell it like it is
- free as a bird
- in the pink
- no sooner said than done
- it goes without saying
- few and far between
- over the hill
- no news is good news
- the life of the party
- keep your shirt on

## Phrasing Sentences

Give the same careful consideration that you give to words to the sentences of your speech as well. Some guidelines follow.

### Use Short Sentences

Short sentences are more forceful and economical. They are also easier for your audience to comprehend and remember. Listeners don't have the time or the inclination to unravel long and complex sentences. Help them to listen more efficiently. Use short rather than long sentences.

### Use Direct Sentences

Direct sentences are easier to understand. They are also more forceful. Instead of saying "I want to tell you of the three main reasons why we should not adopt Program A," say "We should not adopt Program A. There are three main reasons."

### Use Active Sentences

Active sentences—that is, sentences whose verbs are in the active voice—are easier to understand than passive ones. They also make your speech seem livelier and more vivid. Instead of saying "The lower court's decision was reversed by the Supreme Court," say "The Supreme Court reversed the lower court's decision." Instead of saying "The proposal was favored by management," say "Management favored the proposal."

### Use Positive Sentences

Sentences phrased positively are easier to comprehend and remember than sentences phrased negatively. Notice how sentences *a* and *c* are easier to understand than sentences *b* and *d*:

- **a.** The committee rejected the proposal.
- **b.** The committee did not accept the proposal.
- **c.** This committee works outside the normal company hierarchy.
- **d.** This committee does not work within the normal company hierarchy.

### Vary the Types of Sentences

The preceding advice to use short, direct, active, positive sentences is valid most of the time. Yet too many sentences of the same type or length will make your speech sound boring. So follow (generally) the preceding advice, but add variations as well.

# STEP 10: REHEARSE AND PRESENT YOUR SPEECH

Your last step is to rehearse and present your speech. Let's look first at rehearsal.

## Rehearsal

Use your rehearsal time effectively and efficiently for the following purposes:

- To develop a delivery that will help you achieve the objectives of your speech.

- To time your speech; if you time your rehearsals, you'll be able to see if you can add material or if you have to delete something.

- To see how the speech will flow as a whole and to make any changes and improvements you think necessary.

- To test the presentation aids, and to detect and resolve any technical problems.

- To learn the speech thoroughly.

- To reduce any feelings of apprehension and gain confidence.

The following procedures should assist you in achieving these goals.

### Rehearse the Speech as a Whole

Rehearse the speech from beginning to end, not in parts. Rehearse it from getting out of your seat through the introduction, body, and conclusion, to returning to your seat. Be sure to rehearse the speech with all the examples and illustrations (and any audiovisual aids) included. This will enable you to connect the parts of the speech and see how they interact.

### Time the Speech

Time the speech during each rehearsal. Make the necessary adjustments on the basis of this timing. If you're using computer presentation software, you'll be able to time your speech very precisely. Also time the individual parts of your speech so you can achieve the balance you want—for example, you might want to spend twice as much time on the solutions as on the problems, or you might want to balance the introduction and conclusion so that each portion constitutes about 10 percent of your speech.

### Approximate the Actual Speech Situation

Rehearse the speech under conditions as close as possible to those under which you'll deliver it. If possible, rehearse the speech in the same room in which you'll

**TIME PROBLEM**

Your speech has run overtime and you've been given the 30-second stop signal. You wonder if it would be best to ignore the signal and just continue your speech or if you should wrap up in 30 seconds? In either case,

WHAT DO YOU SAY?

present it. If this is impossible, try to simulate the actual conditions as closely as you can—even in your living room or bathroom. If possible, rehearse the speech in front of a few supportive listeners. It's always helpful (and especially for your beginning speeches) that your listeners be supportive rather than too critical. Merely having listeners present during your rehearsal will further simulate the conditions under which you'll eventually speak. Get together with two or three other students in an empty classroom where you can take turns as speakers and listeners.

### See Yourself as a Speaker

Rehearse the speech in front of a full-length mirror. This will enable you to see yourself and see how you'll appear to the audience. This may be extremely difficult at first, and you may have to force yourself to watch. After a few attempts, however, you'll begin to see the value of this experience. Practice your eye contact, your movements, and your gestures in front of the mirror.

### Incorporate Changes and Make Delivery Notes

Make any needed changes in the speech between rehearsals. Do not interrupt your rehearsal to make notes or changes; if you do, you may never experience the entire speech from beginning to end. While making these changes note any words whose pronunciation you wish to check. Also, insert pause notations, "slow down" warnings, and other delivery suggestions into your outline.

If possible, record your speech (ideally, on video-tape) so you can hear exactly what your listeners will hear: your volume, rate, pitch, pronunciation, and pauses. You'll thus be in a better position to improve these qualities.

## Rehearse Often

Rehearse the speech as often as seems necessary. Two useful guides are: (1) Rehearse the speech at least three or four times; less rehearsal than this is sure to be too little. (2) Rehearse the speech as long as your rehearsals continue to result in improvements in the speech or in your delivery. Some suggestions for a long-term delivery improvement program are presented next.

## Undertake a Long-Term Delivery Improvement Program

To become a truly effective speaker, you may need to undertake a long-term delivery improvement program. Approach this project with a positive attitude: Tell yourself that you can do it and that you will do it.

1. First, seek feedback from someone whose opinion and insight you respect. Your public speaking instructor may be a logical choice, but someone majoring in communication or working in a communication field might also be appropriate. Get an honest and thorough appraisal of both your voice and your bodily action.
2. Learn to hear, see, and feel the differences between effective and ineffective patterns. For example, is your pitch too high or your volume too loud? A tape recorder will be very helpful. Learn to feel your rigid posture or your lack of arm and hand gestures. Once you've perceived these voice and/or body patterns, concentrate on learning more effective habits. Practice a few minutes each day. Avoid becoming too conscious of any source of ineffectiveness. Just try to increase your awareness and work on one problem at a time. Do not try to change all your patterns at once.
3. Seek additional feedback on the changes. Make certain that listeners agree that the new patterns you're practicing really are more effective. Remember that you hear yourself through bone conduction as well as through air transmission. Others hear you only through air transmission. So what you hear and what others hear will be different.
4. For voice improvement, consult a book on voice and diction for practice exercises and for additional information on the nature of volume, rate, pitch, and quality.

5. If difficulties persist, see a professional. For voice problems, see a speech clinician. Most campuses have a speech clinic, and you can easily avail yourself of its services. For bodily action difficulties, talk with your public speaking instructor.
6. Seek professional help if you're psychologically uncomfortable with any aspect of your voice or bodily action. It may be that all you have to do is to hear yourself or see yourself on a videotape—as others hear and see you—to convince yourself that you sound and look just fine. Regardless of what is causing this discomfort, however, if you're uncomfortable, do something about it. In a college community there's more assistance available to you at no cost than you'll ever be offered again. Make use of it.

# Presenting Your Speech

If you're like most students, presenting your speech creates more anxiety for you than any other aspect of public speaking. Few speakers worry about organization or audience analysis or style. Many worry about presentation, so you have lots of company. In this section we'll examine general methods and principles of effectiveness in presentation that you can adapt to your own personality.

## Methods of Presentation

Speakers vary widely in their methods of presentation. Some speak off-the-cuff, with no apparent preparation; others read their speeches from manuscript. Some memorize their speeches word for word; others construct a detailed outline, rehearse often, then speak extemporaneously.

**Speaking Impromptu.** In an **impromptu speech** you talk without any specific preparation. You and the topic meet for the first time and immediately the speech begins. On some occasions you will not be able to avoid speaking impromptu. For example, in a classroom, after someone has spoken, you might give a brief impromptu speech of evaluation. In asking or answering questions in an interview situation, you're giving impromptu speeches, albeit extremely short ones. At a meeting, you may find yourself explaining a proposal or defending a plan of action; these too are impromptu speeches. Of course, impromptu speeches don't permit attention to the details of public speaking such as audience adaptation, research, and style.

**Speaking from Manuscript.** In a **manuscript speech** you read aloud the entire speech, which you've written out word for word. The manuscript

## AUDIENCE INACTIVITY

You're giving a speech on the problems of teenage drug abuse and you notice that the entire back rows of your audience have totally tuned you out; they're reading, chatting, working on their laptops.

WHAT DO YOU SAY?

speech allows you to control the timing precisely—a particularly important benefit when you are delivering a speech that will be recorded (on television, for example). Also, there's no risk of forgetting, no danger of being unable to find the right word. Another feature of the manuscript method is that it allows you to use the exact wording that you (or a team of speechwriters) want. In the political arena, this is often crucial. And, of course, because the speech is already written out, you can distribute copies and are therefore less likely to be misquoted.

Many audiences, however, don't like speakers to read their speeches, except perhaps with TelePrompTers on television. In face-to-face situations, audiences generally prefer speakers who interact with them. Reading a manuscript makes it difficult to respond to listener feedback. You cannot easily make adjustments on the basis of feedback. And with the manuscript on a stationary lectern, as it most often is, it's impossible for you to move around.

**Speaking from Memory.** In a **memorized speech** you write out the speech word for word (as in the manuscript method); but instead of reading it, you then commit the speech to memory and recite it or "act it out." Speaking from memory allows you freedom to move about and otherwise concentrate on delivery. It doesn't, however, allow easy adjusting to feedback, and you thus lose one of the main advantages of face-to-face contact.

One potential problem with this method is the risk of forgetting your speech. In a memorized speech, each sentence cues the recall of the following sentence. Thus, when you forget one sentence, you may forget the rest of the speech. This danger, along with the natural nervousness that speakers feel, makes the memorizing method a poor choice in most situations.

**Speaking Extemporaneously.** An **extemporaneous speech** involves thorough preparation but no commitment to the exact wording to be used during the speech. It often involves memorizing your opening lines (perhaps the first few sentences), your closing lines (perhaps the last few sentences), and your main points and the order in which you'll present them. You can also, if you wish, memorize selected phrases, sentences, or quotations. Memorizing the opening and closing lines will help you to focus your complete attention on the audience and will also put you more at ease. Once you know exactly what you'll say in opening and closing the speech, you'll feel more in control.

The extemporaneous method is useful in most speaking situations. Good college lecturers use the extemporaneous method. They prepare thoroughly and know what they want to say and in what order they want to say it, but they've made no commitment to exact wording. This method allows you to respond easily to feedback. Should a point need clarification, you can elaborate on it at the moment when it will be most effective. This method makes it easy to be natural, too, because you're being yourself. It's the method that comes closest to conversation. With the extemporaneous method, you can move about and interact with the audience.

## Making Your Presentation More Effective

Strive for a presentation that is natural, reinforces the message, is varied, and has a conversational tone.

**Be Natural.** Listeners will enjoy and believe you more if you speak naturally, as if you were conversing with a small group of people. Don't allow your delivery to call attention to itself. Your ultimate aim should be to deliver the speech so naturally that the audience won't even notice your presentation. This will take some practice, but you can do it. When voice or bodily action is so prominent that it's distracting, the audience concentrates on the delivery and will fail to attend to your speech.

### Use Presentation to Reinforce Your Message.
Effective presentation should aid instant intelligibility. Your main objective is to make your ideas understandable to an audience. A voice that listeners have to strain to hear, a decrease in volume at the ends of sentences, or slurred diction will obviously hinder comprehension.

### Dress Appropriately.
When you give a public speech, everything about you communicates. You cannot prevent yourself from sending messages to others. The way in which you dress is no exception. In fact, your attire will figure significantly in the way your audience assesses your credibility and even the extent to which they give you attention. In short, the way you present yourself physically will influence your effectiveness in all forms of persuasive and informative speaking. Unfortunately, there are no rules that will apply to all situations for all speakers. Thus, only general guidelines are offered here. Modify and tailor these for yourself and for each unique situation.

- Avoid extremes: Don't allow your clothes, hairstyle, and so on to detract attention from what you're saying.
- Dress comfortably: Be both physically and psychologically comfortable with your appearance so that you can concentrate your energies on what you're saying.
- Dress appropriately: Your appearance should be consistent with the specific public speaking occasion.

### Vary Your Presentation.
Listening to a speech is hard work for the audience. Flexible and varied presentation eases the listeners' task. Be especially careful to avoid **monotonous patterns** and **predictable patterns**.

Speakers who are monotonous keep their voices at the same pitch, volume, and rate throughout the speech. The monotonous speaker maintains a uniform level from the introduction to the conclusion. Like the drone of a motor, this easily puts the audience to sleep. Vary your pitch levels, your volume, and your rate of speaking. In a similar way, avoid monotony in bodily action. Avoid standing in exactly the same position throughout the speech. Use your body to express your ideas, to communicate to the audience what is going on in your head.

A predictable vocal pattern is a pattern in which, for example, the volume levels vary but always in the same sequence. Through repetition, the sequence soon becomes predictable. For example, each sentence may begin loud and then decline to a barely audible volume. In bodily action, the predictable speaker repeatedly uses the same movements or gestures. For example, a speaker may scan the audience from left to right to left to right throughout the entire speech. If the audience can predict the pattern of your voice or your bodily action, your speech will almost surely be ineffective. A patterned and predictable delivery will draw the audience's attention away from what you're saying.

### Be Conversational.
Although more formal than conversation, presentation in public speaking should have some of the most important features of conversation. These qualities include immediacy, eye contact, expressiveness, and responsiveness to feedback.

Just as you can create a sense of immediacy through language, as discussed earlier, you can also create it with your presentation. Make your listeners feel that you're talking directly and individually to each of them. You can communicate immediacy through delivery in a number of ways:

- Maintain appropriate eye contact with the audience members.
- Maintain a physical closeness that reinforces a psychological closeness; don't stand behind a desk or lectern.
- Smile.
- Move around a bit; avoid the appearance of being too scared to move.
- Stand with a direct and open body posture.
- Talk directly to your audience, not to your notes or to your visual aids.

When you maintain eye contact, you make the public speaking interaction more conversational (in addition to communicating immediacy). Look directly into your listeners' eyes. Lock eyes with different audience members for short periods.

When you're expressive, you communicate genuine involvement in the public speaking situation. You can communicate this quality of expressiveness, of involvement, in several ways:

- Express responsibility for your own thoughts and feelings.
- Vary your vocal rate, pitch, volume, and rhythm to communicate involvement and interest in the audience and in the topic.

- Allow your facial muscles and your entire body to reflect and echo this inner involvement.

- Use gestures appropriately; too few gestures may signal lack of interest, but too many can communicate uneasiness, awkwardness, or anxiety.

Read carefully the feedback signals sent by your audience. Then respond to these signals with verbal, vocal, and bodily adjustments. For example, respond to audience feedback signals communicating lack of comprehension or inability to hear with added explanation or increased volume.

**Avoid Common Mistakes.** Be sure to avoid the frequently made mistakes that detract from the power of your speech. Here are a few:

- Don't start your speech immediately. Instead, survey your audience; make eye contact and engage their attention. Stand in front of the audience with a sense of control. Pause briefly, then begin speaking.

- Don't display any discomfort or displeasure. When you walk to the speaker's stand, display enthusiasm and your desire to speak. People much prefer listening to a speaker who seems to enjoy speaking to them.

- Don't race away from the speaker's stand once you've finished your presentation. After your last statement, pause, maintain audience eye contact, and then walk (don't run) to your seat. Show no signs of relief; focus your attention on whatever activity is taking place, glance over the audience, and sit down. If a question period follows your speech and you're in charge of this, pause after completing your conclusion. Ask audience members in a direct manner if they have any questions. If there's a chairperson who will ask for questions, pause after your conclusion, then nonverbally signal to the chairperson that you're ready.

**Use Notes Appropriately.** For many speeches, it may be helpful to use notes. A few simple guidelines may help you avoid some of the common errors made in using notes.

- Keep notes to a minimum. The fewer notes you take with you, the better off you will be. The reason so many speakers bring notes with them is that they want to avoid the face-to-face interaction required. With experience, however, you should find this face-to-face interaction the best part of the public speaking experience.

- Resist the normal temptation to bring with you the entire speech outline. You may rely on it too heavily and lose the direct contact with the audi-

ence. Instead, compose a delivery outline, as discussed earlier in this unit, using only key words. Bring this to the lectern with you—one side of an index card or at most an 8 1/2-by-11-inch sheet should be sufficient. This will relieve any anxiety over the possibility of forgetting your speech but will not be extensive enough to interfere with direct contact with your audience.

- Don't make your notes more obvious than necessary, but at the same time don't try to hide them. For example, don't gesture with your notes—but don't turn away from the audience to steal glances at them, either. Use them openly and honestly but gracefully, with "open subtlety." To do this effectively, you'll have to know your notes intimately. Rehearse with the same notes that you will take with you to the speaker's stand.

- When referring to your notes, pause to examine them; then regain eye contact with the audience and continue your speech. Don't read from your notes, just take cues from them. The one exception to this guideline is an extensive quotation or complex set of statistics that you have to read; immediately after reading, however, resume direct eye contact with the audience.

## Voice

Three dimensions of voice are significant to the public speaker: volume, rate, and pitch. Your manipulation of these elements will enable you to control your voice to maximum advantage.

**Vocal Volume.** *Vocal volume* is the relative intensity of the voice. (Loudness, on the other hand, refers to hearers' perception of that relative intensity.) In an adequately controlled voice, volume will vary according to several factors. For example, the distance between speaker and listener, the competing noise, and the emphasis the speaker wishes to give an idea will all influence volume.

Problems with volume are easy to identify in others, though difficult to recognize in ourselves. One obvious problem is a voice that is too soft. When speech is so soft that listeners have to strain to hear, they will soon tire of expending so much energy. A voice that is too loud can also prove disturbing, because it intrudes on our psychological space. However, it's interesting to note that a voice louder than normal communicates assertiveness (Page & Balloun, 1978) and will lead people to pay greater attention to you (Robinson & McArthur, 1982). On the other hand, it can also communicate aggressiveness and give others the impression that you'd be difficult to get along with.

The most common problem is too little volume variation. Also, as mentioned earlier, a related problem is a volume pattern that, although varied, varies in an easily predictable way. If the audience can predict the pattern of volume changes, they will focus on that pattern and not on what you're saying.

A speaker who tends to fade away at the end of sentences is particularly disturbing to the audience. Here the speaker uses a volume that is largely appropriate but speaks the last few words of sentences at an extremely low volume. Be particularly careful when finishing sentences; make sure the audience is able to hear you without difficulty.

If you're using a microphone, test it first. Whether it's the kind that clips around your neck, the kind you hold in your hand, or the kind that is stationed at the podium, try it out first. Some speakers use the hand microphone as a prop and flip it in the air or from hand to hand as they emphasize a particular point. For your beginning speeches, it's probably best to avoid such techniques and to use the microphone as unobtrusively as you can.

**Vocal Rate.** Your *vocal rate* is the speed at which you speak. About 150 words per minute seems average for speaking as well as for reading aloud. Rate problems include speaking too fast, too slowly, with too little variation, or with too predictable a pattern. If you talk too fast, you deprive your listeners of time they need to understand and digest what you're saying. If the rate is extreme, the listeners will simply not be willing to expend the energy needed to understand your speech.

If your rate is too slow, it will encourage your listeners' thoughts to wander to matters unrelated to your speech. Be careful, therefore, neither to bore the audience by presenting information at too slow a rate, nor to set a pace that is too rapid for listeners to absorb. Strike a happy medium. Speak at a pace that engages the listeners and allows them time for reflection but without boring them.

As with volume, rate variations may be underused or totally absent. If you speak at the same rate throughout the entire speech, you're not making use of this important speech asset. Use variations in rate to call attention to certain points and to add variety. For example, if you describe the dull routine of an assembly line worker in a rapid and varied pace or evoke the wonder of a circus in a pace with absolutely no variation, you're surely misusing this important vocal dimension. Again, if you're interested in and conscious of what you're saying, your rate variations should flow naturally and effectively. Too predictable a pattern of rate variations is sometimes as bad as no variation at all. If the audience can predict—consciously or unconsciously—your rate pattern, you're in a vocal rut. You're not communicating ideas but reciting words you've memorized.

---

## Theory and Research Understanding    Speech Rate

You've probably noticed that advertisers and salespeople generally talk at a rate faster than normal speech. But is this effective? Are people who speak faster more persuasive? The answer is: It depends (Smith & Shaffer, 1991, 1995). The rapid speaker who speaks *against* your existing attitudes is generally more effective than the speaker who speaks at a normal rate. But the rapid speaker who speaks *in favor of* your existing attitudes (say, in an attempt to strengthen them) is actually less effective than the speaker who speaks at a normal rate. The reason for this is quite logical. In the case of the speaker speaking against your existing attitudes, rapid speech doesn't give you the time you need to think of counterarguments to rebut the speaker's position. So you're more likely to be persuaded, because you don't have time to consider why the speaker may be incorrect. In the case of the speaker speaking in favor of your existing attitudes, rapid speech doesn't give you time to mentally elaborate on the speaker's arguments; consequently, they don't carry as much persuasive force as they would if you had the time to add the speaker's arguments to those you already have.

### Working with Theories and Research

*With specific reference to your next speech, how might you apply this research to increase your own persuasiveness?*

## Building Communication Skills   Checking Your Pronunciation

Here are some words that are often mispronounced. Consult a print or online dictionary (ideally, one with audio capabilities) and record the correct pronunciations here.

| Words Often Mispronounced | Correct Pronunciation | Words Often Mispronounced | Correct Pronunciation |
| --- | --- | --- | --- |
| abdomen | _____ | herb | _____ |
| accessory | _____ | hierarchy | _____ |
| arctic | _____ | library | _____ |
| ask | _____ | nausea | _____ |
| buffet | _____ | nuclear | _____ |
| cavalry | _____ | probably | _____ |
| clothes | _____ | prostate | _____ |
| costume | _____ | realtor | _____ |
| diagnosis | _____ | relevant | _____ |
| especially | _____ | repeat | _____ |
| espresso | _____ | salmon | _____ |
| et cetera | _____ | sandwich | _____ |
| February | _____ | similar | _____ |
| foliage | _____ | substantive | _____ |
| forte | _____ | xenophobia | _____ |

*Mispronouncing words in public speaking may significantly damage your credibility. Feeling unsure about how to pronounce any word or words in your speech is also likely to contribute to your communication apprehension.*

**Vocal Pitch.** *Vocal pitch* is the relative highness or lowness of your voice as perceived by your listener. More technically, pitch results from the rate at which your vocal folds vibrate. If they vibrate rapidly, listeners will perceive your voice as having a high pitch. If they vibrate slowly, listeners will perceive your voice as having a low pitch.

Pitch changes often signal changes in the meanings of sentences. The most obvious is the difference between a statement and a question. Thus, vocal inflection or pitch makes the difference between the declarative sentence "So this is the proposal you want me to support" and the question "So this is the proposal you want me to support?"

The obvious problems that arise in relation to pitch are levels that are too high, too low, and too patterned. Neither of the first two problems is common in speakers with otherwise normal voices, and with practice you can correct a pitch pattern that is too predictable or monotonous. With increased

speaking experience, pitch changes will come naturally from the sense of what you're saying. After all, each sentence is somewhat different from every other sentence, so there should be a normal variation—a variation that results not from some conscious or predetermined pattern but rather from the meanings you wish to convey to the audience.

### Pauses

**Pauses** come in two basic types: filled and unfilled. Filled pauses are pauses in the stream of speech that we fill with vocalizations such as *er*, *um*, *ah*, and the like. Even expressions such as *well* and *you know*, when used to fill up silence, are called filled pauses. These pauses are ineffective and weaken the strength of your message. They will make you appear hesitant, unprepared, and unsure of yourself.

Unfilled pauses, in contrast, are silences interjected into the normally fluent stream of speech. Unfilled pauses can be extremely effective if used

correctly. Here are just a few examples of places where unfilled pauses—silences of a few seconds—should prove effective.

- Pause at transitional points. This will signal that you're moving from one part of the speech to another or from one idea to another. It will help the listeners separate the main issues you're discussing.

- Pause at the end of an important assertion. This will allow the audience time to think about the significance of what you're saying.

- Pause after asking a rhetorical question. This will give your listeners time to think about how they would answer the question.

- Pause before an important idea. This will help signal that what comes next is especially significant.

## Bodily Action

Your body is a powerful instrument in your speech. You speak with your body as well as with your mouth. The total effect of the speech depends not only on what you say but also on the way you present it. It depends on your movements, gestures, and facial expressions as well as your words.

Six aspects of bodily action are especially important in public speaking: eye contact, facial expression, posture, gestures, movement, and proxemics.

**Eye Contact.** The most important single aspect of bodily communication is eye contact. The two major problems with eye contact in public speaking are not enough eye contact and eye contact that does not cover the audience fairly. Speakers who do not maintain enough eye contact appear distant and unconcerned and may be seen as less trustworthy than speakers who look directly at their audience. And, of course, without eye contact, you will not be able to secure that all-important audience feedback.

Maintain eye contact with the entire audience. Involve all listeners in the public speaking transaction. Communicate equally with the members on the left and on the right, in both the back and the front.

Use eye contact to secure audience feedback. Are they interested? Bored? Puzzled? In agreement? In disagreement? Use your eyes to communicate your commitment to and interest in what you're saying. Communicate your confidence and commitment by making direct eye contact; avoid staring blankly through your audience or gazing over their heads, down at the floor, or out the window.

**Facial Expression.** Facial expressions are especially important in communicating **emotions**—your anger or fear, boredom or excitement, doubt or surprise. If you feel committed to and believe in your thesis, you'll probably display your emotional messages appropriately and effectively.

Nervousness and anxiety, however, can sometimes prevent you from relaxing enough so that your emotions come through. Fortunately, time and practice will allow you to relax, and the emotions you feel will reveal themselves appropriately and automatically.

Generally, members of one culture will be able to recognize the emotions displayed facially by members of other cultures. But there are differences in what each culture considers appropriate to display. Each culture has its own "display rules" (Ekman, Friesen, & Ellsworth, 1972). For example, Japanese Americans watching a stress-inducing film spontaneously displayed the same facial emotions as did other Americans when they thought they were unobserved. But when an observer was present, the Japanese Americans masked (tried to hide) their emotional expressions more than did the other Americans (Gudykunst & Kim, 1992).

**Posture.** When presenting your speech, stand straight but not stiff. Try to communicate command of the situation without communicating the discomfort that is actually quite common for beginning speakers.

Avoid the common posture mistakes: putting your hands in your pockets or leaning on the desk, the podium, or the chalkboard. With practice, you'll come to feel more at ease and will communicate this by the way you stand before the audience.

**Gestures.** Gestures in public speaking help illustrate your verbal messages. We do this regularly in conversation. For example, when saying "Come here," you probably move your head, hands, arms, and perhaps your entire body to motion the listener in your direction. Your body and your verbal message say "Come here."

Avoid using your hands to preen; for example, restrain yourself from fixing your hair or adjusting your clothing. Avoid fidgeting with your watch, ring, or jewelry. Also avoid keeping your hands in your pockets or clasped in front of you or behind your back.

Effective gestures help you as the speaker, your relationship with the audience, and the subject matter of your speech seem spontaneous and natural. If gestures look planned or rehearsed, they'll appear phony and insincere. As a general rule, don't do anything with your hands that doesn't feel right for you; the audience will recognize it as unnatural. If you feel relaxed and comfortable with yourself and your audience, you'll generate natural bodily action without conscious or studied attention.

**Movement.** Even when speaking behind a lectern, you can give the illusion of movement. You can step back or forward or flex your upper body so you appear to be moving more than you are. It helps to move around a bit. It keeps both the audience and you more alert.

Avoid three potential problems of movement: too little, too much, and too patterned. Speakers who move too little often appear strapped to the podium, afraid of the audience, or too detached to involve themselves fully. At the other extreme, when there's too much movement, the audience begins to concentrate on the movement itself, wondering where the speaker will wind up next. With movement that is too patterned, the audience may become bored—too steady and predictable a rhythm quickly becomes tiring. The audience will often view the speaker as nonspontaneous and uninvolved.

Use whole-body movements to emphasize transitions or to emphasize the introduction of a new and important assertion. Thus, when making a transition, you might take a step forward to signal that something new is coming. Similarly, this type of movement might signal the introduction of an important assumption, a key piece of evidence, or a closely reasoned argument.

If you're using a lectern, you may wish to signal transitions by stepping to the side or in front of it and then behind it again as you move from one point to another. As always, it's best to avoid the extremes; too much movement around the lectern and no movement from the lectern are both to be avoided. You may wish to lean over the lectern when, say, posing a question to your listeners or advancing a particularly important argument. But never lean on the lectern; never use it as support.

**Proxemics.** Proxemics, as discussed in Unit 6, is the study of how you use space in communication. In public speaking the amounts of space between you and your listeners and among the listeners themselves are often a crucial factor. If you stand too close to the people in the audience, they may feel uncomfortable, as if their personal space is being violated. If you stand too far away from your audience, you may be perceived as uninvolved, uninterested, and uncomfortable. Watch where your instructor and other speakers stand, and adjust your own position accordingly.

## Answering Questions

In many public speaking situations, a question-and-answer period will follow the speech. So be prepared to answer questions. Here are a few suggestions for making this Q&A session more effective.

- If you wish to encourage questions, preface the question period with some kind of encouraging statement; for example, "I know you've lots of questions—especially on how the new health program will work and how we'll finance it. I'll be happy to respond to your questions. Anyone?"

- Maintain eye contact with the audience. Let the audience know that you're still speaking with them.

## Building Communication Skills — Responding Strategically and Ethically

Consider the following situations that might arise in a public speaking situation. How would you respond to achieve your purpose and yet not violate any of your own ethical standards?

1. You've just given a speech to a racially diverse high school class on why they should attend your college. One audience member asks how racially diverse your faculty and students are. Your faculty is 94 percent European American, 4 percent Asian American, and 2 percent African American. You do know that the administration aims to recruit a more diverse faculty, but so far no action has been taken. Your student population is approximately 40 percent European American, 40 percent African American, 10 percent Hispanic, and 10 percent Asian American. What do you say?

2. You've just given a speech advocating banning alcohol on campus. In the speech you claimed that more than 70 percent of the students favor banning alcohol. At the end of the speech, you realize that you made a mistake and that only 30 percent favor banning alcohol; you were nervous and mixed up the figures. There's a question-and-answer period, but no one asks about the figures. What do you say?

3. You represent the college newspaper and are asking the student government to increase the paper's funding. The student government objects to giving extra money, because the paper has taken up lots of unpopular causes. You feel that it's essential for the paper to give visibility to minority views and fully expect to continue to do exactly as you have in the past. But if you say this, you won't get the added funding—and the paper won't be able to survive without increased funds. You will get the funding if you say you'll give primary coverage to majority positions. What do you say?

*Because public speeches have effects, they need to be ethically grounded.*

---

- After you hear a question, pause to think about the question and about your answer. If you suspect that some members of the audience didn't hear the question, repeat it; then begin your answer.

- Control defensiveness. Don't assume that a question is a personal attack. Assume, instead, that the question is an attempt to secure more information or perhaps to challenge a position you've taken.

- If appropriate, thank the questioner or note that it's a good question. This will encourage others also to ask questions.

- Don't bluff. If you're asked a question and you don't know the answer, say so.

- Consider the usefulness of a persuasive answer. Question-and-answer sessions often give you opportunities to further advance your purpose by connecting the question and its answer with one or more of your major points: "I'm glad you asked about child care, because that's exactly the differ-

ence between the two proposals we're here to vote on. The plan I'm proposing. . . ."

All of these suggestions are based on the assumption that you want to encourage questions and dialogue. And generally speakers want audience questions, because the dialogue gives them an opportunity to talk more about something they're interested in. In some cases, too, there seems an ethical obligation for the speaker to entertain questions; after all, if the audience sat through what the speaker wanted to say, the speaker should listen to what they want to say.

## CRITICIZING SPEECHES

In learning the art of public speaking, you can gain much insight from the criticism offered by others as well as from your own efforts to critique others' speeches. This section considers the nature of criticism in a learning environment, the influence of culture on criticism, and the standards and principles for evaluating a speech and for making criticism easier and more effective.

## What Is Criticism?

Critics and criticism are essential parts of any art. The word *criticism* comes into English from the Latin *criticus*, which means "able to discern," "able to judge." In the context of public speaking, therefore, **criticism** is the process of evaluating a speech, of rendering a judgment of its value. Note that there is nothing inherently negative about criticism; criticism may be negative, but it also may be positive.

Perhaps the major value of criticism in the classroom is that it helps you improve your public speaking skills. Through the constructive criticism of others, you'll learn the principles of public speaking more effectively. You'll be shown what you do well; what you could improve; and, ideally, how to improve. As a listener–critic, you'll also learn the principles of public speaking through assessing the speeches of others. Just as you learn when you teach, you also learn when you criticize.

When you give criticism—as you do in a public speaking class—you're telling the speaker that you've listened carefully and that you care enough about the speech and the speaker to offer suggestions for improvement.

Of course, criticism can be difficult—for the critic (whether student or instructor) as well as for the person criticized. As a critic, you may feel embarrassed or uncomfortable about offering evaluation. After all, you may think, "Who am I to criticize another person's speech? My own speech won't be any better." Or you may be reluctant to offend, fearing that your criticism may make the speaker feel uncomfortable. Or you may view criticism as a confrontation that will do more harm than good.

But reconsider this view. By offering criticism, you're helping the speaker; you're giving the speaker another perspective that should prove useful in future speeches. When you offer criticism, you're not claiming to be a better speaker; you're simply offering another point of view. It's true that by offering criticism, you're stating a position with which others may disagree. That's one of the things that will make the study of public speaking exciting and challenging.

Criticism is also difficult to receive. After working on a speech for a week or two and dealing with the normal anxiety that comes with giving a speech, the last thing you want is to stand in front

---

# REFLECTIONS
## ON ETHICS

## Criticizing Ethically

Just as speakers and listeners have ethical obligations, so do critics. To be an ethical critic, keep in mind these guidelines:

- Separate personal feelings about the speaker from your evaluations. Liking the speaker should not lead you to evaluate a speech positively, nor should disliking the speaker lead you to evaluate a speech negatively.

- Separate personal feelings about the issues from your evaluation of the validity of the arguments. Recognize the validity of an argument even if it contradicts a deeply held belief; by the same token, recognize the fallaciousness of an argument even if it supports a deeply held belief.

- Demonstrate cultural sensitivity and be conscious of your own ethnocentrism. Beware of evaluating customs and forms of speech negatively simply because they differ from your own. Conversely, be careful not to evaluate a speech positively just because it supports your own cultural beliefs and values. Avoid any inclination to discriminate for or against speakers simply because they're of a particular gender, race, nationality, religion, age group, or affectional orientation.

### Ethical Choice Point

*You and your best friend are taking this course together. Your friend just gave a pretty terrible speech, and unfortunately, the instructor has asked you to offer a critique. The wrinkle here is that the instructor's grades seem to be heavily influenced by what student critics say. So in effect your critique will largely determine your friend's grade. You'd like to give your friend a positive critique so he can earn a good grade—which he badly needs—and you figure you can always tell him the truth later and even help him to improve. What is your ethical obligation in this situation? What would you do?*

of the class and hear others say what you did wrong. Public speaking is ego-involving, and it's normal to take criticism personally. But if you learn how to give and how to receive criticism, it will help you improve your public speaking skills. Constructive criticism also can serve as an important support mechanism for the developing public speaker, a way of patting the speaker on the back for all the positive effort.

## Culture and Criticism

There are vast cultural differences in what is considered proper when it comes to criticism. For example, criticism will be viewed very differently depending on whether members come from an individualist culture (which emphasizes the individual, placing primary value on the individual's goals) or a collectivist culture (which emphasizes the group, placing primary value on the group's goals).

Those who come from cultures that are highly individualist and competitive (the United States, Germany, and Sweden are examples) may find public criticism a normal part of the learning process. Those who come from cultures that are more collectivist and therefore emphasize the group rather than the individual (Japan, Mexico, and Korea are examples) are likely to find giving and receiving public criticism uncomfortable. Thus, people from individualist cultures may readily criticize speakers and are likely to expect the same "courtesy" from listeners. "After all," such a person might reason, "if I'm going to criticize your skills to help you improve, I expect you to help me in the same way." Persons from collectivist cultures, on the other hand, may feel that it's more important to be polite and courteous than to help someone learn a skill. Cultural rules that maintain peaceful relations among the Japanese (Midooka, 1990) and norms of politeness among many Asian cultures (Fraser, 1990) may conflict with the classroom cultural norm that promotes the expression of honest criticism. In some cultures, being kind to the person is more important than telling the truth, so members may say things that are complimentary but that are untrue in a strict literal sense.

Collectivist cultures place a heavy emphasis on face-saving—on allowing people always to appear in a positive light (James, 1995). In these cultures people may prefer not to say anything negative in public. In fact, they may even be reluctant to say anything positive, lest any omission be construed as negative. Japanese executives, for instance, are reluctant to say no in a business meeting for fear of offending the other person. But their yes, properly interpreted in light of the context and the general discussion, may mean no. In cultures in which face-saving is especially important, communication rules such as the following tend to prevail:

- Don't express negative evaluation in public; instead, compliment the person.

- Don't prove someone wrong, especially in public; express agreement even if you know the person is wrong.

- Don't correct someone's errors; don't even acknowledge them.

- Don't ask difficult questions, lest the person not know the answer and lose face or be embarrassed; generally, avoid asking questions.

The difficulties that these differences may cause may be lessened if they're discussed openly. Some people may become comfortable with public criticism once it's explained that the cultural norms of most public speaking classrooms include public criticism, just as they incorporate informative and persuasive speaking and written outlines. Others may feel more comfortable offering written criticism as a substitute for oral and public criticism. Or perhaps private consultations can be arranged.

## Guidelines for Criticizing More Effectively

A useful standard to use in evaluating a classroom speech is the speech's degree of conformity to the principles of the art. Using this standard, you'll evaluate a speech positively when it follows the principles of public speaking established by the critics, theorists, and practitioners of public speaking (as described throughout this text) and evaluate it negatively if it deviates from these principles. These principles include, for example, speaking on a subject that is worthwhile, relevant, and interesting to listeners; designing a speech for a specific audience; and constructing a speech that is based on sound research.

Before reading the specific suggestions for making critical evaluations a more effective part of the total learning process and avoiding some of the potentially negative aspects of criticism, take the following self-test, which asks you to identify what's wrong with selected critical comments.

## TEST YOURSELF

### What's Wrong with These Critical Evaluations?

For the purposes of this exercise, assume that each of the following 10 comments represents the critic's complete criticism. What's wrong with each?

_____ 1. I loved the speech. It was great. Really great.

_____ 2. The introduction didn't gain my attention.

_____ 3. You weren't interested in your own topic. How do you expect us to be interested?

_____ 4. Nobody was able to understand you.

_____ 5. The speech was weak.

_____ 6. The speech didn't do anything for me.

_____ 7. Your position was unfair to those of us on athletic scholarships; we earned those scholarships.

_____ 8. I found four things wrong with your speech. First, . . .

_____ 9. You needed better research.

_____ 10. I liked the speech; we need more police on campus.

**HOW DID YOU DO?** Before reading the discussion that follows, try to explain why each of these statements is ineffective. Visualize yourself as the speaker receiving such comments, and ask yourself if these comments would help you in any way. If not, then they are probably not very effective critical evaluations.

**WHAT WILL YOU DO?** To help you improve your criticism, try to restate the basic meaning of each of these comments but in a more constructive manner.

The following guidelines will help you become a more constructive critic.

### Stress the Positive

Egos are fragile, and public speaking is extremely personal. Speakers understand what Noel Coward meant when he said, "I love criticism just as long as it's unqualified praise." Part of your function as a critic is to strengthen the already positive aspects of someone's public speaking performance. Positive criticism is particularly important in itself, but it's almost essential as a preface to negative comments. There are always positive characteristics about any speech, and it's more productive to concentrate on these first. Thus, instead of saying (as in the self-test), "The speech didn't do anything for me," tell the speaker what you liked first, then bring up a weak point and suggest how it might be improved.

When criticizing a person's second or third speech, it's especially helpful if you can point out specific improvements ("You really held my attention in this speech," "I felt you were much more in control of the topic today than in your first speech").

Remember, too, that communication is irreversible. Once you say something, you can't take it back. Remember this when offering criticism, especially criticism that may be negative. If in doubt, err on the side of gentleness.

### Be Specific

Criticism is most effective when it's specific. General statements such as "I thought your presentation was bad," "I thought your examples were good," or, as in the self-test, "I loved the speech.... Really great" or "The speech was weak" are poorly expressed criticisms. These statements don't specify what the speaker might do to improve his or her presentation or to capitalize on the examples used. In commenting on presentation, refer to such specifics as eye contact, vocal volume, or whatever else is of consequence. In commenting on the examples, tell the speaker why they were good. Were they realistic? Were they especially interesting? Were they presented dramatically?

In giving negative criticism, specify and justify— to the extent that you can—positive alternatives. Here's an example.

> I thought the way you introduced your statistics was vague. I wasn't sure where the statistics came from or how recent or reliable they were. It might have been better to say something like "The U.S. Census figures for 2000 show...." That way we would know that the statistics were as recent as possible and the most reliable available.

## Be Objective

In criticizing a speech, transcend your own biases as best you can, unlike the self-test's example ("Your position was unfair . . . ; we earned those scholarships"). See the speech as objectively as possible. Suppose, for example, that you're strongly for a woman's right to an abortion and you encounter a speech diametrically opposed to your position. In this situation, you'll need to take special care not to dismiss the speech because of your own biases. Examine the speech from the point of view of a detached critic; evaluate, for example, the validity of the arguments and their suitability to the audience, the language, and the supporting materials. Conversely, take special care not to evaluate a speech positively because it presents a position with which you agree, as in "I liked the speech; we need more police on campus."

## Be Constructive

Your primary goal should be to provide the speaker with insight that will prove useful in future public speaking transactions. For example, to say that "The introduction didn't gain my attention" doesn't tell the speaker how he or she might have gained your attention. Instead, you might say, "The example about the computer crash would have more effectively gained my attention in the introduction."

Another way you can be constructive is to limit your criticism. Cataloging a speaker's weak points, as in "I found four things wrong with your speech," will

overwhelm, not help, the speaker. If you're the sole critic, your criticism naturally will need to be more extensive. But if you're one of many critics, limit your criticism to one or perhaps two points. In all cases, your guide should be the value your comments will have for the speaker.

## Focus on Behavior

Focus criticism on what the speaker said and did during the actual speech. Try to avoid the very natural tendency to read the mind of the speaker—to assume that you know why the speaker did one thing rather than another. Compare the critical comments presented in Table 16.3. Note that those in the first column, "Criticism as Attack," try to identify the reasons the speaker did as he or she did; they try to read the speaker's mind. At the same time, they blame the speaker for what happened. Those in the second column, "Criticism as Support," focus on the specific behavior. Note, too, that those in the first column are likely to encourage defensiveness; you can almost hear the speaker saying, "I was so interested in the topic." Those in the second column are less likely to create defensiveness and are more likely to be appreciated as honest reflections of how the critic perceived the speech.

## Own Your Criticism

In giving criticism, own your comments; take responsibility for them. The best way to express this ownership is to use "I-messages" rather than "you-messages." Instead of saying, "You needed better research," say, "I would have been more persuaded if you had used more recent research."

Avoid attributing what you found wrong to others. Instead of saying, "Nobody was able to understand you," say, "I had difficulty understanding you. It would have helped me if you had spoken more slowly." Remember that your criticism is important precisely because it's your perception of what the speaker did and what the speaker could have done more effectively. Speaking for the entire audience ("We couldn't hear you clearly" or "No one was convinced by your arguments") will not help the speaker, and it's likely to prove demoralizing.

Employing I-messages also will prevent you from using "should messages," a type of expression that almost invariably creates defensiveness and resentment. When you say "You should have done this" or "You shouldn't have done that," you assume a superior position and imply that what you're saying is correct and that what the speaker did was incorrect. On the other hand, when you own your evaluations and use I-messages, you're giving your perceptions; it's then up to the speaker to accept or reject them.

## Table 16.3  Criticism as Attack and as Support

Can you develop additional examples to illustrate criticism as attack and as support?

| Criticism as Attack | Criticism as Support |
| --- | --- |
| "You weren't interested in your topic." | "I would have liked to see greater variety in your presentation. It would have made me feel that you were more interested." |
| "You should have put more time into the speech." | "I think it would have been more effective if you had looked at your notes less." |
| "You didn't care about your audience." | "I would have liked it if you had looked more directly at me while speaking." |

## SUMMARY: STYLE AND DELIVERY IN PUBLIC SPEAKING

This unit focused on outlining, style, rehearsal, and presentation. The unit offered suggestions for using preparation, template, and presentation outlines; choosing words and phrasing sentences; and rehearsing and presenting your speech. In addition, this unit discussed guidelines for giving and receiving criticism.

1. An outline is a blueprint that helps you organize and evaluate your speech. The preparation outline is extremely detailed and includes all of your main points, supporting materials, introduction, conclusion, transition, and references. The skeletal outline is a kind of template that can help you see where certain material can be placed. The presentation outline is a brief version of your preparation outline that you use as a guide when presenting your speech.

2. Compared with written style, oral style contains shorter, simpler, and more familiar words; greater qualification; and more self-referential terms.

3. Effective public speaking style is clear (be economical and specific; use guide phrases; and stick to short, familiar, and commonly used terms), vivid (use active verbs, strong verbs, figures of speech, and imagery), appropriate to audience (speak on a suitable level of formality; avoid jargon and technical expressions; avoid slang, vulgarity, and offensive terms), personal (use personal pronouns, ask questions, and create immediacy), and forceful (eliminate weakeners, vary intensity, and avoid trite expressions).

4. In constructing sentences for public speeches, favor short, direct, active, and positively phrased sentences. Vary the type and length of sentences.

5. Use rehearsal to time your speech; perfect your volume, rate, and pitch; incorporate pauses and other delivery notes; and perfect your bodily action.

6. There are four basic methods of presenting a public speech. The impromptu method involves speaking without any specific preparation. The manuscript method involves writing out the entire speech and reading it to the audience. Memorized delivery involves writing out the speech, memorizing it, and reciting it. The extemporaneous method involves thorough preparation and memorizing of the main ideas and their order of appearance but no commitment to exact wording.

7. Effective presentation is natural, reinforces the message, is varied, and has a conversational quality. When you present your speech, regulate your voice for greatest effectiveness. Adjust your vocal volume, rate, and pitch as appropriate.

8. Use unfilled pauses to signal a transition between the major parts of the speech, to allow the audience time to think, to allow the audience to ponder a rhetorical question, or to signal the approach of a particularly important idea. Avoid filled pauses; they weaken your message.

9. Effective body action involves maintaining eye contact with your entire audience, allowing your facial expressions to convey your feelings, using your posture to communicate command of the public speaking interaction, gesturing naturally, and moving around a bit.

10. In answering sessions after the speech, encourage questions, maintain eye contact, repeat the question if necessary, avoid any signs of defensiveness, express thanks for the question (if appropriate), don't bluff, and consider the usefulness of a persuasive answer.

11. Criticism, a process of judging and evaluating a work, is crucial to mastering the principles of public speaking.

12. Criticism can (1) identify strengths and weaknesses and thereby help you improve as a public speaker, (2) identify standards for evaluating all sorts of public speeches, and (3) show that the audience is listening and is concerned about the speaker's progress.

13. Cultures differ in their views of criticism and in the rules they consider appropriate. For example, members of individualist cultures may find public criticism easier and more acceptable than people from collectivist cultures.

14. Among the guidelines for effective criticism are these: Stress the positive, be specific, be objective, be constructive, focus on behavior, and own your criticism.

## KEY TERMS IN STYLE AND DELIVERY IN PUBLIC SPEAKING

appropriateness (p. **369**)

clarity (p. **366**)

clichés (p. **372**)

criticism (p. **383**)

emotions (p. **380**)

extemporaneous speech (p. **375**)

figures of speech (p. **368**)

forcefulness (p. **371**)

impromptu speech (p. **374**)

jargon (p. **369**)

manuscript speech (p. **374**)

memorized speech (p. **375**)

monotonous patterns (p. **376**)

oral style (p. **364**)

outline (p. **356**)

pauses (p. **379**)

personal style (p. **370**)

predictable patterns (p. **376**)

preparation outline (p. **358**)

presentation outline (p. **363**)

slang (p. **369**)

template outline (p. **358**)

vividness (p. **368**)

weakeners (p. **371**)

## THINKING CRITICALLY ABOUT STYLE AND DELIVERY IN PUBLIC SPEAKING

1. **Wording the Speech for Different Audiences.** Francisco is scheduled to give two speeches, one to a predominantly female audience of health professionals and one to a predominantly male audience of small business owners. His topic for both groups is the same: neighborhood violence. What advice—if any—would you give Francisco for tailoring his speech to the two different audiences? If you would not offer advice, why not?

2. **Using Humor.** John has this great joke that is only tangentially related to his speech topic. But the joke is so great that it will immediately get the audience actively involved in his speech; this, John thinks, outweighs the fact that the joke isn't integrally related to the speech. John asks your advice; what do you suggest?

3. **Projecting an Image.** Michael has a very formal type of personality; he's very restrained in everything he does. But he wants to try to project a different image—a much more personable, friendly, informal quality—in his speeches. What advice would you give Michael?

4. **E-Talk and Public Speaking.** How would you describe your language—word and sentence choices—in online and in public speaking communication? How would you describe the "rehearsal" you go through in online messages and in public speeches? How would you compare your willingness to criticize, say, an acquaintance in an e-mail as opposed to a public setting? Would the substance of the criticism change? Would the way you expressed it change? More generally, what are the major differences between online and public communication?

5. **The Two-Minute Speech.** Prepare and deliver a two-minute speech in which you do one of the following:
   • describe the language of a noted personality
   • introduce an excerpt from literature and read the excerpt as you might a manuscript speech
   • analyze an advertisement in terms of one or two of the characteristics of effective style: clarity, vividness, appropriateness, personal style, or forcefulness
   • describe an object in the room using visual, auditory, and tactile imagery

## LogOn! MyCommunicationLab

### WWW.MYCOMMUNICATIONLAB.COM

Visit MCL for 13 template outlines to help you outline a wide variety of speeches. There are also extended discussions of Oral and Written Style, Making Your Speech Easy to Remember, Humor in Public Speaking, and Using Visual Aspects to Reflect Your Organization. Exercises include Organizing a Scrambled Outline, Rephrasing Clichés, Making Concepts Specific, Undertaking a Long-Term Delivery Improvement Program, and Communicating Vocally but Nonverbally. Watch one or more of the speeches; they will help illustrate in concrete fashion the elements of style and techniques of presentation. Also visit the Allyn & Bacon public speaking website (www.ablongman.com/pubspeak) for guidance on delivering the speech and criticizing the speech.

# UNIT 17 The Informative Speech

## MAJOR TOPICS

## Special Features

Many of the speeches you'll deliver will be informative speeches, in which you'll explain to an audience how something works or how to do something.

**In this unit, you'll learn about:**
- the goals and principles for communicating information.
- the types of informative speeches.

**You'll learn to:**
- use the principles for communicating information more effectively and efficiently.
- prepare a variety of informative speeches—speeches of description, definition, and demonstration.

This unit begins a three-part discussion on the types of public speaking. This unit looks at informative speaking, Unit 18 at persuasive speaking, and Unit 19 at the special occasion speech. More specifically, this unit considers the general goals of informative speaking, the principles for communicating information, and the varied types of informative speeches and how you can develop these most effectively.

Before beginning this journey into these three types of speeches—or after giving your next speech—you may want to examine your own satisfaction as a public speaker by taking the self-test "How Satisfying Is Your Public Speaking?"

## TEST YOURSELF

### How Satisfying Is Your Public Speaking?

Respond to each of the following statements by recording the number best representing your feelings after a recent speech, using this scale: 1 = strongly agree; 2 = moderately agree; 3 = slightly agree; 4 = neutral; 5 = slightly disagree; 6 = moderately disagree; and 7 = strongly disagree.

____ **1.** The audience let me know that I was speaking effectively.

____ **2.** My speech accomplished nothing.

____ **3.** I would like to give another speech like this one.

____ **4.** The audience genuinely wanted to get to know me.

____ **5.** I was very dissatisfied with my speech.

____ **6.** I was very satisfied with the speech.

____ **7.** The audience seemed very interested in what I had to say.

____ **8.** I did not enjoy the public speaking experience.

____ **9.** The audience did not seem supportive of what I was saying.

____ **10.** The speech flowed smoothly.

**HOW DID YOU DO?** To compute your score, follow these steps:

1. Add the scores for items 1, 3, 4, 6, 7, and 10.

2. Reverse the scores for items 2, 5, 8, and 9 so that 7 becomes 1, 6 becomes 2, 5 becomes 3, 4 remains 4, 3 becomes 5, 2 becomes 6, and 1 becomes 7.

3. Add the reversed scores for items 2, 5, 8, and 9.

4. Add the totals from steps 1 and 3 to yield your communication satisfaction score.

You may interpret your score along the following scale:

| 10 | 20 | 30 | 40 | 50 | 60 | 70 |
|----|----|----|----|----|----|----|
| Extremely satisfying | Quite satisfying | Fairly satisfying | Average | Fairly unsatisfying | Quite unsatisfying | Extremely unsatisfying |

How accurately do you think this scale captures your public speaking satisfaction?

**WHAT WILL YOU DO?** As you become a more successful and effective public speaker, your satisfaction is likely to increase. What steps can you take to increase your satisfaction?

Source: This test was adapted for public speaking on the basis of the conversational satisfaction test developed by Michael Hecht (1978), "The Conceptualization and Measurement of Interpersonal Communication Satisfaction," *Human Communication Research*, 4, 253–264, and is used by permission of the author and International Communication Association.

## GOALS OF INFORMATIVE SPEAKING

An *informative speech*, as discussed in Unit 14, is a speech in which the speaker tells the audience something it didn't already know. This is the most general goal of all informative speaking. But there are a variety of other more specific goals that can motivate informative speaking. Reviewing these will help explain further the nature and purpose of the informative speech.

One goal of informative speaking may be to *introduce* topics that are totally new to the audience. A sales representative might demonstrate new surgical tools to a group of medical doctors, or an inventor might explain an entirely new toy.

Another goal may be to *clarify* misconceptions that people have about a topic; say, about how an au-tomobile or a cell phone works, or about the ways in which graduate and professional schools select students, or about the criteria for promotion of college professors—all topics that many people assume they understand but about which they actually have lots of misconceptions.

Still another goal may be to *demonstrate* how to use information; the popular cooking shows are good examples of this type of speech. Many of the infomercials on television spend lots of time showing you how to use their new product—whether it's George Foreman's Grilling Machine, Joy Mangano's clothes hangers, or Ron Popeil's slow cooker, baldness fix, or roaster.

Perhaps the most popular goal is to *communicate information* about topics the audience knows something about but not a great deal; your goal here will be to expand on knowledge your listeners already

## THE RESEARCHER

### Communicating and Teaching

*I'm planning to become a high school history teacher, and I'm wondering if there's anything I can start doing now to become a really successful instructor. Are there particular communication skills I should focus on or emphasize?*

Effective teachers are also effective informative speakers. Three informative speechmaking skills that will enhance your ability to teach are learning how to create relevant messages, learning how to make messages clear, and learning how to adapt to your audience.

- *Make messages relevant.* Show students how history will benefit their personal development and professional work lives. Relate history to your audience members' experiences and interests. Be prepared and ready to share yourself with your audience. Explain why you find history fascinating.

- *Make messages clear.* Use language and examples that your audience will understand and find interesting. Teaching history is storytelling. Be prepared to explain and illustrate in a vivid manner the historical context, the setting, the characters, and then pull your students through the story.

- *Adapt to your audience.* Carefully interpret your students' nonverbal behavior. Are they following you? Anticipate confusion, and be prepared to offer multiple examples to illustrate your content. Be prepared to make abstract terms and concepts more concrete.

For further information: See Mottet, T. P., Richmond, V. P., & McCroskey, J. C. (Eds.). (2006). *Handbook of instructional communication: Rhetorical and relational perspectives.* Boston: Allyn and Bacon.

**Timothy P. Mottet** (Ed.D., West Virginia University) holds the Hauser Chair in Communication at the University of Texas-Pan American in Edinburg, Texas. He teaches courses in instructional communication, training and development, and leadership. His research examines the role of communication, personality, and cognition in teaching and learning. He is available to answer your questions at (956) 381-3583.

have. Speeches on such topics as the way pop-ups work or the rules of soccer would likely include information that the audience does not yet know.

As I write this, Microsoft's Vista operating system is making its debut and provides a good example to illustrate that the same topic can be pursued with different goals in mind. So let's say you want to give an informative speech on Vista.

- To an audience of dedicated Mac users, the information might be entirely new, so your goal would be to introduce topics unknown to the audience.

- To an audience of dedicated Mac users who thought there was no or only little difference between the systems, you'd be clarifying misconceptions.

- To an audience of students using Windows, you might demonstrate, for example, the ways in which they could use Vista to accomplish a variety of tasks more efficiently.

- To an audience of Windows XP users, you'd be building on topics they knew a lot about and describing what was new in Vista.

As you can appreciate, your speech on Vista for the dedicated Mac users would have to be different from the speech for the XP users. Though both speeches would cover similar and in some cases the same material, you'd have to approach it very differently depending on the knowledge and experience of your listeners. With this basic principle in mind—a principle you see in operation every time you hear an effective classroom lecture, as you see the principle in violation with every ineffective lecture—we can look at several principles for communicating information.

## PRINCIPLES OF INFORMATIVE SPEAKING

When you communicate "information," you tell your listeners something new, something they don't know. You may tell them about a new way of looking at old things or an old way of looking at new things. You may discuss a theory not previously heard of or a familiar theory not fully understood. You may discuss events that the audience may be unaware of or may have misconceptions about. Regardless of what type of informative speech you intend to give, the following guidelines should help.

In addition, the Public Speaking Sample Assistant boxes illustrate some of the pitfalls you'll want to avoid in a poorly constructed informative speech (below) and some of the principles you'll want to follow in an excellent informative speech (see page 394).

---

## A Poorly Constructed Informative Speech

This poorly constructed informative speech was written by the author to demonstrate some of the faults that beginning speakers sometimes make and that you'll want to avoid.

### Three Jobs

Three Jobs

In general, don't use your title as your opening words. This title seems adequate, though it's not terribly exciting. After reading the speech, try to come up with a more appealing title.

Well, I mean, hello. Er . . . I'm new at public speaking, so I'm a little nervous. I've always been shy. So don't watch my knees shake.

The speaker's nervous opening remarks reveal an anxiety that's understandable but is probably best not shared with the listeners. After all, you don't want the audience to be uncomfortable for you.

Ehm, let me see my notes here. [Mumbles to self while shuffling notes: "One, two, three, four, five—oh, they're all here."] Okay, here goes.

Going through your notes makes the audience feel that you didn't prepare adequately and may be wasting their time.

Three Jobs. That's my title and I'm going to talk about three jobs.

This is the speaker's orientation. Is this sufficient? What else might the speaker have done in the introduction?

## A Poorly Constructed Informative Speech *(Continued)*

The Health Care Field. This is the fastest-growing job in the country, one of the fastest, I guess I mean. I know that you're not interested in this topic and that you're all studying accounting. But there are a lot of new jobs in the health care field. The *Star* had an article on health care and said that health care will be needed more in the future than it is now. And now, you know, like they need a lot of health care people. In the hospital where I work—on the west side, uptown—they never have enough health aides and they always tell me to become a health aide, like, you know, to enter the health care field. To become a nurse. Or maybe a dental technician. But I hate going to the dentist. Maybe I will.

I don't know what's going to happen with the president's health plan, but whatever happens, it won't change the need for health aides. I mean, people will still get sick; so it really doesn't matter what happens with health care.

The Robotics Field. This includes things like artificial intelligence. I don't really know what that is but it's like growing real fast. They use this in making automobiles and planes and I think in computers. Japan is a leading country in this field. A lot of people in India go into this field, but I'm not sure why.

The Computer Graphics Field. This field has a lot to do with designing and making lots of different products, like CAD and CAM. This field also includes computer-aided imagery—CAI. And in movies, I think. Like *Star Wars* and *Terminator 2*. I saw *Terminator 2* four times. I didn't see *Star Wars* but I'm gonna rent the video. I don't know if you have to know a lot about computers or if you can just like be a designer and someone else will tell the computer what to do.

I got my information from a book that Carol Kleiman wrote, *The 100 Best Jobs for the 1990s and Beyond*. It was summarized on the Internet somewhere.

My Conclusion. These are three of the fastest-growing fields in the U.S. And in the world, I think—not in Third World countries, I don't think. China and India and Africa. More like Europe and Germany. And the U.S.—the U.S. is the big one. I hope you enjoyed my speech. Thank you.

I wasn't as nervous as I thought I'd be. Are there any questions?

Such expressions of uncertainty make us question the speaker's competence.

And we begin to wonder, why is the speaker talking about this to us?

Stories in the *Star* may be entertaining, but they don't necessarily constitute evidence. What does this tabloid reference do to the credibility you ascribe to the speaker?

Everything in the speech must have a definite purpose. Asides such as comments about not liking to go to the dentist are probably best omitted.

Here the speaker had an opportunity to connect the topic with important current political events but failed to say anything that was not obvious.

Introducing each topic this way is clear but probably not very interesting. How might the speaker have introduced each of the three main points more effectively?

Notice how vague the speaker is—"includes things like," "and I think in computers," "I'm not sure why." Such statements communicate very little information to listeners and leave them with little confidence that the speaker knows what he or she is talking about.

Again, this part of the speech offers little specific information. CAD and CAM are not defined, and CAI is explained merely as "computer-aided imagery." Unless we already knew what these were, we would have no idea even after hearing the speaker. And again the speaker inserts personal notes (for example, seeing *Terminator 2* four times) that have no meaningful connection to the topic.

The speaker uses only one source and, to make matters worse, doesn't even go to the original source but relies on a summary "somewhere" on the Internet. Especially with a topic like this, listeners are likely to want a variety of viewpoints and additional reliable sources.

Note too that the speech lacked any statistics. This is a subject where statistics are essential. Listeners will want to know how many jobs will be available in these fields, what these fields will look like in 5 or 10 years, how much these fields pay, and so on.

Using the word *conclusion* to signal that you're concluding is not a bad idea, but work it into the text instead of using it as if it were a heading in a book chapter.

Once more, this lack of certainty makes us question the speaker's competence and preparation.

Again, personal comments are best left out.

## An Excellent Informative Speech

This is an excellent informative speech, given by University of Texas at Austin student Jillian Collum.

When Bangladesh achieved its independence in 1971, Vanderbilt University doctoral student Muhammad Yunus decided that it was time to go home. He soon found himself at Chittagong University, teaching complex economic theories involving the transfer of billions of dollars. However, as Yunus explained to Whole Foods Market team members in a March 2006 address, he couldn't help but notice the intense poverty that existed right outside the university's walls. So, Yunus decided to do something about it, and in 1976 he struck his first blow in the battle against poverty, lending 42 people a combined total of $27.

Using a specific story is a good way to gain attention; we all seem interested in personal stories, especially when they're dramatic, like this one.

Did the story gain your attention? In what other ways might the speaker have gained attention?

The recipients used their loans so effectively that Yunus decided to start his own bank, called Grameen, which would give small loans to poor families for income-generating activities, such as buying a cow to sell its milk. Bahrain's *Gulf Daily News* of February 5, 2007, reports that 58 percent of the bank's borrowers have used their loans to rise out of poverty, a success rate so astonishing that it allowed Grameen to launch a global revolution.

The speaker makes the point that a large group (58 percent) used the money to rise out of poverty. In what other ways might you have illustrated the fact that such a large group used the money to rise from poverty?

The *New York Times* of October 14, 2006, asserts that microcredit, or the concept of giving small loans to individuals so that they can work to lift themselves out of poverty, now helps over 100 million of the world's most destitute people in more than 130 countries. And even the Nobel committee was impressed. In an October 13, 2006, press release, the committee awarded Muhammad Yunus the 2006 Nobel Peace Prize, noting that microcredit is an essential and powerful instrument in the worldwide fight against poverty. Because the *Toronto Star* of December 8, 2006, reveals that microcredit leaders plan to use the technique to help half a billion people rise out of poverty by the year 2015, we must examine how this macrorevolution in microcredit is changing the world.

Here the speaker establishes the importance of the topic. Did this part of the introduction convince you that the topic the speaker was about to cover was worth your effort to listen? What specifically convinced you?

To do so, we will first explore the development of microcredit; next, discuss its rationale; and finally, look at the implications of this approach that is transforming lives a few dollars at a time.

In this third part of the introduction, the speaker provides an orientation to what will follow in the rest of the speech. You know from this that there will be three main parts of the speech: the development of microcredit, its rationale, and its implications.

*MacLean's* of November 27, 2006, states that two-thirds of the world's population is too poor to secure funds from traditional banks, which fear that poor borrowers won't repay loans. Muhammad Yunus set out to prove that this view of the poor was completely wrong. In his previously cited speech, Yunus explains that Grameen looks at what a conventional bank does, and then does the opposite. Instead of rich customers, the bank seeks poor ones. Instead of big loans, it gives small ones. And instead of men, the bank more often chooses to lend to women, believing that

Here the speaker explains her first main point: the development of microcredit. This gives those in the audience who didn't know much about this approach to loans and lending a better idea of what microcredit is and how it operates.

Throughout this speech the speaker uses a wide variety of sources. What source material do you find especially helpful? What types of source material would you have liked to see included here?

| | |
|---|---|
| **Public Speaking Sample Assistant** | **An Excellent Informative Speech** *(Continued)* |

money given to women is more likely to directly benefit families. According to the *International Herald Tribune* of October 14, 2006, today, Grameen serves 6.6 million poor people in Bangladesh and enjoys a 98.5 percent repayment rate, almost twice as high as the average rate for traditional Bengali banks. Borrowers use their loans for income-generating activities, such as operating a small food stand or selling handmade crafts. And most astonishingly, *BusinessWeek* of November 27, 2006, notes that Grameen has reached this level of success even though it hasn't accepted any donations since 1995. Grameen remains self-sustaining much the same way traditional banks do—by taking in deposits and issuing loans.

While Muhammad Yunus's initial $27 loans to 42 Bengalis didn't amount to much, the microcredit revolution that this small act launched has changed the lives of millions. To better understand the rationale for this phenomenon, we'll discuss microcredit's driving principles and why the technique is so necessary.

Here the speaker provides a transition from the first to the second main point. As a listener, you now know that you'll hear the rationale for microcredit, and specifically that you'll hear about it in two parts: the program's driving principles and the reason this approach is so necessary.

*Canada's Hamilton Spectator* of November 13, 2006, reports that there are now more than 3,100 microcredit institutions worldwide. These groups provide average loans of $150, and more than 97 percent of the money they lend out is repaid. According to the *Arizona Daily Star* of November 3, 2006, this high repayment rate can be attributed to the group loan principle, in which five people from the community serve as one another's guarantors. Individual borrowers must repay their loans, or the entire group becomes ineligible for more funding. This provides a powerful incentive for individuals to pay on time and help each other meet their obligations. But the true genius of microcredit is that loans are given for income-generating activities that improve the lives of every member of the family. For example, the *Atlanta Journal-Constitution* of November 13, 2006, tells the story of Susan Wangui from Kenya. Abandoned by her parents and her husband after she contracted HIV, Wangui was forced to work as a prostitute to support her two children. But with a series of loans from a local microcredit institution, Wangui was able to start a clothes-mending business, a venture that has been profitable enough to allow her to move her children out of a slum and into a house with a floor and running water.

You've been prepared to hear about the principles of microcredit. After reading this section on the principles, can you now identify the specific principles discussed by the speaker? If you can, what did the speaker do to help you remember them? If you can't, what might the speaker have done to ensure that you would remember the principles?

This section also provides a good example of explaining a concept in terms of abstract and general statements (for example, the fact that 97 percent of the money is repaid) and then following these with specifics (for example, the story of Susan Wangui). This is almost always a useful technique for helping listeners see the issue as a generalization and as uniquely personal as well.

Microcredit is necessary because for many of its recipients, no reasonable alternatives exist. For example, the *New Yorker* of October 30, 2006, reveals that Latin America's largest microcredit institution, Compartamos, serves 500,000 people in Mexico, a country where over 70 percent of the population lacks access to traditional banks. In the absence of microcredit, poor individuals are forced to rely on loan sharks. The Allentown, Pennsylvania, *Morning Call* of December 7, 2006, explains that microcredit groups offer interest rates

Here the necessity for microcredit is considered, the second part of the second main idea. Notice that the speaker uses similar words in introducing these concepts as in previewing them in the introduction. This similarity in wording will help the audience follow the speaker.

between 20 and 30 percent, compared to the 100 percent interest rates local moneylenders charge. In this way, microcredit provides a source of capital that families can actually afford to pay back, allowing them to improve their lives without getting trapped in an unmanageable cycle of debt.

Muhammad Yunus claims that one day the world will only see poverty in museums. While microcredit could make this a reality, it raises several implications for our views on social welfare, the economic role of women, and poverty.

Microcredit could alter our outlook on social welfare. In his 1980 book *Free to Choose*, Nobel Prize–winning economist Milton Friedman argues that the poor benefit more by being empowered to make their own decisions than they do from government handouts. The previously cited *International Herald Tribune* article notes that microcredit reinforces Friedman's belief in free market capitalism by giving the poor control over how they generate income. The success of this approach could provide ammunition to those who rally against social welfare, strengthening attempts to abolish the so-called welfare state and the safety nets that it currently provides.

Additionally, microcredit may not have the expected positive impact on women. According to an April 3, 2006, press release from the United Nations Department of Public Information, 80 percent of microcredit borrowers are women. Microcredit groups seek out female borrowers because they hope to empower women in traditionally patriarchal societies. However, the February 10, 2007, edition of India's *Economic and Political Weekly* argues that sometimes women are forced to hand their loans over to their husbands. The wife ends up worse off than when she started, because she is responsible for repaying the loan but has not received any of its benefits. Thus, microcredit offers women a road to economic empowerment, but if male dominance in a given community is too deeply entrenched, microcredit may not be able to deliver on its promise.

Finally, microcredit could change our understanding of poverty. The 2005 documentary *Small Fortunes: Microcredit and the Future of Poverty* explains that one long-standing perception about the poor is that they just need to work harder. Yet Pakistan's *The Nation* of December 6, 2006, states that microcredit's central message is that people are poor not because they lack ambition, but rather because traditional banking systems are "discriminatory and anti-poor." As microcredit continues to gain legitimacy, it could shift blame away from the impoverished and refocus our attention on the root causes of poverty—the very systems that perpetuate destitution in the first place.

When awarding Muhammad Yunus the Nobel Prize, the committee noted, "Lasting peace can not be achieved un-

Here the speaker provides a transition to the third major point, this one dealing with the implications of microcredit. As you can easily tell, the speaker will cover three implications: those pertaining to social welfare, the role of women, and poverty.

The first implication concerns social welfare. Notice that the speaker effectively establishes the credibility of her source, Milton Friedman, by recalling that he was a Nobel Prize–winning economist. In what other ways does the speaker establish credibility—her own as well as that of her sources?

Here we're jolted a bit. We assume that all microcredit is going to be positive, but here the speaker notes a negative impact—it may make women more vulnerable, not more empowered. Of course, this is an informative speech; it isn't designed to persuade you but to inform you.

We now know the speaker has come to the final point of the speech ("finally"), this one dealing with the implications of microcredit on poverty.

Here the speaker concludes the speech by clearly summarizing the main points of the speech: the development, rationale,

### Public Speaking Sample Assistant

## An Excellent Informative Speech *(Continued)*

less large population groups find ways in which to break out of poverty."

After examining the development of microcredit, its rationale, and the implications of this movement, it seems that this poverty-fighting technique may be a step toward a more peaceful world. In the meantime, Yunus and other microcredit lenders will continue to spread the message that the poor are creditworthy. But the real challenge, in their eyes, is to continue to build banks that are people-worthy.

and implications of microcredit. The speaker then stresses the importance of microcredit by calling it a poverty-fighting technique and suggesting that it may be a step toward a more peaceful world.

The speaker then recalls the introduction by getting back to Yunus and closes by noting the real challenge.

## Limit the Amount of Information

Resist the temptation to overload your listeners with information. Limit the breadth of information you communicate; instead, expand its depth. Limiting the amount of information lets you present a few items of information and explain these with examples, illustrations, and descriptions rather than presenting a wide array of items without this needed amplification. The speaker who attempts to discuss the physiological, psychological, social, and linguistic differences between men and women, for example, is clearly trying to cover too much and is going to be

---

### UNDERSTANDING **Theory and Research**   Information Theory

In the 1940s, engineers working at Bell Telephone Laboratories developed the mathematical theory of communication—which became known as information theory (Shannon & Weaver, 1949). This theory defined **information** as that which reduces uncertainty. For example, if I tell you my name and you already know it, then I haven't communicated information—because my message (my name) didn't reduce uncertainty; you already knew my name and so had no uncertainty in this connection. If, on the other hand, I tell you my salary or my educational background or my fears and dreams, that constitutes information, because these are things you presumably didn't know. Although this theory doesn't explain many of the complexities of human communication very well (see Unit 1), it is helpful when you are thinking about the purpose of the informative speech: to communicate information, to tell the members of the audience something they didn't already know, or to send messages that reduce the uncertainty of your listeners about your speech topic. If you don't communicate enough information, the audience will be bored (they'll already know what you're saying). But if you communicate too much information, they'll be overwhelmed. The art of the effective speaker is to strike an appropriate balance.

---

#### Working with Theories and Research

*Review the speech you're working on now. How much is information? How much does the audience already know? Is this the appropriate balance, or do you need to make adjustments?*

**UNEXPECTED EVENTS**

You're going to speak on the newest Microsoft operating system that you've been using the last few weeks. Unfortunately, the previous speaker turns out to be a Microsoft program designer who gives a speech on exactly your topic.

WHAT DO YOU SAY?

forced to cover these areas only superficially, with the result that little new information will be communicated. Even covering one of these areas is likely to prove too broad. Instead, select one subdivision of one area—say, language development or differences in language problems—and develop that in depth.

## Adjust the Level of Complexity

As you know from attending college classes, information can be presented in a very simplified form or in an extremely complex form. Adjusting the level of complexity on which you communicate is key and should be guided by a wide variety of factors we have already considered: the level of knowledge your audience has, the time you have available, the purpose you hope to achieve, the topic on which you're speaking, and so on. If you simplify a topic too much, you risk boring or, even worse, insulting your audience. If your talk is too complex, you risk confusing your audience and failing to communicate the desired information.

Generally, however, beginning speakers err on the side of being too complex and do not realize that a

5- or 10-minute speech does not allow much time to introduce sophisticated concepts or make an audience understand how a complicated process works. At least in your beginning speeches, try to keep it simple rather than complex. For example, make sure the words you use are familiar to your audience—or, if they're not, explain and define the terms as you use them. Remember too that jargon and technical vocabulary of specialized fields often will need translation. Always see your topic from the point of view of the members of the audience; ask yourself how much they know about your topic and its unique language.

## Stress Relevance and Usefulness

Listeners will remember your information best when they see it as useful and relevant to their own needs of goals. Notice that as a listener you regularly follow the principle of stressing relevance and usefulness. For example, in class you may attend to and remember the stages in the development of language in children simply because you know you'll be tested on the information and you want to earn a high grade. Or you may attend to the information because it will help you make a better impression in your job interview, make you a better parent, or enable you to deal with relationship problems.

Like you, listeners attend to information that will prove useful to them. So if you want the audience to listen to your speech, relate your information to their needs, wants, or goals (Frymier & Shulman, 1995). Throughout your speech, but especially in the beginning, make sure your audience knows that the information you're presenting is relevant and useful to them now—or will be in the immediate future. For example, you might say something like:

> We all want financial security. We all want to be able to buy those luxuries we read so much about in magazines and see every evening on television. Wouldn't it be nice to be able to buy a car without worrying about where you're going to get the down payment or how you'll be able to make the monthly payments? Actually, that is not an unrealistic goal, as I'll demonstrate in this speech. In fact, I will show you several methods for investing your money that will enable you to increase your income by at least 20 percent.

## Relate New Information to Old

Listeners will learn information more easily and retain it longer when you relate it to what they already know. In relating new information to old, link the unfamiliar to the familiar, the unseen to the seen, the untasted to the tasted. Here, for example, Teresa

---

**Theory and Research** — UNDERSTANDING

## Signal-to-Noise Ratio

A useful way of looking at information is in terms of its **signal-to-noise ratio**. *Signal* in this context refers to information that is useful to you, information that you want. *Noise*, on the other hand, is what you find useless; it's what you do not want. So, for example, if a mailing list or newsgroup contained lots of useful information, it would be high on signal and low on noise; if it contained lots of useless information, it would be high on noise and low on signal. Spam is high on noise and low on signal, as is static that interferes with radio, television, or telephone transmission.

From the public speaker's point of view, noise is anything that diverts audience attention away from the speech (the signal)—pictures on the walls, writing on the chalkboard, people talking in the hallways, the rustle of newspapers, and so on. The speaker's task is to keep the audience's focus on the speech instead of the noise.

### Working with Theories and Research

*Look around the classroom in which you give your speeches. What sources of potential noise can you identify? What can you do to prevent the audience from focusing on the noise instead of your speech?*

---

Jacob, a student at Ohio State University (Schnoor, 1997, p. 97), relates the problems of drug interactions (the new) to mixing chemicals in the school lab (the old or familiar):

> During our high school years, most of us learned in a chemistry class the danger of mixing harmless chemicals in lab. Add one drop of the wrong compound and suddenly you've created a stink bomb,

or worse, an explosion. Millions of Americans run the same risk inside their bodies each day by combining drugs that are supposed to help restore or maintain good health.

## Vary the Levels of Abstraction

You can talk about freedom of the press in **abstractions**—for example, by talking about the importance

---

**Building Communication** — SKILLS

## Climbing the Abstraction Ladder

For each of the terms listed below, indicate at least four possible terms that indicate increasing specificity. The first example is provided as an illustration:

| Level 1 | Level 2 | Level 3 | Level 4 | Level 5 |
|---|---|---|---|---|
| | more specific than 1 | more specific than 2 | more specific than 3 | more specific than 4 |
| *Building* | *Masonry building* | *Masonry office building* | *Office skyscraper* | *Chicago's Sears Tower* |
| Transportation | | | | |
| Communication | | | | |
| Toy | | | | |
| Sport | | | | |

*Words exist at different levels of abstraction. As you get more specific, you more clearly communicate your own meanings and more easily direct the listeners' attention to what you wish.*

### TECHNICAL PROBLEMS

You've prepared a great slide show for your informative speech. Unfortunately, the equipment that you need to show the slides never arrives. But you have to give your speech and you have to (or do you?) explain something of what happened.

*WHAT DO YOU SAY?*

of getting information to the public, by referring to the Bill of Rights, and by relating a free press to the preservation of democracy. That is, you can talk about the topic on a relatively high **level of abstraction**. But you can also talk about freedom of the press by citing specific examples: how a local newspaper was prevented from running a story critical of the town council or how Lucy Rinaldo was fired from the *Accord Sentinel* after she wrote a story critical of the mayor. In other words, you can

talk about the topic on a relatively low level of abstraction, a level that is specific and concrete.

Varying the levels of abstraction—combining the abstract and the specific—seems to work best. Too many high abstractions without specifics or too many specifics without high abstractions will generally prove less effective than a combination of the two approaches.

Here, for example, is an excerpt from a speech on the issue of homelessness. Note that in the first para-

# REFLECTIONS
## ON ETHICS

## Speaking Ethically

One interesting approach to ethics that has particular relevance to public speaking identifies four key rules for speakers (Wallace, 1955; Johannesen, 2001). As an ethical speaker, you should be guided by the following principles:

■ Have a thorough knowledge of the topic, an ability to answer relevant questions, and an awareness of the significant facts and opinions bearing on the issues you discuss.

■ Present both facts and opinions fairly, without bending or spinning them to personal advantage. You must allow listeners to make the final judgment.

■ Reveal the sources of these facts and opinions, and help listeners evaluate any biases and prejudices in the sources.

■ Acknowledge and respect opposing arguments and evidence; advocate a tolerance for diversity.

### Ethical Choice Point

*You're giving an informative speech to explain how the new condom machines on campus will work. Among the important items that should logically be covered is their cost, which is going to come from an increase in student fees. Since you are very in favor of these machines, you'd like to eliminate discussing cost largely because the students may vote against installing the machines if they knew their fees would be raised. You figure you don't have time to include all issues, that it's really the responsibility of the audience to ask where the money is coming from, and that the machines will help prevent sexually transmitted diseases. What is your ethical obligation in this situation? What would you do?*

graph we have a relatively abstract description of homelessness. In the second paragraph, we get into specifics. In the last paragraph, the abstract and the concrete are connected.

> Homelessness is a serious problem for all metropolitan areas throughout the country. It's currently estimated that there are more than 200,000 homeless people in New York City alone. But what is this really about? Let me tell you what it's about.
>
> It's about a young man. He must be about 25 or 30, although he looks a lot older. He lives in a cardboard box on the side of my apartment house. We call him Tom, although we really don't know his name. All his possessions are stored in this huge box. I think it was a box from a refrigerator. Actually, he doesn't have very much, and what he has easily fits in this box. There's a blanket my neighbor threw out, some plastic bottles he puts water in, and some Styrofoam containers he picked up from the garbage from Burger King. He uses these to store whatever food he finds.
>
> What is homelessness about? It's about Tom and 200,000 other "Toms" in New York and thousands of others throughout the rest of the country. And not all of them even have boxes to live in.

Now that we've considered these guidelines for informative speaking, let's look at the kinds of informative speeches that you may be called upon to present. Researchers on public speaking have developed numerous classification systems for information speeches, but in this text we'll focus on three broad types: speeches of (1) description, (2) definition, and (3) demonstration. We turn now to the first of these categories: the speech of description.

## SPEECHES OF DESCRIPTION

In a **speech of description**, you're concerned with explaining an object, person, event, or process. Examples of speeches in which you describe an object or person might include "The Structure of the Brain," "The Contributions of Thomas Edison," "The Parts of a Telephone," "The Layout of Philadelphia," "The Hierarchy of a Corporation," or "The Components of a Computer System."

Examples of speeches in which you describe an event or process might include "The Attacks of September 11, 2001"; "The Events Leading to the Iraq War"; "Organizing a Body-Building Contest"; "How a Newspaper Is Printed"; "Purchasing Stock Online"; or "How a Child Acquires Language."

### Thesis

The thesis of a speech, as explained in Unit 15, is your single most important concept; it is what you most want your audience to remember. The thesis of a speech of description simply states what you'll describe in your speech; for example, "The child acquires language in four stages," or "There are three steps to purchasing stock online," or "Four major events led to the Iraq war."

### Main Points

The main points of your speech of description are the major subdivisions of the thesis. You derive your main points from the thesis by asking strategic questions. For example, "What are the four stages in child language acquisition?" "What are the three steps to purchasing stock online?" "What events led to the Iraq war?"

### SPEECH OF DESCRIPTION

You're giving a speech of description on how children acquire language and you notice a woman with a child of the age you're talking about in the audience.

WHAT DO YOU SAY?

## Support

Obviously, you don't want simply to list your main points but rather to flesh them out and to make them memorable, interesting, and most of all clear. You do this by using a variety of materials that amplify and support your main ideas—the examples, illustrations, testimony, statistics, and the like, that have already been explained. So, for example, in describing the babbling stage of language learning, you might give examples of babbling, the age at which babbling first appears, the period of time that babbling lasts, or the differences between the babbling of girls and boys.

Because this is a speech of description, give extra consideration to the types of description you might use in your supporting materials. Try to describe the object or event with lots of different descriptive categories. With physical categories, for example, ask yourself questions such as these: What color is it? How big is it? What is it shaped like? How much does it weigh? What is its volume? How attractive/ unattractive is it? Also consider social, psychological, and economic categories. In describing a person, for example, consider such categories as friendly/ unfriendly, warm/cold, rich/poor, aggressive/meek, and pleasant/unpleasant.

Consider how you might use presentation aids. In describing an object or a person, show your listeners a picture; show them the inside of a telephone, pictures of the brain, the skeleton of the body. In describing an event or process, show them a diagram or flowchart to illustrate the stages or steps; for example, the steps involved in buying stock, in publishing a newspaper, in putting a parade together.

## Organization

Consider using a spatial or a topical organization when describing objects and people. Consider using a temporal pattern when describing events and processes. For example, if you were to describe the layout of Philadelphia, you might start from the north and work down to the south (using a spatial pattern). If you were to describe the contributions of Thomas Edison, you might select the three or four major contributions and discuss each of these equally (using a topical pattern).

If you were describing the events leading up to World War II, you might use a temporal pattern, starting with the earliest and working up to the latest. A temporal pattern would also be appropriate for describing how a hurricane develops or how a parade is put together.

Consider the 5W (who? what? where? when? and why?) pattern of organization discussed in Unit 15. These journalistic categories are especially useful when you want to describe an event or a process. For example, if you're going to describe how to purchase a house, you might want to consider the people involved (who?), the steps you have to go through (what?), the places you'll have to go (where?), the time or sequence in which the steps have to take place (when?), and the advantages and disadvantages of buying the house (why?).

Here are two examples of the main components a descriptive speech might contain. In this first example, the speaker describes four suggestions for reducing energy bills. Notice that the speaker derives the main points from asking a question of the thesis.

**General purpose:**  To inform.

**Specific purpose:**  To describe how you can reduce energy bills.

**Thesis:**  Energy bills can be reduced. (How can energy bills be reduced?)

    **I.** Caulk window and door seams.
    **II.** Apply weather stripping around windows and doors.
    **III.** Insulate walls.
    **IV.** Install storm windows and doors.

In this second example, the speaker describes the way in which fear works in intercultural communication.

**General purpose:**  To inform.

**Specific purpose:**  To describe the way fear works in intercultural communication.

**Thesis:**  Fear influences intercultural communication. (How does fear influence intercultural communication?)

    **I.** We fear disapproval.
    **II.** We fear embarrassing ourselves.
    **III.** We fear being harmed.

In delivering such a speech, a speaker might begin by saying:

Three major fears interfere with intercultural communication. First, we fear disapproval—from members of our own group as well as from members of the other person's group. Second, we fear embarrassing ourselves, even making fools of ourselves, by saying the wrong thing or appearing insensitive. And third, we may fear being harmed—our stereotypes of the other group may lead us to see its members as dangerous or potentially harmful to us.

Let's look at each of these fears in more detail. We'll be able to see clearly how they influence our own intercultural communication behavior. Consider, first, the fear of disapproval. [The speaker would then amplify and support this fear of disapproval, giving examples of disapproval seen in his or her own experience, the testimony of communication theorists on the importance of such fear, research findings on the effects that such fear might have on intercultural communication, and so on.]

## SPEECHES OF DEFINITION

What is leadership? What is a born-again Christian? What is the difference between sociology and psychology? What is a cultural anthropologist? What is safe sex? These are all topics for informative **speeches of definition**.

A *definition*, as explained in Unit 15, is a statement of the meaning or significance of a concept or term. Use definitions when you wish to explain difficult or unfamiliar concepts or when you wish to make a concept more vivid or forceful.

In giving a speech of definition, you may focus on defining a term, defining a system or theory, or pinpointing the similarities and/or differences among terms or systems. A speech of definition may be on a subject new to the audience or may present a familiar topic in a new and different way.

Examples of speeches in which you define a term might include "What Is a Smart Card?" "What Is Machismo?" "What Is Creativity?" "What Is Affirmative Action?" "What Is Multiculturalism?" "What Is Political Correctness?"

Examples of speeches in which you'd define a system or theory might include "What Is the Classical Theory of Public Speaking?" "What Are the Parts of a Generative Grammar?" "Confucianism: Its Major Beliefs," "What Is Expressionism?" "What Is Futurism?" "The 'Play Theory' of Mass Communication."

Examples of speeches in which you'd define similar and dissimilar terms or systems might include "Football and Soccer: What's the Difference?" "What Do Christians and Muslims Have in Common?" "Oedipus and Electra: How Do They Differ?" "Genetics and Heredity," "Animal and Human Rights," and "Key-Word and Directory Searches."

### Thesis

The thesis in a speech of definition is a statement identifying the term or system and your intention to define it or to contrast it with other terms; for example, "Christianity and Islam have much in common" or "You can search for information through key words or through a directory."

### Main Points

You derive the main points for your speech of definition by asking questions of your thesis; for example, "What do Christianity and Islam have in common?" "How do text and online dictionaries differ?" Your main points will then consist of, say, the factors that Christianity and Islam have in common or the several ways in which text and online dictionaries differ.

### Support

Once you have each of your main points, you'll support them with examples, testimony, and the like. For example, one of your main points in the Christianity–Islam example might be that both religions believe in the value of good works. You might then quote from the New Testament and from the Quran to illustrate

### DEFINING

In visualizing your next speech, in which you plan to define the basic tenets of your religion, you know that some members of your audience will have a negative view of your religion while others will hold positive views. You want to acknowledge your understanding of these attitudes.

WHAT DO YOU SAY?

this belief, or you might give examples of noted Christians and Muslims who exemplified this characteristic, or you might cite the testimony of religious leaders who talked about the importance of good works.

Because this is a speech of definition, you'll want to give special attention to different types of definitions, as detailed in Unit 15 (pages 332–333).

## Organization

In addition to the obvious organizational pattern of multiple definitions (see Unit 15, page 348), consider using a topical order, in which each main idea is treated equally. In either case, however, proceed from the known to the unknown. Start with what your audience knows and work up to what is new or unfamiliar. This will help the audience to bring to consciousness the material you want to build on. Let's say you want to explain the concept of phonemics (with which your audience is totally unfamil-

iar). The specific idea you wish to get across is that each phoneme stands for a unique sound. You might proceed from the known to the unknown and begin your definition with something like this:

> We all know that in the written language each letter of the alphabet stands for a unit of the written language. Each letter is different from every other letter. A *t* is different from a *g* and a *g* is different from a *b,* and so on. Each letter is called a "grapheme." In English we know we have 26 such letters.
>
> We can look at the spoken language in much the same way. Each sound is different from every other sound. A *t* sound is different from a *d* and a *d* is different from a *k,* and so on. Each individual sound is called a "phoneme."
>
> Now, let me explain in a little more detail what I mean by a "phoneme."

Here are two examples of how you might go about constructing a speech of definition. In this

**MEDIA WATCH**

## THE KNOWLEDGE GAP

The term *knowledge gap* refers to the difference in knowledge between one group and another; it's the division between those who have a great deal of knowledge about some subject and those who have significantly less. Much of the research in this area has focused on the influence of the media in widening this knowledge gap—a concept known as the knowledge gap hypothesis (Tichenor, Donohue, & Olien, 1970; Severin, 1988; Viswanath & Finnegan, 1995).

Information is valuable; it brings wealth and it gives power. It gives you the means you need to get a high-paid job, to live a healthy life, to plan for retirement, or to accomplish just about any task you set for yourself (Mastin, 1998).

But information is expensive, and not everyone has equal access to it. This is especially true as we live more of our lives in cyberspace. The new communication technologies—computers, CDs, DVDs, high-speed Internet connections, satellite and cable television, for example—are major ways for gaining information. Better-educated people have the money to own and the skills to master the new technologies and thus acquire more information. Less-educated people don't have the money to own or the skills to master the new technologies and thus cannot ac-

quire more information. Thus, the educated have the means for becoming even better educated, and the gap widens.

You also see the knowledge gap hypothesis when you compare different cultures. Developed countries, for example, have the new technologies in schools and offices, and many people in these countries can afford to buy their own computers and satellite systems. Access to the new technologies helps these countries develop even further. Undeveloped countries, with little or no access to such technologies, cannot experience the same gain in knowledge and information as those with this technological access.

Even the language of a culture may influence the extent of the knowledge gap. For example, English dominates the Internet; so the Internet is more easily accessible to people in English-speaking countries, as well as to people in non-English-speaking countries who speak English as a second language.

### Increasing Media Literacy

*Do you see the knowledge gap operating in your community or school? Can you see it in different cultures with which you're familiar?*

first example, the speaker explains the parts of a résumé and follows a spatial order, going from the top to the bottom of the page.

**General purpose:** To inform.

**Specific purpose:** To define the essential parts of a résumé.

**Thesis:** There are four major parts to a résumé. (What are the four major parts of a résumé?)

    **I.** Identify your career goals.
    **II.** Identify your educational background.
    **III.** Identify your work experience.
    **IV.** Identify your special competencies.

In this second example, the speaker selects three major types of lying for discussion and arranges these in a topical pattern.

**General purpose:** To inform.

**Specific purpose:** To define lying by explaining the major types of lying.

**Thesis:** There are three major kinds of lying. (What are the three major kinds of lying?)

    **I.** Concealment is the process of hiding the truth.
    **II.** Falsification is the process of presenting false information as if it were true.
    **III.** Misdirection is the process of acknowledging a feeling but misidentifying its cause.

In delivering such a speech, a speaker might begin the speech by saying:

A lie is a lie is a lie. True? Well, not exactly. Actually, there are a number of different ways we can lie. We can lie by concealing the truth. We can lie by falsification, by presenting false information as if it were true. And we can lie by misdirection, by acknowledging a feeling but misidentifying its cause.

Let's look at the first type of lie—the lie of concealment. Most lies are lies of concealment. Most of the time when we lie we simply conceal the truth. We don't actually make any false statements. Rather we simply don't reveal the truth. Let me give you some examples I overheard recently.

## SPEECHES OF DEMONSTRATION

In a **speech of demonstration** (or in using demonstration within a different type of speech), you show the audience how to do something or how something operates. Examples of speeches in which you demonstrate how to do something might include "How to Give Mouth-to-Mouth Resuscitation," "How to Drive Defensively," "How to Mix Paint Colors," "How to Ask for a Raise," "How to Burglarproof Your House," or "How to Use PowerPoint in Business Meetings."

Examples of speeches in which you demonstrate how something operates might include "How the Body Maintains Homeostasis," "How Perception Works," "How Divorce Laws Work," "How E-Mail Works," "How a Hurricane Develops," or "How a Heart Bypass Operation Is Performed."

### DEMONSTRATING

You want to demonstrate to your audience how some new technology works. Your audience is probably mixed in terms of their knowledge of technology generally—some know a great deal and others know very little. You want to make sure that all audience members will give you their attention and you'd like to accomplish that right at the start of your speech.

WHAT DO YOU SAY?

## Thesis

The thesis for a speech of demonstration identifies what you will show the audience how to do, or how something operates; for example, "E-mail works through a series of electronic connections from one computer to a server to another computer," or "You can burglarproof your house in three different ways," or "Three guidelines will help you get that raise."

## Main Points

You can derive the main points for your speech of demonstration by asking a simple How or What question of your thesis—"How do these electronic connections work?" "What are the methods you can use to burglarproof your house?" "What are the guidelines for asking for a raise?"

## Support

Support each of your main ideas with a variety of materials. For example, you might show diagrams of houses that use different burglarproofing methods, demonstrate how various locks work, or show how different security systems work.

Presentation aids are especially helpful in speeches of demonstration. A good example of this is the signs in restaurants demonstrating the Heimlich maneuver. These signs demonstrate the sequence of steps with pictures as well as words. The combination of verbal and graphic information makes it easy for restaurant-goers to understand this important process. In a speech on this topic, however, it would be best to use only the pictures so that the written words would not distract your audience from your oral explanation.

## Organization

In most cases a temporal pattern will work best in speeches of demonstration. Demonstrate each step in the sequence in which it's to be performed. In this way you'll avoid one of the major difficulties in demonstrating a process—backtracking. Don't skip steps even if you think they're familiar to the audience. They may not be. Connect each step to the next with appropriate transitions. For example, in explaining the Heimlich maneuver, you might say,

> Now that you have your arms around the choking victim's chest, your next step is to....

Assist your listeners by labeling the steps clearly; for example, "the first step," "the second step," and so on.

Begin with an overview. It's often helpful when demonstrating to give a broad general picture and then present each step in turn. For example, suppose you were talking about how to prepare a wall for painting. You might begin with a general overview to give your listeners a general idea of the process, saying something like this:

> In preparing the wall for painting, you want to make sure that the wall is smoothly sanded, free of dust, and dry. Sanding a wall isn't like sanding a block of wood. So let's look at the proper way to sand a wall.

Here are two examples of the speech of demonstration. In this first example, the speaker explains the proper way to paint a wall by rag rolling. As you can see, the speaker uses a temporal organizational pattern and covers three stages in the order in which they would be performed.

**General purpose:** To inform.

**Specific purpose:** To demonstrate how to rag roll.

**Thesis:** Rag rolling is performed in three steps. (What are the three steps of rag rolling?)

   **I.** Apply the base coat of paint.
  **II.** Apply the glaze coat.
 **III.** Roll a rag through the wet glaze.

In the next example, the speaker identifies and demonstrates how to listen actively.

**General purpose:** To inform.

**Specific purpose:** To demonstrate three techniques of active listening.

**Thesis:** We can engage in active listening. (How can we engage in active listening?)

   **I.** Paraphrase the speaker's meaning.
  **II.** Express understanding of the speaker's feelings.
 **III.** Ask questions.

In delivering the speech, the speaker might begin by saying:

> Active listening is a special kind of listening. It's listening with total involvement, with a concern for the speaker. It's probably the most important type of listening you can engage in. Active listening consists of three steps: paraphrasing the speaker's meaning, expressing understanding of the speaker's feelings, and asking questions.
>
> Your first step in active listening is to paraphrase the speaker's meaning. What is a paraphrase? A paraphrase is a restatement in your own words of the speaker's meaning. That is, you express in your own words what you think the speaker meant. For example, let's say that the speaker said....

---

## Building Communication Skills  Preparing an Informative Speech

Consult the Dictionary of Topics (www.mycommunicationlab.com) for suggestions for informative speech topics. Select a topic and develop a preparation outline:

- Formulate a thesis and a specific purpose suitable for an informative speech of approximately 10 minutes;
- Analyze this class as your potential audience, and identify ways that you can relate this topic to their interests and needs;
- Generate at least two main points from your thesis;
- Support these main points with examples, illustrations, definitions, testimony, and so on;
- Construct a conclusion that summarizes your main ideas and brings the speech to a definite close; and
- Construct an introduction that gains attention and orients your audience.

Discuss these outlines in small groups or with the class as a whole. Try to secure feedback from other members on how you can improve these outlines.

*Working repeatedly with the process of preparing a speech will ultimately make the process easier, more efficient, and more effective.*

---

As mentioned earlier, this three-part classification of information speeches into speeches of demonstration, definition, and description is only one way of looking at informative speeches. You may be interested in some alternative classifications of information speeches that other writers in public speaking have devised.

Stephen Lucas (2007), in *The Art of Public Speaking*, uses a four-part classification:

- Speeches about objects, persons, places, or things (for example, the contributions of a noted scientist or philosopher);
- Speeches about processes or series of actions (for example, an explanation of how to do something);
- Speeches about events or happenings (the story of your first date); and
- Speeches about concepts, beliefs, or ideas (for example, a review of theories of economics).

George Grice and John Skinner (2007), in *Mastering Public Speaking*, offer an eight-part system:

- Speeches about people (Cesar Chavez, Margaret Mead);
- Speeches about objects (electric cars, the Great Wall of China);
- Speeches about places (Ellis Island, the Nile);
- Speeches about events (the sinking of the *Titanic*, Woodstock festivals);
- Speeches about processes (cartooning, waterproofing);
- Speeches about concepts (liberty, nihilism);
- Speeches about conditions (McCarthyism, the civil rights movement);
- Speeches about issues (the use of polygraph tests, fetal tissue research).

Rudolph and Kathleen Verderber, in *The Challenge of Effective Speaking* (2006), present a five-part system:

- Speeches of description (speeches about objects, geographical features, settings, or images—a light bulb, a holograph);
- Speeches of definition (speeches that explain something by identifying its meaning—vegetarianism, plane);
- Speeches of comparison and contrast (speeches explaining how something is similar to or different from other things—vegans and vegetarians);
- Speeches of narration (speeches explaining something by recounting events—becoming a vegetarian); and
- Speeches of demonstration (speeches that explain how something is done, the stages of a process, or how something works—how to iron a shirt, the workings of a nuclear reactor).

## SUMMARY: THE INFORMATIVE SPEECH

This unit focused on the informative speech, examining the goals of informative speaking, the guidelines to follow in informing others, and the various types of informative speeches.

1. Informative speaking may have a variety of goals, among them: to introduce new topics, to clarify misconceptions, to demonstrate how to do something, and to expand on information the audience already has.

2. Informative speeches are more likely to be effective when they adhere to the following principles of informative speaking: Limit the amount of information you communicate, adjust the level of complexity, stress the relevance and the usefulness of the information to your audience, relate new information to old, and vary the levels of abstraction.

3. Speeches of description describe a process or procedure, an event, an object, or a person.

4. Speeches of definition define a term, system, or theory or explain similarities and/or differences among terms.

5. Speeches of demonstration show how to do something or how something operates.

## KEY TERMS IN THE INFORMATIVE SPEECH

abstractions (p. **399**)  level of abstraction (p. **400**)  speech of description (p. **401**)  speech of demonstration (p. **405**)

information (p. **397**)  signal-to-noise ratio (p. **399**)  speech of definition (p. **403**)

## THINKING CRITICALLY ABOUT THE INFORMATIVE SPEECH

1. **Communicating Unknown Concepts.** You want to give an informative speech on virtual reality simulation, but most of your audience members have never experienced it. How would you communicate this concept and this experience to your audience?

2. **Informative Strategies.** You're planning to give an informative speech on the history of doctor-assisted suicide and are considering the strategies that you might use. What organizational pattern would be appropriate? What types of presentation aids might you use? How would you define "doctor-assisted suicide"? How would you introduce your speech?

3. **Same-Topic Speech.** You're scheduled to be the third speaker in a series of six presentations today. Unfortu-

nately, the first speaker presented a really excellent speech on the same topic you're speaking on—how the Internet works. What should you do?

4. **Speaking on Technical Issues.** Visit the Society for Technical Communication at www.stc-va.org/ for guides for writing and speaking on technical matters.

5. **Two-Minute Speech.** Prepare a two-minute informative speech on one of the following:
   - Explain a card game.
   - Explain a board game.
   - Explain food preparation.
   - Explain a sport.

## LOGON! MYCOMMUNICATIONLAB

WWW.MYCOMMUNICATIONLAB.COM

An earlier version of the informative speech on microcredit included in a Public Speaking Sample Assistant box in this unit (pages 394–397) is available at MCL. You might find it interesting to compare the two versions. Which do you prefer? Watch the speech "Contemporary Education" and examine it in terms of the principles of informative speaking considered in this chapter. Also view one or both of the demonstration speeches ("Baking a Cake" and "CPR"). The "Hybrid Electric Vehicle" speech provides a good example of the speech of description. Also explore the Definitions activity and visit the suggested websites.

# UNIT 18  The Persuasive Speech

## MAJOR TOPICS

**Goals of Persuasive Speaking**
**Principles of Persuasive Speaking**
**Persuasive Speeches on Questions of Fact**
**Persuasive Speeches on Questions of Value**
**Persuasive Speeches on Questions of Policy**

In addition to informing others, you'll also be called upon to deliver speeches of persuasion—speeches that aim to influence the attitudes and beliefs and sometimes the behaviors of your listeners.

**In this unit you'll learn about:**
- the nature and goals of persuasion and how attitudes, beliefs, values, and behaviors are influenced.
- the major types of persuasive speeches.

**You'll learn to:**
- use the strategies of persuasion in a variety of communication contexts.
- prepare a variety of effective persuasive speeches on questions of fact, value, and policy.
- prevent yourself from being unfairly or unethically persuaded.

The previous unit focused on informative speaking; it examined the goals of such speaking, essential principles for communicating information, and the varied types of informative speeches. This unit looks at persuasive speaking and follows a similar pattern: the goals of persuasive speaking, essential principles of persuasion, and the varied types of persuasive speeches you might give.

## GOALS OF PERSUASIVE SPEAKING

**Persuasion** is the process of influencing another person's attitudes, beliefs, values, and/or behaviors. To review the discussion in Unit 14, here is a brief glossary of the terms in this definition:

- *Attitude:* The tendency to behave in a certain way. For example, if your audience has a positive attitude toward the current administration, then they're likely to favor the policies, proposals, and values of the administration. If they have a negative attitude, they're likely to oppose administration policies and the like.

- *Belief:* The conviction in the existence or reality of something or in the truth of some assertion. For example, if your audience believes that soft drugs lead to hard drugs, then they're likely to oppose legalizing marijuana and perhaps to favor harsher penalties for soft drug use.

- *Value:* An indicator of what people feel is good or bad, ethical or unethical, just or unjust. For example, if your audience positively values "free speech," then they'll likely oppose increased restrictions on what can and cannot be said publicly and will likely oppose increased surveillance of their e-mail or phone calls.

- *Behavior:* Overt, observable actions, such as voting for increased funding for education or for a particular electoral candidate, contributing money to the Red Cross, or buying a Ford.

Your persuasive speeches may focus on influencing listeners' attitudes, beliefs, values, and/or behaviors. You may want to accomplish any one of the following three general goals of persuasive speaking:

- *To strengthen or weaken attitudes, beliefs, or values.* Persuasion often aims to strengthen audience views. For example, religious sermons usually seek to strengthen the existing beliefs of the congregation. Similarly, many public service announcements try to strengthen existing beliefs about, say, recycling, smoking, or safe sex. At times, however, you may want to weaken the existing beliefs of the audience—to suggest that what they currently believe may not be entirely true. For example, you might want to weaken the favorable attitudes people might have toward a particular political party or policy.

- *To change attitudes, beliefs, or values.* Sometimes you'll want to change how your audience feels. You might want to change their attitudes to the college's no-smoking rules, to change their beliefs about television's influence on viewer violence, or to change their values about the efficacy of war.

- *To motivate to action.* Ultimately, your goal is to get people to do something—for example, to vote for one person rather than another, to donate money to a fund for the homeless, or to take a course in personal finance.

It's useful to view the effects of persuasion as a continuum ranging from one extreme to another. Let's say, to take one issue currently in the news, that you want to give a persuasive speech on same-sex marriage. You might visualize your audience as existing on

## CHANGING BEHAVIOR

You're supervising a small work force. Your problem is that some members are just not doing their job and you've been assigned the task of making sure they start working. You decide to tackle this in your weekly meeting with the workers.

WHAT DO YOU SAY?

a continuum ranging from strongly in favor to strongly opposed, as shown in Figure 18.1. Your task is to move your audience in the direction of your persuasive purpose, which you can do in any of three ways (corresponding to the goals of persuasion identified above). You can design your persuasive speech to attempt to:

- Strengthen or weaken your listeners' attitudes, beliefs, or values about same-sex marriage.

- Change your listeners' attitudes, beliefs, or values about same-sex marriage.

- Move your listeners to act—to protest, write letters, or sign a petition.

If your purpose is to persuade the audience to *oppose* same-sex marriage, then in Figure 18.1 on page 412 any movement toward the right will be successful persuasion; if your purpose is to persuade listeners to *support* same-sex marriage, then any movement toward the left will be successful persuasion. Notice, however, that it's quite possible to give a speech in which you hope to move your listeners

## Theory and Research  Balance Theories
## UNDERSTANDING

An especially interesting group of theories of persuasion go under the general term *balance theories*. The general assumption of balance theories is that people strive to maintain consistency between their beliefs and their behaviors. For example, if you believe that people should exercise regularly (because you believe it's the healthy thing to do) but you don't exercise (because you feel exercise is difficult and boring), then you'll be in a state of imbalance or dissonance. According to balance theory, you will then strive either to change your beliefs about exercise (to make them consistent with your behavior) or to change your behavior (to make it consistent with your beliefs).

Applied to persuasion, balance theories claim that people look for information that will maintain or restore balance or consonance. For example, if you as a speaker demonstrate that you offer an easy and enjoyable (not difficult and boring) exercise plan, you stand a good chance of influencing the audience—because they are looking for the very means to restore balance that you are now providing. Conversely, of course, you might assert that exercise is unhealthy; the belief that exercise is unhealthy would be consistent with their no-exercise behavior and also would restore balance.

### Working with Theories and Research

*How might you use the insights of balance theories in preparing a speech on why the audience should start investing, give up junk food, or quit smoking?*

| Strongly in favor of same-sex marriage | __:__:__:__:__:__ | Strongly opposed to same-sex marriage |

**FIGURE 18.1 The Persuasion Continuum**

Any movement along the continuum would be considered persuasion.

in one direction but actually move them in the other direction. This "negative persuasion" effect can occur, for example, if the audience members perceive you as dishonest or self-promoting or if they feel you presented biased evidence or faulty reasoning.

# PRINCIPLES OF PERSUASIVE SPEAKING

To succeed in strengthening or changing attitudes or beliefs and in moving your listeners to action, follow these guidelines for persuasive speaking.

## Anticipate Selective Exposure

Listeners follow the "law of selective exposure." As Unit 3 explained, this principle has two parts: (1) Listeners actively seek out information that supports their opinions, beliefs, values, decisions, and behaviors; and (2) listeners actively avoid information that contradicts their existing opinions, beliefs, attitudes, values, decisions, and behaviors.

Of course, if people are very sure that their opinions and attitudes are logical and valid, then they may not bother to seek out supporting information or to avoid contradictory messages. People exercise selective exposure most often when their confidence in their opinions and beliefs is weak.

So if you want to persuade an audience that holds attitudes different from your own, anticipate selective exposure operating and proceed inductively; that is, hold back on your thesis until you've given them your evidence and argument. Only then relate this evidence and argument to your initially contrary thesis.

If you were to present your listeners with your thesis first, they might tune you out without giving

## THE SPIRAL OF SILENCE

*I have noticed that nothing I have never said ever did me any harm.*

—*Calvin Coolidge*

The spiral of silence theory argues that you're more likely to voice agreement than disagreement (Noelle-Neumann, 1973, 1980, 1991; Windahl, Signitzer, & Olson, 1992). The theory claims that when a controversial issue arises, you try to estimate public opinion on the issue and figure out which views are popular and which are not, largely by attending to the media (Gonzenbach, King, & Jablonski, 1999; Jeffres, Neuendorf, & Atkin, 1999). At the same time, you also judge the likelihood and the severity of punishment for expressing minority opinions. You then use these estimates to regulate your expression of opinions.

The theory continues: When you agree with the majority, you're more likely to voice your opinions than when you disagree. You may avoid expressing minority opinions because you don't want to be isolated from the majority or confront the unpleasant possibility of being proven wrong. Or, you may assume that the majority, because they're a majority, are right.

Not all people seem affected equally by this spiral (Noelle-Neumann, 1991). For example, younger people and men are more likely to express minority opinions than are older people and women. Educated people are more likely to express minority opinions than are those who are less educated. Similarly, the tendency to voice minority opinions will vary from one culture to another (Scheufele & Moy, 2000).

In any case, the "spiral" effect occurs when, as people with minority views remain silent, the media position gets stronger (because those who agree with it are the only ones speaking). As the media's position grows stronger, the voice of the opposition also gets weaker. Thus, the situation becomes an ever-widening spiral of silence.

### Increasing Media Literacy

*In what ways does the spiral of silence operate in your own media life? For example, do you contribute to this spiral of silence? Under what conditions are you most likely to conform to the predictions of this theory? What are its effects on your self-image and on your popularity with peers?*

your position a fair hearing. So become thoroughly familiar with the attitudes of your audience if you want to succeed in making these necessary adjustments and adaptations.

Let's say you're giving a speech on the need to reduce spending on college athletic programs. If your audience is composed of listeners who agree with you and want to cut athletic spending, you might lead with your thesis. Your introduction might go something like this:

> Our college athletic program is absorbing money that we can more profitably use for the library, science labs, and language labs. Let me explain how the money now going to unnecessary athletic programs could be better spent in these other areas.

On the other hand, suppose you're addressing alumni who strongly favor the existing athletic programs. In this case, you may want to lead with your evidence and hold off stating your thesis until the end of your speech.

## Ask for Reasonable Amounts of Change

The greater and more important the change you want to encourage in your audience, the more difficult your task will be. The reason is simple: We normally demand a greater number of reasons and a lot more evidence before we make important decisions such as, say, changing careers, moving to another state, or investing in stocks. On the other hand, we may be more easily persuaded (and demand less evidence) on relatively minor issues—whether to take "Small Group Communication" rather than "Persuasion" or whether to give to the United Heart Fund instead of the American Heart Fund.

Generally, people change gradually, in small degrees over a long period of time. Persuasion, therefore, is most effective when it strives for small changes and works over a period of time. For example, a persuasive speech stands a better chance when it tries to get an alcoholic to attend just one AA meeting rather than asking the person to give up alcohol for life. If you try to convince your audience to change their attitudes radically or to engage in behaviors to which they're initially opposed, your attempts may backfire. In this type of situation, the audience may tune you out, closing its ears to even the best and most logical arguments.

In your classroom speeches, set reasonable goals for what you want the audience to do. Remember that you have only perhaps 10 minutes; in that time you cannot move the proverbial mountain. So ask your listeners for small, easily performed behaviors—signing a petition, voting in the next election, donating a small amount of money.

When you're addressing an audience that is opposed to your position and you're trying to change their attitudes and beliefs, be especially careful to seek change in small increments. Let's say, for example, that your ultimate goal is to get an antiabortion group to favor abortion on demand. Obviously, this goal is too great to achieve in one speech. Therefore, strive for small changes. For example, in the following excerpt the speaker attempts to get an audience that opposes legalized abortion to agree that at least some abortions should be legalized. The speaker begins:

> One of the great lessons I learned in college was that most extreme positions are wrong. Most of the important truths lie somewhere between the extreme opposites. And today I want to talk with you about one of these truths. I want to talk with you about rape and the problems faced by the mother carrying a child conceived in this most violent of all violent crimes we can imagine.

Notice that the speaker does not state a totally pro-choice position, but instead focuses on one area of the abortion issue and attempts to get the audience to ask themselves, "What if my daughter was raped and abortion was unavailable?" and perhaps ultimately to agree that in some cases the possibility of abortion should be available.

When you have the opportunity to persuade your audience on several occasions (rather than simply delivering one speech), two strategies will prove helpful: the foot-in-the-door and door-in-the-face techniques.

### Foot-in-the-Door Technique

As its name implies, the **foot-in-the-door technique** involves requesting something small, something that your audience will easily agree to. Once they agree to this small request, you then make your real request (Cialdini, 1984; Dejong, 1979; Freedman & Fraser, 1966; Pratkanis & Aronson, 1991). People are more apt to comply with a large request after they have complied with a similar but much smaller request. For example, in one study the objective was to get people to put a "Drive Carefully" sign on their lawn (a large request). When this (large) request was made first, only about 17 percent of the people were willing to agree. However, when this request was preceded by a much smaller request (to sign a petition), between 50 and 76 percent granted permission to install the sign. Agreement with the smaller request paves the way for the larger request and puts the audience into an agreeable mood.

# Public Speaking Sample Assistant

# A Poorly Constructed Persuasive Speech

This speech was written by the author to illustrate some really broad as well as some rather subtle errors that a beginning speaker might make in constructing a persuasive speech.

## XXX Has Got to Go

You probably didn't read the papers this weekend, but there's a XXX movie, I mean video, store that moved in on Broad and Fifth Streets. My parents, who are retired teachers, are protesting it, and so am I. My parents are organizing a protest for next weekend.

There must be hundreds of XXX video stores in the country, and they all need to be closed down. I have a lot of reasons.

First, my parents think it should be closed down. My parents are retired teachers and have organized protests over the proposed new homeless shelter and to prevent the city from making that park on Elm Street. So they know what they're doing.

The XXX video place is irreligious. No good person would ever go there. Our minister is against it and is joining in the protest.

These stores bring crime into the neighborhood. I have proof of that. Morristown's crime increased after the XXX video store opened. And in Martinsville, where they got rid of the video store, crime did not increase. If we allow the video store in our own town, then we're going to be like Morristown and our crime is going to increase.

These stores make lots of garbage. The plastic wrappings from the videos will add to our already overextended and overutilized landfill. And a lot of them are going to wind up as litter on the streets.

The XXX Video House stays open seven days a week, 24 hours a day. People will be forced to work at all hours and on Sunday, and that's not fair. And the store will increase the noise level at night with the cars pulling up and all.

The XXX Video House—that's its name, by the way—doesn't carry regular videos that most people want. So, why do we want them?

The XXX Video House got a lease from an owner who doesn't even live in the community, someone by the name of, well, it's an organization called XYX Management. And their address is Carlson Place in Jeffersonville. So, they don't even live here.

What do you think of the title of the speech? Visualizing yourself as a listener, how would the opening comment make you feel? Does the speaker gain your attention? What thesis do you think the speaker will support? Does mentioning "my parents" help or hurt the speaker's credibility?

What is the speaker's thesis? What impression are you beginning to get of the speaker?

How do the speaker's parents sound to you? Do they sound like credible leaders with a consistent cause? Professional protesters (with perhaps a negative agenda)? What evidence is offered to support the assertion that we should believe the speaker's parents? Is this adequate? What would you need to know about people before believing them?

What does this statement assume about the audience? How would this statement be responded to by your public speaking class? What are some reasons why the speaker might not have explained how XXX video stores are against religion?

What do you think of the reasoning used here? Are there other factors that could have influenced Morristown's crime increase? Is there any evidence that getting rid of the video store resulted in the stable crime rate in Martinsville? What assumption about the audience does the speaker make in using Martinsville and Morristown as analogies?

Do you agree with this argument about the garbage? Is this argument in any way unique to the video store? Is it likely that people will open the wrappers and drop them on the street?

What validity do you give to each of these arguments? Given the 24-hour policy, how might you construct an argument against the video store? Are there advantages of a neighborhood store's 24-hour policy that the audience may be thinking of and thus countering the speaker's argument? If there are, how should the speaker deal with them?

Upon hearing this, would you be likely to extend this argument and start asking yourself, "Do we now close up all stores that most people don't want?"

Is there a connection between who the owner is and whether the video store should or shouldn't be closed? Could the speaker have effectively used this information in support of the thesis to close the video store?

### Public Speaking Sample Assistant

## A Poorly Constructed Persuasive Speech *(Continued)*

A neighboring store owner says he thinks the store is in violation of several fire laws. He says they have no sprinkler system and no metal doors to prevent the spread of a fire. So, he thinks they should be closed down, too.

What credibility do you ascribe to the "neighboring store owner"? Do you begin to wonder if the speaker would simply agree to have the store brought up to the fire code laws?

Last week on *Oprah* three women were on and they were in the XXX movie business and they were all on drugs and had been in jail and they said it all started when they went into the porno business. One woman wanted to be a teacher, another wanted to be a nurse, and the other wanted to be a beautician. If there weren't any XXX video stores then there wouldn't be a porn business and, you know, pornography is part of organized crime, and so if you stop pornography you take a bite out of crime.

What is the cause and what is the effect that the speaker is asserting? How likely is it that the proposed cause actually produced the effect? Might there have been causes other than working in pornography that might have led these women into drugs? What credibility do you give to people you see on talk shows? Does it vary with the specific talk show? Do you accept the argument that there would be no pornography business without video stores? What would have to be proved to you before you accepted this connection? How do you respond to the expression "Take a bite out of crime"?

One of the reasons I think it should be closed is that the legitimate video stores—the ones that have only a small selection of XXX movies somewhere in the back—will lose business. And if they continue to lose business, they'll leave the neighborhood and we'll have no video stores.

Is the speaker implying that this is the real reason against XXX video stores? Do you start wondering if the speaker is against XXX video stores—as it seemed in the last argument—or only against stores that sell XXX material exclusively? What effect does this impression have on your evaluation of the speaker's credibility and the speaker's thesis?

That's a lot of reasons against XXX movie houses. I have a quote here: Reason is "a portion of the divine spirit set in a human body." Seneca.

How do you feel about the number of "reasons"? Would you have preferred fewer reasons or reasons more fully developed or more reasons? What purpose does this quotation serve?

In conclusion and to wrap it up and close my speech, I want to repeat and say again that the XXX video stores should all be closed down. They corrupt minors. And they're offensive to men and women and especially women. I hope you'll all protest with the Marshalls—my mother and father—and there'll be lots of others there too.

Might the speaker have introduced this conclusion differently? What is the speaker's thesis now? What do you think of the arguments that XXX video stores are offensive? What is the effect of this argument's being introduced here in the conclusion? Do you think you'd go to the protest? Why or why not?

### Door-in-the-Face Technique

With the **door-in-the-face technique**, the opposite of foot-in-the-door, you first make a large request that you know will be refused and then follow it with a more moderate request. For example, your large request might be "We're asking people to donate $100 for new school computers." When this is refused, you make a more moderate request, the one you really want your listeners to comply with (for example, "Might you be willing to contribute $10?"). In changing from the large to the more moderate request, you demonstrate your willingness to compromise and your sensitivity to your listeners. The general idea here is that your listeners will feel that since you've made concessions, they should also make concessions and at least contribute something. Listeners will probably also feel that $10 is actually quite a small amount considering the initial request and are more likely to donate the $10 (Cialdini, 1984; Cialdini & Ascani, 1976).

### Identify with Your Audience

If you can show your audience that you and they share important attitudes, beliefs, and values you'll clearly advance your persuasive goal. Other similarities are also important in **identification**. For example, in some cases similarity of cultural, educational, or social background may help you identify yourself with your audience. Be aware, however, that insincere or dishonest identification is likely to backfire and create problems for the speaker. So avoid even implying similarities between yourself and your audience that don't exist.

Similarly, as a general rule, never ask the audience to do what you have not done yourself. So demonstrate your own willingness to do what you want the audience to do. If you don't, the audience will rightfully ask, "Why haven't *you* done it?" In addition to making it clear that you have done what you want your listeners to do, show them that you're happy about it. Tell them of the satisfaction you have derived from, for example, donating blood or reading to students with visual difficulties.

## Use Logical Appeals

Logical, emotional, and credibility appeals are all effective tools in persuasion, and we will examine all three. However, it is persuasion from logical argument that proves to be the most effective. When the speaker persuades listeners with **logic**, the listeners are more likely to remain persuaded over time and are more likely to resist counterarguments that may come up in the future (Petty & Wegener, 1998). Let's look at three kinds of reasoning that you can use in logical appeals.

### Reasoning from Specific Instances and Generalizations

In **reasoning from specific instances** (or examples), you examine several specific instances and then arrive at a generalization about the whole. This form of reasoning, known as induction, is useful when you want to develop a general principle or conclusion but cannot examine the whole. For example, you sample a few communication courses and conclude something about communication courses in general; you visit several Scandinavian cities and conclude something about the whole of Scandinavia. Critically analyze reasoning from specific instances by asking the following questions.

*Were enough specific instances examined?* Two general guidelines may help you decide how many instances are enough. First, the larger the group you wish covered by your conclusion, the greater the number of specific instances you should examine. If you wished to draw conclusions about members of an entire country or culture, you'd have to examine a considerable number of people before drawing even tentative conclusions. On the other hand, if you were attempting to draw a conclusion about a bushel of apples, sampling a few apples probably would be sufficient.

Second, the greater the diversity of items in the class, the more specific instances you will have to examine. Some classes or groups of items are relatively homogeneous, whereas others are more heterogeneous; this will influence how many specific instances constitute a sufficient number. Pieces of spaghetti in boiling water are all about the same; thus, sampling one usually tells you something about all the others. On the other hand, communication courses probably differ widely, so valid conclusions about communication courses as a group will require a much larger sample.

*Are there significant exceptions?* When you examine specific instances and attempt to draw a conclusion about the whole, take into consideration the exceptions. Thus, if you examine the GPA of computer science majors and discover that 70 percent have GPAs above 3.5, you may be tempted to draw the conclusion that computer science majors are especially bright. But what about the 30 percent who have lower GPAs? How much lower are these scores? This may be a significant exception that you'll need to take into account and may require you to qualify your conclusion in significant ways. Exactly how many exceptions will constitute "significant exceptions" will depend on the unique situation.

### Reasoning from Causes and Effects

In **reasoning from causes and effects**, you may go in either of two directions. You may reason from cause to effect (from observed cause to unobserved effect) or from effect to cause (from observed effect to unobserved cause). In testing reasoning from cause to effect or from effect to cause, ask yourself the following questions.

*Might other causes be producing the observed effect?* If you observe a particular effect (say, high crime or student apathy), you need to ask if causes other than the one you're postulating might be producing these effects. For example, you might postulate that poverty leads to high crime, but there might be other factors actually causing the high crime rate. Or poverty might be one cause, but it might not be the most important cause. Therefore, explore the possibility of other causes' producing the observed effects.

*Is the causal direction accurate?* If two things occur together, it's often difficult to determine which is the cause and which is the effect. For example, a lack of interpersonal intimacy and a lack of self-confidence are often seen in the same person. The person who lacks self-confidence seldom has intimate relationships with others. But which is the cause and which is the effect? It might be that the lack of intimacy "causes" low self-confidence; it might also be, however, that low self-confidence "causes" a lack of intimacy. Of course, it might also be that some other cause (a history of negative criticism, for example) might be producing both the lack of intimacy and the low self-confidence.

## Reasoning from Sign

**Reasoning from sign** involves drawing a conclusion on the basis of the presence of signs because they frequently occur together. Medical diagnosis is a good example of reasoning by sign. The general procedure is simple. If a sign and an object, event, or condition are frequently paired, the presence of the sign is taken as proof of the presence of the object, event, or condition. For example, fatigue, extreme thirst, and overeating are signs of hyperthyroidism, because they frequently accompany the condition. In reasoning from sign, ask yourself these questions.

*Do the signs necessitate the conclusion drawn?* Given fatigue, extreme thirst, and overeating, how certain can you be of the "hyperthyroid" conclusion? With most medical and legal matters we can never be absolutely certain, but we can be certain beyond a reasonable doubt.

*Are there other signs that point to the same conclusion?* In the thyroid example, the extreme thirst could have been brought on by any number of factors. Similarly, the fatigue and the overeating could have been attributed to other causes. Yet, taken together they seemed to point to only one reasonable diagnosis. Generally, the more signs that point toward the conclusion, the more confidence you can have that it's valid.

*Are there contradictory signs?* Are there signs pointing toward contradictory conclusions? For example, if the butler had a motive and a history of violence (signs supporting the conclusion that the butler was the murderer), but also had an alibi (a sign pointing to the conclusion of innocence), then the conclusion of guilt would have to be reconsidered or discarded.

## Fallacies in Reasoning

Another useful way to approach logical appeals is to become aware of various fallacies you'll want to avoid in your own reasoning and will want to identify in the speeches you hear. Here are 10 such fallacies along with some examples (Lee & Lee 1972, 1995; Pratkanis & Aronson, 1991; Herrick, 2004). As you read these, try to think of examples you've heard or read recently.

- *Anecdotal evidence:* Often you'll hear people use anecdotes to "prove" a point: "Women are like that; I have three sisters" or "That's the way Japanese managers are; I've seen plenty of them." One reason **anecdotal evidence** is inadequate is that it relies on too few observations; it's usually a clear case of overgeneralizing on the basis of too little evidence. A second reason is that one person's observations may be unduly clouded by his or her own attitudes and beliefs; your attitudes toward women or the Japanese, for example, may influence your perception of their behaviors.

- *Straw man:* A **straw man** argument (like a man made of straw) is an argument that's set up merely to be knocked down. In this fallacy a speaker creates an easy-to-destroy oversimplification or distortion of the opposing position (that is, a "straw man") and then proceeds to demolish it. But, of course, if the opposing case were presented fairly and without bias, it wouldn't be so easy to destroy.

- *Appeal to tradition:* Speakers often argue against change by using **appeals to tradition**—that is, by claiming that something is wrong or some change should not be adopted because it was never done before. But, of course, not all tradition is good; in addition, the fact that something has not been done before says nothing about its value or whether it should be done now.

- *Bandwagon:* **Bandwagon** appeals, often referred to as appeals *ad populum* (appeals to the people), attempt to persuade the audience to accept or reject an idea or proposal because "everybody's doing it" or because the "right" people support it. The speaker tries to suggest that you should jump on this large and popular bandwagon—or be left out by yourself. This is a popular technique in political elections, in which campaigns use results of polls to get undecided voters to jump on candidates' bandwagons. After all, you don't want to vote for a loser. Fortunately, mindfulness, discussed in Unit 7, is a good defense against bandwagon appeals (Fiol & O'Connor, 2003).

- *Testimonial:* The **testimonial** technique involves using the image associated with some person to gain your approval (if you respect the person) or your rejection (if you don't respect the person). This is the technique of advertisers who use people dressed up to look like doctors or plumbers or chefs to sell their products. Sometimes testimonial appeals cite only vague and general "authorities," as in "Experts agree," "Scientists say," "Good cooks know," or "Dentists advise."

- *Transfer:* In **transfer** appeals the speaker associates her or his idea with something you respect (to gain your approval) or with something you detest (to gain your rejection). For example, a speaker might characterize a proposal for condom distribution in schools as "saving our children from AIDS" (to encourage acceptance) or as "promoting sexual promiscuity" (to encourage disapproval). Sports car manufacturers try to get you to buy their cars by associating them with high status and sex appeal; exercise clubs and diet plans suggest associations with health, self-confidence, and interpersonal appeal.

■ *Plain folks:* Using the **plain folks** approach, the speaker identifies himself or herself with the audience. The speaker is good—the "reasoning" goes—because he or she is one of the people, just "plain folks" like everyone else. Of course, the speaker who presents himself or herself as one of the plain folks is often not. And even if he or she is one of the plain folks, it has nothing to do with the issue under discussion.

■ *Card stacking:* In **card stacking** the speaker selects only the evidence and arguments that support his or her case and may even falsify evidence or distort facts to better fit the case. Despite these misrepresentations, the speaker presents the supporting materials as "fair" and "impartial."

■ *Thin entering wedge:* In another type of pseudo-argument, a speaker argues against a position on the grounds that it is a **thin entering wedge** that will open the floodgates to all sorts of catastrophes (Chase, 1956). People have used this argument throughout history to argue against change—contending, for example, that school integration and interracial marriage are just the start of the collapse of American education and society, same-sex marriage will destroy the family, computers will lead to mass unemployment, and banning smoking in public places will lead to the collapse of the restaurant industry.

■ *Agenda setting:* In **agenda setting** a speaker indicates that X is the issue and that all others are unimportant and insignificant. This kind of fallacious appeal is heard frequently: "Balancing the budget is the key to the city's survival," or "There's only one issue confronting elementary education in our largest cities, and that is violence." In almost all situations, however, there are many issues and many sides to each issue. Often the person proclaiming that X is the issue really means, "I'll be able to persuade you if you focus solely on X and ignore the other issues."

## Use Emotional Appeals

**Emotional appeals**—appeals to feelings, needs, desires, and wants—can be powerful means of persuasion (Wood, 2000). When you use motivational appeals, you appeal to those forces that energize, move, or motivate people to develop, change, or strengthen their attitudes or ways of behaving. For

example, one motive might be the desire for status. This desire might motivate you to enter a high-status occupation or to dress a certain way.

Developed more than 30 years ago, one of the most useful analyses of motives remains Abraham Maslow's fivefold **hierarchy of needs**, reproduced in Figure 18.2 (Bailey & Pownell, 1998; Kiel, 1999; Maslow, 1970). The theory proposes that you seek to fulfill the needs at the lowest level first and that only when those needs are satisfied do the needs at the next level begin to exert influence on your behavior. For example, you would not concern yourself with the need for security or freedom from fear if you were starving (if your need for food had not been met). Similarly, you would not be concerned with friendship if your need for protection and security had not been fulfilled. The implication for you as a speaker is that you have to know what needs of your audience are unsatisfied. These are the needs you can appeal to in motivating them. Let's look in detail at Maslow's model.

### Physiological Needs

In many parts of the world, and even in parts of the United States, the physiological needs of the people are not fully met and thus, as you can appreciate, are powerful motivating forces. Lech Walesa, former leader of the Polish Solidarity Party, recognized this when he wrote: "He who gives food to the people will win." In many of the poorest countries of the world, the speaker who promises to meet these basic physiological needs is the one the people will follow. Most college students in the United States, however, have their physiological needs for food, water, and air well satisfied—so these needs will not help motivate them. People who already have sufficient food won't be motivated to get more.

### Safety Needs

Those who do not have their basic safety and freedom-from-fear needs met will be motivated by appeals to security, protection, and freedom from physical and psychological distress. You see appeals to this need in advertisements for burglar protection devices for home and car, in political speeches promising greater police protection on the streets and in schools, and in speeches by motivational gurus who promise psychological safety and freedom from anxiety. This freedom from anxiety also seems to be the motive used in the advertisements of psychic services that promise to tell you what is really going on (with, say, your romantic partner) as well as what will happen in the future. With this information, they imply, you'll be free of the anxiety that a lack of knowledge brings. You'll also learn what you

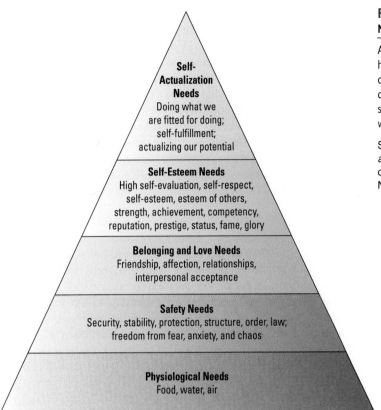

**FIGURE 18.2** Maslow's "Hierarchy of Needs"

Abraham Maslow's model of lower-order and higher-order needs has long influenced theories of persuasion. As you read about these needs, consider which would work best with your specific class members. Are there some that would not work, at least generally?

Source: Maslow & Frager (1987). *Motivation and Personality*, 3rd ed. Adapted by permission of Pearson Education, Inc. Upper Saddle River, New Jersey.

should do—break off your relationship, move to the West Coast, or take that new job. The fact that this information is totally without any factual basis seems not to deter people from spending millions of dollars on psychics.

Sometimes the safety motive takes the form of a desire for order, structure, and organization—motives seen clearly in the advertisements for personal data assistants like the Blackberry, cell phones, and information management software. Many people fear what is unknown, and order and structure make things predictable and, hence, safe.

## Belonging and Love Needs

Belonging and love needs are extremely powerful and comprise a variety of specific motives. For example, most people are motivated to love and be loved. For most persons, love and its pursuit occupy a considerable amount of time and energy. If you can teach your audience how to be loved and how to love, you'll have not only an attentive audience but a grateful one as well.

We also want affiliation—friendship and companionship. We want to be a part of a group, despite our equally potent desire for independence and individuality. Notice how advertisements for singles clubs, cruises, and dating services appeal to this need for affiliation. On this basis alone they successfully gain the attention, interest, and participation of countless people. Again, such affiliation seems to assure us that we are in fact worthy creatures. If we have friends and companions, surely we are people of some merit.

## Self-Esteem Needs

"In his private heart," wrote Mark Twain, "no man much respects himself." And perhaps because of this, we need to develop a positive self-image, to see ourselves in the best possible light. We want to see ourselves as self-confident, worthy, and contributing human beings. Inspirational speeches, speeches of the "you're the greatest" type, never seem to lack receptive and suggestible audiences.

Self-esteem comes, at least in part, from the approval of others (something that is important in all cultures but especially in collectivist cultures). Most people are concerned with peer approval but also want approval from family, teachers, elders, and even children. The approval of others contributes to positive self-esteem. Approval from others also ensures the attainment of related goals. For example, if you have peer approval, you probably also have influence. If you have approval, you're likely to have status. But in relating your propositions to your audience's desire for approval, avoid being too obvious. Few people want to be told that they need or desire approval.

People also want power, control, and influence. They want to have power over their own lives—to be in control of their own destiny, to be responsible for their own successes. As Emerson put it, "Can anything be so elegant as to have few wants, and to serve them one's self?"

Many people also want to have power over other persons, to be influential. Similarly, they may want to increase control over the environment and over events and things in the world. Because of this you'll motivate your listeners when you make them see that they can increase their power, control, and influence as a result of their learning what you have to say or doing as you suggest.

People want to achieve in whatever they do. As a student you want to be a successful student. You also want to achieve as a friend, as a parent, as a lover. This is why books and speeches that purport to tell people how to be better achievers are so successful. At the same time, of course, you also want others to recognize your achievements as real and valuable. In using the achievement motive, be explicit in stating how your speech, ideas, and recommendations will contribute to the listeners' achievements. At the same time, recognize that different cultures will view achievement very differently. To some achievement may mean financial success; to others, group popularity; to still others, security.

Show your audience how what you have to say will help them achieve these goals, and you'll likely have an active and receptive audience.

Although they often deny it, most people are motivated to some extent by the desire for financial gain—for what money can buy, for what it can do. Concerns for lower taxes, for higher salaries, and for fringe benefits are all related to the money motive. Show the audience that what you're saying or advocating will make them money, and they'll listen with considerable interest—much as they read the get-rich-quick books that flood the bookstores.

## Self-Actualization Needs

The self-actualization motive, according to Maslow (1970), influences attitudes and behaviors only after all other needs are satisfied. And because these other needs are very rarely all satisfied, the time a speaker might spend appealing to self-actualization might be better spent on other motives. And yet it seems that, regardless of how satisfied or unsatisfied your other desires are, you have a desire to self-actualize, to become what you feel you're fit for. If you see yourself as a poet, you must write poetry. If you see yourself as a teacher, you must teach. Even if you don't pursue these as occupations, you nevertheless have a desire to write poetry or to teach. Appeals to self-actualization—"to be the best you can be"—encourage listeners to strive for their highest ideals and often are welcomed by the audience.

# REFLECTIONS ON ETHICS

## The Ethics of Emotional Appeals

Emotional appeals are all around. Persons who want to restrict the media's portrayal of violence may appeal to your fear of increased violence in your community; the real estate broker may appeal to your desire for status; the friend who wants a favor may appeal to your desire for social approval; the salesperson may appeal to your desire for sexual rewards. But are such appeals ethical?

Most communication theorists would argue that emotional appeals are ethical when, for example, they are used in combination with logical appeals, used in moderation, and directed at our better selves. Emotional appeals are considered unethical when, for example, they're used instead of logical evidence, directed at our baser selves, or aimed at children. In actual practice,

however, it's often difficult to distinguish between the ethical and unethical use of emotional appeals.

### Ethical Choice Point

*You want to dissuade your teenaged sons and daughters from engaging in sexual relationships. Would it be ethical to use emotional appeals to scare them so that they'll avoid sexual relationships? Would it be ethical to use the same appeals to get them to avoid associating with teens of other races? What ethical obligations do you have in using emotional appeals in these situations? What would you do?*

## Use Credibility Appeals

Your **credibility** is the degree to which your audience sees you as a believable spokesperson. If your listeners see you as competent and knowledgeable, of good character, and charismatic or dynamic, they will think you credible. As a result, you'll be more effective in changing their attitudes or in moving them to do something. Credibility is not something you have or don't have in any objective sense; rather, it's what the audience thinks of you.

What makes a person credible will vary from one culture to another. In some cultures, people would claim that competence is the most important factor in, say, the choice of a teacher for their preschool children. In other cultures, the most important factor might be the goodness or morality of the teacher or perhaps the reputation of the teacher's family.

At the same time, each culture may define each of the characteristics of credibility differently. For example, in defining "character" some cultures may emphasize the rules of a specific religion, whereas others may stress the individual conscience. The

### INTRODUCING CREDIBILITY

You need a brief introduction (about 1 minute in length or about 150 words) about yourself for someone else to use to introduce you and your next speech. You want to use this introduction to establish your competence, character, and charisma.

WHAT DO YOU SAY?

---

**Theory and Research**  **Credibility Impressions**

**UNDERSTANDING**

You form a credibility impression of a speaker on the basis of two sources of information. First, you assess the reputation of the speaker as you know it. This is initial—or what theorists call "extrinsic"—credibility. Second, you evaluate the degree to which that reputation is confirmed or refuted by what the speaker says and does during the speech. This is derived—or "intrinsic"—credibility. In other words, you merge what you know about the speaker's reputation with the more immediate information you get from present interactions in order to form a combined final assessment of credibility.

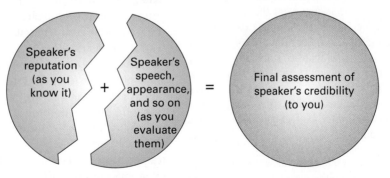

#### Working with Theories and Research

*Does this model adequately explain how you form credibility impressions of others? Can you derive from this model any practical advice for increasing your own credibility?*

Quran, the Torah, and the New Testament, for example, will all have very different levels of credibility ascribed to them depending on the religious beliefs of the audience. And this will be true even when all three religious books say essentially the same thing.

Before reading any further about the ways to establish your credibility, you may wish to take the self-test "How Credible Are You?"

## TEST YOURSELF

### How Credible Are You?

Respond to each of the following phrases to indicate how you think members of your class see you when you deliver a public speech. Use the following scale: Definitely true = 5; probably true = 4; neither true nor untrue = 3; probably untrue = 2; and definitely untrue = 1.

_____ **1.** Knowledgeable about the subject matter

_____ **2.** Experienced

_____ **3.** Informed about the subject matter

_____ **4.** Fair in the presentation of material (evidence and argument)

_____ **5.** Concerned with the audience's needs

_____ **6.** Consistent over time on the issues addressed in the speech

_____ **7.** Assertive in personal style

_____ **8.** Enthusiastic about the topic and in general

_____ **9.** Active rather than passive

**HOW DID YOU DO?** This test focuses on the three qualities of credibility—competence, character, and charisma—and is based on a large body of research (for example, McCroskey, 1997; Riggio, 1987). Items 1 to 3 refer to your perceived competence: How competent or capable does the audience see you when you give a public speech? Items 4 to 6 refer to your perceived character: Does the audience see you as a person of good and moral character? Items 7 to 9 refer to your perceived charisma: Does the audience see you as dynamic and active rather than as static and passive? Scores will range from a high of 45 to a low of 9. If you scored relatively high (say around 32 or higher), then you feel your audience sees you as credible. If you scored relatively low (say below 27), then you feel your audience sees you as lacking in credibility.

**WHAT WILL YOU DO?** Think about how you might go about increasing your credibility. What specific steps can you take to change any audience perception with which you may be unhappy? Are there specific things you can do to strengthen your competence, character, and charisma? A good source to consult is Ronald Riggio's 1987 book *The Charisma Quotient* (New York: Dodd, Mead).

## Competence

**Competence** includes both knowledge and expertise. The more knowledge and expertise the audience sees you as having, the more likely the audience will believe you. Similarly, you're likely to believe a teacher or doctor if you think he or she is knowledgeable on the subject. You can demonstrate your competence to your audience in a variety of ways.

**Tell Listeners of Your Competence.** Let the audience know of any special experience or training that qualifies you to speak on this specific topic. If you're speaking on communal living and you've lived on a commune yourself, then say so in your speech. Tell the audience of your unique and personal experiences when these contribute to your credibility.

This recommendation to tell listeners of your competence generally applies to most audiences you'll encounter in the United States. But in some cultures—notably collectivist cultures such as those of Japan, China, and Korea, for example—stressing your own competence or that of your corporation may be taken to mean that your audience members are inferior or that their corporations are not as good as yours. In other cultures—notably individualist cultures such as those of Scandinavia, the United States, and western Europe, for example—if you don't stress your competence, your listeners may assume it's because you don't have any.

**Cite a Variety of Research Sources.** Make it clear to your audience that you've thoroughly researched your topic. Do this by mentioning some of the books you've read, the persons you've interviewed, the articles you've consulted. Weave these throughout your speech. Don't bunch them together at one time.

**Stress the Competencies of Your Sources.** If your audience isn't aware of them, then emphasize the particular competencies of your sources. In this way, it becomes clear to the audience that you've chosen your sources carefully and with a view toward providing the most authoritative sources possible. For example, saying simply, "Senator Cardova thinks . . ." does nothing to establish the senator's credibility. Instead, consider saying something like "Senator Cardova, who headed the finance committee for three years and was formerly a professor of economics at MIT, thinks. . . ."

## Character

An audience will see you as credible if they perceive you as having high moral **character**: as someone who is honest and someone they can trust. When an audience perceives your intentions as

## ESTABLISHING CREDIBILITY

You're planning a speech on baseball. The problem is that you're a woman and this audience is not going to perceive you as credible, despite your knowing more about baseball that any other person in the room.

WHAT DO YOU SAY?

good for them (rather than for your own personal gain), they'll think you credible and they'll believe you. You can establish your high moral character in several ways.

**Stress Fairness.** In your persuasive speech, show your fairness; stress that you've examined both sides of the issue (if indeed you have). If you're presenting both sides, then make it clear that your presentation is accurate and fair. Be particularly careful not to omit any argument the audience may already have thought of—this is a sure sign that your presentation isn't fair and balanced. Tell the audience that you would not advocate a position if you did not base it on a fair evaluation of the issues.

**Stress Concern for Audience.** Make it clear to the audience that you're interested in their welfare rather than seeking self-gain. If the audience feels that you're "out for yourself," they'll justifiably downgrade your credibility. Make it clear that the audience's interests are foremost in your mind. Tell your audience how the new legislation will reduce *their* taxes, how recycling will improve *their* community, how a knowledge of sexual harassment will make *their* workplace more comfortable and stress free.

**Stress Concern for Enduring Values.** We view speakers who are concerned with small and insignif-

icant issues as less credible than speakers who demonstrate a concern for lasting truths and general principles. Thus, make it clear to the audience that your position—your thesis—is related to higher-order values; show them exactly how this is true.

## Charisma

**Charisma** is a combination of your personality and dynamism as seen by the audience. An audience will perceive you as credible (and believable) if they like you, and if they see you as friendly and pleasant rather than aloof and reserved. Similarly, audiences favor the dynamic speaker over the hesitant, nonassertive individual. They'll perceive you as less credible if they see you as shy, introverted, and soft-spoken rather than as extroverted and forceful. Perhaps people feel that dynamic speakers are open and honest in presenting themselves, whereas shy, introverted individuals may be hiding something. As a speaker there's much that you can do to increase your charisma and hence your perceived credibility.

**Demonstrate a Positive Outlook.** Show the audience that you have a positive orientation to the public speaking situation and to the entire speaker-audience encounter. We see positive and forward-looking people as more credible than negative and backward-looking people. Stress your pleasure at addressing the audience. Stress hope rather than despair; stress happiness rather than sadness.

**Demonstrate Enthusiasm.** The lethargic speaker who somehow plods through the speech is the very opposite of the charismatic speaker. Try viewing a film of Martin Luther King Jr. or Billy Graham speaking—they're totally absorbed with the speech and with the audience. They're excellent examples of the enthusiasm that makes a charismatic speaker.

**Be Emphatic.** Use language that is emphatic rather than colorless and indecisive. Use gestures that are clear and decisive rather than random and hesitant.

Demonstrate a firm commitment to the position you're advocating; the audience will be much more likely to agree with a speaker who believes firmly in the thesis of the speech.

## Credibility Errors

Some speakers try to raise their own credibility by unfairly attacking another's character. For example, here are three types of such attacks. You'll want to avoid using these tactics as a speaker, and you'll want to be alert for these tactics as you listen to others (Lee & Lee, 1972, 1995; Pratkanis & Aronson, 1991; Herrick, 2004).

■ *Personal interest:* **Personal interest** attacks may take either of two forms. In one form, the

# THE RESEARCHER

## Age and Credibility

*I'm a returning student and the oldest (by about 30 years) in the class. The other students seem to regard my views as outdated even before I've explained them, and I fear it's due to my being from their parents' generation. What can I do to enhance my credibility with my classmates and with younger people generally?*

College classrooms in the United States are age-segregated environments. The great majority of students are between 18 and 28 and don't expect to find students from a different age group in the classroom. Therefore, numerous age-related stereotypes will exist. The good news is that time and positive interactions can change these often negative stereotypes. First, it's important to accept that you'll be perceived as significantly different from your younger classmates. Second, it's important to realize that your life experiences, learning styles, cultural likes and dislikes, and responsibilities outside the classroom will not be similar to those of the other students. But these differences can be turned into positives. Listen to the younger students, empathize with their life issues, engage their concerns, accommodate to their styles of interaction, and find interactive strategies that are far from aggressive and "all-knowing." As the course progresses, the negative stereotypes that are evident at initial encounters will disappear, and your credibility as a student will increase.

For further information: Nussbaum, J. F., Thompson, T. L., & Robinson, J. D. (2000). *Communication and aging* (2nd ed.). Mahwah, NJ: Erlbaum. And Baringer, D. K., Kundrat, A. L., & Nussbaum, J. F. (2004). Instructional communication and older adults. In J. F. Nussbaum & J. Coupland (Eds.), *Handbook of communication and aging research* (2nd ed., pp. 543–562). Mahwah, NJ: Erlbaum.

**Jon F. Nussbaum** (Ph.D., Purdue University) is a professor of communication arts and sciences and human development and family studies at Pennsylvania State University. He conducts research and teaches courses on the communicative world of older adults across numerous social contexts. He has recently been elected president of the International Communication Association.

speaker disqualifies someone because he or she isn't directly affected by the issue or doesn't have firsthand knowledge, as would be the case if a speaker dismissed an argument on abortion because it was made by a man. In another form, the speaker disqualifies someone because he or she will benefit in some way from a proposal. But arguing that, for example, someone is rich, middle class, or poor and thus will benefit from a proposed tax cut does not mean that the tax cut proposal is invalid. The legitimacy of an argument can never depend on the gender (or socioeconomic status or culture) of its proponents. Nor can it depend on any gain that a person may derive from the position advocated. The legitimacy of an argument can be judged only on the basis of the evidence and reasoning presented.

■ *Character attacks:* **Character attacks**, often referred to as ad hominem attacks, involve accusing another person (usually an opponent) of some serious wrongdoing or of some serious character flaw. The purpose of this kind of fallacious appeal is to discredit the person or to divert attention from the issue under discussion. Remarks such as "How can we support a candidate who has smoked pot (or avoided the military)?" or "Do you want to believe someone who has been unfaithful on more than one occasion?" are often heard in political discussions but probably have little to do with the logic of the argument.

■ *Name calling:* In **name calling**, often referred to as "poisoning the well," the speaker calls an idea, a group of people, or a political philosophy a bad name ("atheist," "anti-American") to try to get listeners to condemn the idea without analyzing the argument and evidence. The opposite of name calling is the use of the **glittering generality**, in which the speaker tries to make listeners accept some idea by associating it with things they value highly ("democracy," "free speech," "academic freedom"). By using such "virtue words," the speaker tries to lead listeners to ignore the evidence and simply approve of the idea.

---

## Building Communication Skills — Finding the Available Means of Persuasion

What persuasive strategies would you use to convince your class of the validity of either side in any of the following points of view? For example, what persuasive strategies would you use to persuade your class members that interracial adoption should be encouraged? What strategies would you use to persuade them that interracial adoption should be discouraged?

1. *Point of View: Interracial Adoption.* Those in favor of interracial adoption argue that adoption (regardless of race) is good for the child and that the welfare of the child—who might not get adopted if not by someone of another race—must be considered first. Those opposed to interracial adoption argue that children need to be raised in a family of the same race if the child is to develop self-esteem and become a functioning member of his or her own ethnic group.

2. *Point of View: Same-Sex Marriage.* Those in favor of same-sex marriage argue that gay men and lesbians should be accorded exactly the same rights and responsibilities as heterosexuals—no more, no less. Those opposed argue that same-sex marriage will undermine the concept of marriage.

3. *Point of View: Affirmative Action.* Those in favor of affirmative action argue that because of injustices in the way certain groups (racial, national, gender) were treated, they should now be given preferential treatment to correct the imbalance caused by the earlier social injustices. Those opposed argue that merit must be the sole criterion for promotion, jobs, entrance to graduate schools, and so on, and that affirmative action is just reverse discrimination.

*Working with a variety of persuasive strategies will increase your public speaking competence as both speaker and listener.*

## Motivate Your Listeners

If you want to persuade your listeners, you have to motivate them to believe or to act in some way. One way to motivate, as explained in Unit 15, is to use the *motivated sequence*: Gain your audience's attention, demonstrate that a need exists, demonstrate how that need can be satisfied when they believe or do what you say, show them what things will be like once the need is satisfied, and urge them to do something to solve the problem.

Table 18.1 summarizes the motivated sequence as a persuasive strategy and will help you develop your persuasive speeches, whether they deal with questions of fact, value, or policy—the topics to which we now turn.

## PERSUASIVE SPEECHES ON QUESTIONS OF FACT

**Questions of fact** concern what is or is not true, what does or does not exist, what did or did not happen. Some questions of fact are easily answered. These include many academic questions you're familiar with: Who was Aristotle? How many people use the Internet to get news? When was the first satellite launched? Questions of fact also include more mundane questions like: What's on television? When is the meeting? What's Jenny's e-mail address? You can easily find answers to these questions by looking at some reference book, finding the relevant website, or asking someone who knows the answer.

The questions of fact that we deal with in persuasive speeches are a bit different. Although these questions also have answers, the answers are not that easy to find and in fact may never be found. The questions concern controversial issues for which different people have different answers. Daily newspapers and Internet websites abound in questions of fact. For example, on July 21, 2007, Google News (www.googlenews.com) contained articles suggesting such questions of fact as these: Is Iran supporting the militias in Iraq? Did Attorney General Alberto Gonzales pressure then-Attorney General John Ashcroft to recertify President Bush's domestic surveillance program? Has North Korea complied with its promise to dismantle its nuclear plant? Is National Basketball referee Tim Donaghy guilty of betting on the games and providing information to others? Will no-smoking rules save lives? Did FEMA fail in New Orleans? Are the courts in the United States being politicized? Is human activity altering the world's rainfall patterns? Is Apple's iPhone vulnerable to hackers?

## Thesis

For a persuasive speech on a question of fact, you'll formulate a thesis on the basis of a factual statement such as:

- This company has a glass ceiling for women.
- The plaintiff was slandered (or libeled or defamed).
- The death was a case of physician-assisted suicide.
- Gay men and lesbians make competent military personnel.
- Television violence leads to violent behavior in viewers.

## Table 18.1 The Motivated Sequence as a Persuasive Strategy

| Step | Purpose | Audience Question Speaker Should Answer | Audience Response You Want to Avoid |
|------|---------|------------------------------------------|-------------------------------------|
| Attention | Focus listeners' attention on you and your message. | Why should I listen? Why should I use my time listening? | This is boring. This is irrelevant. This is of no interest to me. |
| Need | Demonstrate that there is a problem that affects them. | Why do I need to know or do anything? | I don't need to hear this. Things are fine now. This won't benefit me. |
| Satisfaction | Show listeners how they can satisfy the need (solve the problem). | Can I do anything about this? | I really can't do anything. It's beyond my control. |
| Visualization | Show listeners what their lives will be like with the need satisfied. | How would anything be different or improved? | I can't see how anything would be different. Nothing's going to change. |
| Action | Urge listeners to do something to solve the problem. | What can I do to effect this change? | I can't do anything. I'll be wasting my time and energy. |

If you were preparing a persuasive speech on the first example given above, you might phrase your thesis as "This company discriminates against women." Whether or not the company does discriminate is a question of fact; clearly the company either does or does not discriminate. Whether you can prove it does discriminate or it doesn't, however, is another issue.

## Main Points

Once you've formulated your thesis, you can generate your main points by asking the simple question "How do you know this?" or "Why would you believe this is true (factual)?" The answers to one of these questions will enable you to develop your main points. The essential components of your speech might then look something like this:

**General purpose:** To persuade.

**Specific purpose:** To persuade my listeners that this company discriminates against women.

**Thesis:** This company discriminates against women. (How can we tell that this company discriminates against women?)

  **I.** Women earn less than men.
  **II.** Women are hired less often than men.
  **III.** Women occupy fewer managerial positions than men.

Make sure that you clearly connect your main points to your thesis in your introduction, when introducing each of the points, and again in your summary. Don't allow the audience to forget that the lower salaries that women earn directly supports the thesis that this company discriminates against women.

## Support

Having identified your main points, begin searching for information to support them. Taking the first point, you might develop it something like this:

  **I.** Women earn less than men.
    **A.** Over the past five years, the average salary for editorial assistants was $6,000 less for women than it was for men.
    **B.** Over the past five years, the entry-level salaries for women averaged $4,500 less than the entry-level salaries for men.
    **C.** Over the past five years, the bonuses earned by women were 20 percent below the bonuses earned by men.

The above speech focuses entirely on a question of fact; the thesis itself is a question of fact. In other speeches, however, you may want just one of your main points to center on a question of fact. So, for example, let's say you're giving a speech advocating that the military give gay men and lesbians full equality. In this case, one of your points might focus on a question of fact: You might seek to establish that gay men and lesbians make competent military personnel. Once you've established that, you'd then be in a better position to argue for equality in military policy.

In a speech on questions of fact, you want to emphasize logical proof. Facts are your best support. The more facts you have, the more persuasive you'll be in dealing with questions of fact. For example, the

| Ideal Audience Response | Speech Materials to Use | Cautions to Observe |
|---|---|---|
| This sounds interesting. Tell me more. | Attention-gaining materials, pages 349–350. | Make attention relevant to speech topic. |
| OK, I understand; there's a problem. | Supporting materials (examples, statistics, testimony), pages 329–344. | Don't overdramatize the need. |
| I can change things. | Supporting materials, pages 329–344; logical, emotional, and credibility appeals, pages 416–425. | Answer any objections listeners might have to your plan. |
| Wow! Things look a lot better this way. | Emotional appeals, pages 418–420. Illustrations and language high in imagery, pages 368–369). | Be realistic; don't visualize the world as perfect once your listeners do as you suggest. |
| Let me sign up. Here's my contribution. I'll participate in the effort. | Emotional appeals, pages 418–420. Specific language, pages 366–368. | Be specific. Ask for small attitude changes and easily performed behaviors. |

more evidence you can find that women earn less than men, the more convincing you will be in proving that women do in fact earn less and, ultimately, that women are discriminated against.

Use the most recent materials possible. The more recent your materials, the more relevant they will be to the present time and the more persuasive they're likely to be. Notice, in our example, that if you said that in 1980 women earned on average $13,000 less than men, that fact would be meaningless in relation to the question of whether the company discriminates against women *now*.

## Organization

Speeches on questions of fact probably fit most readily into a topical organizational pattern, in which each reason for your thesis is given approximately equal weight. Notice, for example, that the outline of the speech under "Main Points" uses a topic order in

**Public Speaking Sample Assistant**    An Excellent Persuasive Speech

### Untitled [False Confessions]

Jessy Ohl

Kansas State University

Coached by Craig Brown, Bobby Imbody, and Erica Imbody

Assuming I don't violate the rules, I get 1,800 words to try and change the way you think and feel about some issue. My goal, in a sense, is to get you to confess that my point of view is the "truth" and to do so in around 10 minutes. But what if I really had no time limit, and could speak for say—20 hours? Twenty hours where you had to listen to me. I'd get to badger you, yell at you, no breaks, no judges' lounge, just 20 hours of me. I'm not that bad to listen to for around 10 minutes, but after 20 hours, you'd be ready to sign whatever petition I put in front of you, or confess to practically any crime just to get me to shut up. And I wouldn't blame you. And neither would Kevin Fox. He cracked after only 14 hours. Kevin Fox wasn't a judge in a seriously overtime speech round. Instead, on December 13, 2004, he was a suspect in the murder of his three-year-old daughter Riley. After 14 straight hours of "aggressive persuasion," as the June 21, 2005, *Chicago Tribune* reported, he confessed. The problem is—he didn't do the crime. Only after DNA evidence surfaced did anyone take seriously his claim that he had been coerced into giving a false confession.

There is a fatal flaw with the U.S. legal system—it's too easy to promote and create false confessions. The *Journal of Psychological Science* of August 2005 found that as many as 1 in 5 faulty convictions are from false confessions. Now, you might think, I'm never even going to be in a position to be arrested, let alone give a false confession. OK, but every time someone else is convicted on the basis of a false confession, that means that you and I are still threatened by the real guilty party. It's time to stop the promotion of and abuse of false confessions. And to do so, in what I promise will take a lot less than 20 hours, we must first examine the damage created by false confessions, sec-

Here the speaker refers to the immediate occasion—the speech contest the speaker is now in—and then relates this situation to the topic of the speech; namely, coerced confessions. After you read the entire speech, return to this introduction and consider in what other ways the speaker might gain audience attention and introduce the topic of the speech.

Here the speaker clearly identifies the thesis: The legal system is flawed because it's too easy to create false confessions. The speaker then reinforces this thesis with the finding from a current article in the *Journal of Psychological Science* that 1 out of 5 confessions may be faulty—a statistic that gains our attention. If you were listening to this speech, would you accept this statistic, or would you want more evidence that this large a number of confessions are in fact false? If you would want additional evidence, what would that look like?

Notice how the speaker makes sure that the listeners understand the importance of this topic to them—the topic is not

> **Public Speaking Sample Assistant**
>
> ## An Excellent Persuasive Speech *(Continued)*

ond, explain why anybody would admit to a crime they didn't commit, and finally, discover solutions to get our legal system back on track.

OK, there are going to be the occasional mistakes. But unfortunately, with false confessions they're more than occasional and they're creating damage throughout the process. The *Denver Post* of April 18, 2006, concludes that gross misjudgments in convictions due to coerced confessions create illegitimacy in all prosecutions. And these occurrences are unfortunately far from rare. So let's first look at the scope and then the damage created. The June 4, 2005, issue of *Psychology Today* finds that although it is nearly impossible to determine the exact number of false confessions nationwide, a 2003 review discovered 247 such instances in a single Illinois county over the past 10 years. The *Baltimore Sun* of April 26, 2005, points out that examples range from the juvenile, to adult, to mentally disabled. But the real damage is what happens to those unjustly convicted and to the public; we think we are being protected. For example, Jon Kogut was sentenced to life in prison in 1985 when he confessed to murder. Mr. Kogut spent 17 years before forensic evidence cleared his name. That "solved case" is now a cold case.

An erroneous and problematic legal system that violates the rights of innocent people puts us in danger. The *Chicago Tribune* of June 18, 2005, claims that the United States' prosecution system is constructed in a way that rushes to conviction. But these hasty decisions are threatening the very fabric of justice. As Dr. Joseph Unekis put it in his 2005 book *People, Problems and Power*, the basic principle of the American legal system is the presumed innocence of the accused. You are innocent until proven guilty, not innocent until forced to confess.

I'm sure by now you're wondering one thing about false confessions. Why would you ever admit to a crime that you didn't commit? But remember, what if I had that 20 hours? How we think an interrogation works isn't what really happens. There are two explanations for false confessions: first, interrogation techniques, and second, human tolerance to persuasion. First, police officers are effectively trained to extract confessions, truthful or not. The *Wall Street Journal* of April 15, 2005, reports that "standard interrogation techniques are masterfully designed to leave people with almost no rational choice but confess." The *Christian Science Monitor* of July 20, 2005, explains that "Police can legally lie to suspects, claiming to have physical evidence or witnesses that don't exist." This explains the *Milwaukee Journal Sentinel*'s November 7, 2004, account of the interrogation of a 14-year-old murder suspect. He was told by police that they had witnesses and if

merely important in the abstract, but it's important to these specific audience members. If you were giving this speech to the members of your class, how would you establish the importance of the topic to them? Put differently, how would you answer their question, "Why should I listen to this speech?"

Here the speaker gives an orientation as to the major ideas to be discussed: the damage created by false confessions (the problem), why anyone would admit to a crime he or she didn't commit (some causes that help create the problem), and the ways to get the legal system back on track (the solution). Might this speech have been organized in another pattern? How might you reorganize this speech into the motivated sequence pattern?

This first point explains the problem the frequency of false confessions and the damage that false confessions do to everyone. As a listener, are you convinced? If not, what would convince you?

Here the speaker provides a transition to the second point, namely why anyone would falsely confess to a crime—a question the speaker already began to answer in the introduction. This transition, as all the transitions in this speech, cue the audience into what will be discussed next. Can you identify places in the speech where additional transitions might have been effective?

This second major idea is itself divided into two parts: interrogation techniques and human tolerance.

The argument that interrogation techniques are responsible for these false confessions is supported by the strength and credibility of the *Wall Street Journal* and the *Christian Science Monitor*, two highly respected newspapers. Would members of your class agree that these are respectable and credible sources of such information?

## An Excellent Persuasive Speech *(Continued)*

he didn't confess, he would be raped in prison and given the chair. After six hours with no parent or lawyer, he did confess. Only later was he found innocent.

The second cause for false confessions is the human tolerance to persuasion. Professor Saul Kassin from Williams College in Massachusetts told the *Wall Street Journal* on April 15, 2005, that under traumatic circumstances an individual will confess in order to ensure survival. Being innocent does not protect you from these limits. An experiment published in the winter 2005 edition of *Justice Denied* concluded that 69 percent of participants in the study signed a false confession that they destroyed a government property when confronted with fictitious evidence of their wrongdoing. Despite popular belief, we can all be coaxed into giving a false confession. Richard Ofshe, a sociology professor at the University of California at Berkeley, explained in *Newsday* of May 24, 2005, "most people believe that the innocent won't falsely confess unless they're tortured," but that "psychological coercion" can reduce you to "a state of hopelessness" where you believe confessing is the only alternative.

For example, after 50 hours of interrogation in a small windowless room, Corinthian Bell confessed to murder because he thought that if he told the police what they wanted to hear, they would release him. In the same way, if I legitimately threatened you with a 20-hour persuasion, you'd probably give me a good rank just to shut me up. The *St. Petersburg Times* of December 25, 2005, estimates that nearly 600 Floridians are wrongfully imprisoned, with false confession being both a leading and a preventable cause.

We need to do more to protect the innocent, and get truth back in our legal system. Therefore we will examine solutions on both the federal and personal level. First, on the federal level actions must be taken in order to make interrogations credible. The answer, according to the *New York Times* of April 11, 2006, is mandatory legislation that would require all interrogations to be recorded. Thus, Congress should pass the New York Bar Association's proposed legislation that would give all courtrooms a working history of the interrogation process. Our government must follow the example of Illinois, which as of August 2005 required all interrogations be recorded.

The good news is, cops actually like the idea. A 2004 survey by the Center of Wrongful Convictions found a 98 percent approval rating from the police department using this system. The bad news is that less than 1 percent of interrogation rooms across the country employ such technology. Once implemented this would allow jury members to judge the validity of the remarks and protect police officers who are merely trying to put criminals behind bars. Additionally, modifications must be made to

The story of the 14-year-old boy is a particularly dramatic, example of how unethical interrogation techniques can produce false confessions. Would you have liked to hear more about this particular case? If so, what else might the speaker have included? As you read and respond to comments like this, however, remember the time limits the speaker is up against. If this example were to be increased in length, something else from the speech would have to be deleted. What might that be?

Notice that the next cause of false confessions, human tolerance, is clearly introduced. The audience knows to expect a discussion of how the limits of tolerance can produce such confessions.

This speech contains a particularly good mixture of abstract and general information (for example, the statistic that 69 percent of participants in a study signed false confessions and the fact that a sociologist argued that this can happen to most people) along with specific and concrete examples (for example, the confession of Corinthian Bell). After presenting the specific example, the speaker then returns to more general statistics, noting that in Florida alone some 600 people are wrongfully imprisoned, often based on false confessions.

The speaker here returns to the thesis of the speech—the need to get the legal system back on track—and provides a transition to the third major point, the solution to this clearly demonstrated problem.

The speaker proposes several solutions to the problem. The first solution proposed is that all interrogations be recorded. Another solution is to modify the interrogation training of police officers. Notice, below, that the speaker doesn't leave the audience with solutions that they can do little about but instead suggests that they raise the issue with relevant candidates and contribute to the Center on Wrongful Convictions.

## An Excellent Persuasive Speech *(Continued)*

the interrogation training received by police officers. In nearly all cases false confessions are the product not of bad cops, but rather of good cops wielding bad techniques. The *Boston Globe* of November 27, 2005, believes that requiring interrogators to remain truthful can prevent false confessions and still trap guilty suspects. To help make this a reality, when election time rolls around, raise this issue with candidates running for District Attorney offices in your area. And you don't have to wait for an election to help. Make a tax-deductible donation to the Center on Wrongful Convictions at Northwestern University via their website. Your contributions support the center's mission to identify and rectify wrongful convictions.

On the personal level, you should also be ready to take steps to protect yourself. If you are ever arrested or even a suspect, realize, your best defense is to know your rights. In honor of the movie *Fight Club*, the rules of interrogation are as follows: Rule 1: Don't talk; rule 2: DON'T TALK. Don't say a word without a lawyer. The police can legally lie and attempt to deceive you. So don't talk. And finally, if you're on the other side of this situation, as a jury member, help eliminate the stereotype that a confession is synonymous with truth. If this were true, I would merely confess to being the sexiest speaker in the world.

Today we examined the problem and causes of false confessions in America, and discovered solutions to get truth back in our legal system. If after only 10 minutes of my persuasion you feel like you're ready to crack, think about what Kevin Fox went through before he signed a paper saying he murdered his daughter. And remember that a confessed "truth" will not necessarily set you free.

*Source*: This speech is an edited version of the copy printed in Winning Orations of the Interstate Oratorical Association (Mankata, MN: Interstate Oratorical Association, 2006, pp. 25–27).

Notice that the speaker uses a variety of newspapers, newsmagazines, and professional journals along with testimony from various people. What other supporting materials might the speaker have included?

Additional solutions on a more personal level also are suggested in the event that the audience member ever finds himself or herself a suspect or a juror. Did the inclusion of this personal-level material make you feel that the topic was really important to you? If not, what additional arguments would you have wanted?

Here the speaker wraps up the speech by summarizing the three major ideas discussed (the problem, its causes, and proposed solutions) and closes by recalling the example used in the introduction.

which all of the reasons pointing to discrimination are treated as equal main points.

## PERSUASIVE SPEECHES ON QUESTIONS OF VALUE

**Questions of value** concern what people consider good or bad, moral or immoral, just or unjust. Google News (July 21, 2007), for example, identified such questions of value as these: Are the proposed changes to Medicare beneficial? What should be the legacy of Tammy Faye [Bakker] Messner? What is the value of stopping North Korea's nuclear program? Should the Food and Drug Administration have approved the

new breast cancer drug? Was Tony Blair a good choice for Mideast envoy? Will increasing the minimum wage help workers (or businesses)? Should safeguards be developed to protect consumer privacy on the Internet? Should circumcision be promoted to slow the spread of AIDS? Should Cindy Sheehan have been arrested during her call for President Bush's impeachment? Should the state of Washington have instituted the Domestic Partnership Law? Should Calgary paramedics be permitted to strike? Is funding faith-based education a good idea?

Speeches on questions of value will seek to strengthen audiences' existing attitudes, beliefs, or values. This is true of much religious and political speaking; for example, people who listen to religious speeches usually are already believers, so these speeches strive to strengthen the beliefs and values the people already hold. In a religious setting, the listeners already share the speaker's values and are willing to listen. Speeches that seek to change audience values are much more difficult to construct. Most people resist change. When you try to get people to change their values or beliefs, you're fighting an uphill (though not necessarily impossible) battle.

Be sure that you define clearly the specific value on which you're focusing. For example, let's say that you're developing a speech to persuade high school students to attend college. You want to stress that college is of value, but what type of value do you focus on? The financial value (college graduates earn more money than nongraduates)? The social value (college is a lot of fun and a great place to make friends)? The intellectual value (college will broaden your view of the world and make you a more critical and creative thinker)? Once you clarify the type of value on which you'll focus, you'll find it easier to develop the relevant points. You'll also find it easier to locate appropriate supporting materials.

## Thesis

Theses devoted to questions of value might look something like this:

- The death penalty is unjustifiable.
- Bullfighting is inhumane.
- Discrimination on the basis of affectional orientation is wrong.
- Chemical weapons are immoral.
- Human cloning is morally justified.
- College athletics minimize the importance of academics.

## Main Points

As with speeches on questions of fact, you can generate the main points for a speech on a question of value by asking a strategic question of your thesis, such as "Why is this good?" or "Why is this immoral?" For example, you can take the first thesis given above and ask, "Why is the death penalty unjustifiable?" The answers to this question will give you the speech's main points. The body of your speech might then look something like this:

**General purpose:** To persuade.

**Specific purpose:** To persuade my listeners that the death penalty is unjustifiable.

**Thesis:** The death penalty is unjustifiable. (Why is the death penalty unjustifiable?)

   **I.** The criminal justice system can make mistakes.

   **II.** The death penalty constitutes cruel and unusual punishment.

   **III.** No one has the moral right to take another's life.

## Support

To support your main points, search for relevant evidence. For example, to show that mistakes have been made, you might itemize three or four high-profile cases in which people were put to death and later, through DNA, found to have been innocent.

At times, and with certain topics, it may be useful to identify the standards you would use to judge something moral or justified or fair or good. For example, in the "bullfighting is inhumane" speech, you might devote your first main point to defining when an action can be considered inhumane. In this case, the body of your speech might look like this:

   **I.** An inhumane act has two qualities.

      **A.** It is cruel and painful.

      **B.** It serves no human necessity.

   **II.** Bullfighting is inhumane.

      **A.** It is cruel and painful.

      **B.** It serves no necessary function.

Notice that in the example of capital punishment, the speaker aims to strengthen or change the listeners' beliefs about the death penalty. The speaker is not asking the audience to do anything about capital punishment, but merely to believe that it's not justified. However, you might also use a question of value as a first step toward persuading your audience to take some action. For example, once you got your listeners to see the death penalty as unjustified, you might then ask them to take certain actions—perhaps in your next speech—to support an anti–death penalty politician, to vote for or against a particular proposition, or to join an organization fighting against the death penalty.

## Organization

Like speeches on questions of fact, speeches on questions of value often lend themselves to topical organization. For example, the speech on capital punishment cited earlier uses of topical order. But even within this topical order there is another level of organization, an organization that begins with those items on which there is least disagreement or opposition and moving on to the items on which your listeners are likely to have very different ideas. It's likely that even people in favor of the death penalty would agree that mistakes can be made; and they probably would be willing to accept evidence that mistakes have in fact been made, especially if you cite reliable statistical evidence and expert testimony. By starting

## Building Communication Skills — Constructing Logical, Motivational, and Credibility Appeals

Below are statements suitable as theses for a variety of persuasive speeches. Select any one statement (or its opposite) and construct (a) a logical appeal, (b) an emotional appeal, and (c) a credibility appeal that would prove effective in persuading your class.

1. Sports involving cruelty to animals—such as bullfighting, cockfighting, and foxhunting—should (not) be universally condemned and declared illegal.
2. Gay men and lesbians should (not) be allowed to serve in the military on the same conditions as heterosexuals.
3. Retirement should (not) be mandatory at age 65 for all government employees.
4. The death penalty is (not) morally wrong.
5. Too little (too much) government money is spent on accommodating people with disabilities.

*Practicing the art of persuasion will prove useful in a wide variety of communication situations.*

with this issue, you secure initial agreement and can use that as a basis for approaching areas where you and the audience are more likely to disagree.

## PERSUASIVE SPEECHES ON QUESTIONS OF POLICY

When you move beyond a focus on value to urging your audience to do something about an issue, you're then into a question of policy. For example, in a speech designed to convince your listeners that bullfighting is inhumane, you'd be focusing on a question of value. If you were to urge that bullfighting should therefore be declared illegal, you'd be urging the adoption of a particular policy. Items on Google News (July 21, 2007) that suggested questions of policy included these: How can flooding be prevented? What should be the policy of search engines regarding behaviorally targeted ads? How can prison overcrowding best be reduced? What can be done to improve communication between medical professionals and their older patients? What should be the policy concerning paramedics going on strike? What policy should the National Basketball Association adapt regarding betting by members? How should the United States treat Iran (North Korea)? What safeguards should be developed to protect consumer privacy on the Internet?

**Questions of policy** concern what should be done, what procedures should be adopted, what laws should be changed; in short, what policy should be followed. In some speeches you may want to propose a new policy or to defend an existing policy; in others you may wish to argue that a current policy should be discontinued.

## Thesis

Persuasive speeches frequently revolve around questions of policy and may use theses such as the following:

- Hate speech should be banned in colleges.
- Our community should adopt a zero tolerance policy for guns in schools.
- Abortion should be available on demand.
- Music CDs should be rated for violence and profanity.
- Medical marijuana should be legalized.
- Smoking should be banned from all public buildings and parks.

As you can tell from these examples, questions of policy almost invariably involve questions of values. For example, the argument that hate speech should be banned in colleges is based on the value judgment that hate speech is wrong. To argue for a zero tolerance policy on guns in schools implies that you think it's wrong for students or faculty to carry guns to school.

## Main Points

You can develop your speech on a question of policy by asking a strategic question of your thesis. With policy issues the question will be "Why should the policy be adopted?" or "Why should this policy be

## PERSUASIVE APPEALS

You want to give a speech urging your listeners to vote in favor of establishing a hate speech code at the college. You want to use both logical and emotional appeals.

WHAT DO YOU SAY?

discontinued?" or "Why is this policy better than what we now have?" Taking our first example, we might ask, "Why should hate speech be banned on campus?" From the answers to this question, you would develop your main points, which might look something like this:

    **I.** Hate speech encourages violence against women and minorities.

    **II.** Hate speech denigrates women and minorities.

    **III.** Hate speech teaches hate instead of tolerance.

## Support

Having chosen your main points, you then support each point with a variety of supporting materials that will help convince your audience that hate speech should be banned from college campuses. For example, you might cite the websites put up by certain groups that advocate violence against women and minority members, or quote from the lyrics of performers who came to campus. Or you might cite examples of actual violence that had been accompanied by hate speech or hate literature.

In some speeches on questions of policy, you may simply want your listeners to agree that the policy you're advocating is a good idea. In other cases you may want them to do something about the policy— to vote for a particular candidate, to write to their elected officials, to participate in the walkathon, to wear an AIDS awareness ribbon, and so on.

## Organization

Speeches on questions of policy may be organized in a variety of ways. For example, if you're comparing two policies, consider the comparison-and-contrast method. If the existing policy is doing harm, consider using a cause-to-effect pattern. If your policy is designed to solve a problem, consider the problem-solution pattern. For example, in a speech advocating zero tolerance for guns in school, the problem-solution pattern would seem appropriate; your speech would thus be divided into two basic parts:

    **I.** Guns are destroying our high schools. (problem)

    **II.** We must adopt a zero tolerance policy. (solution)

## SUMMARY: THE PERSUASIVE SPEECH

This unit focused on persuasive speeches and examined the goals of persuasion, several principles of persuasion, and three types of persuasive speeches.

1. Persuasive speeches may have one of three main goals: (1) to strengthen or weaken the attitudes, beliefs, or values of your listeners; (2) to change their attitudes, beliefs, or values; and (3) to motivate them to act in some way, to do something.

2. Among the guidelines for preparing persuasive speeches are the following:
   - Anticipate selective exposure.
   - Ask for reasonable amounts of change.
   - Identify with your audience.
   - Use logical appeals.
   - Use emotional appeals.
   - Use credibility appeals.
   - Motivate your listeners.

3. Several logical fallacies are especially widespread and should be avoided by speakers and recognized by listeners: anecdotal evidence, straw man, appeal to tradition, bandwagon, testimonial, transfer, plain folks, card stacking, thin entering wedge, and agenda setting.

4. Attacks on another's credibility also should be avoided; these include attacks on the grounds of personal interest, character attacks, and name calling.

5. Persuasive speeches can be classified in various ways. One way is in terms of the major question a persuasive speech addresses:
   - Questions of fact focus on what is or is not.
   - Questions of value focus on what is good or bad.
   - Questions of policy focus on what should be done.

## KEY TERMS IN THE PERSUASIVE SPEECH

agenda setting (p. **418**)

anecdotal evidence
(p. **417**)

appeal to tradition
(p. **417**)

bandwagon (p. **417**)

card stacking (p. **418**)

character (p. **422**)

character attacks (p. **425**)

charisma (p. **423**)

competence (p. **422**)

credibility (p. **421**)

door-in-the-face technique
(p. **415**)

emotional appeals (p. **418**)

foot-in-the-door technique
(p. **413**)

glittering generality
(p. **425**)

hierarchy of needs (p. **418**)

identification (p. **415**)

logic (p. **416**)

name calling (p. **425**)

personal interest (p. **424**)

persuasion (p. **410**)

plain folks (p. **418**)

questions of fact (p. **426**)

questions of policy
(p. **433**)

questions of value (p. **431**)

reasoning from causes and
effects (p. **416**)

reasoning from sign
(p. **417**)

reasoning from specific
instances (p. **416**)

straw man (p. **417**)

testimonial (p. **417**)

thin entering wedge
(p. **418**)

transfer (p. **417**)

## THINKING CRITICALLY ABOUT THE PERSUASIVE SPEECH

1. **Gender and Persuasion.** You're planning to give a speech urging more conscientious recycling to two separate audiences. One audience will be composed solely of women and the other audience solely of men. Otherwise the audience members will be similar: college-educated professionals about 30 years old. In what ways would you make the two speeches differ? What general principles or assumptions about gender are you making as you differentiate these two speeches?

2. **Foot-in-the-Door or Door-in-the-Face.** You want to get your listeners to contribute one hour a week to your college's program of helping high school students prepare for college. You're considering using the foot-in-the-door or the door-in-the-face technique. How would you develop each of these strategies? Which would you eventually use?

3. **Fact, Value, and Policy in the News.** Examine one issue of a national newspaper. What are the questions of fact, value, and policy that this newspaper edition covers? Then read the editorials. What types of questions do the editorial address?

4. **The Persuasiveness of Blogs.** Visit a few blogs and analyze them in terms of the principles of persuasion discussed in this unit. How are blogs like persuasive speeches? How are they different?

5. **The Two-Minute Speech.** Prepare and deliver a two-minute speech in which you do one of the following:
   - Explain an interesting attitude, belief, or value that you have come across.
   - Explain how a speech strengthened or changed one of your attitudes or beliefs.
   - Explain an advertisement in terms of the principles of persuasion.

## LOGON! MYCOMMUNICATIONLAB
WWW.MYCOMMUNICATIONLAB.COM

Visit MCL and take the self-test on the ethics of persuasion, When Is Persuasion Unethical? Also, read the discussion Motivational Principles, and try the exercises Analyzing Arguments: The Toulmin Model and Gender, Credibility, and the Topics of Persuasive Speaking.

   Take a look at the video clip on Credibility and the clips War Posters, Responsibility, and Talk to the Elderly and examine these in terms of the principles of persuasion. Also take a look at some of the explore exercises, for example, Proposition Me.

# UNIT 19  The Special Occasion Speech

## MAJOR TOPICS

## Special Features

Another important type of public speech is the special occasion speech: the toast, the presentation of an award, the eulogy, and various others.

**In this unit you'll learn about:**
- the varied types of special occasion speeches, including speeches of introduction, toasts, and euolgies.
- the role of culture in special occasion speaking.

**You'll learn to:**
- prepare and present a variety of special occasion speeches, including speeches to secure goodwill, to praise, or to celebrate.
- apply special occasion insights to all kinds of informative and persuasive speeches.

We can begin our discussion of special occasion speeches with the speech of introduction.

## THE SPEECH OF INTRODUCTION

The **speech of introduction** is usually designed to introduce a speaker or a topic area that a series of speakers will address. For example, before a speaker addresses an audience, another speaker often sets the stage by introducing both the speaker and the topic. At conventions, where a series of speakers address an audience, a speech of introduction might introduce the general topic on which the speakers will focus and perhaps provide connecting links among the several presentations.

In a speech of introduction, your main purpose is to gain the attention and arouse the interest of the audience. Your speech should pave the way for favorable and attentive listening. The speech of introduction is basically informative and follows the general patterns already discussed for the informative speech. The main difference is that instead of discussing a topic's issues, you discuss who the speaker is and what the speaker will talk about. In your speeches of introduction, follow these general principles:

- Establish the significance of the speech. Focus the audience's attention and interest on the main speaker and on the importance of what the speaker will say.
- Establish relevant connections among the speaker, the topic, and the audience and answer your listeners' inevitable question: Why should we listen to this speaker on this topic?

- Stress the speaker's credibility (see Unit 18) by telling the audience what has earned this speaker the right to speak on this topic to this audience.
- Speak in a style and manner that is consistent with the main speech. Introduce the speaker with the same degree of formality that will prevail during the actual speech. Otherwise, the speaker will have to counteract an inappropriate atmosphere created by the speech of introduction.
- Be brief (relative to the length of the main speech). If the main speech is to be brief—say, 10 to 20 minutes—your introduction should be no longer than 1 or 2 minutes. If, on the other hand, the main speech is to be an hour long, then your introduction might last 5 to 10 minutes or even longer.
- Don't cover the substance of the topic the speaker will discuss. Also remember that clever stories, jokes, startling statistics, or historical analogies, which are often effective in speeches of introduction, will prove a liability if the main speaker intended to use this same material.
- Don't oversell the speaker or topic. Present the speaker in a positive light, but don't create an image that the speaker will find impossible to live up to.

## THE SPEECH OF PRESENTATION OR ACCEPTANCE

We'll consider speeches of presentation and speeches of acceptance together, both because they're frequently paired and because the same general principles govern both types of speeches. In a **presentation speech** you seek to (1) place an award or honor in some kind of context and (2) give

# THE RESEARCHER

## Using Humor in Public Speaking

*I enjoy listening to speeches that aren't all doom and gloom and that contain some humor. Can you offer me any suggestions for using humor (or not using it) in special occasion speaking?*

To use humor effectively in special occasion speaking, first ask, "What types of things would my audience find funny?" Appropriate humor choices for college students might include humorous jokes, stories, examples, language, media (for example, comic strips, or video clips), or objects that introduce or reinforce your subject. However, not all types of humor are appropriate in public speaking contexts. Avoid humor that may be perceived as offensive such as sexual, morbid, or vulgar (for example, swearing) humor. Any humor that targets others based on race, sex, intelligence, affectional orientation, or age may also be viewed as inappropriate. Rather than making fun of others, consider using "safe" types of humor that will gain your audience's attention, such as funny nonverbal behaviors (for example, facial expressions, voices, or gestures), props, or word play. Finally, practice your humor attempts in front of your friends, coworkers, and family members, and solicit their feedback. Just be sure to find individuals who will be honest when they evaluate your humor attempts!

For additional information: Wanzer, M. B., Frymier, A. B., Wojtaszczyk, A., & Smith, T. (2006). Appropriate and inappropriate uses of humor by teachers. *Communication Education, 55*(2), 178–196. Also Chesebro, J., & Wanzer, M. B. (2005). Instructional Message Variables. In Mottet, T., Richmond, V. P., & McCroskey, J. C. (Eds). *Instructional Communication: Rhetorical and Relational Perspectives* (89–116). Boston, MA: Allyn & Bacon.

**Melissa Bekelja Wanzer** (Ed.D., West Virginia University) is a professor of communication at Canisius College and teaches undergraduate and graduate courses in interpersonal communication, family communication, and persuasion. Her research focuses on the areas of relational and health communication, and she is currently collaborating with health care providers at Women and Children's Hospital of Buffalo to improve aspects of health care delivery (wanzerm@canisius.edu).

the award an extra air of dignity or status. A speech of presentation may focus on rewarding a colleague for an important accomplishment (being named Teacher of the Year) or on recognizing a particularly impressive performance (winning an Academy Award). It may honor an employee's service to a company or a student's outstanding grades or athletic abilities.

The **acceptance speech** is the other side of this honoring ceremony. Here the recipient accepts the award and attempts to place the award in some kind of context. At times the presentation and the acceptance speeches are rather informal and amount to a simple "You really deserve this" and an equally simple "Thank you." At other times—for example, in the presentation and acceptance of a Nobel Prize—the speeches are formal and are prepared in great detail and with great care. Such speeches are frequently reprinted in newspapers throughout the world. Somewhere between these two extremes lie average speeches of presentation

and acceptance. For fun and for further insight into the acceptance speech, log on to the Academy Award Acceptance Speech Generator (www.chickenhead.com/stuff/oscar/index.asp).

Here is an exceptionally moving and provocative acceptance speech that clearly illustrates how closely tied together are the speaker, audience, and occasion. The speech was given by Elizabeth Taylor in acceptance of the Jean Hersholt Humanitarian Award, given for her humanitarian work on behalf of people with AIDS. The speech was transcribed from television.

I have been on this stage many times as a presenter. I have sat in the audience as a loser. And I've had the thrill and the honor of standing here as a winner. But, I never, ever thought I would come out here to receive this award.

It is the highest possible accolade I could receive from my peers. And for doing something I just have to do, that my passion must do.

## Building Communication Skills — Developing the Speech of Introduction

Prepare a speech of introduction approximately two minutes long. For this experience, you may assume that the speaker you introduce will speak on any topic you wish. Do, however, assume a topic appropriate to the speaker and to your audience—your class. You may wish to select your introduction from one of the following suggestions:

1. Introduce a historical figure to the class.

2. Introduce a contemporary religious, political, or social leader.

3. Prepare a speech of introduction that someone might give to introduce you to your class.

4. Introduce a famous media (film, television, radio, recording, writing) personality—alive or dead.

5. Introduce a series of speeches debating the pros and cons of multicultural education.

I am filled with pride and humility. I accept this award in honor of all the men, women, and children with AIDS who are waging incredibly valiant battles for their lives—those to whom I have given my commitment, the real heroes of the pandemic of AIDS.

I am so proud of the work that people in Hollywood have done to help so many others, like dearest, gentle Audrey. And while she is, I know, in heaven, forever guarding her beloved children, I will remain here as rowdy an activist as I have to be and, God willing, for as long as I have to be. [Applause]

Tonight I am asking for your help. I call upon you to draw from the depths of your being, to prove that we are a human race, to prove that our love outweighs our need to hate, that our compassion is more compelling than our need to blame, that our sensitivity to those in need is stronger than our greed, that our ability to reason overcomes our fear, and that at the end of each of our lives we can look back and be proud that we

## REFLECTIONS ON ETHICS

### Telling the Truth

Telling the truth is something you expect from others, and they expect the same from you. In some cases, as in legal trials, you're legally bound to tell the truth under threat of penalties for perjury. As a physician you're required to tell patients the truth about their illness. These examples provide rather specific guidelines for truth-telling. In other cases, however, it sometimes is not so easy to determine when telling the truth is required and when it isn't. For example, you don't want to tell your friend that she needs a face-lift, even if she asks your opinion. You don't tell your supervisor at work that he lacks a sense of humor or needs to take a bath more often.

### Ethical Choice Point

*You'll be delivering the commencement speech to a graduating class at the high school you attended. In all honesty, you thought the education you received was horrible; the teachers were unconcerned, the science and computer labs were 30 years old, and all the money went to sports and athletic programs. You want to be honest; you want to criticize the poor educational training the high school provided and urge students to approach college with a new perspective. Given that a commencement speech is usually a positive, congratulatory exercise, however, you wonder if you should avoid any mention of negative aspects. And yet you don't want to be dishonest. What is your ethical obligation in this situation? What would you do?*

## PRESENTING AN AWARD

You've been asked to present the award for Student-of-the-Year. The speech is to last no longer than 1 minute (approximately 150 words).

WHAT DO YOU SAY?

have treated others with the kindness, dignity, and respect that every human being deserves.

Thank you and God bless.

In your speeches of presentation, follow these two principles:

- State the reason for the presentation. Make clear why this particular award is being given to this particular person.

- State the importance of the award. The audience (as well as the group authorizing or sponsoring the award) will no doubt want to hear something about this. You might point out the importance of the award by referring to the previous recipients (assuming they're well known to the audience), emphasizing the status of the award (assuming that it's a prestigious award), or describing the award's influence on previous recipients.

In preparing and presenting your speech of acceptance, follow these three principles:

- Thank the people responsible for giving you the award—the academy members, the board of directors, the student body, your teammates.

- Acknowledge those who helped you achieve the award. Be specific without being overly detailed.

- Put the award into personal perspective by telling the audience what the award means to you right now and perhaps what it will mean to you in the future.

---

**Building Communication Skills**

## Developing the Speech of Presentation/Acceptance

Form pairs. One person should serve as the presenter and one as the recipient of a particular award or honor. The two people can select a situation from the following list or make one up themselves. The presenter should prepare and present a 2-minute speech in which she or he presents one of the awards to the other person. The recipient should prepare and present a 2-minute speech of acceptance.

1. Academy Award for best performance

2. Gold watch for service to the company

3. Ms. or Mr. America

4. Five million dollars for the college library

5. Award for contributions to intercultural understanding

6. Book of the year award

7. Mother (Father) of the Year award

8. Honorary Ph.D. in communication for outstanding contributions to the art

9. Award for outstanding achievement in architecture

10. Award for raising a prize hog

## THE SPEECH TO SECURE GOODWILL

The **goodwill speech** is part information and part persuasion. On the surface, the speech informs the audience about a product, company, profession, institution, or person. Beneath this surface, however, lies a more persuasive purpose: to heighten the image of a person, product, or company—to create a more positive attitude toward this person or thing. Many speeches of goodwill have a further persuasive purpose: to get the audience ultimately to change their behavior toward the person, product, or company.

A special type of goodwill speech is the speech of self-justification, in which the speaker seeks to justify his or her actions to the audience. Political figures do this frequently. Richard Nixon's "Checkers Speech," his Cambodia-bombing speeches, and, of course, his Watergate speeches are clear examples of speeches of self-justification. Edward Kennedy's Chappaquiddick speech, in which he attempted to justify what happened when Mary Jo Kopechne drowned, is another example. In securing goodwill, whether for another person or for yourself, consider the following suggestions:

- Demonstrate the contributions that deserve goodwill. Show how the audience may benefit from this company, product, or person. Or at least—in the speech of self-justification—show that the listeners have not been hurt; or, if they have been hurt, that the injury was unintentional.

- Stress uniqueness. In a world dominated by competition, the speech to secure goodwill must stress the uniqueness of the specific company, person, profession, situation, and so on. Distinguish it clearly from all others, otherwise, any goodwill you secure will be spread over the entire field.

- Establish credibility. Speeches to secure goodwill must also establish credibility, thereby securing

### REVERSING MEDIA'S INFLUENCE

*I fear three newspapers more than a hundred thousand bayonets.*

*—Napoleon*

Although you generally think of the media as exerting influence on you, you can also exert influence on the media—on radio, television, newspapers and magazines, film, and the Internet (Jamieson & Campbell, 1997; Postman & Powers, 1992; Media Education Foundation, 2006a, b):

- *Register your complaints.* Write letters, send e-mail, call a television station or advertiser, or fill out the feedback forms available on many websites expressing your views. Write to a public forum, such as a newspaper or newsgroup, or to the Federal Communication Commission or other regulatory agencies. Use any of the variety of websites (**www.vote.com** is perhaps the most popular) that encourage users to voice their opinions and then forward these to the appropriate agencies.

- *Exert group pressure.* Join with others who think the same way you do. Bring group pressure to bear on television networks, newspapers, advertisers, Internet sites, and manufacturers.

- *Protest through an established organization.* There's probably an organization already established for the issue with which you're concerned. Search the Internet for relevant newsgroups, professional organizations, and chat rooms that focus on your topic.

- *Join a social protest movement,* a technique used throughout history to gain civil rights. Such movements have the potential advantage of securing media coverage that might enable you to communicate your message to a large audience.

- *Create legislative pressure.* Exert influence on the state or federal level by influencing your local political representatives (through voting and through calls, letters, and e-mails), who will in turn influence representatives on higher levels of the political hierarchy.

### Increasing Media Literacy

*Let's say that you're unhappy about the way in which the national and local media (television and newspapers) have treated the abortion controversy. How would you go about exerting pressure on the media to better reflect your own position in their coverage?*

goodwill for the individual or commodity. To do so, concentrate on those dimensions of credibility discussed in Unit 18. Demonstrate that the person is competent, of good intention, and of high moral character.

■ Don't be obvious. The effective goodwill speech looks, on the surface, very much like an objective informative speech. It will not appear to ask for goodwill, except on close analysis.

A particularly effective example of the speech to secure goodwill—perhaps *the* classic in the world of business—is the following speech by Lee Iacocca, former CEO of Chrysler Corporation. Iacocca was presented with a particularly difficult problem: Chrysler was accused of disconnecting odometers so that cars would appear to be new despite 40 miles of road testing. This was not a particularly horrible offense; most car buyers know that their cars are put through various tests. Yet it presented Iacocca with a credibility problem. He met this head on with a series of print and television advertisements in which he admitted the error of judgment and spelled out what he would do to correct it.

> Testing cars is a good idea. Disconnecting odometers is a lousy idea. That's a mistake we won't make again at Chrysler. Period.
>
> —Lee Iacocca

Let me set the record straight.

1. For years, spot checking and road testing new cars and trucks that come off the assembly line with the odometers disengaged was standard industry practice. In our case, the average test mileage was 40 miles.
2. Even though the practice wasn't illegal, some companies began connecting their odometers. We didn't. In retrospect, that was dumb. Since October 1986, however, the odometer of every car and truck we've built has been connected, including those in the test program.
3. A few cars—and I mean a few—were damaged in testing badly enough that they should not have been fixed and sold as new. That was a mistake in an otherwise valid quality assurance program. And now we have to make it right.

What we're doing to make things right:

1. In all instances where our records show a vehicle was damaged in the test program and repaired and sold, we will offer to replace that vehicle with a brand new 1987 Chrysler Corporation model of comparable value. No ifs, ands, or buts.
2. We are sending letters to everyone our records show bought a vehicle that was in the test program and offering a free inspection. If anything is wrong because of a product deficiency, we will make it right.
3. Along with free inspection, we are extending their present 5-year or 50,000-mile protection plan on engine and powertrain to 7 years or 70,000 miles.
4. And to put their minds completely at ease, we are extending the 7-year or 70,000-mile protection to all major systems: brakes, suspension, air conditioning, electrical, and steering.

The quality testing program is a good program. But there were mistakes and we were too slow in stopping them. Now they're stopped. Done. Finished. Over.

Personally, I'm proud of our products. Proud of the quality improvements we've made. So we're going to keep right on testing. Because without it we couldn't have given America 5-year, 50,000-mile protection five years ahead of everyone else. Or maintained our warranty leadership with

7-year, 70,000 mile protection. I'm proud, too, of our leadership in safety-related recalls.

But I'm not proud of this episode. Not at all.

As Harry Truman once said, "The buck stops here." It just stopped. Period.

Another type of goodwill speech is the **speech of apology**, a speech in which the speaker apologizes for some transgression and tries to restore his or her credibility. A particularly dramatic example of this type of speech, given by President William Jefferson Clinton, is presented here. The speech was given to the nation on August 17, 1998, after Clinton testified to a grand jury about a variety of issues. The issue that the nation and the media focused on, however, was the president's affair with a White House intern, Monica Lewinsky, including the extent to which he misled the country and the question of whether he obstructed justice. This speech was almost universally criticized for not expressing enough of an apology, for not asking for forgiveness, and for attacking the opposition rather than taking responsibility. (If you wish to learn more about this speech and some of the critical reactions to it, visit *The American Communication Journal* online at www.uark.edu/~aca and go to Volume Two, Issue Two [February, 1999].)

Good evening. This afternoon in this room, from this chair, I testified before the Office of Independent Counsel and a grand jury. I answered their questions truthfully, including questions about my private life, questions no American citizen would ever want to answer.

Still I must take complete responsibility for all my actions, both public and private. And that is why I am speaking to you tonight.

As you know, in a deposition in January, I was asked questions about my relationship with Monica Lewinsky. While my answers were legally accurate, I did not volunteer information. Indeed I did have a relationship with Miss Lewinsky that was not appropriate. In fact, it was wrong.

It constituted a critical lapse in judgment and a personal failure on my part for which I am solely and completely responsible.

But I told the grand jury today, and I say to you now, that at no time did I ask anyone to lie, to hide or destroy evidence, or to take any other unlawful action.

I know that my public comments and my silence about this matter gave a false impression. I misled people. Including even my wife. I deeply regret that.

I can only tell you I was motivated by many factors. First, by a desire to protect myself from the embarrassment of my own conduct. I was also very concerned about protecting my family. The fact that these questions were being asked in a politically inspired lawsuit which has since been dismissed was a consideration too.

In addition, I had real and serious concerns about an independent counsel investigation that began with private business dealings 20 years ago—dealings, I might add, about which an independent federal agency found no evidence of any wrongdoing by me or my wife over two years ago.

The independent counsel investigation moved on to my staff and friends. Then into my private life. And now the investigation itself is under investigation. This has gone on too long, cost too much, and hurt too many innocent people.

Now this matter is between me, the two people I love most—my wife and our daughter—and our God. I must put it right. And I am prepared to do whatever it takes to do so.

Nothing is more important to me personally, but it is private. And I intend to reclaim my family life for my family. It's nobody's business but ours. Even presidents have private lives. It is time to stop the pursuit of personal destruction and the prying into private lives and get on with our national life.

Our country has been distracted by this matter for too long, and I take my responsibility for my part in all of this. That is all I can do. Now it is time, in fact it is past time, to move on. We have important work to do, real opportunities to seize, real problems to solve, real security matters to face.

And so tonight I ask you to turn away from the spectacle of the past seven months, to repair the fabric of our national discourse and to return our attention to all the challenges and all the promise of the next American century.

Thank you for watching and good night.

## THE SPEECH OF DEDICATION

The **dedication speech** is designed to give some specific meaning to, say, a new research lab, a store opening, or the start of the building of a bridge. This speech is usually given at a rather formal occasion. You'll need to do some research on exactly what it is that is being dedicated. For example, if it's a bridge, then you'll want to learn something about why the bridge was built, when it was constructed, and who designed it. In preparing a dedication speech, consider the following suggestions:

- State the reason you're giving the dedication; for example, identify the connection you have to the project.

- Explain exactly what is being dedicated; for example, the opening of the bridge linking Roosevelt Island to Manhattan.

- Tell the audience who is responsible for the project; for example, who designed the bridge, who constructed it, who paid for it.

- Explain why this project is significant—what advantages it will create. For example, to clarify the relevance the bridge has to your audience, describe what changes will occur as a result of the building of this bridge and how the bridge will benefit your listeners.

## THE COMMENCEMENT SPEECH

The **commencement speech** recognizes and celebrates the end of some training period, such as the listeners' school or college years. The commencement speech is designed to congratulate and inspire the recent graduates and is often intended to mark the transition from school to the next stage in life. Usually the person asked to give a commencement speech is a well-known personality. The speakers at college graduations—depending on the prestige of the institution—are often important men and women in the world: presidents, senators, religious leaders, Nobel Prize winners, famous scientists, and people of similar accomplishment. Or a commencement speech may be given by a student who has achieved some exceptional goal; for example, the student with the highest grade point average or the winner of a prestigious award. In giving a commencement speech, consider the following:

- Organize the speech in a temporal pattern, beginning with the past, commenting on the present, and projecting into the future.

- Do your research. Learn something about the school, the student body, the goals and ambitions of the graduates, and integrate these into your speech.

- Be brief. Recognize that your audience has other things on their minds—the graduation party, for example—and may become restless if your speech is too long.

- Congratulate the graduates—but also congratulate the parents, friends, and instructors who also contributed to this day.

- Offer the graduates some kind of motivational message, some guidance, some suggestions for taking their education and using it in their lives.

- Offer your own good wishes to the graduates.

## THE EULOGY

The **eulogy** is a speech of tribute in which you seek to praise someone who has died. In the eulogy you attempt to put the person's life and contributions in perspective and show them in a positive light. This type of speech is often given at a funeral or at the anniversary of the person's birth or death. This is not the time for a balanced appraisal of the individual's life. Rather, it's a time for praise. In developing the eulogy, consider the following:

- Relate the person whose life you're celebrating to yourself, to those in the audience—and, if appropriate, to the larger audience—for example, the scientific community, the world of book lovers, or those who have devoted their lives to peace.

- Be specific; show that you really knew the person, or know a great deal about the person, by giving specific examples from the person's life. Then combine the specifics with the more general so that the audience can see these specifics as being a part of some larger whole—for example, after you mention the several books that the author wrote, frame the author's contribution in a more general way within the mystery genre or contemporary poetry genre.

- Make the audience see that this person is deserving of the praise you are bestowing on him or her by explaining what this person accomplished and how this person influenced—for example— the world of patient care, the design of safer cars, and so on.

- Show the audience what they can learn from this individual.

An excellent example of a eulogy, presented by communication professor and family therapist Bernard J. Brommel at the funeral of his sister, is presented in the Public Speaking Sample Assistant box, opposite. A more complete version of this speech is available online at **www.mycommunicationlab.com**.

## THE INSPIRATIONAL SPEECH

A great many special occasion speeches aim to inspire the audience, as you've seen in the speeches already covered. **Inspirational speeches**, however, are designed primarily to inspire; raising the spirits of an audience is their primary objective. Many religious speeches are of this type. Similarly, speeches given to stockholders when a company introduces a new product or a new CEO, for example, would be designed to inspire investors. A commanding officer might give a speech of inspiration to the troops before going into battle. And of course there are the speeches of professional motivational

## Public Speaking Sample Assistant
### A Eulogy

This eulogy was delivered by communication professor and family therapist Bernard J. Brommel on the occasion of his sister's funeral.

Today we gather to honor the memory of Florence who is at rest from her labors and we rejoice in knowing her love and good deeds remain with us, the living. It's an honor to speak on behalf of her family, especially seven wonderful sons, her husband Bill, my siblings, and our aunt/stepmother, Florence, who was her namesake.

Florence set an example for courage, drive, responsibility, patience, honesty, tolerance, and countless other virtues. Most of all, she set for us an example of how to love, both as a giver and a receiver of it. It took so little to please her and evoke that quiet smile of appreciation. Gentle and kind, never loud or outspoken, she supported each of us by her nurturing nature and that rare ability, seldom found in many humans, to listen without judging. It's easy to understand why it was her heart that kept her alive in the last weeks. Everything in her system failed, but not her heart! Her physical heart was symbolic of her loving heart that reached each of us and was the last to go.

As the oldest of nine, she grew up with far more responsibility than most children. She grew up at the side of her mother as a constant helper. I remember her stirring cakes at five or six; there were no mixes then! She churned butter by hand, washed thousands of dishes, milk pails, diapers, and scrubbed those splintered floors. Mama was frequently ill or having difficult pregnancies. Florence took over! No wonder Florence could later in life manage a bank.

Three years ago this week we buried Dad. Two themes characterized his life: one, that it was a hard life but it got easier, and a second one, work—work—work. Florence's life experiences were similar. In our time Florence represented what has happened to women in transition—a transition for women from a domestic life to combining a professional life with raising a large family. She married at 18. She never planned a career; it just evolved out of necessity! Like her mother, or favorite aunt, Dolly, she might have preferred staying home with her sons. There were no maternity leaves; she saved her two-week vacations to coincide with delivery dates, and then back to work to keep the groceries on the table.

For us, the living, that have loved Florence, it's so hard to accept her death from cancer. Sixty-one years isn't long enough for this gentle soul, but God has called her and we have to accept His decision.

To each of her sons, I express my admiration for the way you helped look after your mom, not only in illness but throughout the years. You stayed out of trouble and made life easier for her because you did. In the hospital, Louie, you rubbed her feet and talked to her about her fears. Greg and Mike, each of you stopped by at noon hour or after work. David—you probably knew your mother best and always brought a special smile to her parched lips. To Will, the farmer, who she said was the loudest of her quiet boys. You could tell that he loved his mom whenever their eyes met. To John and Bob, identical twins who only their mother knew from day one the differences between the two of you. You knew how special you were to her. Finally to my siblings—the time has come for us to say farewell to Florence. Weren't we blessed with a great sister who left us with so much joy to remember? Thanks, Bill, for your love for our sister. Florence will have the last words. I asked her what she wanted me to say on this occasion and she, through tears, said, "Tell each of those at my funeral, 'I love you and I'll miss you, but I'm OK!'"

Source: *Eulogy in honor of my sister, Florence Hraha-Cairo.* Delivered by Bernard J. Brommel, July 30, 1990, St. Marys, Iowa.

speakers, who seek to arouse the audience to feel better about themselves by organizing their lives, taking chances, giving up drugs, or doing any of a variety of things.

Before reading some suggestions for preparing and presenting a speech of inspiration, you may wish to read first the speech by Nikki Giovanni on page 447. This is a particularly impressive inspirational speech given by faculty member and poet Giovanni after 32 students and faculty were killed at Virginia Tech University on April 16, 2007.

To present an effective inspirational speech:

■ Demonstrate your "oneness" with the audience. Try to show in some way that you and your listeners have significant similarities between you. Notice in Giovanni's speech the repeated use of "we," which makes listeners feel connected to the speaker.

## Understanding Theory and Research — A Blurring of Purposes

As you have probably noticed, it's not always easy to distinguish between an informational and a persuasive speech. There is always information that has to be communicated in every persuasive speech. And there is always an element of persuasion in informational speeches—even if it consists merely of encouraging the audience to appreciate the importance of the topic. The distinctions are largely a matter of emphasis: Any given speech is likely to be predominantly informational or predominantly persuasive. In special occasion speaking, however, the purposes of informing and persuading become especially blurred. In a eulogy, you inform your listeners of the individual's accomplishments so as to persuade them to consider this person commendable. In a speech to secure goodwill or a speech of apology, you inform the audience of the specifics of the case so as to persuade them to give you the goodwill or accept your apology and forgive you.

### Working with Theories and Research

*Review the special occasion speeches in this unit and identify the informative and the persuasive purposes that each serve.*

---

- Demonstrate your own enthusiasm, the kind of enthusiasm you want your audience to show. You cannot lead a pep rally without yourself being excited and exciting. The photo opposite aptly captures Giovanni's enthusiasm, as does the language of her speech.

- Stress emotional appeals. Inspiring an audience has to do more with emotions than with logic. Use appeals that are consistent with the nature of the event. In the Giovanni speech you see appeals to courage, loyalty to friends and institution, and empathy for others.

- Stress the positive—and, most important, end your speech on a positive note. Inspirational speeches are always positive. Note the positiveness in Giovanni's speech: "We will prevail. We will prevail. We will prevail."

## THE FAREWELL SPEECH

In the **farewell speech** you say goodbye to an organization or to colleagues and signal that you're moving on. In this speech you'll want to express your positive feelings to those you're leaving. Generally, the farewell speech is given after you've achieved some level of distinction within a company or other group or organization that you're now leaving. In developing a farewell speech, consider the following:

- Thank those who made life interesting, helped you in your position, taught you essential principles, and so on.

- Set your achievements in a positive light, but do it modestly.

- Express your enjoyment of the experience. This is a time for positive reflection, not for critical evaluation, so put aside the negative memories, at least for this speech.

- If appropriate, state your reason for leaving and your plans for the future.

- Express good wishes to those who remain.

- Offer some words of wisdom that you learned and that you now want to pass on to those remaining.

Here is an example of a farewell speech, delivered by Cal Ripken Jr. on his retirement from baseball (www.americanrhetoric.com/speeches/calripkenjr.htm, accessed February 6, 2004):

As a kid, I had this dream.

And I had the parents that helped me shape that dream.

Then, I became part of an organization, the Baltimore Orioles—the Baltimore Orioles, to help me grow that dream. Imagine playing for my hometown team for my whole career.

And I have a wife and children to help me share and save the fruits of that dream.

And I've had teammates who filled my career with unbelievable moments.

And you fans, who have loved the game, and have shared your love with me.

Tonight, we close a chapter of this dream—my playing career.

But I have other dreams.

You know, I might have some white hair on top of this head—well, maybe on the sides of this head. But I'm really not that old.

My dreams for the future include pursuing my passion for baseball. Hopefully, I will be able to share what I have learned. And, I would be happy if that sharing would lead to something as simple as a smile on the face of others.

One question I've been repeatedly asked these past few weeks is, "How do I want to be remembered?" My answer has been simple: to be remembered at all is pretty special.

I might also add that if, if I am remembered, I hope it's because, by living my dream, I was able to make a difference.

Thank you.

### INSPIRING OTHERS

Here, poet and professor Nikki Giovanni delivers an inspirational speech after 32 students and faculty members were killed at Virginia Tech in April, 2007 (see the Public Speaking Sample Assistant below for the full text of the speech). Visualize yourself as the next speaker.

WHAT DO YOU SAY?

## Public Speaking Sample Assistant    An Inspirational Speech

This inspirational speech was delivered by Nikki Giovanni at a convocation at Virginia Tech on April 17, 2007 (www.vt.edu//tragedy/giovanni_transcript.php, accessed April 30, 2007).

We are Virginia Tech.

We are sad today, and we will be sad for quite a while. We are not moving on, we are embracing our mourning.

We are Virginia Tech.

We are strong enough to stand tall tearlessly, we are brave enough to bend to cry, and we are sad enough to know that we must laugh again.

We are Virginia Tech.

We do not understand this tragedy. We know we did nothing to deserve it, but neither does a child in Africa dying of AIDS, neither do the invisible children walking the night away to avoid being captured by the rogue army, neither does the baby elephant watching his community being devastated for ivory, neither does the Mexican child looking for fresh water, neither does the Appalachian infant killed in the middle of the night in his crib in the home his father built with his own hands

being run over by a boulder because the land was destabilized. No one deserves a tragedy.

We are Virginia Tech.

The Hokie Nation embraces our own and reaches out with open heart and hands to those who offer their hearts and minds. We are strong, and brave, and innocent, and unafraid. We are better than we think and not quite what we want to be. We are alive to the imaginations and the possibilities. We will continue to invent the future through our blood and tears and through all our sadness.

We are the Hokies.

We will prevail.

We will prevail.

We will prevail.

We are Virginia Tech.

---

### Theory and Research    Humor

**UNDERSTANDING**

Humor often plays a part in public speaking, and particularly in special occasion speaking. Humor can serve several important purposes. In a speech that is long and somber, humor breaks up the mood and lightens the tone. At times humor serves as a creative and useful transition mechanism. And humor is excellent support material. It can help you emphasize a point, crystallize an idea, or rebut an opposing argument.

Here are a few guidelines for using and not using humor in public speaking.

- *Make it relevant.* Like any other type of supporting material, the humorous anecdote or story must be relevant to your topic and your purpose. If it's not, don't use it.

- *Keep it brief.* If a humorous passage occupies too great a portion of your speech, the audience may question your sincerity or seriousness. Humor in special occasion speeches, however, may logically occupy a greater part of the entire speech than in informative or persuasive speeches.

- *Make it seem spontaneous.* If humor appears studied or too well practiced, it may lose its effectiveness. In telling a humorous anecdote, for example, always keep your eyes on the audience, not on your notes.

- *Keep it tasteful.* If there's even the smallest possibility that your humor might make your listeners uncomfortable, then eliminate it. Avoid sarcasm and ridicule; it's too difficult to predict how an audience will respond. Also, your listeners may well wonder when your sarcasm or ridicule will be directed at them.

- *Be sure it's appropriate.* Humor should be appropriate to you, to your audience, and to the occasion. Be especially careful that your humor does not prove culturally insensitive. You can err less by not using humor than by using it inappropriately. So, when in doubt, leave it out.

---

#### Working with Theories and Research

*Sometimes things don't go as you plan and the audience just doesn't get it. Don't look surprised, hurt, or as though you've lost control of yourself and your material. Instead develop a clever response and keep it in the back of your mind just in case things go amiss.*

---

## THE TOAST

The **toast** is a brief speech designed to celebrate a person or an occasion. You might, for example, toast the next CEO of your company, a friend who just got admitted to a prestigious graduate program, or a colleague on the occasion of a promotion. Often toasts are given at weddings or at the start of a new venture. The toast is designed to say hello or good luck in a relatively formal sense. In developing your toast, consider the following:

- Be brief; realize that people want to get on with the festivities and don't want to listen to an overly long speech.

- Focus attention on the person or persons you're toasting, not on yourself.

- Avoid inside jokes that only you and the person you're toasting understand; remember that the toast is not only for the benefit of the person you're toasting but for the audience as well.

- When you raise your glass in the toast—an almost obligatory part of toasting—make the audience realize that they should drink and that your speech is at an end.

## THE SPECIAL OCCASION SPEECH IN CULTURAL PERSPECTIVE

Like all forms of communication, the special occasion speech must be developed with a clear understanding of the influence of culture. For example, the discussion of the speech of introduction suggested that you not oversell the speaker; excessive exaggeration is generally evaluated negatively in much of the United States. On the other hand, exaggerated praise often is expected in some Latin cultures.

Similarly, the discussion of the speech of goodwill suggested that you present yourself as being worthy of the goodwill rather than as a supplicant begging for it. In some cultures, however, this attitude might be seen as arrogant and disrespectful to the audience. In some Asian cultures, for example, pleading for goodwill would be seen as suitably modest and respectful of the audience.

In introducing or in paying tribute to someone, consider the extent to which you wish to focus on the person's contribution to the group or to individual achievement. An audience with a predominantly collectivist orientation will expect to hear about group-centered achievements, whereas an audience of predominantly individualist orientation will expect to hear about more individually focused achievements.

Culture also will influence the way in which an acceptance should be framed. Not surprisingly, collectivist cultures would suggest that you give a lot of credit to the group, whereas individualist cultures would suggest that taking self-credit is appropriate when it's due. Thus, if you were accepting an award for a performance in a movie, an extreme collectivist orientation would lead you to give great praise to others and to claim that without others you never could have accomplished what you did. An extreme individualist orientation would lead you to accept the award and the praise for yourself; after all, you did it! In the media business, as you see from the numerous televised award shows, everyone gives thanks to almost everyone connected with the project. That's the custom; the collectivist form of expression has become the norm, at least in the context of show business. To examine your own tendencies toward an individual or collectivist orientation, take the accompanying self-test.

## TEST YOURSELF

### How Individualistic Are You?

Indicate how true or false the following statements are of you. Use the following scale: Almost always true = 1; more often true than false = 2; true about half the time and false about half the time = 3; more often false than true = 4; and almost always false = 5.

_____ 1. My own goals rather than the goals of my group (for example, my extended family, my organization) are the more important.

_____ 2. I feel responsible for myself and to my own conscience rather than for the entire group and to the group's values and rules.

_____ 3. Success to me depends on my contribution to the group effort and the group's success rather than on my own individual success or on surpassing others.

_____ 4. Being kind and polite is usually more important than telling the truth, so I might say things that are not true in a literal sense if they allow the other person to appear in a positive light.

_____ 5. In my communications I prefer a direct and explicit communication style; I believe in "telling it like it is," even if it hurts.

**HOW DID YOU DO?** To compute your individualist-collectivist score, follow these steps:

1. Reverse the scores for items 3 and 4: If your response was 1, reverse it to a 5; if your response was 2, reverse it to a 4; if your response was 3, keep it as 3; if your response was 4, reverse it to a 2; and if your response was 5, reverse it to a 1.

2. Add your scores for all 5 items, being sure to use the reverse scores for items 3 and 4 in your calculations. Your score should be between 5 (indicating a highly individualist orientation) and 25 (indicating a highly collectivist orientation).

3. Position your score on the following scale:

5 _____ 12/13 _____ 25

highly individualist | about equally individualist and collectivist | highly collectivist

**WHAT WILL YOU DO?** Do your score and your position on the scale accurately measure the way in which you see yourself on this dimension? Is this orientation going to help you achieve your personal and professional goals? Might it hinder you? What can you do to make your individualist and collectivist attitudes more productive?

## SUMMARY: THE SPECIAL OCCASION SPEECH

This unit discussed special occasion speeches, highlighting a variety of specific types, and placed special occasion speeches in a cultural context.

1. The speech of introduction introduces another speaker or series of speakers. In this speech: Establish a connection among speaker, topic, and audience; establish the speaker's credibility; be consistent in style and manner with the major speech; be brief; avoid covering what the speaker intends to discuss; and avoid overselling the speaker.

2. The speech of presentation explains why the presentation is being made, and the speech of acceptance expresses thanks for the award. In the speech of presentation, state the reason for the presentation and state the importance of the award. In the speech of acceptance, thank those who gave the award, thank those who helped, and state the meaning of the award to you.

3. The speech to secure goodwill attempts to secure or, more often, to regain the listeners' good graces. In this speech: Stress benefits the audience may derive; stress uniqueness; establish your credibility and the credibility of the subject; avoid being obvious and avoid pleading in your effort to secure goodwill.

4. The speech of dedication gives specific meaning to some event or object. In this speech: Explain why you're giving the speech; explain what is being dedicated; state who is responsible for the event or object; and say why this is significant, especially to your specific listeners.

5. The commencement speech celebrates the end of some training period. In this speech: Consider the values of a temporal organizational pattern; learn something about the training organization and demonstrate this knowledge in your speech; be brief; congratulate the larger audience, not only those who went through the training; offer some motivational message; and offer your own good wishes.

6. The eulogy seeks to praise someone who has died. In this speech: Show the connection between yourself and the person you're eulogizing; be specific, then combine specifics with the general; stress that the person is deserving of your praise; and show your listeners what they can learn from this person.

7. The inspirational speech seeks to inspire the audience, to get listeners to think in a positive direction. In this speech: Demonstrate your close connection with the audience, be enthusiastic, stress emotional appeals, and emphasize the positive.

8. The farewell speech signals a transition between what was and what will be. In this speech: Thank those who helped you; portray the positives of the past; explain your reasons for making the transition; and offer good wishes to your audience plus some words of wisdom, some motivational message.

9. The toast celebrates a person or an occasion. In the toast: Be brief; focus attention on the person or event you're toasting; avoid references that listeners may not understand; and make it clear that this is the end of your speech when you raise your glass.

10. The special occasion speech needs to be developed with an awareness of the cultural norms and rules specific to the occasion and to the audience members. Especially relevant here is the distinction between individualist and collectivist cultures.

## KEY TERMS IN THE SPECIAL OCCASION SPEECH

acceptance speech (p. **438**)
commencement speech (p. **444**)
dedication speech (p. **443**)

eulogy (p. **444**)
farewell speech (p. **446**)
goodwill speech (p. **441**)

inspirational speech (p. **444**)
presentation speech (p. **437**)

speech of apology (p. **443**)
speech of introduction (p. **437**)
toast (p. **448**)

## THINKING CRITICALLY ABOUT THE SPECIAL OCCASION SPEECH

1. **The Speech of Goodwill.** Compare and contrast the two speeches designed to secure goodwill—the speech of Lee Iacocca and the speech of President Clinton (pages 442–443). What are the major differences you find in these speeches? If you were hearing the speeches when they were originally delivered, which you would consider the more effective? Which would have the greater persuasive impact on you?

2. **The Toast.** You're scheduled to give a toast at your best friends' commitment ceremony. You were told that it should be about two minutes long. What would you say if your friends were 18 years old? If they were in their 50s?

3. **Speeches of Acceptance.** Read a few speeches of acceptance—that by Elizabeth Taylor (in this unit)—as well as any you find on the Internet. What unifying theme appears throughout speeches of acceptance?

4. **The Eulogy.** Visit the Obituary Daily Times at www .best.com/~shuntsbe/obituary/ to locate information about someone you admire. In what way is an obituary similar to a eulogy? In what ways are they different?

5. **Special Occasion Speaking Practice.** Here are a few examples for special occasion speaking practice. Think about how you would prepare and what you would say in each situation.
   - Introduce any speaker you wish, speaking to any audience you wish, on any subject you wish.
   - Present an award for the best speaker of the year, the best quarterback, the best actor, the best fire-fighter, the best police officer, or the best teacher.
   - Explain how an advertisement is like a speech to secure goodwill.
   - Toast your friend's new relationship commitment.
   - Say thanks to a group of your friends who just surprised you with a birthday party; they're all clapping and yelling "speech, speech."
   - Eulogize a person.
   - Secure the goodwill of your audience toward one of the following: your college (visualize your audience as high school seniors); a particular profession or way of life (teaching, religious life, nursing, law, medicine, bricklaying, truck driving, etc.); this course (visualize your audience as college students who have not yet taken this course); the policies of a particular foreign country now in the news; or a specific multinational corporation.

# LogOn! MyCommunicationLab
## WWW.MYCOMMUNICATIONLAB.COM

Unit 19 of MCL provides an extended example of a eulogy, President William Jefferson Clinton's farewell address, Martin Scorsese's acceptance speech for the John Huston Award for Artists' Rights, and an exercise, Developing the Speech of Tribute.

# GLOSSARY of Human Communication Concepts

**abstraction process** The process by which a general concept is derived from specifics; the process by which some (never all) characteristics of an object, person, or event are perceived by the senses or included in some term, phrase, or sentence.

**abstraction** A general concept derived from a class of objects; a partial representation of some whole.

**accent** The stress or emphasis placed on a syllable when it is pronounced.

**acculturation** The processes by which a person's culture is modified or changed through contact with or exposure to another culture.

**active listening** A process of putting together into some meaningful whole the listener's understanding of the speaker's total message—the verbal and the nonverbal, the content and the feelings.

**adaptors** Nonverbal behaviors that satisfy some personal need and usually occur without awareness; for example, scratching to relieve an itch or moistening your lips to relieve dryness. Three types of adaptors are often distinguished: **self-adaptors**, **alter-adaptors**, and **object-adaptors**.

**adjustment** The principle of verbal interaction that claims that communication takes place only to the extent that the parties communicating share the same system of signals.

**affect displays** Movements of the facial area that convey emotional meaning—for example, expressions showing anger, fear, or surprise.

**affinity-seeking strategies** Behaviors designed to increase our interpersonal attractiveness.

**affirmation** The communication of support and approval.

**ageism** Discrimination based on age, usually against the elderly.

**agenda** A list of the items that a small group must deal with in the order in which they should be covered.

**agenda setting** A persuasive technique in which the speaker states or implies that XYZ is the issue and that all others are unimportant.

**aggressiveness** See **verbal aggressiveness**.

**allness** A language distortion; the assumption that all can be known or is known about a given person, issue, object, or event.

**alter-adaptors** Body movements you make in response to your current interactions; for example, crossing your arms over your chest when someone unpleasant approaches or moving closer to someone you like.

**altercasting** Placing the listener in a specific role for a specific purpose and asking that the listener approach a question or problem from the perspective of this specific role.

**ambiguity** Uncertainty of meaning; the possibility of interpreting a message in more than one way.

**analogy, reasoning from** A type of reasoning in which you compare like things and conclude that since they are alike in so many respects that they are also alike in some previously unknown respect.

**apology** A type of excuse in which you acknowledge responsibility for your behavior, generally ask forgiveness, and claim that this behavior will not happen again.

**apology, speech of** A speech in which the speaker apologizes for some transgression and tries to restore his or her credibility.

**apprehension** See **communication apprehension**.

**arbitrariness** The feature of human language that reflects the absence of a real or inherent relationship between the form of a word and its meaning. If we do not know anything of a particular language, we cannot examine the form of a word and thereby discover its meaning.

**argument** Evidence (for example, facts or statistics) and a conclusion drawn from the evidence.

**argumentativeness** Willingness to argue for a point of view, to speak your mind. Distinguished from **verbal aggressiveness**.

**articulation** The physiological movements of the speech organs as they modify and interrupt the air stream emitted from the lungs.

**artifactual communication** Communication that takes place through the wearing and arrangement of various items made by human hands—for example, clothing, jewelry, buttons, or the furniture in your house and its arrangement.

**assertiveness** Willingness to stand up for your own rights while respecting the rights of others.

**assimilation** A process of distortion in which messages are reconstructed to conform to our own attitudes, prejudices, needs, and values.

**attack** A persuasive technique that involves accusing another person (usually an opponent) of some serious wrongdoing so that the issue under discussion never gets examined.

**attention** The process of responding to a stimulus or stimuli; usually involves some consciousness of responding.

**attitude** A predisposition to respond for or against an object, person, or position.

**attraction** The state or process by which one individual is drawn to another and forms a highly positive evaluation of that other person.

**attraction theory** A theory holding that we form relationships on the basis of our attraction to another person.

**attractiveness** The degree to which a person is perceived to be physically appealing and to possess a pleasing personality.

**attribution theory** A theory concerned with the processes through which we attempt to understand the behaviors of others (as well as our own), particularly the reasons or motivations for those behaviors.

**attribution** A process through which we attempt to understand the behaviors of others (as well as our own), particularly the reasons or motivations for these behaviors.

**audience participation principle** A principle of persuasion stating that persuasion is achieved more effectively when the audience participates actively.

**authoritarian leader** A group leader who determines group policies or makes decisions without consulting or securing agreement from group members.

**avoidance** An unproductive **conflict** strategy in which a person takes mental or physical flight from the actual conflict.

**backchanneling cues** Listener responses to a speaker that do not ask for the speaking role.

**bandwagon** A persuasive technique in which the speaker tries to gain compliance by saying that "everyone is doing it" and urging listeners to jump on the bandwagon.

**barriers to communication** Factors (physical or psychological) that prevent or hinder effective communication.

**behavioral synchrony** The similarity in the behavior, usually nonverbal, of two persons. Generally, it is taken as an index of mutual liking.

**belief** Confidence in the existence or truth of something; conviction.

**beltlining** An unproductive **conflict** strategy in which one person hits at the level at which the other person cannot withstand the blow.

**blame** An unproductive **conflict** strategy in which we attribute the cause of the conflict to the other person or devote our energies to discovering who is the cause and avoid talking about the issues causing the conflict.

**boundary marker** An object that divides one person's territory from another's—for example, a fence.

**brainstorming** A technique for generating ideas either alone or, more usually, in a small group.

**breadth** In the **social penetration theory** of interpersonal relationships, the number of topics about which individuals in a relationship communicate.

**card stacking** A persuasive technique in which the speaker selects only the evidence and arguments that build his or her case and omits or distorts any contradictory evidence.

**causes and effects, reasoning from** A form of reasoning in which you conclude that certain effects are due to specific causes or that specific causes produce certain effects.

**censorship** Restriction on people's rights to produce, distribute, and/or receive various communications.

**central marker** An item that is placed in a territory to reserve it for a specific person—for example, the sweater thrown over a library chair to signal that the chair is taken.

**certainty** An attitude of closed-mindedness that creates a defensiveness among communication participants; opposed to **provisionalism**.

**channel** The vehicle or medium through which signals are sent.

**character** An individual's honesty and basic nature; moral qualities that contribute to **credibility**.

**charisma** An individual's dynamism or forcefulness; one of the qualities that contribute to **credibility**.

**cherishing behaviors** Small behaviors we enjoy receiving from others, especially from our relational partner—for example, a kiss, a smile, or a gift of flowers.

**chronemics** The study of the communicative nature of time—of the way you treat time and use it to communicate. Two general areas of chronemics are **cultural time** and **psychological time**.

**civil inattention** Polite ignoring of others so as not to invade their privacy.

**cliché** An overused expression that has lost its novelty and part of its meaning and that calls attention to itself because of its overuse, such as "tall, dark, and handsome" as a description of a man.

**closed-mindedness** An unwillingness to receive certain communication messages.

**code** A set of symbols used to translate a message from one form to another.

**coercive power** Power derived from an individual's ability to punish or to remove rewards from another person.

**cognitive restructuring** A theory for substituting logical and realistic beliefs for unrealistic ones; used in reducing communication apprehension and in raising self-esteem.

**cohesiveness** The property of togetherness. In group communication situations, cohesiveness has to do with the mutual attraction among members; it's a measure of the extent to which individual group members work together as a group.

**collectivist culture** A culture in which the group's goals are given greater importance than the individual's and in which, for example, benevolence, tradition, and conformity are given special emphasis. Opposed to **individualist culture**.

**color communication** The meanings that different colors communicate in various cultures.

**commencement speech** A speech given to celebrate the end of some training period, often at school graduation ceremonies.

**communication** (1) The process or act of communicating; (2) the actual message or messages sent and received; (3) the study of the processes involved in the sending and receiving of messages.

**communication accommodation theory** Theory holding that speakers adjust their speaking style to their listeners to gain social approval and achieve greater communication effectiveness.

**communication apprehension** Fear or anxiety over communicating; may be "trait apprehension" (fear of communication

generally, regardless of the specific situation) or "state apprehension" (fear that is specific to a given communication situation).

**communication competence** A knowledge of the rules and skills of communication; the term often refers to the qualities that make for effectiveness in communication.

**communication network** The pathways of messages; the organizational structure through which messages are sent and received.

**communicology** The study of communication, particularly the subsection concerned with human communication.

**competence** A person's ability and knowledge; one of the qualities that contribute to **credibility**.

**complementarity** A principle of **attraction** stating that we are attracted by qualities that we do not possess or that we wish to possess and to people who are opposite or different from ourselves; opposed to **similarity**.

**complementary relationship** A relationship in which the behavior of one person (e.g., energetic activity) serves as the stimulus for the complementary behavior of the other (e.g., laziness); in complementary relationships behavioral differences are maximized.

**compliance-gaining strategies** Behaviors that are directed toward gaining the agreement of others; behaviors designed to persuade others to do as we wish.

**compliance-resisting strategies** Behaviors directed at resisting the persuasive attempts of others.

**confidence** A quality of interpersonal effectiveness; a comfortable, at-ease feeling in interpersonal communication situations.

**confirmation** A communication pattern that acknowledges another person's presence and also indicates an acceptance of this person, this person's definition of self, and the relationship as defined or viewed by this other person; opposed to **disconfirmation**.

**conflict** An extreme form of competition in which interdependent persons perceive their respective goals to be incompatible and see each other as interfering with their own attainment of desired goals.

**congruence** A condition in which both verbal and nonverbal behaviors reinforce each other.

**connotation** The feeling or emotional aspect of meaning, generally viewed as consisting of the evaluative (for example, good–bad), potency (strong–weak), and activity (fast–slow) dimensions; the associations of a term. See also **denotation**.

**consensus** A principle of attribution through which we attempt to establish whether other people react or behave in the same way as the person on whom we are now focusing. If the person is acting in accordance with the general consensus, then we seek reasons for the behavior outside the individual; if the person is not acting in accordance with the general consensus, then we seek reasons that are internal to the individual.

**consistency** A perceptual process that influences us to maintain balance among our perceptions; a process that makes us tend to see what we expect to see and to be uncomfortable when our perceptions run contrary to our expectations.

**contact** The first stage of an interpersonal relationship, in which perceptual and interactional contact occurs.

**contamination** A form of territorial encroachment that renders another's territory impure.

**content and relationship dimensions** A principle of communication stating that messages refer both to content (the world external to both speaker and listener) and to the relationship existing between the individuals who are interacting.

**content message** Communication message relating to the objective world—the world external to both speaker and listener.

**context** The physical, psychological, social, and temporal environment in which communication takes place.

**contrast** (principle of) Often-followed rule of perception: If messages or people are very different from each other, they probably don't belong together and do not constitute a set or group.

**controllability** One of the factors we consider in judging whether or not a person is responsible for his or her behavior. If the person was in control, then we judge that he or she was responsible. A principle in **attribution theory**.

**conversation** Communication engaged in by two or three people and usually including an opening, feedforward, a business stage, feedback, and a closing.

**conversational management** The conduct of a conversation by means of **conversational turns**.

**conversational maxims** Principles that are followed in conversation to ensure that the goal of the conversation is achieved.

**conversational turns** The process of exchanging the speaker and listener roles during conversation.

**cooperation** An interpersonal process by which individuals work together for a common end; the pooling of efforts to produce a mutually desired outcome. In communication, an implicit agreement that calls for speaker and listener to work together to achieve mutual comprehension.

**credibility** The degree to which a speaker is perceived to be believable; **competence**, **character**, and **charisma** (dynamism) are its major dimensions.

**critical thinking** The process of logically evaluating reasons and evidence and reaching a judgment on the basis of this analysis.

**critical thinking hats technique** Technique developed by Edward deBono in which a problem or issue is viewed from six distinct perspectives: facts, feelings, negative arguments, positive benefits, creative new ideas, and control of thinking.

**criticism** The reasoned judgment of some work; although often equated with fault finding, criticism can involve both positive or negative evaluations.

**cultural display** Signs that communicate a person's cultural identification, for example, clothing or religious jewelry.

**cultural rules** Rules that are specific to a given cultural group.

**cultural time** The perspective on time shared by members of a particular culture.

**culture shock** The psychological reaction we experience at being placed in a culture very different from our own or from what we are used to.

**culture** The relatively specialized lifestyle of a group of people—consisting of their values, beliefs, artifacts, ways of behaving, and ways of communicating—that is passed on from one generation to the next.

**date** An **extensional device** used to emphasize the notion of constant change and symbolized by a mental subscript: for example, John Smith 1999 is not John Smith 2008.

**deception cues** Verbal or nonverbal cues that reveal the person is lying.

**decoder** Something that takes a message in one form (for example, sound waves) and translates it into another form (for example, nerve impulses) from which meaning can be formulated (for example, in vocal–auditory communication). In human communication the decoder is the auditory mechanism; in electronic communication the decoder is, for example, the telephone earpiece. See also **encoder**.

**decoding** The process of extracting a message from a code—for example, translating speech sounds into nerve impulses. See also **encoding**.

**dedication speech** A special occasion speech in which you commemorate the opening or start of a project.

**defensiveness** An attitude of an individual or an atmosphere in a group characterized by threats, fear, and domination; messages evidencing evaluation, control, strategy, neutrality, superiority, and certainty are assumed to lead to defensiveness; opposed to **supportiveness**.

**delayed reactions** Reactions that are consciously delayed while a situation is analyzed.

**Delphi method** A type of problem-solving group in which questionnaires are used to poll members (who don't interact among themselves) on several occasions so as to arrive at a group decision on, for example, the most important problems a company faces or activities a group might undertake.

**democratic leader** A group leader who stimulates self-direction and self-actualization on the part of the group members.

**denial** One of the obstacles to the expression of emotion; the process by which we deny our emotions to ourselves or to others.

**denotation** Referential meaning; the objective or descriptive meaning of a word. See also **connotation**.

**depenetration** A reversal of penetration; a condition in which the **breadth** and **depth** of a relationship decrease. See **social penetration theory**.

**depth** In the **social penetration theory** of interpersonal relationships, the degree to which the inner personality—the inner core—of an individual is penetrated in interpersonal interaction.

**determinism** The principle of verbal interaction that holds that all verbalizations are to some extent purposeful—that there is a reason for every verbalization.

**dialogue** A form of **communication** in which each person is both speaker and listener; communication characterized by involvement, concern, and respect for the other person; opposed to **monologue**.

**direct speech** Speech in which the speaker states his or her intentions clearly and forthrightly.

**disclaimer** Statement that asks the listener to receive what the speaker says as intended and not to interpret it as reflecting negatively on the image of the speaker.

**disconfirmation** The process by which one person ignores or denies the right of another person even to define himself or herself; opposed to **confirmation**.

**dissolution** The breaking of the bonds holding an interpersonal relationship together.

**door-in-the-face technique** A persuasive strategy in which the speaker first makes a large request that will be refused and then follows with the intended and much smaller request.

**downward communication** Messages sent from the higher levels to the lower levels of an organizational hierarchy; for example, messages sent by managers to workers or by deans to faculty members. See **upward communication**, **lateral communication**.

**dyadic communication** Two-person communication.

**dyadic consciousness** An awareness of an interpersonal relationship or pairing of two individuals; distinguished from situations in which two individuals are together but do not perceive themselves as being a unit or twosome.

**dyadic effect** The process by which one person in a dyad imitates the behavior of the other person, usually used to refer to the tendency of one person's self-disclosures to prompt the other to also self-disclose.

**earmarker** A physical sign that identifies an item as belonging to a specific person—for example, a nameplate on a desk or initials on an attaché case.

**effect** The outcome or consequence of an action or behavior; communication is assumed always to have some effect.

**emblems** Nonverbal behaviors that directly translate words or phrases—for example, the signs for "OK" and "peace."

**emotions** The feelings we have—for example, our feelings of guilt, anger, or sorrow.

**empathy** Feeling another person's feeling; feeling or perceiving something as does another person.

**encoder** Something that takes a message in one form (for example, nerve impulses) and translates it into another form (for example, sound waves). In human communication the encoder is the speaking mechanism; in electronic communication the encoder is, for example, the telephone mouthpiece. See also **decoder**.

**encoding** The process of putting a message into a code—for example, translating nerve impulses into speech sounds. See also **decoding**.

**enculturation** The process by which culture is transmitted from one generation to another.

**E-prime** A form of the English language that omits the verb *to be* except when used as an auxiliary or in statements of existence; also called E'. Designed to eliminate the tendency toward **projection**.

**equality** An attitude that recognizes that each individual in a communication interaction is equal, that no one is superior to any other; encourages supportiveness; opposed to **superiority**.

**equilibrium theory** A theory of **proxemics** holding that intimacy and physical closeness are positively related; as relationship becomes more intimate, the individuals will use shorter distances between them.

**equity theory** A theory of interpersonal relationships claiming that we experience relational satisfaction when there is an equal distribution of rewards and costs between the two persons in the relationship.

**et cetera** An **extensional device** used to emphasize the notion of infinite complexity; because we can never know all about anything, we should end any statement about the world or an event with an explicit or implicit "etc."

**ethics** The rightness or wrongness of actions; the branch of philosophy that studies moral values.

**ethnic identity** A commitment to the beliefs and philosophy of your culture.

**ethnocentrism** The tendency to see others and their behaviors through our own cultural filters, often as distortions of our own behaviors; the tendency to evaluate the values and beliefs of our own culture more positively than those of another culture.

**eulogy** A speech of tribute in which the speaker praises someone who died.

**euphemism** A polite word or phrase used to substitute for some taboo or otherwise offensive term.

**excluding talk** Talk about a subject or in a vocabulary that only certain people understand, often in the presence of someone who does not belong to this group and therefore does not understand; use of terms unique to a specific culture as if they were universal.

**excuse** An explanation designed to lessen the negative consequences of something done or said.

**expectancy violations theory** A theory of **proxemics** holding that people have a certain expectancy for space relationships. When that expectancy is violated (for example, when a person stands too close to you or a romantic partner maintains abnormally large distances from you), the relationship comes into clearer focus and you wonder why this "normal distance" is being violated.

**experiential limitation** The limit of an individual's ability to communicate, as set by the nature and extent of that individual's experiences.

**expert power** Power that a person possesses because others believe the individual to have expertise or knowledge.

**expressiveness** A quality of interpersonal effectiveness that consists of genuine involvement in speaking and listening, conveyed verbally and nonverbally.

**extemporaneous speech** A speech that is thoroughly prepared and organized in detail and in which certain aspects of style are predetermined.

**extensional device** Linguistic device to help make language a more accurate means for talking about the world. Proposed by Alfred Korzybski, the extensional devices include **et cetera**, **date**, and **index**, among others.

**extensional orientation** A tendency to give primary consideration to the world of experience and only secondary consideration to labels. Opposed to **intensional orientation**.

**face-saving** Maintaining a positive public self-image in the minds of others.

**facial feedback hypothesis** The theory that your facial expressions can produce physiological and emotional effects.

**facial management techniques** Techniques used to mask certain emotions and to emphasize others; for example, intensifying your expression of happiness to make a friend feel good about a promotion.

**fact, questions of** Questions that concern what is or is not true, what does or does not exist, what did or did not happen; questions that potentially at least have answers.

**fact–inference confusion** A misevaluation in which a person makes an inference, regards it as a fact, and acts upon it as if it were a fact.

**factual statement** A statement made after observation and limited to what is observed. Opposed to **inferential statement**.

**family** A group of people who consider themselves related and connected to one another and among whom the actions of one have consequences for others.

**farewell speech** A speech designed to say goodbye to a position or to colleagues and to signal that you're moving on.

**fear appeal** The appeal to fear to persuade an individual or group of individuals to believe or to act in a certain way.

**feedback** Information that is given back to the source. Feedback may come from the source's own messages (as when we hear what we are saying) or may come from the receiver(s) in the form of applause, yawning, puzzled looks, questions, letters to the editor of a newspaper, increased or decreased subscriptions to a magazine, and so forth. See also **negative feedback**; **positive feedback**.

**feedforward** Information that is sent prior to a regular message telling the listener something about what is to follow.

**field of experience** The sum total of an individual's experiences, which influences his or her ability to communicate. In some views of communication, two people can communicate only to the extent that their fields of experience overlap.

**flexibility** The ability to adjust communication strategies on the basis of the unique situation.

**focus group** A group designed to explore the feelings and attitudes of its individual members; usually follows a question-and-answer format.

**foot-in-the-door technique** A persuasive strategy in which the speaker first asks for something small (to get a foot in the door) and then, once a pattern of agreement has been achieved, follows with the real and larger request.

**force** An unproductive **conflict** strategy in which a person attempts to win an argument by physical force or threats of force.

**forum** A small group format in which members of the group answer questions from the audience; often follows a symposium.

**free information** Information that is revealed implicitly and that may be used as a basis for opening or pursuing conversations.

**friendship** An interpersonal relationship between two persons that is mutually productive, established and maintained through perceived mutual free choice, and characterized by mutual positive regard.

**fundamental attribution error** The tendency to attribute a person's behavior to the kind of person he or she is (to the person's personality, perhaps) and to give too little importance to the situation the person is in.

**game** A simulation of some situation with rules governing the behaviors of the participants and with some payoff for winning; in transactional analysis, "game" refers to a series of ulterior transactions that lead to a payoff; the term also refers to a basically dishonest kind of transaction in which participants hide their true feelings.

**general semantics** The study of the relationships among language, thought, and behavior.

**glittering generality** Attempt by a speaker to gain listeners' acceptance of an idea by associating it with things they value highly; the opposite of **name calling**.

**goodwill speech** A special occasion speech in which the speaker seeks to make the image of a person, product, or company more positive.

**gossip** Communication about someone not present, some third party; usually concerns matters that are private to this third party.

**grapevine** The informal lines through which messages in an organization may travel; these informal routes resemble a physical grapevine, with its twists and turns and its unpredictable pattern of branches.

**group** A collection of individuals connected to one another by some common purpose and with some structure among them.

**group norms** Rules or expectations of appropriate behavior for members of groups.

**group self-esteem** A person's positive (or negative) evaluation of himself or herself as a member of a particular cultural group.

**groupthink** A tendency observed in some groups in which agreement among members becomes more important than the exploration of the issues at hand.

**gunnysacking** An unproductive **conflict** strategy of storing up grievances—as if in a gunnysack—and holding them in readiness to dump on the opponent in a disagreement.

**halo effect** The tendency to generalize an individual's positive or negative qualities from one area to another.

**haptics** The study of touch communication.

**heterosexist language** Language that assumes all people are heterosexual and thereby denigrates lesbians and gay men.

**high-context culture** A culture in which much of the information in communication is in the context or in the person rather than explicitly coded in the verbal messages. **Collectivist cultures** are generally high context. Opposed to **low-context** culture.

**high-power-distance culture** A culture in which there is a great difference in power between groups; for example, between teachers and students or managers and workers.

**home territories** Territories about which individuals have a sense of intimacy and over which they exercise control—for example, a professor's office.

**home field advantage** The increased power that comes from being in your own territory.

**hostile environment harassment** A form of sexual harassment that includes all sexual behaviors (verbal and nonverbal) that make a worker uncomfortable.

**hyphen** An **extensional device** used to illustrate that what may be separated verbally may not be separable on the event level or on the nonverbal level; although we may talk about body and mind as if they were separable, in reality they are better referred to as body-mind.

**idea-generation group** A group whose purpose is to generate ideas. See also **brainstorming**.

**illustrators** Nonverbal behaviors that accompany and literally illustrate verbal messages—for example, an upward gesture accompanying the verbalization "It's up there."

**I-messages** Messages in which the speaker accepts responsibility for his or her own thoughts and behaviors; messages in which the speaker's point of view is acknowledged explicitly. Opposed to **you-messages**.

**immediacy** A quality of interpersonal effectiveness that creates a sense of contact and togetherness and conveys interest in and liking for the other person.

**implicit personality theory** A theory of personality, complete with rules or systems, that each individual maintains and through which the individual perceives others.

**impromptu speech** A speech given without any explicit prior preparation.

**inclusion principle** In verbal interaction, the principle that all members should be a part of (included in) the interaction.

**inclusive talk** Communication that includes all people; communication that does not exclude certain groups, such as women, lesbians and gays, or members of certain races or nationalities.

**index** An **extensional device** used to emphasize the notion of nonidentity (no two things are the same) and symbolized by a mental subscript—for example, politician$_1$ is not politician$_2$.

**indirect speech** Speech that may hide the speaker's true intentions or that may be used to make requests and observations in a roundabout way.

**indiscrimination** A misevaluation caused by categorizing people, events, or objects into a particular class and responding to them only as members of the class; a failure to recognize that each individual is unique; a failure to apply the **index**.

**individualist culture** A culture in which the individual's goals and preferences are given greater importance than the group's. Opposed to **collectivist culture**.

**inevitability** A principle of communication stating that communication cannot be avoided; all behavior in an interactional setting is communication.

**inferential statement** A statement that can be made by anyone, is not limited to what is observed, and can be made at any time. Opposed to **factual statement**.

**informal time** Approximate rather than exact time, denoted in terms such as "soon," "early," and "in a while."

**information** That which reduces uncertainty.

**information overload** A condition in which the amount of information is too great to be dealt with effectively or the number or complexity of messages is so great that an individual or organization is not able to deal with them.

**information power** Power that a person possesses because others see that individual as having significant information and the ability to communicate logically and persuasively. Also called "persuasion power."

**insulation** A reaction to **territorial encroachment** in which you erect some sort of barrier between yourself and the invaders.

**intensional orientation** A point of view in which primary consideration is given to the way things are labeled and only secondary consideration (if any) to the world of experience. Opposed to **extensional orientation**.

**interaction management** A quality of interpersonal effectiveness; the control of interaction to the satisfaction of both parties. Includes managing conversational turns, fluency, and message consistency.

**interaction process analysis** A content analysis method that classifies messages into four general categories: social emotional positive, social emotional negative, attempted answers, and questions.

**intercultural communication** Communication that takes place between or among persons of different cultures or persons who have different cultural beliefs, values, or ways of behaving.

**interpersonal communication** Communication between two persons or among a small group of persons and distinguished from public or mass communication; communication of a personal nature and distinguished from impersonal communication; communication between or among intimates or those involved in a close relationship; often, dyadic and small group communication in general.

**interpersonal conflict** A conflict or disagreement between two persons.

**interpersonal perception** Our perception of people; the processes through which we interpret and evaluate people and their behavior.

**interviewing** A particular form of interpersonal communication in which two persons interact largely in a question-and-answer format for the purpose of achieving specific goals.

**intimacy** The closest interpersonal relationship; usually, a close **primary relationship**.

**intimacy claims** Obligations incurred by virtue of being in a close and intimate relationship.

**intimate distance** The closest **proxemic distance**, ranging from touching to 18 inches. See also **proxemics**.

**intrapersonal communication** Communication with yourself.

**introduction, speech of** A speech designed to introduce the speaker himself or herself to an audience, or a speech designed to introduce another speaker or group of speakers.

**invasion** The unwarranted entrance into another's territory that changes the meaning of the territory. See also **territorial encroachment**.

**involvement** The stage in an interpersonal relationship that normally follows **contact**; in this stage the individuals get to know each other better and explore the potential for greater intimacy.

**irreversibility** A principle of communication holding that communication cannot be reversed; once something has been communicated, it cannot be uncommunicated.

**jargon** The technical language of any specialized group, often a professional class, that is unintelligible to individuals not belonging to the group; "shop talk."

**Johari window** A diagram of the four selves (open, blind, hidden, and unknown) that details the different kinds of information in each self.

**kinesics** The study of the communicative dimensions of facial and bodily movements.

**laissez-faire leader** A group leader who allows the group to develop and progress (or make mistakes) on its own.

**lateral communication** Messages between equals in an organization—manager to manager, worker to worker. Such messages may move within the same subdivision or department of the organization or across divisions. See **downward communication**, **upward communication**.

**leadership** The quality by which one individual directs or influences the thoughts and/or the behaviors of others. See also **laissez-faire leader**, **democratic leader**, and **authoritarian leader**.

**leave-taking cues** Verbal and nonverbal cues that indicate a desire to terminate a conversation.

**legitimate power** Power that a person possesses because others believe that the individual has a right, by virtue of position, to influence or control their behavior.

**level of abstraction** The relative distance of a term or statement from an actual perception. A low-order abstraction would be a description of the perception, whereas a high-order abstraction would consist of inferences about descriptions of the perception.

**leveling** A process of message distortion in which a message is repeated but the number of details is reduced, some details are omitted entirely, and some details lose their complexity.

**listening** An active process of receiving messages sent orally; this process consists of five stages: receiving, understanding, remembering, evaluating, and responding.

**logic** The science of reasoning; the study of the principles governing the analysis of inference making.

**looking-glass self** The self-concept that results from the image of yourself that others reveal to you.

**loving** An interpersonal process in which one feels a closeness, a caring, a warmth, and an excitement in relation to another person.

**low-context culture** A culture in which most of the information in communication is explicitly stated in the verbal messages. **Individualist cultures** are usually low-context cultures. Opposed to **high-context culture**.

**low-power-distance culture** A culture in which there is little difference in power between groups; for example, between doctors and patients or men and women.

**magnitude of change principle** A principle of persuasion stating that the greater and more important the change desired by the speaker, the more difficult its achievement will be.

**maintenance** A stage of relationship stability at which the relationship does not progress or deteriorate significantly; a continuation as opposed to a dissolution of a relationship.

**maintenance strategies** Specific behaviors designed to preserve an interpersonal relationship. Compare to **relationship repair**.

**manipulation** An unproductive **conflict** strategy in which a person avoids open conflict but instead attempts to divert the conflict by being especially charming and getting the opponent into a noncombative frame of mind.

**manuscript speech** A speech designed to be read verbatim from a script.

**markers** Devices that signify that a certain territory belongs to a particular person. See also **boundary marker**, **central marker**, and **earmarker**.

**mass communication** Communication addressed to an extremely large audience, mediated by audio and/or visual transmitters, and processed by gatekeepers before transmission.

**matching hypothesis** An assumption that we date and mate with people who are similar to ourselves—who match us—in degree of physical attractiveness.

**meaningfulness** A perception principle that refers to your assumption that people's behavior is sensible, stems from some logical antecedent, and is consequently meaningful rather than meaningless.

**mediated communication** Messages sent by a source through some electronic device to a receiver; includes both mass media and computer communication.

**mentoring** The process by which an experienced individual (mentor) helps to train a less experienced person referred to as a mentee or, more often, a protégé.

**mere exposure hypothesis** The theory that repeated or prolonged exposure to a stimulus may result in a change in attitude toward the stimulus object, generally in the direction of increased positiveness.

**message** Any signal or combination of signals transmitted to a **receiver**.

**message isolation** The situation that exists when a worker is given little or no information; may occur when formal messages are not sent to certain people or when some people are excluded from the informal gossip and grapevine messages.

**metacommunication** Communication about communication.

**metalanguage** Language used to talk about language.

**metamessage** A message that makes reference to another message. For example, comments like "Did I make myself clear?" or "That's a lie" refer to other messages and are therefore considered metamessages.

**mindfulness** A state of awareness in which we are conscious of the logic and rationality of our behaviors and the logical connections existing among elements. In a mindless state we are unaware of this logic and rationality.

**mixed messages** Messages that contradict themselves; messages that ask for two different (often incompatible) responses.

**model** A representation of an object or process.

**monochronic time orientation** A view of time in which things are done sequentially; one thing is scheduled at a time. Opposed to **polychronic time orientation**.

**monologue** A form of **communication** in which one person speaks and the other listens; there is no real interaction among participants. Opposed to **dialogue**.

**motivated sequence** An organizational pattern for arranging the information in a speech to motivate an audience to respond positively to the speaker's purpose.

**name-calling** A persuasive tactic in which the speaker gives an idea a derogatory name.

**negative feedback** Feedback that serves a corrective function by informing the source that his or her message is not being received in the way intended. Negative feedback serves to redirect the source's behavior. Looks of boredom, shouts of disagreement, letters critical of newspaper policy, and teachers' instructions on how better to approach a problem are examples of negative feedback. See also **positive feedback**.

**networking** A broad process of enlisting the aid of other people to help you solve a problem or offer insights that bear on your problem.

**noise** Anything that interferes with a person's receiving a message as the source intended the message to be received. Noise is present in a communication system to the extent that the message received is not the message sent.

**nominal group** A collection of individuals who record their thoughts and opinions, which are then distributed to others. Without direct interaction, the thoughts and opinions are gradually pared down until a manageable list (of solutions or decisions) is produced. When this occurs, the nominal group (a group in name only) may restructure itself into a problem-solving group that analyzes the final list.

**nonallness** An attitude or point of view in which it is recognized that one can never know all about anything and that what we know, say, or hear is only a part of what there is to know, say, or hear.

**nondirective language** Language that does not direct or focus our attention on certain aspects; neutral language.

**nonnegotiation** An unproductive **conflict** strategy in which an individual refuses to discuss the conflict or to listen to the other person.

**nonverbal communication** Communication without words; communication by means of space, gestures, facial expressions, touching, vocal variation, and silence, for example.

**nonverbal dominance** Nonverbal behavior through which one person exercises psychological dominance over another.

**norm** See **group norms**.

**object language** Language used to communicate about objects, events, and relations in the world; the structure of the object language is described in a **metalanguage**; the display of physical objects—for example, flower arranging and the colors of the clothes we wear.

**object-adaptors** Movements that involve manipulation of some object; for example, punching holes in or drawing on a Styrofoam coffee cup, clicking a ballpoint pen, or chewing on a pencil.

**olfactory communication** Communication by smell.

**openness** A quality of interpersonal effectiveness encompassing (1) willingness to interact openly with others, to self-disclose as appropriate; (2) willingness to react honestly to incoming stimuli; and (3) willingness to own our own feelings and thoughts.

**oral style** The style of spoken discourse. When compared with written style, consists of shorter, simpler, and more familiar words; more qualification, self-reference terms, allness terms, verbs and adverbs; and more concrete terms and terms indicative of consciousness of projection—for example, "as I see it."

**organization** An organized group of people who work together to achieve compatible goals.

**organizational communication** The process of sending and receiving verbal and nonverbal messages that convey meaning and that occur within an organizational context.

**other-orientation** A quality of interpersonal effectiveness involving attentiveness, interest, and concern for the other person.

**other-talk** Talk about the listener or some third party.

**owning feelings** The process by which you take responsibility for your own feelings instead of attributing them to others.

**panel** A small group format in which "expert" participants speak without any set pattern and respond to questions from an audience.

**paralanguage** The vocal but nonverbal aspect of speech. Paralanguage consists of voice qualities (for example, pitch range, resonance, tempo); vocal characterizers (laughing or crying, yelling or whispering); vocal qualifiers (intensity, pitch height); and vocal segregates ("uh-uh," meaning "no," or "sh" meaning "silence").

**parasocial relationship** Relationship between a real person and an imagined or fictional character; also, relationship between a viewer and a real or fictional television personality.

**pauses** Silent periods in the normally fluent stream of speech. Pauses are of two major types: filled pauses (interruptions in speech that are filled with such vocalizations as "er" or "um") and unfilled pauses (silences of unusually long duration).

**perception** The process of becoming aware of objects and events from the senses. See also **interpersonal perception**.

**perception checking** The process of verifying your understanding of some message or situation or feeling to reduce uncertainty.

**perceptual accentuation** A process that leads you to see what you expect to see and what you want to see—for example, seeing people you like as better looking and smarter than people you do not like.

**personal distance** The second-closest **proxemic distance**, ranging from 18 inches to four feet. See also **proxemics**.

**personal rejection** An unproductive **conflict** strategy in which one individual withholds love and affection and seeks to win the argument by getting the other person to break down under this withdrawal.

**persuasion** The process of influencing attitudes and behavior.

**phatic communication** Communication that is primarily social; communication designed to open the channels of communication rather than to convey substantive information. "Hello" and "How are you?" in everyday interaction are examples.

**pitch** The highness or lowness of the vocal tone.

**plagiarism** The act of passing off the work of someone else as your own without acknowledging the source.

**plain folks** A persuasive tactic in which the speaker seeks to identify himself or herself (and his or her proposal) with the audience.

**polarization** A form of fallacious reasoning in which only two extremes are considered; also referred to as "black-or-white" or "either/or" thinking or as a two-valued orientation.

**policy, questions of** Questions that focus on what should be done (the policy that should be adopted).

**politeness** Good communication manners; a way of interacting that is considerate and respectful.

**polychronic time orientation** A view of time in which several things may be scheduled or engaged in at the same time. Opposed to **monochronic time orientation**.

**positive feedback** Feedback that supports or reinforces the continuation of behavior along the same lines in which it is already proceeding—for example, applause during a speech. See also **negative feedback**.

**positiveness** A characteristic of effective communication involving positive attitudes toward the self and toward the interpersonal interaction. Also can mean complimenting another and expressing acceptance and approval.

**power play** A consistent pattern of behavior in which one person tries to control the behavior of another.

**power** The ability to control the behaviors of others.

**pragmatic implication** An assumption that seems logical but is not necessarily true.

**premature self-disclosures** Disclosures that are made before the relationship has developed sufficiently.

**primacy effect** The condition in which what comes first exerts greater influence in our perceptions than what comes later. See also **recency effect**.

**primacy–recency** Processes of perception in which we give more credence to that which occurs first (primacy) or to that which occurs last or most recently (recency).

**primary relationship** The relationship between two people that they consider their most (or one of their most) important; for example, the relationship between spouses or domestic partners.

**primary territories** Areas that a person can consider his or her own exclusive preserve—for example, someone's room or office.

**problem-solving group** A group whose primary task is to solve a problem or, perhaps more often, to reach a decision.

**problem-solving sequence** A logical step-by-step process for solving a problem that is frequently used by groups; consists of defining and analyzing the problem, establishing criteria for evaluating solutions, identifying possible solutions, evaluating solutions, selecting the best solution(s), and testing the selected solution(s).

**process** Ongoing activity; by thinking of communication as a process, we emphasize that it is always changing, always in motion.

**progressive differentiation** A relational problem caused by the exaggeration or intensification of differences or similarities between individuals.

**projection** A psychological process whereby we attribute characteristics or feelings of our own to others; often, the process whereby we attribute our own faults to others.

**pronunciation** The production of syllables or words according to some accepted standard; for example, as presented in a dictionary.

**protection theory** A theory of **proxemics** referring to the fact that people establish a body-buffer zone to protect themselves from unwanted closeness, touching, or attack.

**provisionalism** An attitude of open-mindedness that leads to the creation of supportiveness; opposed to **certainty**.

**proxemic distances** The spatial distances that people maintain in communication and social interaction.

**proxemics** The study of the communicative function of space; the study of how people unconsciously structure their space—the distances between people in their interactions, the organization of spaces in homes and offices, and even the design of cities.

**proximity** Physical closeness; one of the qualities influencing **attraction**. Also, as a principle of **perception**, the tendency to perceive people or events that are physically close as belonging together or representing some unit.

**psychological time** The importance you place on past, present, or future time.

**public distance** The longest **proxemic distance**, ranging from 12 to more than 25 feet. See also **proxemics**.

**public speaking** Communication in which a speaker presents a relatively continuous message to a relatively large audience in a unique context.

**public territories** Areas that are open to all people—for example, restaurants or parks.

**punctuation of communication** The breaking up of continuous communication sequences into short sequences with identifiable beginnings and endings or stimuli and responses.

**punishment** Noxious or aversive stimulation.

**pupillometrics** The study of communication through changes in the size of the pupils of the eyes.

**purr words** Highly positive words that express the speaker's feelings rather than referring to any objective reality; opposite of **snarl words**.

**quality circle** Group of workers whose task it is to investigate and make recommendations for improving the quality of some organizational function.

**quid pro quo harassment** A form of workplace sexual harassment in which employment opportunities (as in hiring and promotion) are made dependent on the granting of sexual favors.

**quotes** An **extensional device** to emphasize that a word or phrase is being used in a special sense and should therefore be given special attention.

**racist language** Language that denigrates or is derogatory toward members of a particular racial or ethnic group.

**rate** The speed with which you speak, generally measured in words per minute.

**reasoning from causes and effects** See **causes and effects**.

**reasoning from sign** See **sign**.

**reasoning from specific instances** See **specific instances**.

**receiver** Any person or thing that takes in messages. Receivers may be individuals listening to or reading a message, a group of persons hearing a speech, a scattered television audience, or machines that store information.

**recency effect** The condition in which what comes last (that is, most recently) exerts greater influence in our perceptions than what comes first. See also **primacy effect**.

**redundancy** The quality of a message that makes it totally predictable and therefore lacking in information. A message of zero redundancy would be completely unpredictable; a message of 100 percent redundancy would be completely predictable. All human languages contain some degree of built-in redundancy, generally estimated to be about 50 percent.

**referent power** Power that a person possesses because others desire to identify with or be like that individual.

**regulators** Nonverbal behaviors that regulate, monitor, or control the communications of another person, such as nods or changes in body posture.

**reinforcements** In **attraction theory**, rewards or favors that tend to promote interpersonal relationships.

**rejection** A response to an individual that rejects or denies the validity of that individual's ideas or actions.

**relational communication** Communication between or among intimates or those in close relationships; used by some theorists as synonymous with **interpersonal communication**.

**relationship deterioration** The stage of a relationship during which the connecting bonds between the partners weaken and the partners begin drifting apart; can lead to **dissolution**.

**relationship development** The stages of a relationship that lead up to **intimacy**; in the model of relationships presented here, relationship development includes the **contact** and **involvement** stages.

**relationship dialectics theory** A theory that describes relationships in terms of the tensions between a series of competing opposite desires or motivations, such as the desire for autonomy versus the desire to belong to someone, desires for novelty versus predictability, and desires for closedness versus openness.

**relationship maintenance** The processes by which individuals attempt to keep an interpersonal relationship stable and satisfying.

**relationship message** Message that comments on the relationship between the speakers rather than on matters external to them.

**relationship repair** Efforts to reverse the process of **relationship deterioration**.

**response** Any overt or covert behavior.

**reward power** Power derived from an individual's ability to reward another person.

**rigid complementarity** The inability to break away from a **complementary relationship** that once was appropriate but is no longer.

**role** The part an individual plays in a group; an individual's function or expected behavior.

**round table** A small group format in which members arrange themselves in a circular or semicircular pattern and interact informally, with or without a moderator.

**rules theory** A theory that describes relationships as interactions governed by series of rules that couples agree to follow. When the rules are followed, a relationship is maintained; when they are broken, the relationship experiences difficulty.

**schemata** Mental templates or structures that help us organize the millions of items of information we come into contact with every day (singular: schema).

**script** A general idea of how an event should unfold; a rule governing the sequence of occurrences in some activity. A type of **schema**.

**secondary territories** Areas that do not belong to a particular person but that have been occupied by that person and are therefore associated with her or him—for example, the seat you normally take in class.

**selective attention** A principle of **perception** that states that listeners attend to those things that they anticipate will fulfill their needs or will prove enjoyable.

**selective exposure** A principle of **perception** and **persuasion** that states that listeners actively seek out information that supports their opinions and actively avoid information that contradicts their existing opinions, beliefs, attitudes, and values.

**self-acceptance** Being satisfied with ourselves, our virtues and vices, and our abilities and limitations.

**self-adaptors** Movements that usually satisfy a physical need, especially a need to be more comfortable; for example, scratching your head to relieve an itch, moistening your lips because they feel dry, or pushing your hair out of your eyes.

**self-attribution** A process through which we seek to account for and understand the reasons and motivations for our own behaviors.

**self-awareness** The degree to which a person knows himself or herself.

**self-concept** An individual's self-evaluation; an individual's self-appraisal.

**self-disclosure** The process of revealing something about ourselves to another; usually, revealing information that would normally be kept hidden.

**self-esteem** The value you place on yourself; your self-evaluation; usually, the positive value you place on yourself.

**self-fulfilling prophecy** The situation in which we make a prediction or prophecy and fulfill it ourselves—for example, expecting a class to be boring and then fulfilling this expectation by not listening and thus becoming bored.

**self-monitoring** The manipulation of the image we present to others in interpersonal interactions so as to create the most favorable impression.

**self-serving bias** A bias that operates in the **self-attribution** process and leads us to take credit for the positive consequences and to deny responsibility for the negative consequences of our behaviors.

**self-talk** Talk about oneself.

**semantics** The area of language study concerned with meaning.

**sexist language** Language derogatory to one sex, usually women; also, language that seems to prefer one gender over the other, as in the use of "man" for "humankind."

**sexual harassment** Unsolicited and unwanted sexual messages.

**shyness** The condition of discomfort and uneasiness in interpersonal situations.

**sign, reasoning from** A form of reasoning in which the presence of certain signs (clues) are interpreted as leading to a particular conclusion.

**signal reaction** A conditioned response to a signal; a response to some signal that is immediate rather than delayed.

**signal-to-noise ratio** In verbal interaction, the relative amounts of signal (meaningful information) and noise (interference). Messages high in information and low in noise would have a high signal/noise ratio; messages low in information and high in noise would have a low signal/noise ratio.

**silence** The absence of vocal communication. Often mistakenly thought to be the absence of any and all communication, silence actually can communicate feelings or can serve to prevent communication about certain topics.

**similarity** A principle of **attraction** holding that we are attracted to qualities similar to those we possess and to people who are similar to ourselves; opposed to **complementarity**. Also, in **perception**, rule stating that things that look alike belong together and form a unit.

**slang** Language used by particular groups that is highly informal, nonstandard, and often considered improper.

**small group communication** Communication among a collection of individuals small enough in number that all members may interact with relative ease as both senders and receivers, the members being connected to one another by some common purpose and with some degree of organization or structure.

**snarl words** Highly negative words that express the feelings of the speaker rather than referring to any objective reality; opposite to **purr words**.

**social clock** An internalized schedule—based on cultural teachings—for the ages at which important events should be done; for example, the approximate ages for getting married or for buying a house.

**social comparison processes** The processes by which you compare yourself (for example, your abilities, opinions, and values) with others and then assess and evaluate yourself; one of the sources of **self-concept**.

**social distance** The third **proxemic distance**, ranging from 4 to 12 feet; the distance at which business is usually conducted. See also **proxemics**.

**social exchange theory** A theory hypothesizing that we develop relationships in which our rewards or profits will be greater than our costs and that we avoid or terminate relationships in which the costs exceed the rewards.

**social penetration theory** A theory describing how relationships develop from the superficial to the intimate level and from few to many areas of interpersonal interaction.

**source** Any person or thing that creates messages. A source may be an individual speaking, writing, or gesturing or a computer sending an error message.

**spatial distance** Physical distance that signals the type of relationship you are in: intimate, personal, social, or public.

**specific instances, reasoning from** A form of reasoning in which several specific instances are examined and then a conclusion about the whole is formed.

**speech** Messages utilizing a vocal–auditory channel.

**spontaneity** Communication pattern in which a person verbalizes what he or she is thinking without attempting to develop strategies for control; encourages **supportiveness**; opposed to **manipulation**.

**stability** Principle of **perception** that refers to the fact that our perceptions of things and of people are relatively consistent with our previous perceptions.

**static evaluation** An orientation that fails to recognize that the world is characterized by constant change; an attitude that sees people and events as fixed rather than as constantly changing.

**status** The relative level a person occupies in a hierarchy; because status always involves a comparison, one individual's status is only relative to the status of another.

**stereotype** In communication, a fixed impression of a group of people through which we then perceive specific individuals; stereotypes are most often negative but also may be positive.

**stimuli** External or internal changes that impinge on or arouse an organism (singular: stimulus).

**subjectivity** The principle of **perception** that refers to the fact that our perceptions are not objective but are influenced by our wants and needs and our expectations and predictions.

**supportiveness** An attitude of an individual or an atmosphere in a group that is characterized by openness, absence of fear, and a genuine feeling of equality.

**symmetrical relationship** Relationship between two or more persons in which one person's behavior prompts the same type of behavior in the other person(s). For example, anger in one person may encourage or serve as a stimulus for anger in another person, or a critical comment by one person may lead the other person to criticize in return.

**symposium** A small group format in which each member of the group delivers a relatively prepared talk on some aspect of the topic. Often combined with a **forum**.

**systematic desensitization** A theory and technique for dealing with fears (such as communication apprehension) in which you gradually expose yourself to and develop a comfort level with the fear-causing stimulus.

**taboo** Forbidden; culturally censored. Taboo language is language that is frowned on by "polite society." Topics and specific words may be considered taboo—for example, death, sex, certain forms of illness, and various words denoting sexual activities and excretory functions.

**temporal communication** The messages communicated by a person's time orientation and treatment of time.

**territoriality** A possessive or ownership reaction to an area of space or to particular objects.

**testimonial** A persuasive tactic in which the speaker tries to use the authority or image of some positively evaluated person to gain your approval—or the image of some negatively evaluated person to gain your rejection.

**theory** A general statement or principle applicable to related phenomena.

**thesis** The main assertion of a message—for example, the theme of a public speech.

**toast** A brief speech designed to celebrate a person or an occasion.

**touch avoidance** The tendency to avoid touching and being touched by others.

**touch communication** Communication through tactile means.

**transactional** Characterizing the relationship among elements whereby each influences and is influenced by each other element; communication, in which no element is independent of any other element, is a transactional process.

**transfer** A persuasive tactic in which a speaker associates an idea with something you respect to gain your approval or with something you dislike to gain your rejection.

**uncertainty reduction strategies** Passive, active, and interactive ways of increasing accuracy in interpersonal perception.

**uncertainty reduction theory** The theory holding that as relationships develop, uncertainty is reduced; relationship development is seen as a process of reducing uncertainty about each other.

**universal of communication** A feature of communication common to all communication acts.

**unrepeatability** Principle of communication stating that no communication can ever be re-created in quite the same way, because circumstances are never the same.

**upward communication** Messages sent from the lower levels of a hierarchy to the upper levels—for example, line worker to manager, or faculty member to dean. See **downward communication**, **lateral communication**.

**value** Relative worth; a quality that makes something desirable or undesirable; an ideal or custom about which we have emotional responses, whether positive or negative.

**value, questions of** Questions that focus on the goodness or badness, the morality or immorality of an act.

**verbal aggressiveness** An unproductive **conflict** strategy that involves trying to win an argument by attacking the other person's **self-concept**. Often considered opposed to **argumentativeness**.

**visual dominance** The use of the eyes to maintain a superior or controlling position; for example, when making an especially important point, you might look intently at the other person.

**voice qualities** Aspects of **paralanguage**—specifically, pitch range, vocal lip control, glottis control, pitch control, articulation control, rhythm control, resonance, and tempo.

**volume** The relative loudness of the voice.

**withdrawal** (1) A reaction to territorial encroachment in which we leave the territory. (2) A tendency to close oneself off from conflicts rather than confront the issues.

**you-messages** Messages in which you deny responsibility for your own thoughts and behaviors; messages that attribute your perception to another person; messages of blame. Opposed to **I-messages**.

# GLOSSARY of Human Communication Skills

**abstractions** Use both abstract and specific terms when describing or explaining.

**accommodation** Accommodate to the speaking style of your listeners with moderation: Too much mirroring of the other person's manner of communicating may appear too obvious and even manipulative.

**active interpersonal conflict** Engage in interpersonal conflict actively; generally, don't rely on silence as a way of avoiding the issues.

**active listening** To listen actively, paraphrase the speaker's meaning, express understanding of the speaker's feelings, and ask questions when you need something clarified.

**advantages and disadvantages of relationships** In evaluating your own relationship choices, consider both the advantages and the disadvantages of relationships generally and of your specific relationships.

**allness** Avoid allness statements (for example, statements containing such words as *all*, *never*, or *always*); they invariably misstate the reality and often will offend other people.

**amplifying informative speeches** For an informative speech, select a variety of amplifying materials: examples, illustrations, and narratives; testimony, definitions, statistics, and visual aids.

**amplifying persuasive speeches** Support the main points of a persuasive speech with amplifying materials such as examples, statistics, and visual aids and with logical, emotional, and ethical proofs.

**analyze your perceptions** Increase accuracy in interpersonal perception by (1) identifying the influence of your physical and emotional state; (2) making sure that you're not drawing conclusions from too little information; and (3) identifying any perceptions that may be the result of your mindreading.

**anger management** Manage your anger by calming down as best you can and then reflecting on the fact that communication is irreversible, reviewing your communication options, and considering the relevant communication skills for expressing your feelings.

**appreciating cultural differences** Look at cultural differences not as deviations from the norm or as deficiencies but simply as the differences they are. At the same time, remember that recognizing differences and considering these as you communicate does not necessarily mean accepting them.

**appropriateness of self-disclosure** In self-disclosure consider the legitimacy of your motives, the appropriateness of the disclosure, the listener's responses (is the dyadic effect operating?), and the potential burdens such disclosures might impose.

**argumentativeness** During conflict aim for argumentativeness, not aggressiveness. That is, avoid attacking the other person's self-concept; instead focus logically on the issues; emphasize finding solutions; and work to ensure that what is said will result in positive self-feelings for both individuals.

**articulation and pronunciation** Avoid the articulation and pronunciation errors of omission, substitution, addition, accent, and pronouncing sounds that should be silent.

**artifactual communication** Use artifacts (such as color, clothing, body adornment, space decoration) to communicate your desired messages. But check that the messages you think are being communicated are the same that others see.

**audience analysis** Analyze your audience in terms of its sociological and psychological characteristics and adapt your speech based on these findings.

**before and after the conflict** Prepare for interpersonal conflict by arranging to fight in private, knowing what you're fighting about, and fighting about things that can be solved. After the conflict, profit from it by learning what worked and what didn't, by keeping the conflict in perspective, and by increasing the exchange of rewards.

**body movements** Use body and hand gestures to reinforce your communication purposes.

**brainstorming** In brainstorming follow these general rules: Avoid negative criticism, strive for quantity, combine and extend the contributions of others, and contribute ideas that are as wild as possible.

**channel** Assess your communication channel options (such as face-to-face conversation, e-mail, or leaving a voice mail message when you know the person won't be home) before communicating important messages.

**checking perceptions** Increase accuracy in perception by (1) describing what you see or hear and the meaning you assign to it and (2) asking the other person if your perceptions and meanings are accurate.

**communicating appropriately interculturally** Communicate interculturally with appropriate openness, empathy, positiveness, immediacy, interaction management, expressiveness, and other-orientation.

**communicating assertively** To use an assertive approach, describe the problem, say how the problem affects you, propose solutions, confirm your understanding, and reflect on your own assertiveness.

**communicating power** Communicate power by avoiding mannerisms such as hesitations, too many intensifiers, disqualifiers, tag questions, one-word answers, self-critical statements, overly polite statements, and vulgar and slang expressions.

**communicating with the grief-stricken** With someone who is grieving, use confirming messages, give the person permission to grieve, avoid directing the person, encourage the expression of feelings, and communicate empathy and support.

**communication apprehension management** To manage apprehension acquire communication skills and experiences, focus on your prior successes, reduce unpredictability, and put apprehension in perspective.

**communication options** Assess your communication options before communicating, remembering that communication is inevitable, irreversible, and unrepeatable.

**conclusions** Conclusions to speeches should summarize the main points and bring the speech to a crisp close.

**confirmation** When you wish to be confirming, acknowledge (verbally and/or nonverbally) others in your group and their contributions.

**conflict, culture, and gender** Approach conflict with an understanding of cultural and gender differences in what constitutes conflict and in how it should be pursued.

**conflict styles** Adjust your conflict style to the specific conflict in which you find yourself.

**connotative meanings** As a speaker, clarify your connotative meanings if you have any concern that your listeners might misunderstand you; as a listener, ask questions if you have doubts about the speaker's connotations.

**content and relationship** Listen to both the content and the relationship aspects of messages, distinguish between them, and respond to both.

**content and relationship conflicts** Analyze conflict messages in terms of content and relationship dimensions and respond to each accordingly.

**context adjustment** Adjust your messages to the unique communication context, taking into consideration its physical, cultural, social–psychological, and temporal aspects.

**conversational maxims** Follow (generally) the basic maxims of conversation, such as those governing quantity, quality, relations, manner, and politeness.

**conversational rules** Observe the general rules for conversation (for example, using relatively short speaking turns and avoiding interruptions), but break them when there seems logical reason to do so.

**conversational turns** Maintain relatively short conversational turns; when appropriate, pass the speaker's turn to another person nonverbally or verbally.

**credibility appeals** Seek to establish credibility by displaying competence, high moral character, and dynamism or charisma.

**critical analysis** Critically analyze reasoning from specific instances to generalizations, causes and effects, and sign.

**critical thinking** Use Edward deBono's critical thinking hats technique: Evaluate problems in terms of facts, feelings, negative arguments, positive benefits, creative ideas, and control of thinking.

**cultural differences in listening** When listening in multicultural settings, realize that people from different cultures may give very different listening cues and may operate with different rules for listening.

**cultural identifiers** Use cultural identifiers that are sensitive to the desires of others; when appropriate, make clear the cultural identifiers you prefer.

**cultural influences** Communicate with an understanding that culture influences communication in all its forms.

**cultural sensitivity** Increase your cultural sensitivity by learning about different cultures, recognizing and facing your own fears of intercultural interaction, recognizing differences between yourself and others, and becoming conscious of the cultural rules and customs of other cultures.

**culture and groups** Recognize and appreciate cultural differences in relation to aspects of group membership and leadership.

**culture and perception** Increase accuracy in perception by learning as much as you can about the cultures of those with whom you interact.

**dating statements** Mentally date your statements to avoid thinking and communicating that the world is static and unchanging. Be sure that your messages reflect the inevitability of change.

**deciding to self-disclose** In deciding to self-disclose, consider the potential benefits (for example, self-knowledge) as well as the potential personal, relationship, and professional risks.

**Delphi method** Use the Delphi method (polling by questionnaire) to solve problems when members are separated geographically.

**dialogic conversation** Treat conversation as a dialogue rather than a monologue; show concern for the other person, and for the relationship between you, with other-orientation.

**disclaimers** Preface your comments with disclaimers if you feel you might be misunderstood. But avoid disclaimers when they aren't necessary; too many disclaimers can make you appear unprepared or unwilling to state an opinion.

**disconfirming language** Avoid sexist, heterosexist, racist, and ageist language, which is disconfirming and insulting and invariably contributes to communication barriers.

**downward communication** To improve downward communication, use a vocabulary known to the workers, keeping technical jargon to a minimum; provide workers with sufficient information; and be especially careful not to damage others' image or face.

**emotional appeals** In persuasive speaking use emotional appeals—for example, appeals to fear; power, control, and influence; safety; achievement; and financial gain—as appropriate to the speech and the audience.

**emotional communication** To communicate emotions effectively, (1) describe feelings, (2) identify the reasons for the feelings, (3) anchor feelings to the present, and (4) own your feelings and messages.

**emotional display** Express your emotions and interpret the emotions of others in light of the cultural rules dictating what is and what isn't "appropriate" emotional expression.

**emotionality in interpersonal communication** Include the inevitable emotionality of your thoughts and feelings in your interpersonal communication, verbally and nonverbally.

**emotional understanding** Be able to identify and describe emotions (both positive and negative) clearly and specifically. Learn the vocabulary of emotional expression.

**empathic and objective listening** To listen empathically, punctuate the interaction from the speaker's point of view, engage in dialogue, and understand the speaker's thoughts and feelings. To listen objectively, be careful that you don't hear what you want to hear.

**empathic conflict** Engage in interpersonal conflict with empathy rather than with blame. And express this empathy ("I can understand how you must have felt").

**empathy** When appropriate, communicate empathy: Resist evaluating the person's behaviors, focus concentration on the person, express active involvement through facial expressions and gestures, reflect back the feelings you think are being expressed, self-disclose, and address any mixed messages.

**ethnocentric thinking** Recognize your own ethnocentric thinking and how it influences your verbal and nonverbal messages.

**evaluating** In evaluating messages, try first to understand fully what the speaker means; also try to identify any biases and self-interests that may lead the speaker to give an unfair presentation of the material.

**expressiveness** Expressiveness means communicating active involvement in the interaction: Use active listening, address mixed messages, use I-messages, and use appropriate variations in paralanguage and gestures.

**eye movements** Use eye movements to seek feedback, exchange conversational turns, signal the nature of your relationship with others, and compensate for increased physical distance. At the same time, look for such meanings in the eye movements of others.

**face-saving strategies** In a conflict use strategies that allow your opponent to save face; for example, avoid beltlining (hitting your opponent with attacks that he or she will have difficulty absorbing and will resent).

**facial messages** Use facial expressions to communicate that you're involved in the interaction. As a listener, look to the emotional expressions of others as additional cues to their meaning.

**facts and inferences** Distinguish facts (verifiably true past events) from inferences (guesses, hypotheses, hunches), and act on inferences with tentativeness.

**fallacy identification** When listening to a persuasive speech, detect such fallacies as name-calling, transfer, testimonial, plain folks, card stacking, bandwagon, and character attacks; avoid using these in your own speeches.

**feedback** Be alert to both verbal and nonverbal feedback—from yourself and from others—and use these cues to adjust your messages for greatest effectiveness.

**feedforward** Preface your messages with some kind of feedforward when you feel your listener needs some background or when you want to ease into a particular topic, such as bad news.

**flexibility** Because no two communication situations are identical, because everything is in a state of flux, and because everyone is different, cultivate flexibility and adjust your communication to the unique situation.

**friendships** Establish friendships to help serve such needs as utility, ego support, stimulation, and security. At the same time, seek to serve your friends' similar needs.

**fundamental attribution error** Avoid the fundamental attribution error, whereby you attribute someone's behavior solely to internal factors, by focusing on possible situational influences.

**gaining perspective on problems and solutions** To gain perspective on problems and solutions, analyze them in terms of facts, feelings, negative arguments, positive benefits, creative new ideas, and control of thinking.

**gender differences in listening** Communicate with men and women with an understanding that women give more cues that they're listening and appear more supportive in their listening than men.

**giving space** Give others the amount of space they need, which will vary on the basis of culture, gender, and emotional state. Look to the other person for any signs of spatial discomfort.

**grapevine communication** To deal with the office grapevine, understand the variety of purposes the grapevine serves and listen to it carefully, treat grapevine information as tentative, repeat only what you know or believe to be true, tap into the grapevine frequently, and always assume that what you say in grapevine communication will be repeated to others.

**group norms** Actively seek to discover the norms of the group, and take these norms into consideration when interacting in the group.

**group participation** Be group oriented rather than individually oriented, center any conflict on issues rather than on personalities, be critically open-minded, and make sure that group members' meanings are clearly understood.

**groupthink** Recognize the symptoms of groupthink and actively counter any groupthink tendencies evidenced in groups you participate in.

**high- and low-context cultures** Adjust your messages and your listening in light of the differences between high- and low-context cultures.

**I-messages** Use I-messages when communicating your feelings; take responsibility for your own feelings ("I get angry when you . . .") rather than attributing them to others ("You make me angry").

**immediacy** Maintain nonverbal immediacy through close physical distances, eye contact, and smiling; maintain verbal immediacy by using the other person's name and focusing on the other's remarks.

**implicit personality theory** Bring to your mindful state your implicit personality theory to subject your perceptions and conclusions to logical analysis.

**increasing assertiveness** Increase your own assertiveness by analyzing the assertive messages of others, rehearsing assertive messages, and communicating assertively.

**indirect messages** Use indirect messages when a more direct style might prove insulting or offensive; but be aware that indirectness can create communication problems, because indirect statements are easier to misunderstand than direct ones.

**indiscrimination** Avoid indiscrimination; that is, treat each situation and each person as unique (when possible) even when they're covered by the same label or name. "Index" your key concepts.

**individualist and collectivist cultures** Adjust your messages and your listening on the basis of the differences between individualist and collectivist cultures.

**individual roles** In a small group, avoid playing the popular but dysfunctional individual roles—the roles of aggressor, blocker, recognition seeker, self-confessor, or dominator.

**information overload** To prevent or manage information overload, pass on only messages that the other person needs to have, use messages as they come to you, organize your messages, rid yourself of extra copies, and periodically review and eliminate the sources of unnecessary messages.

**informative speaking** Follow the principles of informative speaking: Stress the information's usefulness, relate new information to information the audience already knows, present information through several senses, adjust the level of complexity, vary the levels of abstraction, avoid information overload, and recognize cultural variations.

**initial impressions** Guard against drawing impressions too quickly or on the basis of too little information; initial impressions can function as filters and prevent you from forming more accurate perceptions on the basis of more information.

**intensional orientation** Avoid intensional orientation. That is, respond to things first and to labels second; for example, the way a person is talked about is not the best measure of who that person really is.

**interaction management** Speak in relatively short conversational turns, avoid long and frequent pauses, and use verbal and nonverbal messages that are consistent.

**intercultural communication** When communicating interculturally, become mindful of (1) the differences between yourself and the member of a different culture, (2) the differences within every cultural group, (3) the differences in meanings for both verbal and nonverbal signals that you and the other person may have, and (4) the differences in cultural rules and customs.

**introductions** Introductions to speeches should gain attention and preview what is to follow.

**lateral communication** To improve lateral communication, reduce jargon and clarify terminology as needed, recognize the importance of all areas, and balance the needs of an organization that relies on cooperation and a system that rewards competition.

**leadership style** Adjust your leadership style to the task at hand and the needs of group members.

**leading a group** It is a leader's responsibility to start group interaction, maintain effective interaction throughout the discussion, keep members on track, ensure member satisfaction, encourage ongoing evaluation and improvement, and prepare members for the discussion as necessary.

**listening to the feelings of others** In listening to the feelings of others, avoid the tendency to try to solve their problems; instead, listen, empathize, focus on the other person, and encourage the person to explore his or her feelings.

**making excuses** Repair conversational problems by offering excuses (apologies) that (1) demonstrate that you understand the problem, (2) acknowledge your responsibility, (3) acknowledge your displeasure at what you did, (4) request forgiveness, and (5) make it clear that this will never happen again.

**managing relationship deterioration** When a relationship ends, break the loneliness–depression cycle, take time out, bolster your self-esteem, seek the support of nourishing others, and avoid repeating negative patterns.

**markers** Become sensitive to the markers (central, boundary, and ear) of others, and learn to use these markers to define your own territories and to communicate the desired impression.

**masculine and feminine cultures** Adjust your messages and your listening to differences in cultural "masculinity" and "femininity."

**meanings depend on context** When deciphering messages, look at the context for cues as to how you should interpret the meanings.

**meanings in people** When you are deciphering meaning, the best source is the person; meanings are in people. So, when in doubt, find out—from the source.

**metacommunication** Metacommunicate when you want to clarify the way you're talking or what you're talking about; for example, give clear feedforward and paraphrase your own complex messages.

**mindfulness** Increase your mindfulness by creating and recreating categories, being open to new information and points of view, and avoiding excessive reliance on first impressions.

**mixed messages** Avoid emitting mixed messages by focusing clearly on your purposes when communicating and by increasing conscious control over your verbal and nonverbal behaviors.

**negatives and positives of conflict** Approach conflict to minimize negative outcomes and to maximize the positive benefits of conflict and its resolution.

**networking** To network effectively, begin with people you already know and then branch out; establish relationships that are mutually beneficial; create folders, files, and directories of potentially useful sources; be proactive; consider the possible value of the variety of Web-based organizations devoted to networking; and be willing to lend your expertise to the networks of others.

**noise management** Reduce the influence of physical, physiological, psychological, and semantic noise to the extent that you can; use repetition and restatement and, when in doubt, ask if you're being clear.

**nominal group** Use the nominal group technique (compilation of unsigned written opinions) to solve problems when anonymity may be desirable.

**nonjudgmental and critical listening** To listen nonjudgmentally, keep an open mind, avoid filtering out difficult messages, and recognize your own biases. When listening to evaluate, listen extra carefully, ask questions if in doubt, and check your perceptions before offering criticism.

**nonverbal communication and culture** As far as possible, interpret the nonverbal cues of others not with the meanings assigned by your culture but with the meanings assigned by the speaker's culture.

**online conflict** Avoid common causes of online conflict such as sending out unsolicited commercial messages, spamming, and flaming.

**open expression in conflict** In interpersonal conflict try to facilitate open expression on the part of your combatant. Avoid power tactics that inhibit expression; these not only will not help resolve the conflict but also may have lasting negative effects on the relationship.

**openness** Increase openness when appropriate by self-disclosing, responding spontaneously and honestly to those with whom you're interacting, and owning your own feelings and thoughts.

**organizational message competence** To achieve organizational message competence, listen actively, empathically, critically, and in depth; apologize for errors; avoid contributing to information overload or information isolation; follow the rules of netiquette; use the grapevine; demonstrate the communication skills of group leadership and membership; avoid racist, heterosexist, ageist, or sexist language; help reduce conflict; use power effectively; use the expected channels of communication; treat all your messages as if they were being graded by your instructor.

**organizational relationship competence** To deal effectively with organizational relationships, be a mentor and a network giver as well as a protégé and network seeker; be supportive of your coworkers, and avoid being either overly critical or unconcerned with their specific jobs; exercise caution in the development of office romances, and understand your company's policies regarding such relationships; self-disclose selectively; avoid bringing relationship problems into work with you; follow the cultural rules of the organization, and break them only for an outstanding reason; stress the positive.

**organizing a speech** To organize the main points of a speech; select a thought pattern appropriate to the subject matter, the purpose of the speech, and the audience.

**organizing learning discussions** In educational or learning groups, use an organizational structure—chronological or spatial, for example—to give order to the discussion.

**other-orientation** Demonstrate other-orientation by acknowledging the importance of the other person; using focused eye contact and appropriate facial expressions; smiling, nodding, and leaning toward the other person; and expressing agreement when appropriate.

**overattribution** Avoid overattribution; rarely is any one factor an accurate explanation of complex human behavior.

**packaging** Make your verbal and nonverbal messages consistent; inconsistencies between, say, verbal and nonverbal messages often create uncertainty and misunderstanding.

**paralanguage** Vary paralinguistic features such as rate, pauses, pitch, and volume to communicate your meanings and to add interest and color to your messages.

**pauses** Use pauses to signal transitions, to allow listeners time to think, and to signal the approach of a significant idea.

**perceptual shortcuts** Be mindful of your perceptual shortcuts (for example, rules, schemata, and scripts) so that they don't mislead you and result in inaccurate perceptions.

**persuasive speaking** Apply (where relevant) the principles of persuasion, including selective exposure, audience participation, and magnitude of change.

**polarization** Avoid thinking and talking in extremes by using middle terms and qualifiers. At the same time, remember that using too many qualifiers may make you appear unsure of yourself.

**positiveness** Communicate positiveness: Express your own satisfaction with the interaction and compliment others by expressing your positive thoughts and feelings about and to the other person.

**power distance** Adjust your messages and listening based on the power-distance orientation of the culture in which you find yourself.

**power communication** Communicate power through forceful speech; avoidance of weak modifiers and excessive body movement; and demonstration of your knowledge, preparation, and organization relative to the matters at hand.

**power plays** Respond to power plays with cooperative strategies: (1) Express your feelings, (2) describe the behavior to which you object, and (3) state a cooperative response.

**presentation** During the presentation of a speech, maintain eye contact with the entire audience, allow facial expressions to convey feelings, gesture naturally, and incorporate purposeful body movements.

**presentation method** In general, use the extemporaneous method of delivery for speeches.

**present-focus conflict** Focus conflict resolution messages on the present; avoid dredging up old grievances and unloading them on the other person (gunnysacking).

**problem solving** Follow these six steps in group problem-solving situations: (1) Define and analyze the problem, (2) establish the criteria for evaluating solutions, (3) identify possible solutions, (4) evaluate solutions, (5) select the best solution(s), and (6) test selected solution(s).

**problem-solving conflicts** Treat interpersonal conflicts as problems to be solved systematically: (1) Define the problem, (2) examine possible solutions, (3) test the solution, (4) evaluate the solution, and (5) accept or reject the solution.

**quality circles** Use the quality circle technique to improve organizational functions.

**receiving** In receiving messages, focus your attention on both the verbal and the nonverbal messages, because both communicate meaning.

**reducing uncertainty** To increase accuracy in perception, reduce your uncertainty, using passive, active, and interactive strategies.

**rehearsal** Rehearsal guidelines for speeches are the following: Rehearse often, perfect presentation, rehearse the speech as a whole, time the speech at each rehearsal, approximate the specific speech situation as much as possible, see and think of yourself as a public speaker, and incorporate any presentation notes that may be of value on the occasion of the actual speech.

**relationship messages** Formulate messages that are appropriate to the stage of the relationship. Also, listen to messages from relationship partners that may reveal differences in perception about your relationship stage.

**relationship repair** To repair a deteriorating relationship, recognize the problem, engage in productive conflict resolution, pose possible solutions, affirm each other, integrate solutions into normal behavior, and take risks as appropriate.

**relationship rules** Follow the rules for maintaining relationships (such as sharing activities, sharing values, being faithful, and communicating openly and positively) when you do in fact wish to maintain and even strengthen a relationship.

**remembering** To enhance your ability to remember messages, identify the central ideas, summarize the message in an easy-to-retain form, and repeat (aloud or to yourself) key terms and names.

**research** Research topics effectively and efficiently, and critically evaluate the reliability of the research material.

**responding** In responding to messages, express support for the speaker using I-messages ("I didn't understand the point about . . .") instead of you-messages ("You didn't clarify what you meant about . . .").

**responding to others' disclosures** Respond appropriately to the disclosures of others by listening actively, supporting the discloser, and keeping the disclosures confidential.

**restimulating brainstorming** If appropriate, restimulate a brainstorming group that has lost its steam by asking for additional contributions or for further extensions of previously contributed ideas.

**romantic workplace relationships** Approach any romantic relationship at work with a clear understanding of the potential problems.

**selecting main points** After generating the possible main points for a speech, eliminate those that seem least important to the thesis, combine those that have a common focus, and select those most relevant to the purpose of the speech and the audience.

**self-awareness** Increase self-awareness: Listen to others, increase your open self as appropriate, and seek out information (discreetly) to reduce any blind spots.

**self-concept** Learn who you are: See yourself through the eyes of others; compare yourself to similar (and admired) others; examine the influences of culture; and observe, interpret, and evaluate your own message behaviors.

**self-esteem** Raise your self-esteem: Challenge self-destructive beliefs, seek out nurturing people with whom to interact, work on projects that will result in success, and seek affirmation.

**self-fulfilling prophecy** Take a second look at your perceptions when they correspond very closely to your initial expectations; the self-fulfilling prophecy may be at work.

**self-serving bias** Become mindful of any self-serving bias—any tendency to give too much weight to internal factors when explaining your positives but too much weight to external factors when explaining your negatives.

**sentence style** In preparing a speech construct sentences that are short, direct, active, and positive, and vary the type and length of sentences.

**sexual harassment management** First, talk to the harasser; if this doesn't stop the behavior, then consider collecting evidence, using appropriate channels within the organization, and filing a complaint. Do not blame yourself.

**sexual harassment messages** Avoid behaviors that could be interpreted as sexual harassment: behavior that's sexual in nature, that might be considered unreasonable, that is severe or pervasive, and that is unwelcome and offensive.

**silence** Silence can communicate lots of different meanings (e.g., anger or a need for time to think), so examine silence for meanings just as you would eye movements or body gestures.

**spatial and proxemic conversational distances** Let your spatial relationships reflect your interpersonal relationships. Maintain spatial distances that are comfortable (neither too close nor too far apart) and that are appropriate to the situation and to your relationship with the other person.

**speech of definition** For a speech of definition, consider using a variety of definitions, choose credible sources, and proceed from the known to the unknown.

**speech of demonstration** For a speech of demonstration, consider using a temporal pattern, employ transitions to connect the steps, present a broad overview and then the specific steps, and incorporate visual aids.

**speech of description** For a speech of description, consider using a spatial, topical, or 5W organizational pattern, a variety of descriptive categories, and visual aids.

**speech rate** Use variations in rate to increase communication efficiency and persuasiveness as appropriate.

**stereotypes** Be careful of thinking and talking in stereotypes; recognize that members of all groups are different, and focus on the individual rather than on the individual's membership in one group or another.

**surface and depth listening** To listen in depth: Focus on both verbal and nonverbal messages and on both content and relationship messages, and take special note of statements that refer back to the speaker. At the same time, do not avoid the surface or literal meaning.

**talk versus force** Talk about your problems rather than trying to use physical or emotional force.

**thesis and main points** Expand the thesis or main assertion of the speech by asking strategic questions to develop the main points or propositions.

**time cues** Interpret time cues from the perspective of the person with whom you're interacting. Be especially sensitive to leave-taking cues such as comments that "it's getting late" or glances at the person's watch.

**topic and purpose** Select speech topics and purposes that are appropriate to speaker, audience, and occasion, and narrow them to manageable proportions.

**touch and touch avoidance** Respect the touch-avoidance tendencies of others; pay special attention to cultural and gender differences in touch preferences and touch avoidance.

**transitions** Use transitions and internal summaries to connect the parts of a speech and to help listeners remember the speech.

**turn-taking cues** Respond to both the verbal and the nonverbal conversational turn-taking cues given to you by others, and make your own cues clear to others.

**understanding** To enhance your ability to understand messages, relate new information to what you already know, ask questions, and paraphrase what you think the speaker said.

**upward communication** To improve upward communication, set up a nonthreatening system that is acceptable to the cultural norms of the workforce; be open to hearing worker comments (even criticisms), and eliminate unnecessary gatekeepers; avoid disconfirming messages; avoid information overload; reduce ambiguity.

**vocal variation** Vary vocal volume and rate to reflect and reinforce verbal messages. Avoid a volume that is too low to understand and rates that are monotonous, too slow, or too fast.

**win–win solutions** In interpersonal conflict strive for win–win solutions rather than solutions in which one person wins and the other loses.

**word style** Word your speeches so they are clear, vivid, appropriate, and personal.

# BIBLIOGRAPHY

Acor, A. A. (2001). Employers' perceptions of persons with body art and an experimental test regarding eyebrow piercing. (Doctoral dissertation, Marquette University, 2001). *Dissertation Abstracts International, 61*, 3885B.

Adams, S. (1997). *The Dilbert principle*. New York: Harper-Collins.

Adler, R. B. (1977). *Confidence in communication: A guide to assertive and social skills*. New York: Holt, Rinehart & Winston.

Adrianson, L. (2001). Gender and computer-mediated communication: Group processes in problem solving. *Computers in Human Behavior, 17*, 71–94.

Akert, R. M., & Panter, A. T. (1988). Extraversion and the ability to decode nonverbal communication. *Personality & Individual Differences, 9*, 965–972.

Akinnaso, F. N. (1982). On the differences between spoken and written language. *Language and Speech, 25* (Part 2), 97–125.

Albas, D. C., McCluskey, K. W., & Albas, C. A. (1976). Perception of the emotional content of speech: A comparison of two Canadian groups. *Journal of Cross-Cultural Psychology, 7* (December), 481–490.

Alessandra, T. (1986). *How to listen effectively, speaking of success* (Video Tape Series). San Diego, CA: Levitz Sommer Productions.

Allan, K., & Burridge, K. (2006). *Forbidden words*. Cambridge: Cambridge University Press.

Al-Simadi, F. A. (2000). Detection of deception behavior: A cross-cultural test. *Social Behavior & Personality, 28*, 455–461.

Altman, I. (1975). *The environment and social behavior*. Monterey, CA: Brooks/Cole.

Altman, I., & Taylor, D. (1973). *Social penetration: The development of interpersonal relationships*. New York: Holt, Rinehart & Winston.

Amato, P. R. (1994). The impact of divorce on men and women in India and the United States. *Journal of Comparative Family Studies, 25*, 207–221.

Andersen, P. (1991). Explaining intercultural differences in nonverbal communication. In L. A. Samovar & R. E. Porter (Eds.), *Intercultural communication: A reader* (6th ed., pp. 286–296). Belmont, CA: Wadsworth.

Andersen, P. A., & Leibowitz, K. (1978). The development and nature of the construct touch avoidance. *Environmental Psychology and Nonverbal Behavior, 3*, 89–106.

Anderson, K. J. (1998). Meta-analysis of gender effects on conversational interruption: Who, what, when, where, and how. *Sex Roles, 39* (August), 255–252.

Angier, N. (1995a, February 14). Powerhouse of senses: Smell, at last, gets its due. *New York Times*, pp. C1, C6.

Angier, N. (1995b, May 9). Scientists mull role of empathy in man and beast. *New York Times*, pp. C1, C6.

Angier, N. (2003, July 8). Opposites attract? Not in real life. *New York Times*, pp. F1, F6.

Argyle, M. (1986). Rules for social relationships in four cultures. *Australian Journal of Psychology, 38* (December), 309–318.

Argyle, M. (1988). *Bodily communication* (2nd ed.). New York: Methuen.

Argyle, M., & Henderson, M. (1984). The rules of friendship. *Journal of Social and Personal Relationships, 1* (June), 211–237.

Argyle, M., & Henderson, M. (1985). *The anatomy of relationships: And the rules and skills needed to manage them successfully*. London: Heinemann.

Argyle, M., & Ingham, R. (1972). Gaze, mutual gaze, and distance. *Semiotica, 1*, 32–49.

Arliss, L. P. (1991). *Gender communication*. Englewood Cliffs, NJ: Prentice-Hall.

Aronson, E., Wilson, T. D., & Akert, R. M. (1999). *Social psychology: The heart and the mind* (3rd ed.). New York: Longman.

Aronson, E., Wilson, T. D., & Akert, R. M. (2002). *Social psychology: The heart and the mind* (4th ed.). New York: Longman.

Aronson, J., Cohen, J., & Nail, P. (1998). Self-affirmation theory: An update and appraisal. In E. Harmon-Jones & J. S. Mills (Eds.), *Cognitive dissonance theory: Revival with revisions and controversies* (pp. 127–147). Washington, DC: American Psychological Association.

Asch, S. (1946). Forming impressions of personality. *Journal of Abnormal and Social Psychology, 41*, 258–290.

Aune, R. K., & Kikuchi, T. (1993). Effects of language intensity similarity on perceptions of credibility, relational attributions, and persuasion. *Journal of Language and Social Psychology, 12* (September), 224–238.

Authier, J., & Gustafson, K. (1982). Microtraining: Focusing on specific skills. In E. K. Marshall, P. D. Kurtz, and Associates (Eds.), *Interpersonal helping skills: A guide to training methods, programs, and resources* (pp. 93–130). San Francisco: Jossey-Bass.

Axtell, R. E. (1990). *Do's and taboos of hosting international visitors*. New York: Wiley.

Axtell, R. E. (1993). *Do's and taboos around the world* (3rd ed.). New York: Wiley.

Ayres, J. (1986). Perceptions of speaking ability: An explanation for stage fright. *Communication Education, 35*, 275–287.

Ayres, J., & Hopf, T. S. (1992). Visualization: Reducing speech anxiety and enhancing performance. *Communication Reports, 5*, 1–10.

Ayres, J., & Hopf, T. S. (1993). *Coping with speech anxiety*. Norwood, NJ: Ablex.

Ayres, J., Hopf, T. S., & Ayres, D. M. (1994). An examination of whether imaging ability enhances the effectiveness of an intervention designed to reduce speech anxiety. *Communication Education, 43* (July), 252–258.

Bach, G. R., & Wyden, P. (1968). *The intimate enemy*. New York: Avon.

Bailey, G., & Pownell, D. (1998). Technology staff-development and support programs: Applying Abraham Maslow's hierarchy of needs. *Learning and Leading with Technology, 26* (November), 47–51.

Bales, R. F. (1950). *Interaction process analysis: A method for the study of small groups*. Cambridge, MA: Addison-Wesley.

Banerjee, N. (2005, January 23). Few but organized, Iraq veterans turn war critics. *New York Times*, National Report, 16.

Barbato, C. A., & Perse, E. M. (1992). Interpersonal communication motives and the life position of elders. *Communication Research, 19*, 516–531.

Baringer, D. K., & McCroskey, J. C. (2000). Immediacy in the classroom: Student immediacy. *Communication Education, 49*, 178–186.

Barker, L. L., & Gaut, D. (2002). *Communication* (8th ed.). Boston: Allyn & Bacon.

Barna, L. M. (1985). Stumbling blocks in intercultural communication. In L. A. Samovar & R. E. Porter (Eds.), *Intercultural communication: A reader* (4th ed., pp. 330–338). Belmont, CA: Wadsworth.

Barna, L. M. (1997). Stumbling blocks in intercultural communication. In L. A. Samovar & R. E. Porter (Eds.), *Intercultural communication: A reader* (7th ed., pp. 337–346). Belmont, CA: Wadsworth.

467

Barnard, C. I. (2005). *The functions of the executive: 30th anniversary edition*. Cambridge, MA: Harvard University Press.

Barnlund, D. C. (1970). A transactional model of communication. In J. Akin, A. Goldberg, G. Myers, & J. Stewart (Eds.), *Language behavior: A book of readings in communication*. The Hague: Mouton.

Barnlund, D. C. (1989). *Communicative styles of Japanese and Americans: Images and realities*. Belmont, CA: Wadsworth.

Baron, R. A., & Byrne, D. (1984). *Social psychology: Understanding human interaction* (4th ed.). Boston: Allyn & Bacon.

Barr, M. J. (2000). Mentoring relationships: A study of informal/formal mentoring, psychological type of mentors, and mentor/protégé type combinations. *Dissertation Abstracts International, 60*, 2568A.

Barrett, G. (2006, December 24). Glossary. *New York Times*, Wk 4.

Barrett, L., & Godfrey, T. (1988). Listening. *Person-Centered Review, 3* (November), 410-425.

Basso, K. H. (1972). To give up on words: Silence in Apache culture. In P. P. Giglioli (Ed.), *Language and social context*. New York: Penguin.

Barry, D. T. (2003). Cultural and demographic correlates of self-reported guardedness among East Asian immigrants in the U.S. *International Journal of Psychology 38* (June), 150-159.

Bassellier, G., & Benbasat, I. (2004). Business competence of information technology professionals: Conceptual development and influence on IT-business partnerships. *MIS Quarterly 28* (December), 673-694.

Baxter, L. A. (1983). Relationship disengagement: An examination of the reversal hypothesis. *Western Journal of Speech Communication, 47*, 85-98.

Baumeister, R. F., Bushman, B. J., & Campbell, W. K. (2000). Self-esteem, narcissism, and aggression: Does violence result from low self-esteem or from threatened egotism? *Current Directions in Psychological Science, 9* (February), 26-29.

Baxter, L. A. (1984). An investigation of compliance-gaining as politeness. *Human Communication Research, 10*, 427-456.

Baxter, L. A. (1986). Gender differences in the heterosexual relationship rules embedded in break-up accounts. *Journal of Social and Personal Relationships, 3*, 289-306.

Baxter, L. A. (1988). A dialectical perspective on communication strategies in relationship development. In S. Duck (Ed.), *Handbook of Personal Relationships*. New York: Wiley.

Baxter, L. A. (1990). Dialectical contradictions in relationship development. *Journal of Social and Personal Relationships, 7* (February), 69-88.

Baxter, L. A., & Simon, E. P. (1993). Relationship maintenance strategies and dialectical contradictions in personal relationships. *Journal of Social and Personal Relationships, 10* (May), 225-242.

Beach, W. A. (1990-91). Avoiding ownership for alleged wrongdoings. *Research on Language and Social Interaction, 24*, 1-36.

Beatty, M. J. (1988). Situational and predispositional correlates of public speaking anxiety. *Communication Education, 37*, 28-39.

Beatty, M. J., Rudd, J. E., & Valencic, K. M. (1999). A re-evaluation of the verbal aggressiveness scale: One factor or two? *Communication Research Reports, 16*, 10-17.

Bechler, C., & Johnson, S. D. (1995). Leadership and listening: A study of member perceptions. *Small Group Research, 26*, 77-85.

Becker, S. L., & Roberts, C. L. (1992). *Discovering mass communication* (3rd ed.). New York: HarperCollins.

Beebe, S. A., & Masterson, J. T. (2006). *Communicating in small groups: Principles and practices* (8th ed.). Boston: Allyn & Bacon.

Beier, E. (1974). How we send emotional messages. *Psychology Today, 8* (October), 53-56.

Bell, R. A., & Daly, J. A. (1984). The affinity-seeking function of communication. *Communication Monographs, 51*, 91-115.

Bell, S. T., Kuriloff, P. J., & Lottes, I. (1994). Understanding attributions of blame in stranger rape and date rape situations: An examination of gender, race, identification, and students' social perceptions of rape victims. *Journal of Applied Social Psychology, 24* (October), 1719-1734.

Bellafiore, D. (2005). *Interpersonal conflict and effective communication*. Retrieved May 7, 2006, from http://www.drbalternatives.com/articles/cc2.html.

Benne, K. D., & Sheats, P. (1948). Functional roles of group members. *Journal of Social Issues, 4*, 41-49.

Bennett, M. (1990). Children's understanding of the mitigating function of disclaimers. *Journal of Social Psychology, 130* (February), 29-37.

Bennis, W., & Nanus, B. (1985). *Leaders: The strategies for taking charge*. New York: Harper & Row.

Ben-Ze'ev, A. (2003). Primacy, emotional closeness, and openness in cyberspace. *Computers in Human Behavior 19* (July), 451-467.

Berg, J. H., & Archer, R. L. (1983). The disclosure-liking relationship. *Human Communication Research, 10*, 269-281.

Berger, C. R., & Bradac, J. J. (1982). *Language and social knowledge: Uncertainty in interpersonal relations*. London: Edward Arnold.

Bernstein, W. M., Stephan, W. G., & Davis, M. H. (1979). Explaining attributions for achievement: A path analytic approach. *Journal of Personality and Social Psychology, 37*, 1810-1821.

Berry, J. W., Poortinga, Y. H., Segall, M. H., & Dasen, P. R. (1992). *Cross-cultural psychology: Research and applications*. New York: Cambridge University Press.

Bierhoff, H. W., & Klein, R. (1991). Dimensionen der Liebe: Entwicklung einer Deutschsprachigen Skala zur Erfassung von Liebesstilen. *Zeitschrift for Differentielle und Diagnostische Psychologie 12*, 53-71.

Bishop, S. (2006). *Develop your assertiveness*. London: Kogan Page.

Blake, R. R., & Mouton, J. S. (1984). *The managerial grid III* (3rd ed.). Houston, TX: Gulf Publishing.

Blieszner, R., & Adams, R. G. (1992). *Adult friendship*. Thousand Oaks, CA: Sage.

Blumstein, P., & Schwartz, P. (1983). *American couples: Money, work, sex*. New York: Morrow.

Bochner, A. (1984). The functions of human communication in interpersonal bonding. In C. C. Arnold & J. W. Bowers (Eds.), *Handbook of rhetorical and communication theory* (pp. 544-621). Boston: Allyn & Bacon.

Bochner, A., & Kelly, C. (1974). Interpersonal competence: Rationale, philosophy, and implementation of a conceptual framework. *Communication Education, 23*, 279-301.

Bochner, S., & Hesketh, B. (1994). Power, distance, individualism/collectivism, and job-related attitudes in a culturally diverse work group. *Journal of Cross-Cultural Psychology, 25* (June), 233-257.

Bodon, J., Powell, L., & Hickson, M., III. (1999). Critiques of gatekeeping in scholarly journals: An analysis of perceptions and data. *Journal of the Association for Communication Administration, 28* (May), 60-70.

Bok, S. (1978). *Lying: Moral choice in public and private life*. New York: Pantheon.

Bok, S. (1983). *Secrets*. New York: Vintage.

Bok, S. (1998). *Mayhem: Violence as public entertainment*. Reading, MA: Perseus Books.

Bond, C. F., Jr., & Atoum, A. O. (2000). International deception. *Personality & Social Psychology Bulletin, 26* (March), 385-395.

Borden, G. (1991). *Cultural orientation: An approach to understanding intercultural communication*. Englewood Cliffs, NJ: Prentice-Hall.

Bourland, D. D., Jr. (1965-66). A linguistic note: Writing in E-prime. *General Semantics Bulletin, 32-33*, 111-114.

Bower, B. (2001). Self-illusions come back to bite students. *Science News, 159*, 148.

Brauer, M., Judd, C. M., & Gliner, M. D. (1995). The effects of repeated expressions on attitude polarization during group discussions. *Journal of Personality and Social Psychology, 68* (June), 1014-1029.

Bravo, E., & Cassedy, E. (1992). *The 9 to 5 guide to combating sexual harassment*. New York: Wiley.

Brennan, M. (1991). Mismanagement and quality circles: How middle managers influence direct participation. *Employee Relations, 13*, 22–32.

Bridges, C. R. (1996). The characteristics of career achievement perceived by African American college administrators. *Journal of Black Studies, 26* (July), 748–767.

Brilhart, J., & Galanes, G. (1992). *Effective group discussion* (7th ed.). Dubuque, IA: Brown & Benchmark.

Brody, J. E. (1991, April 28). How to foster self-esteem. *New York Times Magazine*, pp. 26–27.

Brody, J. E. (1994, March 21). Notions of beauty transcend culture, new study suggests. *New York Times*, p. A14.

Brown, P. (1980). How and why are women more polite: Some evidence from a Mayan community. In S. McConnell-Ginet, R. Borker, & M. Furman (Eds.), *Women and language in literature and society* (pp. 111–136). New York: Praeger.

Brownell, J. (1987). Listening: The toughest management skill. *Cornell Hotel and Restaurant Administration Quarterly, 27*, 64–71.

Brownell, J. (2002). *Listening: Attitudes, principles, and skills* (2nd ed.). Boston: Allyn & Bacon.

Brownell, J. (2006). *Listening: Attitudes, principles, and skills* (3rd ed.). Boston: Allyn & Bacon.

Bruneau, T. (1985). The time dimension in intercultural communication. In L. A. Samovar & R. E. Porter (Eds.), *Intercultural communication: A reader* (4th ed., pp. 280–289). Belmont, CA: Wadsworth.

Bull, R., & Rumsey, N. (1988). *The social psychology of facial appearance*. New York: Springer-Verlag.

Buller, D. B., LePoire, B. A., Aune, K., & Eloy, S. (1992). Social perceptions as mediators of the effect of speech rate similarity on compliance. *Human Communication Research, 19* (December), 286–311.

Bullock, C., McCluskey, M., Stamm, K., Tanaka, K., Torres, M. & Scott, C. (2003). Group affiliations, opinion polarization, and global organization: Views of the World Trade Organization before and after Seattle. *Mass Communication & Society, 5*(4), 433–450.

Burgoon, J. K. (1978). A communication model of personal space violations: Explication and an initial test. *Human Communication Research, 4*, 129–142.

Burgoon, J. K. (1991). Relational message interpretations of touch, conversational distance, and posture. *Journal of Nonverbal Behavior, 15* (Winter), 233–259.

Burgoon, J. K., & Bacue, A. E. (2003). Nonverbal communication skills. In J. O. Greene & B. R. Burleson (Eds.), *Handbook of communication and social interaction skills* (pp. 179–220). Mahwah, NJ: Lawrence Erlbaum.

Burgoon, J. K., Berger, C. R., & Waldron, V. R. (2000). Mindfulness and interpersonal communication. *Journal of Social Issues, 56*, 105–127.

Burgoon, J. K., Buller, D. B., & Woodall, W. G. (1996). *Nonverbal communication: The unspoken dialogue* (2nd ed.). New York: McGraw-Hill.

Burgoon, J. K., & Hoobler, G. D. (2002). Nonverbal signals. In M. L. Knapp & J. A. Daly (Eds.), *Handbook of interpersonal communication* (3rd ed., pp. 240–299). Thousand Oaks, CA: Sage.

Burke, N. D. (1993). Restricting gang clothing in the public schools. *West's Education Law Quarterly, 2* (July), 391–404.

Burleson, B. R., Holmstrom, A. J., & Gilstrap, C. M. (2005). "Guys can't say *that* to guys": Four experiments assessing the normative motivation account for deficiencies in the emotional support provided by men. *Communication Monographs 72* (December): 468–501.

Burleson, B. R., Kunkel, A. W., & Birch, J. D. (1994). Thoughts about talk in romantic relationships: Similarity makes for attraction (and happiness, too). *Communication Quarterly, 42* (Summer), 259–273.

Burleson, B. R., Samter, W., & Luccetti, A. E. (1992). Similarity in communication values as a predictor of friendship choices: Studies of friends and best friends. *Southern Communication Journal, 57*, 260–276.

Burnard, P. (2003). Ordinary chat and therapeutic conversation: Phatic communication and mental health nursing. *Journal of Psychiatric and Mental Health Nursing, 10* (December), 678–682.

Bushman, B. J., & Baumeister, R. F. (1998). Threatened egotism, narcissism, self-esteem, and direct and displaced aggression: Does self-love or self-hate lead to violence? *Journal of Personality and Social Psychology, 75*, 219–229.

Butler, P. E. (1981). *Talking to yourself: Learning the language of self-support*. New York: Harper & Row.

Byers, E. S., & Demmons, S. (1999). Sexual satisfaction and sexual self-disclosure within dating relationships. *Journal of Sex Research, 36*, 180–189.

Cai, D. A., & Fink, E. L. (2002). Conflict style differences between individualists and collectivists. *Communication Monographs, 69* (March), 67–87.

Callan, V. J. (1993). Subordinate-manager communication in different sex dyads: Consequences for job satisfaction. *Journal of Occupational & Organizational Psychology, 66* (March), 1–15.

Canary, D. J., Cody, M. J., & Manusov, V. L. (2000). *Interpersonal communication: A goals-based approach* (2nd ed.). Boston: Bedford/St. Martins.

Canary, D. J., Cupach, W. R., & Messman, S. J. (1995). *Relationship conflict*. Thousand Oaks, CA: Sage.

Canary, D. J., & Hause, K. S. (1993). Is there any reason to research sex differences in communication? *Communication Quarterly, 41* (Spring), 129–144.

Castleberry, S. B., & Shepherd, D. D. (1993). Effective interpersonal listening and personal selling. *Journal of Personal Selling and Sales Management, 13*, 35–49.

Cate, R., Henton, J., Koval, J., Christopher, R., & Lloyd, S. (1982). Premarital abuse: A social psychological perspective. *Journal of Family Issues, 3*, 79–90.

Cathcart, D., & Cathcart, R. (1985). Japanese social experience and concept of groups. In L. A. Samovar & R. E. Porter (Eds.), *Intercultural communication: A reader* (4th ed., pp. 190–197). Belmont, CA: Wadsworth.

Cawthon, S. W. (2001). Teaching strategies in inclusive classrooms with deaf students. *Journal of Deaf Studies and Deaf Education, 6*, 212–225.

Chadwick-Jones, J. K. (1976). *Social exchange theory: Its structure and influence in social psychology*. New York: Academic Press.

Chaney, R. H., Givens, C. A., Aoki, M. F., & Gombiner, M. L. (1989). Pupillary responses in recognizing awareness in persons with profound mental retardation. *Perceptual and Motor Skills, 69* (October), 523–528.

Chang, H.-C., & Holt, G. R. (1996). The changing Chinese interpersonal world: Popular themes in interpersonal communication books in modern Taiwan. *Communication Quarterly, 44* (Winter), 85–106.

Chanowitz, B., & Langer, E. (1981). Premature cognitive commitment. *Journal of Personality and Social Psychology, 41*, 1051–1063.

Chase, S. (1956). *Guides to straight thinking: With 13 common fallacies*. New York: Harper & Brothers.

Chen, G.-M. (1992). *Differences in self-disclosure patterns among Americans versus Chinese: A comparative study*. Paper presented at the annual meeting of the Eastern Communication Association, Portland, ME.

Cheney, G., & Tompkins, P. K. (1987). Coming to terms with organizational identification and commitment. *Central States Speech Journal, 38* (Spring), 1–15.

Cho, H. (2000). Asian in America: Cultural shyness can impede Asian Americans' success. *Northwest Asian Weekly, 19* (December 8), 6.

Chung, L. C., & Ting-Toomey, S. (1999). Ethnic identity and relational expectations among Asian Americans. *Communication Research Reports, 16* (Spring), 157–166.

Cialdini, R. T. (1984). *Influence: How and why people agree to things*. New York: Morrow.

Cialdini, R. T., & Ascani, K. (1976). Test of a concession procedure for inducing verbal, behavioral, and further compliance with a request to give blood. *Journal of Applied Psychology, 61*, 295-300.

Coates, J., & Sutton-Spence, R. (2001). Turn-taking patterns in deaf conversation. *Journal of Sociolinguistics, 5* (November), 507-529.

Cohen, J. (2002, May 9). An e-mail affliction: The long goodbye. *New York Times*, p. G6.

Cole, T., & Leets, L. (1999). Attachment styles and intimate television viewing: Insecurely forming relationships in a parasocial way. *Journal of Social and Personal Relationships, 16* (August), 495-511.

Coleman, P. (2002). *How to say it for couples: Communicating with tenderness, openness, and honesty*. Paramus, NJ: Prentice-Hall.

Collier, M. J. (1991). Conflict competence within African, Mexican, and Anglo-American friendships. In S. Ting-Toomey & F. Korzenny (Eds.), *Cross-cultural interpersonal communication* (pp. 132-154). Thousand Oaks, CA: Sage.

Comadena, M. E. (1984). Brainstorming groups: Ambiguity tolerance, communication apprehension, task attraction, and individual productivity. *Small Group Behavior, 15*, 251-254.

Comer, L. B., & Drollinger, T. (1999). Active emphatic listening and selling success: A conceptual framework. *Journal of Personal Selling and Sales Management, 19*, 15-29.

Cooley, C. H. (1922). *Human nature and the social order* (Rev. ed.). New York: Scribners.

Coombes, A. (2003). E-termination: Employees are getting fired for e-mail infractions. CBSMarketWatch.Com (accessed 9/3/04).

Cooper, A., & Sportolari, L. (1997). Romance in cyberspace: Understanding online attraction. *Journal of Sex Education and Therapy, 22*, 7-14.

Coover, G. E., & Murphy, S. T. (2000). The communicated self: Exploring the interaction between self and social context. *Human Communication Research, 26*, 125-147.

Copeland, L., & Griggs, L. (1985). *Going international: How to make friends and deal effectively in the global marketplace*. New York: Random House.

Cornwell, B., & Lundgren, D. C. (2001). Love on the Internet: Involvement and misrepresentation in romantic relationships in cyberspace vs. realspace. *Computers in Human Behavior, 17*, 197-211.

Cragan, J. F., & Wright, D. W. (1990). Small group communication research of the 1980s: A synthesis and critique. *Communication Studies, 41* (Fall), 212-236.

Crampton, S. M., Hodge, J. M., & Mishra, J. M. (1998). The informal communication network: Factors influencing grapevine activity. *Public Personnel Management, 27* (Winter), 569-584.

Crusco, A. H., & Wetzel, C. G. (1984). The Midas touch: The effects of interpersonal touch on restaurant tipping. *Personality and Social Psychology Bulletin, 10* (December), 512-517.

Daly, J. A., McCroskey, J. C., Ayres, J., Hopf, T., & Ayres, D. M. (1997). *Avoiding communication: Shyness, reticence, and communication apprehension* (2nd ed.). Cresskill, NJ: Hampton Press.

Davis, K. (1980). Management communication and the grape vine. In S. Ferguson & S. D. Ferguson (Eds.), *Intercom: Readings in organizational communication* (pp. 55-66). Rochelle Park, NJ: Hayden Books.

Davis, M. S. (1973). *Intimate relations*. New York: Free Press.

Davison, W. P. (1983). The third-person effects and the differential impact in negative political advertising. *Journalism Quarterly, 68*, 680-688.

Davitz, J. R. (Ed.). (1964). *The communication of emotional meaning*. New York: McGraw-Hill.

Deal, J. E., & Wampler, K. S. (1986). Dating violence: The primacy of previous experience. *Journal of Social and Personal Relationships, 3*, 457-471.

Deaux, K., & LaFrance, M. (1998). Gender. In D. Gilbert, S. Fiske & G. Lindzey (Eds.), *The Handbook of Social Psychology*, Vol. 1. (4th ed., pp. 788-828). New York: Freeman.

deBono, E. (1973). *Lateral thinking: Creativity step by step*. New York: Harper Paperbacks.

deBono, E. (1976). *Teaching thinking*. New York: Penguin.

deBono, E. (1987). *The six thinking hats*. New York: Penguin.

DeJong, W. (1979). An examination of self-perception mediation of the foot-in-the-door effect. *Journal of Personality and Social Psychology, 37*, 2221-2239.

Derlega, V. J., Winstead, B. A., Wong, P. T. P., & Greenspan, M. (1987). Self-disclosure and relationship development: An attributional analysis. In M. E. Roloff & G. R. Miller (Eds.), *Interpersonal processes: New directions in communication research* (pp. 172-187). Thousand Oaks, CA: Sage.

Derlega, V. J., Winstead, B. A., Wong, P. T. P., & Hunter, S. (1985). Gender effects in an initial encounter: A case where men exceed women in disclosure. *Journal of Social and Personal Relationships, 2*, 25-44.

Derne, S. (1999). Making sex violent: Love as force in recent Hindi films. *Violence against Women, 5* (May), 548-575.

DeStephen, R., & Hirokawa, R. (1988). Small group consensus: Stability of group support of the decision, task process, and group relationships. *Small Group Behavior 19*, 227-239.

DeTurck, M. A. (1987). When communication fails: Physical aggression as a compliance-gaining strategy. *Communication Monographs, 54*, 106-112.

DeVito, J. A. (1974). *General semantics: Guide and workbook* (Rev. ed.). DeLand, FL: Everett/Edwards.

DeVito, J. A. (1989). *The nonverbal communication workbook*. Prospect Heights, IL: Waveland Press.

DeVito, J. A. (1996). *Brainstorms: How to think more creatively about communication (or about anything else)*. New York: Longman.

Dewey, J. (1910). *How we think*. Boston: Heath.

DeZoysa, R., & Newman, O. (2002). Globalization, soft power and the challenge of Hollywood. *Contemporary Politics, 8*, 185-202.

Dietz, T. L. (1998). An examination of violence and gender role portrayals in video games: Implications for gender socialization and aggressive behavior. *Sex Roles, 38* (March), 425-442.

Dindia, K., & Fitzpatrick, M. A. (1985). Marital communication: Three approaches compared. In S. Duck & D. Perlman (Eds.), *Understanding personal relationships: An interdisciplinary approach* (pp. 137-158). Thousand Oaks, CA: Sage.

Dindia, K., & Timmerman, L. (2003). Accomplishing romantic relationships. In J. O. Greene & B. R. Burleson (Eds.), *Handbook of communication and social interaction skills* (pp. 685-722). Mahwah, NJ: Lawrence Erlbaum.

Dion, K. K., & Dion, K. L. (1993a). Individualistic and collectivist perspectives on gender and the cultural context of love and intimacy. *Journal of Social Issues 49*, 53-69.

Dion, K. L., & Dion, K. K. (1993b). Gender and ethnocultural comparisons in styles of love. *Psychology of Women Quarterly 17*, 464-473.

Dion, K. K., & Dion, K. L. (1996). Cultural perspectives on romantic love. *Personal Relationships 3*, 5-17.

Dion, K., Berscheid, E., & Walster, E. (1972). What is beautiful is good. *Journal of Personality and Social Psychology, 24*, 285-290.

Dodd, C. H. (1995). *Dynamics of intercultural communication* (4th ed.). Dubuque, IA: William C. Brown.

Dolgin, K. G., Meyer, L., & Schwartz, J. (1991). Effects of gender, target's gender, topic, and self-esteem on disclosure to best and middling friends. *Sex Roles, 25*, 311-329.

Donohue, W. A. (with Kolt, R.). (1992). *Managing interpersonal conflict*. Thousand Oaks, CA: Sage.

Dovidio, J. F., Gaertner, S. E., Kawakami, K., & Hodson, G. (2002). Why can't we just get along? Interpersonal biases and interracial distrust. *Cultural Diversity and Ethnic Minority Psychology, 8*, 88-102.

Dresser, N. (1996). *Multicultural manners: New rules of etiquette for a changing society*. New York: Wiley.

Drews, D. R., Allison, C. K., & Probst, J. R. (2000). Behavioral and self-concept differences in tattooed and nontattooed college students. *Psychological Reports, 86*, 475-481.

Dreyfuss, H. (1971). *Symbol sourcebook*. New York: McGraw-Hill.

Drucker, S. J., & Gumpert, G. (1991). Public space and communication: The zoning of public interaction. *Communication Theory, 1* (November), 294-310.

Dsilva, M. U., & Whyte, L. O. (1998). Cultural differences in conflict styles: Vietnamese refugees and established residents. *The Howard Journal of Communications, 9* (January–March), 57-68.

Duck, S. (1986). *Human relationships*. Thousand Oaks, CA: Sage.

Duncan, S. D., Jr. (1972). Some signals and rules for taking speaking turns in conversation. *Journal of Personality and Social Psychology, 23*, 283-292.

Duval, T. S., & Silva, P. J. (2002). Self-awareness, probability of improvement, and the self-serving bias. *Journal of Personality and Social Psychology 82*, 49-61.

Eagly, A. H., & Crowley, M. (1986). Gender and helping behavior: A meta-analytic review of the social psychological literature. *Psychological Bulletin, 100* (November), 283-308.

Eakins, B., & Eakins, R. G. (1978). *Sex differences in communication*. Boston: Houghton Mifflin.

Eckstein, D., & Goldman, A. (2001). The couple's gender-based communication questionnaire (CGCQ). *Family Journal: Counseling and Therapy for Couples and Families 9*, 62-74.

Eden, D. (1992). Leadership and expectations: Pygmalion effects and other self-fulfilling prophecies in organizations. *Leadership Quarterly, 3* (Winter), 271-305.

Eder, D., & Enke, J. L. (1991). The structure of gossip: Opportunities and constraints on collective expression among adolescents. *American Sociological Review, 56*, 494-508.

Ehrenhaus, P. (1988). Silence and symbolic expression. *Communication Monographs, 55* (March), 41-57.

Einhorn, L. (2006). Using e-prime and English minus absolutisms to provide self-empathy. *Etc.: A Review of General Semantics 63* (April), 180-186.

Einstein, E. (1995). Success or sabotage: Which self-fulfilling prophecy will the stepfamily create? In D. K. Huntley (Ed.), *Understanding stepfamilies: Implications for assessment and treatment*. Alexandria, VA: American Counseling Association.

Ekman, P. (1985). *Telling lies: Clues to deceit in the marketplace, politics, and marriage*. New York: Norton.

Ekman, P., & Friesen, W. V. (1969). The repertoire of nonverbal behavior: Categories, origins, usage, and coding. *Semiotica, 1*, 49-98.

Ekman, P., Friesen, W. V., & Ellsworth, P. (1972). *Emotion in the human face: Guidelines for research and an integration of findings*. New York: Pergamon Press.

Elfenbein, H. A., & Ambady, N. (2002). Is there an in-group advantage in emotion recognition? *Psychological Bulletin, 128*, 243-249.

Ellis, A. (1988). *How to stubbornly refuse to make yourself miserable about anything, yes anything*. Secaucus, NJ: Lyle Stuart.

Elmes, M. B., & Gemmill, G. (1990). The psychodynamics of mindlessness and dissent in small groups. *Small Group Research, 21*, 28-44.

Emmert P. (1994). A definition of listening. *Listening Post, 51*, 6.

Exline, R. V., Ellyson, S. L., & Long, B. (1975). Visual behavior as an aspect of power role relationships. In P. Pliner, L. Krames, & T. Alloway (Eds.), *Nonverbal communication of aggression*. New York: Plenum Press.

Fehr, B. (2004). Intimacy expectations in same-sex friendships: A prototype interaction-pattern model. *Journal of Personality and Social Psychology 86* (February), 265-284.

Felson, R. B. (2002). Violence and gender reexamined. *Law and public policy*. Washington, DC: American Psychological Association.

Fengler, A. P. (1974). Romantic love in courtship: Divergent paths of male and female students. *Journal of Comparative Family Studies*, 134-139.

Fernald, C. D. (1995). When in London ...: Differences in Disability Language Preferences Among English-Speaking Countries. *Mental Retardation, 33* (April), 99-103.

Festinger, L. (1954). A theory of social comparison processes. *Human Relations, 7*, 117-140.

Fiol, C. M., & O'Connor, E. J. (2003). Waking up! Mindfulness in the face of bandwagons. *Academy of Management Review, 28* (January), 54-70.

Fisher, D. R. (1998). Rumoring theory and the Internet: A framework for analyzing the grass roots. *Social Science Computer Review 16*, 158-168.

Fitzpatrick, M. A. (1983). Predicting couples' communication from couples' self-reports. In R. N. Bostrom (Ed.), *Communication Yearbook 7* (pp. 49-82). Thousand Oaks, CA: Sage.

Fitzpatrick, M. A. (1988). *Between husbands and wives: Communication in marriage*. Thousand Oaks, CA: Sage.

Fitzpatrick, M. A. (1991). Sex differences in marital conflict: Social psychophysiological versus cognitive explanations. *Text, 11*, 341-364.

Fitzpatrick, M. A., Jandt, F. E., Myrick, F. L., & Edgar, T. (1994). Gay and lesbian couple relationships. In Ringer, R. J. (Ed.), *Queer words, queer images: Communication and the construction of homosexuality* (pp. 265-285). New York: New York University Press.

Flocker, M. (2006). *Death by Power Point: A modern office survival guide*. Cambridge, MA: DaCapo Press.

Fodor, I. G., & Collier, J. C. (2001). Assertiveness and conflict resolution: An integrated Gestalt/cognitive behavioral model for working with urban adolescents. In M. McConville & G. Wheeler (Eds.), *The heart of development: Vol. II: Adolescence: Gestalt approaches to working with children, adolescents and their worlds* (pp. 214-252). Cambridge, ME: Analytic Press.

Folger, J. P., Poole, M. S., & Stutman, R. K. (1997). *Working through conflict: A communication perspective* (3rd ed.). New York: Longman.

Folkerts, J., & Lacy, S. (2001). *The media in your life: An introduction to mass communication* (2nd ed.). Boston: Allyn & Bacon.

Forbes, G. B. (2001). College students with tattoos and piercings: Motives, family experiences, personality factors, and perception by others. *Psychological Reports, 89*, 774-786.

Franklin, C. W., & Mizell, C. A. (1995). Some factors influencing success among African-American men: A preliminary study. *Journal of Men's Studies, 3*, 191-204.

Fraser, B. (1990). Perspectives on politeness. *Journal of Pragmatics, 14* (April), 219-236.

Fraser, Christopher O. (2000). The social goals of excuses: Self-serving attributions or politeness strategies. *Journal of Applied Social Psychology, 30* (March), 599-611.

Freedman, J., & Fraser, S. (1966). Compliance without pressure: The foot-in-the-door technique. *Journal of Personality and Social Psychology, 4*, 195-202.

French, J. R. P., Jr., & Raven, B. (1968). The bases of social power. In D. Cartwright & A. Zander (Eds.), *Group dynamics: Research and theory* (3rd ed., pp. 259-269). New York: Harper & Row.

Frentz, T. (1976). *A general approach to episodic structure*. Paper presented at the Western Speech Association Convention, San Francisco, CA. Cited in Reardon (1987).

Frey, K. J., & Eagly, A. H. (1993). Vividness can undermine the persuasiveness of messages. *Journal of Personality and Social Psychology, 65* (July), 32-44.

Friedkin, N. E. (1999). Choice shift and group polarization. *American Sociological Review, 64* (December), 856-875.

Frieze, I. H. (2000). Violence in close relationships—development of a research area: Comment on Archer (2000). *Psychological Bulletin, 126* (September), 681-684.

Frymier, A. B., & Shulman, G. M. (1995). "What's in it for me?": Increasing content relevance to enhance students' motivation. *Communication Education, 44* (January), 40-50.

Furlow, F. B. (1996). The smell of love. *Psychology Today* (March/April), 38-45.

Galvin, K., Bylund, C., & Brommel, B. J. (2004). *Family communication: Cohesion and change* (6th ed.). Boston: Allyn & Bacon.

Geffner, R., Braverman, M., Galasso, J., & Marsh, J. (Eds.). (2004). *Aggression in organizations*. Binghamton, NY: Haworth Maltreatment and Trauma Press.

Gelfand, M. J., Nishii, L. H., Holcombe, K. M., Dyer, N., Ohbuchi, K., & Fukuno, M. (2001). Cultural influences on cognitive representations of conflict: Interpretations of conflict episodes in the United States and Japan. *Journal of Applied Psychology, 86*, 1059-1074.

Gergen, K. J., Greenberg, M. S., & Willis, R. H. (1980). *Social exchange: Advances in theory and research*. New York: Plenum Press.

Giles, D. C. (2001). Parasocial interaction: A review of the literature and a model for future research. *Media Psychology, 4*, 279-305.

Giles, H., Mulac, A., Bradac, J. J., & Johnson, P. (1987). Speech accommodation theory: The first decade and beyond. In M. L. McLaughlin (Ed.), *Communication yearbook 10* (pp. 13-48). Thousand Oaks, CA: Sage.

Giordano, J. (1989). *Telecommuting and organizational culture: A study of corporate consciousness and identification*. Unpublished doctoral dissertation, University of Massachusetts, Amherst.

Gladstone, G. L., & Parker, G. B. (2002). When you're smiling, does the whole world smile for you? *Australasian Psychiatry, 10* (June), 144-146.

Glucksberg, S., & Danks, J. H. (1975). *Experimental psycholinguistics: An introduction*. Hillsdale, NJ: Erlbaum.

Goffman, E. (1971). *Relations in public: Microstudies of the public order*. New York: HarperCollins.

Goldin-Meadow, S., Nusbaum, H., Kelly, S. D., & Wagner, S. (2001). Gesture—Psychological aspects. *Psychological Science, 12*, 516-522.

Goldsmith, D. J., & Fulfs, P. A. (1999). "You just don't have the evidence": An analysis of claims and evidence. In M. E. Roloff (Ed.), *Communication yearbook, 22* (pp. 1-49). Thousand Oaks, CA: Sage.

Goleman, D. (1995, February 14). For man and beast, language of love shares many traits. *New York Times*, pp. C1, C9.

Gonzalez, A., & Zimbardo, P. G. (1985). Time in perspective. *Psychology Today, 19*, 20-26.

Gonzenbach, W. J., King, C., & Jablonski, P. (1999). Homosexuals and the military: An analysis of the spiral of silence. *Howard Journal of Communication, 10* (October-December), 281-296.

Goode, E. (2000, August 8). How culture molds habits of thought. *New York Times*, pp. F1, F8.

Goode, E. (2003, September 2). Power of positive thinking may have a health benefit, study says. *New York Times*, p. E5.

Goodwin, R., & Findlay, C. (1997). "We were just fated together". Chinese love and the concept of yuan in England and Hong Kong. *Personal Relationships 4*, 85-92.

Goodwin, R., & Lee, I. (1994). Taboo topics among Chinese and English friends: A cross-cultural comparison. *Journal of Cross-Cultural Psychology, 25*, 325-338.

Gorden, W. I., & Nevins, R. J. (1993). *We mean business: Building communication competence in business and professions*. New York: Longman.

Gordon, T. (1975). *P.E.T.: Parent effectiveness training*. New York: New American Library.

Gosling, S. D., Ko, S. J., Mannarelli, T., & Morris, M. E. (2002). A room with a cue: Personality judgments based on offices and bedrooms. *Journal of Personality and Social Psychology, 82* (March), 379-398.

Goss, B., Thompson, M., & Olds, S. (1978). Behavioral support for systematic desensitization for communication apprehension. *Human Communication Research, 4*, 158-163.

Gottman, J. (2004). 12-year study of gay & lesbian couples. Retrieved March 25, 2006, from http://www.gottman.com/research/projects/gaylesbian.

Gottman, J. M., & Carrere, S. (1994). Why can't men and women get along? Developmental roots and marital inequities. In D. J.

Canary & L. Stafford (Eds.), *Communication and relational maintenance* (pp. 203-229). San Diego, CA: Academic Press.

Gottman, J. M., & Levenson, R. W. (1999). Dysfunctional marital conflict: Women are being unfairly blamed. *Journal of Divorce and Remarriage, 31*, 1-17.

Gould, S. J. (1995, June 7). No more "wretched refuse." *New York Times*, p. A27.

Graham, E. E. (1994). Interpersonal communication motives scale. In R. B. Rubin, P. Palmgreen, & H. E. Sypher (Eds.), *Communication research measures: A sourcebook* (pp. 211-216). New York: Guilford.

Graham, E. E., Barbato, C. A., & Perse, E. M. (1993). The interpersonal communication motives model. *Communication Quarterly, 41*, 172-186.

Graham, J. A., & Argyle, M. (1975). The effects of different patterns of gaze, combined with different facial expressions, on impression formation. *Journal of Human Movement Studies, 1* (December), 178-182.

Graham, J. A., Bitti, P. R., & Argyle, M. (1975). A Cross-cultural study of the communication of emotion by facial and gestural cues. *Journal of Human Movement Studies, 1* (June), 68-77.

Greene, J. O., & Burleson, B. R. (Eds.). (2003). *Handbook of communication and social interaction skills*. Mahwah, NJ: Lawrence Erlbaum.

Grice, G. L., & Skinner, J. F. (2007). *Mastering public speaking* (6th ed.). Boston: Allyn & Bacon.

Griffin, E., & Sparks, G. G. (1990). Friends forever: A longitudinal exploration of intimacy in same-sex friends and platonic pairs. *Journal of Social and Personal Relationships 7*, 29-46.

Grobart, S. (2007, January). Allow me to introduce myself (properly). *Money, 36*, 40-41.

Gross, L. (1991). The contested closet: The ethics and politics of outing. *Critical Studies in Mass Communication, 8* (September), 352-388.

Gross, T., Turner, E., & Cederholm, L. (1987, June). Building teams for global operation. *Management Review*, 32-36.

Grossin, W. (1987). Monochronic time, polychronic time and policies for development. *Studi di Sociologia, 25* (January-March), 18-25.

Gudykunst, W. B. (1994). *Bridging differences: Effective intergroup communication* (2nd ed.). Thousand Oaks, CA: Sage.

Gudykunst, W. B., & Kim, Y. Y. (1992). *Communicating with strangers: An approach to intercultural communication* (2nd ed.). New York: Random House.

Gudykunst, W., & Nishida, T. (1984). Individual and cultural influence on uncertainty reduction. *Communication Monographs, 51*, 23-36.

Gudykunst, W. B., & Ting-Toomey, S., with Chua, E. (1988). *Culture and interpersonal communication*. Thousand Oaks, CA: Sage.

Gudykunst, W., Yang, S., & Nishida, T. (1985). A cross-cultural test of uncertainty reduction theory: Comparisons of acquaintance, friend, and dating relationships in Japan, Korea, and the United States. *Human Communication Research, 11*, 407-454.

Gueguen, N. (2003). Help on the Web: The effect of the same first name between the sender and the receptor in a request made by e-mail. *Psychological Record, 53* (Summer), 459-466.

Guerrero, L. K. (1997). Nonverbal involvement across interactions with same-sex friends, opposite-sex friends, and romantic partners: Consistency or change? *Journal of Social and Personal Relationships 14*, 31-58.

Guerrero, L. K., & Andersen, P. A. (1991). The waxing and waning of relational intimacy: Touch as a function of relational stage, gender and touch avoidance. *Journal of Social and Personal Relationships, 8*, 147-165.

Guerrero, L. K., & Andersen, P. A. (1994). Patterns of matching and initiation: Touch behavior and touch avoidance across romantic relationship stages. *Journal of Nonverbal Behavior, 18* (Summer), 137-153.

Guerrero, L. K., DeVito, J. A., & Hecht, M. L. (Eds.). (1999). *The nonverbal communication reader: Class and contemporary readings* (2nd ed.). Prospect Heights, IL: Waveland Press.

Guerrero, L. K., Eloy, S. V., & Wabnik, A. I. (1993). Linking maintenance strategies to relationship development and disengagement: A reconceptualization. *Journal of Social and Personal Relationships, 10,* 273–282.

Gumpert, G., & Drucker, S. J. (1995). Place as medium: Exegesis of the cafe drinking coffee, the art of watching others, civil conversation—with excursions into the effects of architecture and interior design. *The Speech Communication Annual, 9* (Spring), 7–32.

Haar, B. F., & Krabe, B. (1999). Strategies for resolving interpersonal conflicts in adolescence: A German-Indonesian comparison. *Journal of Cross-Cultural Psychology, 30* (November), 667–683.

Hackman, M. Z., & Johnson, C. E. (1991). *Leadership: A communication perspective.* Prospect Heights, IL: Waveland Press.

Haferkamp, C. J. (1991–92). Orientations to conflict: Gender, attributions, resolution strategies, and self-monitoring. *Current Psychology Research and Reviews, 10* (Winter), 227–240.

Haga, Y. (1988). Traits de langage et caractere Japonais. *Cahiers de Sociologie Economique et Culturelle, 9,* 105–109.

Hall, E. T. (1959). *The silent language.* Garden City, NY: Doubleday.

Hall, E. T. (1963). A system for the notation of proxemic behavior. *American Anthropologist, 65,* 1003–1026.

Hall, E. T. (1976). *Beyond culture.* Garden City, NY: Doubleday.

Hall, E. T., & Hall, M. R. (1987). *Hidden differences: Doing business with the Japanese.* New York: Doubleday.

Hall, J. A. (1998). How big are nonverbal sex differences? The case of smiling and sensitivity to nonverbal cues. In D. J. Canary & K. Dindia (Eds.), *Sex differences and similarities in communication: Critical essays and empirical investigations of sex and gender in interaction* (pp. 155–178). Mahwah, NJ: Lawrence Erlbaum.

Hall, J. K. (1993). Tengo una bomba: The paralinguistic and linguistic conventions of the oral practice Chismeando. *Research on Language and Social Interaction, 26,* 55–83.

Halmari, H. (1995). The organization of episode structure in Finnish/Finnish and Finish/Anglo-American business telephone conversations: An intercultural perspective. ERIC Clearinghouse: FL022794 (Accession No. ED386914).

Haney, W. (1973). *Communication and organizational behavior: Text and cases* (3rd ed.). Homewood, IL: Irwin.

Haridakis, P. M., & Rubin, A. M. (2003). Motivation for watching television violence and viewer aggression. *Mass Communication and Society, 6* (February), 29–56.

Harris, M., & Johnson, O. (2007). *Cultural anthropology,* 7th ed. Boston: Allyn & Bacon.

Hart, F. (1990). The construction of masculinity in men's friendships: Misogyny, heterosexuality, and homophobia. *Resources for Feminist Research, 19,* 60–67.

Hart, R. P., Carlson, R. E., & Eadie, W. F. (1980). Attitudes toward communication and the assessment of rhetorical sensitivity. *Communication Monographs, 47,* 1–22.

Hatfield, E., & Rapson, R. L. (1996). *Love and sex: Cross-cultural perspectives.* Boston: Allyn & Bacon.

Hayakawa, S. I., & Hayakawa, A. R. (1990). *Language in thought and action* (5th ed.). New York: Harcourt Brace Jovanovich.

Hays, R. B. (1989). The day-to-day functioning of close versus casual friendships. *Journal of Social and Personal Relationships, 6,* 21–37.

Heap, J. L. (1992). Seeing snubs: An introduction to sequential analysis of classroom interaction. *Journal of Classroom Interaction, 27,* 23–28.

Heasley, J. B., Babbitt, C. E., & Burbach, H. J. (1995). Gender differences in college students' perceptions of "fighting words." *Sociological Viewpoints, 11* (Fall), 30–40.

Hecht, M. L., Collier, M. J., & Ribeau, S. (1993). *African American communication: Ethnic identity and cultural interpretation.* Thousand Oaks, CA: Sage.

Hecht, M. L., Jackson, R. L., & Ribeau, S. (2003). *African American communication: Exploring identity and culture* (2nd. ed.). Mahwah, NJ: Erlbaum.

Heenehan, M. (1997). *Networking.* New York: Random House.

Hellweg, S. A. (1992). Organizational grapevines. In K. L. Hutchinson (Ed.), *Readings in organizational communication* (pp. 159–172). Dubuque, IA: William C. Brown.

Hendrick, C., & Hendrick, S. (1990). A relationship-specific version of the love attitudes scale. In J. W. Heulip (Ed.), *Handbook of replication research in the behavioral and social sciences* [Special issue]. *Journal of Social Behavior and Personality, 5,* 239–254.

Hendrick, C., Hendrick, S., Foote, F. H., & Slapion-Foote, M. J. (1984). Do men and women love differently? *Journal of Social and Personal Relationships 1,* 177–195.

Herrick, J. A. (2004). *Argumentation: Understanding and shaping arguments* (updated edition). State College, PA: Strata.

Hersey, P., Blanchard, K. H., & Johnson, D. E. (2001). *Management of organizational behavior: Leading human resources* (8th ed.). Upper Saddle River, NJ: Prentice-Hall.

Hess, E. H. (1975). *The tell-tale eye.* New York: Van Nostrand Reinhold.

Hess, E. H., Seltzer, A. L., & Schlien, J. M. (1965). Pupil response of hetero- and homosexual males to pictures of men and women: A pilot study. *Journal of Abnormal Psychology, 70,* 165–168.

Hess, U., Kappas, A., McHugo, G. J., Lanzetta, J. T., et al. (1992). The facilitative effect of facial expression on the self-generation of emotion. *International Journal of Psychophysiology, 12* (May), 251–265.

Hewitt, J. P. (1998). *The myth of self-esteem: Finding happiness and solving problems in America.* New York: St. Martin's Press.

Hewitt, J., & Stokes, R. (1975). Disclaimers. *American Sociological Review, 40,* 1–11.

Hickson, M. L., Stacks, D. W., & Moore, N. J. (2003). *Nonverbal communication: Studies and applications.* Los Angeles: Roxbury.

Hilton, L. (2000). They heard it through the grapevine. *South Florida Business Journal, 21* (August), 53.

Himle, J. A., Abelson, J. L, & Haghightgou, H. (1999). Effect of alcohol on social phobic anxiety. *American Journal of Psychiatry, 156* (August), 1237–1243.

Hirokawa, R. Y., & Wagner, A. E. (2004). Superior–subordinate influence in organizations. In J. S. Seiter & R. H. Gass (Eds.), *Perspectives on persuasion, social influence, and compliance gaining* (pp. 337–351). Boston: Allyn & Bacon.

Hirokawa, R. Y., & Miyahara, A. (1986). A comparison of influence strategies utilized by managers in American and Japanese organizations. *Communication Quarterly, 34,* 250–265.

Hirsch, E. D., Jr., Kett, J. F., & Trefil, J. (Eds.). (2002). *The new dictionary of cultural literacy.* Boston: Houghton Mifflin.

Hocker, J. L., & Wilmot, W. W. (1985). *Interpersonal conflict* (2nd ed.). Dubuque, IA: William C. Brown.

Hoffner, C., Plotkin, R. S., Buchanan, M., Anderson, J. D., Kamigaki, S. K., Hubbs, L. A., Kowalczyk, L., Silberg, K., & Pastoret, A. (2001). The third-person effect in perceptions of the influence of television violence. *Journal of Communication, 51* (June), 283–299.

Hofstede, G. (1997). *Cultures and organizations: Software of the mind.* New York: McGraw-Hill.

Hofstede, G. (Ed.). (1998). *Masculinity and femininity: The taboo dimension of national cultures.* Thousand Oaks, CA: Sage.

Hoft, N. L. (1995). *International technical communication: How to export information about high technology.* New York: Wiley.

Holden, J. M. (1991). The most frequent personality priority pairings in marriage and marriage counseling. *Individual Psychology Journal of Adlerian Theory, Research, and Practice, 47* (September), 392–398.

Holmes, J. (1995). *Women, men and politeness.* New York: Longman.

Hopper, R., Knapp, M. L., & Scott, L. (1981). Couples' personal idioms: Exploring intimate talk. *Journal of Communication 31,* 23–33.

Horenstein, V. D., & Downey, J. L. (2003). A cross-cultural investigation of self-disclosure. *North American Journal of Psychology 5*, 373-86.

Hosman, L. A. (1989). The evaluative consequences of hedges, hesitations, and intensifiers: Powerful and powerless speech styles. *Human Communication Research, 15*, 383-406.

Hunt, M. O. (2000). Status, religion, and the "belief in a just world": Comparing African Americans, Latinos, and whites. *Social Science Quarterly, 81* (March), 325-343.

Huston, M., & Schwartz, P. (1995). The relationships of lesbians and gay men. In J. T. Wood, & S. Duck (Eds.) *Under-studied relationships: Off the beaten track* (pp. 89-121).Thousand Oaks, CA: Sage.

Iizuka, Y. (1993). Regulators in Japanese conversation. *Psychological Reports, 72* (February), 203-209.

Imahori, T. T., & Cupach, W. R. (1994). A cross-cultural comparison of the interpretation and management of face: U.S. American and Japanese responses to embarrassing predicaments. *International Journal of Intercultural Relations, 18* (Spring), 193-219.

Infante, D. A. (1988). *Arguing constructively.* Prospect Heights, IL: Waveland Press.

Infante, D. A., & Rancer, A. S. (1982). A conceptualization and measure of argumentativeness. *Journal of Personality Assessment, 46*, 72-80.

Infante, D. A., & Rancer, A. S. (1995). Argumentativeness and verbal aggressiveness: A review of recent theory and research. In B. R. Burleson (Ed.), *Communication Yearbook 19*. Thousand Oaks, CA: Sage.

Infante, D. A., Rancer, A. S., & Womack, D. F. (2002). *Building communication theory* (4th ed.). Prospect Heights, IL: Waveland Press.

Infante, D. A., & Wigley, C. J. (1986). Verbal aggressiveness: An interpersonal model and measure. *Communication Monographs, 53*, 61-69.

Jablin, F. M. (1981). Cultivating imagination: Factors that enhance and inhibit creativity in brainstorming groups. *Human Communication Research, 7*, 245-258.

Jacobson, D. (1999). Impression formation in cyberspace: Online expectations and offline experiences in text-based virtual communities. *Journal of Computer-Mediated Communication, 5*, n.p.

Jaksa, J. A., & Pritchard, M. S. (1994). *Communication ethics: Methods of analysis* (2nd ed.). Belmont, CA: Wadsworth.

Jambor, E., & Elliott, M. (2005). Self-esteem and coping strategies among deaf students. *Journal of Deaf Studies and Deaf Education 10* (Winter), 63-81.

James, D. L. (1995). *The executive guide to Asia-Pacific communications*. New York: Kodansha International.

Jamieson, K. H., & Campbell, K. K. (1992). *The interplay of influence* (3rd ed.). Belmont, CA: Wadsworth.

Jandt, F. E. (2004). *Intercultural communication* (4th ed.). Thousand Oaks, CA: Sage.

Janis, I. (1983). *Victims of group thinking: A psychological study of foreign policy decisions and fiascoes* (2nd ed.). Boston: Houghton Mifflin.

Janus, S. S., & Janus, C. L. (1993). *The Janus report on sexual behavior*. New York: Wiley.

Jaworski, A. (1993). *The power of silence: Social and pragmatic perspectives*. Thousand Oaks, CA: Sage.

Jecker, J., & Landy, D. (1969). Liking a person as a function of doing him a favor. *Human Relations, 22*, 371-378.

Jeffres, L. W., Neuendorf, K. A., & Atkin, D. (1999). Spirals of silence: Expressing opinions when the climate of opinion is unambiguous. *Political Communication, 16* (April-June), 115-131.

Johannesen, R. L. (1974). The functions of silence: A plea for communication research. *Western Speech, 38* (Winter), 25-35.

Johannesen, R. L. (2001). *Ethics in human communication* (6th ed.). Prospect Heights, IL: Waveland Press.

Johansson, W., & Percy, W. A. (1994). *Outing: Shattering the conspiracy of silence*. New York: Harrington Park Press.

Johnson, K. (1998, May 5). Self-image is suffering from lack of esteem. *New York Times*, p. F7.

Johnson, M. P. (1973). Commitment: A conceptual structure and empirical application. *Sociological Quarterly, 14*, 395-406.

Johnson, M. P. (1982). Social and cognitive features of the dissolution of commitment to relationships. In S. Duck (Ed.), *Personal Relationships: 4. Dissolving personal relationships* (pp. 51-73). New York: Academic Press.

Johnson, M. P. (1991). Commitment to personal relationships. In W. H. Jones & D. Perlman (Eds.), *Advances in personal relationships* (Vol. 3, pp. 117-143). London: Jessica Kingsley.

Johnson, S. A. (1993). *When "I love you" turns violent: Emotional and physical abuse in dating relationships*. Far Hills, NJ: New Horizon Press.

Johnson, S. D., & Bechler, C. (1998). Examining the relationships between listening effectiveness and leadership emergence: Perceptions, behaviors, and recall. *Small Group Research, 29* (August), 452-471.

Joinson, A. N. (2001). Self-disclosure in computer-mediated communication. The role of self-awareness and visual anonymity. *European Journal of Social Psychology, 31* (March-April), 177-192.

Joinson, A. N. (2004). Self-esteem, interpersonal risk, and preference for e-mail to face-to-face communication. *CyberPsychology and Behavior 7* (August), 472-478.

Jones, Q., Ravid, G., & Rafaeli, S. (2004, June). Information overload and the message dynamics of online interaction spaces: A theoretical model and empirical exploration. *Information Systems Research, 15*, 194-210.

Jones, S., & Yarbrough, A. E. (1985). A naturalistic study of the meanings of touch. *Communication Monographs, 52*, 19-56. A version of this paper appears in DeVito and Hecht (1990).

Jourard, S. M. (1968). *Disclosing man to himself*. New York: Van Nostrand Reinhold.

Jourard, S. M. (1971a). *Self-disclosure*. New York: Wiley.

Jourard, S. M. (1971b). *The transparent self* (Rev. ed.). New York: Van Nostrand Reinhold.

Joyner, R. (1993). An auto-interview on the need for E-prime. *Etc.: A Review of General Semantics, 50* (Fall), 317-325.

Kanner, B. (1989, April 3). Color schemes. *New York Magazine*, pp. 22-23.

Kapoor, S., Wolfe, A., & Blue, J. (1995). Universal values structure and individualism-collectivism: A U.S. test. *Communication Research Reports, 12* (Spring), 112-123.

Kelly, M. S. (2006). *Communication@work: Ethical, effective, and expressive communication in the workplace*. Boston: Allyn & Bacon.

Kelly, P. K. (1994). *Team decision-making techniques*. Irvine, CA: Richard Chang Associates.

Kennedy, C. W., & Camden, C. T. (1988). A new look at interruptions. *Western Journal of Speech Communication, 47*, 45-58.

Ketcham, H. (1958). *Color planning for business and industry*. New York: Harper.

Keyes, R. (1980). *The height of your life*. New York: Warner Books.

Kiel, J. M. (1999). Reshaping Maslow's hierarchy of needs to reflect today's education and managerial philosophies. *Journal of Instructional Psychology, 26* (September), 167-168.

Kim, M.-S., & Sharkey, W. F. (1995). Independent and interdependent construals of self: Explaining cultural patterns of interpersonal communication in multi-cultural organizational settings. *Communication Quarterly, 43* (Winter), 20-38.

Kim, S. H., & Smith, R. H. (1993). Revenge and conflict escalation. *Negotiation Journal, 9* (January), 37-43.

Kim, Y. Y. (1988). Communication and acculturation. In L. A. Samovar & R. E. Porter (Eds.), *Intercultural communication: A reader* (4th ed., pp. 344-354). Belmont, CA: Wadsworth.

Kindler, H. S. (1996). *Managing disagreement constructively* (Rev. ed.). Menlo Park, CA: Crisp Publications.

Kirkpatrick, C., & Caplow, T. (1945). Courtship in a group of Minnesota students. *American Journal of Sociology 51*, 114-125.

Klein, J. (Ed.). (1992). The E-prime controversy: A symposium [Special issue]. *Etc.: A Review of General Semantics, 49*(2).

Kleinke, C. L. (1986). *Meeting and understanding people.* New York: W. H. Freeman.

Kleinke, C. L., & Dean, G. O. (1990). Evaluation of men and women receiving positive and negative responses with various acquaintance strategies. *Journal of Social Behavior and Personality, 5*, 369-377.

Knapp, M. L., Ellis, D., & Williams, B. A. (1980). Perceptions of communication behavior associated with relationship terms. *Communication Monographs 47*, 262-278.

Knapp, M. L., & Hall, J. (1997). *Nonverbal behavior in human interaction* (4th ed.). New York: Holt, Rinehart & Winston.

Knapp, M. L., Hart, R. P., Friedrich, G. W., & Shulman, G. M. (1973). The rhetoric of goodbye: Verbal and nonverbal correlates of human leave-taking. *Communication Monographs, 40*, 182-198.

Knapp, M. L., & Taylor, E. H. (1995). Commitment and its communication in romantic relationships. In A. L. Weber & J. H. Harvey (Eds.), *Perspectives on close relationships* (pp. 153-175). Boston: Allyn & Bacon.

Knapp, M. L., & Vangelisti, A. L. (2000). *Interpersonal communication and human relationships* (4th ed.). Boston: Allyn & Bacon.

Knobloch, L. K., & Solomon, D. H. (1999). Measuring the sources and content of relational uncertainty. *Communication Studies, 50* (Winter), 261-278.

Knox, D., Daniels, V., Sturdivant, L., & Zusman, M. E. (2001). College student use of the Internet for mate selection. *College Student Journal 35*, 158-160.

Kochman, T. (1981). *Black and white: Styles in conflict.* Chicago, IL: University of Chicago Press.

Koerner, A. F., & Fitzpatrick, M. A. (2002). You never leave your family in a fight: The impact of family of origin on conflict behavior in romantic relationships. *Communication Studies 53* (fall), 234-252.

Kohn, A. (1989). Do religious people help more? Not so you'd notice. *Psychology Today* (December), 66-68.

Kollock, P., & Smith, M. (1996). Managing the virtual commons: Cooperation and conflict in computer communities. In S. Herring (Ed.), *Computer-mediated communication: Linguistic, social, and cross-cultural perspectives* (pp. 109-128). Amsterdam: John Benjamins.

Komarovsky, M. (1964). *Blue collar marriage.* New York: Random House.

Koppelman, K. L., with Goodhart, R. L. (2005). *Understanding human differences: Multicultural education for a diverse America.* Boston: Allyn & Bacon.

Korzybski, A. (1933). *Science and sanity.* Lakeville, CT: International Non-Aristotelian Library.

Kramarae, C. (1999). The language and nature of the Internet: The meaning of Global English. *New Media & Society, 1* (April), 47-53.

Kramer, R. (1997). Leading by listening: An empirical test of Carl Rogers's theory of human relationship using interpersonal assessments of leaders by followers. *Dissertation Abstracts International: Section A. Humanities and Social Sciences, 58* (August), 0514.

Krebs, G. L. (1990). *Organizational communication* (2nd ed.). New York: Longman.

Krivonos, P. D., & Knapp, M. L. (1975). Initiating communication: What do you say when you say hello? *Central States Speech Journal, 26*, 115-125.

Kurdek, L. A. (1994). Areas of conflict for gay, lesbian, and heterosexual couples: What couples argue about influences relationship satisfaction. *Journal of Marriage and the Family, 56* (November), 923-934.

Kurdek, L. A. (1995). Developmental changes in relationship quality in gay and lesbian cohabiting couples. *Develop mental Psychology, 31* (January), 86-93.

Kurdek, L. A. (2003). Differences between gay and lesbian cohabiting couples. *Journal of Social and Personal Relationships 20* (August), 411-436.

Kurdek, L. A. (2004). Are gay and lesbian cohabitating couples really different from heterosexual married couples? *Journal of Marriage and Family 66* (November), 880-900.

Laing, M. (1993). Gossip: Does it play a role in the socialization of nurses? *Journal of Nursing Scholarship, 25* (Spring), 37-43.

Lamb, G. M. (2005). Product placement pushes into print. Retrieved March 30, 2006, from http://www.csmonitor.com.

Langer, E. J. (1989). *Mindfulness.* Reading, MA: Addison-Wesley.

Lantz, A. (2001). Meetings in a distributed group of experts: Comparing face-to-face, chat and collaborative virtual environments. *Behaviour and Information Technology, 20*, 111-117.

Lanzetta, J. T., Cartwright-Smith, J., & Kleck, R. E. (1976). Effects of nonverbal dissimulations on emotional experience and autonomic arousal. *Journal of Personality and Social Psychology, 33*, 354-370.

Larsen, R. J., Kasimatis, M., & Frey, K. (1992). Facilitating the furrowed brow: An unobtrusive test of the facial feedback hypothesis applied to unpleasant affect. *Cognition and Emotion, 6* (September), 321-338.

Lauer, C. S. (2003). Listen to this. *Modern Healthcare, 33* (February 10), 34.

Lea, M., & Spears, R. (1995). Love at first byte? Building personal relationships over computer networks. In J. T. Wood & S. Duck (Eds.), *Under-studied relationships: Off the beaten track* (pp. 197-233). Thousand Oaks, CA: Sage.

Leaper, C., & Holliday, H. (1995). Gossip in same-gender and cross-gender friends' conversations. *Personal Relationships, 2* (September), 237-246.

Leathers, D. G. (1997). *Successful nonverbal communication: Principles and applications* (3rd ed.). New York: Macmillan.

Lederer, W. J. (1984). *Creating a good relationship.* New York: Norton.

Lee, A. M., & Lee, E. B. (1972). *The fine art of propaganda.* San Francisco: International Society for General Semantics.

Lee, A. M., & Lee, E. B. (1995). The iconography of propaganda analysis. *Etc.: A Review of General Semantics, 52* (Spring), 13-17.

Lee, C., & Gudykunst, W. B. (2001). Attraction in initial interethnic interactions. *International Journal of Intercultural Relations, 25* (July), 373-387.

Lee, F. (1993). Being polite and keeping MUM: How bad news is communicated in organizational hierarchies. *Journal of Applied Social Psychology, 23*, 1124-1149.

Lee, H. O., & Boster, F. J. (1992). Collectivism-individualism in perceptions of speech rate: A cross-cultural comparison. *Journal of Cross-Cultural Psychology, 23*, 377-388.

Lee, J. A. (1976). *The colors of love.* New York: Bantam.

Lee, K. (2000, November 1). Information overload threatens employee productivity. *Employee Benefit News* (Securities Data Publishing, Inc.), p. 1.

Lee, R. L. M. (1984). Malaysian queue culture: An ethnography of urban public behavior. *Southeast Asian Journal of Social Science, 12*, 36-50.

Leon, J. J., Philbrick, J. L., Parra, F., Escobedo, E., et al. (1994). Love styles among university students in Mexico. *Psychological Reports 74*, 307-310.

Leung, K. (1988). Some determinants of conflict avoidance. *Journal of Cross-Cultural Psychology, 19* (March), 125-136.

Lever, J. (1995, August 22). The 1995 *Advocate* survey of sexuality and relationships: The women, lesbian sex survey. *The Advocate, 687/688*, pp. 22-30.

Levesque, M. J. (1995). Excuses as a method of impression management: Toward an understanding of the determinants of excuse effectiveness. *Dissertation Abstractions International Section B: The Sciences and Engineering, 56* (August), 1150.

Levine, D. (2000). Virtual attraction: What rocks your boat. *CyberPsychology & Behavior, 3* (August), 565-573.

LeVine, R., & Bartlett, K. (1984). Pace of life, punctuality, and coronary heart disease in six countries. *Journal of Cross-Cultural Psychology, 15*, 233-255.

Levine, M. (2004, June 1). Tell the doctor all your problems, but keep it to less than a minute. *New York Times*, F6.

LeVine, R., Sato, S., Hashimoto, T., & Verma, J. (1994). Love and marriage in eleven cultures. Unpublished manuscript. California State University, Fresno. Cited in Hatfield & Rapson (1996).

Levine, T. R., Beatty, M. J., Limon, S., Hamilton, M. A., Buck, R., & Chory-Assad, R. M. (2004, September). The dimensionality of the verbal aggressiveness scale. *Communication Monographs, 71*, 245-268.

Lewin, K. (1947). *Human relations*. New York: Harper & Row.

Lewis, D. (1989). *The secret language of success*. New York: Carroll & Graf.

Lewis, P. H. (1995, November 13). The new Internet gatekeepers. *New York Times*, pp. D1, D6.

Li, C., & Shi, K. (2003). Transformational leadership and its relationship with leadership effectiveness. *Psychological Science, 26* (January), 115-117.

Li, H. Z. (1999). Communicating information in conversations: A cross-cultural comparison. *International Journal of Intercultural Relations, 23* (May), 387-409.

Lindeman, M., Harakka, T., & Keltikangas-Jarvinen, L. (1997). Age and gender differences in adolescents' reactions to conflict situations: Aggression, prosociality, and withdrawal. *Journal of Youth and Adolescence, 26* (June), 339-351.

Lloyd, S. R. (2001). *Developing positive assertiveness* (3rd ed.). Menlo Park, CA: Crisp Publications.

Lu, S. (1998, October 9). *Critical reflections on phatic communication research: schematizations, limitations and alternatives*. Paper delivered at the New York State Speech Communication Association, Monticello, New York.

Lucas, S. (2007). *The art of public speaking* (9th ed.). New York: McGraw-Hill.

Lumsden, G., & Lumsden, D. (1996). *Communicating in groups and teams* (2nd ed.). Belmont, CA: Wadsworth.

Lustig, M. W., & Koester, J. (2006). *Intercultural competence: Interpersonal communication across cultures* (5th ed.). New York: Longman.

Ma, K. (1996). *The modern Madame Butterfly: Fantasy and reality in Japanese cross-cultural relationships*. Rutland, VT: Charles E. Tuttle.

Ma, R. (1992). The role of unofficial intermediaries in interpersonal conflicts in the Chinese culture. *Communication Quarterly, 40* (Summer), 269-278.

MacLachlan, J. (1979). What people really think of fast talkers. *Psychology Today, 13* (November), 113-117.

Main, F., & Oliver, R. (1988). Complementary, symmetrical, and parallel personality priorities as indicators of marital adjustment. *Individual Psychology Journal of Adlerian Theory, Research, and Practice, 44* (September), 324-332.

Malandro, L. A., Barker, L., & Barker, D. A. (1989). *Nonverbal communication* (2nd ed.). New York: Random House.

Malinowski, B. (1923). The problem of meaning in primitive languages. In C. K. Ogden & I. A. Richards, *The meaning of meaning* (pp. 296-336). New York: Harcourt Brace Jovanovich.

Mallen, M. J., Day, S. X., & Green, M. A. (2003). Online versus face-to-face conversation: An examination of relational and discourse variables. *Psychotherapy: Theory, Research, Practice, Training, 40* (Spring-Summer), 155-163.

Mandese, J. (2006). When product placement goes too far. Retrieved March 30, 2006, from http://www.broadcastingcable.com.

Manes, J., & Wolfson, N. (1981). The compliment formula. In F. Coulmas (Ed.), *Conversational routines* (pp. 115-132). The Hague: Mouton.

Mao, L. R. (1994). Beyond politeness theory: "Face" revisited and renewed. *Journal of Pragmatics, 21* (May), 451-486.

Marien, M. (1992). *Vital Speeches of the Day* (March 15), 340-344.

Markman, H. J., Silvern, L., Clements, M., & Kraft-Hanak, S. (1993). Men and women dealing with conflict in heterosexual relationships. *Journal of Social Issues, 49* (Fall), 107-125.

Marsh, P. (1988). *Eye to eye: How people interact*. Topfield, MA: Salem House.

Marshall, A. (2005). *Confronting sexual harassment: The law and policies of everyday life*. Burlington, VT: Ashgate.

Marshall, E. (1983). *Eye language: Understanding the eloquent eye*. New York: New Trend.

Marshall, L. L., & Rose, P. (1987). Gender, stress, and violence in the adult relationships of a sample of college students. *Journal of Social and Personal Relationships, 4*, 299-316.

Marston, P. J., Hecht, M. L., & Robers, T. (1987). True love ways: The subjective experience and communication of romantic love. *Journal of Personal and Social Relationships 4*, 387-407.

Martin, G. N. (1998). Human electroencephalographic (EEG) response to olfactory stimulation: Two experiments using the aroma of food. *International Journal of Psychophysiology, 30*, 287-302.

Martin, M. M., & Anderson, C. M. (1995). Roommate similarity: Are roommates who are similar in their communication traits more satisfied? *Communication Research Reports, 12* (Spring), 46-52.

Martin, M. M., & Rubin, R. B. (1994). Development of a communication flexibility measure. *The Southern Communication Journal, 59* (Winter), 171-178.

Maslow, A. (1970). *Motivation and personality*. New York: HarperCollins.

Mastin, T. (1998). Employees' understanding of employer-sponsored retirement plans: A knowledge gap perspective. *Public Relations Review, 24* (Winter), 521-534.

Matsumoto, D. (1991). Cultural influences on facial expressions of emotion. *Southern Communication Journal, 56* (Winter), 128-137.

Matsumoto, D. (1994). *People: Psychology from a cultural perspective*. Pacific Grove, CA: Brooks/Cole.

Matsumoto, D. (1996). *Culture and psychology*. Pacific Grove, CA: Brooks/Cole.

Matsumoto, D., & Kudoh, T. (1993). American-Japanese cultural differences in attributions of personality based on smiles. *Journal of Nonverbal Behavior, 17*, 231-243.

McCall, D. L., & Green, R. G. (1991). Symmetricality and complementarity and their relationship to marital stability. *Journal of Divorce and Remarriage, 15*, 23-32.

McCarthy, M. (2003). Talking back: Small interactional response tokens in everyday conversation. *Research on Language and Social Interaction 36* (January), 33-63.

McCown, J. A., Fischer, D., Page, R., & Homant, M. (2001). Internet relationships: People who meeting people. *CyberPsychology & Behavior 4* (October), 593-596.

McCroskey, J. C. (1997). *Introduction to rhetorical communication* (7th ed.). Englewood Cliffs, NJ: Prentice-Hall.

McCroskey, J., & Wheeless, L. (1976). *Introduction to human communication*. Boston: Allyn & Bacon.

McDonald, E. J., McCabe, K., Yeh, M., Lau, A., Garland, A., & Hough, R. L. (2005). Cultural affiliation and self-esteem as predictors of internalizing symptoms among Mexican American adolescents. *Journal of Clinical Child and Adolescent Psychology 34* (February), 163-171.

McGill, M. E. (1985). *The McGill report on male intimacy*. New York: Harper & Row.

McGregor, D. (1980). *The human side of enterprise*. New York: McGraw-Hill.

McGregor, D. (2005). *The human side of enterprise: Annotated edition*. New York: McGraw-Hill.

McKerrow, R. E., Gronbeck, B. E., Ehninger, D., & Monroe, A. H. (2000). *Principles and types of speech communication* (14th ed.). Boston: Allyn & Bacon.

McLaughlin, M. L. (1984). *Conversation: How talk is organized*. Thousand Oaks, CA: Sage.

McNatt, D. B. (2001). Ancient Pygmalion joins contemporary management: A meta-analysis of the result. *Journal of Applied Psychology, 85*, 314-322.

Media Education Foundation. (2006a). 20 Ways to be a media activist. Retrieved June 23, 2006, from http://www.mediaed.org.

Media Education Foundation. (2006b). 10 reasons why media education matters. Retrieved June 23, 2006, from http://www.mediaed.org.

Medora, N. P., Larson, J. H., Hortacsu, N., & Dave, P. (2002). Perceived attitudes towards romanticism: A cross-cultural study of American, Asian-Indian, and Turkish young adults. *Journal of Comparative Family Studies, 33* (Spring), 155-178.

Mehrabian, A. (1976). *Public places and private spaces.* New York: Basic Books.

Meier, A. (2000). Offering social support via the Internet: A case study of an online support group for social workers. *Journal of Technology in Human Services, 1,* 237-267.

Meier, A. (2002). An online stress management support group for social workers. *Journal of Technology in Human Services, 20,* 107-132.

Merton, R. K. (1957). *Social theory and social structure.* New York: Free Press.

Messick, R. M., & Cook, K. S. (Eds.). (1983). *Equity theory: Psychological and sociological perspectives.* New York: Praeger.

Metts, S., & Planalp, S. (2002). Emotional communication. In M. L. Knapp & J. A. Daly (Eds.), *Handbook of interpersonal communication* (3rd ed., pp. 339-373). Thousand Oaks, CA: Sage.

Meyer, J. R. (1994). Effect of situational features on the likelihood of addressing face needs in requests. *Southern Communication Journal, 59* (Spring), 240-254.

Midooka, K. (1990). Characteristics of Japanese style communication. *Media, Culture and Society, 12* (October), 477-489.

Miller, G. R. (1978). The current state of theory and research in interpersonal communication. *Human Communication Research, 4,* 164-178.

Miller, M. J., & Wilcox, C. T. (1986). Measuring perceived hassles and uplifts among the elderly. *Journal of Human Behavior and Learning, 3,* 38-46.

Moghaddam, F. M., Taylor, D. M., & Wright, S. C. (1993). *Social psychology in cross-cultural perspective.* New York: W. H. Freeman.

Molloy, J. (1975). *Dress for success.* New York: P. H. Wyden.

Molloy, J. (1977). *The woman's dress for success book.* New York: Warner Books.

Molloy, J. (1981). *Molloy's live for success.* New York: Bantam.

Monin, B. (2003). The warm glow heuristic: When liking leads to familiarity. *Journal of Personality and Social Psychology, 85* (December), 1035-1048.

Monk, A., Fellas, E., & Ley, E. (2004). Hearing only one side of normal and mobile phone conversations. *Behaviour & Information Technology 23* (September/October), 301-306.

Montagu, A. (1971). *Touching: The human significance of the skin.* New York: Harper & Row.

Moon, D. G. (1996). Concepts of "culture": Implications for intercultural communication research. *Communication Quarterly, 44* (Winter), 70-84.

Moore, A., Masterson, J. T., Christophel, D. M., & Shea, K. A. (1996). College teacher immediacy and student ratings of instruction. *Communication Education, 45,* 29-39.

Morahan-Martin, J. & Schumacher, P. (2003). Loneliness and social uses of the Internet. *Computers in Human Behavior 19* (November), 659-671.

Morrow, G. D., Clark, E. M., & Brock, K. F. (1995). Individual and partner love styles: Implications for the quality of romantic involvements. *Journal of Social and Personal Relationships 12,* 363-387.

Mullen, B., Tara, A., Salas, E., & Driskell, J. E. (1994). Group cohesiveness and quality of decision making: An integration of tests of the groupthink hypothesis. *Small Group Research, 25,* 189-204.

Mullen, B., Salas, E., & Driskell, J. (1989). Salience, motivation, and artifact as contributions to the relation between participation rate and leadership. *Journal of Experimental Social Psychology, 25* (November), 545-559.

Murstein, B. I., Merighi, J. R., & Vyse, S. A. (1991). Love styles in the United States and France: A cross-cultural comparison. *Journal of Social and Clinical Psychology 10,* 37-46.

Naifeh, S., & Smith, G. W. (1984). *Why can't men open up? Overcoming men's fear of intimacy.* New York: Clarkson N. Potter.

Napier, R. W., & Gershenfeld, M. K. (1992). *Groups: Theory and experience* (5th ed.). Boston: Houghton Mifflin.

National Institute of Mental Health. (1982). *Television and behavior: Ten years of scientific progress and implications for the eighties.* Rockville, MD: National Institute of Mental Health.

Neff, K. D., & Harter, S. (2002). The authenticity of conflict resolutions among adult couples: Does women's other-oriented behavior reflect their true selves? *Sex Roles, 47* (November), 403-417.

Neugarten, B. (1979). Time, age, and the life cycle. *American Journal of Psychiatry, 136,* 887-894.

Neuliep, J. W., & Grohskopf, E. L. (2000). Uncertainty reduction and communication satisfaction during initial interaction: An initial test and replication of a new axiom. *Communication Reports, 13,* 67-77.

Ng, S. H., Loong, C. S. F., He, A. P., Liu, J. H., & Weatherall, A. (2000). Communication correlates of individualism and collectivism: Talk directed at one or more addressees in family conversations. *Journal of Language and Social Psychology, 19* (March), 26-45.

Nice, M. L., & Katzev, R. (1998). Internet romantics: The frequency and nature of romantic on-line relationships. *CyberPsychology and Behavior, 1* (Fall), 217-223.

Noble, B. P. (1994, August 14). The gender wars: Talking peace. *New York Times,* p. 21.

Noelle-Neumann, E. (1973). Return to the concept of powerful mass media. In H. Eguchi & K. Sata (Eds.), *Studies in broadcasting: An international annual of broadcasting science* (pp. 67-112). Tokyo: Nippon Hoso Kyokai.

Noelle-Neumann, E. (1980). Mass media and social change in developed societies. In G. C. Wilhoit & H. de Bock (Eds.), *Mass communication review yearbook* (Vol. 1, pp. 657-678). Thousand Oaks, CA: Sage.

Noelle-Neumann, E. (1991). The theory of public opinion: The concept of the spiral of silence. In J. A. Anderson (Ed.), *Communication yearbook 14* (pp. 256-287). Thousand Oaks, CA: Sage.

Noller, P. (1993). Gender and emotional communication in marriage: Different cultures or differential social power? In *Emotional communication, culture, and power* [Special issue]. *Journal of Language and Social Psychology, 12* (March-June), 132-152.

Noller, P., & Fitzpatrick, M. A. (1993). *Communication in family relationships.* Englewood Cliffs, NJ: Prentice-Hall.

Northouse, P. G. (1997). *Leadership: Theory and practice.* Thousand Oaks, CA: Sage.

Ober, C., Weitkamp, L. R., Cox, N., Dytch, H., Kostyu, D., & Elias, S. (1977). HLA and mate choice in humans. *American Journal of Human Genetics, 61,* 494-496.

Oggins, J., Veroff, J., & Leber, D. (1993). Perceptions of marital interaction among black and white newlyweds. *Journal of Personality and Social Psychology, 65* (September), 494-511.

O'Hair, D., Cody, M. J., Goss, B., & Krayer, K. J. (1988). The effect of gender, deceit orientation and communicator style on macro-assessments of honesty. *Communication Quarterly, 36,* 77-93.

O'Keefe, D. J. (1999). How to handle opposing arguments in persuasive messages: A meta-analytic review of the effects of one-sided and two-sided messages. In M. E. Roloff (Ed.), *Communication yearbook 22* (pp. 209-249). Thousand Oaks, CA: Sage.

Olday, D., & Wesley, B. (1990). Intimate relationship violence among divorcees. *Free Inquiry in Creative Sociology, 18* (May), 63-71.

O'Sullivan, P. B., & Flanagin, A. J. (2003). Reconceptualizing "flaming" and other problematic messages. *New Media and Society 5* (March), 69-94.

Osborn, A. (1957). *Applied imagination* (Rev. ed.). New York: Scribners.

Ouchi, W. G. (1981). *Theory Z: How American business can meet the Japanese challenge.* Reading, MA: Addison-Wesley.

Page, R. A., & Balloun, J. L. (1978). The effect of voice volume on the perception of personality. *Journal of Social Psychology, 105,* 65-72.

Palmer, M. T. (1989). Controlling conversations: Turns, topics, and interpersonal control. *Communication Monographs 56,* 1-18.

Parks, M. R. (1995). Webs of influence in interpersonal relationships. In C. R. Berger & M. E. Burgoon (Eds.), *Communication and social influence processes* (pp. 155–178). East Lansing: Michigan State University Press.

Parks, M. R., & Floyd, K. (1996). Making friends in cyberspace. *Journal of Communication, 46* (Winter): 80–97.

Parsons, C. K., Liden, R. C., & Bauer, T. N. (2001). Personal perception in employment interviews. In M. London (Ed.), *How people evaluate others in organizations* (pp. 67–90). Mahwah, NJ: Lawrence Erlbaum.

Patton, B. R., Giffin, K., & Patton, E. N. (1989). *Decision-making group interaction* (3rd ed.). New York: HarperCollins.

Paul, A. M. (2001). Self-help: Shattering the myths. *Psychology Today, 34*, 60ff.

Payne, K. E. (2001). *Different but equal: Communication between the sexes*. Westport, CT: Praeger.

Pearson, J. C. (1993). *Communication in the family* (2nd ed.). New York: Harper & Row.

Pearson, J. C., & Spitzberg, B. H. (1990). *Interpersonal communication: Concepts, components, and contexts* (2nd ed.). Dubuque, IA: William C. Brown.

Pearson, J. C., West, R., & Turner, L. H. (1995). *Gender and communication* (3rd ed.). Dubuque, IA: William C. Brown.

Penfield, J. (Ed.). (1987). *Women and language in transition*. Albany, NY: State University of New York Press.

Pennebaker, J. W. (1991). *Opening up: The healing power of confiding in others*. New York: Avon.

Perse, E. M., & Rubin, R. B. (1989). Attribution in social and parasocial relationhips. *Communication Research, 16* (February), 59–77.

Persell, C. H. (1990). *Understanding society*, 3rd ed. New York: Harper & Row.

Peter, L. J., & Hull, R. (1969). *The Peter principle*. New York: Bantam.

Peterson, C. C. (1996). The ticking of the social clock: Adults' beliefs about the timing of transition events. *International Journal of Aging and Human Development, 42*, 189–203.

Petrocelli, W., & Repa, B. K. (1992). *Sexual harassment on the job*. Berkeley, CA: Nolo Press.

Petty, R. E., & Wegener, D. T. (1998). Attitude change: Multiple roles for persuasion variables. In D. T. Gilbert, S. T. Fiske, & G. Lindzey (Eds.), *The handbook of social psychology* (4th ed., Vol. 1, pp. 323–390). New York: McGraw-Hill.

Pierce, C. A., & Aquinis, H. (2001). A framework for investigating the link between workplace romance and sexual harassment. *Group and Organization Management, 26* (June), 206–229.

Pilkington, C. J., & Richardson, D. R. (1988). Perceptions of risk in intimacy. *Journal of Social and Personal Relationships, 5*, 503–508.

Pilkington, C., & Woods, S. P. (1999). Risk in intimacy as a chronically accessible schema. *Journal of Social and Personal Relationships, 16*, 249–263.

Pittenger, R. E., Hockett, C. F., & Danehy, J. J. (1960). *The first five minutes*. Ithaca, NY: Paul Martineau.

Place, K. S., & Becker, J. A. (1991). The influence of pragmatic competence on the likeability of grade school children. *Discourse Processes, 14* (April–June), 227–241.

Placencia, M. E. (2004). The Online Disinhibition Effect. *Journal of Sociolinguistics 8* (May), 215–245.

Pornpitakpan, C. (2003). The effect of personality traits and perceived cultural similarity on attraction. *Journal of International Consumer Marketing, 15*, 5–30.

Porter, R. H., & Moore, J. D. (1981). Human kin recognition by olfactory cues. *Physiology and Behavior, 27*, 493–495.

Porter, S., Brit, A. R., Yuille, J. C., & Lehman, D. R. (2000). Negotiating false memories: Interviewer and rememberer characteristics relate to memory distortion. *Psychological Science, 11* (November), 507–510.

Postman, N., & Powers, S. (1992). *How to watch TV news*. New York: Penguin.

Pratkanis, A. R. (2000). Altercasting as an influence tactic. In D. J. Terry & M. A. Hogg (Eds.), *Attitudes, behavior, and social context: The role of norms and group membership* (pp. 201–226). Mahwah, NJ: Erlbaum.

Pratkanis, A. R., & Aronson, E. (1991). *Age of propaganda: The everyday use and abuse of persuasion*. New York: W. H. Freeman.

Prosky, P. S. (1992). Complementary and symmetrical couples. *Family Therapy, 19*, 215–221.

Prusank, D. T., Duran, R. L., & DeLillo, D. A. (1993). Interpersonal relationships in women's magazines: Dating and relating in the 1970s and 1980s. *Journal of Social and Personal Relationships, 10* (August), 307–320.

Rabinowitz, F. E. (1991). The male-to-male embrace: Breaking the touch taboo in a men's therapy group. *Journal of Counseling and Development, 69* (July–August), 574–576.

Radford, M. L. (1998). Approach or avoidance? The role of nonverbal communication in the academic library user's decision to initiate a reference encounter. *Library Trends, 46* (Spring), 699–717.

Ragins, B. R., & Kram, K. E. (2007). *The handbook of mentoring at work: Research, theory, and practice*. Thousand Oaks, CA: Sage.

Rancer, A. S. (1998). Argumentativeness. In J. C. McCroskey, J. A. Daly, M. M. Martin, & M. J. Beatty (Eds.), *Communication and personality: Trait perspectives* (pp. 149–170). Cresskill, NJ: Hampton Press.

Rancer, A. S., & Avtgis, T. A. (2006). *Argumentative and aggressive communication: Theory, research, and application*. Thousand Oaks, CA: Sage.

Raven, R., Centers, C., & Rodrigues, A. (1975). The bases of conjugal power. In R. E. Cromwell & D. H. Olson (Eds.), *Power in families* (pp. 217–234). New York: Halsted Press.

Rawlins, W. K. (1983). Negotiating close friendship: The dialectic of conjunctive freedoms. *Human Communication Research 9*, 255–266.

Rawlins, W. K. (1989). A dialectical analysis of the tensions, functions, and strategic challenges of communication in young adult friendships. In J. A. Andersen (Ed.), *Communication yearbook 12* (pp. 157–189). Thousand Oaks, CA: Sage.

Rawlins, W. K. (1992). *Friendship matters: Communication, dialectics, and the life course*. Hawthorne, NY: Aldine DeGruyter.

Regan, P. C., Kocan, E. R., & Whitlock, T. (1998). Ain't love grand! A prototype analysis of the concept of romantic love. *Journal of Social and Personal Relationships, 15*, 411–420.

Reardon, K. K. (1987). *Where minds meet: Interpersonal communication*. Belmont, CA.: Wadsworth.

Rector, M., & Neiva, E. (1996). Communication and personal relationships in Brazil. In W. B. Gudykunst, S. Ting-Toomey, & T. Nishida, *Communication in personal relationships across cultures* (pp. 156–173). Thousand Oaks, CA: Sage.

Reisman, J. M. (1979). *Anatomy of friendship*. Lexington, MA: Lewis.

Reisman, J. M. (1981). Adult friendships. In S. Duck & R. Gilmour (Eds.), *Personal relationships. 2: Developing personal relationships* (pp. 205–230). New York: Academic Press.

Rhee, K. Y. & Kim, W-B. (2004). The adoption and use of the Internet in South Korea, *Journal of Computer Mediated Communication 9* (4).

Rice, M. (2007). Domestic violence. Retrieved May 7, 2007, from www.ncptsd.va.gov/ncmain/ncdocs/fact_shts/fs_domestic _violence.html.

Rich, A. L. (1974). *Interracial communication*. New York: Harper & Row.

Richards, I. A. (1951). Communication between men: The meaning of language. In H. von Foerster (Ed.), *Cybernetics, transactions of the eighth conference*.

Richmond, V. P., & McCroskey, J. C. (1998). *Communication: Apprehension, avoidance, and effectiveness* (5th ed.). Boston: Allyn & Bacon.

Richmond, V. P., McCroskey, J. C., & McCroskey, L. L. (2005). *Organizational communication for survival: Making work, work*. Boston: Allyn & Bacon.

Riggio, R. E. (1987). *The charisma quotient*. New York: Dodd, Mead.

Robbins, S. P., & Hunsaker, P. L. (2006). *Training in interpersonal skills: Tips for managing people at work* (4th ed.). Boston: Allyn & Bacon.

Roberts, W. (1987). *Leadership secrets of Attila the Hun*. New York: Warner.

Robinson, J., & McArthur, L. Z. (1982). Impact of salient vocal qualities on casual attribution for a speaker's behavior. *Journal of Personality and Social Psychology, 43*, 236-247.

Robinson, W. P. (1993). Lying in the public domain. *American Behavioral Scientist, 36* (January), 359-382.

Rodman, G. (2001). *Making sense of media: An introduction to mass communication*. Boston: Allyn & Bacon.

Roebuck, D. B. (2001). *Improving business communication skills* (3rd ed.). Upper Saddle River, NJ: Prentice-Hall.

Rogers, C. (1970). *Carl Rogers on encounter groups*. New York: Harrow Books.

Rogers, C., & Farson, R. (1981). Active listening. In J. A. DeVito (Ed.), *Communication: Concepts and processes* (3rd ed., pp. 137-147). Englewood Cliffs, NJ: Prentice-Hall.

Rohlfing, M. E. (1995). "Doesn't anybody stay in one place anymore?" An exploration of the under-studied phenomenon of long-distance relationships. In J. T. Wood & S. Duck (Eds.), *Under-studied relationships: Off the beaten track* (pp. 173-196). Thousand Oaks, CA: Sage.

Rollman, J. B., Krug, K., & Parente, F. (2000). The chat room phenomenon: Reciprocal communication in cyberspace. *CyberPsychology and Behavior, 3* (April), 161-166.

Ronfeldt, H. M., Kimerling, R., & Arias, I. (1998). Satisfaction with relationship power and the perpetration of dating violence. *Journal of Marriage & the Family, 60* (February), 70-78.

Rosenthal, R. (2002). Covert communication in classrooms, clinics, courtroom, and cubicles. *American Psychologist, 57*, 839-849.

Rosenthal, R., & DePaulo, B. M. (1979). Sex differences in accommodation in nonverbal communication. In R. Rosenthal (Ed.), *Skill in nonverbal communication: Individual differences* (pp. 68-103). Cambridge, MA: Oelgeschlager, Gunn & Hain.

Rosenthal, R., & Jacobson, L. (1968). *Pygmalion in the classroom*. New York: Holt, Rinehart & Winston.

Rosenthal, R., & Jacobson, L. (1992). *Pygmalion in the classroom*. New York: Holt, Rinehart & Winston.

Rosnow, R. L. (1977). Gossip and marketplace psychology. *Journal of Communication, 27* (Winter), 158-163.

Ross, J. L. (1995). Conversational pitchbacks: Helping couples bat 1000 in the game of communications. *Journal of Family Psychotherapy, 6*, 83-86.

Rotello, G. (1995, April 18). The inning of outing. *The Advocate, 679*, p. 80.

Rowland-Morin, P. A., & Carroll, J. G. (1990). Verbal communication skills and patient satisfaction: A study of doctor-patient interviews. *Evaluation and the Health Professions, 13*, 168-185.

Ruben, B. D. (1985). Human communication and cross-cultural effectiveness. In L. A. Samovar & R. E. Porter (Eds.), *Intercultural communication: A reader* (4th ed., pp. 338-356). Belmont, CA: Wadsworth.

Rubenstein, C. (1993, June 10). Fighting sexual harassment in schools. *New York Times*, p. C8.

Rubin, A. M., Perse, E., & Powell, R. (1985). Loneliness, parasocial interaction, and local television news viewing. *Human Communication Research, 12*, 155-180.

Rubin, R. B. (1982). Assessing speaking and listening competence at the college level: The communication competency assessment instrument. *Communication Education, 31* (January), 19-32.

Rubin, R. B. (1985). The validity of the communication competency assessment instrument. *Communication Monographs, 52*, 173-185.

Rubin, R. B., Fernandez-Collado, C., & Hernandez-Sampieri, R. (1992). A cross-cultural examination of interpersonal communication motives in Mexico and the United States. *International Journal of Intercultural Relations, 16*, 145-157.

Rubin, R. B., & Martin, M. M. (1994). Development of a measure of interpersonal communication competence. *Communication Research Reports, 11*, 33-44.

Rubin, R. B., & Martin, M. M. (1998). Interpersonal communication motives. In J. C. McCroskey, J. A. Daly, M. M. Martin, & M. J. Beatty (Eds.), *Communication and personality: Trait perspectives* (pp. 287-307). Cresskill, NJ: Hampton Press.

Rubin, R. B., & McHugh, M. (1987). Development of parasocial interaction relationships. *Journal of Broadcasting and Electronic Media, 31*, 279-292.

Rubin, R. B., Perse, E. M., & Barbato, C. A. (1988). Conceptualization and measurement of interpersonal communication motives. *Human Communication Research, 14*, 602-628.

Rubin, R. B., & Rubin, A. M. (1992). Antecedents of interpersonal communication motivation. *Communication Quarterly, 40*, 315-317.

Rubin, Z. (1973). *Liking and loving: An invitation to social psychology*. New York: Holt.

Rundquist, S. (1992). Indirectness: A gender study of Fluting Grice's maxims. *Journal of Pragmatics, 18* (November), 431-449.

Ruscher, J. B. (2001). *Prejudiced communication: A social psychological perspective*. New York: Guilford.

Sabatelli, R. M., & Pearce, J. (1986). Exploring marital expectations. *Journal of Social and Personal Relationships, 3*, 307-321.

Sapadin, L. A. (1988). Friendship and gender: Perspectives of professional men and women. *Journal of Social and Personal Relationships 5*, 387-403.

Sarwer, D. B., Kalichman, S. C., Johnson, J. R., Early, J., et al. (1993). Sexual aggression and love styles: An exploratory study. *Archives of Sexual Behavior 22*, 265-275.

Sayre, S. (1992). T-shirt messages: Fortune or folly for advertisers? In S. R. Danna (Ed.), *Advertising and popular culture* (pp. 73-82). Bowling Green, OH: Bowling Green State University Popular Press.

Scandura, T. (1992). Mentorship and career mobility: An empirical investigation. *Journal of Organizational Behavior, 13*, 169-174.

Schaap, C., Buunk, B., & Kerkstra, A. (1988). Marital conflict resolution. In P. Noller & M. A. Fitzpatrick (Eds.), *Perspectives on marital interaction* (pp. 203-244). Philadelphia: Multilingual Matters.

Schaefer, C. M., & Tudor, T. R. (2001). Managing workplace romances. *SAM Advanced Management Journal* (Summer), 4-10.

Schafer, M., & Crichlow, S. (1996). Antecedents of groupthink. *Journal of Conflict Resolution, 40* (September), 415-435.

Scherer, K. R. (1986). Vocal affect expression. *Psychological Bulletin, 99*, 143-165.

Scheufele, D. A., & Moy, P. (2000). Twenty-five years of the spiral of silence: A conceptual review and empirical outlook. *International Journal of Public Opinion Research, 12* (Spring), 3-28.

Schlenker, B. R., Pontari, B. A., & Christopher, A. N. (2001). Excuses and character: Personal and social implications of excuses. *Personality and Social Psychology Review, 5*, 15-32.

Schnoor, L. G. (Ed.). (1999). *Winning orations of the interstate oratorical association*. Mankato, MN: Interstate Oratorical Association.

Schott, G., & Selwyn, N. (2000). Examining the "male, antisocial" stereotype of high computer users. *Journal of Educational Computing Research, 23*, 291-303.

Schramm, W., & Porter, W. E. (1982). *Men, women, messages and media: Understanding human communication*. New York: Harper & Row.

Schultz, B. G. (1996). *Communicating in the small group: Theory and practice* (2nd ed.). New York: HarperCollins.

Schwartz, M., and the Task Force on Bias-Free Language of the Association of American University Presses. (1995). *Guidelines for bias-free writing*. Bloomington, IN: Indiana University Press.

Seiter, J. S., & Sandry, A. (2003). Pierced for success?: The effects of ear and nose piercing on perceptions of job candidates' credibility, attractiveness, and hirability. *Communication Research Reports, 20* (Fall), 287-298.

Severin, W. J., with Tankard, J. W., Jr. (1988). *Communication theories* (2nd ed.). New York: Longman.

Shannon, J. (1987). Don't smile when you say that. *Executive Female, 10,* 33, 43.

Shaw, M. E., & Gouran, D. S. (1990). Group dynamics and communication. In G. Dahnke & G. W. Clatterbuck (Eds.), *Human communication: Theory and research.* Belmont, CA: Wadsworth.

Shimanoff, S. (1980). *Communication rules: Theory and research.* Thousand Oaks, CA: Sage.

Shockley-Zalabak, P. (2006). *Fundamentals of organizational communication: Knowledge, sensitivity, skills, values* (6th ed.). Boston: Allyn & Bacon.

Siegert, J. R., & Stamp, G. H. (1994). "Our first big fight" as a milestone in the development of close relationships. *Communication Monographs, 61* (December), 345-360.

Silverman, T. (2001). Expanding community: The Internet and relational theory. *Community, Work and Family, 4,* 231-237.

Singh, N., & Pereira, A. (2005). *The culturally customized Web site.* Oxford, UK: Elsevier Butterworth-Heinemann.

Skinner, M. (2002). In search of feedback. *Executive Excellence* (June), 18.

Slade, M. (1995, February 19). We forgot to write a headline. But it's not our fault. *New York Times,* p. 5.

Smith, B. (1996). Care and feeding of the office grapevine. *Management Review, 85* (February), 6.

Smith, D. (2003, December 2). Doctors cultivate a skill: Listening. *New York Times,* p. 6.

Smith, S. M., & Shaffer, D. R. (1991). Celerity and cajolery: Rapid speech may promote or inhibit persuasion through its impact on message elaboration. *Personality and Social Psychology Bulletin, 17* (December), 663-669.

Smith, S. M., & Shaffer, D. R. (1995). Speed of speech and persuasion: Evidence for multiple effects. *Personality and Social Psychology Bulletin, 21* (October), 1051-1060.

Smoreda, Z., & Licoppe, C. (2000). Gender-specific use of the domestic telephone. *Social Psychology Quarterly, 63,* 238-252.

Snyder, C. R. (1984). Excuses, excuses. *Psychology Today, 18,* 50-55.

Snyder, C. R., Higgins, R. L., & Stucky, R. J. (1983). *Excuses: Masquerades in search of grace.* New York: Wiley.

Snyder, M. (1992). A gender-informed model of couple and family therapy: Relationship enhancement therapy. *Contemporary Family Therapy: An International Journal, 14* (February), 15-31.

Solomon, G. B., Striegel, D. A., Eliot, J. F., Heon, S. N., et al. (1996). The self-fulfilling prophecy in college basketball: Implications for effective coaching. *Journal of Applied Sport Psychology, 8* (March), 44-59.

Song, I, LaRose, R., Eastin, M. S., & Lin, C. A. (2004). Internet gratifications Internet addiction: On the uses and abuses of new media. *CyberPsychology & Behavior 7* (August), 384-394.

Sorenson, P. S., Hawkins, K., & Sorenson, R. L. (1995). Gender, psychological type and conflict style preferences. *Management Communication Quarterly, 9* (August), 115-126.

Sprecher, S. (1987). The effects of self-disclosure given and received on affection for an intimate partner and stability of the relationship. *Journal of Social and Personal Relationships 4,* 115-127.

Sprecher, S., & Toro-Morn, M. (2002). A study of men and women from different sides of earth to determine if men are from Mars and women are from Venus in their beliefs about love and romantic relationships. *Sex Roles 46* (March), 131-147.

Spitzberg, B. H. (1991). Intercultural communication competence. In L. A. Samovar & R. E. Porter (Eds.), *Intercultural communication: A reader* (pp. 353-365). Belmont, CA: Wadsworth.

Spitzberg, B. H., & Cupach, W. R. (1989). *Handbook of interpersonal competence research.* New York: Springer.

Spitzberg, B. H., & Hecht, M. L. (1984). A component model of relational competence. *Human Communication Research, 10,* 575-599.

Sprecher, S., & Metts, S. (1989). Development of the "romantic beliefs scale" and examination of the effects of gender and gender-role orientation. *Journal of Social and Personal Relationships, 6,* 387-411.

Steil, L. K., Barker, L. L., & Watson, K. W. (1983). *Effective listening: Key to your success.* Reading, MA: Addison-Wesley.

Stein, M. M., & Bowen, M. (2003). Building a customer satisfaction system: Effective listening when the customer speaks. *Journal of Organizational Excellence, 22* (Summer), 23-34.

Stephan, W. G., & Stephan, C. W. (1985). Intergroup anxiety. *Journal of Social Issues, 41,* 157-175.

Stephan, W. G., & Stephan, C. W. (1992). *Improving intergroup relations.* Thousand Oaks, CA: Sage.

Stephen, R., & Zweigenhaft, R. L. (1986). The effect on tipping of a waitress touching male and female customers. *Journal of Social Psychology, 126* (February), 141-142.

Stewart, L. P., Cooper, P. J., Stewart, A. D., with Friedley, S. A. (2003). *Communication and gender,* 4th ed. Boston: Allyn & Bacon.

Strassberg, D. S., & Holty, S. (2003). An experimental study of women's Internet personal ads. *Archives of Sexual Behavior 54* (June), 253-260.

Strecker, I. (1993). Cultural variations in the concept of "face." *Multilingua 12,* 119-141.

Stromer-Galley, J. (2003). Diversity of political conversation on the Internet: User's perspectives. *Journal of Computer Mediated Communication 8.* Retrieved June 21, 2006, from http://jcmc .indiana.edu/vol8/issue3/stromergalley.html.

Suler, J. (2004). The online disinhibition effect. *CyberPsychology and Behavior 7* (June), 321-326.

Swim, J. K., & Hyers, L. L. (1999). Excuse me—what did you say?!: Women's public and private responses to sexist remarks. *Journal of Experimental Social Psychology, 35* (January), 68-88.

Tanaka, K. (1999). Judgments of fairness by just world believers. *Journal of Social Psychology, 139* (October), 631-638.

Tang, S., & Zuo, J. (2000). Dating attitudes and behaviors of American and Chinese college students. *The Social Science Journal, 37* (January), 67-78.

Tannen, D. (1990). *You just don't understand: Women and men in conversation.* New York: Morrow.

Tannen, D. (1994a). *Gender and discourse.* New York: Oxford University Press.

Tannen, D. (1994b). *Talking from 9 to 5: How women's and men's conversational styles affect who gets heard, who gets credit, and what gets done at work.* New York: Morrow.

Tannen, D. (2006). *You're wearing that? Understanding mothers and daughters in conversation.* New York: Random House.

Taraban, C. B., & Hendrick, C. (1995). Personality perceptions associated with six styles of love. *Journal of Social and Personal Relationships 12,* 453-461.

Tardiff, T. (2001). Learning to say "no" in Chinese. *Early Education and Development 12,* 303-323.

Tardy, C. H., & Dindia, K. (2006). Self-disclosure: Strategic revelation of information in personal and professional relationships. In O. Hargie (Ed.), *The handbook of communication skills* (3rd ed., pp. 229-266). New York: Routledge.

Tersine, R. J., & Riggs, W. E. (1980). The Delphi technique: A long-range planning tool. In S. Ferguson & S. D. Ferguson (Eds.), *Intercom: Readings in organizational communication* (pp. 366-373). Rochelle Park, NJ: Hayden Books.

Thibaut, J. W., & Kelley, H. H. (1986). *The social psychology of groups.* New Brunswick, NJ: Transaction.

Thompson, C. A., & Klopf, D. W. (1991). An analysis of social style among disparate cultures. *Communication Research Reports, 8,* 65-72.

Thompson, C. A., Klopf, D. W., & Ishii, S. (1991). A comparison of social style between Japanese and Americans. *Communication Research Reports, 8,* 165-172.

Thorne, B., Kramarae, C., & Henley, N. (Eds.). (1983). *Language, gender and society.* Rowley, MA: Newbury House.

Tichenor, P. J., Donohue, G. A., & Olien, C. N. (1970). Mass media flow and differential growth in knowledge. *Public Opinion Quarterly, 34,* 159-170.

Timm, P. R., & DeTienne, K. B. (1995). *Managerial communication: A finger on the pulse* (3rd ed.). Upper Saddle River, NJ: Prentice-Hall.

Ting-Toomey, S. (1981). Ethnic identity and close friendship in Chinese-American college students. *International Journal of Intercultural Relations, 5*, 383–406.

Ting-Toomey, S. (1985). Toward a theory of conflict and culture. *International and Intercultural Communication Annual, 9*, 71–86.

Tinsley, C. H., & Brett, J. M. (2001). Managing workplace conflict in the United States and Hong Kong. *Organizational Behavior and Human Decision Processes 85*, 360–381.

Trager, G. L. (1958). Paralanguage: A first approximation. *Studies in Linguistics, 13*, 1–12.

Trager, G. L. (1961). The typology of paralanguage. *Anthropological Linguistics, 3*, 17–21.

Trower, P. (1981). Social skill disorder. In S. Duck & R. Gilmour (Eds.), *Personal relationships 3* (pp. 97–110). New York: Academic Press.

Turner, M. M., Mazur, M. A., Wendel, N., & Winslow, R. (2003). Relational ruin or social glue? The joint effect of relationship type and gossip valence on liking, trust, and expertise. *Communication Monographs, 70* (June), 129–141.

Ueleke, W., et al. (1983). Inequity resolving behavior as a response to inequity in a hypothetical marital relationship. *A Quarterly Journal of Human Behavior, 20*, 4–8.

Unger, F. L. (2001). Speech directed at able-bodied adults, disabled adults, and disabled adults with speech impairments. (Doctoral dissertation, Hofstra University, 2001). *Dissertation Abstracts International, 62*, 1146B.

Uris, A. (1986). *101 of the greatest ideas in management.* New York: Wiley.

Veenendall, T. L., & Feinstein, M. C. (1995). *Let's talk about relationships: Cases in Study* (2nd ed.). Prospect Heights, IL: Waveland Press.

Velting, D. M. (1999). Personality and negative expectations: Trait structure of the Beck Hopelessness Scale. *Personality and Individual Differences, 26*, 913–921.

Verderber, R. (2006). *The challenge of effective speaking* (13th ed.). Belmont, CA: Wadsworth.

Victor, D. (1992). *International business communication.* New York: HarperCollins.

Viswanath, K., & Finnegan, J. R., Jr. (1995). The knowledge-gap hypothesis: Twenty-five years later. In B. R. Burleson (Ed.), *Communication yearbook 19.* Thousand Oaks, CA: Sage.

Vrij, A., & Mann, S. (2001). Telling and detecting lies in a high-stake situation: The case of a convicted murderer. *Applied Cognitive Psychology, 15* (March–April), 187–203.

Wallace, K. (1955). An ethical basis of communication. *Communication Education, 4* (January), 1–9.

Walster, E., & Walster, G. W. (1978). *A new look at love.* Reading, MA: Addison-Wesley.

Walster, E., Walster, G. W., & Berscheid, E. (1978). *Equity: Theory and research.* Boston: Allyn & Bacon.

Walster, E., Walster, G. W., & Traupman, J. (1978). Equity and premarital sex. *Journal of Personality and Social Psychology 36*, 82–92.

Watzlawick, P. (1977). *How real is real? Confusion, disinformation, communication: An anecdotal introduction to communications theory.* New York: Vintage.

Watzlawick, P. (1978). *The language of change: Elements of therapeutic communication.* New York: Basic Books.

Watzlawick, P., Beavin, J. H., & Jackson, D. D. (1967). *Pragmatics of human communication: A study of interactional patterns, pathologies, and paradoxes.* New York: Norton.

Weathers, M. D., Frank, E. M., & Spell, L. A. (2002). Differences in the communication of affect: Members of the same race versus members of a different race. *Journal of Black Psychology, 28*, 66–77.

Weinberg, H. L. (1958). *Levels of knowing and existence.* New York: Harper & Row.

Weinstein, E. A., & Deutschberger, P. (1963). Some dimensions of altercasting. *Sociometry, 26*, 454–466.

Weitzman, P. F., & Weitzman, E. A. (2000). Interpersonal negotiation strategies in a sample of older women. *Journal of Clinical Geropsychology, 6*, 41–51.

Weitzman, P. F. (2001). Young adult women resolving interpersonal conflicts. *Journal of Adult Development, 8*, 61–67.

Wennerstrom, A., & Siegel, A. F. (2003). Keeping the floor in multiparty conversation: Intonation, syntax, and pause. *Discourse Processes, 36* (September), 77–107.

Westwood, R. I., Tang, F. F., & Kirkbride, P. S. (1992). Chinese conflict behavior: Cultural antecedents and behavioral consequences. *Organizational Development Journal, 10* (Summer), 13–19.

Wetzel, P. J. (1988). Are "powerless" communication strategies the Japanese norm? *Language in Society, 17*, 555–564.

Wheeless, L. R., & Grotz, J. (1977). The measurement of trust and its relationship to self-disclosure. *Human Communication Research, 3*, 250–257.

Whitty, M. (2003). Cyber-flirting. *Theory and Psychology 13*, 339–355.

Whitty, M., & Gavin, J. (2001). Age/sex/location: Uncovering the social cues in the development of online relationships. *CyberPsychology and Behavior, 4*, 623–630.

Wiederman, M. W., & Hurd, C. (1999). Extradyadic involvement during dating. *Journal of Social and Personal Relationships 16*, 265–274.

Wigley, C. J., III. (1998). Verbal aggressiveness. In J. C. McCroskey, J. A. Daly, M. M. Martin, & M. J. Beatty (Eds.), *Communication and personality: Trait perspectives* (pp. 191–214). Cresskill, NJ: Hampton Press.

Wilkins, B. M., & Andersen, P. A. (1991). Gender differences and similarities in management communication: A meta-analysis. *Management Communication Quarterly, 5* (August), 6–35.

Wilmot, W. W. (1987). *Dyadic communication* (3rd ed.). New York: Random House.

Wilson, J. H., & Taylor, K. W. (2001). Professor immediacy as behaviors associated with liking students. *Teaching of Psychology, 28*, 136–138.

Wilson, R. A. (1989). Toward understanding E-prime. *Etc.: A Review of General Semantics, 46*, 316–319.

Windahl, S., & Signitzer, B. (with Olson, J. T.). (1992). *Using communication theory: An introduction to planned communication.* Thousand Oaks, CA: Sage.

Winquist, L. A., Mohr, C. D., & Kenny, D. A. (1998). The female positivity effect in the perception of others. *Journal of Research in Personality, 32* (September), 370–388.

Witcher, S. K. (1999, August 9–15). Chief executives in Asia find listening difficult. *Asian Wall Street Journal Weekly*, 21, p. 11.

Withecomb, J. L. (1997). Causes of violence in children. *Journal of Mental Health, 5* (October), 433–442.

Witt, P. L., & Wheeless, L. R. (2001). An experimental study of teachers' verbal and nonverbal immediacy and students' affective and cognitive learning. *Communication Education, 50*, 327–342.

Wolak, J., Mitchell, K. J., & Finkelhor, D. (2003). Escaping or connecting? Characteristics of youth who form close online relationships. *Journal of Adolescence 26* (February), 105–119.

Wolpe, J. (1957). *Psychotherapy by reciprocal inhibition.* Stanford, CA: Stanford University Press.

Won-Doornink, M.-J. (1985). Self-disclosure and reciprocity in conversation: A cross-national study. *Social Psychology Quarterly, 48*, 97–107.

Won-Doornink, M. (1991). Self-disclosure and reciprocity in South Korean and U.S. male dyads. In Stella Ting-Toomey & Felipe Korzenny (Eds.), *Cross-cultural interpersonal communication* (pp. 116–131). Newbury Park, CA: Sage.

Wood, W. (2000). Attitude change: Persuasion and social influence. *Annual Review of Psychology, 51*, 539–570.

Wrench, J. S., & McCroskey, J. C. (2003). A communibiological examination of ethnocentrism and homophobia. *Communication Research Reports, 20*, 24–33.

Wright, P. H. (1978). Toward a theory of friendship based on a conception of self. *Human Communication Research 4*, 196–207.

Wright, P. H. (1984). Self-referent motivation and the intrinsic quality of friendship. *Journal of Social and Personal Relationships 1*, 115–130.

Wright, P. H. (1988). Interpreting research on gender differences in friendship: A case for moderation and a plea for caution. *Journal of Social and Personal Relationships 5*, 367–373.

Wright, J. W., & Hosman, L. W. (1983). Language style and sex bias in the courtroom: The effects of male and female use of hedges and intensifiers on impression formation. *Southern Speech Communication Journal, 48*, 137–152.

Young, K. S., Griffin-Shelly, E., Cooper, A., O'Mara, J., & Buchanan, J. (2000). Online infidelity: A new dimension in couple relationships with implications for evaluation and treatment. *Sexual Addiction and Compulsivity, 7*, 59–74.

Young, K. S., Griffin-Shelley, E., Cooper, A., O'Mara, J., & Buchanan, J. (2000). Online infidelity: A new dimension in couple relationships with implications for evaluation and treatment. *Sexual Addiction and Compulsivity 7*, 59–74.

Yun, H. (1976). The Korean personality and treatment considerations. *Social Casework, 57*, 173–178.

Zane, N., & Yeh, M. (2002). The use of culturally-based variables in assessment: Studies on loss of face. In K. S. Kurasaki (Ed.), *Asian American mental health: Assessment theories and methods* (pp. 123–138). New York: Kluwer Academic/Plenum Publishers.

Zimmerman, A. (2000, November 10). If boys just want to have fun, this may bring them down. *Wall Street Journal*, pp. A1, A12.

Zornoza, A., Ripoll, P., & Peiró, J. M. (2002). Conflict management in groups that work in two different communication contexts: Face-to-face and computer-mediated communication. *Small Group Research 33* (October), 481–508.

Zuckerman, M., Klorman, R., Larrance, D. T., & Spiegel, N. H. (1981). Facial, autonomic, and subjective components of emotion: The facial feedback hypothesis versus the externalizer-internalizer distinction. *Journal of Personality and Social Psychology, 41*, 929–944.

# INDEX

The letters b, f, and t following page numbers indicate boxes, figures, and tables, respectively.

# CREDITS

## Text Credits

Pages 438–440: Acceptance Speech for the Jean Hersholt Humanitarian Award by Elizabeth Taylor.
Page 442–443: "Testing Cars" by Lee Iacocca. Reprinted by permission.
Page 446: By kind permission of Ripken Baseball Inc. and Cal Ripken, Jr.
Page 447: © 2007 Nikki Giovanni, by permission.

## Photo Credits

Page 2: © image 100/CORBIS;   Page 4: © Tom Stewart/CORBIS;   Page 15: © Charles Gupton/Stock Boston;   Page 22: © Royalty-Free/CORBIS;   Page 24: © Richard Lord/PhotoEdit;   Page 29: © Lara Jo Regan/Getty Images;   Page 33: © Kathy McLaughlin/The Image Works;   Page 38: © Bloomimage/CORBIS;   Page 45: © Bernard Lang/Getty Images;   Page 46: © Steve Niedorf/Getty Images;   Page 51: © R W Jones/CORBIS;   Page 55: © Brand X Pictures/JupiterImages;   Page 58: © Bob Daemmrich/The Image Works;   Page 61: © Stone/Getty Images;   Page 63: © PhotoDisc/Getty Images;   Page 65: © Jessica Martinez/PhotoEdit;   Page 67: © Artiga Photo/CORBIS;   Page 70: © Peter Beavis/Getty Images;   Page 81: © Walter Hodges/CORBIS;   Page 90: © Digital Vision/Getty Images;   Page 92: © Chuck Savage/CORBIS;   Page 93: © Richard Lord/PhotoEdit;   Page 96: Jim Whitmer;   Page 100: © PhotoDisc/Getty Images;   Page 105: © Gary Conner/PhotoEdit;   Page 111: © Digital Vision/age fotostock;   Page 114: © Rosa & Rosa/CORBIS;   Page 116: © PhotoDisc/Getty Images;   Page 123: © Robert Frerck/Odyssey Productions/Chicago. All Rights Reserved;   Page 129: © Steven Begleiter/Pictor/ImageState;   Page 133: © Zefa RF/Alamy;   Page 135: © Robert Mizono/Getty Images;   Page 137: © Photolibrary;   Page 150: © Karen Moskowitz/Getty Images;   Page 161: © Yellow Dog Production/Getty Images;   Page 163: © Stuart Cohen/The Image Works;   Page 167: © Bob Falcetti/Getty Images;   Page 168: © Michael Doolittle/The Image Works;   Page 171: © Rhoda Sidney/PhotoEdit;   Page 176: © PhotoDisc/Getty Images;   Page 177: © Bob Daemmrich Photography;   Page 188: © Mary Kate Denny/PhotoEdit;   Page 191: © Tomas Van Houtryve/CORBIS;   Page 195: © Bob Daemmrich/The Image Works;   Page 202: © Ingram Publishing/SuperStock;   Page 204: © Larry Dale Gordon/Photolibrary;   Page 214: © Skjold Photographs;   Page 219: © Walter Hodgers/Getty Images;   Page 221: © David Young-Wolff/PhotoEdit;   Page 223: © Dan Bosler/Getty Images;   Page 227: © David Young-Wolff/PhotoEdit;   Page 233: © Helen King/CORBIS;   Page 237: © PhotoDisc/Getty Images;   Page 238: © Sotograph/Getty Images;   Page 242: © JupiterImages/BananaStock/Alamy;   Page 245: © Michael Newman/PhotoEdit;   Page 248: © David Joel/Getty Images;   Page 251: © Dirk Anschutz/Getty Images;   Page 256: © Kayte M Deioma/PhotoEdit;   Page 262: © CORBIS;   Page 269: © Bob Daemmrich Photography;   Page 272: © Jose Luis Pelaez, Inc./CORBIS;   Page 275: © Paddy Eckersley/Pictor/ImageState;   Page 281: © Image Source/Getty Images;   Page 284: © Martyn Vickery/Alamy;   Page 291: © Bill Aron/PhotoEdit;   Page 297: © Michael Newman/PhotoEdit;   Page 301: © JupiterImages/BananaStock/Alamy;   Page 309: © A. Ramey/PhotoEdit;   Page 315 © DiMaggio/Kalish/CORBIS;   Page 320: © PhotoDisc/Getty Images;   Page 326: © Russell Underwood/CORBIS;   Page 332: © Bill Aron/PhotoEdit;   Page 349: © Paul Conklin/PhotoEdit;   Page 350: © Barbara Stitzer/PhotoEdit;   Page 355: © JupiterImages/Comstock Images/Alamy;   Page 373: © image100/age fotostock;   Page 375: © image100/CORBIS;   Page 380, 384: © Barbara Stitzer/PhotoEdit;   Page 389: © Susan Van Etten/PhotoEdit;   Page 398: © Chip Simons/Getty Images;   Page 400: © Russell Underwood/CORBIS;   Page 401: © Michael Newman/PhotoEdit;   Page 403: © Bruce Ayres/Getty Images;   Page 405: © Jeff Greenburg/PhotoEdit;   Page 409: © Marilyn Humphries/The Image Works;   Page 411: © K. Shamsi-Basha/The Image Works;   Page 421: © Jim Franco/Getty Images;   Page 423: © Stockbyte/Getty Images;   Page 434: © Bob Daemmrich Photography;   Page 436: © Digital Vision/age fotostock;   Page 440: © Axel Koester/CORBIS;   Page 442: © Richard Hutchings/PhotoEdit;   Page 447: © AP Photo/Peoria Journal Star, Ron Johnson.